The Palgrave Handbook of Education Law for Schools

Karen Trimmer • Roselyn Dixon
Yvonne S. Findlay
Editors

The Palgrave Handbook of Education Law for Schools

palgrave
macmillan

Editors
Karen Trimmer
Faculty of Business, Law, Education & Arts
University of Southern Queensland
Toowoomba, QLD, Australia

Roselyn Dixon
School of Education
University of Wollongong
Wollongong, NSW, Australia

Yvonne S. Findlay
Faculty of Business, Law, Education & Arts
University of Southern Queensland
Toowoomba, QLD, Australia

ISBN 978-3-030-08529-2 ISBN 978-3-319-77751-1 (eBook)
https://doi.org/10.1007/978-3-319-77751-1

Softcover re-print of the Hardcover 1st edition 2018

Printed on acid-free paper

This Palgrave Macmillan imprint is published by the registered company Springer International Publishing AG part of Springer Nature.
The registered company address is: Gewerbestrasse 11, 6330 Cham, Switzerland

Preface

Tensions, paradoxes and uncertainty are hallmarks of the operating environments in which professionals undertake their practices. Handy (1994) suggests that such tensions and paradoxes are "endemic" given the complex, uncertain, and turbulent world of constant change in all aspects of contemporary organisations. The education sector has not been immune from such dynamics. Policy makers, decision makers, parents, school leaders, teachers and broad stakeholder and interest groups undertake professional practices, interactions and decision making that is ever growing in terms of complexity of the law. Principals and teachers who are at the core of the delivery of school provision are faced with ever increasing demands on their roles and associated responsibilities as a result (Trimble et al. 2012). It is essential that educators feel equipped with the appropriate knowledge and skills to enable them to respond to current and emerging issues of a legal nature.

Many countries are endeavouring to establish systemic approaches to the governance of education systems that balance 'responsiveness to local diversity with the ability to ensure national objectives' (Burns and Koster 2016, p. 3). This is typified by such trends as greater discretion and autonomy in relation to decision making; increased accountability for school performance; enhanced transparency in relation to student data and more inclusive approaches to the provision of schooling. This approach in turn generates an increased policy, legislative and legal framework that school leaders and teachers are required to engage with and manage. McKinsey & Company (2007) in their study of the world's best performing education systems note that one of the common interventions in shaping the next phase of any systemic schooling reform are the instruments of policy documents and educational laws. Such mechanisms applied in this manner are seen as enablers and support to the aspirations, objectives and priorities of governments and policy makers. Moreover, the espoused intention and rhetoric of such changes to the operating principles of any schooling system is encapsulated as supportive of schools, their leaders and primary stakeholders such as parents. Good, well thought out policy and associated implementation is necessary to meet the key purposes of the educative process. In reality the execution of policy to practice ('praxis') provides significant challenges and concerns for school leaders and schools in general. Typically these include the sheer amount and rate of change; the associated increase in managerial workloads; the apparent disconnected nature of the policies and the capacities of the workforce.

The development of effective executive management capabilities is seen as a key dimension of the role of key school leaders such as principals, headmasters or school heads. A review of school leadership standards from a selection of international education systems is evidence of this. In Australia, the Australian Professional Standard for Principals developed by the Australian Institute for Teaching and School Leadership (AITSL) notes that one of the roles and responsibilities of a principal is to lead the management of the school including the human, physical and financial resources effectively, ensuring good governance and meeting policy, legal and accountability requirements (AITSL 2011, p. 77). In Scotland, the Standards for Leadership and Management (2012) developed by the General Teaching Council (GTC) also privileges the centrality of management capability as crucial to the role and associated responsibilities of school heads (GTC 2012). The Ontario Leadership Framework (2012) acknowledges the importance of school leaders having an awareness of the legal requirements of their role.

Given the centrality and importance of executive management to successfully undertaking school leadership and specifically, school principals or headship, it is concerning that many aspiring to or in such roles reported little or no preparation or support to enable this or other leaders capabilities to be developed:

> Some 35 per cent of surveyed principals in Australia have no school administration or principal training, and 30 per cent have not undertaken any instructional leadership training. In fact, 45 per cent reported receiving average or weak leadership training as part of their formal education. (OECD, TALIS 2014)

The case therefore exists for a much more concerted and proactive approach to the enhancement of capability in this crucial area of school leadership practice. AITSL (2015) in a report reviewing effective preparation for aspiring school principals noted that the development of management skills prior to taking up the role of principal was one of three (3) priority areas for any preparation program for such a role. This sense of urgency about executive leadership management knowledge and skill development is reflected in other contexts. In a report entitled *The Making of the Principal: Five Lessons in Leadership Training*, The Wallace Foundation key exemplary programs requires course work in areas such as management of resources and operations, ethical practices and political, social, economic, legal and cultural contexts (2012, p. 13). Critically, current and future school leaders require and need knowledge in the area of the law and the legal context in which they discharge their increasingly complex roles. Despite such a case being immutable, the access to such knowledge tailored for such leadership roles is not uniform.

At the core or heart of the work of an educator should be the best interests of the children in their care. Teachers and school leaders are imbued with a sense of moral purpose-a desire to improve the lives of all children through learning. Despite this underpinning commitment by educators to this ideal, the complexity and diversity of issues related to students continues to increase. In the ever increasing legal and litigious operating environment that educators undertake their work it brings into question what is a realistic view or definition of moral purpose.

I commend the contributors of *The Palgrave Handbook of Education Law for Schools* for bringing a much needed focus on a crucial aspect of the provision of schooling and education in post-modern times.

Victorian Department of Education and Early Childhood Development
and Queensland Education Leadership Institute
Brisbane, Australia

Stephen Brown

References

Australian Institute for Teaching and School Leadership. (2011). *Australian Professional Standard for Principals,* Education Services Australia, Carlton.

Australian Institute for Teaching and School Leadership (AITSL). (2015). *Accreditation of initial teacher education programs: Standards and procedures.* Melbourne: Education Services Australia.

Burns, T., & Koster, F. (Eds.). (2016). *Governing education in a complex world, educational research and innovation.* Paris: OECD Publishing.

General Teaching Council for Scotland. (2012). *The standards for leadership and management.* http://www.gtcs.org.uk/web/FILES/the-standards/standards-for-leadership-and-management-1212.pdf. Accessed 7 Mar 2017.

Handy, C. (1994). *The empty raincoat: Making sense of the future*. London: Random House.

McKinsey & Company. (2007). *How the world's most improved school systems keep getting better*. Washington, DC/New York: McKinsey & Company/The Wallace Foundation.

Organisation for Economic Cooperation and Development (OECD). (2014). TALIS 2013 results: An international perspective on teaching and learning, TALIS, OECD Publishing.

The Wallace Foundation. (2012, June). *Perspective: The making of the principal: Five lessons in leadership training*.

Trimble, A., Cranston, N., & Allen, J. (2012). School principles and education law: What do they know, what do they need to know? *Leading & Managing, 18*(2), 46–51.

Acknowledgements

- Ms. Eleanor Christie, Ms. Laura Aldridge and the editorial team at Palgrave Macmillan for all their work in getting this publication to press
- Ms. Katrina Wilson for her attention to detail and patience in copy-editing the manuscript and composing the index
- Dr. Stephen Brown for writing the Preface to the book
- The chapter authors for their respective chapters and for engaging wholeheartedly with feedback from editors and peer reviewers
- The scholars who provided double blind peer reviews of one or more submitted chapters:
  - Associate Professor Lindy-Anne Abawi, University of Southern Queensland, Australia
  - Ms. Christine Adams, Australian National University, Canberra
  - Professor Michael Arthur-Kelly, University of Newcastle, Australia
  - Dr. Vito Breda, University of Southern Queensland, Australia
  - Dr. Susan Bruck, Autism Australia (Aspect), Australia
  - Professor Suzanne Carrington, Queensland University of Technology, Australia
  - Associate Professor Mark Carter, Macquarie University, Australia
  - Dr. Philip Crane, University of the Sunshine Coast, Australia
  - Dr. Linda Devlin, University of Wolverhampton, UK
  - Dr. Robert Doherty, University of Glasgow, UK
  - Associate Professor David Evans, University of Sydney, Australia
  - Dr. Giuliana Ferri, University of West London, UK
  - Professor Gregg Gassman, Southern Oregon University, USA
  - Dr. Christine Grima-Farrell, University of New South Wales, Australia

  - Mr. David Ford, Emil Ford Lawyers, Sydney, Australia
  - Dr. Amanda Heffernan, University of Southern Queensland, Australia
  - Ms. Bronwyn Herbertson, Independent scholar, Australia
  - Dr. Anne Jasman, Independent scholar, Australia
  - Dr. Paula Jervis-Tracey, Griffith University, Australia
  - Dr. Nicky Jones, University of Southern Queensland, Australia
  - Ms. Hannah McConaghy, Iona College, Queensland, Australia
  - Dr. Katie Murray, University of Southern Queensland, Australia
  - Associate Professor Linda Newman, University of Newcastle, Australia
  - Professor Shirley O'Neill, University of Southern Queensland, Australia
  - Professor Jacqui Roberts, Griffith University, Australia
  - Professor Carmen Robertson, University of Regina, Canada
  - Ms. Nyree Scott, Canterbury Christ Church University, UK
  - Dr. Danielle Tracey, Western Sydney University, Australia
  - Dr. Viv Wilson, Canterbury Christ Church University, UK
  - Professor Simon Young, University of Southern Queensland, Australia

- Our colleagues for their continuing encouragement and interest
- Our families and friends for their inexhaustible love and support.

Karen Trimmer, Roselyn Dixon and
Yvonne S. Findlay
Editors

Contents

List of Contributors

Jose Luis Alvarado California State University Monterey Bay, Seaside, CA, USA

Marie Battiste University of Saskatchewan, Saskatoon, SK, Canada

Elisabetta Biffi University of Milano-Bicocca, Milan, Italy

Stephen Brown Queensland Education Leadership Institute, Brisbane, Australia

Hazel Bryan University of Gloucestershire, Cheltenham, UK

India Bryce University of Southern Queensland, Toowoomba, QLD, Australia

Mark Butlin University of Southern Queensland, Toowoomba, Australia

Neil Cranston University of Tasmania, Launceston and Hobart, Australia

Joy Cumming Australian Catholic University, Brisbane, QLD, Australia

Therese M. Cumming University of New South Wales, Sydney, NSW, Australia

Elizabeth Dickson Queensland University of Technology, Brisbane, QLD, Australia

Roselyn Dixon University of Wollongong, Wollongong, NSW, Australia

Sally Elton-Chalcraft University of Cumbria, Carlisle, UK

Franziska Felder University of Birmingham, Birmingham, UK

Yvonne S. Findlay University of Southern Queensland, Toowoomba, QLD, Australia

Jonathan H. Green University of Southern Queensland, Toowoomba, Australia

James [Sa'ke'j] Youngblood Henderson University of Saskatchewan, Saskatoon, SK, Canada

Karen Embry Jenlink Stephen F. Austin State University, Nacogdoches, TX, USA

Patrick M. Jenlink Stephen F. Austin State University, Nacogdoches, TX, USA

Patrick Meehan Canterbury Christ Church University, Canterbury, UK

Joseph John Morgan University of Nevada, Las Vegas, NV, USA

Sarah J. Murphy University of Nevada, Las Vegas, NV, USA

Eszter Anna Nyúl University of Pécs, Pécs, Hungary

Sue O'Neill University of New South Wales, Sydney, NSW, Australia

Fernando F. Padró University of Southern Queensland, Toowoomba, Australia

Scott Peter Wallacestone Primary School, Brightons, Falkirk, UK; School of Education, University of Aberdeen, Aberdeen, UK

Shiralee Poed University of Melbourne, Parkville, VIC, Australia

Lynn Revell Canterbury Christ Church University, Canterbury, UK

Francine Rochford La Trobe University, Bundoora, Australia

Cathi Draper Rodriguez California State University Monterey Bay, Seaside, CA, USA

Charles J. Russo University of Dayton, Dayton, OH, USA

Jacquie Seemann Thomson Geer Lawyers, Sydney, NSW, Australia

Rachel Shanks University of Aberdeen, Aberdeen, UK

Ilektra Spandagou The University of Sydney, Camperdown, NSW, Australia

Tracy Griffin Spies University of Nevada, Las Vegas, NV, USA

Linda Steele University of Technology Sydney, Sydney, NSW, Australia

Iva Strnadová University of New South Wales, Sydney, NSW, Australia

Mui Kim Teh Deakin University, Geelong, VIC, Australia

Allison Trimble University of Tasmania, Launceston and Hobart, Australia

Karen Trimmer University of Southern Queensland, Toowoomba, Australia

Sally Varnham University of Technology Sydney, Haymarket, NSW, Australia

Amanda A. Webster University of Wollongong, Wollongong, NSW, Australia

Kristopher H. Yeager University of Nevada, Las Vegas, NV, USA

List of Figures

List of Tables

Section I

The Need for Legal Literacy by School Principals and Educational Leaders

1

The Need for an Understanding of Education Law Principles by School Principals

Mark Butlin and Karen Trimmer

1.1 Introduction

> *We live in a dangerous time for teachers. The American mentality of 'If it moves, sue it' has been imported along with fast food and videos. Australia is now the second most litigious country in the world. Allowing for population differences, it now ranks behind only the United States. Teachers, principals and schools are now legal targets in a way that was unthinkable two decades ago.* (Tronc 1996, p. 3)

Dr. Keith Tronc, one of the prominent pioneers in this relatively new area of education law research, presaged us some two decades ago about this growing phenomenon in Australia. Tronc also warns us about bush-lawyer parents who like to, often erroneously, claim their rights against a teacher or school because their child is not receiving the treatment that they are seeking (Tronc 1996; Tronc and Sleigh 1989). He also expresses concern about bush-lawyer children who stand up in classrooms and confidently state to the teacher in authority what they think they can and cannot do or say. The prevalence of this behaviour is, according to Tronc, on the increase (Tronc 1996).

There is no doubt that there is more discussion about legal matters in schools now than there was twenty years ago. It is our contention that more teachers and principals in schools are increasingly aware that their everyday activities and decisions can be the subject of a legal claim or action being

M. Butlin (✉) • K. Trimmer
University of Southern Queensland, Toowoomba, Australia
e-mail: Mark.Butlin@usq.edu.au; Karen.trimmer@usq.edu.au

K. Trimmer et al. (eds.), *The Palgrave Handbook of Education Law for Schools*,
https://doi.org/10.1007/978-3-319-77751-1_1

brought against them by a disgruntled student and/or parent. Birch and Richter (1990, as cited in Teh 2014) observed a significant increase in cases reaching Australian courts. Our experience in engaging in conversations within a community of practice strongly suggests that many teachers are not aware of the legal protection that is afforded to them in carrying out their duties in the course of their employment. Furthermore, there are many in the teaching profession who are worried about possible legal redress being sought against them when, in fact, the law is on their side. This is not only in legal defences available to them, or in legal principles that place the liability on their employer, but moreover in the manner that judges in our Australian courts usually side with teachers and school authorities who are acting in the course of their undertakings with the best interests of the children in their care in mind (Tronc and Sleigh 1989).

It is from this premise that the authors suggest that school principals should have a sound working knowledge of the legal issues and principles that affect their daily operations as the leader in charge of managing their school community. Principals and teachers now work in increasingly uncertain and challenging environments involving complex legislative frameworks (Trimble et al. 2012). As the roles and responsibilities of principals and teachers change to meet new demands and capabilities, especially for dealing with safety and security issues, so too does the need for a sound knowledge of emerging legal issues in schools such as the impact of court orders, competing parental rights, and issues around children with disabilities; information confidentiality, records and the internet; accident and incident risk management. The legal matters that can be raised are multi-faceted and complex. These can vary from more simple cases of negligence to more complicated disputes of disability discrimination. They are numerous, costly, exhausting and potentially damaging to the reputation of the school irrespective of whether or not the plaintiff (aggrieved person) is successful.

It is becoming essential for educators to adapt, and acquire new knowledge and skills relating to child protection and aspects of criminal law, to the school management environment. Educators are being required to gain confidence and expertise in identifying possible legal problems before and as they arise based on their knowledge of various statutory, contractual and common law duties, especially the duty to take reasonable care, which underpin the educational process. They are being challenged on a daily basis to critically examine and evaluate the legal rights and obligations of various stakeholders, including students and parents, educators and administrators associated with the role of management within schools.

Consequently, there is a need for school staff, and in particular school principals, to have an appropriate level of legal literacy (Stewart and Knott 2002; Teh 2009). Stewart and Knott (2002) suggest that many principals have an inadequate level of knowledge and legal understanding because principals manage complex organisations and while they are usually time poor, they make decisions on the run and sometimes, due to competing interests, without the due care and diligence that is required. A survey of 253 public school principals in Western Australia found that the dichotomy created by decentralisation, in combination with increased external accountability, creates a perturbing dilemma for school principals who have the dual task of being instructional leaders and managers (Trimmer 2011). As instructional leaders principals have to ensure that students attain achievement standards. Simultaneously they must lead and manage the school, including compliance with requirements imposed through legislation and policy, for both educational and business aspects of management.

1.2 Education Law Principles

These requirements on educators to be knowledgeable of legal issues are not confined to Australia. Many books, journal articles, specific publications, websites and even annual conferences are being focused on education law globally. Publications by Butler and Mathews (2007), Jackson and Varnham (2007), Ramsay and Shorten (1996), Stewart and Knott (2002), Tronc (1996) and Tronc and Sleigh (1989) are being used by both educational and legal practitioners to respond to legal questions related to school law. In addition, there are journals on education and the law published in Australia, the United Kingdom, Canada, and Europe that specialise in educational law matters in their various jurisdictions (e.g. Australia and New Zealand Education Law Association (ANZELA) journal; Hopkins 2008; Knott 2010; Mawdsley and Cumming 2008; Weegen 2013), and other professional publications that provide advice to school principals on their legal responsibilities in relation to managing their educational community.

However, the predominant focus with these publications is that they espouse the position of legal findings based on either common law or from legislation. That is, they explain the law or legal principles that schools and other educational authorities need to follow to be legally compliant, and in doing so, avoid having an actionable matter brought against them. However, they do not address the question of the legal knowledge required by principals and other school leaders to be able to effectively fulfil their roles. Nor do they comment on the impact of having (or of not having) such legal literacy on their capacity or effectiveness as school leaders. This book aims to address this gap by providing an examination of legal and policy perspectives in an approach aimed at developing awareness and understanding for readers of the impact of legislative frameworks in the context of school based education and educational systems internationally. The book is organised around three main themes which are used as the organising framework for the chapters in each section. The first section of the book focuses on examination and evaluation of the legal rights and obligations of various stakeholders, including students and parents, educators and administrators and the issues and impacts experienced by educational leaders in making decisions that are legally compliant and in the educational interest of students in their care. Trimble and Cranston (in Chap. 2) examine the external and internal legal environments of schools within which principals practice in Tasmania, Australia, the legal areas they deal with, current legal preparation and development arrangements, principals' legal knowledge and consciousness, and the legal support frameworks available to them.

As academics working in postgraduate education we are receiving increasing requests from education systems, regulatory bodies, school principals and teacher leaders for courses to assist educators to have an understanding of legislation to be able to have an understanding of the personal context of their students' lives; meet the regulatory obligations concerning the health and safety of the students in their care; be fully aware of the correct procedures to report suspected incidents of child abuse; and know who to contact regarding the emotional health and well-being of their students.

1.3 Developing Trends

When education law was beginning to be spoken about amongst legal professionals and academics, (much earlier than when school administrators and teachers were considering such issues) the focus lay solely on the risk of physical injury to students. This meant that if students were injured in the playground while on a lunch break, or if they suffered an injury, for example while involved in a science experiment, they could then seek legal advice asking if they could sue the careless teacher for negligence. There are innumerable examples of where this has occurred and paved the way for what some researchers call the "Suing Mentality" (Nolan and Spencer 1997) that we have today.

In such cases, and, indeed, many more, judicial decisions have clarified the legal position in relation to this notion of a duty of care being owed to school students. This included and helped to define, inter alia: legal liability in and out of the classroom, before and after school, what level, or standard of care is owed, and what constituted a breach of the duty of care. The duty of care principle has continued and will undoubtedly continue to be shaped by legal cases involving students who suffer both physical and emotional injury in a variety of ways that are brought before the courts of this land and no doubt internationally as well.

Touching students to stop physical fights and also in the use of discipline became part of the education law dialogue in the 1980s (Williams 1995). The issue of discrimination followed and became part of the education law vernacular as students and their parents became increasingly aware of their rights under both federal and state law that provides protection for students being discriminated against on a number of grounds in education. For example, failing to enrol certain students due to gender or failing to allow students of a certain gender to participate in activities such as sports predominately played by the other gender (Salidu 1994). Seemann (in Chap. 10) considers the parameters placed on religious schools by relevant discrimination and other laws, and some of the issues that arise in seeking to balance all these competing expectations.

Workplace health and safety laws (Forlin 1995) were closely followed by defamation laws in the educational context (Walker 1995). Wider employment law issues relating to schools and teachers employed in those schools were then debated and trialled in various jurisdictions (Edwards 1996). Students' rights was the next topic to be introduced into the legal framework concerning schools (Knott 2010; Rayner 1996). Criminal law matters have possibly always been a matter for schools and the law, particularly when schools have had to consider how to manage miscreant pupils. Having sound behaviour management policies and techniques has been imperative in the effective administration of educational communities (Stewart and Cope 1996).

The changes to family law and how custody of, and access to, children in the mid-1980s (and later changes in 2006) then became an important issue for schools in handling the legal arrangements of children when parents became separated (Christie and Christie 2008; Conte-Mills 2010; Davies 1997). This has and probably will remain a fixture on the education law landscape as divorce rates continue to rise. Acrimonious breakups and the legal arguing over children will continue, and often involve, unfortunately, and sometimes, unnecessarily, the child(ren)'s school.

Discrimination moved to include age discrimination, creating novel grounds for such actions, where students started to accuse schools of unfair and unjust dealings when asking students who turned 18 years of age to leave educational facilities; or refusing to allow brighter students to advance year levels in order to be taught the unfamiliar and as such, only allowing such students to follow their chronological age development in school years (Lindsay 1997). Along with this area came the introduction of mandatory reporting and the early legal provisions concerning child protection (Best 2001; Farrell 2001; Mathews et al. 2006; Murray 1997). Bryce (in Chap. 5) provides an overview of legal issues encountered by school leaders in relation to mandatory reporting obligations. The complexities encountered by schools can pose conflicting moral and ethical issues for principals in protecting children in their care from abuse and neglect.

The next major topic introduced in education law was the whole area of bullying. This later metamorphosed into cyber bullying, using electronic devices and social media to exact hurtful messages to others (Bolton 2002; Campbell et al. 2008; Farrell 1998; Healy 1998; Knott 1998; Slee 1998; Winram 2008).

In the latter part of last century, another two areas in regulating the affairs of schools developed. One of these is the notion of 'non-delegable duties' where schools and educational authorities are not legally permitted to absolve themselves in law of their liability to take care of students by placing all responsibility onto another authority such as a camp site or local council. The other area which needs highlighting here is the principle of 'vicarious liability' where the school employer is held liable at law and therefore has to pay for the damages and injuries suffered by the student(s) caused by the actions of its agents, in this case, namely the teachers (Tronc 1999).

Throughout all this time, further developments to the duty of care owed by teachers to students were being made. The definition of actual foreseeable risks of harm (Williams 2002) was being framed in the students' favour, while a clearer understanding of what level of care owed to students in a playground fight was being clarified (Hamilton and Smith 2002). Varnham (in Chap. 4) discusses how responsibilities of school authorities under duty of care may now extend beyond physical harm to include expectations around mental and emotional harm arising from bullying, cyberbullying and sexual abuse. The implications of risk and responsibility for school leaders and potential liability is emerging as an area where initiatives around restorative practice may have value in assisting schools to reduce threats of harm to students.

Privacy, both in government and non-government schools, became an issue and was something on the radar of most school principals and educational authorities. This came at the time when new legislation was introduced protecting the privacy of individuals. It also coincided with disability discrimination actions where students with disabilities attempted to keep their special needs private (Simmonds 2005).

One of the more recent issues raised in the law involving schools lies in the area of consumer protection legislation where, in particular, independent or private schools have a duty not to mislead students and their paying parents in the provision of educational services to young people (Squelch and Goldacre 2009). As can be gathered from the developing trends over the years in education law, this discipline has developed significantly, moving from straight forward duty of care claims (which will always be a significant part of the school law backdrop) to include more vexing and complicated areas of the law. Stewart and McCann (1995, as cited in Teh 2014, p. 398) observed that education law issues "were not just limited to physical safety of students, but there were increasing legislation as well as common law and equity issues associated with children's rights". Teh and Russo (in Chap. 3) also question whether cases of educational negligence or malpractice could be brought if students fail to meet expected educational outcomes. They suggest that the setting of professional standards for teaching may have implications for interpretation of duty of care. We will undoubtedly see further nascent problems which will became part of school law where would-be litigants decide to sue to gain redress from school authorities for alleged harms.

The work of educators takes place within national legislative structures, including the constitution, legislation and rulings and common law arising from them. These enactments have had significant impact on corporate governance of public sector agencies including schools (Bauer and Bogotch 2006; Collier and Roberts 2001; Allison 1983). Wirtz, Cribb and Barber (2005, p. 335) found that public sector policy makers, "felt accountable to provide decisions which are politically and legally defensible" and "which could be defended in public, including in court". Similarly, the influence of legislative structures as a determinant in decision-making in the school environment has become an increasing concern for school principals (Trimmer 2003, 2011). The move towards standards and accountability has influenced the governance of schools and the move towards distributed models of leadership has increased the complexity of responsibilities and expectations of school leadership (Bauer and Bogotch 2006). Starr (2008, as cited in Wirtz et al. 2005, p. 335) indicates that consideration of risk in schools "has risen dramatically in stakes and prominence" and that the increase in litigation, insurance and compensation claims have resulted in education systems and principals needing to respond by "identifying, managing and delegating responsibility for risk". Increased knowledge of legal issues and the application of the law has become essential to avoid decision-making where "procedural safeguards are being valued more than the content of the decision" (Wirtz et al. 2005, p. 335). The focus on avoiding legal liability however may lead to decisions that do not align with professional ethics. Jenlink and Jenlink (in Chap. 6) examine the ethical implications of decision-making that needs to take account of law, policy and also the potential for breaches of ethics. The implications are significant if principals are not aware of and sensitive to the impact on ethical behaviour. It is also a concern where educators are deterred from pursuing innovative educative strategies due to potential litigation risks.

Disability discrimination became part of the education law argot at the beginning of this century with the development of respective legislation in the Disability Discrimination Act (DDA) (Australian government 1992) and the interpretation of same in case law before the courts (Dempsey 2003; Dickson 2003, 2004, 2006; Hamilton 2002; Johnson 2002; Keeffe 2003; Lindsay and Keeffe-Martin 2002; Stafford 2004; Stewart 2003; Varnham 2002). The introduction of inclusive education policy has required school leaders to adapt to ensure that they and their teaching staff are able to meet the needs of all children attending their school. Webster (in Chap. 11) reviews the difficulties school leaders have faced in dealing with the demands of this legislation and conflicting priorities that arise in the context of high-stakes accountability. Whilst, there are regulatory requirements in some Australian states for all teachers to be familiar with the DDA, particularly with the Disability Standards for Education (Australian Government Department of Education and Training 2005), and be able to apply this on a daily basis in their classroom, schools and systems are sometimes only giving the illusion of compliance with the legislation. The Disability Standards for Education attempt to clarify expectations and legal obligations under the DDA. All teachers in Australia are being encouraged to complete an on-line module about the Disability Standards for Education (Kilham 2014) to further enhance their understanding.

Section two of this book focuses on inclusive schooling and the impacts of the DDA and DSE on inclusion and participation of students with disabilities in Australia, and on areas of the application or non-application of antidiscrimination legislation for students with disabilities both in Australia and in the USA. These areas include accountability in assessment, the impact of problem behaviour on court decisions and the negative impact of a lack of case law in the Australian legal system.

1.4 Principals' Understanding of Education Law

Birch (1990, as cited in Stewart 1996) presaged that although there was a paucity of education law matters before the courts here in Australia, there are sufficient to suggest that school law in and of itself is an established area of interest for both legal and educational professionals. Moreover, Mr. Justice Dowsett of the Queensland Supreme Court (1994, as cited in Stewart 1996, p. 114) cautioned that "there is likely to be more consumer litigation in the education field and that this would reflect growing community demands for greater accountability in the professions generally." Stewart (1996) also adds that in particular novitiate principals are grossly inadequately prepared for the administrative and management responsibilities that this high level position requires. Their understanding of the law as it applies to the education setting is unacceptably scarce (Stewart 1996).

A comparative study (Teh 2009) of the types of legal issues that principals, in both Singapore and Australia, had encountered as part of their principalship found that not only were they wide ranging, but that a level of legal literacy amongst principals is needed to avoid multifarious legal scenarios. Similarly, Stewart's (1998) quantitative study of state school principals' level of understanding of school law found a generally low level of knowledge held by Queensland state school principals.

1.4.1 Education Practitioners' Fear of Legal Consequences

The authors have heard both teachers and principals say on many occasions that they would not participate in an activity such as a school camp or sporting event because of the fear of being sued (Trimmer 2003, 2011). This has become a commonly held view of members of the teaching profession with educators expressing professional concerns about being a party of a legal dispute and therefore declining to be involved in or allow school events that they believe would be educationally beneficial to students. In a review of Australian curriculum (Wilson 2014), teachers reported that they are avoiding school excursions and field trips, notwithstanding their imperative educational value and importance, because of the threat of being sued. Fear of legal liability and litigation risks are high and consequently these important co-curricular activities are being shunned, even by more experienced practitioners (Wilson 2014). In this review, the federal Education Minister stated that educational standards could "be at risk if kids are bound to their desks" (Wilson 2014, p. 12). The released report went on to remark that "state and federal governments needed to provide better training and professional support so teachers would feel comfortable exposing pupils to important out-of-classroom lessons" (Wilson 2014, p. 12). The Australian Education Union president stated "For some subject areas, excursions and field trips are vital in getting a better understanding of the content being covered… But we are living in an increasingly litigious society and schools bear the brunt of that litigiousness" (Wilson 2014, p. 12). Ford (2004, p. 1) puts it this way:

> *A balancing act is involved: schools must strike some balance between meticulous supervision of children every moment of the time when they are under their care, and the very desirable object of encouraging the sturdy independence of children as they grow up. Nevertheless, there are cases which suggest that the courts are less likely to find negligence where the activity is intended to develop independence.*

There are a number of cases where judges have had to decide on whether the law should side with the education provider doing its job or should protect an injured student who allegedly falls foul of schools not protecting them whilst under their care (Ford 2004).

1.4.2 The Need for Some Legal Literacy by Principals

An essential premise for this book is the need for school principals and administrators to have a basic understanding of how the law standardises the everyday activities of schools. This is sometimes referred to as having legal literacy.

Nolan and Spencer (1997), Stewart and Knott (2002) and Teh (2009) all believe that teachers and school leaders should have some basic legal knowledge and understanding as it relates to their roles in schools. Unfortunately, it has been our experience that in practice this is simply not the case, and those in the profession that do sprout some legalise from time to time often do so speciously. This view has been supported by Pell (1994, as cited in Stewart 1996, p. 122) when he stated that "not only do most educators have a lack of knowledge of school law but what knowledge they do have is often distorted, inaccurate or based on misinformation. Such knowledge Pell maintains not only affects one's understanding of the law but also can be the basis for poor decision-making." This difficult maze of regulations and rules and how it may be navigated by school leaders in making decisions is discussed by Padró and Green (in Chap. 7). This chapter outlines an approach that administrators can apply in their school context to make decisions on legal and policy matters that are regulatory compliant. In Chap. 8 Padró and Green use Total Quality Management (TQM) as a lens to explore the impact of administrative law schemes and strategic decision making in education.

Accountability, risk assessment and compliance are increasingly a priority for educational organisations and governments. Rochford (in Chap. 9) considers the relationship between law and 'quasi law' such as codes of practice and professional standards for teachers. Stewart and Knott (2002) suggest that having an understanding of education law is only one highly specialised area that principals and school leaders are being held more and more accountable for. It is mooted therefore that principals and teachers in schools should have a deeper working understanding of how the law protects and regulates their everyday work activities to help prevent legal matters being brought against them. Rossow (1990) advises (as cited in Stewart 1996, p. 111) that principals should have enough legal understanding to "know initially what questions to ask when confronted with a potential problem". Similarly, Haller and Strike (1986) suggest (as cited in Stewart 1996, p. 111) that school administrators "need a basic sense of what kinds of problems and situations generate litigation and what kinds of actions are more likely to generate legal difficulties". Sungaila (1988, as cited in Stewart 1996, p. 111) summarises this imperative:

> *... there are two things educators need to know about the law. The first is that he or she should have an appreciation of the law as one of our most precious social institutions. The second is that he or she should have an understanding of that law which infringes on professional educational practice sufficient to recognise whether a problem which has arisen is one about which professional legal advice should be sought or not.*

Having a basic understanding of the legal matters that potentially come before a principal is not only prudent but also helpful in dispelling possible legal cases early before they gain momentum. Principals can then field off potential cases by saying the right things or garnering the relevant materials early on to suggest to would-be parent litigants that their case will not be a one sided matter. Nolan and Spencer (1997, p. 14) put it this way by stating that principals and "teachers should be aware of situations and activities where negligence would be difficult to disprove and order their personal behaviour and supervisory role accordingly."

Leschied et al. (2000, as cited in Teh 2014) have argued that the explosion of information technology, changes in domestic living patterns and related values, the fact that children are at risk of physical and sexual abuse and the escalation in youth crime collectively combine and result in an increased reliance on laws and the courts; all of which have an impact on the role of teachers and principals, and the school system. According to research conducted in the United States, Teh (2014) reports that teachers perceive themselves to be legally illiterate. Another survey indicated that over 75 percent of American school teachers (Teh 2014) had no exposure to school law courses at all and over 50 percent were either wrong or unsure about questions relating to teachers' rights and responsibilities. Yet another study performed in the United States suggested that 85 percent of secondary school principals said that they would change their behaviour if they knew more about the rights and responsibilities of teachers and students associated with education law (Teh 2014). Teh (2014) puts forward a similar position in Canada where principals surveyed achieved less than half of the correct responses when tested.

In Australia, the situation is much the same. Teh (2014) considers some research conducted here in 1996, 2006 and 2012. All studies revealed many areas of law which principals had to deal with but lack sufficient knowledge or understanding to deal with them. A prominent recent case Oyston v St Patrick's College (2013), as cited in Teh (2014) is apposite in this discussion as it was noted from the judges who sat on the New South Wales Court of Appeal that many schools in Australia have policies and practices in written form largely as a consequence of mandates from education cases or legislation. When these are complied with, they may well provide a strong defence against legal claims. Conversely, they noted that where schools have written policies but do not take steps to follow them, the defence against a legal claim will be significantly weakened. They went on to say:

> *What was required of the College was not a system of impractical perfection. Rather, what was required was the practical implementation of its own system, to bring ongoing bullying to an end and to monitor the victim to ensure such behaviour did not continue. That, it failed to do.* (Teh 2014, p. 405)

The example of Oyston illustrates the need for teachers and school leaders to keep abreast of developments, not only of legislation, but also of the decisions arrived at by our courts.

It is expected that principals have an understanding of, and be experts in, all matters pertaining to schools. "Such expectations, along with a growing movement towards increased accountability in the professions generally, provide compelling reasons for principals to be more highly literate in school law than currently appears to be the case" (Stewart 1996, p. 112).

Stewart (1996, p. 115) goes on to plead:

While there has been a noted increase in both judicial decisions and statute law that may impact on school leadership and management, there has not been a commensurate level of research in Australia to determine schools' actual involvement with legal matters. As a consequence there has been a dearth of information concerning principals' need for, and extent of, knowledge of the law that affects the principalship.

1.5 Research Findings

In a recent research study (Butlin 2014) involving a number of Australian principals and their level of legal literacy, the authors found that whilst the principals see it as an important issue to be familiar with, they do not possess a confident level of legal understanding when it comes to managing their school environment. This discovery reflects the literature referred to above. The evidence was demonstrated through responses to survey questions about common legal situations confronting schools where the majority of principals scored lower than 35 percent of the responses correctly. During interviews held with the principal participants, this low level of legal literacy was explored in more detail with most of them shocked to discover their level was so low. They thought that they had a more correct and developed understanding of their legal duty than in fact they actually did have. This has been highlighted above in an earlier section of this chapter and is (sadly) probably reflective of most principals in this country and possibly even principals internationally.

This led on conveniently to the next major question under review considering whether or not school principals should, in fact, have a level of legal understanding as it relates to running their school. When asked about the concept of having an acceptable understanding of school law matters to minimise litigious activity and to help manage risk, all principals interviewed acknowledged that some understanding, even at a limited level, was indeed imperative (Butlin 2014).

The agreement of principals interviewed of the importance for the school leader to have some degree of familiarity with school law aligns with Nolan and Spencer (1997) and Stewart and Knott (2002) who argue that all school principals should have some degree of legal literacy to better lead and function in this demanding role. One participant proposed that whilst legal matters are not the main focus of the role, nor should they be, suggesting that they are not 'top of mind as a principal', and only tend to enter your thinking when an issue raises its ugly, litigious head.

When challenged with the question about how much knowledge principals need to effectively lead their schools, the respondents offered different levels of legal understanding. One respondent stated the principal is less of a teacher and more of a CEO and hence has to know a sufficient amount to adequately protect his/her school from the legal arrows that are fired towards it. Another participant alluded to the fact that as principal, you need to know as much as you can so as to avoid legal traps in the school. Another indicated that a law degree is probably not required, but total ignorance is putting the organisation at huge risk. She surmised that you need to have some idea of the law governing schools and importantly need to understand the basic principles and intention of those laws.

As indicated by one respondent: for the profession at large to be successful, principals will need a heightened awareness of legal matters as they relate to the school setting. This concept, coupled with the notions of protection of both students and the school, in addition to the philosophical view that we are becoming more litigious as a society all mean that tomorrow's school leaders will need to become more legally literate in order to maintain a safe and well managed educational environment.

1.6 The International Context

More broadly, education authorities in jurisdictions internationally are required to establish guidelines for their school educators in increasingly complex societies. For example, in 2015 Europe experienced the highest movement of displaced people across multiple borders since the end of World War II (WWII). The vast migration of refugees and their acceptance in new communities is compounded by the underlying current of fear generated by terrorist attacks such as the Paris shootings and bombings of 13 November, 2015. The third and final section of this book considers what the response of educators internationally might be in the face of the conflicting challenges posed globally. The principal international legislation for working with children and young people is the United Nations Convention on the Rights of the Child (UNCRC) which provides the base from which each signatory nation can build a response. The convention clearly sets out our responsibilities in regards to the children trapped in adult created circumstances. All young people under the age of 18 are considered to come under the protection of the convention – unless a specific country has set the age of majority earlier. Articles 28 and 29 of the UNCRC have particular significance for education authorities and educators. Both articles could provide a global education foundation of rights, responsibilities and core curriculum. A knowledge and understanding of the UNCRC provisions becomes essential for educators if they are to meet the global challenge of educating the world's children. Principals and teachers in Australia and internationally need to adopt and adapt the UNCRC provisions to meet the needs of all children in their care, whether permanent resident, citizen or refugee seeking shelter.

Section three of this book focuses on these international legislative frameworks including educators' knowledge and understanding of their obligations under the UNCRC, and also awareness of how their national and local policies both support and contravene the domestic and international legislation. Chapters in this section explore issues surrounding the development of citizenship, the rights and education of the children of native peoples and of refugees, and legislation internationally that is impacting on the safety, care and education of young people.

References

Allison, G. (1983). Public and private management: Are they fundamentally alike in all unimportant respects? In J. Perry & K. Kramer (Eds.), *Public management, public and private perspectives*. Palo Alto: Mayfield Publishing.

Australian Government. (1992). *Disability discrimination act*. Canberra: Governor General's Department. Retrieved from https://www.legislation.gov.au/Series/C2004A04426

Australian Government Department of Education and Training. (2005). Disability standards for education. Canberra: Attorney-General's Department, Department of Education, Science and Training. Retrieved from https://education.gov.au/disability-standards-education

Bauer, S., & Bogotch, I. (2006). Modeling site-based decision making: School practices in the age of accountability. *Journal of Educational Administration, 44*(5), 446–470.

Best, R. (2001). Where child protection systems and schools meet. (K. Lindsay, Ed.) *Australia and New Zealand Journal of Law and Education, 6*(1 & 2), 3–14.

Bolton, B. (2002). Schools, the internet and the law. (A. Knott, & D. Stewart, Eds.) *ANZELA Reporter, 8*(1), 29–52.

Butler, D., & Mathews, B. (2007). *Schools and the law*. Sydney: Federation Press.

Butlin, M. (2014). *Legal principles for school principals: An investigation into the impact of education law on school leaders*. Unpublished master's thesis, University of Southern Queensland, Australia.

Campbell, M., Butler, D., & Kift, S. (2008). A school's duty to provide a safe learning environment: Does this include cyberbullying? (J. Cumming, & E. Dickson, Eds.) *Australia and New Zealand Journal of Law and Education, 13*(2), 21–32.

Christie, P., & Christie, S. (2008, October). *Family law and the school.* Paper presented at the 17th Annual Conference of the Australia and New Zealand Education Law Association, Christchurch.

Collier, J., & Roberts, J. (2001). An ethic for corporate governance. *Business Ethics Quarterly, 11*(1), 67–71.

Conte-Mills, K. (2010, October). Family law issues and the school: Views from the school and court. Paper presented at the 19th Annual Conference of the Australia and New Zealand Education Law Association, Sydney.

Davies, A. (1997). Family law reform act, 1995. (D. Stewart, Ed.) *ANZELA Reporter, 4*(1), 3–20.

Dempsey, I. (2003). The Impact of the disability discrimination act on school students with a disability in Australia. (K. Lindsay, Ed.) *Australia and New Zealand Journal of Law and Education, 8*(1), 35–44.

Dickson, E. (2003). Understanding disability: An analysis of the influence of the social model of disability in the drafting of the anti-discrimination act 1991 (Qld) and in its interpretation and application. (K. Lindsay, Ed.) *Australia and New Zealand Journal of Law and Education, 8*(1), 45–68.

Dickson, E. (2004). Disability discrimination, unjustifiable hardship and students with disability-induced problem behaviour. (K. Lindsay, Ed.) *Australia and New Zealand Journal of Law and Education, 9*(2), 37–52.

Dickson, E. (2006). Disability standards for education and the obligations of reasonable adjustment. (J. Cumming, & E. Dickson, Eds.) *Australia and New Zealand Journal of Law and Education, 11*(2), 23–42.

Edwards, J. (1996). Swings and roundabouts: Changing state and federal laws regulating employment and its termination. *Education, law and the future: Proceedings of the fifth ANZELA national conference* (pp. 73–84). Brisbane: Australia and New Zealand Education Law Association (Inc.) Qld Chapter.

Farrell, A. (1998). Bullying in early childhood settings. (A. Knott, & D. Stewart, Eds.) *ANZELA Reporter, 5*(1), 14–17.

Farrell, A. (2001). Legislative responsibility for child protection and human rights in Queensland. (K. Lindsay, Ed.) *Australia and New Zealand Journal of Law and Education, 6*(1 & 2), 15–24.

Ford, D. (2004, December 1). *Emil Ford & Co.* Retrieved from School excursions: Are they worth the risk? http://www.emilford.com.au/imagesDB/wysiwyg/Excursions%20Article.pdf

Forlin, P. (1995). Health and safety law in Australia: Identifying a standard of liability in Australia from an international perspective. In D. Hopkins (Ed.), *Fourth national conference of the Australian and New Zealand education law association* (pp. 120–132). Melbourne: Australian and New Zealand Education Law Association (Inc.).

Hamilton, J. (2002). Discrimination and the enrolment process – Who is in the wrong? In D. Stewart (Ed.), *Legal risk management safety, security and success in education: Proceedings of the 11th annual conference of the Australia and New Zealand education law association* (pp. 329–350). Brisbane: GSM Press.

Hamilton, J., & Smith, F. (2002). The schoolyard fight: Duty of cared owed by teachers. (K. Lindsay, Ed.) *Australia and New Zealand Journal of Law and Education, 7*(1), 88–90.

Healy, K. (1998). *Addressing bullying at the school level through multiple systems.* (A. Knott, & D. Stewart, Eds.) *ANZELA Reporter, 5*(1), 18–22.

Hopkins, D. (2008, April). *The legal obligations of a teacher.* Retrieved from http://www.vit.vic.edu.au/SiteCollectionDocuments/PDF/Legal-obligations-of-a-teacher.pdf

Jackson, J., & Varnham, S. (2007). *Law for educators: School and university law in Australia.* Sydney: LexisNexis Butterworths.

Johnson, P. (2002). Disability discrimination law and occupational health and safety law: How to reconcile the two? In D. Stewart (Ed.), *Legal risk management safety, security and success in education: Proceedings of the 11th annual conference of the Australia and New Zealand education law association* (pp. 277–286). Brisbane: GSM Press.

Keeffe, M. (2003). The principal's governance of inclusion and the requirements of the disability discrimination legislation: Are they words apart? (K. Lindsay, Ed.) *Australia and New Zealand Journal of Law and Education, 8*(1), 69–76.

Kilham, C., & Watson, L. (2014, December). *The Impact of online learning about the disability standards for education on Australian school staff.* Paper presented at the Australian Association for Research in Education Conference, Brisbane.

Knott, A. (1998). Bullying, harassment and violence in schools – Legal options for victims. (A. Knott, & D. Stewart, Eds.) *ANZELA Reporter, 5*(1), 23–31.

Knott, A. (2010). Regulation of the school teaching profession 1970–2010 (Mid-career reflections). In *Australian & New Zealand education law association 19th annual conference* (pp. 51–52). Sydney: ANZELA.

Lindsay, K. (1997). Age discrimination in education: A critique of law and policy. (D. Stewart, Ed). *Australia and New Zealand Journal of Law and Education, 2*(1), 59–68.

Lindsay, K., & Keeffe-Martin, M. (2002). Issues in Australian disability discrimination case law and strategic approaches for the lawful management of inclusion. (K. Lindsay, Ed.) *Australia and New Zealand Journal of Law and Education, 7*(2), 141–160.

Mathews, B. P., Walsh, K. M., Butler, D. A., & Farrell, A. M. (2006). Mandatory reporting by Australian teachers of suspected child abuse and neglect: Legislative requirements and questions for future direction. *Australia and New Zealand Journal of Law and Education, 11*(2), 7–22.

Mawdsley, R. D., & Cumming, J. J. (2008). The origins and development of education law as a separate field of law in the United States and Australia. *Australia and New Zealand Journal of Law & Education, 13*(2), 7–20.

Murray, B. (1997). Failing to report: Potential action for breach of the statutory duty to report child abuse in Victoria. (D. Stewart, Ed.) *Australia and New Zealand Journal of Law and Education, 2*(1), 89–100.

Nolan, B. C., & Spencer, J. D. (Eds.). (1997). *Schools and litigation: Developing legal policies*. Toowoomba: P.C.S. Publications.
Oyston v St Patrick's College [2013] NSWCA 135.
Ramsay, I., & Shorten, A. (1996). *Education and the law*. Sydney: Butterworths.
Rayner, M. (1996). Student's rights. *Education, law and the future: Proceedings of the fifth ANZELA national conference* (pp. 19–30). Brisbane: Australia and New Zealand Education Law Association (Inc.) QLD Chapter.
Salidu, M. (1994). Discrimination and schools: The legislation and its effects. In D. Stewart (Ed.), *Third annual conference of the Australian and New Zealand education law association* (pp. 173–193). Brisbane: Qld University of Technology Press.
Simmonds, R. (2005). Is our right to privacy at risk in a technology world? In *Free speech, privacy and property rights in education* (pp. 11–35). Fremantle: Promaco Conventions Pty Ltd.
Slee, P. (1998). Bullying in Australian Schools. (A. Knott, & D. Stewart, Eds.) *ANZELA Reporter, 5*(1), 3–6.
Squelch, J., & Goldacre, L. (2009). School prospectuses and the potential liability of private schools under section 52 of the trade practices act 1974 (Cth). (J. Cumming, & E. Dickson, Eds.) *International Journal of Law and Education, 14*(1), 39–50.
Stafford, N. (2004, September). *What can a school do to ensure student and staff wellbeing and safety in light of the Australian high court's decision in Purvis v State of NSW*. Paper presented at the 13th Annual Conference of the Australia and New Zealand Education Law Association, Wellington.
Stewart, D. (1996). Principals' knowledge of law affecting schools. (D. Stewart, Ed.) *Australia and New Zealand Journal of Law and Education, 1*(1), 111–129.
Stewart, D. (1998). Legalisation of education: Implications for principals' professional knowledge. *Journal of Educational Administration, 36*(2), 129–145.
Stewart, D. (2003). Inclusion: How far does a school have to go? Ensuring best practice: The case of 'I'. (K. Lindsay, Ed.) *Australia and New Zealand Journal of Law and Education, 8*(1), 77–86.
Stewart, D., & Cope, B. (1996). Judicious behaviour management. *Education, law and the future: Proceedings of the fifth ANZELA national conference* (pp. 173–180). Brisbane: Australia and New Zealand Education Law Association (Inc.) Qld Chapter.
Stewart, D., & Knott, A. (2002). *Schools, courts and the law: Managing student welfare*. Sydney: Pearson Education Australia.
Teh, M. (2009). *Principals and legal risk: Complacency or concern?* Paper presentated as the 18th Annual Conference of the Australia and New Zealand Education Law Association, Melbourne.
Teh, K. (2014). The case for legal literacy for educators. *Australian & New Zealand education law association 23rd annual conference* (pp. 387–412). Adelaide: ANZELA.
Trimble, A. J., Cranston, N., & Allen, J. M. (2012). School principals and education law: What do they know, what they need to know? *Leading & Managing, 18*(2), 46–61.

Trimmer, K. (2003). *Review of the West Australian department of education regulatory framework.* Paper read at Australian Association of Research in Education Conference, Auckland.

Trimmer, K. (2011). *Non-compliance by school principals: The effects of experience, stakeholder characteristics and governance mechanisms on reasoned risk-taking in decision-making.* Thesis for award of Doctor of Business Administration, Curtin University of Technology, Australia.

Tronc, K. (1996). *You, your school and the law.* Brisbane: Fernfawn Publications.

Tronc, K. (1999, September). *Schools and the law: Some backdates, updates and mandates.* Paper presented at the 8th Annual Conference of the Australia and New Zealand Education Law Association, Brisbane.

Tronc, K., & Sleigh, D. (1989). *Australian teachers and the law.* Sydney: Butterworths.

Varnham, S. (2002). Mainstreaming or Maindumping? Daniels v the attorney general. Equality of access to education for children with special needs in New Zealand. In D. Stewart (Ed.), *Legal risk management safety, security and success in education: Proceedings of the 11th annual conference of the Australia and New Zealand education law association* (pp. 239–254). Brisbane: GSM Press.

Walker, S. (1995). Schools and defamation. In D. Hopkins (Ed.), *Fourth national conference of the Australian and New Zealand education law association* (pp. 15–25). Melbourne: Australian and New Zealand Education Law Association (Inc.).

Weegen, C. (2013). Defining 'reasonable force' in the modern school environment. *International Journal of Law & Education, 18*(1), 83–97.

Williams, P. (1995). Touching students: A legal dilemma for teachers. (A. Knott, & D. Stewart, Eds.) *ANZELA Reporter, 3*(1), 17–23.

Williams, P. (2002). Educational employers and foreseeable risks of harm. (K. Lindsay, Ed.) *Australia and New Zealand Journal of Law and Education, 7*(1), 81–83.

Wilson, L. (2014, October 14). Frightened teachers avoiding excursions. *The Courier Mail.* Brisbane.

Winram, M. (2008). Lawyers and educators working together to protect schools, teachers and students from You-Tube and other websites that malign them, *Achieving excellence: Lawyers and educators working together* (pp. 133–150). Christchurch.

Wirtz, V., Cribb, A., & Barber, N. (2005). Reimbursement decisions in health policy-extending our understanding of the elements of decision-making. *Health Policy, 73*, 330–338.

2

Education Law, Schools and School Principals: What Does the Research Tell Us?

Allison Trimble and Neil Cranston

2.1 Introduction and Background

This chapter overviews some key aspects of recent Australian research in Education Law,[1] that is, "those areas of jurisprudence that bear on the operation of … schools" (Alexander and Alexander 2011, p. 2). In Australia, the field of Education Law research in schools[2] is composed of two broad streams of interest, one of which is law-focused, examining the application of particular areas of the law to the education context, and the other, education-focused, concentrating primarily upon the impact of law on, and the responses of, educational institutions and actors. This chapter is education-focused, specifically concerned with school principals in Tasmania,[3] the impact of Education Law on them, their theoretical knowledge and practical understanding of the law, and the ways they consider their legal support might be improved.

[1] *Education Law* is the term generally adopted in Australia and equates with *School Law* more commonly adopted in the United States and Canada.

[2] In addition to school-based Education Law, the term *Education Law* may also refer to law impacting the operation of non-school institutions in higher and vocational training. For the purposes of this chapter, however, the use of the term is limited to law affecting schools.

[3] Tasmania is one of six States and two Territories in Australia. It has a population of about half a million, the majority of which are located in four major cities and towns. By sector, most students attend government schools, with the remainder in independent/non-government, Catholic and other faith-based institutions.

A. Trimble (✉) • N. Cranston
University of Tasmania, Launceston and Hobart, Australia
e-mail: allison.trimble@utas.edu.au; n.c.cranston@utas.edu.au

K. Trimmer et al. (eds.), *The Palgrave Handbook of Education Law for Schools*,
https://doi.org/10.1007/978-3-319-77751-1_2

The research was undertaken in a context where the importance of law and legal issues in the working lives of school principals, and the operation of their schools, has never been higher (Trimble et al. 2012). Whether a principal is dealing with a complaint about disability discrimination, counselling staff for unprofessional conduct, reporting a case of a student's neglect or abuse, managing the school's copyright exemptions, ensuring that photographs in promotional materials are the subject of appropriate permissions, or assessing the risks of an out-of-school activity, the school leader's legal decisions are potentially critical to the safety and welfare of students, their families, and members of staff, as well as the smooth and effective running of the school. Indeed, the importance of school leaders' engagement with legal matters in the course of their roles and responsibilities has now been recognised nationally in Australia as a central aspect of principalship practice under the *Australian Professional Standard for Principals* (the *Professional Standard*) (AITSL 2012).

Australian research regarding the impact of Education Law on the working lives of school principals is limited, with two major studies undertaken some years ago, by Stewart (1996) and McCann (2006), both located in Queensland. While not the earliest Education Law research pursued in this country, Stewart's (1996) survey-based inquiry was the first to comprehensively examine the legal burdens borne by Government school principals. That study was followed up a decade later by the McCann (2006) research, largely replicating the Stewart methodology but focused on the experiences of Catholic school principals. In addition, a small-scale study was conducted by the researcher in Northern Tasmania in 2011, with Government primary school principals (Trimble et al. 2012). The Stewart and McCann studies in particular provided important background for the research reported here.

Despite the growing impact of law on schools, and the changing legal landscape within which principals operate, the empirical knowledge base regarding school principals and Education Law in Australia has remained limited across more than two decades. The present research provides important contemporary base-line data not only for Tasmania, but also for Australian schools more broadly.

2.2 Focus and Design of the Research

Drawing on a larger research study (Trimble 2017), this chapter examines the impact of legal issues on the working lives of principals in Tasmania in schools across all schooling sectors, particularly in relation to legal literacy and legal consciousness, the legal context of principalship, negative impacts from their dealings with legal matters, and possibilities for improving the situation as perceived by educators themselves.

The study used a mixed methods design, based on both quantitative and qualitative data collection, analysis, and findings. Quantitative data was collected using a 44 item, on-line survey developed specifically for this study, which drew on ideas used in previous research. This was accompanied by a series of semi-structured, in-depth interviews with school principals, supervisors of principals, senior system leaders, administrators, as well as an Education Law lawyer.

As part of the on-line survey, participants were asked a number of True/False/Don't Know questions in relation to Tasmanian disability, sexual and racial discrimination law (*Anti-Discrimination Act* 1998 [Tas]). The answers were used to assess the accuracy of participants' legal knowledge. This approach has been applied in previous Australian research and in almost every reported study from the United States and Canada, although the content and form of the questions has varied. The limitations of this approach are, however, acknowledged: participants may have had only minimal experience and training in the relevant legislation; knowledge about one particular area of the law does not necessarily apply to other legal areas; and the on-line nature of the survey meant that participants could have consulted a more expert source to determine the correct answers. As such, the accuracy of Tasmanian school principals' legal knowledge, so identified, should be treated with some caution. The survey also sought data on the professional and personal impacts of Education Law, and the participants' legal learning engagement and needs.

Participants in the survey phase constituted a non-random convenience sample. From 35 people who accessed the survey, 34 indicated their eligibility to participate (as appointed or acting principals of Tasmanian schools) and went on to complete the survey. Their participation turned on awareness of the survey through notices from various educational organisations (the Tasmanian Principals' Association, Independent Schools Tasmania and the Association of Heads of Independent Schools Australia, Tasmanian branch), their employment status, and their willingness to respond to the on-line survey. The self-selected volunteer sample of participants increased the likelihood of obtaining useful data because the participants were more likely to be engaged with the topic of research than might be the case with a random sample. Further details of the survey are available elsewhere (Trimble 2017).

The sample of participants interviewed for the study covered a wider mix of persons, including school principals, principal supervisors, senior system leaders and administrators. That sample was constituted from volunteers from the survey phase – a small nested component (Collins and O'Cathain 2009) – as well as persons identified purposively and by recommendation (Brundrett and Rhodes 2014; Cresswell and Plano Clark 2007). A total of 26 interviews were conducted across these groups. Further details of the interviews are available elsewhere (Trimble 2017).

All the interviews were conducted by the researcher, face-to-face, generally with a single participant. The interviews were semi-structured in nature, in that they followed a general framework to ensure critical points were covered (Bell 2005). However, the interviewer remained free to reformulate questions, give prompts, and follow-up points of interest (Morgan 1998; Sarantakos 2005). In all instances, the schedules of interview questions were provided to participants prior to the interview, so that they had an opportunity to consider the material, and their responses, before the interview itself.

2.3 Research Findings and Discussion

Although the following discussion overviews the research findings under a number of headings, it should be noted that issues raised under one heading are invariably relate to those discussed under other headings.

2.3.1 Areas of Law Dealt with by Principals and the Context of Law in Schools

While the general nature of Education Law matters dealt with by school principals in Western countries appears to be relatively constant and universal, principals are, nevertheless, faced with novel legal situations from time to time, deriving from differences in the legal environment of schools, including the jurisdictional legal structure. Moreover, elements of the legal context of a school vary with changes in technology, social developments, and the like. As such, the educational legal environment can be considered to be both fluid and unpredictable.

It is clear from this research that Tasmanian school principals deal with a broad range of legal issues, which may arise with little or no prior warning. Many of these matters involve the safety and welfare of students and their families, and school staff. One system leader observed that, in recent years, "The big ticket ones in schools are Family Law, it certainly has a significant impact on a school", which view was echoed by a number of participants. Other matters raised by principals concerned duty of care (negligence) and child welfare, employment and discrimination. Of course, many of these are not single-issue matters, but rather have potentially complex legal implications. These findings, made a decade or two after the previous Australian studies, closely reflect the previous research with Queensland school principals (McCann 2006; Stewart 1996), as well as the studies from New Zealand (Wardle 2006), Canada (Findlay 2007), and the United States (Eberwein 2008).

This research proposed that the legal issues arising in any particular school depend to a large extent on the institution's internal and external legal environments, both of which are individual to that particular school. As a result, the legal problems that a principal must deal with, and the manner of dealing, are as unique as the school itself. The situation will, in all likelihood, be further complicated by the involvement of the school's primary stakeholders including students and their parents (and their past and present relationship with the principal, teachers, and the school as a whole), school boards (where they exist) and staff members (Connolly et al. 2017). The religious influence in some faith-based schools is also reported as a factor.

The principals' core legal concerns involving safety and welfare arise predominantly, although not entirely, from the internal legal environment. The principal's task, however, also requires that the boundary between the school and its external environment be continuously monitored (Boyd 2016), so that the school leader becomes aware of any change in the environment that may constitute an opportunity or a threat. This environmental scanning enables a principal to proactively manage changes to the regulation and compliance regimes, institute action to resolve a dispute at its earliest stages, and if unsuccessful, seek expert legal support as soon as appropriate.

2.3.2 Principals' Level of Legal Knowledge

While it is not expected that principals have formal legal qualifications, it is widely accepted that school principals need some legal knowledge in order to adequately fulfill their legal responsibilities, as acknowledged by the *Professional Standard* (Australian Institute for Teaching and School Leadership 2012). This research examined a number of issues impacting on a principal's legal knowledge, including:

- legal preparation and development;
- legal confidence;
- the accuracy and adequacy of legal knowledge; and,
- sources of legal information.

2.3.2.1 Legal Preparation and Development

Not surprisingly, preparation and development of school principals in relation to Education Law impacts their overall capacity to deal appropriately with legal matters. However, participants reported legal training as absent or limited, with one in this research noting, "Something I wasn't trained for. Something I've had to learn on the job." Another commented, "You learn it as you go" while yet another confessed, "I'm rattled to see so many areas in which I am definitely under-educated".

This research revealed a very low rate of tertiary legal study among participants, lower than reported in previous Australian research (McCann 2006; Stewart 1996). This general absence of tertiary legal training may be a cause for concern. It is possible that a principal of a Tasmanian school may have had as little as three hours formal training in relation to Education Law, typically received as a pre-service teacher. However, even in the United States, where pre-license tertiary Education Law study is widely mandated, the evidence indicates that school principals nevertheless continue to lack adequate legal knowledge (Eberwein 2008).

Most principals across all three schooling sectors reported having attended legal professional development in the previous year, although a considerable proportion of older principals had not, with some very experienced principals holding the view that they had sufficient knowledge and neither wanted nor needed extra training. One noted, "I'm pretty experienced and well over most things." This finding appears not to have been reflected previously in the literature. It can, however, be argued that the participation of older principals in such professional development is important on two counts. Firstly, it enables more experienced principals to maintain the currency of their knowledge in light of the dynamic nature of the legal environments they deal with, and secondly, it provides an opportunity for them to share their experiences with younger principals.

2.3.2.2 Legal Confidence

Almost two thirds of principals in this study reported feeling a positive level of confidence when dealing with legal issues. However, that sense of confidence was not supported by the accuracy of their legal knowledge as demonstrated by their responses to the legal knowledge questions in the survey. Clearly, some principals may be over-confident about their own legal knowledge. This may be problematic, where a principal's over-confidence contributes to their relying on their own intuition or judgment when it is inappropriate to do so (Strahilevitz et al. 2015).

2.3.2.3 Accuracy and Adequacy of Principals' Legal Knowledge

In terms of the legal knowledge questions in the survey, participants' mean score (average 53% correct responses) fell short of the 70% proficiency level generally applied in Education Law research. Catholic and government school principals scored higher than did Independent school leaders. Despite continuing improvements in training technology, information access, legal training opportunities, and the requirements of the *Professional Standard* (AITSL 2012), the overall results on the accuracy of principals' legal knowledge were generally equivalent to the knowledge levels of Queensland principals reported by Stewart (1996) and McCann (2006) and were within the range of results reported from around the globe.

While principals are not, and are not expected to be, lawyers, it is suggested that a principal should have sufficient basic legal knowledge to deal appropriately with most *routine* education law matters that arise within a school, and understand the need to seek support when appropriate, such as in more complex *non-routine* matters (Gallant 2004; Stewart and McCann 1999). This issue of decision support introduces the fundamentally important concept of the school leaders' legal support network.

2.3.2.4 Legal Sources Accessed by Principals

This research identified that the mix of decision support accessed by a principal is contingent on a number of matters, such as the context of the legal problem (including the parties involved and the seriousness of the likely consequences), the principal's own "internal state", and the accessibility of advisors within the legal support framework (subject to restrictions like time and money). A principal faced with a *routine* legal issue may consider that it is sufficient to rely on their own knowledge and experience perhaps augmented by a check of relevant policy, the views of a colleague, or a law handbook/reference if available. This approach accommodates situations involving quick decisions on essentially structured problems within a relatively stable environment (Heyden et al. 2013). Principals report such legal situations to be common, and, more often than not, they are adequately dealt with. However, for *non-routine* matters, falling beyond the principal's previous experience and with the capacity for serious long-term consequences, principals more appropriately seek the support of systemic or school advisors and/or consult a lawyer, if available and thought to be required (Collins et al. 2011). And, of course, there is every position in between.

In large systems and schools a principal is likely to be supported by an extensive legal support framework, encompassing lawyers familiar with the school and its context, specialist advisers in functional areas like student welfare, staff development, and work health and safety, as well as a comprehensive suite of policies and guidelines. However, in smaller Independent schools, such as some faith-based schools represented in this research, the level of support is likely to be much less than described above, potentially exposing the principal and the school to legal pressures.

Importantly, as this research demonstrated, a principal's legal support framework may be used differently from one legal issue to another. The sources constituting the legal support frameworks differ among principals, among schools within a system, and among schooling systems. The constitution of the frameworks inevitably changes over time as principals' levels of experience grow, legal requirements change, school policies are amended, and novel issues arise (Arendt et al. 2005).

The findings in this study suggest that, because the accuracy of principals' legal knowledge may be limited, it is important that they participate in relevant professional development to improve the standard of their knowledge, they have reasonable access to a sound legal support framework, and that they recognise the need, in some circumstances, to seek decision support from sources more legally expert than themselves (Bonaccio and Dalal 2006). It also needs to be acknowledged that principals may face dispositions (for example, over-confidence) and practical barriers (for example, lawyers' fees) that potentially militate against their seeking legal decision support (Blackburn et al. 2010).

Given the limitations in some principals' legal knowledge identified here and supported by research elsewhere, and the importance of the legal decision support they receive from legally-qualified and non-legally-qualified advisors and resources, it is clear that the capacity for legal decision-making within a school should be considered holistically rather than focusing only on the principals' legal knowledge test result. Such an approach would take the results of a legal knowledge test into account along with principals' legal consciousness as well as looking at the decision support available to the principal through his or her legal support framework.

2.3.3 Legal Consciousness of Principals

Legal consciousness is a concept adopted from research in the field of Law and Society (Cooper 1995) and relates to the beliefs held by non-lawyers (such as school principals) about the law and its operation (Hoffmann 2003). The findings from this research recognised participants' beliefs that the law would not apply to certain kinds of acts that were carried out for some higher motivation; for example, if they were done in the interest of safety, or because they were ethical, or made good sense in the circumstances or were good for the school. Several principals in this research acknowledged that they considered such matters when dealing with legal issues.

Whether principal's beliefs about the law are legally accurate or not – and some views reported in the study were not – it appears that such beliefs may have the capacity to influence principals' legal decision making. This research has highlighted legal consciousness as a potentially new aspect of school principals' legal decision-making, and one that warrants further inquiry.

2.3.4 The Legal Environment Faced by Principals

As noted earlier, principals' dealings with legal issues are impacted by a diverse, varied and constantly changing set of influences located within the schools' internal legal environments as well as their external legal environments. Internal factors identified as relevant to principals' legal dealings involved matters concerning the primary stakeholders of the school (students and families, staff, school boards and others) such as the demands of legal risk management (Starr 2012), school legalisation, especially the willingness of disgruntled stakeholders to threaten or indeed institute legal action (D'Cruz 2016), and the general rights awareness and activism of students, parents and staff (Butler and Mathews 2007). External factors identified in this research included matters from the international arena, national concerns, Tasmanian State issues as well as issues relating specifically to the education sector.

Notwithstanding their shared environmental influences, it is important to recognise that every school has its own individual legal context (Guthrie and Schuermann 2010) that reflects among other things: its mission, the community it serves, its history and background and the experiences and backgrounds of the school principal, students and their families, and staff. Within each school the principal can be expected to place differing priorities on the various legal environmental factors (Cummings and Worley 2014) and make decisions to bridge or buffer the environmental changes (Bush 2017). The considerations and decisions made by one principal are unlikely to exactly match those of another. As such, legal decisions taken by principals need to be carefully considered in light of the school's internal and external legal environments.

2.3.5 Impacts on Principals from Dealing with Legal Issues

This research identified several direct and indirect negative consequences flowing from principals' dealings with legal matters. These included the financial costs paid by non-government schools to obtain legal advice,[4] and the sterilisation of learning activities from an application of an inappropriate standard of risk. Important issues related to principals' personal and professional lives were also noted, such as the time consumed by legal issues, and the levels of stress involved. The issue of legal stress was identified in earlier research (McCann 2006; Stewart 1996; Teh 2008).

Several principals in non-government schools identified the financial costs as an important factor when dealing with legal issues. Where the school is seen as an open system, the potential cost of obtaining legal advice – if that is the path taken by the school – becomes a resource-dependency issue (Ballantine and Spade 2011) in which the cost is weighed against the likely benefit, judged in light of the values and priorities of the school. A number of principals identified this as a tension within their leadership decisions. The research identifies (perhaps unsurprisingly) that small schools with limited resources feel the impact more keenly.

Of course, it is not always necessary for a principal to seek expert advice from a lawyer on every legal issue that arises. As noted earlier, where the law is relatively stable principals reported that their personal legal knowledge was sufficient to deal with many routine legal matters, particularly when decision-making was supported by consultation with policies, a law manual, and functional specialists from the principal's legal support framework. Where expert legal advice is necessary, there are options such as group legal arrangements that can be pursued by schools seeking to limit their legal costs.

The other costs identified, such as the sterilisation of learning activities, and principals' time and stress, are important issues for the core activities of the school, potentially impacting negatively on teaching and learning generally

[4] In Tasmania, at the time of data collection (2014–2015), government schools had open and free access to advice on legal matters provided by the Department of Education's Legal Services Unit.

and the principal's many other responsibilities in particular A misapplication of the principles of legal risk management or an unfounded fear of litigation may lead to principals unnecessarily removing valuable student learning opportunities from the school program, and some principals reported being uncertain as to whether their approach to risk management was appropriate. Several noted that teachers often indicated that they thought the risk management processes were excessive and unnecessary.

If the legal stress experienced by a school principal reaches an unhealthy level (Maxwell and Riley 2017), then the negative impacts on their well-being are likely to affect the principal's leadership roles in a variety of ways. In some circumstances this may be unavoidable, simply because the principal is the school's legal decision-maker, but is not a lawyer. Nevertheless, it is clear that negative impacts, which may ultimately affect the students and staff of the school, should be limited wherever possible.

2.3.6 Principals' Suggestions to Enhance Their Education Law Support

The findings of this study concerning principals' suggestions to improve their legal support largely reflected the previous Australian research (McCann 2006; Stewart 1996), as well as recommendations made in studies from the United States (e.g., Eberwein 2008) and Canada (e.g., Cooper 2011). In the broadest terms, principals proposed strengthening professional legal preparation and development, as well as the provision of legal training for teachers and pre-service teachers. It was argued that the priority for additional training should be given to core legal topics, focusing on the safety and welfare as well as the legal rights of students and their families, and school staff. In particular, principals suggested that legal professional learning should be offered on an in-service or on-line basis, be shorter, more tightly focused, and more frequent, use real-life scenarios, and emphasise the stages when it may be appropriate to seek expert legal support.

While there have been developments along these lines in Tasmania and elsewhere, there remains some way to go for many schools and school leaders. Of course additional legal training and decision support for principals would impose financial costs and a toll in terms of time and training resources on principals, schools and schooling systems that may prove to be challenging in the short term. However, such costs need to be balanced against the longer term benefits of better quality legal decision making on the part of principals

(McCann 2006; Stewart 1996), the recognition and protection of legal rights of students and their families, and schools themselves (Eberwein 2008), and the assessment of legal risk in academic and co-curricular activities to ensure both that personal safety is not compromised and that student learning is maximised (Starr 2012).

It is likely that schooling authorities in Australia have been, or should have been, aware for some time of the professional and personal impacts on school principals caused by legal stress (Riley 2017). Such stress is contributed to, at least in part, by weaknesses in principals' legal preparation and development, and their legal support frameworks. This research argues that there is at least an ethical obligation (in addition to any legal responsibility under Workplace Health and Safety legislation), on credentialing authorities such as universities, and employers, to provide appropriate levels of training and resources to reduce legal job stress within the principalship. By doing so, they may contribute to principals' wellbeing and help to ensure that school leaders do not suffer physical, emotional, or psychological injury.

The views of participants in this research indicate that the legal knowledge held by a school principal should be basic, but accurate. Principals should know enough about the law to appropriately deal with most routine, recurrent problems, and understand when to seek support in dealing with other non-routine issues. This is consistent with most decision-makers in the business world, who typically do not make important, complex, decisions in isolation, but rather accept advice received from others within, or outside, the organisational structure (Bonaccio and Dalal 2006). It is unrealistic to expect a school principal who does not hold a legal qualification to make decisions regarding novel and complex legal issues, with the likelihood of serious consequences, and perhaps involving multiple disputing parties, without appropriate legal decision support. The research (based in Australia and elsewhere) strongly suggests that every school principal should have access to a formal legal support framework, which includes up-to-date information resources together with qualified experienced functional specialist advisors and lawyers.

The significance of deficits in principals' legal preparation and training is not limited to individual principals and their schools, but may have longer-term impacts on the future recruitment of principals from the profession. It is clear from the literature that the legal responsibilities and workloads of school leaders may contribute to reluctance on the part of potential principals to take on the role of school leader (Lock and Lummis 2014). Perceptions of legal job stress in the principalship may contribute to potential candidates deciding not to pursue promotion (Klocko and Wells 2015).

2.4 Summary and Conclusions

In recent years the legal environment within which Australian school principals operate has become increasingly legalised. School leaders now face an ever-expanding range of legal issues; areas of law are becoming more complex; and there is a widely-held perception that school stakeholders, internal and external, increasingly turn to the law to settle disputes (Teh 2008; Trimble et al. 2012). Principal preparation and development in Education Law – across all education sectors – has not kept pace with these growing legal demands. Generally, school leaders in this study and in other research have been found to possess a low level of legal literacy, despite (in some cases) an unwarranted level of confidence in their own legal knowledge. For *routine* legal matters requiring a standard response or continuation of the status quo, this may not present great difficulties. However, when a principal must deal with a *non-routine* legal matter, reliance on past personal experience or that of a colleague principal, coupled with an unwillingness to seek expert advice, may prove problematic. In such circumstances, the availability of accurate legal advice through a legal support framework, particularly legal advice from a qualified legal advisor, and a willingness to accept advice is crucial. Further, the legal decisions taken by school principals do not always depend solely on their knowledge *of the law*. As identified in this research, many will be guided also, or even instead of, by their legal consciousness *about the law*, which may not accord with the law.

The legal element of contemporary principalship clearly creates significant levels of stress for many school leaders. This is contributed to by deficits in their own legal understandings, but may also be exacerbated by: financial costs of legal advice; time consumed in dealing with legal problems; the degree to which such issues distract from the principal's central leadership role; and the potential impact on teaching and learning in the school.

This research, and other Education Law studies, indicates that all schooling sectors in Australia should be actively using the statement about Education Law in the *Professional Standards* (AITSL 2012) to drive focused legal professional learning for principals. This research highlights that such professional development should, as a priority, address matters that impact the safety and welfare of students and their families, and school staff, including: duty of care (negligence); employment; discrimination; and Family Law issues.

This research has provided some useful (base-line) data for Tasmania, and highlights a need for the exploration of similar issues in other educational jurisdictions to develop better and more broadly based understandings of the impact of Education Law on schools and school leaders. At the outset it was noted that, to date, Education Law has been an under-researched area, yet it remains a critical one for school principals as they navigate the changing and challenging operational contexts for their schools. On-going research in the area is indicated, with the importance of developing a better understanding illustrated by the comments of a Tasmanian system leader from this study:

> *If I think back 10 or 15 years ago, our principals … didn't have to be as savvy in this space … They didn't have to deal with these areas (of law). But we do now, so I suppose we have to keep pace.*

References

Alexander, K., & Alexander, M. (2011). *American public school law* (8th ed.). Belmont: Thomson West.

Anti-Discrimination Act 1998 (Tas).

Arendt, L., Priem, R., & Ndofor, H. (2005). A CEO-adviser model of strategic decision making. *Journal of Management, 31*(5), 680–699.

Australian Institute for Teaching and School Leadership (AITSL). (2012). Australian professional standard for principals. Melbourne: AITSL Retrieved from http://www.aitsl.edu.au/australian-professional-standard-forprincipals

Ballantine, J., & Spade, J. (2011). *Schools and society: A sociological approach to education.* Thousand Oaks: Pine Forge Press.

Bell, J. (2005). *Doing your research project.* Maidenhead: Open University Press.

Blackburn, R., Tanewski, G., & Carey, P. (2010). *Advice seeking strategies: Entrepreneurs' and accountants' perspectives.* London: Kingston University.

Bonaccio, S., & Dalal, R. (2006). Advice taking and decision-making: An integrative literature review, and implications for the organizational sciences. *Organizational Behavior and Human Decision Processes, 101*(2), 127–151. https://doi.org/10.1016/j.obhdp.2006.07.001.

Boyd, R. (2016). The "gatekeeper principle". *Perspectives, 2016*(1), 3–4.

Brundrett, M., & Rhodes, C. (2014). *Researching educational leadership and management.* London: Sage.

Bush, T. (2017). Governing schools and colleges. *Educational Management Administration & Leadership, 45*(1), 3–4. https://doi.org/10.1177/1741143216671044.

Butler, D., & Mathews, B. (2007). *Schools and the law.* Sydney: The Federation Press.

Collins, E., Percy, E., Smith, E., & Kruschke, J. (2011). Integrating advice and experience: Learning and decision making with social and nonsocial cues. *Journal of Personality and Social Psychology, 100*(6), 967–982. https://doi.org/10.1037/a0022982.

Collins, K., & O'Cathain, A. (2009). Ten points about mixed methods research to be considered by the novice researcher. *International Journal of Multiple Research Approaches, 3*(1), 2–7.

Connolly, M., Farrell, C., & James, C. (2017). An analysis of the stakeholder model of public boards and the case of school governing bodies in England and Wales. *Educational Management Administration & Leadership, 45*(1), 5–19. https://doi.org/10.1177/1741143215607879.

Cooper, D. (1995). Local government legal consciousness in the shadow of juridifcation. *Journal of Law and Society, 22*(4), 506–526.

Cooper, T. (2011). The legal literacy levels of educators in one family of schools in Ontario. M.Ed. Unpublished, Nipissing University, North Bay. Retrieved from http://search.proquest.com.ezproxy.utas.edu.au/pqdt/docview/904667231/abstract/D8047370663E496APQ/1?accountid=14245. ProQuest Dissertations & Theses A&I database (MR80926).

Cresswell, J., & Plano Clark, V. (2007). *Designing and conducting mixed methods research*. Thousand Oaks: Sage.

Cummings, T., & Worley, C. (2014). *Organization development and change* (10th ed.). Mason: Cengage Learning.

D'Cruz, C. (2016). Legal actions against schools: Is your school prepared? *School Governance, 28*, 1–4.

Eberwein, H. (2008). Raising legal literacy in public schools, a call for principal leadership: A national study of secondary school principals' knowledge of public school law. Ed.D. Unpublished, University of Massachusetts Amherst, Amherst. Retrieved from http://search.proquest.com.ezproxy.utas.edu.au/pqdt/docview/304576529/previewPDF/C5B8D3C3D11A40D7PQ/1?accountid=14245. ProQuest Dissertations and Theses A&I database (3325154).

Findlay, N. (2007). *Ignorance of the law is no excuse: School administrators' knowledge of education law*. Regina: Saskatchewan School Boards Association.

Gallant, J. (2004). Advising principals: Using law to improve schools and support school leaders. In R. Flynn (Ed.), *Law in education: Help or hindrance?* (pp. 403–429). Markham: Bluestone Print.

Guthrie, J., & Schuermann, P. (2010). *Successful school leadership: Planning, politics, performance, and power*. Boston: Allyn & Bacon.

Heyden, M., van Doorn, S., Reimer, M., Van Den Bosch, F., & Volberda, H. (2013). Perceived environmental dynamism, relative competitive performance, and top management team heterogeneity: Examining correlates of upper echelons' advice-seeking. *Organization Studies, 34*(9), 1327–1356. https://doi.org/10.1177/0170840612470229.

Hoffman, E. (2003). Legal consciousness and dispute resolution: Different disputing behaviour at two similar taxicab companies. *Law & Social Inquiry, 28*(3), 691–716.

Klocko, B., & Wells, C. (2015). Workload pressures of principals: A focus on renewal, support, and mindfulness. *NASSP Bulletin, 99*(4), 332–355. https://doi.org/10.1177/0192636515619727.

Lock, G., & Lummis, G. (2014). Complying with school accountability requirements and the impact on school leaders. *Australian Journal of Teacher Education, 39*(2), 58–69.

Maxwell, A., & Riley, P. (2017). Emotional demands, emotional labour and occupational outcomes in school principals. *Educational Management Administration & Leadership, 45*(3), 484–502. https://doi.org/10.1177/1741143215607878.

McCann, P. (2006). Principals' understanding of aspects of the law impacting on the administration of Catholic schools: Some implications for leadership. PhD Published, Australian Catholic University, Melbourne. Retrieved from http://dlibrary.acu.edu.au/digitaltheses/public/adt-acuvp129.17052007/index.html Available from National Library of Australia Trove database (174389481).

Morgan, D. (1998). Practical strategies for combining qualitative and quantitative methods: Applications to health research. *Qualitative Health Research, 8*(3), 362–376. https://doi.org/10.1177/104973239800800307.

Riley, P. (2017). The Australian principal occupational, safety and well-being survey: 2016. Institute for Positive Psychology & Education, Faculty of Education & Arts, Australian Catholic University, Fitzroy.

Sarantakos, S. (2005). *Social research* (3rd ed.). Basingstoke: Palgrave Macmillan.

Starr, K. (2012). Problematizing "risk" and the principalship: The risky business of managing rick in schools. *Educational Management Administration & Leadership, 40*(4), 464–479.

Stewart, D. (1996). Principals' knowledge of law affecting schools. (D. Stewart, Ed.) *Australia and New Zealand Journal of Law and Education, 1*(1), 111–129.

Stewart, D. (1996). School principals and the law: A study of the legal knowledge needed and held by principals in government schools in Queensland. PhD Unpublished, Queensland University of Technology, Brisbane. Available from National Library of Australia Trove database (24587328).

Stewart, D., & McCann, P. (1999). Educators and the law: Implications for the professional development of school administrators and teachers. *Professional Development in Education, 25*(1), 135–150.

Strahilevitz, M., Harvey, J., & Ariely, D. (2015). Understanding consumer financial behaviour: Spending, saving, investing and debt. *Advances in Consumer Research, 43*, 90–94.

Teh, M. (2008). Schools and the law: Legal issues internationally with implications for school leaders in Singapore. PhD Published, University of Southern Queensland, Toowoomba. Retrieved from http://eprints.usq.edu.au/4439/. Available from National Library of Australia Trove database (153062505)

Trimble, A. (2017). Education law, schools and school principals: A mixed methods study of the impact of law on Tasmanian school principals. PhD Unpublished, University of Tasmania, Launceston.

Trimble, A., Cranston, N., & Allen, J. (2012). School principals and Education Law: What do they know, what do they need to know? *Leading and Managing, 18*(2), 46–61.

Wardle, D. (2006). School related law: Do principals know what they need to know? Masters of Educational Administration Unpublished, Massey University, Palmerstone North.

3

Educational Negligence: Is It a Viable Form of Action?

Mui Kim Teh and Charles J. Russo

3.1 Introduction

In Australia, it has been established that educational authorities owed their students a non-delegable duty of care. Generally, this duty of care typically referred to taking responsibility for students' physical well-being while they are in school, with the result that negligence in doing so may result in liability (Ramsay v Larsen (1964), Geyer v Downs (1977) and Commonwealth v Introvigne (1982) 150 CLR 258). Over the years, though, legal responsibility for educators has changed significantly. There are now many areas of responsibility of which educators need to have an overall understanding and for which they carry a duty. Often, educators must deal with the specifics of the law for issues such as students with disability (in terms of equity and access), custody in family law, and even regulatory control of the use of social media and technology rather than just the general duty of care for health and safety.

For many years, negligence cases involving schools covered mainly student supervision involving a wide range of school activities, such as before and after

M. K. Teh (✉)
Deakin University, Geelong, VIC, Australia
e-mail: kim.teh@deakin.edu.au

C. J. Russo
Panzer Chair in Education and Research Professor of Law, University of Dayton, Dayton, OH, USA

K. Trimmer et al. (eds.), *The Palgrave Handbook of Education Law for Schools*,
https://doi.org/10.1007/978-3-319-77751-1_3

school supervision, school excursions, sports and classroom management (Babie et al. 2004). It is now also recognised that this duty extends not only to physical injury but also to psychiatric injury (Cox v. State of New South Wales 2007; Oyston v St Patrick's College 2013).

Thus, the tort of negligence, by definition, an unintentional act, relating to physical and/or psychiatric injuries suffered in schools, is well recognised by Australian courts. Indeed, cases have escalated to the extent that, in many jurisdictions – for example, the United States (US), England and Australia – education law communities, comprising organisations, law firms, educational law journals and textbooks which deal specifically with education law matters, have emerged to deal with them (Mawdsley and Cumming 2008a, b). At the same time, claims such as those for inadequate supervision resulting in physical injury, failure to prevent bullying, and exposing students to unnecessary risks of injury (including risks of sexual assault) have been successful. Even so, litigation has demonstrated the general judicial reluctance to impose a similar duty of care in relation to educational negligence or malpractice, as it is referred to in the US. In most Australian cases, the allegation of a breach of duty of care does not involve a breach of a "duty to educate". Educational negligence thus forms a novel type of negligence claim, but, interestingly, in 2002, Justice R. Atkinson of the Supreme Court in Queensland said:

> In thirty years' time, an experienced lawyer will be able to chart the development of the law in Australia with regard to educational negligence, discrimination in the provision of educational services and liability for educational outcomes. At present, we can but survey the international trends and local developments to try to determine where these developments might lead. (p. 14)

It is now halfway to Justice Atkinson's target date. In light of Justice Atkinson's comment, this chapter charts the development of educational negligence, examining whether such claims will eventually be allowed in Australia. The next section looks briefly at the law of negligence. The following two parts explore the development of educational negligence where it was first raised, namely the US, and then in England. The final sections discuss educational negligence claims in Australia, along with examining the impact of setting professional standards for teaching. The chapter concludes with speculation about the future of educational negligence or malpractice claims.

3.2 Negligence

Torts are civil wrongs, comprising acts or omissions, committed by people on others, and the infringement of a legally recognised interest of a person will give rise to a right of civil action. Negligence is classified under the law of torts and it is generally accepted as the most wide-ranging among the numerous torts. In order to be successful in claims against defendants for the tort of negligence, plaintiffs must establish the following four elements:

- Duty of care;
- The standard of care and breach;
- Breach of duty;
- Damage: causation and remoteness.

Further, defendants must not be able to counter with such defences as immunity, contributory/ comparative negligence, and assumption of risk to avoid liability.

3.3 Duty of Care

The element of duty of care is a threshold requirement meaning that, before lawyers can advise plaintiffs to proceed with negligence claims, they must be satisfied that a duty of care existed. The duty, in school settings, arises out of some legal relationship or proximity, and in determining who is owed a duty of care, the oft-cited words of Lord Atkin in Donoghue v. Stevenson (1932) provide the answer:

> *You must take reasonable care to avoid acts or omissions which you can reasonably foresee would be likely to injure your neighbour. Who, then, in law is my neighbour? The answer seems to be – persons who are so closely and directly affected by my act that I ought reasonably to have them in contemplation as being so affected when I am directing my mind to the acts or omissions which are called in question.* (p. 580)

For schools, Williams v. Eady (1893) established the principle that a duty of care exists between teachers or school systems, in the form of their officials and/or boards, and a student whenever the former has care or custody of students. In this case, Lord Esher stated that "the schoolmaster was bound to take such care of his boys as a careful father would take of his boys" (p. 42).

However, while establishing a duty of care for physical injury is not difficult, imposing a duty for claims of non-physical injury has proven to be more challenging.

3.4 The Standard of Care

If plaintiffs succeed in establishing a duty of care, they must then prove that the acts or omissions of the defendants failed to meet the standard of care required by law. The standard of care required in litigation is a question of law for the court to determine. This is an objective standard, considering what reasonable persons in the defendants' positions ought to have done in like or similar circumstances. Where schools are concerned, the High Court in Trustees of the Roman Catholic Church for the Diocese of Canberra and Goulburn v Hadba (2005) held that, while the courts impose a duty of care on them, the standard expected is not one of 'unrealistic and impractical perfection' (para 26).

3.5 Breach of Duty

The next element plaintiffs must prove is whether defendants breached the standard of care owed to the plaintiffs. Civil liability legislation in Australia restates the common law position set out by the High Court in Wyong Shire Council v Shirt (1980). The factors the courts consider in deciding whether there is a breach of the standard of care in a particular case are:

- Was the risk foreseeable?
- Was the probability of the risk more than insignificant?
- Would a reasonable person in the position of the defendant have taken the precautions? (Wyong Shire Council v Shirt, pp. 47–48)

3.6 Damage: Causation and Remoteness

Finally, plaintiffs must prove that the defendants' breaches of duty caused their damages (causation) (March v E & M H Stramare Pty Ltd. (1991); Roads and Traffic Authority v Royal (2008)), and that it was reasonably foreseeable that the defendant's negligence could cause that kind of damage (remoteness) (Overseas Tankship (UK) Ltd. v Miller Steamship Co Pty Ltd.

(Wagon Mound (No 2)) (1967)). In the education context, on the evidence, a judge has to determine whether it is logical and reasonable to infer that what teachers did or should not have done in the performance of their duties caused the injury or harm that the student complains of – the notion of causal connection. Not only must plaintiffs prove that defendants' conduct was, in fact, the cause of the injury (factual causation), they must also satisfy the court that the defendants should be held liable for their ensuing injuries (legal causation – scope of liability).

Having provided some background knowledge of the law of negligence, we now look at the development of educational negligence in the US, where it all started, followed by England, where this area of law was subsequently explored by the courts, and finally Australia, which saw similar claims arise in lower courts, mainly starting in the early part of this century. A comparison of these three nations is also warranted, because they share the common law tradition out of which "regular" negligence claims emerged in Nineteenth Century England.

3.7 Educational Malpractice Claims in the US

Starting in the 1970s, parents in the US sought to impose liability on school boards and educators for perceived educational shortcomings, allegedly due to the poor instruction their children received. Malpractice, a term of art, meaning it defies a precise definition, applicable to negligence by professionals, is usually applied to those who work in one-to-one relationships with clients such as physicians or lawyers. To date, as detailed in this section, efforts to establish educational malpractice in regular education have failed because it is '…a tort theory beloved of commentators, but not of courts.' In other words, while academicians support this notion, the courts are unwilling to do so because it is too vague a notion to apply. This dichotomy exists because, as discussed below, of public policy considerations. It is unclear who has what duty to whom, when it may have been breached, and what the measure of damages should be as a remedy for alleged harms.

Peter W v. San Francisco Unified School District (1976) (Peter W.) was the first case in the US where parents took school officials to court for inadequate or incompetent teaching and for promoting their son to a higher level each year despite his lack of progress. The claim failed, not because his argument was not substantiated, but because of public policy considerations. The court was not prepared to open the floodgates and place an undue burden on the limited resources of schools. An appellate court in California concluded that there was no general duty of care owed by educators to students in respect of educational outcomes, because classroom methodology affords no readily acceptable standards of care, or cause, or injury.

Public policy considerations, therefore, include concerns about placing an undue burden upon the limited resources of schools, the possibility of putting the judiciary into improper positions of interfering with the day-to-day policies entrusted to school authorities, and a flood of cases inundating the courts.

A string of similar cases followed. In Donohue v. Copiague Union Free School District (1979), the student plaintiff made a similar claim as in Peter W. but further alleged that his low literacy level even prevented him from completing applications for employment. While the student's claim failed, due to policy considerations, New York's highest court left the door ajar by this comment: 'if doctors, lawyers, architects, engineers and other professionals are charged with a duty owing to the public whom they serve, it could be said that nothing in the law precludes similar treatment of professional educators' (Donohue v. Copiague Union Free School District, p. 391). The implication is that a suit for 'educational malpractice' could be made to fit the traditional negligence principles if, as in special education, school officials owe students a clear duty to teach.

Hoffman v. Board of Education (1979), another suit from New York, had a significant effect on the meaning of 'educational malpractice'. In contrast to the earlier two cases, the student alleged specific incidents of negligence, namely the incorrect assessment of his IQ level and failure to reassess him two years after the first assessment, as recommended by the clinical psychologist. As a result, he spent twelve years in education facilities for 'mentally retarded children', resulting in emotional and intellectual injury, and a much reduced ability to obtain employment. The state's highest court agreed that this was a case that could have been classified as one of 'educational malpractice', but, unfortunately for the plaintiff, it was rejected due to public policy considerations.

A notable exception to typical educational malpractice litigation in the US is B.M. v State (1982). The Supreme Court of Montana held that school authorities owed a child a duty of care to test and place him or her in an appropriate special education program by virtue of state statute. As this duty arose from the state Constitution and a relevant statute, the court decided that there was no common law duty of care.

At this point, it is important to recognise a significant distinction. While American courts have been unwilling to recognise a tort for educational malpractice for regular students, they have been more receptive to claims filed on behalf of children with special needs. The courts treat these two classes of students, those in regular education as compared with their peers in special education, differently because the educational courses of study for the latter group of children are identified specifically in their written Individualised Educational Programs, which are akin to contracts, thereby establishing a specific duty, albeit one that is targeted rather than guaranteed.

In Hunter v Board of Education of Montgomery County (1982), Maryland's highest court found that the student plaintiff was allowed to proceed to a higher grade each year without being able to read. Even so, the court affirmed that '[t]he field of education is simply too fraught with unanswered questions for the courts to constitute themselves as a proper forum for resolution of those questions' (p. 685).

The question concerning measuring educational injuries was addressed in D.S.W. v Fairbanks North Star Borough School District (1981) and Torres v Little Flower (1984), where courts rejected claims for the same public policy reasons given by the earlier seminal cases. In Smith v Alameda County Services Agency (1979), the claim failed due to the lack of a satisfactory standard of care by which to evaluate an educator. Further, in Moore v Vanderloo (1986), the cause of action was denied because of the potential it presents for a flood of litigation against schools.

It can be seen from these cases that even potentially valid educational negligence claims are repeatedly rejected on grounds of public policy.

In Bell v Board of Education of the City of West Haven (1999), the student plaintiff claimed the school was negligent in 'impos[ing] on the children a teaching method (responsive classroom method) that…emphasize[d] social skills at the expense of discipline and academics' (p. 403). An appellate court in Connecticut refused to recognise a duty of care, because the tort principles of 'duty, standard[s] of care, and reasonable conduct…are difficult, if not impossible, to apply in the academic environment' (p. 406).

Most recently, in New York, an appellate court continued the trend and reversed an earlier judgment in favour of the plaintiffs, denying a claim it described as being akin to educational malpractice, albeit in a non-public, religious, rather than public, school, as a claim still not cognisable in the state (Sisters of the Holy Child Jesus at Old Westbury v. Corwin (2016)). The court rejected the parental claim that school personnel were unqualified to address the alleged special needs of their daughter, because the standards applicable to evaluate the qualifications of educators in non-public schools is a matter for the state department of education rather than the judiciary. The court also upheld the liquidated damages clause in a registration contract requiring parents to pay tuition and fees for the full year after they withdrew their daughter from the school, because it was not an impermissible penalty.

In a 2012 study (Eckes et al. 2012), US scholars reported that where negligence cases succeeded, they related to specific harms, such as student physical injuries resulting from lack of supervision or improper maintenance of equipment. Arguably, these types of injuries are not as damaging as harm that may be suffered by students as a result of educational malpractice. Yet, public policy continually prevents claims for educational malpractice from succeeding.

The public policy concerns of the US courts have revolved around finding a workable standard of care against which to measure an educator's conduct, the difficulty in proving or disproving the proximate causes of the injuries, and in measuring such harms. American courts generally agree that recognition of educational malpractice actions would be blatant judicial interference in the regulation of educational programs or pedagogical methods. While these concerns seem reasonable, what is puzzling is the judicial reluctance to impose liability on specific incidents of educational malpractice, such as in Hoffman v. Board of Education (1979) discussed earlier. Conversely, English courts have not demonstrated such a persistent reluctance. Indeed, there have been various indications that the courts should address negligence in the delivery of education more seriously, and we therefore now look at the development of educational negligence claims in England and where the law stands.

3.8 Educational Negligence Claims in England

The first educational negligence case in England was a consolidated appeal of five separate claims brought by students against local education authorities for negligence, three of which related to educational negligence in failing to address their special learning needs; the other two related to child abuse (X (minors) v Bedfordshire County Council); M (a minor) and another v Newham London Borough Council and others; E (a minor) v Dorset County Council; and other appeals [1995] 2 AC 633 (X (minors) v Bedfordshire County Council). Insofar as these claims were based on the breach of statutory duty, the plaintiffs were not successful because, as explained by Lord Browne-Wilkinson, allowing private tort actions against local authorities would make it difficult for authorities to carry out their statutory duties efficiently.

However, the House of Lords did not exclude the possibility of educational negligence claims in the right circumstances. Lord Brown-Wilkinson said since 'the education of the pupil is the very purpose for which the child goes to school' (X (minors) v Bedfordshire County Council, p. 766), a school assumes responsibility for a pupil's educational as well as physical needs. Thus, 'if it comes to the attention of the headmaster that a pupil is under-performing, he does owe a duty to take such steps as a reasonable teacher would consider appropriate to try to deal with such under-performance' (X (minors) v Bedfordshire County Council, p. 766). Also, subsequently, in Phelps v London Borough of Hillingdon (2001), the House of Lords stated that public policy reasons are not sufficient grounds to exclude educational negligence claims.

In Phelps v London Borough of Hillingdon (2001), school authorities employed an educational psychologist who did not diagnose the plaintiff's dyslexia but instead reported that the testing revealed no specific weaknesses. After leaving school, the plaintiff obtained a job but was subsequently dismissed because she had difficulties with anything requiring literacy. The plaintiff claimed that due to the failure of school officials, including the psychologist, she failed to receive the necessary educational provision for her dyslexia and did not learn to read and write as well as she could have done had she received proper diagnosis and instruction.

The plaintiff thus sued the Local Education Authority (LEA) in the High Court, which held the LEA vicariously liable for the psychologist's negligence. The LEA was ordered to pay compensation to the plaintiff. The Court of Appeal, though, determined that the function of the psychologist was to provide information to the LEA and thus there was no direct duty owed to the child. The first requirement, namely, the duty of care owed to the plaintiff, for bringing a negligence case was not satisfied. The Court was also concerned that 'the immunity of the LEA from suit granted for powerful policy reasons will be completely circumvented' if an individual psychologist or teacher can be sued and the employer held vicariously liable (Phelps v Hillingdon London Borough Council (1999), p. 516, per Lord Justice Stuart-Smith). For these reasons, the High Court's ruling was reversed. The plaintiff then appealed to the House of Lords.

The House of Lords disagreed with the Court of Appeal. Instead, the House of Lords concurred with the principle laid down by Lord Browne-Wilkinson in X (minors) v. Bedfordshire. The House held unanimously that claims for education negligence could be brought against the teacher/ psychologist/ LEA. The Lords were of the view that the educational psychologist owed a direct duty of care to the plaintiff, because she was specifically asked to give advice on the child's needs and was to recommend suitable educational provision for that child. It was also clear that the plaintiff's parents and teachers would follow that advice. According to the Lords, there was therefore no reason why the LEA, as employer of the psychologist, could not be vicariously liable for the breach of duty of care by the educational psychologist. The decision of the Court of Appeal was overturned and damages of almost £50,000 were awarded to the plaintiff.

This approach taken by the English courts, unlike their American counterparts, recognises that teachers owe their students a duty of care for their educational well-being, and allows the law to 'provide a remedy in damages when there is manifest incompetence or negligence comprising specific, identifiable mistakes' (Phelps v London Borough of Hillingdon (2001), p. 667). The House of Lords also did not limit the duty of care to special needs children when saying:

> The law would be in an extraordinary state if, in carrying out their teaching responsibilities, teachers owed duties to some of their pupils but not others... The principal objection raised to this conclusion is the spectre of a rash of 'gold-digging' actions brought on behalf of under-achieving children by discontented parents...and the time of teaching staff will be diverted away from teaching and defending unmeritorious legal claims...I am not persuaded by these fears. I do not think they provide sufficient reason for treating work in the classroom as territory which the courts must never enter. 'Never' is an unattractive absolute in this context. (Phelps v London Borough of Hillingdon (2001), p. 667)

This is a landmark statement. Unlike courts in the US, which have made it almost impossible for even the most compelling and meritorious claims to succeed, the judiciary in England has clearly opened the door to granting such claims serious attention. The fear of a flood of 'gold-digging' actions brought by discontented parents did not eventuate, as most cases brought after Phelps did not succeed (Mawdsley and Cumming 2008a, b). Later cases were unsuccessful because, even though a duty of care could be established, the plaintiffs could not persuade the courts that the other elements of breaching the standard of care had taken place, nor was the cause of the injury proven convincingly.

While the English courts are more open to considering sound educational negligence claims, their chances of success are minimal. As in the US, outside the special needs context, liability for educational negligence will probably only be imposed in cases of specific and manifestly negligent mistakes, such as teaching the wrong syllabus. In one case, a teacher neglected to use the correct syllabus and prepared the students for only two of the three exams (BBC 2001). Insofar as the case was settled out of court, no legal opinions were available. Nevertheless, the outcome suggests that the door may be slowly opening to allegations of 'negligent teaching' as parents become more knowledgeable about classroom practice through increased communication with schools.

While educational negligence has been the subject of detailed discussion in the US and England, in Australia, such claims are not couched under this term, as will be seen in the next two sections, which examine litigation arising in Australia, discussing the position the appellate courts might take should they be asked to review such cases.

3.8.1 Educational Negligence Claims in Australia

The landmark case of Commonwealth of Australia v Introvigne (1982) imposed a non-delegable duty of care on school officials to exercise reasonable care and supervision to prevent injury to students. However, the emphasis in the judgment was a legal duty to ensure the physical safety of students, not a duty to educate (Commonwealth of Australia v Introvigne, p. 267 para 10). Even so, in an address to a group of educators in South Australia in 1982, the then Justice Kirby wrote:

> But I do think it likely that increasing community concern about educational standards will evidence itself one day … and we will then see whether the teacher's legal duty of care goes beyond protecting pupils from physical injury in the playground and science laboratory to what is perhaps the more relevant and usually more profound professional injury that can result from indifferent, ill-motivated, incompetent or just plain lazy teaching. (Kirby, pp. 14–15)

Justice Kirby's prediction came to fruition in 1996 when two former high school students sued the New South Wales Department of School Education for an apparent failure to teach the appropriate curriculum in 1993 for their art course, which, in turn, affected their performance in the Higher School Certificate examination (Raethel 1996). The case was settled out of court for an undisclosed sum.

In another case against the New South Wales Department of School Education (Tronc, para 20–303), students in a secondary school took action because their English results were in the lowest twenty percent. They attributed the poor results to 'negligent' teaching for that subject, since their results for other subjects were in the top twenty percent. Again, the case was settled out of court. Yet, not all challenges against schools are framed in the tort of negligence, as the following cases show.

In 2006 a mother obtained a payout from a top private school, Brighton Grammar School, for failing to teach her son to read properly (Hannan 2006). The case brought by the mother to the Victorian Civil and Administrative Tribunal was based on the allegation that Brighton Grammar had breached the Trade Practices Act 1974 (Cth) for failing to deliver the service it promised. Perhaps encouraged by the success of this case, in 2008, another parent of Brighton Grammar filed a case in a Victorian court for the repayment of up to $400,000 in fees paid for his twin boys' education from kindergarten to Year 12. It was alleged that at the end of Year 12, the boys did not achieve the academic results that were expected from having studied at the elite private school (Hudson 2008). The case was settled upon payment of an undisclosed sum of money (Sarre 2008).

In yet another case in New South Wales (Mears v Sydney Anglican Schools Corporation (No. 2) (2013)), parents of four children were sued for outstanding school fees after they withdrew their children from the school. The parents counterclaimed against the school for breach of s 52 of the Trade Practices Act 1974 (Cth), breach of the statutory warranties implied in the contract, and a breach of a common law duty of care in failing to "address or correct" problems with one of their daughters' academic work, ultimately leading to her underperforming in the 2006 Higher School Certificate. The judgment of the magistrate in 2011 was in favour of the school, because the magistrate was satisfied that officials provided educational and pastoral services at a reasonable standard of care. The decision was successfully appealed in 2013 because of procedural issues and the judge ordered the matter to be reheard in the District Court, with the parties first submitting their dispute to mediation (Mears v Sydney Anglican Schools Corporation (No. 2) (2013); Dale 2011). At the time of writing, this dispute has not been resolved (Grant Mears v Sydney Anglican Schools Corporation (2016)).

In 2012, a student and her mother sued school authorities for failing to provide the academic support she needed. This failure, it was alleged, resulted in the student's not being able to study law at the University of Sydney (Weir v Geelong Grammar School (Civil Claims) (2012)). The claim was not based on educational negligence. Instead, the plaintiffs relied on the law of contract as well as misrepresentation and breach of consumer guarantees under the State's Fair Trading Act (Vic). The plaintiffs also claimed that the representations of officials about the quality of education services available were not matched by what they delivered. In dismissing the claim, DP Lulham referred to the judgment of FM Neville in Yee Tak On v Dr. Linda Hort (ANU College) (2012), who held that dissatisfaction of the delivery of a course does not provide a basis in law to claim relief.

In 2013, the Federal Court of Australia dismissed an action by a plaintiff, now an adult, who claimed that the Education Department in Victoria failed to teach him properly by allowing him to pass through the system, even though he failed to meet the required academic levels (Abela v State of Victoria

(2013)). Because the plaintiff was diagnosed as having an intellectual disability, the claim was not couched in negligence. Rather, the charge alleged that the Education Department contravened the Disability Discrimination Act 1992 by denying him access to proper education and for failure to reasonably adjust to his educational needs. On the facts of the case, the court found that there was no breach of the disability standards, and the application was dismissed.

As seen in the way claims against educational institutions are brought in Australia, one can conclude that there are no authoritative cases endorsing educational negligence claims. Nevertheless, the litigation demonstrates an expanding interest in the nature of professionalism and accountability of the teaching profession. This is especially so for fee paying parents, who naturally expect value for money. But there is also a noticeable change in societal culture, one characterised by rights and entitlements, and recent decades have seen an expanding willingness to challenge institutions and individuals, sometimes in the courts.

Against this backdrop, then, the question remains: if professional groups, such as the medical, legal and accounting professions can be liable for negligence, is there scope for educators to be liable similarly for failing to meet defined expectations? The general consensus is that, even if there is a duty to educate, establishing a breach of that duty and the proximate cause of injury will be difficult.

Another consideration is this: while professionals such as doctors, lawyers, and accountants typically deal with one client at a time, teachers have to meet the needs of a large group of students with varying educational needs. This poses further complications to the issue of liability when determining where the fault lies for a student's poor academic performance.

3.8.2 The Impact of Setting Professional Standards for Teaching

While claims for incompetent teaching have not met with judicial success, scholars and commentators have argued for its recognition (see Elson 1978; Funston 1980–81; Ramsay 1988; Jamieson 1991; Mawdsley and Cumming 2008a, b; DeMitchell et al. 2012; Hutt and Tang 2013). Many suggestions have been put forward to support a cause of action for educational negligence. Mawdsley and Cumming argued that the setting of professional standards, teacher evaluations and outcomes measures 'should allow point-in-time identification of teachers who are failing…at least by the end of the year of instruction' (p. 37). Hutt and Tang (2013) discussed the use of complex statistical techniques to calculate and differentiate teacher effectiveness using data on student growth as a significant factor.

Professionals are defined by the Australian and New Zealand Standard Classification of Occupations as those who 'perform analytical, conceptual and creative tasks through the application of theoretical knowledge and experience' (Australian Bureau of Statistics 2013), and the fields listed include education. In Victoria, section 59 of the Wrongs Act 1958 (Vic) provides a defence for professionals or persons claiming to possess a particular skill. Section 59(1) states:

> A professional is not negligent in providing a professional service if it is established that the professional acted in a manner that (at the time the service was provided) was widely accepted in Australia by a significant number of respected practitioners in the field (peer professional opinion) as competent professional practice in the circumstances.

A similar statutory test applies in the other states: Civil Liability Act 2002 (Tas) s 22(1); Civil Liability Act 2003 (Qld) s 22(1), Civil Liability Act 2002 (NSW) s 5O(1); Civil Liability Act 1936 (SA) s 41(1); Civil Liability Act 2002 (WA) s 5PA and B (applies only to health professionals).

This section suggests that teachers will not be found negligent if they have acted in accordance with practices accepted by the teaching profession. Given the various pedagogical and teaching methods, and the 'great diversity in the working conditions encountered by educators' (Foster 1985, p. 223), it is no wonder that the courts have taken the position that 'classroom methodology affords no readily acceptable standards of care' (Peter W, p. 860). Still, it is pointed out by Cumming (2009) that the current climate of setting professional standards for the teaching profession through policy or legislation precludes such arguments.

Tokic (2014, p. 125), on the other hand, suggested that instead of placing the conduct of teachers at the centre of analyses, an alternative cause of action – 'institutional negligence' – can overcome that. He argued that institutional negligence in the education context focuses on 'processes' rather than putting the teachers' conduct or students' learning at the centre of attention. Similarly, Mawdsley and Mawdsley (2012, p. 225) maintained that even if students' failure results entirely from poor instruction, 'the problem is more likely to be systemic than the fault of a single incompetent teacher'.

In Tokic's (2014) view, the claims, if proven, should succeed, since the universities failed to put in place mechanisms for preventing the 'educational missteps' from occurring (p. 128). Similarly, in primary and secondary educational institutions, Hutt and Tang (2013) argued that, with the data available concerning teacher effectiveness and impact on student learning, educational authorities should be liable for negligence if school officials knowingly assign ineffective teachers to classrooms. Of course, this begs the question of evaluating teacher effectiveness. Perhaps without realising it, decision makers are making rods for their own backs through the increasing use of narrowly defined standards.

Indeed, standards have become prevalent in many systems. The Teachers' Standards in England (Department of Education 2011), the Value-Added Modeling evaluation system in the US (DeMitchell et al. 2012), and the National Professional Standards for Teachers in Australia (Australian Institute for Teaching and School Leadership 2011) all purport to raise the standard of teaching, and some go so far as to link the standards to pay. In such circumstances, to continue the deployment of teachers who fail to meet acceptable standards is fraught with legal danger, particularly in countries wherein courts dismissed the primacy of public policy in relation to educational negligence, for it makes it easier for plaintiffs to locate the blame for inadequate performance. However, as reflected by a recent controversy from Minnesota, plaintiffs face a long, uphill battle in trying to prove that educational officials intentionally assigned ineffective teachers to schools, particularly those in poor, urban areas (Maglan 2016; Matos 2016).

3.9 Conclusion

An often quoted passage by Keeton et al. (1984) has this to say about valid claims:

> *It is the business of the law to remedy wrongs that deserve it, even at the expense of a "flood of litigation", and it is a pitiful confession of incompetence on the part of any court of justice to deny relief on such grounds. That a multiplicity of actions may follow is not a persuasive objection; if injuries are multiplied, actions should be multiplied, so injured parties may have recompense. So far as distinguishing true claims from false ones is concerned, what is required is rather a careful scrutiny of the evidence supporting the claim; and the elimination of trivialities calls for nothing more than the same common sense which has distinguished serious from trifling injuries in other fields of the law.* (p. 56)

By putting aside policy arguments and concentrating on the evidence, it is not difficult to establish a duty of care and even a breach of the standard of care, thereby establishing valid claims for educational negligence-malpractice. Yet, causation remains a challenge. As reflected in some cases, there is no guarantee that the plaintiffs would have achieved higher grades. In fact, it must be kept in mind that the plaintiff's own lack of intelligence, ability, diligence, aptitude or 'general educability' (Funston 1980–81, p. 789) or personal problems may well have led to their poor results. As pointed out by Lord Nicholls in Phelps:

> Proof of under-performance by a child is not by itself evidence of negligent teaching. There are many, many reasons for under-performance. A child's ability to learn from what he is taught is much affected by a host of factors which are personal to him and over which a school has no control. (p. 667)

Assuming there is a legal duty of care, and that courts are able to rely on expert evidence to find that educators' conduct as instructors fell below accepted professional levels; or if there is conclusive evidence that those employing and managing the work of teachers had continued to assign responsibility to those who are defined as incompetent or unsatisfactory, only factual causation is established. The question remains about whether there is legal causation. Another question remains over the scope of the liability. In resolving this issue, the courts will likely have regard to policy considerations in deciding whether responsibility for the harm should be imposed on the negligent party.

The public policy considerations that could preclude findings of educational negligence or malpractice include preventing defensive practices by teachers, the undesirability of interfering with the statutory duties of the education ministries (such as meeting special educational needs of students with learning disabilities) or imposing undue burdens on limited school resources, and that the courts are not the appropriate forum for determining educational issues. Further, the 'multiplicity of factors affecting the learning process' (Funston 1980–81, p. 786), such as home environment, personality, motivation, aptitude, class size, attitude, and many others make it almost impossible to prove that the defendant had in fact caused a student's illiteracy.

In other professional negligence or malpractice cases, for example, such as those involving medicine, plaintiffs are able to point to specific events in single incidents that caused their injuries. In educational contexts, though, teaching occurs over extended periods of time and involves classes of students rather than individuals. So, if whole classes received the same instruction, it would seem odd that only one pupil should fail, thereby raising the question of whether teachers and school officials should be liable if students either lack the skill or desire to succeed. Thus, educational negligence or malpractice claims for incompetent teaching per se are highly unlikely to succeed.

At the same time, it is true that school authorities and teachers should not be guarantors of the success of their students. Still, as rightly pointed out by Ramsay, there is a duty to ensure the attainment of basic skills to enable students to survive in the world, and failure to do so should lead to accountability (Ramsay 1988). However, applying the legal principles in Phelps, such an assertion is only feasible if a claimant is able to identify a professional error rather than simply alleging inadequate education. As observed by Lord Nicholls,

> A style of teaching which suits one child, or most children in a class, may not be as effective with another child and so on. Suffice to say the existence of a duty of care owed by teachers to their pupils should not be regarded as furnishing a basis on which generalised 'educational malpractice' claims can be mounted. (p. 804)

As discussed herein, many have argued that in the age of professional accountability, there should be judicial recognition of educational negligence or malpractice, with the time now being ripe for courts to consider claims for inadequate teaching. Even so, such novel cases have not been recognised in the US, as litigious as the country is, since the first case was brought in 1976. In England, damages have been awarded only where specific and identifiable professional errors caused personal injuries. In Australia, this area of law has not been tested. But, unless and until the courts are able to set practicable and workable standards to measure educators' professional conduct, the difficult question of causation remains a significant hurdle to cross. The upshot is that educational negligence or malpractice for inadequate teaching is highly likely to remain out of reach of students.

References

Abela v State of Victoria [2013] FCA 832.

Australian Bureau of Statistics. (2013). *1220.0 – ANZSCO – Australian and New Zealand standard classification of occupations, version 1.2*. Retrieved from http://www.abs.gov.au/ausstats/abs@.nsf/Lookup/1220.0Chapter612013%20Version%201.2

Australian Institute for Teaching and School Leadership (AITSL). (2011). *National professional standards for teachers*. Retrieved from http://www.aitsl.edu.au/verve/_resources/AITSL_National_Professional_Standards_for_Teachers.pdf

B.M. v State, 649 P.2d 425 (Mont. 1982).
Babie, P., Russo, C. J., & Dickinson, G. M. (2004). Supervision of students: An exploratory comparative analysis. *Australia & New Zealand Journal of Law and Education, 9*(1), 41–70.
BBC. (2001, October 1). *School sued over poor results.* Retrieved from http://news.bbc.co.uk/2/hi/uk_news/education/1573033.stm
Bell v Board of Educ. of the City of W.Haven, 739 A.2d 321(Conn. Ct. App. 1999).
Civil Liability Act 1936 (SA).
Civil Liability Act 2002 (NSW).
Civil Liability Act 2002 (Tas).
Civil Liability Act 2002 (WA).
Civil Liability Act 2003 (Qld).
Commonwealth v Introvigne. (1982). 150 CLR 258.
Cox v. State of New South Wales (2007) NSWSC 471.
Cumming, J. J. (2009). Assessment challenges, the law and the future. In C. Wyatt-Smith & J. J. Cumming (Eds.), *Educational assessment in the 21st century – Connecting theory and practice* (pp. 157–179). London: Springer.
D.S.W. v Fairbanks North Star Borough Sch. Dist., 628 P.2d 554 (Alaska 1981).
Dale, A. (2011, June 1). Parents must pay up – Court rules Roseville college did enough to help daughters. *The Daily Telegraph.* Retrieved from http://www.news.com.au/top-stories/parents-must-pay-up-court-rules-private-school-did-enough-to-help-daughters/story-e6frfkp9-1226066808945
DeMitchell, T. A., DeMitchell, T. A., & Gagnon, D. (2012). Teacher effectiveness and value-added modelling: Building a pathway to educational malpractice? *Brigham Young University Education and Law Journal, 2,* 257–301.
Department of Education. (2011). *Teachers' standards: Guidance for school leaders, school staff and governing bodies.* Retrieved from https://www.gov.uk/government/uploads/system/uploads/attachment_data/file/301107/Teachers__Standards.pdf
Disability Discrimination Act. (1992). Retrieved from http://www.austlii.edu.au/au/legis/cth/consol_act/dda1992264/
Donohue v. Copiague Union Free Sch. Dist., 418 N.Y.S.2d 375 (N.Y. 1979).
Donoghue v Stevenson [1932] AC 562.
Eckes, S. E., Decker, J. R., & Richardson, E. N. (2012). Trends in court opinions involving negligence in K-12 schools: Considerations for teachers and administrators. *West's Education Law Reporter, 275,* 505.
Elson, J. (1978). A common law remedy for the educational harms caused by incompetent or careless teaching. *Northwestern University Law Review, 73,* 641–771.
Foster, W. F. (1985). Educational malpractice: A Tort for the untaught? *University of British Columbia Law Review, 19,* 161–244.
Funston, R. (1980–1981). Educational malpractice: A cause of action in search of a theory. *San Diego Law Review, 18,* 743–812.
Geyer v Downs. (1977). 138 CLR 90.
Grant Mears v Sydney Anglican Schools Corporation [2016] NSWCA 39.

Hannan, E. (2006, August 15). School payout for boy's reading failure. *The Australian*, p. 1.
Hoffman v. Board of Educ., 424 N.Y.S.2d 376 (N.Y. 1979).
Hudson, F. (2008, March 16). Father wants refund on Brighton Grammar school fees. *Sunday Herald Sun*. Retrieved from http://www.theaustralian.com.au/news/sons-flunk-school-dad-demands-a-refund/storye6frg6n6-1111115809105
Hunter v. Board of Educ. of Montgomery Cnty., 439 A.2d 582 (Md.1982).
Hutt, E., & Tang, A. (2013). The new education malpractice litigation. *Virginia Law Review, 99*(3), 419–492.
Jamieson, L. S. (1991). Educational malpractice: A lesson in professional accountability. *Boston College Law Review, 32*(4), 899–965.
Keeton, W. P., Dobbs, D. B., Keeton, R. E., & Owen, D. G. (1984). *Prosser and Keeton on the law of Torts* (5th ed.). St Paul: West Publishing Co.
Maglan, C. (2016, October 27). Judge dismisses lawsuit challenging Minnesota teachers union protections. *Duluth News Tribune* (MN) at A 9, 2016 WLNR 32881528.
March v E & M H Stramare Pty Ltd (1991) 171 CLR 506.
Matos, A. (2016, April 14). Lawsuit accuses Minnesota of protecting bad teachers at expense of students. Minneapolis-St. Paul, *Star Tribune*. Retrieved from http://www.startribune.com/suit-says-minnesota-protects-bad-teachers-at-expense-of-students/375609941
Mawdsley, R. D., & Cumming, J. J. (2008a). Educational malpractice and setting damages for ineffective teaching: A comparison of legal principles in the USA, England and Australia. *Education and the Law, 20*(1), 25–46.
Mawdsley, R. D., & Cumming, J. J. (2008b). The origins and development of education law as a separate field of law in the United States and Australia. *Australia and New Zealand Journal of Law & Education, 13*(2), 7–20.
Mawdsley, R. D., & Mawdsley, J. L. (2012). Should educational malpractice be actionable? In C. J. Russo (Ed.), *School law* (pp. 213–227). Thousand Oaks: SAGE Publications.
Mears v Sydney Anglican Schools Corporation [2013] NSWSC 535; Mears v Sydney Anglican schools corporation (No. 2)[2013] NSWSC 876.
Moore v Vanderloo, 386 N.W.2d 108 (Iowa 1986).
Overseas Tankship (UK) Ltd v Miller Steamship Co Pty Ltd (Wagon Mound (No 2)) [1967] AC 617.
Oyston v St Patrick's College [2013] NSWCA 135.
Peter W v. San Francisco Unified Sch. Dist., 131 Cal. Rptr. 854 (Cal. Ct. App. 1976).
Phelps v Hillingdon London Borough Council [1999] 1 W.L.R. 500.
Phelps v London Borough of Hillingdon [2001] 2 AC 619.
Raethel, S. (1996, April 11). Pupils sue over missing lessons. *Sydney Morning Herald*, p. 3.

Ramsay, I. (1988). Educational negligence and the legalisation of education. *University of New South Wales Law Journal, 11*, 184–218.
Ramsay v Larsen. (1964). 111 CLR 16.
Roads and Traffic Authority v Royal [2008] HCA 19.
Sarre, R. (2008). Fairness in trading: Trade practices law and school governance. *AISSA School Board Governance Journal, 11*, 1–4.
Sisters of the Holy Child Jesus at Old Westbury v. Corwin, 29 N.Y.S.3d 736 (N.Y. App. Div. 2016).
Smith v. Alameda Cnty. Social Servs. Agency, 153 Cal.Rptr. 712 (Cal. Ct. App. 1979).
Tokic, S. (2014). Rethinking educational malpractice: Are educators rock stars? *Brigham Young University Education and Law Journal, 3*(1), 105–133.
Torres v Little Flower, 485 N.Y.S.2d 15 (N.Y.1984).
Trade Practices Act 1974 (Cth).
Trustees of the Roman Catholic Church for the Diocese of Canberra and Goulburn v Hadba [2005] HCA 31.
Weir v Geelong Grammar School (Civil Claims) [2012] VCAT 1736.
Williams v. Eady. (1893). 10 TLR 41 CA.
Wrongs Act (Vic) 1958.
Wyong Shire Council v Shirt (1980) 146 CLR 40.
Yee Tak On v Dr Linda Hort (ANU College) [2012] FMCA 391.

4

Risk and Responsibility: Liability of School Authorities for Harm to Pupils

Sally Varnham

4.1 Introduction

Duty of care and risk are ever-present and sometimes overwhelming concepts for educators in Australia as elsewhere. This chapter considers the law in relation to school safety by examining the circumstances which may render school authorities liable for student harm based on the legal duty of care within the tort of negligence (Morrison and Vaandering 2012). Negligence is a branch of private law which essentially establishes duties owed to one another and remedies for breaches of those duties when harm results. It is combination of law from decided cases (referred to as common law) and the Civil Liability legislation (known as the Tort Law Reforms) enacted by all States and Territories following the Review of the Law of Negligence (Ipp Report 2002).

First, the chapter explores school responsibility and the implications for risk management within this context. It aims to clarify the parameters of liability, and to follow the trend of the courts towards a pragmatic approach in considering a school's standard of care and the assumption of risk. Secondly, the chapter takes a proactive approach towards safe school environments and considers restorative practices now being instituted across the sector.

Any such discussion is necessarily underpinned by the development of safe practice and the role played by the *National Safe Schools Framework*,

S. Varnham (✉)
University of Technology Sydney, Ultimo, NSW, Australia
e-mail: Sally.Varnham@uts.edu.au

K. Trimmer et al. (eds.), *The Palgrave Handbook of Education Law for Schools*,
https://doi.org/10.1007/978-3-319-77751-1_4

and health and safety legislation. The Framework provides a set of principles accompanied by practical resources to enable schools to develop positive and effective policies and procedures to build a safe school cultures. The occupational health and safety legislation sets out a range of statutory requirements aimed at ensuring safety of the school environment and the elimination of risks. The most relevant provisions are within the *Work Health and Safety Act 2011* (Cth) (section 3), and most jurisdictions have enacted the model law and their own corresponding legislation. It is beyond the scope of this chapter to deal with these in detail but it is important to point to the importance of their facilitation and enabling functions within the context of school safety.

The reality is that policies and regulations are one thing but putting them into practice effectively in the hurly-burly of a school environment with its many competing demands, is another. The overarching vision of the National Safe Schools Framework is that: 'All Australian schools are safe, supportive and respectful school communities'. The focus is on having strict standards to ensure the 'elimination or minimisation of risks'. All schools have this goal uppermost and most achieve a high standard of safety. Sadly however things go wrong and the question of liability arises.

Children and young people are inevitably exposed to many risks within schools, in classrooms and laboratories, within playgrounds, during games, sporting activities and school excursions. They face many hazards outside the school gates such as getting to and from school, and when taken on sporting trips, excursions, volunteer activities and work experience. It would be impossible and arguably counterproductive for all potential dangers to be eliminated. Educators must reach a balance between eliminating unacceptable perils while still affording the opportunity for young people to learn the important qualities of managing risk and personal responsibility, core elements of their education.

Societal problems inevitably enter the school environment. Students' behavioural issues, sometimes related to the use of drugs and alcohol, confront schools on a daily basis. So do matters pertaining to security, for example, the bringing of weapons on to school grounds (Perry-Hazan and Birnhack 2016). Varying methods of searching and surveillance are now entrenched in school systems abroad and Australian schools are following.

While the injuries suffered by children remain most commonly a result of misadventure or carelessness, recent years have seen a greater focus on harm caused by the intentional conduct of others, such as violence, bullying and abuse by both peers and teachers. There is a new recognition of long term historical failure to respond to complaints and suspicions of conduct such as sexual abuse and its devastating effect on the lives of many (significantly by the Royal Commission on Institutional Responses to Child Sexual Abuse referred to below). In addition, technology is now giving rise to phenomena such as text and online bullying and questions as to the extent of a school's responsibility include now dangers arising in cyberspace (Shariff and Hoff 2007).

When harm happens it is in the direction of the school that students and their parents look for redress. While in reality the majority of school negligence cases reach settlement before progressing to litigation, this chapter discusses those actions which have reached the courts. These are valuable for legal guidance but most often are at considerable financial and emotional expense, particularly for the plaintiffs and their parents as media and law reports attest (a stark example is *Chaina* (2003), *"Nathan Chaina's family ordered to pay Scots College $8 million in legal fees"* SMH 31/07/14).

As discussed in this chapter, harm occurring within a school's control may legally be the responsibility of the school or its employees, but often it is perpetrated by students towards each other. It is beyond doubt that school environments characterised by cultures of caring, responsibility and respect, often referred to as 'restorative schools', are worth striving for and there is evidence of moves in this direction (Varnham et al. 2014–2015a, b). The chapter concludes on this note.

4.2 The Tort of Negligence: Personal Injury Liability Generally

Negligence is now a combination of case law and civil liability legislation in all states and territories (CLAs). This chapter refers primarily to the Civil Liability Act (NSW) and while the provisions are generally universal in essence there are minor differences and the reader should refer to the legislation of their state or territory where necessary. Any significant differences will be referred to specifically. The CLAs aim to clarify the principles which apply to actions for damages for personal injury and death through negligence. Liability rests on a legal duty of care being owed and determination of this remains the precinct of common law (one exception is in the case of mental harm when s 32 CLA NSW applies also). The legislation then sets out the further requirements to establish negligence – breach of the duty, causation and damages and other matters.

The Tort Law Reforms were driven essentially by a need to limit liability for personal injury (pushed partly by the insurance industry) and to move society towards individual responsibility for safety. Many CLA provisions codify the basic elements of the tort of negligence laid down by the courts with limitations for this purpose (discussed below). Previous cases remain important aids for interpretation of the statutory provisions. The suite of new provisions dealing with 'obvious risk' and 'recreational activities' have clear significance in determining school liability, and how educators respond to risk particularly in relation to sports and school recreational excursions. Issues of age and understanding may be of practical importance in considering a student's knowledge and assumption of risk and personal responsibility as provided by the CLAs.

It is important to note that harm from intentional acts is excluded specifically (s3b CLA NSW). Actions in this area, such as trespass to the person – assault and battery and false imprisonment – are still within the precinct of common law and not subject to the provisions of the CLAs. Such actions, for example in sexual assault, would be taken against the perpetrator specifically and not the school and are not examined here (see Stewart and Stuhmcke 2017).

4.2.1 The Tort of Negligence in Practice in School Liability

A negligence case has four elements, all of which must be proven on the facts. These are:

1. The school authority or the employee/agent owed to the student a duty of care.
2. The school or employee/agent fell below the standard of care required in such a situation, so as to be in breach of the duty of care; and
3. The breach of the duty of care caused the injury to the student and the injury was not caused by some intervening factor; and
4. The plaintiff's injury is one for which compensation should rightly be paid, for example, not too remote.

4.2.2 The Duty of Care

The term 'duty of care' is commonly referred to in a variety of contexts, but it has a precise meaning in law. It is derived from the principle in *Donoghue v*

Stevenson (1932) which asks the question: was the risk foreseeable by a reasonable person in the position of the defendant? The initial answer may be reinforced or diminished by the 'salient features' test' *Hill* (1997) which directs consideration of matters of the relationship between the parties, such as control and vulnerability.

However, since the decision of the High Court in *Commonwealth v Introvigne* (1982) the inquiry to determine whether a duty is owed by the school may not be necessary as a school clearly owes a non-delegable duty. Determination of duty or otherwise is required however in situations where it is questionable whether the action or inaction occurred within the school's jurisdiction (for example, cyber bullying discussed below).

Where the claim relates to mental harm, the CLAs make special provision for the establishment of a duty of care. There must be proof of 'recognised psychiatric harm' or a 'recognised psychiatric illness' suffered by the Plaintiff, and that it was foreseeable harm to a person of 'normal fortitude' (ss 31, 32 CLA NSW). This is of obvious importance in bullying/sexual assault cases.

4.2.3 The Non-delegable Duty of Care

The High Court of Australia said in *Commonwealth v Introvigne:*

> *A school authority owes to its pupils a duty to ensure that reasonable care is taken of them whilst they are on the school premises during hours when the school is open for attendance ... The duty is not discharged by merely appointing competent teaching staff and leaving it to the staff to take appropriate steps for the care of the children. It is a duty to ensure that reasonable steps are taken for the safety of the children, a duty the performance of which cannot be delegated.* (269)

The school authority was found directly liable for the student's physical injury suffered while swinging on a halyard attached to a flagpole in the school grounds. The Court said the duty was to provide suitable and safe premises, and to ensure that adequate systems were in place and carried out so children were not exposed to unnecessary risks. This applied even though the school day had not yet begun.

The 'non-delegable duty' has not been extended to harm resulting from intentional criminal acts committed by school employees (*Lepore* (2003), affirmed recently in *Prince Alfred College Inc.* (2016)). However school authorities may be vicariously liable in this situation (discussed in the context of sexual harassment and abuse below).

4.2.4 Vicarious Liability

Vicarious liability ensures that an employer is held liable for the torts of its employee or agent committed in the course of employment or agency. Vicarious liability is established when (Salmond 1907):

- the person was employed; and
- he or she was acting within the scope of their employment at the time of the injury.

It arises from the relationship of the parties and the notion of control. A school would not be vicariously liable if, for example, the person who acted carelessly was an independent contractor, but they would owe a non-delegable duty in any event.

Teachers and suchlike are clearly employees or agents, including 'supply' or relief teachers employed on a short-term or casual basis or to perform specific tasks. This was clearly established by the House of Lords in the UK educational negligence cases, *X (Minors)* (1995). There are two parts to this enquiry. First, were they acting in the course of carrying out their duties? Second, could it be said that they doing so in a way that was so wrong it could not be said to be within their duties at all? In simple terms, where the motivation behind the action or inaction can be logically connected to his or her duties, the school could be liable, but if there is personal motivating factor on the part of the employee or agent, the school may not be held to account vicariously.

Vicarious liability encourages educators to ensure their policies are effective, known and implemented by all. However the effect of a school owing a non-delegable duty may often remove many of the issues surrounding vicarious liability. A school would not be able to point the finger at independent contractors who created the risk in question to absolve itself from liability, although the errant contractor may be added as co-defendant by the defendant school or may be subject to a 'contribution' action pursuant to the 'solidary principle' (*Law Reform (Miscellaneous Provisions)* Act *1944* NSW).

Whatever the basis of the duty, the primary focus of the court's enquiry is the action or inaction of the school's employee or agent in response to the risk. In reality the question is: was the duty of care breached? The civil liability legislation of New South Wales provides specifically in Section 5Q that the determination of liability of a defendant for non-delegable duty is considered in the same way as vicarious liability (s 5Q CLA NSW).

A teacher will rarely be held personally liable to a student unless it is clearly shown that they acted outside their authority or where serious or wilful misconduct is found (*Deaton* 1949). The law endeavours to provide fair and efficient system of compensation for a wronged plaintiff and to take a pragmatic view the school authority has the 'deepest pocket'. Among the many policy grounds for vicarious liability are loss spreading and ensuring the adherence to strict standards. Generally such claims are negotiated with the Department of Education of the particular state or territory, or the school proprietor and with the school's insurer.

Moving from establishment of duty, the next examination is of the standard of care required in the circumstances and whether the educator fell short.

4.2.5 Breach of the Duty of Care

The principles by which this is determined in each situation are now within the CLAs (s 5B CLA NSW). While essentially a codification of the existing common law there are seemingly slight but important differences. The foreseeable risk must now be 'not insignificant' which is higher than the previous common law: 'not far-fetched or fanciful' (*Wyong Shire* 1980).

A duty of care will not be breached unless:

- the risk is foreseeable, meaning a risk of which the person knew or ought to have known; and
- the risk was not insignificant; and
- a reasonable person in that position would have taken precautions.

In deciding whether a reasonable person would have taken precautions, the factors which a court is to consider are:

- probability of harm;
- likely seriousness of harm;
- burden of taking precautions to avoid the risk;
- the social utility or potential net benefit of the activity that creates the risk.

A determination is made by a balance of these factors on the facts. The following are examples of situations where the equivalent questions in common law were considered in the school context.

4.2.6 Supervision

What is reasonable supervision is often a vexed question, clearly depending on circumstances such as the age of the child. The level of supervision realistically required was stated as 'a fine balance between discipline and supervision on the one hand and freedom of action and inculcation of independence on the part of students, on the other' (*H* (1987) at 163). Importantly the plaintiff must satisfy the court that, in the circumstances, the injury would have been prevented had the school done more in terms of supervision. This was affirmed by High Court of Australia in *Hadba* (2005). Farrah Hadba, aged 8, was injured by the actions of another child while playing on a flying fox in the school playground. It was standard procedure for use of the flying fox to be closely supervised and there was a 'hands-off rule' of which all the children were made well aware. As Farrah was leaving the platform two other students grabbed her legs, she was pulled off the flying fox, suffering significant injury as she hit her head on the platform and fell to the ground. The supervising teacher had momentarily moved away to deal with some other misbehaving students.

The plaintiff's case turned on the question of supervision and the Court held there was no breach. The school had strict practices and procedures for supervision and safety of children using this apparatus and to impose any greater requirement was unrealistic. In addition, they found that it was unlikely that even a teacher watching the equipment uninterruptedly would have been able to prevent the events that led to the accident. The plaintiff had not demonstrated that any alternative system of supervision would have been more effective.

While there is a higher standard in the case of very young children and where the child concerned has special needs (*Miller* 1980; *Kretschmar v* 1989), the courts are reluctant to set an age for when children achieve the competence to be able to either protect themselves or be aware of the potential for injury of their actions.

4.2.7 School Transport and Getting to and from School

A duty arises when transport is specially organised by the school. Arguably would be different if it was merely sanctioned. The key determining factors are whether the school has assumed control over the activities of the student and whether the school had actual constructive knowledge or ought to have known of the risk, even though outside the school gates.

4.2.8 Activities Outside the School, Sports and School Excursions

The CLA 'recreational activity' and 'obvious risk' provisions (discussed below) clearly apply here. Traditional forms of education are now combined with activities outside the classroom and the school, designed to provide opportunities for the students to experience and learn things for themselves. This is as it should be – not governed unrealistically by risk aversion. A school owes a duty to make careful investigation of the excursion to be undertaken and to plan it accordingly in recognition of the possible dangers. It must take into account all the circumstances surrounding the excursion, including the age and experience of the children, the type of excursion, the conditions of terrain, weather and so on, which are likely to prevail, and prepare for all reasonable eventualities (*Chaina* 2003).

The test is reasonableness. For example, when a student was injured when his foot went into a hole on the school oval while playing touch football, the school was liable as the hole would not have been there if the school had undergone regular inspections which it was reasonable to expect (*Bujnowicz* 2005). Difficulties arise when the sporting activity is provided by an independent body and/or outside school grounds and school hours. Any student who engages in a sporting activity must assume a certain level of risk of injury and the test is whether there were deficiencies on the part of the school which in some way indicated carelessness in respect of its duty to its sporting students. Particularly tragic is the recent case of *Miller* (*Uniting Church v* 2015), where the plaintiff suffered spinal injuries practising racing dives in her own time following instructions of the school coach. The unsuccessful plaintiff was unable to show that the school should have done anything different to the technique set out in the guidance literature.

When using student helpers in a sporting activity, the teacher has a duty to ensure that instructions are understood and applied. A school will be liable to a student who suffers harm as a result of a breach of this duty.

A school ensures a discharge of its duty by some fundamental guidelines which include:

- team coaches are appropriately trained and able;
- players are aware of the rules of each game and ensuring that as far as possible those rules are adhered to;
- in contact sports team sizes are, as far as possible, evenly matched;

- when students are assisting in sporting activities they are given clear and proper instructions so there can be no misunderstanding or confusion as to their roles; and
- sports are not played in conditions that render them so dangerous as to be beyond what could be reasonably expected in a sport of the kind.

A school's prior knowledge of the way in which an injury can occur will render the risk foreseeable and a failure to take precautions a breach. Thus a school was liable when a student who had a long thin neck became paraplegic when he was positioned in the front row of a scrum while playing school rugby because the education authority knew of research which pointed to this risk (*Watson* 1987).

4.2.9 Obvious Risks, Recreational Activities and Dangerous Recreational Activities: The CLAs and Their Impact on Duty and Breach

4.2.9.1 Obvious Risks

The CLAs contain a general provision to the effect that there will be no liability for manifestation of a risk which was or should have been obvious (s 5F (1) CLA NSW). In the words of Mason JA (*Wyong Shire Council* 2004):

> 'Obvious' means that both the condition and the risk are apparent to and would be recognised by a reasonable man, in the position of the [plaintiff], exercising ordinary perception, intelligence and judgment. (para 35)

A person is presumed to have been aware of an obvious risk unless they can prove otherwise (s 5G(1) CLA NSW). The effect of this provision is uncertain in the school environment. It is speculated that successful application of a defence based on this provision would depend largely on the age and maturity of the child concerned (*Dederer* 2007), and arguably it would be diminished in any event if the activity was compulsory.

In addition, there is no liability when the injury suffered was the manifestation of an 'inherent risk'. This is defined as a risk of something occurring which cannot be avoided by the exercise of reasonable care and skill (s 5I CLA NSW). Here there is a clear overlap with whether the school breached the duty or not.

4.2.9.2 Recreational Activities

Recreational activities receive special treatment in the CLAs. A 'recreational activity' is defined as 'any sport (whether or not the sport is an organised activity) any pursuit or activity engaged in for enjoyment, relaxation or leisure, or any pursuit or activity engaged in at a place (such as a beach, park or other public open space) where people ordinarily engage in sport or any pursuit or activity for enjoyment, relaxation or leisure' (s 5 K CLA NSW). A 'dangerous recreational activity' is one which involves a significant risk of physical harm. An increasingly large number of sports such as rugby, water polo, netball, rugby league, football and gymnastics are played by students in schools today. All come within the definition of recreational activity and arguably many could be considered 'dangerous'. As they involve some level of contact and often high levels of physicality.

A school is not liable for harm suffered 'as a result of a materialisation of an obvious risk of a dangerous recreational activity' (s 5 L CLA NSW). There is no duty to warn and no possibility for a plaintiff to argue that the risk was not obvious to them. The courts have wrestled with the concept of dangerousness and 'obvious risk', particularly whether the harm caused was in fact a 'manifestation' of this risk (*Fallas* 2006).

Many blurred lines have emerged. Education establishments, in common with sporting and coaching clubs and providers of recreational facilities have risk warnings to prevent any such questions arising (s 5 M CLA NSW). It is clear that a warning may operate to absolve a school from liability even though its nature may be general. It is important to note in this context that where a person is 'incapable' by age or disability, the risk warning must be given to the parent or other person in that position. State and territory departments of education provide information sheets for risk warnings to assist schools in this regard. It is debatable whether a school may rely on a risk warning when the activity which created the risk was compulsory so it could not be said that the student and his or her parents were aware of the risk but proceeded voluntarily with the activity in an event. Similarly the courts will closely examine a situation where the breach complained of was so grossly negligent as to be outside any accepted risk (*Fallas* 2006).

CLAs provide for a contractual waiver which would allow the supplier of recreational services to escape liability altogether (s 5 N CLA NSW). It is generally standard for parents to sign such waivers before allowing students to take part in school excursions. Once again, there are questions, for example whether such a waiver would absolve a school when its actions were so grossly negligent they could be considered to be outside the consented activity.

Proving a duty of care and breach is one thing but the plaintiff must prove that the breach caused the loss (causation).

4.2.10 Causation

Causation has been historically referred to as the 'but for' test. Would the injury not have been suffered but for the breach of duty complained of?

s 5D CLA NSW requires that:

- it be determined that the fault of the defendant was a necessary condition of the occurrence of the harm; and
- it is appropriate for the scope of the tortfeasor's duty to extend to the harm so caused.

The establishment of a causal connection between a failure to provide adequate supervision and the injury may prove insurmountable for the plaintiff. For example in *El Sheik* (2000) there was no liability when a 'play fight that got serious' would have caused the plaintiff relatively minor injury except for a congenital condition which led to serious lasting harm. The Federal Court said that the plaintiff had failed to establish that the injury was sustained from a cause that could have been foreseen and prevented by reasonable supervision. The duty could not be extended to protection from apparently normal student behaviour.

Illustrated by the decision of the High Court of Australia in *Hadba* (above), the onus is on the plaintiff to show that the school's failure to do more caused the accident. The spontaneity and impulsiveness of children frequently means that accidents happen quickly. The cases demonstrate a trend towards taking a practical approach in considering first, whether there has been a breach of duty and, second, whether such a breach could reasonably be said to have caused the injury suffered.

4.2.11 Plaintiff's Loss Must Be Compensable at Law

The CLAs generally have introduced a policy factor by stating, that the court is to consider whether or not and why responsibility for the harm should be imposed on the party in breach (s 5 D(4) CLA NSW) This provision directs a court to apply all existing factors and circumstances in making its decision on liability.

As raised above, redress for the mental harm suffered as a result of bullying and abuse is a developing area pointing to a multitude of issues and provides an example where the above section may be invoked (in addition to the operation of ss 31,32 CLA NSW).

4.2.12 A School's Defences

Clearly a school's defence may rest on evidence that a duty of care was not owed in the particular situation (for example, the event happened outside the school's control or knowledge), or that it was not breached and/or the breach did not cause the harm. While keen to provide redress for harm where justified it is clear that a court will stress the realities of the situation and will not impose impossible expectations. In addition, the 'obvious risk' provisions of the CLAs may be invoked. Other defences are contributory negligence, or limitation if appropriate.

4.2.13 Contributory Negligence

This argues that the student contributed to their injury by their own failure to take care. While previously a 'partial defence' the CLAs of some states provide that a court may decide on 100 per cent reduction in damages if it considers it 'just and equitable to do so' (s 5S CLA NSW). However, because an acceptance of a need for protection for young people unable to take care for their own safety provides strong rationale for imposing a duty of care, it follows that here are limited situations in which such a defence may be successfully pleaded. It may be different where the child is older and in cases of physical harm, the courts have attributed them with some ability to take care for their own safety. In *Abrahams* (2007) while the school was liable, damages were reduced by 10 per cent for the 9-year-old boy's contribution to his own harm by sliding down the bannister.

In the case of mental harm as a result of bullying, the court is unlikely to find contributory negligence. In *Oyston* (2013) even though the school argued that Jazmine was particularly vulnerable, the court held that her injuries were the direct result of the college's failure to take the very steps it had devised to prevent such injury being inflicted by one student upon another.

4.2.14 Limitation

Where a student commences an action against his or her school authority some period of time after the alleged negligence occurred, it may be argued that the action is statute-barred due to the limitation periods contained in legislation. The legislation of the various states provides that actions in tort must be commenced within either 3 or 6 years from when the cause of action accrued (s 14 CLA NSW). In the case of mental harm caused by bullying or sexual abuse (below), a plaintiff may be in his or her adult life before they are in a psychological or emotional state to confront the events which took place during their school years. Frequently also the evidence shows that complaints made by the students at the time 'fell on deaf ears'. Very seldom has commencement of an action outside the limitation period disqualified a student's action (*Gregory* 2009). Generally courts and statutes provide that the limitation period commences from when the student was reasonably able to discover the wrong, or from the removal of the student's disability due to age. Recently however the High Court of Australia was not prepared to grant a time extension thus precluding a plaintiff's action for harm from sexual abuse on the grounds of limitation (*Prince Alfred College Inc.* 2016). Importantly though the court did accept the potential for vicarious institutional liability for the intentional criminal acts of others (below).

This and other emerging challenges facing schools are now discussed.

4.3 Exploration of Current Issues

4.3.1 Bullying and Harassment

Bullying, both physical violence and emotional abuse, historically entrenched in school environments was considered to be part and parcel of school life. Happily, this culture is changing and thanks to both school and national educative campaigns, a strong intolerance of bullying has developed. Such behaviour is now rightly recognised as antisocial and damaging, causing long lasting mental harm and impacting on the exercise of the right to education of all. Despite this recognition there is now 'cyber bullying' carried out through social media, online or text which poses new problems. The key to dealing with all bullying is not only recognising it as such and having effective preventative policies and processes and using them, but most importantly developing school cultures which are the antitheses to such behaviour (below).

A school will be liable when it has or should have knowledge and fails to take effective action to stop the bullying. The same principles of negligence apply, established first in Australia in *Eskinazi* (2003). Two later cases demonstrate the extent of a school's responsibility. The school authority was liable to

Benjamin Cox, who while a pupil at a New South Wales school, suffered continual bullying over years by another student in the same class (*Cox* 2007). It was important to this finding that the bullying was ongoing, not an isolated incident and the school had actual knowledge of its occurrence. It was not enough for the school to point to its policies but its knowledge required all possible steps to have been taken to stop the behaviour and thus eliminate the risk.

A recent case demonstrates the devastating harm caused not only by the bullying but by the prolonged quest for redress. *Oyston* (2013) was finally decided by the NSW Court of Appeal in September 2013. Jazmine Oyston had suffered bullying over a number of years and the school was well aware. Although it argued that it had policies and that it was active in attempts to address a bullying problem, this was shown to be ad hoc and not systematic. The final court decided that the school's attempts were inadequate and it was liable for the harm suffered.

Cyber-bullying poses increasing threats to student safety and calls for educators to think of new responses. It is defined as '...the use of information and communication technologies to support deliberate, repeated and hostile behaviour by an individual or group, that is intended to harm others' (Belsey 2007). Various jurisdictions have introduced legislation which attracts criminal penalties for perpetrators of menacing, harassing or offensive use of internet, some of which applies specifically within the context of 'attending the school' (eg s 60E inserted by *Crimes Amendment (School Protection) Act 2002* (NSW) into the *Crimes Act 1900* (NSW)).

By restricting the application of provisions to matters within the school premises or entering or leaving school for school activities, it could be said that there is an implied limitation to a school's duty of care. With no boundaries in cyberspace it is exceedingly difficult to delineate an area of a school's responsibility for harm arising in this way. However liability is not inconceivable, for example when the bully uses technology within the school or provided by the school, and where the school has or ought to have knowledge that it is being used for this purpose, inside or outside the school. Although there is much discussion a lead is yet to be taken from the Australian courts on the extent of a school's duty of care in this area (Pelletier et al. 2015). Notable however is Alistair Nicholson, the former Chief Justice of the Family Court of Australia, adding his voice to the call for school liability whether or not the bullying occurs during school hours (Dwyer and Easteal 2013).

4.3.2 Intentional Criminal Acts: Liability of School Authorities for School Employee/Student Sexual Abuse

The liability of school authorities to compensate a student who suffers physical or psychiatric harm as a result of intentional criminal acts of a school employee is now receiving considerable national and international attention. This is within the wider consideration of sexual abuse in all manner of institutions which includes schools. Redress for survivors is now for determination by bodies such as the Royal Commission on Institutional Responses to Child Sexual Abuse and comprehensive discussion is beyond the scope of this Chapter (http://www.childabuseroyalcommission.gov.au/).

The High Court of Australia in a landmark decision held that a school authority may be vicariously liable for the intentional criminal acts of its employees (*Lepore* 2003). While rejecting the plaintiffs' argument that a school's non-delegable duty may extend into this area, the majority nevertheless held there could be vicarious liability, following the decisions of *Lister* (2002) in the UK House of Lords and *Bazley* (1999) in the Supreme Court of Canada. This principle was affirmed in *Prince Alfred College Inc.* (2016) (although declining liability on limitation grounds).

Important in *Lepore* is Kirby J's emphasis on policy as a powerful rationale for imposing vicarious liability on school authorities. He said 'fair and efficient' compensation requires a solvent defendant; 'enterprise risk' extending to public schools means the community bears the cost; and the potential liability of employers may effectively encourage them to take effective precautions and initiatives to reduce risks to protect vulnerable children.

The case for direct liability of school authorities for breach of their duty of care under the ordinary principles of negligence will arise when it is shown that they knew or ought to have known of the abuse and took no action (*S* [2001]).

Whatever the basis for liability, there is potential application to new challenges relating to criminal conduct within schools, for example, the use of weapons.

4.3.3 Weapons at School

There are not infrequent reports of weapons such as guns, knives, screwdrivers, and clubs being brought into schools and sometimes used. Arguably it is only a matter of time before a student injured in such an assault takes action against a school authority in Australia (Mazerolle et al. 2011). If a lead is to be taken from the United States, these problems will inevitably raise new issues for the courts to resolve.

This disturbing trend enhances and expands the duty of care of schools from the traditional standard which rested on matters such as supervision. What is foreseeable harm which the school must guard against, for example: what is the extent of a school's duty to implement procedures aimed at preventing such weapons being brought on to the school property? In addition to the age old and controversial measures such as body and locker searching, this threat has led many schools to implement surveillance procedures such as close-circuit television (CCTV) (Perry-Hazan and Birnhack 2016; Rooney 2010). These all give rise to significant human rights issues, particularly those concerning privacy and body integrity. Currently in Australia, it may only be speculated as to how this area could play out in the courts (Fronius et al. 2016).

The chapter now moves to the positive: to focus specifically on reducing student to student behaviour occasioning harm, and on the creation of safe environments conducive to learning while keeping all young people in schools. There is an emergent trend in Australia as elsewhere towards community or 'whole school approaches' to school discipline and safety, referred to as 'restorative justice' or more widely, 'restorative practice' (Varnham et al. 2014–2015a, b; Anders 2015).

4.4 Restorative Practice: An Approach to Keeping Schools Safe and Young People in School

> *Restorative justice sees things differently ... Crime is a violation of people and relationships ... It creates obligations to make things right. Justice involves the victim, the offender and the community in a search for solutions which promote repair, reconciliation, and reassurance.* (Zehr 1990, 181)

There is now much evidence of success in education sectors abroad (see for example Anders 2015; Buckley and Maxwell 2007). Begun in individual schools, restorative justice is now reflected in some education department policies. It has become a strong focus of Australian Catholic school systems (see, for example Catholic Education Office Archdiocese of Melbourne 2007, http://web.spgww.catholic.edu.au/documents/policies/restorativejusticeresearch.pdf) (Varnham 2015). On a reactive level, restorative justice is a response to wrongdoing that focuses on people and relationships rather than on retribution (Morrison and Vaandering 2012). The aim is not to punish but to assist students to take responsibility for their actions and the rebuilding of relationships. It works on the basis that in all but the most serious cases the detrimental effects of exclusion from school outweigh any positives.

Most importantly on a proactive level, restorative practice focuses on conflict resolution and relationship-building in the school community and is directed at a reduction in anti-social behaviour, conflict and disciplinary issues by changing school cultures. It aims to reduce suspensions and exclusions and to improve academic performance by as far as is possible keeping all young people in school. It is within the frame of practising citizenship and is based on responsibility, relationships and respect to ultimately work towards improving student behaviour generally to benefit the wider school community. The attention now being paid to restorative approaches in Australian schools is evidenced by a number of organisations set up for this purpose (for example, the Centre for Restorative Justice in South Australia, RealJustice, Restorative Practices Australia). Recent research in New South Wales schools pointed to powerful benefits (Varnham et al. 2014–2015a, b).

In common usage, restorative practice involves 'circles', peer mediation or the convening of a conference of all parties with a stake in the particular event for the purpose of working towards a collective resolution. The development of a restorative 'culture' in a school may however include a wider variety of initiatives.

The practice of 'circles' is not necessarily used to address particular wrongdoings but as a forum for open discussion as a means of community-building to enhance students' learning environment. Peer mediation is seen as a constructive problem-solving approach – empowering students to work out differences constructively and to work towards solutions on their own rather than through school disciplinary mechanisms.

Conferencing is a meeting targeted to address a particular issue. New Zealand was a forerunner in this area with conferencing developed in schools there based on the indigenous Maori practice of community problem solving through the 'hui' process (Buckley and Maxwell 2007; Hayden 2001). It may be a small meeting to address student wrongdoing, with all involved parties, or a large conference including the whole school to consider a serious incident of wrongdoing or a wider school problem.

While there is still disagreement as to where the emphasis should lie with restorative practice and some still lean towards the more reactive and retributive, most accept that a whole school approach is needed. Many schools eliminate the term 'justice' to move away from retributive language and to emphasize the approach they are taking to address the core of their functioning. This is to make educational policy and practice more responsive to the needs and concerns of the school community. 'Practising citizenship' is seen to be key – removing the 'them and us' mindset and establishing responsibility of all for the safety of the school environment (Osher et al. 2010; Sullivan et al. 2014).

Initiatives based on 'positive behaviour support' are also emerging now in some Australian states. These involve frameworks for preventing and responding to anti-social student behaviour and one example is Victoria's School-Wide Positive Behaviour Support (SWPBS). While clearly articulating the use of restorative practice also, this program aims to create a positive school climate, a culture of student competence and an open, responsive management system for all school community members.

4.5 Conclusion

Schools are responsible for maintaining a safe environment and in Australia they face the same challenges as education systems elsewhere. Within the wide range of activities carried out both in a school and outside, it is inevitable that risks will be manifested in harm. This may be physical injury or psychiatric harm as a result of bullying, harassment or abuse.

Frequently, children and parents seek to hold the school liable for the child's injury. Determination of liability depends upon the application of the principles of the tort of negligence to the facts of each particular case. The law is now a combination of previously existing common law from decided cases, the provisions of the Civil Liability Acts of each state and territory, and guidance from the courts as to the application of these provisions.

In *Introvigne* the High Court established the direct liability of schools pursuant to a non-delegable duty of care to protect their pupils against foreseeable harm. However this liability is not absolute, it is dependent on breach. The central inquiry focuses on the action which would be expected in the particular situation and the extent to which the school fell short of this standard. Courts are now adopting a pragmatic approach as to what is practicable and are drawing back from imposing unreasonable expectations. In cases of bullying and cyber-bullying a school's liability for harm rests on the tests of foreseeability and whether it could be said to have taken place within the school's jurisdiction and it was in a position to both know of it and to take action. If so, courts will not shrink from imposing liability.

In all the areas considered above, the elimination as far as possible of risks both within and outside a school environment is a clear priority. Equally pressing is how to respond to the much greater recognition in recent years of the devastating and sometimes catastrophic effects of bullying and harassment and to eliminate it. Schools have a responsibility to educate their students as to what is unacceptable behaviour and to implement policies and procedures to ensure that such behaviour is eradicated from the school environment (Varnham 2015). Many Australian schools now are taking steps to develop cultures of respect and responsibility where antisocial behaviour such as bullying cannot flourish. This is frequently referred to as 'restorative practice' (Varnham et al. 2014–2015a, b). Such a system requires a fundamental shift in the thinking of educators and makers of educational policy – in the way in which they perceive their roles and how the education function is perceived by others. The results are encouraging.

References

Anders, J. (2015). *Keeping kids in school and out of court: A study of education – Youth justice collaboration in the US, Scotland and Denmark*. Canberra: Winston Churchill Memorial Trust of Australia.

Australia Capital Territory Schools Authority v El Sheik (2000) FCA 931 (11 July 2000).

Bazley v Curry. (1999). 2 SCR 534.

Belsey, B. (2007). Always on, always aware! bullying.org. 17 January www.cyberbullying.ca

Buckley, S., & Maxwell, G. (2007). *Respectful schools: Restorative practices in education a summary report*. Office of the Children's Commissioner and the Institute of Policy Studies, School of Government, Victoria University, Wellington.

Bujnowicz v Trustees Roman Catholic Church [2005] NSWCA 457.

Catholic Education Office Archdiocese of Melbourne, Student Wellbeing Central to Learning and School Improvement. (2007, October). http://web.spgww.catholic.edu.au/documents/policies/restorativejusticeresearch.pdf

Commonwealth v Introvigne. (1982). 150 CLR 258.

Cox v New South Wales [2007] NSWCA 471.

Deatons Pty Ltd v Flew (1949) 79 CLR 370.

Donoghue v Stevenson [1932] AC 562.

Dwyer, A., & Easteal, P. (2013). Cyber bullying in Australian schools: The question of negligence and liability. *Alternative Law Journal, 38*(2), 92.

Fallas v Mourlas [2006] NSWCA 32.

Fronius, et al. (2016). *Restorative justice in US schools: A research review*. San Francisco: Wested Justice and Prevention Research Centre.

Gregory v New South Wales [2009] NSWSC 559.

H v Pennell and South Australia. (1987). 46 SASR 158.
Hayden, A. (2001). *Restorative conferencing manual of Aotearoa New Zealand.* Wellington: Department for Courts.
Hill v Van Erp. (1997). 188 CLR 159.
Ipp, J. (2002). *Report of the panel for the review of the law of negligence* (the Ipp report). http:revofneg.treasury.gov.au/content/reports.asp
Kretschmar v Queensland. (1989). Aust Torts Reports ¶80–272.
Lisa Eskinazi v Victoria (County Court (Vic), Lewitan J, No 06471/99, 20 June 2003, unreported).
Lister v Hesley Hall Ltd [2002] 1 AC 215.
Mazerolle, P., Legosz, M., & Finighan, P. Weapons in schools in Queensland: The nature, causes and responses (2011) Griffith University, Brisbane. www.behaviour.education.qld.gov.au/SiteCollectionDocuments/.../weapons-in-schools.pdf
Miller v South Australia. (1980). 24 SASR 416.
Morrison, B., & Vaandering, D. (2012). Restorative justice: Pedagogy, praxis, and discipline. *Journal of School Violence, 11*(2), 138.
New South Wales v Lepore. (2003). 195 ALR 412; Samin v Queensland and Rich v Queensland (2003) 195 ALR 412.
Osher, D., Bear, G., Sprague, J., & Doyle, W. (2010). How can we improve school discipline? *Educational Researcher, 39*(1), 48.
Oyston v St Patrick's College (No 2) [2013] NSWCA 310.
Pelletier, R., Handal, B., Khalil, J., & Francis, T. (2015). Cyberbullying – When does a school authority's liability in Tort end? *The Western Australian Jurist, 6*, 93.
Perry-Hazan, L., & Birnhack, M. (2016). The hidden human rights curriculum of surveillance cameras in schools: Due process, privacy and trust. *Cambridge Journal of Education, 48*(1), 47–64.
Prince Alfred College Incorporated v ADC [2016] HCA 37.
Roads and Traffic Authority of New South Wales v Dederer. (2007). 234 CLR 330.
Rooney, T. (2010). Trusting children: How do surveillance technologies alter a child's experience of trust, risk and responsibility? *Surveillance & Society, 7*(3/4), 344.
Salmond, J. (1907). Salmond on Torts (1st ed.). London: Sweet & Maxwell. Schools should be sued for cyberbullying: Experts. *Sydney Morning Herald*, August 15 2013.
Shariff, S., & Hoff, D. L. (2007). Cyberbullying: Clarifying the legal boundaries for school supervision in cyberspace. *International Journal of Cyber Criminology, 1*(1), 76.
St Mark's Orthodox Coptic College v Abraham [2007] NSWCA 185.
Sullivan, A., Johnson, B., Owens, L., & Conway, R. (2014). Punish them or engage them? Teachers' views of unproductive student behaviours in the classroom. *Australian Journal of Teacher Education, 39*(6), 43.
Trustees of the Roman Catholic Church for the Diocese of Canberra and Goulburn v Hadba [2005] HCA 31.
Uniting Church in Australia Property Trust (NSW) v Miller, Miller v Lithgow City Council [2015] NSWCA 320.

Varnham, S. (2015, November). *The role of Catholic schools in Australia in educating for human rights and social justice: An overview*. Paper presented at the annual conference of the European education law association, within educating for today and tomorrow: A renewing passion, The World Catholic Education Congress, The Vatican, 18–21. (International Journal of Education Law and Policy Special Issue forthcoming).

Varnham, S., Evers, M., & Booth, T. (2014–2015a). Valuing their voices: Encouraging responsibility and citizenship through student participation in school decision making. *International Journal of Law and Education, 19*(2) & *20*(1), 23.

Varnham, S., Evers, M., Booth, T., & Avgoustinos, C. (2014–2015b). Democracy in schools: Encouraging responsibility and citizenship through student participation in school decision making. *International Journal of Law and Education, 19*(1) & *20*(1), 73.

Watson v Haines. (1987). Aust Torts reports 80–094.

Wyong Shire Council v Shirt (1980) 146 CLR 40.

Wyong Shire Council v Vairy [2004] NSWCA 247.

X (minors) v Bedfordshire County Council; M (a minor) and another v Newham London Borough Council and others; E (a minor) v Dorset County Council; and other appeals [1995] 2 AC 633.

Zehr, H. (1990). *Changing Lenses: A New Focus for Crime and Justice*. Herald Press: North Dakota.

5

Child Protection for Educators and Principals: A Moral and Legal Obligation

India Bryce

5.1 Introduction

Child maltreatment has reached 'epidemic' proportions globally. Defined in the Australian context child maltreatment refers to,

> *any non-accidental behaviour by parents, caregivers, other adults or older adolescents that is outside the norms of conduct and entails a substantial risk of causing physical or emotional harm to a child or young person. Such behaviours may be intentional or unintentional and can include acts of omission (i.e., neglect) and commission (i.e., abuse).* (Bromfield 2005; Christoffel et al. 1992)

Whilst it is difficult to ascertain the exact incidence of child maltreatment, overwhelming evidence indicates the magnitude of the problem is significant. Studies highlight that 25–70% of children around the world experience physical abuse, 20% of female children and 5–10% of male children suffer sexual abuse and 24–30% of children experience emotional abuse (ISPCAN International Congress on Child Abuse and Neglect 2012). In Australia from 2014 to 2015, 320,169 child protection notifications were received, of those, 152,086 were investigated with 56,423 substantiated, resulting in 48,730 children on child protection orders and of those, 43,399 children entering out

I. Bryce (✉)
School of Linguistics, Adult and Specialist Education, University of Southern Queensland, Toowoomba, QLD, Australia
e-mail: India.Bryce@usq.edu.au

K. Trimmer et al. (eds.), *The Palgrave Handbook of Education Law for Schools*,
https://doi.org/10.1007/978-3-319-77751-1_5

of home care (Australian Institute of Health and Welfare, 2016). In recent years, there has been an influx of media attention, government inquiries into departmental responses to child abuse and neglect and a host of research identifying the prevalence of abuse and neglect in our society. Schools are arguably on the front-line, holding a front row seat to the detection and reporting of child maltreatment. As our society becomes more complex, and the responsibilities of educators more diverse and welfare oriented, the legal terrain for educators and educational leaders becomes more ambiguous. Educators are perfectly positioned to detect, respond to and advocate for vulnerable children, prior to the point of crisis. It is of great importance that educators and educational leaders are equipped with the necessary knowledge and skills to navigate their legal and moral obligations.

This chapter aims to provide education professionals with an overview of the legal issues commonly encountered in the professional context, the nature of mandatory reporting obligations and the often-conflicting moral and ethical considerations. The chapter will explore the attitudes and deterrents to educators fulfilling these obligations and role of preservice education in adequately preparing professionals for the complexities of their role on the front line of child protection.

5.2 On the Front Line: The Role of Educators

Educators are in the invaluable position to identify and respond to suspected child maltreatment, in many cases, prior to statutory involvement and intrusive tertiary interventions. Schools afford students, especially those most vulnerable, a place of safety and security, of routine and predictability; likewise, educators hold a position of trust with children and their families. As caretakers, educators often maintain a close and consistent relationship with children and their families and can receive a great deal of personal and privileged information. Alternatively, when there is limited history available to the educator, the professional must rely on their skills of observation and their understanding of development and attachment in order to be effective in responding to child maltreatment in the first instance. This perspective strengthens the argument for the value of comprehensive child protection education for pre service and practicing teachers.

This information offers insight on which to base assessment of needs and risk and allows educators to advocate for children and access programs and services, which may strengthen vulnerable families. With children spending most of their waking hours in the care of education professionals and with education departments identified as the second most common notifier of child abuse and neglect, an education institution's role in child protection seems clear (Australian Institute of Health and Welfare 2015).

A range of factors have been identified in research to highlight the key role educators hold in child protection. The body of time teachers spend with children is greater than any other professional or non-familial adult and is comparable to that of the child's own family (Riley 2009). Due to their specific knowledge and skills, including targeted observation and comprehensive understanding of human development, teachers are well placed to identify delays, changes and anomalies in behaviour, appearance and progress. They are also well positioned to detect indicators or risk factors of abuse and neglect (Walsh et al. 2005). Rapport and accessibility are also factors which often result in teachers receiving disclosures of maltreatment directly from children, as well as from family and other concerned community members. A British study of adolescents' experiences of social work services found that for many young people, teachers were a preferred confidante, as compared to social workers (Triseliotis et al. 1995, p. 140). Seidman et al. identified educators as a group of "unrelated adults who are able to serve as 'listeners' and 'valuers' for young people" (1994, p. 519). Schools and educational staff within these institutions have become such an acknowledged source of monitoring and support for children that child protection departments recognise schools as a 'protective factor' in risk assessment practices (Centre for Disease Control 2016; Queensland Government 2015).

There is a clear and definite link between the duration, frequency and severity of abuse and its impact on the child (Bromfield and Miller 2007). 'Cumulative harm' is experienced by a child as a result of "a series or pattern of harmful events and experiences that may be historical, or ongoing, with the strong possibility of the risk factors being multiple, inter-related and co-existing over critical developmental periods" (Victorian Government 2007, p. 1). According to Higgins (2004) there is a growing body of evidence suggesting that a significant proportion of maltreated individuals experience not just repeated episodes of one type of maltreatment, but are likely to be the victim of other forms of abuse or neglect. The Adverse Childhood Experiences Study (ACEs) conducted in the United States of America from 1995 to 1997, one of the largest investigations of child abuse and neglect and lifespan well-being, identified that 87% of maltreated individuals had experienced two or more types of adverse childhood experiences (CDC 2016). They also concluded that the more ACEs a person has, the higher the risk of medical, mental and social issues as an adult (CDC 2016). Nurcombe et al. (2000) argue that due to the important relationship between duration and frequency of maltreatment and the negative impact on the individual, the timing of the action taken by educators is critical to interrupting the cycle of abuse and neglect. Identifying and responding to early indicators of maltreatment and disadvantage may lower the risk of reoccurring maltreatment and negate the need for intrusive tertiary level interventions. Similarly, educational institutions have been identified as 'capacity builders' for children, with schools adopting a "social inoculation role in strengthening the capacity of children to cope effectively with adversity and to resist the impact of negative experiences" through school-based prevention programs (Gilligan 1998, p. 15). The value of early detection, prevention and intervention by educational institutions, prior to the invasive involvement of statutory child protection departments, lies in addressing concerns prior to the issues becoming enduring and entrenched (Walsh et al. 2005).

Arguably, the most crucial role of education professionals in child protection is that of reporting suspected maltreatment to necessary statutory authorities. Educators in many countries around the world are mandated to report allegations of abuse and neglect. This process of reporting concerns is termed 'notifying'. According to Warner and Hansen "notifying is considered a 'critical antecedent' to addressing the harm and injustices caused by child abuse and neglect." (1994, p. 11).

Research in the field (Taylor 1997; Taylor and Hodgkinson 2001; Kenny 2004; Walsh and Farrell 2008; Baginsky 2003; Bourke and Maunsell 2015) has long argued for the inclusion of child protection 'training' in teacher education due the escalating prevalence of child abuse and neglect in Australia and globally. With the rise of statistics, comes an equally widespread intensification of responsibilities of educators, due to their placement at the forefront of detection of and response to children identified as 'at risk' or vulnerable to abuse and neglect. Research loudly articulates educators experiences of 'weighing up' the consequences of failing to meet the legal obligations versus the impact of mandatory reporting on the teacher, the family and the parent-child-teacher relationship. Educators are situated within a confusing and daunting intersection of moral and legal obligation.

Educators are bound by a vast array of legislation and policy, outlining their conflicting responsibilities. The UN Convention on the Rights of the Child (1989) outlines a social justice perspective, a 'decent human-being' perspective so to speak, highlighting a moral and ethical obligation to ensure the wellbeing and safety of all children. Legalisation, often both federal and state, and institutional policy outline the legal and statutory demands placed on teachers, including mandatory reporting requirements and duty of care. Health promotion initiatives such as the National framework for Protecting

Australia's Children (2009), lies somewhere in between, offering a middle ground between moral and legislative requirements, however offering yet another perspective to further confuse education professionals attempting to traverse the vague landscape.

5.3 Legal Concerns and Professional Responsibilities

5.3.1 A Legislated Perspective

There are often three sources of authority dictating an educators obligations regarding child protection, these include common law duty of care, policy associated with the educational institutions and their governing bodies and state and federal legalisation.

5.3.1.1 Duty of Care

The legal concept of duty of care is historically derived from the common law of torts, specific to the field of tort law referred to as negligence and operated within civil liability legislation (Mathews and Walsh 2014). The essence of this multifaceted legal area, with regard to the educational context, is that an education professional owes a student a duty of care and must not breach that duty and harm the student by their actions or omissions (Mathews 2011; Mathews and Walsh 2014). If the educator's duty of care includes a duty to report suspected child maltreatment, failure to do so may render the educator liable, should the omission result in further harm to the child (Mathews 2011; Mathews and Walsh 2014). This scenario may unfold when an educator has knowledge or reasonable suspicion of abuse or neglect of a child, fails to report the concerns to the relevant authorities and the maltreatment continues, further compounding the impact on the child, physically and emotionally.

In the Royal Commission into Institutional Responses to Child Sexual Abuse in Australia in 2014, a Queensland primary school was investigated regarding the adequacy of their responses to allegations of child sexual abuse (Commonwealth of Australia 2015). A public hearing was held to inquire whether the staff had upheld their duty of care and legislated responsibilities in responding to the allegations made against a teacher. The alleged abuse had taken place in a school which had both internal procedures and legally mandated reporting obligations for responding to suspected abuse. Multiple allegations were made to the principal, who attempted to contact the governing education authority in the district regarding the reports, however did not report the allegations to police. The findings of this incident confirm the principal failed to meet his duty of care and obligations to report and avoided his responsibilities by attempting to pass the information to the local education authority. Subsequent allegations were made to the school leadership staff and were also not recorded or reported to necessary authorities. The school did not take any disciplinary action against the teacher against whom the allegations were made; he was in fact reemployed as a relief teacher following his retirement. The teacher was later arrested after a parent reported concerns to police, he was sentenced to 10 years imprisonment after pleading guilty to 44 sexual abuse offenses against 13 girls aged eight to ten years. The principal's employment was terminated due to his breach of duty of care and failure to meet his reporting obligations. It is reported in the findings of the Inquiry regarding this case that more than $2.25 million has been paid in damages, costs and administration fees to nine victims and some of their families (Commonwealth of Australia 2015).

5.3.1.2 Policy

An educational institution and their governing bodies, such as the colleges and boards which regulate standards of practice, will usually have a host of policies and procedures regarding student protection and wellbeing, which run parallel to both duty of care and legislated obligations. The occupation-based policies often replicate, but also broaden the scope of the legislative obligations and closely reflect common law duty of care (Mathews and Walsh 2014). Failure to abide by student protection policies may result in institutional disciplinary action (Mathews 2011) as well as breach common law duties and liability may ensue. A review of Australian student protection policies indicates they align with both state child protection and education legislation and reflect relevant codes of conduct and standards of practice. The policies generally cover reporting obligations, student support and wellbeing, record keeping, training and adult conduct (Department of Education Queensland 2016; Department of Education and Training Victoria 2016; Department of Education and Child Development South Australia 2016; Department of Education Northern Territory 2016; Department of Education Western Australia 2016; New South Wales Department of Education 2016; Department of Education, Australian Capital Territory 2016). Non-State school such as faith-based and independent institutions align closely with the policies outlined in State documentation. Generally, non-state institutions demand compliance with child protection legislation, and employ processes which reflect the legal and pastoral responsibilities of the staff (Queensland Catholic Education Commission 2016; Catholic Education Commission NSW 2016). Policies encompass both legal responsibilities as well as broader student wellbeing considerations. Governing education bodies, responsible for regulation and registration, such as the Queensland College of Teachers in Australia, also have requirements which dictate the actions employees must take when a students is deemed at risk of harm. These regulatory bodies align with the legislated requirements of mandatory reporting but also require professionals to 'report' their concerns directly to the regulatory body.

5.3.1.3 Legislation

The United Nations Convention on the Rights of the Child (UNCRC) (Unicef, 1989) names government as the body responsible for upholding and safeguarding children's rights to protection, participation and provision. Bourke and Maunsell state "in the case of education, schools and teachers may be seen as the 'arms' and 'eyes' of the government, both in terms of ensuring children's rights are upheld and identifying situations where these rights have been violated" (2015, p. 3). In order to consistently and effectively meet these obligations to uphold the rights of children to protection and safety, educators, along with a host of helping professionals, are bound by government legislation, which underpins their roles and responsibilities. In Australia, education professionals are bound by both education legislation and child protection legislation, which differs somewhat, from state to state. In Queensland, for example, teachers are guided by the Education (General Provisions) Act (2006) which stipulates the obligations to report child sexual abuse and the Child Protection Act (1999) which is a legal framework guiding child protection across all agencies providing services to children and their families. This child protection legislation also outlines the mandatory reporting obligations of educators.

Mandatory reporting laws require designated persons to report suspected child maltreatment to government authorities. Mathews and Walsh (2015) identify the motivating principle underlying these laws as a desire to increase the likelihood that vulnerable children experiencing significant harm will be brought to the attention of helping professionals. Mandatory reporting was first implemented in Australia in response to the murder of Daniel Valerio

(Saunders and Goddard 2002). The goal was to increase the number of cases of child maltreatment reported to encourage earlier intervention (Matthews and Kenny 2008). Legal protection was applied in order to safeguard notifiers from breaches of privacy and dilemmas of professional ethics, thus removing obstacles that may have hindered the reporting of suspected maltreatment (Denham 2008).The desired outcome of mandatory reporting is to protect children from harm as well as to reduce recidivism by supporting parents and caregivers (Mathews and Walsh 2015). Failure to comply with mandatory reporting legislation can result in monetary penalty and possibly imprisonment. Mathews, Walsh, Butler and Farrell clarify "all statutes confer immunity for mandatory reporters from legal liability in any proceeding brought concerning the report, provided the repot is made in good faith" (2006, p. 9).

Mandatory reporting laws were initially established in the United States in the 1960s, following the identification of "the battered child syndrome" by paediatrician Henry C Kempe and his colleagues in 1962. "Battered child syndrome" referred to the intentional harm inflicted on young children, causing severe physical injury (Kempe et al. 1962). Kempe and his colleagues (1962) also noted the reluctance of medical professionals to acknowledge parental responsibility for non-accidental injury to a child and thus an aversion to report suspicions. This prompted the first mandatory reporting laws requiring medical professionals to report physical abuse.

According to Mathews and Kenny (2008) the International Society for the Prevention of Child Abuse and Neglect (ISPCAN) surveyed 161 countries regarding their reporting obligations. Forty nine of the seventy two countries who responded, indicated they had legislated reporting requirements and 12 countries specified voluntary reporting for professionals. The United Kingdom (England, Wales and Scotland) and New Zealand have chosen not to legislate mandatory reporting and countries including Brazil, France, Israel, Malaysia, Mexico, South Africa and many Scandinavia countries have broad and generalised legislative reporting duties (Mathews and Kenny 2008). Similarly, the General Teaching Council for Scotland Standards for Registration outline mandated knowledge and understanding of "the legal and professional aspects of a teacher's position of trust in relation to learners" (2012, p. 10). Australia first imposed mandatory reporting obligations in South Australia in 1969, with each state and territory retaining autonomy in child protection legislation. Whilst all states and territories in Australia have enacted mandatory reporting laws, this has created some dysfunction across jurisdictions due to variances in reporting responsibilities (Matthews et al. 2009). This is a consistent theme across jurisdictions internationally, resulting in a broad spectrum of mandatory reporting approaches. The main differences lie in who is obligated to report and what abuse types have to be reported (CFCA 2016). Countries such as Saudi Arabia apply the legislation only to health professionals (Mathews 2014). In contrast, USA, Canada and Australia, the nations who have given significant attention to the implementation of these laws, have an extensive range of mandated reporters, in some cases applying the legislation to all citizens (Mathews and Kenny 2008). There are also differences, most notably in Australian legislation, in the 'state of mind', which motivates the reporting duty and the authority to which the report must be delivered (Hayes and Higgins 2014). These inconsistencies have contributed to the debate regarding the validity and effectiveness of mandatory reporting.

5.3.2 Mandatory Reporting: A Policy of Worth?

Mandatory reporting legislation is one approach to identifying and responding to significant child maltreatment. Few academics have focused their research on mandatory reporting (Ainsworth 2002; Harries and Clare 2002; Mathews 2012) however, there is an almost equally distributed debate regarding the validity and value of mandatory reporting in managing the endemic nature of abuse and neglect. Mathews et al. (2015) identify a lack of consensus regarding the global merits of the laws with contrasting arguments commonly proposed on the same themes. Arguments promoting mandatory reporting state it can prevent child death and injury, identify at risk children, protect children's rights, increase community awareness of positive child treatment and provide reporters with a safety net (Harries and Clare 2002). Opposing arguments stress the approach can cause increased inaccurate and false reports, burden the child protection system, cause undue trauma to wrongly accused families, breach privacy and trust in communities, inhibit self-disclosure and discriminate against vulnerable persons (Harries and Clare 2002).

The most significant criticism of mandatory reporting is the notion that they increase the number of inaccurate and unsubstantiated reports of abuse and neglect, overloading an already overburdened child protection system. Critics argue that the ripple effect of this increased workload results in a reduction in the quality of service delivery and resources for vulnerable families (Mathews and Bross 2008). As the United States broadened the scope of their policies, increasing the types of abuse and reporting professionals included in legislation, a surge in notifications was received, less than half of which were substantiated (McDaniel 2006). This raised the question as to the effectiveness of the legislation and whether mandated reporting drained an already diminished pool of resources, at the expense of those most in need (Ainsworth 2002; Lindsey 2004). Melton referred to mandated reporting as a "policy without reasoning" and argued that empirical research illustrates a "bankrupt policy" (2005, p. 15). Melton (2005) draws our attention to a review conducted by the US Advisory Board on Child Abuse and Neglect in the 1990s, which laid blame on mandatory reporting for the "chronic and critical multiple organ failure" of the child protection system (1990, p. 2).

> *The most serious shortcoming of the nation's system of intervention on behalf of children is that it depends upon a reporting and response process that has punitive connotations and requires massive resources dedicated to the investigation of allegations. ....it has become far easier to pick up the telephone to report one's neighbour for child abuse than it is for that neighbour to pick up the telephone and receive help before the abuse happens.* (US Advisory Board on Child Abuse and Neglect 1990, p. 80)

Scott (2012) argues that mandatory reporting does result in an overloaded system, creating lengthy timeframes for investigations or a triage system, which results in high false positives, due to the focus of statutory intervention on evidence rather that statistical risk. A submission made to the Child Protection Review in South Australia in 2003 by the Richard Hillman Foundation stated;

> *...whilst important to ensuring early intervention in child abuse, mandatory reporting as it is currently used/acted upon is resulting in the "fish net" being cast so far and so wide as to now be useless in catching predominantly/exclusively those persons who are a genuine risk to children.* (Layton 2003, p. 10.5)

Briggs and Hawkins (1997) stressed the extra pressure that would be applied to educators under this legislation may in fact result in fear-based over-reporting, motivated by the threat of prosecution or disciplinary action for failing to report. Mathews and Walsh (2004) also make mention of the criticisms which focus on the impact on families who are unjustly accused, because of the over reporting phenomenon. The argument made against extending the mandated obligation to educators, highlights the potential damage to reputation, career and family because of false and inaccurate reports (Mathews and Walsh 2004).

Whilst the opposing arguments illustrate an imperfect system, with the best interest of the child paramount, as is outlined in the UNCRC, and drawing on global research, mandatory reporting holds a position of value as a means of identifying at-risk families and directing them to helping professionals. The most vocal critic of mandatory reporting, Melton (2005), proposed voluntary help-seeking as an alternative to legislation. However, he went on to acknowledge that a potential consequence of relying solely on voluntary reporting, would be accepting that severe abuse and neglect would be experienced by those children who would remain hidden from the helping professions (Melton 2005). The introduction of mandatory reporting in Western Australia, the last state in Australia to adopt the legislation, was considered a "significant milestone in strengthening the child protection system" (Government of Western Australia 2008, p. 3).

Mandatory reporting is recognised as a critical aspect of child protection practice and is deemed necessary to protecting the rights of children who are unable to advocate for themselves (Mathews and Walsh 2004). The role mandatory reporting plays in protecting children who are unable to self-protect, due to age, status, disability or general circumstance, is a sentiment reflected in much of the theoretical arguments supporting mandatory reporting and is consistent with the articles of the UNCRC and reflected in common law duty of care. Mathews and Bross state "without proven alternatives in place, abandoning mandated reporting would ignore children's subjective experience and sacrifice many children's rights to dignity and security" (2008, p. 10).

It is widely agreed that childhood trauma and adversity results in a significant social and financial burden on the individual, society and state. A commissioned report in Australia concluded that the annual cost of childhood trauma to the government is $16 billion (Kezelman Am et al. 2015).

> Early, active, and comprehensive intervention could result in a minimum saving of $6.8 billion from addressing of the impacts of child sexual, emotional and physical abuse in adults, alone. A minimum of $9.1 billion could be gained from addressing the problem of childhood trauma more generally in the 5 million Australian adults affected by it. (Kezelman Am et al. 2015, p. 43)

There is a direct relationship between the economic cost of abuse and neglect and the impact trauma has on the individual across the lifespan, with adverse childhood experiences affecting physical and mental health, substance use, graduation rates, academic achievement, employment and poverty (Felitti et al. 1998). Therefore mandatory reporting plays a significant role in ensuring the detection and thus early intervention, of abuse and neglect, lessening the contribution to the national cost of childhood trauma. Smallbone and Wortley (2001) acknowledge the role of mandatory reporting in reducing criminal recidivism especially in child sexual offending, through prevention of repeat victimisation of a particular child and other children. Mathews and Walsh (2004) argue that the overwhelming prevalence of child sexual abuse presents the strongest argument for legislated mandatory reporting.

Whilst mandatory reporting legislation has been enacted in many countries, recent research indicates reporting inconsistencies, with many educators unaware of their legal duties or reluctant to adhere to their reporting obligations, due to a range of attitudes and deterrents.

5.4 Teachers' Attitudes, Behaviour and Hesitations in Detecting and Responding to Child Maltreatment

Despite the majority of countries worldwide enacting some form of legislated mandatory reporting, professionals often fail to comply with this obligation. According to Walsh et al. (2005), 75% of Australian primary school educators had suspected child maltreatment during their careers, however only 49% of the educators who had suspected child abuse and neglect had ever reported their suspicions. In The United States, 84% of suspected child abuse cases are not reported to the mandated authorities (Kesner and Robinson 2002). Numerous studies in the US reflect these inconsistencies in compliance with mandated reporting, with up to 40% of staff across the United States acknowledging a reluctance or avoidance of the their reporting obligations (Romano et al. 1990; Abrahams et al. 1992; Crenshaw et al. 1995; Kenny 2001). This is consistent with findings from Ireland, where despite significant support and guidance offered in relation to legislated mandatory reporting, educators struggled with decision making in matters of child maltreatment, resulting in non-compliance (Francis et al. 2012). In Dublin, a study of educators' understanding of child maltreatment identified that 23% had suspected child sexual abuse but only half (50%) of these teachers had reported their suspicions to mandated authorities (Smyth 1996). In Taiwan, most professionals have never reported a case of child abuse or neglect and many admit to failing to report when they have suspicions of maltreatment (Feng et al. 2010; Feng and Levine 2005).

The prevalence for non-compliance with mandatory reporting stems from dilemmas that educators face when balancing their legal obligations with what they consider to be the best interests of the child or family (Francis et al. 2012). A host of research endeavours have explored the deterrents and motivators associated with meeting mandatory reporting obligations which range from understanding and knowledge, moral and ethical dilemmas, fear of repercussion, limitations in agency feedback following reporting, concerns for privacy and a lack of confidence in the child protection system (Walsh et al. 2005; Blaskett and Taylor 2003; Kenny 2001; Goebbells et al. 2008; Alvarez et al. 2004; Francis et al. 2012).

5.4.1 Attitudes and Behaviour as a Deterrent to Meeting Legislated Obligations

Goddard (1996) suggested, in references to practices in Australia, that the unwillingness of professionals to report suspected child maltreatment often stems from entrenched social myths surrounding child abuse. Beliefs, values and perceptions of abuse and neglect continue to inform responses to child maltreatment internationally. Blaskett and Taylor (2003) argue discriminatory attitudes have been shown to influence reporting responses of mandated professionals, including educators. Perpetuated stereotypes regarding family types, victims and perpetrators of abuse heavily influenced decisions to report, especially in cases of child sexual abuse (Portwood 1998; Kean and Dukes 1991). Beliefs regarding 'culpability' of a victim to provoke or incite maltreatment, especially relating to sexual abuse, contributes to the degree of empathy felt for the victim, therefore influencing the reporting behaviour of the professional (Blaskett and Taylor 2003).

Similarly, individual perceptions regarding severity and 'reportability' of abuse types influences professionals' decisions to report. Child neglect is often overlooked due to the subtle and often hidden nature of the maltreatment, with many educators citing 'no physical evidence' as their reason for not reporting suspicions of maltreatment (Alvarez et al. 2004). An American study identified a pattern in which educators had ranked sexual abuse as the most severe abuse type and highest priority to respond to in a timely manner, neglect was identified as the lowest priority with physical and emotional abuse falling somewhere in the middle (Morejohn 2006). When making judgements regarding child abuse, educators rely on professional discretion and this behaviour often results in underreporting, especially in cases which involve physical abuse, an older child or a child with positive behaviour (Webster et al. 2005). A child who exhibits high personal resilience may be overlooked, however Bromfield, Lamont, Antcliff and Parker argue "we must not focus on resilience to the extent we ignore the risk for the child" and misinterpret internalising or normalising as coping (2014, p. 8). Interestingly, Blaskett and Taylor (2003) emphasise the influence of the media on reporting behaviours, arguing that the visibility of child abuse in the media can heighten awareness of child protection issues and motivate professionals to report. Lonne and Gillespie (2014) also argue the Australian media plays a pivotal role in public opinion and in generating political support for policy reform.

Educators are largely motivated by a desire to act in the best interests of the child, therefore concerns for a negative consequence or outcome for the child, as a result of reporting, is a powerful deterrent. Educators commonly hold concerns that their report may exacerbate an already volatile familial situation and destabilise the family structure should prosecution or removal of a child result from their notification (Alvarez et al. 2004). Concerns regarding the potential removal of a child also influence educators reporting behaviour due to negative perceptions of child protection agencies and services. Educators have acknowledged perceived systemic inadequacies, such as lengthy response timeframes, inconsistent screening and decision making and general inaction, as deterrents to reporting (Alvarez et al. 2004; Melton 2005; O'Toole and Webster 1999). An Australian study identified a lack of confidence in responses by child protection services, contributed to non-compliance by mandated reporters (Goddard et al. 2002).

Due to the nature of the teacher-child-family relationship, educators are often reluctant to meet their mandated obligations for fear reporting concerns may damage these partnerships and alliances and have ongoing consequences for all involved. Educators build rapport with both the child and the caregiver and often feel a sense of loyalty to all parties involved, causing the professional to feel conflicted and influencing their reporting behaviour. Feng et al. (2012) highlight the challenge of sympathy versus responsibility, in which professional's often sympathise with a family's hardship or circumstance and engage in rationalisation of intentions to justify unacceptable behaviour. Kenny (2001) found that many educators are concerned for the legal repercussions should their suspicions be inaccurate. Hawkins and McCallum (2001) assert teachers are often concerned with the validity of their suspicions and tend to postpone reporting in favour of gathering further evidence to support their concerns.

Professional attitudes to reporting have been likened to 'whistleblowing' (Taylor 1998) and educators often perceive reporting as a breach of a family's privacy and a violation of the trust relationship (Blaskett and Taylor 2003). Confusion regarding their professional duty to maintain confidentiality versus their legal responsibility to report suspected maltreatment undermines decision making. The fear of reprisal and retaliation in response to making a report also promotes hesitation in reporting, especially in rural, remote and small communities. Francis et al. (2012) identified that the increased visibility experienced by teachers in small communities exacerbated apprehension regarding reporting suspected child abuse and neglect. In a study conducted by Jervis-Tracey et al. (2012), difficulty in managing professional identify was identified as a common theme in all of the tensions identified by professionals undertaking statutory roles in rural and remote communities. Blaskett and Taylor (2003) concur with this perspective, stating recrimination resulting from the making of a mandatory report influences reporting behaviours and is exacerbated in rural communities. Studies conducted in rural communities in both Australia and in the United States emphasise the impact of locale on reporting behaviour, due to the lack of anonymity, close relationship between professionals and families, visibility in the community and multiplicity of roles (Blaskett and Taylor 2003; Jervis-Tracey et al. 2012).

Characteristics of the reporter have also been known to influence reporting behaviours. Gender, parental status and professional experience have all been identified as potential influencing factors in decision making in relation to mandatory reporting (Walsh et al. 2005). Some US studies argue that males are less tolerant of abuse and more likely to detect and report it more readily (O'Toole et al. 1999). In contrast, conflicting US research has found females to be more likely to report and assist others to make reports (Kenny 2001). Conversely, Sundell (1997) concludes there are no significant gender related differences in reporting and non-reporting tendencies. According to O'Toole et al. (1999), parental status lessens the likelihood that teachers will detect or report abuse and teachers who have interacted with large cohorts of children can more accurately detect abuse but will be less inclined to report it. In comparison, Kenny (2001) argues the more experienced a teacher is, the more likely they are to report and assist others, with special education teachers particularly inclined to meet their reporting obligations. Culture also contributes to reporting behaviours and presents potential contradictions between ethical and legal duties. Feng et al. state "in a culture emphasizing parental rights and family privacy, reporting child abuse can contradict societal norms and values" (2012, p. 278). Physical discipline is identified as a particularly sensitive terrain for educators to navigate, considering the vast array of cross cultural discipline practices and approaches to admonishment. Professionals often feel powerless and hesitant to involve themselves in such matters of culture-specific parenting practice, adding to the confusion between parental rights and mandatory reporting obligations (Feng et al. 2012).

In summarising, the conflicting demands faced by teachers in their mandated reporting obligations, Feng et al. (2009) identified four dominant categorical themes; preserving relationships, avoiding harm, obligation and maintaining balance; they aptly labelled their model 'dancing on the edge'. A host of deterrents to educators complying with mandatory reporting obligations have been identified and evidence clearly indicates a significant number of professionals experience hesitation and reluctance in meet their legal obligations. However, a vast number of professionals adhere to their legislated requirements and are motivated by the belief that schools play an important role in child protection. Hawkins and McCallum (2001) argue a teacher's desire to fulfil their reporting obligations in order to serve their role in critical child protection, has strong positive influences on reporting tendencies.

5.4.2 Understanding and Knowledge: A Case for Preservice Teacher Education and Training

Research exploring teachers' failure to adhere to mandatory reporting legislation highlights the significant influence knowledge and education have on reporting behaviours. Inadequate knowledge of the signs and symptoms of child abuse and neglect and in reporting procedures presents significant barriers to detecting and reporting suspected maltreatment (Alvarez et al. 2004). Research indicates teacher reporting practices are heavily influenced by the extent and nature of teacher education in recognising abuse and instilling confidence in educators' abilities and accuracy (Hawkins and McCallum 2001; Goebbels et al. 2008). In South Australia, Hawkins and McCallum (2001) discovered that teachers with recent training had increased confidence in recognising abuse, were adequately aware of the nature of their reporting responsibilities and were more inclined to adhere to their obligations. In comparison, their untrained colleagues exhibited significant gaps in knowledge of both procedure and indicators of abuse (Hawking and McCallum 2001). A study of educators in the United States found comparable results when they surveyed 568 elementary and middle school teachers, identifying that two thirds experienced inadequate training and lacked the necessary knowledge to accurately detect and report abuse and neglect (Abrahams et al. 1992). There appears to be a strong consensus within educators and education professionals, including principals, that there are significant inadequacies in the quality and quantity of training and education to equip professionals in detecting and responding to child abuse and neglect (Kenny 2001, 2004; Mathews and Kenny 2008). A major finding from a study by Walsh and Farrell (2008) highlighted an absence of knowledge of content in relation to abuse and neglect, including the definitions, causes, impacts, laws and policies relating to child abuse and neglect. Walsh and Farrell (2008) give emphasis by addressing this absence, teachers will be better equipped to intervene appropriately within their professional context. An appropriate response to this gap is two-pronged; firstly, the dissemination of child abuse and neglect research into education literature and secondly comprehensive pre and in-service teacher education (Walsh and Farrell 2008; Mathews 2011; Mathews and Walsh, 2015).

Despite the increasing complexities of the role educators hold in child protection and student wellbeing, teacher education programs have been unhurried in their adoption of a discipline specific knowledge base for child maltreatment (Taylor and Hodgkinson 2001). In Northern Ireland preservice child protection training has been identified as a means of addressing inadequate knowledge of child abuse and neglect in practicing educators (McKee and Dillenburger 2009). In the UK (England and Wales) educational context institutions have implemented core courses in undergraduate and postgraduate programmes for teacher education (McKee and Dillenburger 2012). Walsh et al. (2011) have identified several universities across Australia who have integrated child protection content into their courses within teacher education programs with some offering elective courses devoted to child abuse and neglect. Ireland has followed suit, with Bachelor of Education programs being lengthened and restructured to accommodate the evidence supporting the inclusion of child protection content in preservice teacher education (Bourke and Maunsell 2015).

Baginsky (2003) warns training must occur again when teachers are practicing in their field experienced by newly qualified educators may cause their learnings to fade or be forgotten. It is a requirement of practicing education professionals in Australia to undertake some compulsory child protection training as an accompaniment to their mandatory reporting obligations. In England and Wales, the report, Safeguarding Children: A Joint Chief Inspectors' Report on Arrangements to Safeguard Children, recommended child protection training be integrated into core education for all professionals working with children (The Directorate for Children, Older People and Social Care Services Department of Health 2002). The National Guidance for Child protection in Scotland also emphasises the critical importance of child protection training across disciplines including education, stating "training should recognise and support the unique contribution each service has to make to meeting children's wellbeing needs and protecting them" (2014, p. 24). Baginsky (2003) concurs with this approach, suggesting in-service training be implemented as a requirement of employment, much like Australia has done in their adoption of training as a parallel process with mandatory reporting for educators. Buckley and McGarry (2011) provided a similar perspective, highlighting the need for more comprehensive child protection training for teachers in Ireland as a response the minimal offering provided in teacher education courses. Bourke and Maunsell (2015) argue teacher education must target the obstacles to meeting mandatory reporting obligations, including lack of knowledge of maltreatment as well as the insufficient understanding of reporting procedures and policies.

5.5 Conclusion

As child maltreatment continues to permeate all socio-economic and cultural groups worldwide, educators are faced with escalating complexity in their role on the front line of student protection and wellbeing. Educators possess both the knowledge and position to detect, respond to and advocate for vulnerable children, prior to the point of crisis and are acknowledged in research and in practice as a crucial source of monitoring and protection. Kesner suggests "perhaps there is no other non-familial adult that is more significant in a child life than his or her teacher" (2000, p. 134).

Educators, due to their position in the lives of vulnerable families, are required to respond to abuse and neglect from a legal and ethical perspective. Whilst governed and informed by legislation, common law duty of care and policies and procedures specific to the employing organisations and regulatory bodies, these sources of authority can prove complex and confusing for the education professional. In order to navigate this daunting terrain, educators must possess a comprehensive knowledge of child abuse and neglect and have a strong understanding of their legal and ethical obligations, in order to act in the best interests of the child and adhere to their legislated responsibilities. Ultimately, mandatory reporting was introduced to protect children from harm and to reduce recidivism, by supporting parents and caregivers (Mathews and Walsh 2015). An understanding of the motivation behind mandatory reporting legislation and an acknowledgement of and respect for the potential obstacles to compliance, especially in small communities, will assist the professional in decision making and managing the tensions associated with statutory obligations.

In order to fulfil their multifaceted and valuable role, educators need to be adequately equipped, through preservice and in-service training and ongoing professional development in discipline specific child protection. Armed with knowledge, skills and a respect for the role they occupy in the lives of vulnerable children and their families, professionals will be more adequately equipped to respond to child maltreatment. Education professionals will be able to address student protection and wellbeing in a way, which not only adheres to legislative requirements, but improves outcomes for at-risk children and families.

References

Abrahams, N., Casey, K., & Daro, D. (1992). Teachers' knowledge, attitudes, and beliefs about child abuse and its prevention. *Child Abuse & Neglect, 16*(2), 229–238.

Ainsworth, F. (2002). Mandatory reporting of child abuse and neglect: Does it really make a difference? *Child & Family Social Work, 7*(1), 57–63.

Alvarez, K. M., Kenny, M. C., Donohue, B., & Carpin, K. M. (2004). Why are professionals failing to initiate mandated reports of child maltreatment, and are there any empirically based training programs to assist professionals in the reporting process? *Aggression and Violent Behaviour, 9*, 563–578.

Australian Institute of Health and Welfare (AIHW). (2015). *Youth justice fact sheet no. 47. Types of community-based youth justice supervision: 2013–14*. Cat. no. JUV 66. Canberra: AIHW.

Australian Institute of Health and Welfare. (2016). *Child protection Australia 2014–15*. Child welfare series no. 63. Cat. no. CWS 57. Canberra: AIHW.

Baginsky, M. (2003). Newly qualified teachers and child protection. *Child Abuse Review, 12*, 119–127.

Blaskett, B., & Taylor, C. (2003). *Facilitators and inhibitors of mandatory reporting of suspected child abuse*. Ballarat: University of Ballarat.

Bourke, A., & Maunsell, C. (2015). 'Teachers matter': The impact of mandatory reporting on teacher education in Ireland. *Child Abuse Review*. doi: https://doi.org/10.1002/car.2379.

Briggs, F., & Hawkins, R. (1997). *Child protection: A guide for teachers and child care professionals*. St Leonards: Allen St Unwin.

Bromfield, L. M. (2005). *Chronic child maltreatment in an Australian statutory child protection sample*. Unpublished doctoral dissertation, Deakin University, Geelong.

Bromfield, L., & Miller, R. (2007). *Specialist practice guide: Cumulative harm*. Melbourne: Victorian Government Department of Human Services.

Bromfield, L., Lamont, A., Antcliff, G., & Parker, R. (2014). *Practice guide 7: Cumulative harm*. Sydney: The Benevolent Society.

Buckley, H., & McGarry, K. (2011). Child protection in primary schools: A contradiction in terms or a potential opportunity? *Irish Educational Studies, 30*(1), 113–128.

Catholic Education Commission NSW. (2016). *Annual report 2016*. NSW: Author.

Centers for Disease Control and Prevention. (2016). *Adverse childhood experiences study*. Retrieved September 20, 2016, from https://www.cdc.gov/violenceprevention/acestudy/ child abuse: An analysis of the decision to report. *Child Abuse & Neglect, 19*(9), 095–1113. Child Protection Act (Qld) 1999.

CFCA. (2016). *Reporting child abuse and neglect – CFCA resource sheet*. Victoria: Australian Institute of Family Studies.

Christoffel, K. K., Scheidt, P. C., Agran, P. F., Kraus, J. F., McLoughlin, E., & Paulson, J. A. (1992). Standard definitions for childhood injury research: Excerpts of a conference report. *Pediatrics, 89*(6), 1027–1034.

Commonwealth of Australia. (2015). *Reports of case study 6: The response of a primary school and the Toowoomba Catholic education office to the conduct of Gerard Byrnes.* NSW: Commonwealth of Australia Education (General Provisions) Act (Qld) 2006.

Crenshaw, W. B., Crenshaw, L. M., & Lichtenberg, J. W. (1995). When educators confront difference? *Child and Family Social Work, 7*(1), 57.

Denham, G. (2008). Mandatory reporting of child abuse requirements for medical imaging professionals throughout Australia. *The Radiographer, 55*(3), 9–12.

Department of Health. (2002). *Safeguarding children: A joint chief inspectors' report on arrangements to safeguard children.* London: Department of Health.

Department of Education and Child Development South Australia. (2016). *Child protection in schools, early childhood education and care.* South Australia: Author.

Department of Education and Training Victoria. (2016). *Child protection – Reporting obligations.* Victoria: Author.

Department of Education Northern Territory. (2016). *Student safety and wellbeing.* Northern Territory: Author.

Department of Education Queensland. (2016). *Student protection procedure.* Queensland: Author.

Department of Education Western Australia. (2016). *Child protection.* Western Australia: Author

Department of Education, Australian Capital Territory. (2016). *Safe and supportive schools.* WA: Author.

Felitti, V. J., Anda, R. F., Nordenberg, D., Williamson, D. F., Spitz, A. M., Edwards, V., & Koss, M. P. (1998). Relationship of childhood abuse and household dysfunction in many of the leading causes of death in adults. *American Journal of Preventive Medicine, 14*(4), 245–258.

Feng, J.-Y., & Levine, M. (2005). Factors associated with nurses' intention to report child abuse: A national survey of Taiwanese nurses. *Child Abuse & Neglect, 29*(7), 783–795.

Feng, J. Y., Chen, S. J., Wilk, N. C., Yang, W. P., & Fetzer, S. (2009). Kindergarten teachers' experience of reporting child abuse in Taiwan: Dancing on the edge. *Children and Youth Services Review, 31*(3), 405–409.

Feng, J. Y., Huang, T. Y., & Wang, C. J. (2010). Kindergarten teachers' experience with reporting child abuse in Taiwan. *Child Abuse & Neglect, 34*(2), 124–128.

Feng, J. Y., Chen, Y. W., Fetzer, S., Feng, M. C., & Lin, C. L. (2012). Ethical and legal challenges of mandated child abuse reporters. *Children and Youth Services Review, 34*(1), 276–280.

Francis, K., Chapman, Y., Sellick, K., James, A., Miles, M., Jones, J., & Grant, J. (2012). The decision-making processes adopted by rurally located mandated professionals when child abuse or neglect is suspected. *Contemporary Nurse, 41*(1), 58–69.

Gilligan, R. (1998). The importance of schools and teachers in child welfare. *Child and Family Social Work, 3*, 13–25.

Goddard, C. (1996). *Child abuse and child protection a guide for health, education and welfare professionals*. South Melbourne: Churchill Livingstone.

Goddard, C., Saunders, B., Stanley, J., & Tucci, J. (2002). *A study in confusion: Factors which affect the decisions of community professionals when reporting child abuse and neglect*. Australians Against Child Abuse, Melbourne.

Goebbels, A., Nicholson, J., Walsh, K., & De Vries, H. (2008). Teachers' reporting of suspected child abuse and neglect: Behaviour and determinants. *Health Education Research, 23*(6), 941–951.

Government of Western Australia. (2008). *Mandatory reporting of child sexual abuse*. Western Australia: Government of Western Australia, Department of Child Protection.

Harries, M., & Clare, M. (2002). *Mandatory reporting of child abuse: Evidence and options*. Perth: University of Western Australia.

Hawkins, R., & McCallum, C. (2001). Mandatory notification training for suspected child abuse and neglect in South Australian schools. *Child Abuse & Neglect, 25*(12), 1603–1625.

Hayes, A., & Higgins, D. (Eds.). (2014). *Families, policy and the law: Selected essays on contemporary issues for Australia*. Melbourne: Australian Institute of Family Studies.

Higgins, D. (2004). Differentiating between child maltreatment experiences. *Family Matters, 69*, 50–55.

Jervis-Tracey, P., Chenoweth, L., McAuliffe, D., O'Connor, B., & Stehlik, D. (2012). Managing tensions in statutory professional practice: Living and working in rural and remote communities. *Australian and International Journal of Rural Education, 22*(2), 97.

Kean, R. B., & Dukes, R. L. (1991). Effects of witness characteristics on the perception and reportage of child abuse. *Child Abuse & Neglect, 15*(4), 423–435.

Kempe, C. H., Silverman, F., Steele, B., Droegemueller, W., & Silver, H. (1962). The battered-child syndrome. *JAMA: Journal of the American Medical Association, 181*, 17–24.

Kenny, M. C. (2001). Child abuse reporting: Teachers' perceived deterrents. *Child Abuse & Neglect, 25*(1), 81–92.

Kenny, M. C. (2004). Teachers' attitudes toward and knowledge of child maltreatment. *Child Abuse & Neglect, 28*(12), 1311–1319.

Kesner, J. E. (2000). Teacher characteristics and the quality of child–teacher relationships. *Journal of School Psychology, 38*(2), 133–149.

Kesner, J. E., & Robinson, M. (2002). Teachers as mandated reporters of child maltreatment: Comparison with legal, medical, and social services reporters. *Children & Schools, 24*(222), 231.

Kezelman Am, C., Hossack, N., Stavropoulos, P., & Burley, P. (2015). *The cost of unresolved childhood trauma and abuse in adults in Australia*. Sydney: Adults Surviving Child Abuse.

Layton, R. (2003). *Child protection review*. Adelaide: Government of South Australia.

Lindsey, D. (2004). *The welfare of children* (2nd ed.). New York: Oxford University Press.

Lonne, R., & Gillespie, K. (2014). How do Australian print media representations of child abuse and neglect inform the public system reform. *Child Abuse & Neglect, 38*(5), 837–850. https://doi.org/10.1016/j.chiabu.2014.04.021.

Mathews, B. (2011). Teacher education to meet the challenges of child sexual abuse. *Australian Journal of Teacher Education, 36*(11), 13–32.

Mathews, B. (2012). Mandatory reporting laws in the. *Current legal issues*, Law and childhood studies (Vol. 14, pp. 302).

Mathews, B. (2014). Mandatory reporting laws and identification of child abuse and neglect: Consideration of differential maltreatment types, and a cross-jurisdictional analysis of child sexual abuse reports. *Social Sciences, 3*(3), 460–482.

Mathews, B., & Bross, D. (2008). Mandated reporting is still a policy with reason: Empirical evidence and philosophical grounds. *Child Abuse & Neglect, 32*(5), 511–516.

Mathews, B., & Kenny, M. C. (2008). Mandatory reporting legislation in the USA, Canada and Australia: A cross-jurisdictional review of key features, differences and issues. *Child Maltreatment, 13*(1), 50–63.

Mathews, B., & Walsh, K. (2004). Queensland teachers' new legal obligation to report child sexual abuse. *Australia and New Zealand Journal of Law and Education, 9*(1), 25–40.

Mathews, B. P., & Walsh, K. M. (2014). Mandatory reporting laws. In A. Hayes & D. Higgins (Eds.), *Families, policy and the law: Selected essays on contemporary issues for Australia* (pp. 131–142). Melbourne: Australian Institute of Family Studies.

Mathews, B. P., & Walsh, K. M. (2015). *Submission to Queensland Law Reform Commission WP 73 Review of child protection mandatory reporting laws for the early childhood education and care sector.* Brisbane: Queensland Law Reform Commission.

Mathews, B. P., Walsh, K. M., Butler, D. A., & Farrell, A. M. (2006). Mandatory reporting by Australian teachers of suspected child abuse and neglect: Legislative requirements and questions for future direction. *Australia and New Zealand Journal of Law and Education, 11*(2), 7–22.

Mathews, B., Goddard, C., Lonne, B., Short, S., & Briggs, F. (2009). Developments in Australian laws requiring the reporting of suspected child sexual abuse. *Children Australia, 34*(3), 18–23.

Mathews, B. P., Bromfield, L., Walsh, K. M., & Vimpani, G. (2015). *Child abuse and neglect: A socio-legal study of mandatory reporting in Australia – Report for the Australian government.* Commonwealth of Australia, Canberra, A.C.T. (In Press).

McDaniel, M. (2006). In the eye of the beholder: The role of reporters in bringing families to the attention of child protective services. *Children and Youth Services Review, 28*, 306–324.

McKee, B. E., & Dillenburger, K. (2009). Child abuse and neglect: Training needs of student teachers. *International Journal of Educational Research, 48*(5), 320–330.

McKee, B. E., & Dillenburger, K. (2012). Effectiveness in child protection training for pre-service early childhood educators. *International Journal of Educational Research, 53*, 348–359.

Melton, G. (2005). Mandated reporting: A policy without reason. *Child Abuse & Neglect, 29*(1), 9–18.

Morejohn, N. B. (2006). *Reporting child maltreatment: Challenges faced by teachers*. Berkeley: California State University.

New South Wales Department of Education. (2016). *Guide to teaching and protecting young people*. NSW: Author.

Nurcombe, B., Wooding, S., Marrington, P., Bickman, L., & Roberts, G. (2000). Child sexual abuse II: Treatment. *Australian & New Zealand Journal of Psychiatry, 34*, 92–97.

O'Toole, R., & Webster, S. W. (1999). Teachers' recognition and reporting of child abuse: Factorial survey. *Child Abuse & Neglect, 23*(11), 1083–1101.

O'Toole, R., Webster, S. W., O'Toole, A. W., & Lucal, B. (1999). Teachers' recognition and reporting of child abuse: A factorial survey. *Child Abuse & Neglect, 23*(11), 1083–1101.

Portwood, S. (1998). The impact of individuals' characteristics and experiences on their definitions of child maltreatment. *Child Abuse & Neglect. 22*(5), 437–452. Professionals. St Leonards: Allen & Unwin.

Queensland Government. (2015). *Queensland child safety practice manual*. Brisbane: Department of Communities, Child Safety and Disabilities.

Queensland Catholic Education Commission. (2016). *Annual report 2016*. Queensland: Author.

Riley, P. (2009). An adult attachment perspective on the student–teacher relationship & classroom management difficulties. *Teaching and Teacher Education, 25*(5), 626–635.

Romano, N., Casey, K., & Daro, D. (1990). *Schools and child abuse: A national survey of principals' attitudes, beliefs and practices*. Chicago: National Centre on Child Abuse Prevention Research.

Saunders, B. J., & Goddard, C. (2002). *The role of mass media in facilitating community education and child abuse prevention strategies*. Melbourne: Australian Institute of Family Studies.

Scott, D. A. (2012). *Improving the measurement and surveillance of child abuse in Queensland emergency departments*. Doctoral dissertation, Queensland University of Technology.

Seidman, E., Allen, L., Aber, J. L., Mitchell, C., & Feinman, J. (1994). The impact of school transitions in early adolescence on the self-system and social context of poor urban youth. *Child Development, 65*, 507–522.

Smallbone, S., & Wortley, R. (2001). Child sexual abuse in Queensland: Offender characteristics and modus operandi. *Trends and issues in crime and criminal justice 193*. Canberra: Australian Institute of Criminology.

Smyth, K. (1996). An investigation into teachers' knowledge and awareness of child sexual abuse in singe sex national schools in Dublin. *Journal of Child Centred Practice, 3*(1), 23–44.

Sundell, K. (1997). Child care personnel's failure to report child maltreatment: Some Swedish evidence. *Child Abuse & Neglect, 21*(1), 93–105.

Taylor, A. S. (1997). From survival to reflection: Locating child protection in teacher education. In J. Davies & P. Garner (Eds.), *At the crossroads: Special education needs and teacher education* (pp. 61–74). London: David Fulton Publishers.

Taylor, A. (1998). Hostages to fortune: The abuse of children in care. In G. Hunt (Ed.), *Whistleblowing in the social services: Public accountability and professional practice*. London: Arnold.

Taylor, A. S., & Hodgkinson, K. (2001). Subjecting the initial teacher training curriculum for England and Wales to the test of child protection. *Teacher Development, 5*(1), 75–86.

Triseliotis, J. P., Sellick, C., & Short, R. (1995). *Foster care: Theory and practice.* London: Batsford.

Unicef. (1989). Convention on the Rights of the Child. *Child Labor*, 8.

U.S. Advisory Board on Child Abuse and Neglect. (1990). *Child abuse and neglect: Critical first steps in response to a national emergency.* Washington, DC: U.S. Department of Health and Human Services and Office of Human Developmental Services.

Victoria Government, Department of Human Services. (2007). *Cumulative harm: A conceptual overview*. Melbourne: Victorian Government.

Walsh, K., & Farrell, A. (2008). Identifying and evaluating teachers' knowledge in relation to child abuse and neglect: A qualitative study with Australian early childhood teachers. *Teaching and Teacher Education, 24*(3), 585–600.

Walsh, K., Farrell, A., Schweitzer, R., & Bridgstock, R. (2005). *Critical factors in teachers' detecting and reporting child abuse and neglect: Implications for practice.* Brisbane: Queensland University of Technology.

Walsh, K. M., Laskey, L., McInnes, E., Farrell, A., Mathews, B. P., & Briggs, F. (2011). Locating child protection in preservice teacher education. *Australian Journal of Teacher Education, 36*(7), 1–20.

Warner, J. E., & Hansen, D. J. (1994). The identification and reporting of physical abuse by physicians: A review and implications for research. *Child Abuse & Neglect, 18*(1), 11–25.

Webster, S. W., O'Toole, R., O'Toole, A. W., & Lucal, B. (2005). Overreporting and underreporting of child abuse: Teachers' use of professional discretion. *Child Abuse & Neglect, 29*(11), 1281–1296.

6

Education, Ethics, and the Law: Examining the Legal Consequences of Unethical Judgment

Patrick M. Jenlink and Karen Embry Jenlink

In civilized life, law floats in a sea of ethics. Each is indispensable to civilization. Without law, we should be at the mercy of the least scrupulous; without ethics, law could not exist. (US Supreme Court Chief Justice Earl Warren 1962, p. 2)

Chief Justice Warren argued the importance of ethics and law in civil society, drawing into specific relief the intentional relationship of ethics to law and the instrumental role that ethics and law play in the judicial system. We are a society of laws that requires ethics to enable the courts, as a legal system, to be ever mindful of the public it serves. Chief Justice Warren's argument of the indispensable nature of law and ethics set a precedent for high ethical standards predicated on the necessity of public trust in the professionals that enter courtrooms and argue the law. The very nature of ethics as assurances to the enactment of the law warrants specific attention to the nature of arguing the law and the predatory nature of those who would breach ethical codes of conduct to favor themselves and/or those they represent. As Chief Justice Warren argued, "there are always people who, in the conflict of human interest, ignore their responsibility to their fellow man" (1962, p. 2).

Today, a fundamental commitment to high ethical standards pervades professional rhetoric (Bazerman and Gino 2012; Perlman 2015; Sezer et al. 2015; Tenbrunsel and Messick 2004; Woolley and Wendel 2010). Educational,

P. M. Jenlink (✉) • K. E. Jenlink
Department of Secondary Education and Educational Leadership, Stephen F. Austin State University, Nacogdoches, TX, USA
e-mail: pjenlink@sfasu.edu; kjenlink@sfasu.edu

K. Trimmer et al. (eds.), *The Palgrave Handbook of Education Law for Schools*,
https://doi.org/10.1007/978-3-319-77751-1_6

legal, and political/policy ethics codes exhort professionals to maintain the highest degree of ethical conduct and declare that the integrity of an institution and the security of a democratic society depend upon whether the conduct and the motives of the members of the education, legal, and politics/policy profession are such as to merit public trust and belief in ethical conduct and integrity (see Bon 2012; Bon and Bigbee 2011; DeVito 2007). The point made is that in matters of ethics in education there is a legal and political/policy concern when unethical behavior is determined. The essential characteristics of professionals and fidelity to ethics and integrity as a meaningful commitment are quintessential in the spirit of enlarging and enhancing the practice, and awareness, of ethics as first among the elements of professionalism (Pearce 1998).

Examining the intersection of law and ethics in education is critical given the fundamental importance of education as a social institution. Equally important is the intersection of law and policy in education.[1] DeVito (2007) claims that most Americans assume that educational rights are protected under the U.S. Constitution. However, education is not a protected right; instead, it is primarily a function of state laws and governance. Thus, it is often left to the courts to interpret and define the parameters of statutory law to determine the extent of children's educational rights pursuant to the law. This interpretation of statutory law frequently occurs in the state courts, but when constitutional rights are implicated, the U.S. Supreme Court plays a significant role in public schools, ensuring that children's constitutional rights, especially equal educational opportunities, are protected (see Bon 2012).

Concerns about ethics cut across all categories of professions and practice. Educational professionals, both administrators and policy-makers, as well as legal professionals are expected to make decisions and take actions based on ethics and laws; codes of ethics and laws that function as a subset of public morality (Murphy and Nagel 2002). Jones (1978) is instructive on this point

[1] As contributing authors to an edited work that reflects a cross-national or diverse global perspective on education and the law, we are sensitive that the discussion set forth in this chapter on education, ethics, and law and the legal consequences of unethical behavior will be viewed differently by educational and legal professionals as well as political/policy professionals from nation states in other regions of the world, and equally sensitive to the different perspectives that define the legal consequences of unethical behavior in educational institution/settings in those nation states. With this in mind, the positions on ethics and legal consequences of unethical behavior that we discuss are based on a belief that other countries or national states, in similar fashion to the United States, have educational institutions and court systems as well as political/policy frameworks that function in cultural contexts. In terms of the legal system in other nation states, it is Recognise that whereas the United States has a judicial branch of its government, other national states have a comparable legal system pursuant to the constitutions and workings of those nation states. That said, we believe the points presented in our discussion have merit for educational, legal, and political/policy professionals in the U.S. and other nation states.

in arguing that "law and morality can be kept entirely and antiseptically separate only by a closet legal philosopher who is willfully blind to legal reality" (pp. 957–958). Public morality is clearly aligned with ethics and law. Concerning professionalism, Wagner (2012) has posited, "the professionalism of educators cannot be adequately captured in any laws, codes, regulations, or policies" (p. 33). This is equally valid whether the educator is in higher education or pre-K-12 public schools. "Such directives must always be seen through the prism of one's professional commitments and duties. True professionalism requires more moral commitment than can be secured by the threat of sanctions" (p. 33).

When the professionalism of educators is called into question due to ethical misconduct – such as partisanship that yields to political or positional power, breech of professional ethics codes, falsification of records, manipulating research data, intentional accounting and auditing irregularities, disavowing or limiting educational services for special needs students, plagiarism, conflict of interest, discrimination, harassment – policy and law become avenues used to address the behavior and adjudicate actions as deemed necessary (see Bluhm and Heineman 2007; Bon and Bigbee 2011; Lincoln and Homes 2007; Moore et al. 2010; Nagorcka et al. 2005; Rotunda 2002; Wagner 2012).

When ethics, laws, or policies are breeched, broken, or ignored, unethical behavior is involved. Ethical misconduct "is influenced by a person-situation interaction. Specifically, the tendency of people to engage in unethical behavior depends on both characteristics of the environment and characteristics of the individual" (Gino and Margolis 2011, p. 146). The reasons for unethical behavior on the part of individuals or groups within educational settings is complex and often compounded by actions of others, pressures from others internal or external to the educational setting, self-deceit, etc. As Moore and Gino (2013) explained, individuals " … can morally disengage either actively or unconsciously. For example, when conditions permit disadvantageous social comparisons, individuals may actively employ justifications" (p. 64) for unethical behavior. As well, individuals "may be aware of the moral content of their actions, make accurate judgments about what is right and wrong, and still be unable to follow through with desirable action" (p. 64). Regardless of the reason for ethical misconduct, when behavior usurps ethics, law, or policy, there is a consequence.

Research focusing specifically upon how people make ethical (and unethical) decisions or engage in unethical actions, characterised as "ethical drift", "ethical fading", "ethical misconduct", "ethical lapses", "moral myopia", has created an entirely new field called *behavioural ethics* (also "empirical ethics" or "scientific ethics")[2] that adds important dimensions to the study of ethical decision making (see Drumwright et al. 2015). Behavioural ethics, as Bazerman and Gino (2012) argued "is better suited than traditional approaches to addressing the increasing demand from society for a deeper understanding of what causes even good people to cross ethical boundaries" (p. 85). Concerning professionalism in education, law, politics/policy, understanding the nature of ethics is critical; ethics, as Regan (2003) explained, "is involved not simply in making choices between two courses of action in an atmosphere of high moral drama…. we … have to think of ethics as the intersection of individual character and organisational structure" (p. 365).

Considering the legal consequence of unethical behavior in educational institutions and organisations requires an examination of the relationship between ethics, law, and politics/policy as each relate to education. While ethics can be discussed and debated on many different levels, perhaps only the narrow realm of professional ethics seems 'legal' in any sense within education; professional ethics attempts to distinguish between personal moral responsibilities in one's life outside the workplace and professional moral and legal responsibilities within the workplace. The balance of this chapter will examine two questions: What is ethics? And how does it sustain and interplay with law in the educational setting, or more specifically for the purposes of this chapter, interplay with education and law? And what constitutes unethical behavior in education and what is the legal consequence of unethical missteps, both professional and legal consequences.

In the sections that follow, the authors will examine first the relationship between ethics, law, and policy. This examination is intended to present distinction between as well as the intersection of ethics, law, and policy as situated in education. The next section will examine the nature of ethics, distinguishing between legal and professional ethics; legal ethics as practiced in adherence to the law and professional ethics as adherence to professional and/or institutional codes of ethics specific to educational cultures (i.e., higher education and public education in pre-K-12 school systems). Following is a section on ethical awareness and ethical sensitivity as related to ethical behavior in contrast to ethical deceit and ethical self-interest. The next section examines the nature of unethical behavior or ethical misconduct, focusing on ethical drift, ethical fading, ethical mirage, ethical missteps, conflict of interest, partisanship, and psychological basis for unethical behavior. Exemplars of ethical misconduct are presented. Drawing forward from the discussion of

[2] For further discussion of behavioural ethics see Ariely (2012), Bazerman and Tenbrunsel (2011), De Cremer (2009), Green (2013), Gino (2013), Heffernan (2011), Johnson (2014).

unethical behavior, the next section examines the legal consequences of unethical behavior in education. This section presents exemplars in education germane to Pre-K-12 and higher education. The concluding section presents the authors' final thoughts on education, ethics, and the law, drawing attention to the ethical responsibilities of professionals.

6.1 The Relationship Between Ethics, Law,[3] and Policy[4]

Ethics, law, and policy are closely intertwined yet distinctively different in terms of purpose in society in general, and in institutions and organisations in particular. Professional ethics codes in education are designed by the different professional organisations to guide professional ethical behavior. Importantly, ethics, law, and policy establish standards of conduct and professional behavior.

Law establishes legal normative standards for the public and is of particular importance to educational professionals responsible for all aspects of the educational organisation, higher education and public pre-K-12 schools alike. Just as ethics has different interpretations, so too does law. In and across nation states, much like the United States, law may be delineated into different categories, often interconnected. Law may be delineated as statutory law, case law, regulatory law, constitutional law, and executive order.[5] For purposes

[3] Law is a general term that serves as an umbrella for several types of law that impact professionals in education. Civil law comprises a wide variety of laws that govern a nation or state and deal with the relationships and conflicts between organisational entities and people. Criminal law addresses activities and conduct harmful to society, and is actively enforced by the state. Law can also be categorized as private or public. Private law encompasses family law, commercial law, and labor law, and regulates the relationship between individuals and organisations. Public law regulates the structure and administration of government agencies and their relationships with citizens, employees, and other governments. Public law includes criminal, administrative, and constitutional law. When considering the relationship between ethics and law it is important to distinguish between the subject of the law (i.e., application of law), the practice of law (i.e., attorneys and legal counsel in a court of law), and the consequence illegal and unethical behavior (i.e., adjudication of an act that fails to meet the intent of the law).

[4] For purposes of this chapter, the authors' focus is on policy as directly related to education and specific to pre-K-12 and higher education. Policy may be understood as decision rule used to guide decision making in relation to all aspects of the educational organisation. Policy in this sense is designed for both the employees of an educational organisation and for the individuals served by the educational organisation. With respect to policy within educational organisations, it is noted that public education, and to a large degree, private education, policy has substantive implication for the pubic and therefore is a normative standard for making decisions.

[5] The following is provided to further explain the types of law (see Dzienkowski 2016):

- **Statutory law, e.g., the United States** Congress and state laws enacted by legislatures, affect educators. Examples include statutes governing educators' obligation to report suspected abuse and neglect of children; requirements for educators to address needs of special needs students; federal requirements

of this chapter, statutory law, regulatory law, and constitutional law (both state and federal) have more direct bearing in terms of professional practice in education. The intersection point between law and ethics is often found in policy as constituted in organisations and institutions in general and education in particular.

6.1.1 Ethics and Law

The distinction between ethics and laws is that ethics are social guidelines based on moral principles and values whereas laws are rules and regulations that have specific penalties and consequences when violated (see Bon 2012; Bottery 2001). The law has traditionally been considered a subset of public morality (Murphy and Nagel 2002). Laws are rules established by legislative branch of government that are normalising in nature, that is, laws mandate or prohibit certain behavior and provide for consequences of unacceptable behavior. The intersectionality of law and ethics is that law is drawn from ethics; ethics define socially acceptable behaviors. Importantly, a defining difference between laws and ethics is that laws carry the authority of a governing body, federal, state, local in nature, and ethics do not. Whereas, ethics in contrast are based on historical, cultural values and beliefs: the fixed and accepted moral attitudes or customs of a particular group (Bottery 2001). Both laws and ethics set standards of expected societal behavior, which give way to the normative nature of both, but whereas laws enforce, ethics set social guidelines based on values and beliefs.

---

for researchers to submit applications to Institutional Review Boards (IRB) for review of research including human subjects.

- **Case law** is typically considered in adjudicating cases in the courtroom. For example, a judge may need to interpret the meaning or application of existing law, resolve conflicts between laws, or fill gaps in existing laws. Such rulings by the court become legal precedent or case law.
- **Regulatory law in education speaks to** regulations promulgated by federal and state government agencies. As example such under the United States system of law, federal and state agencies have the authority to establish enforceable regulations. Public agencies must follow strict procedures when they create regulations (e.g., providing public notice and opportunity for public comment about drafts of regulations).
- **Constitutional law, e.g.,** the U.S. Constitution and state constitutions, include numerous provisions that pertain to social work practice. Examples concern citizens' right to privacy and protections against improper search and seizure (which are important in residential treatment programs) and protections against cruel and unusual punishment (which are important in juvenile and adult correctional facilities).
- **Executive orders are the responsibility of** chief executives in federal, state, and local governments (e.g., a president, governor, mayor, or county executive) may issue orders that resemble regulations. This authority is usually based in federal and state statute.

The intersection of laws and ethics enable each to work in concert to ensure that individuals, the public, acts in a certain manner, and likewise coordinate efforts to protect the health, safety and welfare of the citizens (Jones 1991). Although most ethics established at the national level do not set penalties for violations of civil codes, many individual organisations and agencies can choose to establish and require remedial actions for breaches of ethics rules. In some instances, schools, companies and other organisations have rules that coordinate with a code of ethics, and these institutions may impose penalties and/or sanctions for individuals who violate those rules. It is important to note that sanctions or penalties at the organisational level may be viewed as secondary when misconduct is viewed as a violation of law and is adjudicated in court. In some instances, laws are established at the state or local levels based on ethics, principles or morals. In these instances, morals help to establish a minimal level of safety or expected behavior, which in turn facilitates the act of establishing organisational policies and societal laws.

6.1.2 Policy and Law

A policy is a decision rule that guides decision-making and in this sense is normative in nature, whereas law is a rule established by federal, state, local entities that have jurisdictive power of the court. A policy established by an organisation such as a school or university aligns with the entity's purpose. In this sense, policy serves to establish an infrastructure of decision rules by which the individuals within the organisation function on a day-to-day basis. Whereas a law is an established procedure or legal standard set in place to guide society, there is an intersection of policy and law. Policies are used to guide the decisions of an organisation or institution, while laws are used to implement justice and order (see Bluhm and Heineman 2007). When a policy or decision rule is violated and an individual or individuals are determine in violation, the severity of the violation may set in motion the need for adjudication in a court of law. Simply stated, policy is informal in nature and is a written document that states the purpose and intentions of an institution such as a school or university, while laws are formalised in society and are used to ensure fairness and equity in society.

In some cases, policy serves to inform and guide the development of new laws. However, current policy must always comply with existing laws. Although these two aspects of society are interrelated, each has a distinct function. Laws are enforced by the penalties of the judicial system and help regulate the actions of members in society (see Cerar 2009; Dzienkowski 2016).

6.1.3 Ethics and Policy

Education (Pre-K-12 public education as well as higher education) is a highly political endeavor as well as ethical undertaking; the politics of education require political ethics (sometimes called public ethics) to guide educators. Political ethics, in terms of education, is the practice of making moral judgments about political action, and the study of that practice (Thompson 1987, 2013). As a field of study, it is divided into two branches, each with distinctive problems (see Gutmann and Thompson 2006; Luban et al. 1992; Mendus 2009; Wolff 2011). One branch, the ethics of process (or the ethics of office), focuses on public officials and the methods they use. In the case of a school or university, the ethics of office relates to the administrator and his/her ethical enactment roles and responsibilities as designated under contract of employment. The other branch, the ethics of policy (or ethics and public policy) focuses on judgments about policies and laws (Thompson 2013). It is the second branch that has more direct influence in and on education and educational professionals, however the first branch may have bearing when public officials, such as local, state, and federal elected or appointed officials enter into relationships with educational professionals for political purposes (Thompson 2013). The key problem in policy ethics does not reside in conflicts between ends and means, or between the process and outcomes, rather, the key problems arise between the values of the ends or outcomes themselves. This point of intersection is where education professionals often find themselves challenged. It is the ends or outcomes themselves that are generally called in question and serve as points for legal action. Many of the salient issues in policy ethics are driven by the general tension between partial and impartial claims or obligations. Partisanship is an example where the ethics of process (or office) and the ethics of policy may present points of concern as to political ethics. Partisanship in this case reflects political or other allegiance to an individual who uses the allegiance to sway decisions or actions or garner favors. When a principal or university administrator crosses the line in terms ethics of office and his/her actions or decisions result in scrutiny of outcomes due to perceived violations of ethics of policy, perceived malfeasance[6] may lead to a legal consequence.

[6] Malfeasance as used in this context of education is the commission of an act that is illegal or wrongful and intentional. Improper and/or illegal acts by a public official in an educational setting such as a school or university are determined as an act of malfeasance when the act violates public official's duty to follow the law and act on behalf of the public good (see Woods 2013).

6.1.4 Nature of Ethics

The word *ethics* is derived from the Greek word *ethos*, which means "character," and from the Latin word *mores*, which means "customs." Ethics permeate the cultures of all institutions and organisations, taking different forms and meanings. While differences exist regarding the meaning of ethics, " ... it is useful to think about ethics as the behavioural extension of morals. Morals are beliefs about right versus wrong. Ethics, then, are the behavioural practices which put morals into action" (Ballard 1990, p. 35).

Bazerman and Gino (2012) note that discussions of ethics tend to focus "... either on a moral development perspective or on philosophical approaches and used a normative approach by focusing on the question of how people should act when resolving ethical dilemmas" (p. 39). Ethics applied to decision making in educational cultures, not unlike the cultures of other institutions and organisations, "commonly involve trade-offs between the decision maker's well-being (e.g., not risking losing a job for blowing the whistle) and that of others (e.g., creating harm to potential consumers by not stopping the production of an unsafe product)" (Bazerman and Gino 2012, p. 91).

Equally important, ethical awareness, being sensitive to when the ethicality of a person or situation, is an important factor in educational professionals making ethical decisions at the right time, for the right reasons given the circumstances surrounding the situation.

6.1.5 Legal Ethics Verses Professional Ethics

Distinguishing between legal and professional ethics is an extension of discussions on the nature of ethics. The examination of legal issues in education plays a major role in these discussions, in particular emphasizing the intersection between law, ethics, and administration in educational institutions and organisations (Bon 2012).

Extrapolating "ethics" into institutional and organisational contexts and cultures, it is evident that "ethics" has many and varied connotations and no precise and unequivocal meaning; the variances in meaning are aligned with both the moral philosophical groundings as well as the practical application of ethics within and across professions, for example in medicine, law, education, military, and corporate settings (see DalPont 2006; Drumwright et al. 2015; Parker 2010; Wagner 2012).

While differences exist in the literature regarding the definition of *ethics,* for our purposes it is useful to think of ethics as the behavioural extension of morals. Morals are beliefs about right versus wrong. Ethics, then, are the behavioural practices that interpret morals into action. With this in mind, the distinction between legal and professional ethics reflects application of ethics in relation to professionalism in education (professional ethical codes) versus application of ethics relation to law (following the law, jurisdictive in criminal and civil proceedings).

Legal Ethics The term "legal ethics" refers to ethics rules, bar (Law Bar) opinions, the vast body of case law relevant to the conduct of lawyers and "the role of lawyers in our society," as well as development of students' "capacity for reflective judgment" (ABA 1996 as cited in Pearce 1998, p. 720). Parker (2010) argues that "legal ethics should never be concerned with the morality of *lawyers* or of *clients*; rather it should be concerned only with the morality of the acts lawyers or clients do (or propose to do)" (p. 169) is of importance. This argument is made in concert with a belief that normative theories are of more importance than philosophical considerations of the moral person. In contrast, Woolley and Wendel (2010) argue that moral character in legal ethics is of concern; attention should be paid to "personal features—about, *inter alia*, her dispositions, personality, character, cognition, emotions, or virtues—that correlate with (or inhere in)" (p. 1066, italics in original). Legal ethics play a critical role in the courtroom as well as outside, whether the enactment of legal ethics is juridical or counseling. Rather than purely normative theories of the ideal lawyer, Woolley and Wendel argue that asking "how the person is likely to fare as an ethical decision-maker in actual legal practice" (p. 1067) is of importance.

Legal ethics are logically situated in the law profession and concern the attorney, lawyer, and legal counsel's professional behavior in matters of education (Rhode and Luban 2008). In many educational institutions a general counsel is employed in higher education, or an attorney is on retainer in public pre-K-12 schools. Employment of legal professionals is a part of the culture and context of education in general (Pearce 1998; Wagner 2012).

The distinction of legal ethics lies largely in understanding of ethics pursuant to legal or law practice and understanding that, while educational professionals are required to adhere to law, adjudicating a legal issue is the province of the juridical. Importantly, educational professionals often find themselves situation in a matter of law that requires them to act with prudence in seeking legal assistance (see Woolley 2010a, b). The intersection of legal ethics and professional ethics on one level, is that lawyers are professionals and therein have an ethics code established by the legal profession (Dzienkowski 2016;

Regan 2003). On another level, professional ethics speaks to the moral character[7] of the individual. Different professions have ethics codes that require professionals to govern their practice according to the ethics code.

Professional Ethics A code of ethics provides members of a profession with standards of behavior and principles to be observed regarding their moral and professional obligations toward one another, their clients, and society in general. The primary function of a code of ethics is to provide guidance to employers and employees in ethical dilemmas, especially those that are particularly ambiguous (Moore and Gino 2013).

A code of ethics is often developed by a professional society within a particular profession. The higher the degree of professionalism required of society members, the stronger and, therefore, more enforceable the code; medicine, law, corporations develop ethics codes that align with their professional purpose and practice (see Bazerman and Gino 2012; Messick and Bazerman 1996; Messick and Tenbrunsel 1996). For instance, in medicine, the behavior required is more specific and the consequences are more stringent in the code of ethics for physicians than in the code of ethics for nurses. Similarly, in law, the behavior required of attorneys is distinctly different than that of judges or law clerks. For education, the behavior required of educational administrators/leaders differs from that expected of teachers. More specifically, ethics codes for educational professionals in higher education as opposed to public pre-K-12 public schools require distinctly different ethical behavior.

All professional codes of ethics can be considered quasi-public because of the effect they may have on legal judgments during litigation. Many states adopt accrediting associations' codes of ethics, thereby establishing those standards as public codifications. Failure to comply with a code can, in some professions, result in expulsion from the profession. Ethical misconduct can also result in incarceration and legal penalties. The response of many professions to the challenging and demanding problem of institutionalising ethics is to implement codes of ethics, develop statements of organisational or institutional goals, provide educational programs in ethics, install internal judiciary bodies that hear cases of improprieties, and access points through which employees can anonymously report possible ethical violations.

[7] By moral character we mean a collection of virtues or vices that enable or inhibit the accomplishment of good conduct (see MacIntyre 2007, for further discussion of moral character).

6.1.6 Ethical Awareness, Sensitivity to Unethical Behaviors

Educational professionals, not unlike professionals in the field of medicine, law, accounting, face ethical dilemmas daily. Sensitivity to an ethical dilemma, in particular when one's behavior or the behavior of another drifts away from what is considered ethically acceptable, is important. Discussion of ethical awareness and ethical sensitivity in the context of education practice and addressing ethical dilemmas requires a conception of unethical behavior (ethical misconduct) (Reynolds 2006). Here we rely on Jones' (1991) broad conceptualisation of unethical behavior as reflecting any action that is "… either illegal or morally unacceptable to the larger community" (p. 367). Examples include violations of ethical norms or standards (whether they are legal standards or not), stealing, cheating, falsifying test scores, or other forms of dishonesty. Gino and Bazerman (2009) argue that "… one unexamined, critical factor that could affect when people report others' ethical misconduct is the nature of the wrongdoers' behavior" (p. 709).

Awareness of ethical misconduct, unethical behavior of an individual, is a factor in ethical decision making. Messick and Bazerman (1996) suggested that ethical decisions are compromised by the same systematic errors that characterise our thinking and decision-making processes overall, of which some are beyond our conscious awareness (Chugh et al. 2005). According to this view, unethical actions result from unintentional behavior that is fueled by implicit biases and automatic cognition (Kern and Chugh 2009). Banaji et al. (2003) use the term "bounded ethicality" to refer to individuals' limits in recognising the ethical challenge inherent in a situation or decision.

The absence of conscious awareness of ethical misconduct, Banaji et al. (2003) and Bazerman and Banaji (2004) argue, suggests that much unethical behavior is unintentional and inconsistent with the preferred action that someone would engage in if he/she had greater awareness of his/her own behavior. Based on this argument, in the case of educational professionals, an individual may believe that his/her behavior follows the professional ethics code and is not biased; at the same time, many individuals also are subject to "unconscious biases in ethically relevant domains—for instance, succumbing to implicit forms of prejudice, in-group favoritism, conflicts of interest, and the tendency to over-claim credit" (Gino and Bazerman 2009, p. 710). Discussion of ethical lapses or ethical fading in suggests that moral awareness may not always be activated at the time of decision making (see Tenbrunsel et al. 2010; Tenbrunsel and Messick 2004).

Ethical awareness, such as being sensitive to the unethical behavior of others or when one is drifting of his/her ethical course of professional behavior or when an ethical dilemma is experienced is critical for the educational professional. Wagner (2012) is instructive on this point, stating "professional educators are expected by the publics they serve to exhibit virtue and wisdom and not act simply out of fear of legalistic sanction or other sources of personal and professional distraction" (p. 28). The intersection of ethics, law, and policy for the educational professional requires a high level of ethical awareness, sensitivity to when ethics codes, law, or policy are being disregarded or ignored.

6.1.7 Unethical Behavior: Ethical Misconduct

There are differing perspectives on the psychological basis for unethical behavior or ethical misconduct. Educational professionals, much like individuals in other professions are subject to the psychological influences on ethical behavior and, in turn, on ethical decision making.

Ethical Drift With the slow, shifting of ethical conduct in concert with the challenges of ethical practices in education, professionals are confronted with what is termed ethical drift in the behavior of others that are primary to day-to-day work within the educational setting (Bledsoe et al. 2007; Sternberg 2012a, b; Tenbrunsel and Messick 2004). Ethical drift connotes a significant problem in educational practice. The terms generally reflect when an individual or individuals do not follow an ethical path in decision-making (see Kleinman 2006; Moore and Gino 2013; Sternberg 2012a, b for further discussion).

Kleinman (2006) is particularly instructive, noting that the importance of ethical drift cannot be overestimated because of people's universal susceptibility to it and the gravity of its potential consequences. Educational professionals, not unlike professionals across many fields of study, experience ethical drift in meeting their ethical responsibilities. Moore and Gina (2013) note that ethical drift can be interpreted as moving away from one's moral compass, so to speak. Given the political nature of education and the complex and dynamic nature of ethical dilemmas and problems, compounded by external tensions from government agencies (i.e., state and federal funding sources, accreditation entities, standards and accountability, etc.) and internal tensions (i.e., cultural and political resistance to top-down decisions), the educational practice and decision-making processes are subject to those tensions and therefore subject to "ethical drift".

Recognition that all individuals are subject to ethical drift, just as they are to experiencing ethical dilemmas, Kleinman (2006) notes that the very essence of ethical drift is that it often occurs before individuals Recognise the seriousness of a dilemma as it evolves and takes shape or before the conflict is even perceived. At the same time, individuals "make an imperceptible adjustment to the situation or make a minor exception to their ethical code due to the pressure of the situation, most often with no awareness that this has occurred" (p. 75). Drift occurs, albeit "... not apparent to them that the farther they go down a new path, the farther they get from their original course" (p. 75).

Ethical Fading Ethical fading occurs when ethical blindspots and the contours of the slippery slope of ethical decision making contribute to a process of *ethical fading* or *moral disengagement* in which decision makers "do not 'see' the moral components of an ethical decision, not so much because they are morally uneducated, but because psychological processes *fade* the 'ethics' from an ethical dilemma" (Tenbrunsel and Messick 2004, pp. 223–224). A variety of additional psychological processes also play a role in fading ethical considerations from view, making unethical decisions more likely.

Robbennolt and Sternlight (2013, p. 1120) note that the *scripts* – memory patterns containing knowledge structures that guide our understanding of how events typically unfold – that govern a particular situation and has similarities to a previous event may determine whether or not ethical considerations are taken into account. One "may approach a particular [decision] with a script that has moral content, triggering moral judgment processes, or with one that is devoid of moral content, triggering non-moral judgment processes" (Butterfield et al. 2000, p. 1120). The script relevant to the current situation may characterise a particular decision – such as whether a conflict is an obstacle to taking on representation of a new client – as a *business* decision as opposed to an ethical decision, fading the ethical implications from view (Tenbrunsel and Messick 2004).

Misrepresentations and expectations of misrepresentations in ethical dilemmas may cause what Tenbrunsel et al. (2010) term ethical mirage. Not unlike the mirage one would see on the horizon after walking for a length of time in the desert, the ethical mirage is a psychological phenomenon where individuals predictions and post-hoc recollections of their behavior are dominated by the thinking of their "should" self, but, at the time of the decision, their actual actions are dominated by the thinking of their "want" self. Again, as the individual in the desert walks further toward a mirage of say water, over time the individual's sense of reality is fading. In like fashion, as an individual's ethical awareness fades over time, so too are the ethical implications of the decision during the action phase of decision making (Tenbrunsel and Messick 2004), which is partially responsible for the dominance of the "want" self during this time (O'Connor et al. 2002).

When ethical fading occurs – a process by which a person does not realise that the decision he/she is making has ethical implications and thus ethical criteria do not enter into her decision – the "should" self has no reason to be activated. Ethical mirage suggests that our predictions of how we will behave and our recollections of our past behavior are at odds with how we actually behave. Specifically, people tend to mispredict how they will behave in the future, often overestimating the extent to which they would engage in socially desirable behaviors (Epley and Dunning 2000).

Consequently, the "want" self is allowed to freely dominate the decision and unethical behavior ensues. Bazerman et al. (1998) note that negotiating with yourself often ends in losing, making decisions with competing internal preferences. The "want/should" conflict,[8] "coupled with the temporal dimension inherent in the phases of prediction, behavior, and recollection, allow for the sustained belief that we are more ethical than our actions demonstrate, a faulty misperception of ourselves that is difficult to self-correct. ... highlight how our misperceptions are perpetuated over time" (see Tenbrunsel et al. 2010, p. 154).

Ethical Blind Spots Many professionals make decisions that are questionable, ethically, due to the existence of ethical blind spots – a lack of awareness that impairs the ability to identify the ethical implications of a situation (Bazerman 2014; Bazerman and Tenbrunsel 2011; Chugh et al. 2005). Ethical blindness occurs when "... self-interest is pitted against being honest" and " ... ambiguity serves as a justification to do wrong but feel moral. That is, people's attention is more easily shifted toward tempting information in ambiguous settings than in unambiguous settings, and this tempting information then shapes their self-serving lies" (Pittarello et al. 2015). When professionals face ethically tempting situations, their attention is bounded by ethical blind spots guided by their self-serving motivation (Bazerman 2014; Bazerman and Tenbrunsel 2011). Unethical decisions are most likely to occur in educational "settings in which ethical boundaries are blurred. In ambiguous

[8] Bazerman et al. (1998) proposed the "want/should" distinction to describe intrapersonal conflicts that exist within the human mind.

settings, people's attention drifts toward tempting information, which shapes their lies" (Pittarello et al. 2005, p. 803).

Outcome Bias Outcome bias occurs when people judge the quality of a decision based on its outcome – for example, decisions resulting in negative consequences are judged to have been bad decisions (Robbennolt and Sternlight 2013). The perceived moral intensity of a decision can also be influenced by the ease with which the nature, magnitude, probability, and timing of any potential consequences can be drawn to mind (Tversky and Kahneman 1973). For example, decisions are seen as more unethical when they result in observable harm (the outcome bias) and when they harm identifiable victims (Gino et al. 2010). In contrast, when harm is perceived as less likely to occur or more removed in time, the decision will feel less ethically fraught (see Hayibor and Wasieleski 2009; Robbennolt and Sternlight 2013).

Socialisation Socialisation, as Moore and Gino (2013) explain, is a process internal to the institutional or organisational culture that "sets up role expectations for individuals that communicates which organisational goals are important, and establishes appropriate ways to achieve them" (p. 59). With respect morality, socialisation processes tend to be "agnostic about questions of morality" (p. 59). Unethical behavior and practices often exist in organisational and institutional cultures, taking long periods to pervade a culture (Moore 2009). Socialisation to unethical practices in these cultures "can happen both consciously, when an individual resists objectionable practices until finally *surrendering* to them as inevitable, and unconsciously, when an individual becomes *seduced* by the positive material or psychological benefits of participating in corrupt behavior" (Moore and Gino 2012, p. 59). Socialisation directs individuals to look for cues from others to identify appropriate behavior when they are new to an organisation, or when a pre-existing organisational culture re-socialises individuals to new institutional demands, socialisation directs them to look for cues from others to identify appropriate behavior.

Conflict of Interest Professionals are often called on in many situations to play dual roles that require different perspectives. As example, " … attorneys embroiled in pretrial negotiations may exaggerate their chances of winning in court to extract concessions from the other side. But when it comes time to advise the client on whether to accept a settlement offer, the client needs objective advice. Professors, likewise, have to evaluate the performance of graduate students and provide them with both encouragement and criticism" (Moore et al. 2010, p. 37).

Given the frequency with which professionals are called upon to fulfill multiple roles, "their different roles demand that they pursue conflicting objectives" (Moore et al. 2010, p. 38). While it might seem, at the time, desirable that multiple aspects of the self inform each other in judgment and choice, such mutual influence also undermines individuals' ability to play multiple roles. What Chugh et al. (2005) call bounded ethicality creates a psychological barrier to recognising conflicts of interest. Due to this bounded ethicality, a professional's " ... inability to switch between roles without having them influence each other can partly explain the corrosive effect of conflicts of interest on professional judgment" (Moore et al. 2010, p. 38).

6.1.8 Exemplars of Ethical Misconduct

Ethical misconduct takes many forms and does not discriminate in terms of educational professionals' roles and responsibilities. Ethical lapses occur more easily and less intentionally than we might imagine. While most of us desire to act ethically, psychological processes often lead individuals and groups to engage in ethically questionable behaviors that are inconsistent with their own preferred ethics (Bazerman and Moore 2008; Moore and Gino 2013).

Unethical decisions are more likely when the decision maker does not see the decision at hand as involving ethical issues or when he/she believes that any potential ethical challenges can easily be overcome. Each of us tends to believe that we see the world objectively; to see ourselves as more fair, unbiased, competent, and deserving than average; and to be overconfident about our abilities and prospects (see Robbennolt and Sternlight 2013, p. 1116).

Special Education: Failure to Meet the Needs of Students The legal ramifications of not meeting the basic needs of special needs students with disabilities, as well as the ethical responsibilities of school principals and district administrators present increasing problems in schools today. Attention Deficit Disorder (ADD), Attention Deficit Hyperactive Disorder (ADHD), Emotionally Disabled (E,D), and Severely and Profoundly Mentally Retarded (SPMR), Autism, Bi-polar, and Asperger syndrome are examples of disabilities afflicting children today. The school has a legal responsibility to meet the needs students diagnosed with disorders that affect learning. The identification of learning disabilities is primary responsibility of the school, as well as providing for the specific learning needs of the students (see IDEA 2004).[9] The cost of providing for students with learning disabilities has increased astronomically for public schools in recent years in the United States. IDEA (2004) requires that pre-K-12 students with disabilities be educated in the least restrictive environment and, to the minimum extent appropriate with students who do not have disabilities. Seclusion of special needs students with disabilities in isolation, removal from the least restrictive environment, is one of many situations that pervade schools. As well, failure to provide the diagnostic and related services to identify students with disabilities, particularly when school personnel have evidence and/or reason to know a student with suspected disabilities resides in the community represents another pervasive problem. Whereas school districts are required to have appropriate polices in place to address the needs of students with disabilities, the ethical responsibility of the principal and/or school superintendent or designated district personnel is to follow school district policy as well as state and federal laws concerning special education and students with disabilities. When the principal and/or superintendent elect to disregard their ethical responsibilities due to perceived demands on the district – i.e., fiscal burden for special education programs, additional personnel, transportation, equipment for certain disabilities, etc. – the legal framework established to ensure a fair and equitable education of students with disabilities is a recourse for parents and guardians.

Crossing Professional Boundaries–Sexual Misconduct Sexual misconduct incorporates a range of behaviors including sexual assault, sexual harassment, stalking, voyeurism, sexual relations between an adult and an underage child, and any other conduct of a sexual nature that is inappropriate ethically and morally as well as legally. Sexual misconduct is an act of malfeasance.[10] A teacher and student sexual relationship is an example of misconduct that is present schools (Shakeshaft 2004, 2013; Zarra 2013, 2016). Cases of both

[9] Legal responsibility of schools:

Under the law, schools have an affirmative duty to identify, locate, and evaluate students who they suspect may have a disability, in order to evaluate them for potential eligibility for special education services (see IDEA 2004, 20 U.S.C. § 1412(a) and 334 C.F. R. § 300.111). Schools must maintain a system of notices, outreach efforts, staff training, and referral processes designed to ascertain when there are reasonable grounds to suspect disability and the potential need for special education services. (http://www.rtinetwork.org/learn/ld/legal-implications-of-response-to-intervention-and-special-education-identification)

[10] The distinction between sexual misconduct and sexual abuse is significant in legal and other terms, however the two terms may be used interchangeably in certain contexts. The prevalence of sexual misconduct in schools is of concern to students, parents, school administrators and the courts (Shakeshaft 2004, 2013). An intentional act of sexual misconduct on the part of a teacher toward a student is considered malfeasance and actionable in courts of law.

male and female teachers engaged in sexual relations with a student have been documented. Professional codes of conduct as well as professional ethics speak to moral turpitude and clearly delineate the lines of professional behavior. Crossing the professional boundaries on the part of a teacher with his/her student may result in physical and emotional harm to the student (Aultman et al. 2009). The phrase "do no harm" is an ethical as well as legal boundary that teachers are expected to embrace as a code of ethics. A breach of ethics on the part of a teacher who engages in seductive behavior that results in sexual activity with a minor is also viewed as an illegal act as defined in local, state, and federal law Title IX.[11] The principal and the school district are faced with the ethical dilemma of reporting or not reporting an incident where a teacher violates the professional boundary and engages in a sexual relationship with student. Local and state as well as federal laws require the reporting of child abuse. A principal deciding not to report an incident of sexual misconduct to purportedly protect the school, the teacher, or the child's family compounds the problem and violates his/her ethical and legal responsibilities. Importantly, the safety of the student is of paramount concern for the principal in his/her determination of appropriate actions to take, respective to the teacher's actions of sexual misconduct.

Social Media The prevalence of social media in society and in particular in the access to and use of social media on the part of students are increased exponentially in the past five years. Papandrea (2012), writing on social media and public school teachers noted that educational administrators are grappling with issues surrounding public school teachers' use of social media. As a new generation grows up with social networks as an integral part of life, there is an increasing challenge to ensure that using social networks does not open students up to vulnerabilities. Personal information that was once considered private is increasingly being shared online. School districts are advancing new policies on the use of social media networks in schools and classrooms, policies that stipulate restrictions on teacher and student interactions. Whereas the public sharing of information obscures the normal boundaries between teacher and student and teacher and colleagues, district policies are focused

[11] Title IX of the United States Education Amendments of 1972 ("Title IX"), Public Law No. 92–318, 86 Stat. 235 (June 23, 1972), codified at 20 U.S.C. §§ 1681–1688 is a Federal civil rights law that prohibits discrimination on the basis of sex in education programs and activities. All public and private elementary and secondary schools, school districts, colleges, and universities receiving and Federal funding must comply with Title IX. Under Title IX, discrimination on the basis of sex can include sexual harassment or sexual violence, such as rape, sexual assault, sexual battery, and sexual coercion. Sexual violence is inclusive of sexual misconduct such as engaging in sexual relations with a minor (see https://www2.ed.gov/about/offices/list/ocr/docs/tix_dis.html)

on professional boundaries. Social media has provided a virtual access and communication portal between teachers and students. Young teachers are especially vulnerable to the consequences of putting out personal information and pictures that may implicate them morally and professionally. Papandrea (2012) acknowledges that in question is the First Amendment[12] rights to freedom of speech as a point of contention in a number of legal cases pursuant to teachers use of social media and their right to use of social media (Levin 2016).

Crossing professional boundaries and violating professional ethics via social media has compounded the problems that schools and school administrators face (Simpson 2015). In the same way that email and texting communications between educators and students has resulted in the crossing of the boundaries of appropriate relationships, educators must also recognise the dangers of social network sites in contributing to this as well. Facebook, Twitter, SnapChat, Instagram and other contemporary social media networks have increased the pressure on principals and school districts as they sort out teacher rights under the First Amendment versus district policy and the safety of students. Equally perplexing, school districts are faced with ensuring that their social media use does not violate FERPA.[13] A concern as present is focused on ensuring that teachers' use of digital technology and social media for communication and interactions is does not violate FERPA.

School districts are faced with parents drawn into new and increasingly difficult challenges in monitoring their children's social media activity and ensuring that sexual predators and related activity does not endanger their children. The school and school administration has an ethical responsibility to design and implement district policy and procedure that establishes a safe and protective environment for students. The intersectionality of policy, ethics, and law in matters of social media is of particular importance in a digitally advanced society (Papandrea 2012). The number of social media network access portals for students has increased the security and safety concerns for school districts. As well, the concern for maintaining professional boundaries

[12] First Amendment, found in the Bill of Rights in the U.S. Constitution guarantees freedoms concerning religion, expression, assembly, and the right to petition (see https://www.law.cornell.edu/wex/first_amendment).

[13] The Family Educational and Rights and Privacy Act (FERPA) (20 U.S.C. § 1232 g; 34 CFR Part 99) is a Federal law that protects the privacy of student education records. The law applies to all schools that receive funds under an applicable program of the U.S. Department of Education. (see https://www2.ed.gov/policy/gen/guid/fpco/ferpa/index.html)

between teacher and students has exponentially increased due to the proliferation of social media.

Malfeasance Malfeasance is an intentional act that an individual knows is ethically wrong and which violates policy and law (Woods 2013). School districts have anti-nepotism policies and are generally derived from state and federal law. The purpose of a district's anti-nepotism policy is to ensure employees are selected fairly, and that the best candidates for the position are selected. Eliminating nepotism, which is the practice of hiring or granting favor to relatives or friends, also does away with the problems inherent in having a person in a position of authority directly supervising a relative or close friend. As an example, a principal has a position in the school cafeteria and knowingly hires his sister-in-law for position because the she has experienced difficulty in securing a new position. The principal intentionally falsifies his sister-in-law's employment history of salary and benefits in previous places of employment in order to pay her at a rate higher than normal for the position. In this case the principal violates the intent of the nepotism policy resulting in an act of malfeasance, an act that is unethical and potentially actionable in a court of law.

A second example of malfeasance is when a teacher intentionally hurts or causes bodily harm to a student. There are situations in classrooms where a teacher has a student that constantly acts out in belligerent and disrespect ways, perhaps verbally or with offensive gestures, at times physical contact. Teachers are typically prepared to deal with classroom management issues. However, after repeated offenses with the individual student where the student uses inappropriate language with another student, the teacher intervenes, and the student then turns his verbal assault on the teacher. As an act of inappropriate behavior, the teacher intentionally grabs the student and presses the student against the wall, striking that student, and then drops the student to the floor. While perhaps a momentary lapse of professional decorum, this action not only violates school policy and professional ethics, is an act of malfeasance. Teachers, like principals, are in positions of power, and whether it is acting on behalf of a sister-in-law or striking a student, these actions are inappropriate and/or illegal acts by a public employee in an educational setting (Woods 2013).

Self-Deception*[14] *in Administrative Decisions Professional integrity is a corner stone of ethical behavior. Ethical misconduct may emerge as a result of self-deception, which " … allows one to behave self-interestedly while, at the same time, falsely believing that one's moral principles were upheld" (Tenbrunsel and Messick 2004, p. 223). The university administrator who promotes on-line programs at the expense of a long history of success with face-to-face programs because the administrator is a strong proponent of technology fails to see the institutional image as important. Disregard for program quality and success and the advocacy for on-line programs is an example where self-interest (i.e., technology and online program delivery) drives decisions. This self-interest is compounded when universities faced with fiscal constraints and the need to reallocate budget lines allow an administrator's decisions to take precedent over the quality and success of high profile programs, shifting programs to on-line delivery at the expense of students and faculty and the quality of existing programs.

Contrasting in nature, a school principal that selectively supports certain programs over other programs in his school in order to garner support from parents in the community and secure his position demonstrates self-interest. A principal has a duty-bound obligation to ensure that all students are provided appropriate learning opportunities in a least restrictive environment. Allocating resources to programs that are elective or extracurricular, as an example, where student enrollment is not mandatory than in other programs required by the state for graduation, where enrollment is high can result in inequities in the allocation and use of school fiscal and personnel resources and can impact in student learning. The case where select parents and patrons of the school have vested interests in a specific program, perhaps their child or grandchild is in the programs, and these vested interests reflect an "old guard" politics in the community, this sets the stage for ethical misconduct on the part of the principal. When the principal plays to the "old guard" politics and pressures of parents and patrons, as an act of self-interest to secure the "old guard's" favor, the principals' actions and decisions may result in a breach of professional ethics. Self-interest as to one's position and power can lead to ethical misconduct.

---

[14] On self-deception, Dolovich (2002) notes:

> This tendency to self-deception may be the single biggest obstacle to integrity. It prevents honest scrutiny of our own motives, requires that certain ideas be permanently excluded from our minds, and prevents us from fitting comfortably, without tension, into ourselves. The practice of self-deception thus precludes the possibility of becoming an integrated whole, a state of being which is the essence of integrity. (p. 1658). .

The psychology of the self-interest overpowers ethics and self-deception convinces the administrator that his/her decisions are in the best interest of the university. The educational professional does not "see" the moral components of an ethical decision, not so much because they are morally uneducated, but because psychological processes *fade* the "ethics" from an ethical dilemma (Tenbrunsel and Messick 2004, p. 224, emphasis in original).

Partisanship and Politics A vast body of research reveals that situational factors, like placing a university council,[15] administrator, accountant or auditor in a partisan[16] role, can result in behavior that is inconsistent with conventional ethical theories. Placing a person in a partisan role results in the person remaining objective under partisan circumstances. For instance, university administrators have a tendency to offer different assessments of a problem or situation in a case depending on whether they are asked to defend a person's action or find fault in the action and hold the person responsible. In like fashion, university accountants and auditors conducting audits on academic units "are more likely to find that a [university or academic unit's] financial reports comply with generally accepted accounting principles when the accountants are placed in a role of the [university's] accountant that when they are assigned the role of the accountant for an outside [entity] ..." (Perlman 2015, p. 1639). Simply stated, the accountants or auditors placed in a partisan role have some level of difficulty remaining objective. Similarly, a university council acting on behalf of the university may find the partisan position he/she is placed in has an effect on judgment (Moore et al. 2010). Distorted professional judgment may occur when a university council is involved in a case dealing with a student who is victim of a rape attack, or with a faculty member filing suit against the university resulting from unfair political pressure exacted on the faculty member by a well-known politician that also is a strong supporter of the university. Lawyers (university council) have a tendency to offer different assessments on what should be maintained as objective judgment due to the profile of the case, the implication of the case in terms of the university's reputation,

[15] The term university counsel as used herein is treated as synonymous with attorney or lawyer. University counsel holds a law degree from an accredited institution.

[16] Partisan is commonly used to describe people who fit a dictionary definition of a "partisan," that is, those who are adherents to, or aligned with, a specific "political party, faction, cause, or person". Legal professionals (lawyers, university counsel) and educational professionals (administrators, researchers) may be partisans in the social-psychology sense (i.e., adhering to a specific political, financial, ideological affiliation) without complying with the partisanship principle (i.e., pursuing that client's cause as far as the law allows). The distinction is significant because critics of the dominant view reject the partisanship principle but acknowledge that lawyers are partisans in the sense of being aligned with a particular side of a matter. For purposes of this chapter, partisan and partisanship speak to being in a position or relationship subjectively due to positions of power or politics (see Perlman 2015, p. 1643).

or when the political pressure exacted by a politician is too close to upper administration in the university.

Confidentiality in Research Conducting research with human subjects requires that protection of privacy for participants in the research begin with the planning of the research project. Protecting human subjects and maintaining confidentiality and anonymity is crucial to the way research on human subjects is conducted (see, NIH 1998; OHRP 2010). This protection assurance extends through the review of research results (on both human) for publication and the sharing of data sets. Everyone involved – researchers, human subjects, support personnel, editors, reviewers, and data managers – should be aware of the ethical and legal requirements regarding privacy and should not compromise confidentiality for any reason.

Institutional review boards (IRBs) must be consulted about any research involving human subjects, and informed consent forms must be obtained and honored. Human subjects have a right to expect that their personal information will not be divulged when the results of a study are published or when data sets from a research project are shared with other investigators. Protecting the privacy of research subjects is an obligation for all those who are involved in the research.

Falsifying Research Manufacturing or falsifying data to present findings in research is an example of ethical misconduct. Universities often place pressure on faculty to conduct research and publish findings; often times the publish or perish phenomenon drifts off the ethical path, particularly if the researcher is focused on writing grants and pursuing higher profile research. Ethical drift is the erosion of ethical behavior that occurs in individuals below their level of self-awareness. Manufacturing or falsifying data takes many forms. When a researcher is conducting quantitative research against a tight timeline on a grant-funded project and pressure from university administrators is exacted in order to demonstrate to the funding entity that the research findings are in alignment with the original project proposal, researchers manipulate data and/or create false data to ensure the findings are what was promised. Kleinman (2006) explained that ethical drift is "an incremental deviation from ethical practice that goes unnoticed by individuals who justify the deviations as acceptable and who believe themselves to be maintaining their ethical boundaries" (p. 73). Often, ethical drift occurs below a level of awareness, to the individual and to others, and "facilitates doing that which fosters self-serving needs" (p. 73). When the perceived costs to the researcher outweigh adhering to principled ethical conduct, and the researcher elects to place the needs of 'self' above the ethical responsibility to the research, the subjects, the institution, and society, ethical drift occurs. Educational researchers are faced with ethical dilemmas and concerns are part of the everyday practice of doing research; when the benefit to 'self' outweighs ethical behaviors, ethics codes for researchers are breached.

Student Privacy Issues There are many academic programs that prepare audiologists and speech-language pathologists for entry into the field of communication sciences and disorders. At all levels of professional education, students and student clinicians have privacy rights that educators must respect. These rights are specifically protected by federal law (Family Educational Rights and Protection Act FERPA,[17] for example, in the United States), and there may also be relevant state statutes. But, once again, safeguarding the privacy of information entrusted to a teacher, program administrator, or institution is an ethical and not just a legal obligation. When personnel at any level have responsibility for access to records and either intentionally neglect that responsibility or violate federal, state, and organisational/institutional law and policy, such as granting access to the personnel records of a faculty member in a university department, to unauthorised persons, for non-department purposes, it is not only a gross violation of ethics but a legal regulations. Whether students or employees in an educational setting, individuals are required to follow the legal and ethical responsibilities to the profession and their relationships with colleagues and students.

Falsifying Assessment Results for Accountability Purposes Standards and accountability have placed educational professionals under enormous pressure; standardised tests in pre-K-12 schools and the accountability ratings of schools have resulted in breach of ethical codes for school administrators, test coordinators, and teachers across the United States. This phenomenon is paralleled in other nation statues where PISA[18] and comparable systems for assessing and rating educational systems are in effect.

[17] The Family Educational Rights and Privacy Act (*FERPA*) (20 U.S.C. § 1232 g; 34 CFR Part 99) is a Federal law that protects the privacy of student education records. The law applies to all schools and educational organisations that receive funds under an applicable program of the U.S. Department of Education.

[18] The Programme for International Student Assessment (PISA) is a worldwide study by the Organisation for Economic Co-operation and Development (OECD) in member and non-member nations of 15-year-old school pupils' scholastic performance on mathematics, science, and reading (see https://www.oecd.org/pisa/test/). Its influence on countries' policy of student assessment is the range of ways in which PISA is influencing countries education policy choices. Policy-makers in most participating countries see PISA

The growing concern in the United States in public schools is with school administrators falsifying assessment results on reports to the governing board of directors. Equally problematic is test coordinators and teachers making versions of the assessment instrument available to students prior to test dates, allowing the students prepare for the test with unauthorised access to testing materials. As example, more than five years after Michelle Rhee took over Washington, D.C., public schools as chancellor, and nearly three years after she left her position as chancellor, critics are still looking for closure and demanding a more rigorous investigation of the seeming rise in student test scores under her reign. Washington D.C. school administrators released an investigation into the district's 2012 standardised tests. The report concluded that 11 schools had "critical" test security violations – and in some cases, teacher cheating – on last year's DC Comprehensive Assessment System (U.S. Department of Education 2013).

6.2 Legal Consequences of Unethical Behavior

Professional ethics and codes of conduct have become an important part of the education, legal, corporate, and professional world. Ethics and codes of conduct are created to help a profession define minimum and expected standards of ethical conduct by its members. Professional ethics are usually created by a state or national organisation, and typically enforced according to guidelines within the organisation. A wide range of groups has adopted ethics codes, including lawyers, doctors, accountants, teachers, journalists, social workers and engineers. The ethical standards set forth in the ethics codes allow the public as clients as well as professional peers to rely on the fitness and honor of that professional's conduct in the workplace, and confident that remedies will be available when those standards are not upheld. Boldizar and Korthonen (1999) succinctly stated:

> *The ethical task is to encounter the problems of life as they come: open, indeterminate, uncontainable, irreducible. 'Authenticity' in this pragmatic world is about facing the problems in their full complexity, without simplification or abdication of responsibility to higher unverified authorities, ideals or standards, in a manner*

as an important indicator of system performance; PISA reports can define policy problems and set the agenda for national policy debate; policymakers seem to accept PISA as a valid and reliable instrument for internationally benchmarking system performance and changes over time; most countries – irrespective of whether they performed above, at, or below the average PISA score – have begun policy reforms in response to PISA reports.

> *which builds a relation of significance between what we do, both in terms of our work and our personal actions, and what we are and currently want to be as people.* (p. 284)

The consequence of unethical behavior lies in three courts, so to speak. The first court is that of the person and the profession to which he/she belongs. The moral questions that pursue an unethical behavior or ethical misconduct are bound in the 'self' of the individual and must be adjudicated accordingly; the 'self' must come to terms with the misconduct. The second court is that of the profession and the employing institution or organisation wherein the ethical misconduct or transgression took place. The adjudication of unethical behavior falls under the ethics codes for the profession at large, and the ethics codes set within the employing entity; the ethics codes of the profession and employing entity are not generally estranged, rather codes are intertwined. Professional behavior is clearly defined and unethical behavior is judged by the codes. The third court of adjudication is the legal court system, civil or criminal, local or state or federal. The bearing of the ethical transgression and the weight of statutory, regulatory, and constitutional law falls accordingly to the severity of the case.

The legal consequence of unethical behavior or ethical misconduct is determined, in part by the regulatory standards set in place and aligned with ethics codes and codes of conduct. These standards and codes differ, in some respects, between higher education institutions and pre-K-12 public schools. Whereas, the law – statutory and constitutional – tends to be more uniform in applications and the adjudication of unethical act weighted according to severity of the case, i.e., if a state or federal regulation or law was broken, if the security of individuals, communications, or records is placed at risk, or if the case represents a clear violation of legal precedent (case law) the supercedes other regulatory standards set in place by an institution or organisation wherein the regulation is at odds with legal standing.

In light of the type of unethical behavior and the consequential filing of legal action to determine legality or illegality, the outcome varies according to the severity of case. Reflecting on the different exemplars presented in the previous section of this chapter, it is important to denote that the exemplars are only a few amidst a larger volume of points of concern when considering ethics and the law in education.

The special education exemplar presents historical as well as more contemporary ethical and legal issues that plaque public education and its schools. The statutory requirements to meet the needs of all students presents important in often times difficult challenges for school districts. IDEA (2004) has established specific parameters that school administrators are required to work within, as well clearly delineating the policy/procedure expectations for ensuring all children have equitable learning opportunities in the least restrictive environment. In addition the ethical responsibilities of school administrators in terms of meeting the needs of students with disabilities, schools are expected to provide necessary programs and services. When a school administrator or school district fails to meet the legal intent of IDEA (2004) the consequences could include legal sanctions against personnel, fiscal penalties for the district, and ultimately, depending on the nature of misconduct and/or malfeasance, adjudication in the courts, both state and federal.

The legal consequence for self-deception misconduct could result in loss of position (termination), and civil court procedures could be brought. In the self-deception exemplars the university administrator and/or the public school principal could be removed his/her administrative position. In select cases, legal action could be brought if it is determined that the unethical behavior was not properly vetted with key individuals. Self-deception, if determined as an intentional act of misconduct could be rendered to a court of law and tried as a case of malfeasance. Specifically, in public schools and universities, personnel found guilty may lose their position as face penalty of law.

In matters of student privacy and violations of FERPA, as presented, the legal consequence could extend beyond termination if the severity of the unethical acts is proven; individuals could face criminal and/or civil charges. FERPA violations are technically federal in nature, although enforcement tends to be upon the State, and legal action pursuant to the policy parameters may result in court trial and possible penalty of law.

Sexual misconduct, as exemplified in dozens of court cases pending in the United States and/or that have been rendered as guilty by the courts, are intentional breaches of professional ethics on the part of teachers and legally considered acts of malfeasance in the courts (see Clark 2011; Shakeshaft 2004). Teachers found guilty of sexual misconduct face loss of certification or licensure as well as incarceration for a felony carrying imprisonment. Also, teachers found guilty of sexual misconduct will bear the burden of being labeled, under law, as sex offenders and /or sexual predators.

Social media presents a contemporary and prevalent problem for schools and universities, as well as the public courts (see Papandrea 2012). Inappropriate use of social media on the part of a public employee or official, in particular when use includes violating school district policy concerning restrictions on school personnel from communicating with students or posting in appropriate photos or personal information, may result in termination and possible adjudication in a court of law (see Russo 2012).[19] The sanctions set forth in school district policy are intended to protect students and the district. When policy and procedure is violated, the school district may seek legal recourse.

Concerning the exemplar confidentiality of research and falsifying research, a researcher or persons affiliated with conducting research found guilty of unethical behavior or research misconduct will face loss of research funding, loss of academic position, termination and may face civil charges in court based on the severity of the case. In many cases the external funding entity withdraws funding and may file charges. The researchers' professional career may come to an end. Finally, in the falsifying of educational assessment data for accountability purposes, loss of employment is eminent as exemplified in the Washington DC case. Civil and criminal charges are likely and certainly the individual's professional career will be permanently and negatively impacted.

6.3 Final Thoughts

One of the most demanding tasks of every society, regardless of which country or nation state, is to continuously attempt to establish and maintain an appropriate balance between politics, policy, ethics and law. When focused on an institution such as education, maintaining a balanced perspective ethics in relation to the politics of education is difficult; education professionals find themselves entrenched in the politics and subject to ethical tensions that often give way to unethical behavior. This relationship is always, without question, different in an authoritarian or totalitarian state as compared to a democratic state based on the rule of law.

Importantly, law and ethics are the scaffolding or supporting framework that guide the practice of the education profession. Without either law or ethics, the profession could not exist. Policy plays an instrumental role in interpreting law and aligning law with ethical standards set in place by professional codes of ethics. The normative dimension of professional behavior is expressed by the term policy and entails the creation of normative ideas or ideals that define basic societal values and objectives geared towards a practical realisation of such.

[19] Title IX, as discussed previously, sets Federal guidelines for sexual misconduct and provides for appropriate institutional action. A review of this law should be considered in concert with local and state laws pertaining to illicit relations between a teacher and student.

Malfeasance on the part of educators (as with any individual) may lead to criminal and/or civil action in a court of law (see Bon 2012). Breach of ethical codes of conduct may be determined in a court of law as an act of malfeasance. When professionalism of lawyers and legal counsel is called into question due to perceived unethical behavior, the consequence could lead to disbarment from the legal profession (see Perlman 2015; Robbennolt and Sternlight 2013). When professionalism of politicians and policy makers comes under public scrutiny for unethical behavior, the consequence could lead to incarceration, failure to be reelected or reappointed to office. Professionals in education, law, and politics/policy, as servants of the public, are uniquely responsible to the public for ethical behavior above reproach; ethical behavior on the part of education professionals is a voice of public morality.

In all of the uncertainty of human behavior, education professionals should remain aware that professional ethics, as standards for ethical conduct, may have legal consequences. Behaving ethically may not only avoid professional discipline, but civil litigation as well. Education professionals rarely set out to become corrupt, engage in ethical misconduct. However, many of these professionals "face powerful conflicting motives that make it difficult to maintain perfect professional integrity" (Moore et al. 2010, p. 47). Examining unethical behavior or ethical misconduct draws the psychology of human behavior into question, giving way to recognition that unethical behavior may be both intentional and unintentional, conscious and unconscious in nature.

Wagner (2012) provides an important final thought concerning the relationship between ethics, law, and policy in the professional world and work of educators.

> *The professionalism of educators cannot be adequately captured in any laws, codes, regulations, or policies. Such directives must always be seen through the prism of one's professional commitments and duties. True professionalism requires more moral commitment than can be secured by the threat of sanctions.* (p. 33)

References

Ariely, D. (2012). *The (honest) truth about dishonesty.* New York: HarperCollins.

Aultman, L. P., Williams-Johnson, M. R., & Schutz, P. A. (2009). Boundary dilemmas in teacher-student relationships: Struggling with "the line". *Teaching and Teacher Education, 25*, 636–646.

Balizar, A., & Korthonen, O. (1999). Ethics, morals and international law. *EJIL, 10*(2), 279–311.

Ballard, S. (1990, September 17). *Ethics, public policy and civic education*. Speech delivered at the national public policy education conference, Salt Lake City, Utah.

Banaji, M. R., Bazerman, M. H., & Chugh, D. (2003). How (un)ethical are you? *Harvard Business Review, 81*(12), 56–64.

Bazerman, M. H. (2014). *The power of noticing: What the best leaders see*. New York: Simon & Schuster.

Bazerman, M. H., & Banaji, M. R. (2004). The social psychology of ordinary ethical failures. *Social Justice Research, 17*(2), 111–115.

Bazerman, M. H., & Gino, F. (2012). Behavioral ethics: Toward a deeper understanding of moral judgment and dishonesty. *Annual Review of Law and Social Science, 8*, 85–104.

Bazerman, M. H., & Moore, D. A. (2008). *Judgment in managerial decision making* (7th ed.). New York: Wiley.

Bazerman, M. H., & Tenbrunsel, A. E. (2011). *Blind spots: Why we fail to do what's right and what to do about it*. Princeton: Princeton University Press.

Bazerman, M. H., Tenbrunsel, A. E., & Wade-Benzoni, K. (1998). Negotiating with yourself and losing: Making decisions with competing internal preferences. *Academy of Management Review, 23*(2), 225–241.

Bledsoe, C. H., Sherin, B., Galinsky, A. G., et al. (2007). Regulating creativity: Research and survival in the IRB iron cage. *Northwestern Law Review, 101*(2), 593–642.

Bluhm, W. T., & Heineman, R. A. (2007). *Ethics and public policy: Method and cases*. Upper Saddle River: Pearson Prentice Hall.

Bon, S. C. (2012). Examining the crossroads of law, ethics, and education leadership. *Journal of School Leadership, 22*, 285–308.

Bon, S. C., & Bigbee, A. (2011). Special education leadership: Integrating professional and personal codes of ethics to serve the best interest of the child. *Journal of School Leadership, 21*(3), 324–359.

Bottery, M. (2001). *Education: Policy and ethics*. New York: Continuum.

Butterfield, K. D., Trevin, L. K., & Weaver, G. R. (2000). Moral awareness in business organizations: Influences of issue-related and social context factors. *Human Relations, 53*(7), 981–1018.

Cerar, M. (2009). Relationship between law and politics. *Annual Survey of International & Comparative Law, 15*(1), 19–40.

Chugh, D., Bazerman, M. H., & Banaji, M. B. (2005). Bounded ethicality as a psychological barrier to recognizing conflicts of interest. In D. A. Moore, D. M. Cain, G. Lowewenstein, & M. H. Bazerman (Eds.), *Conflicts of interest: Challenges and solutions in business, law, medicine, and public policy* (pp. 74–95). New York: Cambridge University Press.

Clark, J. P. (2011). *A legislative and judicial analysis of sexual relationships between American secondary students and their teachers*. Unpublished dissertation, Kent State University.
DalPont, G. E. (2006). *Lawyers' professional responsibility in Australia and New Zealand* (3rd ed.). Pyrmont: Lawbook Co.
De Cremer, D. (2009). *Psychological perspectives on ethical behavior and decision making*. Charlotte: Information Age Press.
DeVito, D. (2007). The gap between the real and the ideal: The right to education amid fiscal equity legislation in a democratic culture. *Ethics and Education, 2*(2), 173–180.
Dolovich, S. (2002). Ethical lawyering and the possibility of integrity. *Fordham Law Review, 70*(5), 1629–1687.
Drumwright, M., Prentice, R., & Biasucci, C. (2015). Behavioral ethics and teaching ethical decision making. *Decision Sciences Journal of Innovative Education, 13*(3), 431–458.
Dzienkowski, J. (2016). *Professional responsibility, standards, rules and statutes, abridged (selected statutes)*. Kansas: West Academic Publishing.
Epley, N., & Dunning, D. (2000). Feeling "holier than thou": Are self-serving assessments produced by errors in self- or social prediction. *Journal of Personality and Social Psychology, 79*(6), 861–875.
Gino, F. (2013). *Sidetracked*. Boston: Harvard Business Review Press.
Gino, F., & Bazerman, M. H. (2009). When misconduct goes unnoticed: The acceptability of gradual erosion in others' unethical behavior. *Journal of Experimental Social Psychology, 45*, 708–719.
Gino, F., & Margolis, J. D. (2011). Bringing ethics into focus: How regulator focus and risk preferences influence (un)ethical behavior. *Organizational Behavior and Human Decision Processes, 115*(2011), 145–156.
Gino, F., Shu, L. L., & Bazerman, M. H. (2010). Nameless + harmless = blameless: When seemingly irrelevant factors influence judgment of (un)ethical behavior. *Organizational Behavior and Human Decision Processes, 111*(2), 102–115.
Green, J. (2013). *Moral tribes: Emotion, reason, and the gap between us and them*. New York: Penguin Press.
Gutmann, A., & Thompson, D. (2006). *Ethics and politics: Cases and comments* (4th ed.). Chicago: Nelson-Hall.
Hayibor, S., & Wasieleski, D. M. (2009). Effects of the use of the availability heuristic on ethical decision-making in organizations. *Journal of Business Ethics, 84*, 151–165.
Heffernan, M. (2011). *Willful blindness*. New York: Walker & Co.
Individuals with Disabilities Improvement Education ACT (IDEA). (2004). Available from http://idea.ed.gov
Johnson, M. (2014). *Morality for humans*. Chicago: University of Chicago Press.
Jones, H. W. (1978). Lawyers and justice: The uneasy ethics of partisanship. *Villanova Law Review, 23*(5–6), 957–976.

Jones, T. M. (1991). Ethical decision making by individuals in organizations: An issue contingent model. *Academy of Management Review, 16*, 366–395.
Kern, M. C., & Chugh, D. (2009). Bounded ethicality: The perils of loss framing. *Psychological Science, 20*(3), 378–384.
Kleinman, C. S. (2006). Ethical drift: When good people do bad things. *JONA's Healthcare Law, Ethics, and Regulation, 8*(3), 72–76.
Levin, C. S. (2016). *Legal analysis: How far can schools go in limited student speech online?* Retrieved from http://www.splc.org/article/2016/06/legal-analysis-student-speech
Lincoln, S. H., & Homes, E. K. (2007, October). *A need to know: An ethical decisions-making model for research administrators*. Paper presented at the annual society of research administrators international meeting, Nashville.
Luban, D., Strudler, A., & Wasserman, D. (1992). Moral responsibility in the age of bureaucracy. *Michigan Law Review, 90*, 2348–2392.
MacIntyre, A. (2007). *After virtue: A study in moral theory* (3rd ed.). Notre Dame: University of Notre Dame Press.
Mendus, S. (2009). *Politics and morality*. Cambridge: Polity.
Messick, D. M., & Bazerman, M. H. (1996). Ethics for the 21st century: A decision making approach. *Sloan Management Review, 37*, 9–22.
Messick, D. M., & Tenbrunsel, A. E. (Eds.). (1996). *Codes of conduct*. New York: Russell Sage Foundation.
Moore, C. (2009). Psychological perspectives on corruption. In D. De Cremer (Ed.), *Psychological perspectives on ethical behavior and decision making* (pp. 35–71). Charlotte: Information Age Publishing.
Moore, C., & Gino, F. (2013). Ethically adrift: How others pull our moral compass from true North, and how we can fix it. *Research in Organizational Behavior, 33*, 53–77.
Moore, D., Tanlu, L., & Bazerman, M. H. (2010). Conflict of interest and the intrusion of bias. *Judgment and Decision making, 5*(1), 37–53.
Murphy, L., & Nagel, T. (2002). *The myth of ownership: Taxes and justice*. New York: Oxford University Press.
Nagorcka, F., Stanton, M., & Wilson, M. (2005). Stranded between partisanship and the truth? A comparative analysis of legal ethics in the adversarial and inquisitorial systems of justice. *Melbourne University Law Review, 29*(2), 448–477.
National Institute of Health (NIH). (1998). *NIH policy for data and safety monitoring*. Retrieved from https://grants.nih.gov/grants/guide/notice-files/not98-084.html
O'Connor, K. M., deDreu, C. K. W., Schroth, H., Barry, B., Lituchy, T., & Bazerman, M. H. (2002). What we want to do versus what we think we should do. *Journal of Behavioral Decision Making, 15*, 403–418.
Office for Human Research Protection (OHRP). (2010). *IRB continuing review of research*. Retrieved from https://www.hhs.gov/ohrp/regulations-and-policy/guidance/guidance-on-continuing-review-2010/index.html

Papandrea, M.-R. (2012). Social media, public school teachers, and the first amendment. *North Carolina Law Review, 90*, 1597–1642.

Parker, C. (2010). Forum: Philosophical legal ethics, morals and jurisprudence. *Legal Ethics, 13*(2), 165–208.

Pearce, G. R. (1998). Teaching legal ethics seriously: Legal ethics as the most important subject in law school. *Loyola University Chicago Law Journal, 29*(4), 719–739.

Perlman, A. M. (2015). A behavioral theory of ethics. *Indiana Law Journal, 9*, 1639–1669.

Pittarello, A., Leib, M., Gordon-Hecker, T., & Shalvi, S. (2015). Justifications shape ethical blind spots. *Psychological Science, 26*(6), 794–804.

Regan, M. C. (2003). Ethics, law firms, and legal education. *Maine Law Review, 55*(2), 363–372.

Reynolds, S. J. (2006). Moral awareness and ethical predispositions: Investigating the role of individual differences in the recognition of moral issues. *Journal of Applied Psychology, 91*(1), 233–243.

Rhode, D., & Luban, D. (2008). *Legal ethics* (5th ed.). New York: Foundation Press.

Robbennolt, J. K., & Sternlight, J. R. (2013). Behavioral legal ethics. *Arizona State Law Journal, 45*, 1107–1182.

Rotunda, R. D. (2002). *Professional responsibility* (6th ed.). St. Paul: West.

Russo, C. J. (2012). *Reutter's the law of public education* (9th ed.). St. Paul: Foundation Press.

Sezer, O., Gino, F., & Bazerman, M. H. (2015). Ethical blind spots: Explaining unintentional unethical behavior. *Current Opinion in Psychology, 6*, 77–81.

Shakeshaft, C. (2004). *Educator sexual misconduct: A synthesis of existing literature.* Washington, DC: U.S. Department of Education, Department of the Under Secretary, Policy and Program Studies Service.

Shakeshaft, C. (2013). Knowing the warning signs of educator sexual misconduct. *Phi Delta Kappan, 94*(5), 8–13.

Simpson, M. (2015). *Social networking nightmares.* Retrieved from www.nea.org/home/38324.htm

Sternberg, R. J. (2012a). Ethical drift. *Liberal Education, 98*(3), 58–60.

Sternberg, R. J. (2012b). A model of ethical reasoning. *Review of General Psychology, 16*(4), 319–326.

Tenbrunsel, A. E., & Messick, D. M. (2004). Ethical fading: The role of self-deception in unethical behavior. *Social Justice Research, 17*, 223–236.

Tenbrunsel, A. E., Diekman, K. A., Wade-Benzoni, K. A., & Bazerman, M. H. (2010). The ethical mirage: A temporal explanation as to why we are not as ethical as we think we are. *Research in Organizational Behavior, 30*, 153–173.

Thompson, D. F. (1987). *Political ethics and public office.* Cambridge, MA: Harvard University Press.

Thompson, D. F. (2013). Political ethics. In H. LaFollette (Ed.), *International encyclopedia of ethics.* Oxford: Wiley-Blackwell.

Tversky, A., & Kahneman, D. (1973). Availability: A heuristic for judging frequency and probability. *Cognitive Psychology, 5*(2), 207–232.

United States Department of Education. (2013). Closing memorandum for file 11-000491, Steven D. Anderson, special agent in charge. Office of Inspector General, Investigative Services. Washington, DC: Author.

Wagner, P. A. (2012). Legal ethics no paradigm for educational administrators. *Journal of Thought, 47*(1), 21–27.

Warren, E. (1962). *Special address to the Louis Marshall award dinner of the Jewish theological seminary, Americana hotel.* New York. November 11.

Wolff, J. (2011). *Ethics and public policy: A philosophical inquiry.* New York: Routledge.

Woods, N. L. (2013). Educational malfeasance: A new cause of action for failure in education. *Tulsa Law Review, 14*(2), 383–409.

Woolley, A. (2010a). The psychology of good character: The past, present and future of good character regulation in Canada (with Jocelyn Stacey). In K. Tranter et al. (Eds.), *Re-affirming legal ethics* (p. 165–187). New York: Routledge.

Woolley, A. (2010b). Legal ethics and regulatory legitimacy: Regulating lawyers for personal misconduct. In F. Bartlett et al. (Eds.), *Alternative perspectives on legal ethics: Reimagining the profession* (pp. 241–268). New York: Routledge.

Woolley, A., & Wendel, W. B. (2010). Legal ethics and moral character. *Georgetown Journal of Legal Ethics, 23*(4), 1065–1100.

Zarra, E. J., III. (2013). *Teacher-student relationships: Crossing into the emotional, physical, and sexual realms.* Lanham: Rowman & Littlefield Publishers.

Zarra, E. J., III. (2016). Addressing appropriate and inappropriate teacher-student relationships: A secondary education professional development model. *CLEARvoz Journal, 3*(2), 15–29.

7

Education Administrators in Wonderland: Figuring Out Policy-Making and Regulatory Compliance When Making Decisions

Fernando F. Padró and Jonathan H. Green

7.1 Introduction

Associate (later Chief Justice) of the U.S. Supreme Court William Rehnquist wrote in his majority opinion in Board of Curators of the University of the University of Missouri et al. v. Horowitz (435 U.S. 78 (1978)) that a "school is an academic institution, not a courtroom or administrative hearing room." This is true for primary and secondary schools (P/SS) as it is for higher education institutions (HEIs). However, for school and university administrators, many times it feels as if it is the reverse: that court and regulatory compliance considerations need to be much in the forefront of day-to-day administration and decision-making. Complicating matters is the myriad intersecting regulations that directly impact school decisions and actions.

While for many administrators thinking of court cases and potential adjudication pertaining acts and decisions within the institution is in practicality a forward-looking event, it is the application of regulatory compliance and oversight that is of immediate concern.

Looking at the effects of litigation only represents one segment of school law and, even then – compounding matters – administrators tend to have limited information how these cases apply to specific aspects of their responsibilities (Zierkel 2006). The experiences of the authors suggest this has

F. F. Padró (✉) • J. H. Green
University of Southern Queensland, Toowoomba, QLD, Australia
e-mail: Fernando.Padro@usq.edu.au; Jonathan.Green@usq.edu.au

K. Trimmer et al. (eds.), *The Palgrave Handbook of Education Law for Schools*,
https://doi.org/10.1007/978-3-319-77751-1_7

become even more so, as rulemaking within regulatory compliance has been having the effect of making a different, decentred form of public law (Black 2001 as cited in Porter and Ronit 2006).

For school or university administrators, a decentred legal environment generates many challenges in decision-making. Unfortunately, the impact of decentralisation of public law is not often brought to the fore in the literature, especially from the lens of where law and policy meet. Often, the focus of attention is on the court cases and secondarily on decisions from government regulatory bodies or equivalent self-regulating organisations (or both). And when focusing on court cases, the major areas of interest are:

- how to navigate the areas of due process relating to fundamental student rights;
- pursuance of good faith in decision-making;
- torts pertaining students and staff;
- contracts and employment law;
- criminal acts – committed by students and employees;
- risk management relating to safety concerns resulting from external actors; and
- property law.

Just looking at court cases specific to educational institutions is not sufficient. There are many instances where findings in cases outside education may apply, requiring education administrators to contextualise the potential impact (as exemplified in the impact of the USA's Palsgraf case).

There are overlaps between all of the areas of law listed above, but the locus of the basis of law does differ, which does have bearing on administrator considerations (cf. Rogers 2010). For example, one differentiation between torts – the law of civil wrongdoing – and contracts is in regards to liability. In torts, duties are fixed by law, while under contract law, they arguably sit within the contract itself, although statutes can define specific contractual obligations (Rogers 2010). Overlap with criminal law happens when the breach of duty (through an act or its omission) can give rise to both tort and criminal actions. Different priorities are involved; however, thus while both can be seen as protecting society and deterring wrongful behaviour, punishment is secondary to compensation in tort (Harpwood 2009).

One area that is not often directly considered is the field of administrative law. Administrative law provides the basis for procedural and substantive law, emphasising the former. Although the emphasis is on executive administration, in some jurisdictions administrative law leans more toward judicial review of decisions rather than the processes of agency-based law.

Also not often directly linked by school and university administrators are politics and legislative actions, policy formation and enactment. The decoupling makes it more difficult to see developing trends or understand some of the rationale behind compliance. Simply put, the deeper implications of how philosophies became normative references through this process and are then enacted in regulatory practice are not fully conceptualised to generate an understanding of why certain things must be done in certain ways. The complexity of the interrelationships and process in administering government requires an understanding of the procedural aspects of law which, according to Epstein (2016):

> *... determines how "organic" statutes (which set out the relevant substantive statutory scheme) actually distribute power to public officials and impose obligations on the ground. But the very complexity of the substantive commands of most modern regulatory schemes requires the creation of an intermediate system to complete the governance cycle from government command to private compliance. That intermediate function necessarily falls to government officials, who sometimes respond in formal ways and other times in informal ones.* (p. 48)

It is difficult to argue against the view that the regulatory state has become the dominant form of governance in the developed and developing worlds. The agenda regulatory governance represents "requires substantial learning on the part of the public sector and key stakeholders who interact in a new dynamic of public-private problem-solving and accountability" (Jacobs 2007, p. 18). The key issues are that (1) regulatory schemes are not unbiased and may be dependent on political interplay within government structures (cf. de Figueiredo and Vanden Bergh 2004) and (2) the location of ultimate authority may rest elsewhere outside the agency or agencies one thinks are at play.

As a consequence of the complex interrelationships of the overlapping areas of the law that have been outlined, school and university administrators find themselves in a Wonderland situation, trying to figure out what is what, if what you see is what you get, how to navigate through the myriad regulatory entanglements (sometimes conflicting) to effectively perform duties and responsibilities without getting in trouble. At times, the effect of wanting to do the right thing and then navigate through the legal quagmire of regulations and legal rules leads to the quandary evoked by Lewis Carroll:

> If I had a world of my own, everything would be nonsense. Nothing would be what it is, because everything would be what it isn't. And contrary wise, what is, it wouldn't be. And what it wouldn't be, it would. You see?

Thus, for example, what is an educational institution to do when it comes to an academic decision being challenged through the now expected conduits of a complaints process? From the end of the 1990s onward, educational policy schemes directly or indirectly (often through other regulatory nets overseen by other agencies)have demanded or at least expected an intra-institutional complaints process for students and/or parents to pursue, as suggested in total quality management (TQM)/quality management system (QMS—hereafter TQM) literature and processes.

The basis for TQM is customer focus and satisfaction, often treated as indicators for quality performance, and it can be seen as a calming mechanism in uncertain and unsettled environments as it emphasises the notion of a symmetrical value exchange based on how students and their parents validate school actions (cf. Grant and Schlesinger 1995). Focusing on students is not an issue: making sure that they are given their due academically and procedurally from an operational perspective is a recognised long-standing interest and raison d'etre for administrators and teachers alike. However, what is meant by customer focus in educational settings, especially as it is defined and used in regulatory language? Mark (2013) suggests that theoretical developments around the concept of the customer render appropriateness of the customer focus moot, but the practical point still remains about the legal boundaries framing rights and expectations in the exercise of the student's and school's interests.

The legal boundaries suggested by TQM in turn have practical implications when internal due process is completed and dissatisfaction remains, with the student (and/or parents) moving their complaint not to court but to a regulatory agency, either (1) in preparation of going to court (e.g., access to information through a petition for information under various guises), (2) an attempt at getting the school to reverse the decision or (3) getting the agency to intervene as a resolver (and hence creating an extra-institutional appeals process). In other words, likening TQM to legal frameworks rather than standards emanating from self-regulating professional organisations, which is more the norm (i.e., ISO standards such as the 9000 series), is not something typically found in the legal or quality literature strands. However, making such a comparison provides a basis to analyse and understand the shaping of policy, particularly in regards to collective consumption (typical public welfare services such as education, healthcare, welfare, transportation, etc.) and the political processes and policy changes impacting how the services are provided and consumed (Dunleavy 1980).

This chapter suggests a framework or roadmap that administrators can use to identify key elements in both policy-making and administrative law based regulatory compliance. This approach helps administrators better understand how regulatory activity is taking on the imprimatur of law alongside legislation (statutes) and court cases. It aspires to provide an anticipatory capacity for those difficult decisions that have to be made and try to find a way out of the rabbit hole. What will be seen is that the processes and components can be represented by an hourglass configuration. The hourglass is made up of two conjoined funnels: one funnel leads in to policy formation and legislation, and a second funnel leads out (really overlapping policy jurisdictional funnels) through the rulemaking process and its various components. Navigating the process can be a vexing exercise.

7.2 Policy-Making Funnel: From Value to Law

Policy formation begins with ideas that become norms within the community. They then, through the negotiated environment of the political process become laws. Norms shape purpose and purpose relates to policy type (cf. Lowi 1972). Public policy can be described as the state in action, with different types of policy, each its own regime, each generating its own political interactions (Lowi 1985). Lowi's perspective is that policy causes politics, rather than the other way around:

> In operational terms, the causal arrows run from a policy proposal to its implementation, and back again through a group reaction to policy and administrative adaptation. The policy becomes the boundary conditions within which political action takes place. (p. 68)

For those wanting to navigate this labyrinth and understand the impact of policy-steering – the ability to influence policy formation to achieve a desired approach and outcome(s) – Carter et al. (2015) suggest adapting and using the Mazmanian and Sabatier (1983 as cited in Sabatier 1986) "generally necessary conditions for the effective implementation of legal objectives" (p. 23):

- clarity, consistency, and closeness of outputs and outcomes;
- adequate causal theory ("the sequence of activities formulated in the policy that, presumably, lead to achievement of the outputs" – Carter et al. 2015, p. 161);
- consistency of the government agency mission with policy objectives and outcomes;
- adequate allocation of financial resources;
- hierarchical integration within and among implementing organizations ("the extent to which a government agency controls the decisions generating outputs... identifying veto points where those subject to regulations can stall policy output attainment, and distinguishing the incentives that encourage compliance" – p. 162);

- decision rules by implementing agencies (there are two forms of decision rules: [a] burden of proof rules stipulating criteria or evidence required to make a decision and [b] rules stipulating decision-making procedural criteria);
- formal access by outsiders; and
- policy adaptability ("formal procedures by which an administrative agency can adapt a policy to the local context or after learning during implementation" – p. 163).

From a more pragmatic and risk-based compliance strategic perspective that is becoming more prevalent in this era of heightened uncertainty, Black and Baldwin (2010) suggest also evaluating regulatory performance based on responsiveness to these five factors:

- behaviour, attitudes, and cultures of regulatory actors ("motivational postures, conceptions of interests, and cognitive frameworks of regulated firms (and regulators) heavily influence the regulatory relationship and the regulator's capacity to influence or regulate behaviour" – p. 186);
- institutional setting of the regulatory regime ("the position that each organization (regulator or regulatee) occupies with regard to other institutions can have a critical effect on the actual and potential operation of regulation" – p. 186);
- the different logic behind regulatory tools, strategies and their interaction (as these impact on regulatory performance);
- the regime's performance track record over time (self-assessment as an indicator of their capacity to enact the furthering of their objectives); and
- changes to each of these elements as an indicator of ability and agility to changing conditions and environments.

Hofferbert's (1974 as cited in Wilder 2016) funnel of causality model provides a starting point for looking at policy formation, as it places attention on convergence of circumstances, developmental sequence, effects, events, participants, prospects and purpose within a dynamic framework. The idea of the funnel is useful as it illustrates the narrowing of the process to achieve a particular policy. Nonetheless, this model is not complete because it does not focus on:

- who can be involved (stakeholders in contrast to political elites);
- what the prospects (outcomes and effects) are in relation to purpose of policy;

- headwinds slowing the process such as risk and uncertainty; and
- the effects of the negotiated environment driven by feedback loops that can also slow the process up.

Therefore, there is a need to take a look at antecedent concepts such as philosophies and how these influence norms or are influenced by norms.

7.2.1 The Background Considerations: Philosophies and Norms

Policy can be defined as an articulation of principles defining action taken by government and organisations. Policy represents the philosophies from deliberations, principles and values of a particular point-of-view. Philosophies often articulate norms of preferred approaches to getting things done and, often, not done. These norms are informal in nature, but often define an imperative, potentially subjecting actions and persons to regulation (Raz 1999). There is a tautological relationship between norms, philosophies and policies because norms define what ought to happen by systematically interpreting meaning derived from human acts or texts (Ávila 2007; Degani and Wiener 1991; Kelsen 1967).

Burton Clark's (1983) triangle of coordination, although focused on higher education, sets the framework of the three philosophies and related norms shaping policies and laws relating to education:

- government (traditional police power based on the public good or welfare);
- markets (neoliberalism and preference for self-regulation); and
- academic oligarchs, which translates to sector leaders (and is thus analogous to a corporatist, market sector interest-government oversight partnership of sorts).

These three philosophies translate [converge?]to maintain a strong interest in government oversight (government) or a reaction against it in the form of a sector representing the interests of specific societal arena and government seeing them as partners in policy formation (corporatist) or self-regulation without government interference (neoliberal). The philosophies, in general are responses to the prevailing norm that regulation under policy "is obviously only one of several ways governments seek to control society and individual conduct" (Lowi 1972, p. 299).

Education is one of those societal entities whose function and structure changes according to which of the three elements of the triangle prevails. As one of the leading neoliberal thinkers, Milton Friedman (1955) wrote:

A stable and democratic society is impossible without widespread acceptance of some common set of values and without a minimum degree of literacy and knowledge on the part of most citizens. Education contributes to both (p. 124).

Even for neoliberals, education is the engine of economic development as enacted by, for example, The World Bank (2011) and the OECD (2013). In sum, as Callahan (1959) put it, education is essential to the preservation of the state. With the prevalence of the neoliberal philosophy regarding governance matters, Clark (1983) noted the following tendencies of bureaucratic coordination have become more acute in this era of corporatist accountability:

- layering (the increase of governmental or quasi-governmental bureaucratic oversight);
- jurisdictional expansion (scope of responsibilities);
- rule expansion (in numbers and complexity for preforming decisions and compliance);
- ascending and deepening political priority (preference for centralisation and involvement by legislators); and
- hardening of internal interests (by those wanting to be seen as participants in decision-making).

7.2.2 High-Touch Government Oversight

An old definition of police power from Black's Law Dictionary exemplifies the high-touch government approach to educational oversight. However, it also shows its age as it does not reflect the changes resulting from agency-based "lawmaking." Police power, in this definition, refers to a legislature's capacity to "make, ordain, and establish all manner of wholesome and reasonable laws for the good and welfare" of citizens (Padró 2004, p. 1). Emphasis is placed on the government's ability to be the better guarantor of the public good (equity, fairness, social justice) through the maintenance of a social safety net or what for some is a welfare state (Padró 2004). Most of the policies under these conditions are seen as redistributive through high taxation in what, in many instances, are issues of personal integrity and responsibility. As Keynes (1936) wrote:

... in the task of adjusting ... the propensity to consume and the inducements to invest... as the only practicable means of avoiding the destruction of existing economic forms in their entirety and as the condition of the successful functioning of individual initiative. (p. 239/263)

The controversy of determining whether education is a personal or public good was noted by Machlup (1962) back in the 1950s and 1960s. A couple of issues are at play: (1) the notion of public good based on public interest as a clear, identifiable concept lacks a comprehensive normative focus; and (2) that the value of the public good is bounded by having to be demonstrated and highly linked to current normative consensus shaping public policy over individual preferences (Bozeman 2002; Noll 1985).

7.2.3 Neoliberalism

Neoliberalism, while ill-defined as a concept, describes "demands for market deregulation, as well as the public sector reforms which aim at making government agencies more similar to private companies" (Thorsen 2010, p. 189). As North (1991), noted, "an essential part of the institutional evolution entails a shackling of the arbitrary behavior of the state over economic activity" (p. 109). Or, as Karl Polanyi (2001/1944) stated, "[nothing] must be allowed to inhibit the formation of markets... no measure or policy must be countenanced that would influence the action of these markets" (p. 72). Thus, there is a concomitant preference to consider education from market-based and utilitarian viewpoints.

Neoliberalism can take on forms from the left and right ends of the political spectrum, as Thorsen (2010) points out. The ends of the neoliberal spectrum can be seen in terms of the role of government, rules and rulemaking play in the shaping of personal affairs and making of individual choices. Neoliberalism in this chapter is treated from the perspective of F.A. Hayek. Hayek represents the libertarian, self-regulation approach to government end of the spectrum. While suggesting that government possesses "enormous powers for good and evil" (1944, p. 19), he sees personal liberty encroached because "the transformation of governmental edicts from general rules enacted by the legislature to the ad hoc directives of regulatory agencies, whose decisions in any particular instance are unpredictable, enlarges and intensifies the arbitrary nature of our interactions with the state" (Hamowi 2011, p. 9). The government's capacity to coerce should be limited to "instances where it is required to prevent coercion by private persons" (Hayek 2011/1960, p. 72).

Duly, self-governance (bounded or expanded) under the neoliberal regime tends to exhibit the following tendencies:

- major cuts to the state's fiscal and administrative resources to rescale government efforts (do more with less) under the premises of competition enhancement and increased efficiencies;
- devolution of regulatory responsibilities to lower levels of government (typically to the lowest levels) without proportional transfers of power or capacity, [except when it comes to the various education sectors where the national economic interest seems to centralise regulatory oversight to assure success];
- devolution to lower government levels is at times accompanied by increased acceptance of increasingly international agencies with little or no accountability or transparency; and
- a preference for voluntary rather than binding regulatory frameworks of non-binding standards and rules, public-private cooperation, self-regulation and greater participation from citizen coalitions [once again with the exception of education of all but participation from citizen coalitions] (McCarthy and Prudham 2004).

7.2.4 Corporatism

Corporatism is a concept that lost favour after the inception of the European Union, but arguably it still is representative of social democratic systems. The reason for using this label is that it is more representative of Foucault's (2000, 2007/1978, 2008/1979) notion of governmentality more tolerant to government regulation. There is the paradoxical preference for bureaucracy in what could be termed corporatist (cooperation between the government and relevant socio-economic interest groups considered stakeholders) approach to government, even though Foucault tried to walk away from these ideas in his work (Flew 2014; Woldendorp 1997 as cited in Siaroff 1999).

Similar in the sense that neoliberalism is based on the existence of the self-interested, market-based homo economicus (cf. Hamann 2009), there is a concern of governing the self and others through the presence of an apparatus, i.e. governance (Foucault 2000). Governmentality refers to the art of governing through a network of government, political and social networks (Foucault 2007). Fundamentally, there is separation between freedom and the domain of governmentality which leads to the concern about the effects of the actions of those governing (2008/1979). For Foucault (2000) there is a paradox of accepting a role for government rather than full self-regulation: government is what has allowed for the survival of the state.

Foucault postulates that the ultimate end of government is the welfare of the population. This is achieved by either acting directly by through large-scale campaigns or indirectly by using techniques of which people may not be fully aware to achieve specific aims. As empirical evidence has demonstrated, privatisation and regulation to work alongside each other in the long term needs complementary policies that promote competition and regulatory capacity (Parker and Kirkpatrick 2005). Power (2010) suggested this creates a dual structure, existing "side-by-side engaging in a continuous dialectic" (p. 197). The result is having parallel bureaucracies.

7.2.5 Total Quality Management (TQM)

TQM principles support the corporatist and neoliberal apparatus (e.g., Padró 1988). Notions of consumer-defined inferences regarding performance and satisfaction are now at the forefront of desired outcomes: Seymour (1993), for example, saw students – along with parents and the state – purchasing a service: a student "pays money for the course, buys the books, attends classes, writes reports, studies, takes examinations, and wants a grade" (p. 42). Meanwhile, technical performance modes – difficult as they are to identify, quantify and measure – operate in a background mode (Oliver 1997).

TQM sets the behaviour expectations, while the body imparting the regulatory scheme sets sanction from non-compliance based on statutory limitations. Much of the language of current policy is couched within the frame of ensuring, assuring and improving quality. Governments support TQM as a philosophy (through general policy statements) and as an improvement tool built into regulatory rules (Farazmand 2005). Quality assurance (QA) and standards broadly or specifically are increasingly embedded within rules to regulate behaviours and practices (Padró 2015). The difficulty in translating TQM into an educational setting stems from the difficulty in measuring learning because the core processes of learning are too subtle to be measured meaningfully (Harvey 1995). Paradoxically, for those not enamoured of managerial cultures within educational systems, the rationale behind looking at how TQM has replaced both the cultural and normative references within legally supported regulatory schemes can be summed up by Elliott Eisner (1979):

> Because educational practice at the realization of certain values, the educational significance of educational inquiry must first be appraised in relation to the virtues the enterprise seeks to attain (p. ix).

7.2.6 Stakeholders and Coalition Formation

One area of interest within TQM is stakeholder involvement. Policy formation is a double contingency situation, one in which a social problem requires a selected solution in order to achieve and maintain social interaction and social order (Vanderstraeten 2002). The result is not a merger of interests as much as it is a response to observation and feedback of the resulting policy (Luhmann 1995). More important, however, is that double contingency places an emphasis on the reciprocity of contributory influences in policy development and later on with the degree to which ensuing regulatory regime(s) recognise and are able to work with the regulations and rules bounding or defining the activities and performance of those being regulated.

Identifying stakeholders depends on recognising and accepting them as context-dependent (Lorini et al. 2009). There are two schools of thought specific to stakeholder identification: the broad and narrow schools, based on direct or indirect association with the organisation in question. The narrow approach is more contractually based influence while the broader school believes that stakeholders can be any individual or group that can influence or be impacted by an institution's actions, and thus has to be taken into account (Fassin 2009).

Stakeholders can be identified demographically (identifying key stakeholder attributes) and/or structurally, based on key individuals within the organisation (Frooman and Murrell 2005). The demographic approach identifies stakeholders based on three dichotomies highlighting salience (recognition, priority) as power, legitimacy and urgency (Mitchell et al. 1997):

- claimant v. influencer;
- actual v. potential relationship; and
- power, dependence and reciprocity in relationships

Another approach looks at organisational structure as a means of identifying stakeholder relationships and their influence on decisions. This pays attention to the interactions of stakeholder cultural components impact on sector policy formation and framing (de Bakker and den Hond 2008). Phillips (2003) proposed a middle ground approach based on derivative stakeholder legitimacy; this approach rests on recognising the relationship of moral obligation and pragmatic, power-based considerations. It merits consideration because, as Fuller (1969) asserts, morals of aspiration focus on creative acts to create achievements rather than merely on aversion.

Prioritization of stakeholders seems to be dependent on context and the eye of the beholder (Parent and Deephouse 2007). Salience manifests the amount of attention and priority given to different stakeholder claims by organisational leaders (Mitchell et al. 1997). As such, it is a value statement of the prevalent organisational cultures (Jones et al. 2007). A typical approach toward prioritization is matrix-like, based on perceived levels of importance, impact, influence, interest, or power. A caveat: don't treat stakeholders simply (and ironically) as isolated economic actors but as social actors "who acquire, select, and share information in the mesh of their social networks" (Kim et al. 2010, p. 127).

Important as identifying and prioritising stakeholders are, more crucial is how they become actors, particularly through forming coalitions. Sabatier's (1988) advocacy coalition framework (ACF), which treats stakeholders broadly, identifies the potential impact of coalition strategies. When together in a coalition, the main "glue" is the held key policy beliefs that shape their norms and empirical commitments. Secondary or ancillary beliefs may demonstrate some differences, but these can be attenuated based on contextual changes as the policy process unfolds.

7.2.7 Policy Purpose

At the end of the policy funnel is the making of policy through either legislative statutory acts, changes to regulation, or a combination of both (Fig. 7.1). Education administrators should understand are the procedural and substantive knowledge found within policy to provide attention and identified solution(s) to problems (Lasswell 1971). What one looks for is which norms have been given legal status. There is an inter-relationship between these norms (with higher and lower forms) to ensure validity and appropriateness based on policy type. What began as a preference based on Clark's (1983) coordination triangle now is the legal way of doing things.

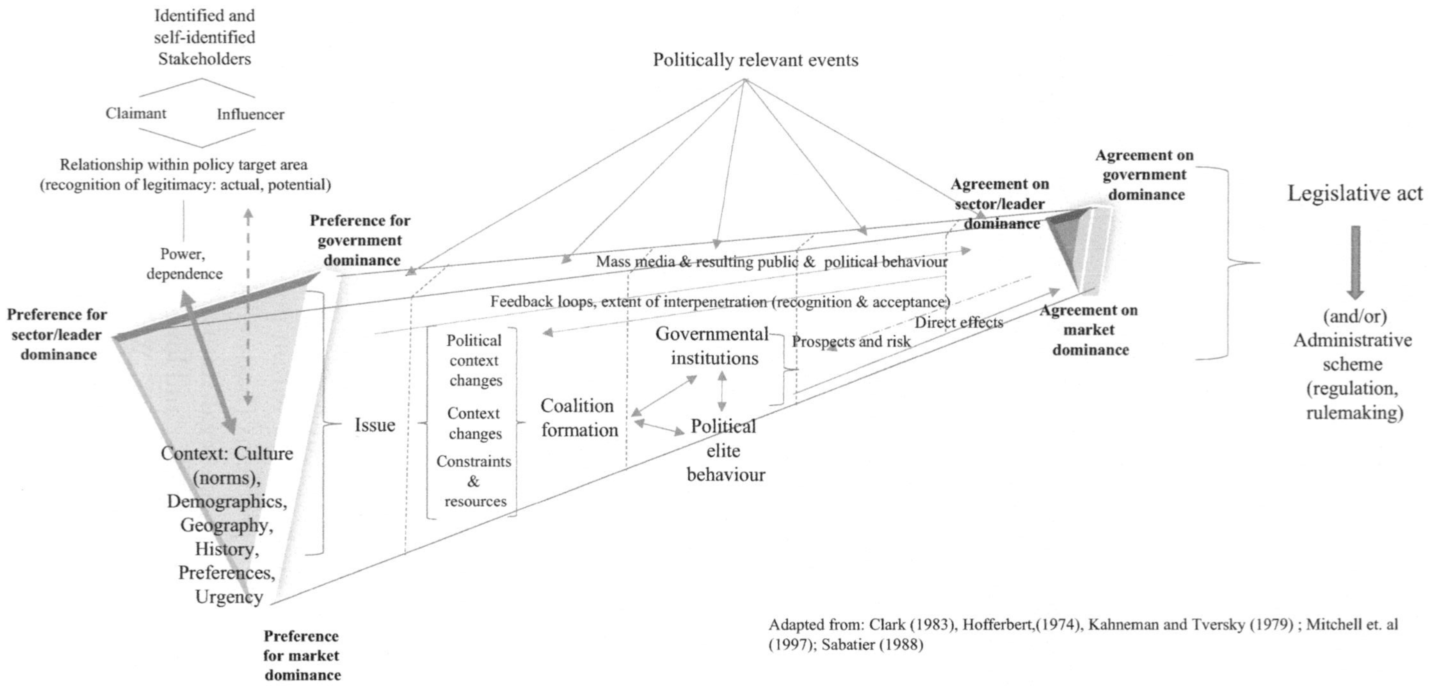

Fig. 7.1 Policy development to rulemaking model: policy development funnel (Adapted from: Clark (1983), Hofferbert (1974), Kahneman and Tversky (1979), Mitchell et al. (1997), Sabatier (1988))

7.3 The Rulemaking Funnel: From Legislation to Agency Oversight and Regulation

Once policy is formally created through legislation or administrative decision-making within a governmental agency, regulations and rules operationalise policy by identifying expectations, obligations and sanctions (repercussions) from noncompliance. In effect, this "other side of the process" generates a new funnel that can be appended alongside (but slightly off-line) Hofferbert's model, fashioning an hourglass configuration (Fig. 7.2). Within this reverse funnel is driven by policy type and on notions of rulemaking. It is like going from the Mad Hatter's tea party to the court of the Red Queen.

This outward funnel begins with the determination of which philosophy prevailed from Clark's triangle. The next step is determining which policy type (regulatory, redistributive, distributive or constituent – Lowi 1972) and then the overlapping premises of rules and rulemaking within the different administrative agencies.

7.3.1 Administrative Law

The state and its officers are limited by laws (Tamanaha 2012). As Dicey (1982/1915) said, rule of law means three things: (1) the exercise of government's power is not arbitrary, (2) everyone is subject to the law regardless of status (equality under the law) and (3) the rules based on constitutional codes "are not the source but the consequence of the rights of individuals" (p. 121). Policy formation as enacted into law has a deontic logic operational element to it that needs to be taken into account in as far as action, agency and rights are concerned (Ávila 2007). The deontic elements come from policy being the formal enactment of with normative concepts such as obligation, permission, and prohibition (Hansen et al. 2007). These norms define what ought to be, and whether ought is a command or a suggested act or omission pertaining to the behaviour of others (Kelsen 1967), having the effect of directing officials "to apply certain sanctions if certain conditions are satisfied" (Hart 1997, p. 36). There is a downside, – which adds to the difficulty in understanding policy – of fragmenting rules and obscuring what is possible within the larger framework of compliance (Hart 1997).

Once legislation is passed, one method governments use to control decisions by non-government entities is:

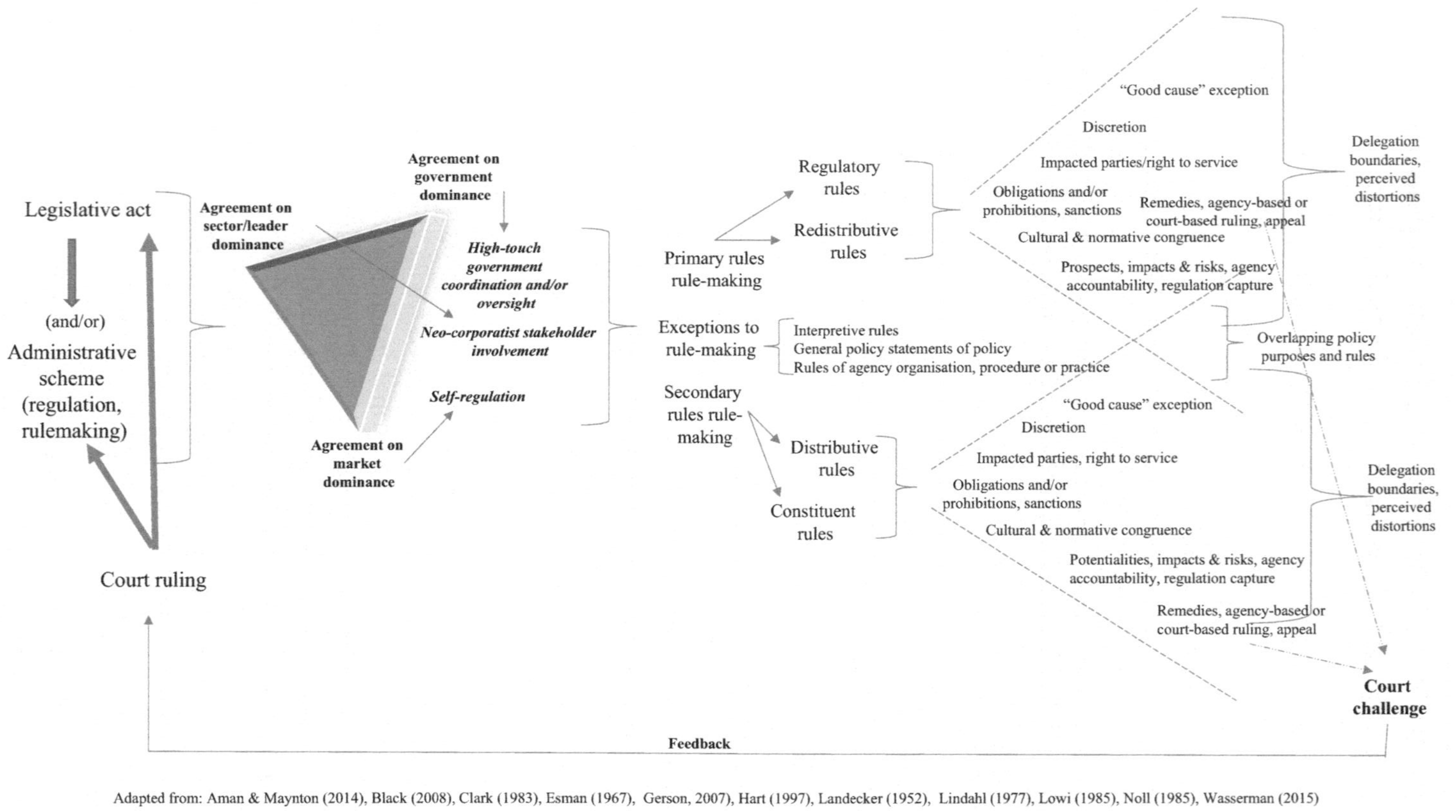

Fig. 7.2 Policy development to rulemaking model: rulemaking and regulation funnel (Adapted from: Aman and Maynton (2014), Black (2008), Clark (1983), Esman (1967), Gerson (2007), Hart (1997), Landecker (1952), Lindahl (1977), Lowi (1985), Noll (1985), Wasserman (2015))

> ... *to assign to a government agency the responsibility of writing rules...using a quasi-judicial administrative process to administer these rules [based on satisfying] elaborate procedural and evidentiary rules... The reason for this focus on regulation is more practical than theoretical... [Regulation] is a distinct kind of policy....* (Noll 1985, p. 9, 10)

Failure occurs when:

1. failing to make rules;
2. failing to publicise the rules to be followed;
3. abuse of retroactive legislation (as it undermines the integrity of the rules when they could be retroactively overturned);
4. failing to make rules understandable;
5. enacting contradictory rules;
6. rules requiring conduct beyond the capabilities of the affected party;
7. introduction of so many changes that those required to observe the rules cannot orient themselves properly; and
8. failure of congruence between the rules as announced and actual administration (Fuller 1969).

Although not limited to government agencies, regulation is defined by the OECD as "an imposition of rules by government, backed by the use of penalties that are intended specifically to modify the economic behaviour of individuals and firms in the private sector" (Khemani and Shapiro 1993, p. 73). Regulation instils a course of conduct in addressing collective problems or achieving an identified end, usually enforced through a combination of legal or non-legal rules or norms (Aman and Mayton 2014; Black 2008). Regulation, moreover, defines opportunities and pathways organisations and their networks should follow to maintain political stability and capture potential benefits (North 1991). A "good" regulatory framework "establishes an incentive structure that reduces uncertainty and promotes efficiency" (Kirkpatrick 2014, p. 161). A countervailing concern, nonetheless, and that that requires consideration, is that of what is termed regulatory capture on the part of stakeholders, which can lead to drift or reduced effectiveness from intended application, perspective, results and legitimacy (Black 2008; Noll 1985).

Administrative law provides the basis for procedural and substantive law, emphasising the former. To Head (2012), administrative law:

> ... *regulates the relationship between the executive government and those it governs... It involves understanding the way governments operate, the nature of*

> *administrative power and processes, the function of those who participate in the system, and the practices, procedures, manuals, guidelines and other internal policies or rules which may influence the way they behave.* (p. 2)

While emphasis is on executive administration, in some jurisdictions administrative law leans more toward judicial review of decisions rather than the processes of agency-based law. An understanding of the procedural aspects of law is required by the complexity of the interrelationships and process in administering government: "The very complexity of the substantive commands of most modern regulatory schemes requires the creation of an intermediate system to complete the governance cycle from government command to private compliance" (Epstein 2016, p. 48). In a number of countries, administrative law is grounded on Administrative Procedure Acts. These acts codify administrative procedures through statute, defining the formal and informal mechanisms and processes the executive branch uses to enforce the laws and support policies laws represent. Credibility and effectiveness of the regulatory framework vary with a country's political and social institutions along with its capacity to adapt to modern realities (Barnes 2010). Regulation impact analysis (RIA) is technique to evaluate effectiveness by systematically analysing costs and benefits, effectiveness in achieving policy goals and determining better alternative approaches as noted in Table 7.1 (OECD 2009).

7.3.2 Rule Making and Rules

Agencies can create law, and rules are the preferred means of agency lawmaking (Aman and Mayton 2014). Where present, APAs provide the framework for rulemaking. The stages in rulemaking are:

1. Setting the agenda and forming a proposal. Notice is required for informal, hybrid and formal (trial-type) hearing processes, with final rule emanating from this process subject to the "logical outgrowth" of the rule as proposed in the original notice (Aman and Mayton 2014; Burrows and Garvey 2011; Levinson 1977; 5 U.S.C. §553). Agencies are required to provide adequate opportunity to comment on rule content (submission of facts, arguments and offers of settlements – 5 U.S.C. §554(c)).
2. Publicise the decision, providing a general overview allowing the public to understand the gist of what the rule is about before 30 days before the rule goes into effect (unless allowable exceptions are met). For formal rules, a direct-final rulemaking order finalising "routine" or "non-controversial

Table 7.1 Research impact analysis parameters

	Appropriate to regulate	Justification of regulation	Maximising social welfare	Cost (burden) appropriateness
Information needed	What groups in society are being affected? What is the size of each group? What is the nature of the impact on each group? How large are these effects? How long will these effects persist?	Limited ability of government to make and enforce regulations effectively Size of identified problems as compared to others being considered as possibly requiring regulation Ability of affected groups to take actions themselves to address identified problems Whether problems likely to be long-lasting or may change relatively quickly due to external factors	Market failure Equity and other social goals Regulatory capture (by stakeholders) and other failures (design & implementation) Capacity to identify risk in above	Direct Indirect Competition-related costs (difficulty entering the market, preventing strong competition capacity, negative impression of regulation) Substitution effects

Source: OECD (2008)

rules"; however, one adverse comment leads to the withdrawal of the proposed rule (Burrows and Garvey 2011).

A regulatory system attempts to administer legislation in an equitable and rational manner, using rules as the instruments to set the framework of rights to service, obligations of what has to be done and/or the prescriptions of how the obligation ought to be done and the conferring of power (who is responsible for what) as countered by a right to liberty from the setting of the obligation. Rules, in sum, have the purpose of conforming to an accepted standard of conduct (Hart 1997). Legal rules are specific in contrast to broader legal principles which are reflected in the normative referencing found in the broader regulatory scheme. Rules are "justified as time-saving devises and as devices to reduce the risk of error in deciding what ought to

Table 7.2 Lowi's (1985) categorisation of public policies on Hart's primary and secondary rules

Forms of expressed intention		
	Works through individual conduct	Works through environment of conduct
Primary rule (imposing obligations or positions)	Regulatory policies Rules imposing obligations; Rules of individual conduct (criminal in form) Synonyms: Police power, government intervention Examples: Public health laws, industrial safety, traffic laws, antitrust	Redistributive policies Rules imposing classification Or status; rules categorising Activities Synonyms: Fiscal and monetary policy, overall budget policies Examples: Income tax, safety net elements (e.g., retirement, welfare support)
Secondary rule (conferring power or privileges)	Distributive policies Rules conferring facilities or Privileges unconditionally Synonyms: Patronage, subsidy, "pork barrel" Examples: Public works, land grants	Constituent policies Rules confer power; rules About rules and about authority Synonyms: Overhead, auxiliary, government organisation Examples: Agencies for budgetary and personnel policy, laws establishing judicial jurisdiction

Adapted from: Lowi (1985, p. 74)

be done" (Raz 1999, p. 59). Hart (1997) labels legal obligations or duties as primary rules, while power-conferring rules are secondary. Rules of obligation (primary) generate a command or prohibition and reference to beneficiaries.

Lowi (1985) distinguished his four policy types within Hart's primary and secondary rules categories (Table 7.2). One notable item is that these are not distinctly different categories, explaining (1) different policy interests present within the rulemaking scheme and (2) jurisdictional overlap by different agencies pertaining different organisational action. Attending to the differences between the other types and how rules create the map for obligations, prohibitions, sanctions and procedure/processes does provide a rationale for understanding and deconstructing policy jurisdictional overlaps. Knowing the differences also provides a mechanism for understanding how and why the overlapping regulatory frameworks act differently and how to reconcile these differences within institutional governance decision-making.

7.4 Conclusion

This chapter has taken a position similar to Lowi's 2002 article regarding the relationships between policy and law. Administrators in all education sectors should pay attention to remember that "[law] is formal: policy is real" (p. 500). Legislation and rulemaking also are formal processes, but are ultimately subordinate to the informal, dynamic interest-based process often driven by philosophy (vision) and/or practicality (specific outcomes). On the other hand, the meaning of rule of law is a contested area. Much of what has been discussed is a demonstration of some of the issues related to how to interpret the application of the rule of law into quotidian educational practice – curricular and operational.

Although the Australian context is taken into consideration, much of this chapter in informed by legal issues and practices from the USA and the UK. This is not surprising because (1) the field of education law is more developed in the USA and the UK and (2) these countries share similar educational issues and traditions even if context can be somewhat different legally, politically and structurally. The centre of attention has been administrative law vis a vis regulatory compliance and agency-based law (policies, regulations and rules). One area not discussed is the notion of sovereignty. This has been treated as a given based on the idea that government structures (overall form of government, legislative and executive bodies) are the repositories of sovereignty, as suggested by Foucault (2008/1979) and dealt with by Dicey (1982/1915).

The reason this is a "Wonderland" situation as the chapter's title indicates is the myriad players, philosophies, jurisdictions and possibilities in terms of obligations, prospects, results, impact of results and potential application of sanctions based on improper, incomplete, or no compliance. In the unfolding of the tale, some minor distortions to some connecting ideas within legal theory have been committed for the purpose of providing greater clarity both in establishing a "big picture" perspective and in providing for granular level analysis on legal ramifications on decisions education administrators need to make. Care needs to be given in framing the exercise properly, asking the right question and identifying key incidents and milestones. Care is also needed in remembering that the proposed model may only capture parts and not all of what happened or is happening. As Carroll said:

> 'Would you tell me, please, which way I ought to go from here?' 'That depends a good deal on where you want to get to,' said the Cat. 'I don't much care where –' said Alice. 'Then it doesn't matter which way you go,' said the Cat. '- so long as I get SOMEWHERE,' Alice added as an explanation. 'Oh, you're sure to do that,' said the Cat, 'if you only walk long enough'.

References

Aman, A. C., & Mayton. (2014). *Administrative law* (3rd ed.). St. Paul: West Academic Publishing.

Ávila, H. (2007). *Theory of legal principles*. Dordrecht: Springer.

Barnes, J. (2010). Towards a third generation of administrative procedure. In S. Rose-Ackerman & P. L. Lindseth (Eds.), *Comparative administrative law* (pp. 336–356). Cheltenham/Northampton: Edward Elgar.

Black, J. (2008). Constructing and contesting legitimacy and accountability in polycentric regulatory regimes. *Regulation & Governance, 2*, 137–164.

Black, J., & Baldwin, R. (2010). Really responsive risk based regulation. *Law and Policy, 32*, 181–213.

Bozeman, B. (2002). Public-value failure: When efficient markets may not do. *Public Administration Review, 62*(2), 145–161.

Burrows, V. K., & Garvey, T. (2011). *A brief overview of rulemaking and judicial review. CRS report for congress – Prepared for members and committees of congress*. Washington, DC: U.S. Government.

Callahan, R. E. (1959). *An introduction to education in American society*. New York: Alfred A. Knopf.

Carter, D. P., Weible, C. M., Siddiki, S. N., Brett, J., & Chonaiew, S. M. (2015). Assessing policy divergence: How to investigate the differences between a law and a corresponding regulation. *Public Administration, 93*(1), 159–176.

Clark, B. R. (1983). *The higher education system: Academic organization in cross-national perspective*. Berkeley: University of California Press.

de Bakker, F. G. A., & den Hond, F. (2008). Introducing the politics of stakeholder influence: A review essay. *Business & Society, 47*(1), 8–20.

de Figueiredo, R. J. P., Jr., & Vanden Bergh, R. G. (2004). The political economy of state-level administrative procedure acts. *The Journal of Law & Economics, 47*(2), 569–588.

Degani, A., & Wiener, E. L. (1991). *Philosophy, policies and procedures: The three P's of flight deck operations*. Paper presented at the sixth international symposium on aviation psychology, April 1992, Columbus.

Dicey, A. V. (1982/1915). *Introduction to the study of the law of the constitution* (8th ed.). Indianapolis: Liberty Press.

Dunleavy, P. (1980). *Urban politics analysis: The politics of collective consumption*. London: The Macmillan Press.

Eisner, E. W. (1979). *The educational imagination: On the design and evaluation of school programs*. New York: Macmillan Publishing Co., Inc.

Epstein, R. A. (2016). The role of guidance in modern administrative procedure: The case for *de novo* review. *Journal of Legal Analysis, 8*(1), 47–93.

Esman, M. J. (1967). *The institution building concepts: An interim appraisal*. Pittsburgh: University of Pittsburgh.

Farazmand, A. (2005). Role of government in an era of Total Quality Management (TQM) and globalization: Challenges and opportunities. *Public Organization Review: A Global Journal, 5*, 201–217.

Fassin, Y. (2009). The stakeholder model refined. *Journal of Business Ethics, 84*, 113–135.

Flew, T. (2014). Six theories of neoliberalism. *Thesis Eleven, 122*(1), 49–71.

Foucault, M. (2000). Governmentality. In J. D. Faubion (Ed.), *Michel Foucault: Power* (trans: Hurley, R. and others). (pp. 201–222). New York: The New Press.

Foucault, M. (2007/1978). *Security, territory, population: Lectures at the Collège de France, 1977–1978*. (trans: Burchell, G.). New York: Palgrave Macmillan.

Foucault, M. (2008/1979). *The birth of biopolitics: Lectures at the Collège de France 1979–1979*. In M. Sellenart (Ed.), (trans: Burchell, V.). New York: Picador.

Friedman, M. (1955). The role of government in education. In R. A. Solo (Ed.), *Economics fox, C., and the public interest* (pp. 123–144). New Brunswick: Rutgers University Press.

Frooman, J., & Murrell, A. J. (2005). Stakeholder influence strategies: The roles of structural and demographic determinants. *Business & Society, 44*(1), 3–31.

Fuller, L. L. (1969). *The morality of law* (Revised ed.). New Haven: Yale University Press.

Gersen, J. (2007). Overlapping and underlapping jurisdiction in administrative law. *Supreme Court Review, 2006*(1), 201–247.

Grant, A. W. H., & Schlesinger, L. A. (1995). Realize your customers' full profit potential. *Harvard Business Review, 73*(5), 59–72.

Hamann, T. H. (2009). Neoliberalism, governmentality, and ethics. *Foucault Studies, 6*, 37–59.

Hansen, J., Pigozzi, G., & van der Torre, L. (2007). Ten philosophical problems in deontic logic. In G. Boella, L. van der Torre, & H. Verhagen (Eds.), *Normative multi-agent systems Dagstuhl seminar proceedings* (Vol. 07122, p. 26). Waden: Schloss Dagstuhl Leibniz-Zentrum für Informatik GmbH (IBFI). Retrieved from http://icr.uni.lu/pubs/han07a.pdf

Harpwood, V. (2009). *Modern Tort law* (7th ed.). London: Routledge-Cavendish.

Hart, H. L. A. (1997). *The concept of law* (2nd ed.). Oxford: Oxford University Press.

Harvey, L. (1995). *Quality assurance systems, TQM, and the new collegialism*. Birmingham: Centre for Research into Quality, University of Central England.

Hayek, F. A. (2011/1960). The constitution of liberty. In R. Hamowy (Ed.), *The collected works of F.A. Hayek*, Volume 17: The constitution of liberty. The definitive edition. Chicago: University of Chicago Press.

Head, M. (2012). *Administrative law: Context and critique* (3rd ed.). Anndale: Federation Press.

Hofferbert, R. (1974). *The study of public policy*. Indianapolis: Bobbs-Merrill.

Jacobs, S. H. (2007). Current trends in the process and methods of regulatory impact assessment: Mainstreaming RIA into policy processes. In C. Kirkpatrick &

D. Parker (Eds.), *Regulatory impact assessment: Towards better regulation?* (pp. 17–35). Cheltenham: Edward Elgar.
Jones, T. M., Felps, W., & Bigley, G. A. (2007). Ethical theory and stakeholder-related decisions: The role of stakeholder culture. *The Academy of Management Review, 32*(1), 137–155.
Kahneman, D., & Tversky, A. (1979). Prospect theory: An analysis of decisions under risk. *Econometrica, 47*(2), 263–291.
Kelsen, H. (1967). *Pure theory of law* (Revised ed.). (trans: Knight, M.). Clark: The Lawbook Exchange, Ltd.
Keynes, J. M. (1936). *The general theory of employment, interest, and money*. London: Macmillan & Co. Retrieved from http://cas2.umkc.edu/economics/people/facultypages/kregel/courses/econ645/winter2011/generaltheory.pdf
Khemani, R. S., & Shapiro, D. M. (1993). *Glossary of industrial organisation economics and competition law*. Paris: OECD.
Kim, J.-N., Grunig, J. E., & Ni, L. (2010). Reconceptualizing the communicative action of publics: Acquisition, selection, and transmission of information in problematic situations. *International Journal of Strategic Communication, 4*(2), 126–154.
Kirkpatrick, C. (2014). Assessing the impact of regulatory reform in developing countries. *Public Administration and Development, 24*, 161–167.
Landecker, W. S. (1952). Integration and group structure: An area for research. *Social Forces, 30*, 394–400.
Lasswell, H. D. (1971). *A preview of policy sciences*. New York: Elsevier.
Levinson, L. H. (1977). Elements of the administrative process: Formal, semi-formal, and free-form models. *The American University Law Review, 26*, 872–941.
Lindahl, L. (1977). *Position and change*. Dordrecht: Reidel Publishing Company.
Lorini, E., Longin, D., Gaudou, B., & Herzig, A. (2009). The logic of acceptance: Grounding institutions on agents' attitudes. *Journal of Logic and Computation, 19*(6), 901–940.
Lowi, T. J. (1972). Four systems of policy, politics, and choice. *Public Administration Review, 32*(4), 298–310.
Lowi, T. J. (1985). The state in politics: The relationship between policy and administration. In R. G. Noll (Ed.), *Regulatory policy and the social sciences* (pp. 67–104). Berkeley: University of California Press.
Lowi, T. J. (2002). Law vs. public policy: A critical exploration. *Cornell Journal of Law and Public Policy, 12*(3), 493–501.
Luhmann, N. (1995) *Social systems*. (trans: Bednarz, J. Jr. & Baecker, D.). Stanford: Stanford University Press.
Mark, E. (2013). Student satisfaction and the customer focus in higher education. *Journal of Higher Education Policy and Management, 35*(1), 2–10.
McCarthy, J., & Prudham, S. (2004). Neoliberal nature and the nature of neoliberalism. *Geoforum, 35*, 275–283.

Machlup, F. (1962). *The production and distribution of knowledge in the United States*. Princeton: Princeton University Press.
Mitchell, R. K., Agle, B. R., & Wood, D. J. (1997). Toward a theory of stakeholder identification and salience: Defining the principle of who and what really counts. *The Academy of Management Review, 22*(4), 853–886.
Noll, R. G. (1985). Government regulatory behaviour: A multidisciplinary survey and synthesis. In R. G. Noll (Ed.), *Regulatory policy and the social sciences* (pp. 9–63). Berkeley: University of California Press.
North, D. C. (1991). Institutions. *The Journal of Economic Perspectives, 5*(1), 97–112.
OECD. (2008). *Introductory handbook for undertaking regulatory impact analysis (RIA). Version 1.0*. Paris: Author.
OECD. (2009). *Regulatory impact analysis: A tool for regulatory coherence*. Paris: Author. Retrieved from http://www.keepeek.com/Digital-Asset-Management/oecd/governance/regulatory-impact-analysis_9789264067110-en#.WSIbNH2-YSk#page4
Oliver, R. L. (1997). *Satisfaction: A behavioral perspective on the consumer*. New York: The McGraw-Hill Companies, Inc.
Organisation for Economic Cooperation and Development (OECD). (2013). *Education today 2013: The OECD perspective*. Paris: Author.
Padró, F. F. (1988). *Quality circles and their existence in present-day high schools*. Unpublished doctoral dissertation, University of Arizona, Tucson, AZ.
Padró, F. F. (2004). *Statistical handbook on the social safety net*. Westport: Greenwood Publishers.
Padró, F. F. (2015). Quality in primary and secondary education. In S. M. Dahlgaard-Park (Ed.), *The SAGE encyclopedia of quality and the service economy* (pp. 592–596). Thousand Oaks: SAGE.
Parent, M. M., & Deephouse, D. L. (2007). A case study of stakeholder identification and prioritization by managers. *Journal of Business Ethics, 75*, 1–23.
Parker, D., & Kirkpatrick, C. (2005). Privatisation in developing countries: A review of the evidence and the policy lessons. *The Journal of Development Studies, 41*(4), 513–541.
Phillips, R. (2003). Stakeholder legitimacy. *Business Ethics Quarterly, 13*(1), 25–41.
Polanyi, K. (2001/1944). *The great transformation: The political and economic origins of our times*. Boston: Beacon Press.
Porter, T., & Ronit, K. (2006). Self-regulation as policy process: The multiple and criss-crossing stages of private rule-making. *Policy Sciences, 39*, 41–72.
Power, M. (2010). *Organized uncertainty: Designing a world of risk management*. Oxford: Oxford University Press.
Raz, J. (1999). *Practical reasons and norms*. Oxford: Oxford University Press.
Rogers, W. V. H. (2010). *Winfield & Jolowicz Tort* (18th ed.). London: Sweet & Maxwell.

Sabatier, P. A. (1986). Top-down and bottom-up approaches to implementation research: A critical analysis and suggested synthesis. *Journal of Public Policy, 6*(1), 21–48.

Sabatier, P. A. (1988). An advocacy coalition framework of policy change and the role of policy-oriented learning therein. *Policy Sciences, 21*, 129–168.

Seymour, D. T. (1993). *On Q: Causing quality in higher education*. New York: Macmillan.

Siaroff, A. (1999). Corporatism in 24 industrial democracies: Meaning and measurement. *European Journal of Political Research, 36*, 175–205.

Tamanaha, B. Z. (2012, December). The history and the elements of the rule of law. *Singapore Journal of Legal Studies*, 232–247.

Thorsen, D. E. (2010). The neoliberal challenge: What is neoliberalism? *Contemporary Readings in Law and Social Justice, 2*(2), 188–214.

Vanderstraeten, D. (2002). Parsons, Luhmann and the theorem of double contingency. *Journal of Classical Sociology, 2*(1), 78–92.

Von Hayek, F. (1944). *The road to serfdom*. Abingdon: Routledge.

Wasserman, M. F. (2015). Defense asymmetries: Distortions in the evolution of regulatory law. *Texas Law Review, 93*, 625–679.

Wilder, M. (2016). Whither the funnel of causality? *Canadian Journal of Political Science, 49*(4), 721–741.

World Bank. (2011). *Learning for all: Investing in people's knowledge and skills to promote development: World Bank group education strategy 2020*. Washington, DC: The International Bank for Reconstruction and Development/The World Bank.

Zierkel, P. A. (2006). Paralyzing fear? Avoiding distorted assessments of the effect of law on education. *Journal of Law and Education, 35*(4), 461–495.

8

TQM's Impact on the Legal Apparatus: Informing and Directing Compliance Practices

Fernando F. Padró and Jonathan H. Green

8.1 Introduction

> *A "source" of law, is on the one hand, a procedure by which norms are created; on the other hand, the reason why norms are valid.* (Kelsen 1952, p. 406)

In his book *Management Fads in Higher Education: Where they come from, what they do, why they fail*, Robert Birnbaum (2000) termed TQM a managerial fad that failed. He viewed continued support reciting the few examples of success and claims of failure being the result of misapplication. He also noted the USA's public sector's continued interest in its application, although he agreed with Radin and Coffee's (1993) earlier sceptical observations that the interest has been based on:

- Government interest in responding to live with greatly diminished resources and diffusing the reality of the cutbacks;
- A desire to emulate successes in the private sector;
- Avoid criticism because other agencies are using TQM;
- Top government officials want it;
- "TQM provides a way for an agency to look as if it is taking action and dispels criticism… [by appearing that] the agency is addressing its problems" (p. 44).

F. F. Padró (✉) • J. H. Green
University of Southern Queensland, Toowoomba, Australia
e-mail: Fernando.Padro@usq.edu.au; Jonathan.Green@usq.edu.au

K. Trimmer et al. (eds.), *The Palgrave Handbook of Education Law for Schools*,
https://doi.org/10.1007/978-3-319-77751-1_8

Yet, as we near the end of the second decade of the 21st century, the education sector is still talking about TQM (or quality management systems as is becoming known in reference to the ISO 9000 series of standards). As implicit in the legal philosopher Hans Kelsen's (1952) comment above, TQM has been accepted as an 'inferior' source of legal norms in numerous countries, based on what Hart (1997) saw as 'rule of recognition'. This does not mean that TQM is seen as of lesser value, but as dependent of and supporting or undergirding the 'superior' legal norms espoused in administrative procedure acts and enacted through regulatory schemes. In other words, TQM serves what Hart (1997) saw as an internal point of view and Kelsen termed justified normativity (Raz 1974). TQM can be said to validly influence rule-making because there is a similarity between it and administrative law (Kelsen 1982).

Why has TQM made such inroads within the regulatory schemes of government and why should teachers and administrators within all levels of the education sector have to concern themselves with it? Although, commenting for the higher education sector, the sentiments of Coaldrake and Stedman (2016) in providing an answer to these questions can apply to all levels of education, "[over the last two decades] universities (and many others) have developed new industries around quality (TQM, QA, Six sigma, triple bottom line, and so on) and risk" (p. 231). Proponents of TQM argue for an even more influential role for TQM. For example, Farazmand (2005) argues that government should support TQM as a movement or philosophy and as a tool for improvement in quality governance and management. For him – and what can be noted in the literature – is that TQM provides governments a means to achieve strategic international and national goals and improve the life of citizens. Adopting TQM adds emphasis to the impact globalisation has had on nations and their management of their activities vis-à-vis enhancement.

According to Bhat's analysis (2006), countries with English, German and Scandinavian legal origins have higher instances of TQM application when compared to French and other socialist countries. The question is a simple one: "how so?" The answer and the search for it are not. Direct oversight is at times complemented with buffered direct and indirect oversight and regulation at the national and state government levels, made up of a complex of interlocking levels of regulation from more than one source impacting institutional administrative and educational activities, decisions and performance outcomes.

Becoming aware of TQM's presence in the regulatory environment helps make sense of demands and expectations from the external environment as represented by government and other key stakeholders, even if these are unwritten or embedded in a de-constituted form within the layers of primary and secondary rules educators are required to follow. TQM, rather than being treated as a fad, should be seen as a normative "source" of law as viewed by Kelsen (1952) or as a "paradigm" which filters the interpretation and acceptance of the norm (Dworkin 1986). TQM is often seen in terms of a leadership or management framework, but in actuality it is more frequently adopted for the sake of utility by politicians and regulators. The result: economic theory and managerialism have become more widespread in administrative rules while at the same time providing challenges to, among other things, earlier accepted standards of practice in administrative procedures and decision review concepts (McAuslan 1988).

For the educational leader, understanding the interplay between TQM, legislation and regulation allows for the discovery of signposts in otherwise uncertain environments (political, sectoral, socio-economic). Adding to that uncertainty is the clash between the current regulatory regime and traditional notions of institutional mission; philosophy; approach to assessment, interactions with students, learning, teaching; and operational activities. This is not to say that long-held beliefs are sacrosanct; for example, operational activities in education tend to be seen by insiders and outsiders as a world needing improvement. Indeed, the *Peter Principle: Why things always go wrong* was based on Laurence Peter's dissertation on the vagaries of education administration.

In addition to identifying signposts from the interplay of elements, coping with uncertainty is assisted by thinking of and building resilience, especially when there is an erosion of sense and an understanding of the organisation's sense of structural integrity (Berkes 2007; Weick 1993). Building this resilience means (1) learning to live with change and uncertainty, (2) nurturing diversity in its various forms, (3) combining different types of knowledge for learning and (4) creating opportunity for self-organisation (Folke et al. 2003). With this awareness, looking for and finding the TQM elements in the legal and political framework allows educational leaders to at least create a functioning détente with the regulatory scheme. It puts the clash between long-term accepted standards of practice and thinking within the education community and the political and other stakeholder groups in the perspective that this diversity has to be accounted for in the decision-making process. This does not mean overturning long-held beliefs, necessarily, but it does mean enhancing the memory and understanding of the external environment (ecological) memory. Figuring out where and how the TQM norms influence external perception as well as regulation fosters complementarity and builds process knowledge that, in aggregate, accounts for the effects of these external drivers on institutional decisions.

8.2 Defining TQM

Discussing the meaning of TQM is different from arguing over the definition of *quality* in its essential form, especially in education. In essence, *quality* from the perspective of the field of Quality goes beyond the perceptual elements that help someone judge what is good and what is bad, which is why Juran's (1989) *Fitness for Use* acts as a baseline only, as reflected in the Harvey and Green (1993) definition of quality for higher education which has become for all intents and purposes the normative reference in education. The field of Quality thus looks to how fitness for use is operationalised, based on leadership and management, process and psychology (Padró et al. 2016).

Diverging from the essence of *quality* itself TQM, which has been around since the end of World War II, is based principally on value, conformance to requirements, customer satisfaction, defect avoidance, fitness for use, and statistical process control developed during this period as identified by the top names in the field of Quality (Crosby, Deming, Feigenbaum, Ishikawa, Juran, Taguchi, etc.). The term *total quality control* (TQC) was first coined by Armand Feigenbaum in 1961, but it was changed to *total quality management* in the 1980s to reflect that quality is something to be managed rather than controlled (Sahney 2016; Walton 1986).

There are different definitions of TQM, depending on the user's perspective (Kontoghiorghes 2003). However, the definition of the American Society for Quality (ASQ – http://asq.org/learn-about-quality/total-quality-management/overview/overview.html) probably reflects the most standard view of the model:

> … a management system for a customer-focused organization that involves all employees in continual improvement. It uses strategy, data, and effective communications to integrate the quality discipline into the culture and activities of the organization.

Vlăsceanu et al. (2007) created a more detailed definition of TQM in their glossary on quality assurance and accreditation in higher education that unpacks the above:

> … [a] comprehensive approach to quality management that places emphasis on factors such as continuous improvement, customer focus, strategic management, need for explicit systems to assure quality of higher education, and a view of leadership and supervision that stresses employee empowerment and

delegation. Such an approach... emphasizes assessment that is undertaken of: (i) defined objectives or standards (set internally or by external funding bodies); (ii) measures of customer satisfaction; (iii) expert and professional judgment; and (iv) comparator organizations. (p. 76)

The focus of TQM is the organisation *as part of* and *as a* system: "Thus, the overall effectiveness of the system is higher than the sum of the individual outputs from the subsystems" (Swift et al. 1998, p. 5). TQM includes three components: a managerial philosophy; an improvement process; and a set of tools (Tague 2005), reflecting the approach from the field of Quality as presented by Padró et al. (2016). All told, TQM links the following concepts into a coherent operational framework that have to be taken into account (cf. Kanji and Asher 1993):

- All work as a process (people make quality);
- Continuous improvement;
- Delighting the customer/customer satisfaction (external and internal);
- Management by fact/measurement;
- People-based management;
- Prevention/[and more recently risk management];
- Teamwork;
- Top-down leadership.

There are two particular perspectives that educators and education administrators will pay attention to – and not necessarily to their preference: "One of the most significant features brought about by TQM models was the rediscovery of the central role of customer/stakeholder perceived results" (Conti 2007, p. 117). And, per the view of the Union of Japanese Scientists and Engineers (JUSE), TQM works best under strong top-management leadership (Godfrey 1999).

8.3 Why a Formal Approach to Quality and Its Management Fits Government Purpose

R. Freeman Butts noted as far back as 1947 that the built-in variance emanating from localised autonomy in schools in the USA – and this applies to universities as well – means a sector weakness in terms of unequal "quality and quantity" of education provided to students (p. 628). This view, more widespread internationally than not, translated early on to a loss of credibility in the sector that is still noted in political statements and news coverage. Still seeming to prevail is Berliner's (1982) observation in the USA from back in the 1980s about how the community (and government) sees schools "as places where learning takes place relatively haphazardly" (p. 7), as happens within family environments and communities in general – that with which the majority of citizens and politicians are most familiar. The criticism toward schools remains even in Finland, whose PISA success identifies the country as having one of the most successful educational systems in the planet. Komulainen et al. (2011) asserted, for example, that critics of the Finnish system complain of underachievement by boys possibly due to the "feminisation of schools" resulting from 70 percent of the teachers being female and that the curriculum is too abstract and not sufficiently real world-focused.

Education in the 21st century has maintained the early 20th century structure based on the industrial model emphasising the "Taylorian" or "Scientific" school of management. Approaches and tools from the field of Quality thus receive more than a passing interest because of the belief that these will improve performance while, at the same time increasing effectiveness in learning and efficiency of administration (cf. Padró 1988). Ironically, legislative interest and regulatory rulemaking schemes overshadow and minimise the employee-oriented focus in favour of the traditional, top-down control model that is a key component of general practice within the field of quality such as TQM because it is deemed more efficient *and* effective. The top-down mindset also reinforces the preference for regulatory compliance in education as benchmarks, guidelines and standards are used to bound institutional and sector autonomy as well as acts as a rationale for centralised, national oversight over more localised forms of oversight and accountability. This last, in particular, conflicts with the neoliberal view of decentralisation – but education seems to be working against neoliberal tenets outside the call for privatisation opportunity for schools. As Sallis (2002) argued:

> Leadership and commitment to quality must come from the top. This is the 'iron law' of quality. All models of quality emphasize that, without the drive of senior management, quality initiatives will be short lived. (p. 136)

Quality has played a role in the public sector, at least implicitly, shifting from a focus on norms and procedures, to effectiveness, to customer satisfaction (Löffler 2001). The central role of quality ties in with the view that rule-making yields higher-quality policy decisions by generating greater efficiency and fairness (cf. Pierce 1988). There is also a pragmatism accrued to having quality as a focus of regulation because it opens up additional sources of information providing additional light to key issues with a sector or agency or department jurisdiction (cf. Shapiro 2005).

The importance of TQM to the public sector emanates from a number of issues. Swiss (1992) indicated that in a modified form, TQM serves government agencies because of its emphasis on client feedback, emphasis on tracking performance, principles of continuous improvement and worker participation. Parenthetically, Houston (2007) agreed with Swiss regarding the need to adapt TQM to make it fit higher education. Rago (1994), in partially disagreeing with some of Swiss's arguments regarding TQM's fitness for purpose in government agencies, adds other points (actually, re-inserting them) seen in regulations and regulatory compliance schemes such as work processes, government culture (the function of secondary rules within administrative law structures as suggested by Hart 1997; Lowi 1985) and policy deployment through considerations of inputs and outcomes. McAdam et al. (2002) add cost reduction to the complex. While the tenets of TQM are visible, it can be argued, in the legal and regulatory context within which school leaders work, that modification has occurred in the sense that administrative law does require solutions that bring together intent and context to ensure sustained application of regulations and minimisation of appeals based on improper construction or application of rules.

Neoliberalism and its link to globalisation have driven the adoption of TQM as the basis for performance in meeting the mandates of legislated actions. In a sense, and perhaps paradoxically, neoliberalism acted as a catalyst because it requires techniques in auditing, accounting and management to distance organisations and sectors away from central control (Barry et al. 1996). Neoliberalism has also changed the social expectations regarding the purpose and role of education, as well as that of the students themselves (as posited by Sahney et al. 2004). But the reality is somewhat the opposite as "[neoliberalism], in these terms, involves less a retreat from governmental 'intervention' than a re-inscription of the techniques and forms of expertise required for the exercise of government" (p. 14). There may be a sense of ignoring or overcoming regulatory "administrative fatigue," as Stewart (2003) argued, based on the growing sense of an inverse relations between regulatory results (falling short of expectations) and the increased burden of regulatory requirement that suggests the bypassing of rulemaking. However, education seems to be immune to this "fatigue". For education administrators at any level, there is a sense of over-much governing rather than an intended opposite.

8.4 Where's TQM?

A look at the literature to investigate the nexus between TQM and the legal system will prove disappointing. Fried (1995) noted as far back as 1995 that little could be found, and this remains the case. Parenthetically, the same can be said about the psychological aspects of quality, even though motivation is an important component of W.E. Deming's *System of Profound Knowledge* (Padró 2009). What little can be found is from the early 1990s when TQM was being touted as the next big paradigm to fix education's woes, found, for example, in Harold Federow's 1993 article 'Total Quality Management and the law: A survey of legal issues relating to implementation of TQM' in the Commercial Law Journal, ergo Fried's lament. Even under TQM's updated name, *quality management systems* (QMS), there is nothing that we have found that discusses how TQM is represented within the legal structures of a country, let alone countries.

There has seemed to have been little interest in the connection between quality management and the law, and one can speculate that this is the result of its being labelled a fad, which is what a look at the literature on TQM and education can suggest. Can it also be a result of the limitations of what Hayek (1998/1973) termed *constructivistic rationalism* – "a conception which assumes that all social institutions are, and ought to be, the product of deliberate design" (p. 5) – or a simple failure of what Popper (2002/1959) called *naïve* belief of inductive logic? However, Shapiro (2005) suggested that as new reforms of the legal system are piled on previous ones, what emerges is a jumble that makes identification and application of TQM elements difficult because they may co-exist with other reforms that are contradictory and may have inconsistent results. This presents a challenge for educators in trying to navigate a cohesive roadmap towards meeting demands from a legal – and regulatory – perspective in that it helps to find the source or sources of the rationale for the schemes impacting education. It is critical not only to note explicit TQM tenets themselves: understanding the juxtapositions and overlaps that are often embedded and somewhat implicit provides a means to establish an institutional or at least personal *modus operandi*.

Tenets of TQM in the legal system can be found, therefore, but mainly in an indirect, de-constructed form as intermediate systems or approaches supporting the procedural aspects of law (Epstein 2016). Governmental agencies and departments, in what some have termed "soft law", rely on codes and guidelines and other non-legislative materials (Metcalfe 2010). While these soft law elements are in plain sight, TQM is not often immediately identifiable because of where the elements are embedded and the slightly modified language.

As a guide, the easiest way in which to find TQM in a more complete form is in national quality award (NQA) schemes. In addition, elements of TQM are found in accreditation schemes at the national level (e.g., USA) and in program level accreditation or similar activity by professional and voluntary sector associations; however, one can argue that a number of these schemes have other legal requirements as well as previous, historically accepted tenets that are placed alongside TQM, either modifying TQM (or the reverse) or adding additional layers to the process. More difficult to discern are the regulatory rules because these are at times applied to the regulator (secondary rules) as well as to the intended regulated sector (primary rules). The presence of TQM in this structure should be seen in terms of Stewart's (2003) observation that:

> In liberal democratic societies, administrative regulation is itself regulated by administrative law. This law defines the structural position of administrative agencies within the governmental system, specifies the decisional procedures those agencies must follow, and determines the availability and scope of review of their actions by the independent judiciary. It furnishes common principles and procedures that cut horizontally across the many different substantive fields of administration and regulation. (p. 438)

Some critical legislation itself reflects the paradigm, if not the actual terminology, of TQM. But for these last two sources, the issue becomes one of jurisdiction, i.e., the type of law and regulator directly or indirectly impacting institutional behaviour. It is one thing to think in terms of educational agencies, but it is another consideration when dealing with employment law issues, environmental law questions, procurement contracts, for example, as these fall outside what is considered direct oversight and add to the notion of regulatory burden that education and other sectors often complain about.

8.4.1 National Quality Awards

The aim of National Quality Awards (NQAs) is to promote awareness and share information about successful strategies, and the literature has some calls for using these awards to document performance (Chen et al. 2017). TQM's approach toward systems thinking, fitness for purpose, focus on the "voice of the customer", management-by-fact (measurement), continuous improvement, leadership and planning are what are being touted by these national frameworks as not just good practice but best practice. Relatively few countries have these (e.g., China, Japan, Korea, Poland, Russia, Sweden, Taiwan, U.K., USA) and most of these do not target education directly; however, where in place, the idea behind them is to promote business excellence practices more broadly, which, as Chen et al. (2017) argued, should also be applied toward educational institutions.

When looking at the NQAs, educators should be examining the language that is used. Rather than focusing on the "business language" as a means of discounting the implications, consider the concepts that are being put forward. These act as a lodestone to providing an understanding of the legal and supporting regulatory structures and to determining a course of action.

An example of an NQA that has been targeted to education (primary/secondary as well as tertiary and higher education) is the USA's Malcolm Baldrige National Quality Award Education Criteria. The Award, legislatively created in 1987, has had as its purpose the promotion of quality so as to improve the American economy. Although, arguably, a one-size-fits-all mentality prevails, the Baldrige criteria decided to branch out to education and health care in 1999 to promote the use of quality, i.e., TQM approaches, in these two sectors. Originally a publicly supported program, it is now a joint private-public venture (due to budget cuts eliminating federal government funding for the Program in 2014) whose recipients are recognised in an award ceremony typically attended by the President of the United States who gives the Award to the winners.

Table 8.1 identifies the 2015–2016 version of the Educational Criteria's set of seven criteria reflective of TQM (Baldrige Performance Excellence Program [BPEP] 2015a). It is worth noting that Badri et al. (2006) found that all of the hypothesised causal relationships on which the Baldrige criteria are based showed statistical significance. While these results would be expected from USA institution, the study was based on colleges and universities in the United Arab Emirates.

Consider, for example, the values that emerge in the 2018 version of the Deming Prize guide. It indicates that evaluation is based on the following 5 items.

(i) Formulation of proactive customer-driven business objectives and strategies.
(ii) Role of top management and its exhibition.

Table 8.1 Categories and items making up the Baldrige excellence framework in the Malcolm Baldrige national quality award criteria for education

Categories	Items
P. Organisational profile	P.1 Organisational description P.2 Organisational situation
1. Leadership	1.1 Senior leadership 1.2 Governance and societal responsibilities
2. Strategy	2.1 Strategy development 2.2 Strategy implementation
3. Customers	3.1 Voice of the customer 3.2 Customer engagement
4. Measurement, analysis, and knowledge management	4.1 Measurement, analysis, and improvement of organisational performance 4.2 Knowledge management, information, and information technology
5. Workforce	5.1 Workforce environment 5.2 Workforce engagement
6. Operations	6.1 Work processes 6.2 Operational effectiveness
7. Results	7.1 Student learning and process Results[a] 7.2 Customer-focused results 7.3 Workforce-focused results 7.4 Leadership and governance results 7.5 Budgetary, financial, and market Results[a]

[a]Only items within the Education Criteria that differ from the Criteria applied to manufacturing, service, small business, non-profit or government (cf. BPEP 2015b)

Source: BPEP 2015a, p. 3; BPEP 2015b, p. 3. Japan's Deming Prize is an example of how an NQA is linked with policy steering, either directly through regulatory compliance or indirectly with legislation. After World War II, the passing of the *Foreign Exchange and Foreign Trade Law* of 1949 connected capital flows with industrial policy, with quality control becoming a key element in the rebuilding and expansion of the business sector (Tabb 1995). Consequently, in 1951, the Japanese Union of Scientists and Engineers (JUSE) established the prize to recognise organisational success in the implementation of TQM. Named after W.E. Deming, it is a recognition of his contributions to Japan in understanding the value of statistical quality control, which in turn acted as one of the catalysts for the nation's post-war economic revival. This NQA serves as a more typical example of *intended* application, i.e., in this case, application to education is not a consideration. However, what it emphasises does demonstrate values that governments associate with excellence and value and as such, is worth consideration

(iii) Suitable utilisation and implementation of TQM for the realisation of business objectives and strategies.
(iv) Effects obtained regarding business objectives and strategies through utilisation and implementation of TQM.
(v) Outstanding TQM activities and acquisition of organisational capabilities. (p. 34)

Table 8.2 Evaluation items and points used in Japan's 2018 Deming prize application guide

Evaluation items	Evaluation points
A. Establishment of business objectives and strategies and top management's leadership	I. Establishment of proactive customer-oriented business objectives and strategies II. Role of top management and its fulfilment
B. Suitable utilisation and implementation of TQM	III. Suitable utilisation and implementation of TQM for the realisation of business objectives and strategies 1. Organisational deployment of business objectives and strategies 2. Creation of new values based on understanding of customer and social needs and innovation of technology and business model 3. Management and improvement of quality of products and services and/or work process 4. Establishment and operation of cross-functional management systems such as quality, quantity, delivery, cost, safety, environment, etc. across the supply chain 5. Collection and analysis of information and accumulation and utilisation of knowledge 6. Development and active utilisation of human resource and organisational capability 7. Initiatives for social responsibility of the organization
C. Effects of TQM	IV. Effects obtained regarding business objectives and strategies through utilisation and implementation of TQM V. Outstanding TQM activities and acquisition of organisational capabilities

Source: JUSE (2018, pp. 35–36)

Tellingly, Table 8.2 identifies the items and key points that are used to evaluate whether or not an organisation is worthy of consideration for the Prize, and thus reveals some key values.

Of course, there are some concerns about the appropriateness of the criteria in an educational context. Asif et al. (2013) recently agreed with earlier concerns of Badri et al. (2006) and Winn and Cameron (1998) about the need to modify the criteria themselves because while there is demonstrable validity on the whole, the validity of the criteria to each other is another concern. Indirectly, this suggests that there is a gap in the research relating to the appropriateness of TQM as embodied in the criteria to an educational context. For the cynic from within the education sectors, this gap between TQM and institutional context and practice augurs and supports the view of their lack of fitness for purpose; however, as these values are embedded within the oversight and regulatory structures controlling the education sectors, educational leaders cannot ignore their presence and understanding of implications to maintain viability and acceptance.

To find proponents of these awards, look at other claims in the literature indicating that TQM models, especially for higher education, are consistent with models frequently used in the business, manufacturing or service sectors (Chen et al. 2017).

8.4.2 Professional Associations and Accrediting Bodies

In addition to NQAs there are national and international organisations that generate benchmarks, criteria, guidelines or standards applicable to education that provide another avenue of "soft law". Organisations such as the International Organization for Standardization (ISO) bring "together experts to share knowledge and develop voluntary, consensus-based, market relevant International Standards that support innovation and provide solutions to global challenges" (https://www.iso.org/about-us.html). The ISO 9000 set of standards, due to their scope, has an effect similar to NQAs (Chen et al. 2017) and "[a]pplying ISO 9000 in universities is deemed useful because of its similarities to TQM" (p. 132). In some countries, Ministries of Education provide strong support to implementing the 9000 series at this level (e.g., Cheng et al. 2004). However, interest in ISO 9000 for primary and secondary schools is noted throughout the literature, although the results are not positive, with one study indicating there is no relationship between ISO 9000 application and student learning outcomes as measured by state-mandated tests (Bae 2007; Thornhauser and Passmore 2006).

ISO is comprised of national standards bodies from over 160 countries. Of their many standards, the one that has the broadest implications and application to all education sectors is ISO 9000 (quality management standards fundamentals and vocabulary – TQM) and its supporting standards, ISO 9001 (quality management systems requirements) and ISO 9004 (managing for the sustained success of an organisation). ISO 9000 and 9001 went through a major rewrite in 2015 and efforts are still underway to update supporting documentation and adaptation processes. This last has interest for education as the ISO 9001:2000 version had international workshop agreements (IWA) spelling out how to apply ISO 9001 to educational institutions without adding, changing or modifying ISO 9001:2000 requirements (Caraman et al. 2008; ISO 2007).[1] Creating the IWA was needed because of difficulties encountered in applying and interpreting the standard in educational settings (El Abbaddi et al. 2013). The current ISO 9000:2015 and ISO 9001:2015 are based on seven quality principles identified in Table 8.3.

There are other international organisations such as the International Monetary Fund, Organisation for Economic Cooperation and Development (OECD), The World Bank, UNDP and UNESCO, for example, that provide policies, effective practice and quality assurance recommendations and monitoring and reporting that also inform national approaches related to education. Overall, their belief is that there is a need for a common framework, data collection/analysis and language that can be applied to national systems through practice and regulation as well as legislation when appropriate. There are different documents, the majority related to higher education that focus on standards that should be followed to ensure that national economic and social goals are achievable and achieved. From a practical perspective what these organisations suggest is an amalgam where the concepts of "quality assessment", "quality evaluation" and "quality assurance" are used within the wider processes of managing quality (Vlăsceanu et al. 2007).

A good example of their influence is the OECD's Programme for International Student Assessment (PISA) for secondary school students aged 15 years initiated in 1997 performed in different countries every three years to assess performance on the core school subjects of reading, mathematics and science. Again, while indirect, the language reflects a TQM perspective and tool utilisation that is being applied to the educational setting through policy formation and steering as can be seen in the quote below.

> Policy makers around the world use PISA findings to gauge the knowledge and skills of students in their own country/economy in comparison with those in other participating countries/economies, establish benchmarks for improvements in the education provided and/or in learning outcomes, and understand the relative strengths and weaknesses of their own education systems. (OECD 2017, p. 12)

Accreditation is a process through which status, legitimacy or appropriateness of an institution, program, course or modules of study are adjudged (Harvey 2004). Agencies or private or quasi-private organisations exist or expand their professional jurisdiction to provide these binary (or at times

---

[1] One of the authors has been aware of the interest to update the IWA after the 2015 SIO 9000 and 9001 rewrites, but these seem to still be in process at the time of this writing.

Table 8.3 ISO 9000:2015 and ISO 9001:2015 seven quality principles

Quality Principle	Elements
1. Customer focus	Understand the needs of existing and future customers Align organisational objectives with customer needs and expectations Meet customer requirements Measure customer satisfaction Manage customer relationships Aim to exceed customer expectations
2. Leadership	Establish a vision and direction for the organization Set challenging goals Model organisational values Establish trust Equip and empower employees Recognise employee contributions
3. Engagement of people	Ensure that people's abilities are used and valued Make people accountable Enable participation in continual improvement Evaluate individual performance Enable learning and knowledge sharing Enable open discussion of problems and constraints
4. Process approach	Manage activities as processes Measure the capability of activities Identify linkages between activities Prioritize improvement opportunities Deploy resources effectively
5. Improvement	Improve organisational performance and capabilities Align improvement activities Empower people to make improvements Measure improvement consistently Celebrate improvements
6. Evidence-based decision making	Ensure the accessibility of accurate and reliable data Use appropriate methods to analyze data Make decisions based on analysis Balance data analysis with practical experience
7. Relationship management	Identify and select suppliers to manage costs, optimize resources, and create value Establish relationships considering both the short and long term Share expertise, resources, information, and plans with partners Collaborate on improvement and development activities Recognise supplier successes

Source: ISO website http://asq.org/learn-about-quality/iso-9000/overview/overview.html

trinary if one wants to consider conditional/probationary judgments as the in-between step) recognition of achievement or denial. These private or quasi-private bodies are given either formal or informal recognition by government to help assess and evaluate educational institutions at all levels, almost in a reciprocal *foedus aequum* arrangement. In the USA, accreditation at the institutional level is granted by regional voluntary accrediting organisations for schools as well as universities. Formal legal recognition, however, is performed by governmental agencies at the state level. Elsewhere, formal recognition rests with governmental agencies and accreditation by professional associations or equivalents only occurs at the program level. However, in either, for education, the set-up is a symbiotic relationship in that formal legal recognition (highly) recommends having accreditation from professional associations or accreditation bodies made up of the institutions they review (e.g., Massachusetts Department of Elementary and Secondary Education [DESE] 2016, p. 28).[2] The relationship is even stronger in professions requiring licensure and additional governmental agencies become involved. However, where there is no accrediting body involved in the review and recognition process the governmental agency is responsible for all aspects of the review, approval and recognition process.[3]

---

[2] As a sidebar example, in the State of Massachusetts the influence of TQM can be seen in teacher preparation programs recognition requirements in 603 CMR 7.00, Educator Licensure and Preparation Program Approval Regulations (http://www.doe.mass.edu/lawsregs/603cmr7.html?section=03):

> **7.03: Educator Preparation Program Approval**
>
> (2) Program Approval Standards. Each sponsoring organization seeking approval of its preparation program(s) shall provide evidence addressing the following Program Approval Standards, in accordance with the Guidelines for Program Approval.
>
> (a) Continuous Improvement: Demonstrate continuous improvement by conducting an annual evaluation to assess program compliance, effectiveness, and impact using an evidence-based system that includes the analysis of state available data.
> (b) Collaboration and Program Impact: Collaborate with school districts to ensure positive impact in meeting the needs of the districts.
> (c) Capacity: Create, deliver and sustain effective preparation programs.
> (d) Subject Matter Knowledge: …
> (e) Professional Standards for Teachers: …
> (f) Professional Standards for Administrative Leadership: …
> (g) Educator Effectiveness: Demonstrate effectiveness of program completers using aggregate evaluation ratings data of program completers, employment data on program completers employed in the Commonwealth of Massachusetts, results of survey data, and other available data.

[3] An example of this related to the accreditation (recognition) of initial teacher education programs from the State of Queensland, Australia can be seen in the legislation authorizing the creation of the Queensland College of Teachers [QCT] in the Education (Queensland College of Teachers) Act 2005. The statute only refers to accreditation in Schedule 3 (Dictionary), stating that the terms "**higher education course** means an accredited course under the *Tertiary Education Quality and Standards Agency Act 2011* (Cwlth)" (p. 237). The QCT uses the 2015 *Accreditation of initial teacher education programs in Australia Standards and Procedures* written by the Australian Institute for Teaching and School Leadership (AITSL) as a

Accreditation has traditionally concentrated on institutions meeting threshold standards, typically *de minimis* in nature, i.e., must haves. What has changed coincidental to the rise in TQM is a change from a focus on inputs (what the institution provides for programming) to outputs (student engagement and learning). In the USA, probably the most direct example of TQM application in accreditation at the institutional level – in this case higher education – is The Higher Learning Commission's Academic Quality Improvement Program (AQIP) pathway toward achieving accreditation. It "blends the philosophy and techniques of the Malcolm Baldrige National Quality Award program with traditional accreditation" (Lindborg and Spangehl 2011, p. 5/7). Currently, the AQIP pathway is guided by six principles that provide a framework for higher education institutions (HEIs) to use as examining frame of references (Table 8.4). Looking at these the similarities are not difficult to find. With a similar background and timeline (developed in the late 1990s as a means of aligning educational practices with quality models such as the Baldrige Award), the Council for the Accreditation of Educator Preparation (CAEP) serves as an example of TQM influence of program level accreditation. One of the two pathways toward accreditation of teacher education programs now-a-days embodied by CAEP also developed along the

means of detailing the accreditation process. TQM influence can be particularly noted in its first, second, and fourth principles:

1. Impact – the accreditation process relies on evidence about the program's impact. Evidence of impact is drawn from both pre-service teacher performance and graduate outcomes.
2. Evidence-based – evidence must underpin all elements of initial teacher education, from the design and delivery of programs to the teaching practices taught within programs. Evidence is the basis on which panels make accreditation recommendations.
3. Rigour – a relentless focus on rigour across all elements of the accreditation process is vital in assuring robust and nationally consistent decisions, as well as the quality of programs and their graduates.
4. Continuous improvement – accreditation contributes to the improvement of the quality of initial teacher education and consequently of teaching and learning in Australia. The ongoing cycle of review and re-accreditation will provide assurance of graduate teacher quality and building public confidence in the profession.
5. Flexibility, diversity and innovation – accreditation encourages the capacity of providers to be innovative in the delivery of programs to meet the diverse needs of students and the profession, as long as the program can demonstrate a positive impact.
6. Partnerships – national accreditation is built around partnerships involving shared responsibilities and obligations among initial teacher education providers, education settings, teachers, employers, and Authorities and a shared commitment to improve initial teacher education and work in partnership to positively affect student learning and graduate outcomes.
7. Transparency – the accreditation process requires transparency across all elements of initial teacher education, from entrant selection to program outcomes. This results in publically available data that is valid and comparable, as well as clarity for pre-service teachers about what to expect from initial teacher education and, in turn, what is expected of them throughout their course. 8. Research – accreditation generates and relies upon a strong research base that informs program design and delivery, and informs the continual improvement of teacher education programs by providers.

Table 8.4 The higher learning commission AQIP pathway framework's six categories

Category	Description
Helping students learn	[Focusing] on the design, deployment, and effectiveness of teaching-learning processes (and on the processes required to support them) that underlie the institution's credit and non-credit programs and courses
Meeting student and other key stakeholder needs	[Addressing] the key processes (separate from instructional programs and internal support services) through which the institution serves its external stakeholders in support of its mission
Valuing employees	[Exploring] the institution's commitment to the hiring, development, and evaluation of faculty, staff, and administrators
Planning and leading	[Focusing] on how the institution achieves its mission and lives its vision through direction setting, goal development, strategic actions, threat mitigation, and capitalising on opportunities
Knowledge management and resource stewardship	[Addressing] management of the fiscal, physical, technological, and information infrastructures designed to provide an environment in which learning can thrive
Quality overview	[Focusing] on the continuous quality improvement culture and infrastructure of the institution. This category gives the institution a chance to reflect on all its quality improvement initiatives, how they are integrated, and how they contribute to improvement of the institution

Source: Adapted from http://www.hlcommission.org/Accreditation/aqip-categories.html

idea of aligning educational practices with quality models. The impact is particularly noticeable in the language in Standards 3, 4 and 5 (Table 8.5).

8.4.3 Examples of Statutes and Regulations

Australia's Tertiary Education Quality and Standards Agency Act of 2011 (No. 73, 2011) [TEQSA] provides a clear example of TQM principles used as the basis for the creation of an education agency (https://www.legislation.gov.au/Details/C2017C00271). The basis for it, however, at the *prima facie* level is risk management as this is the main driving framework. But as Williams et al. (2006) noted, risk and quality frameworks help each other and, for the most part work alongside each other directly or indirectly when these are present in an organisation. Looking at the Baldrige Criteria from that time on to the present time, one notes the increasing amount of prominence of risk within this recognised TQM model. Their key term is *intelligent risk*: "Opportunities for which the potential gain outweighs the potential

Table 8.5 2013 CAEP standards

Category	Description
Content and pedagogical knowledge	The provider ensures that candidates develop a deep understanding of the critical concepts and principles of their discipline and, by completion, are able to use discipline-specific practices flexibly to advance the learning of all students toward attainment of college- and career-readiness standards
Clinical partnerships and practice	The provider ensures that effective partnerships and high-quality clinical practice are central to preparation so that candidates develop the knowledge, skills, and professional dispositions necessary to demonstrate positive impact on all P-12 students' learning and development
Candidate quality, recruitment, and selectivity	The provider demonstrates that the quality of candidates is a continuing and purposeful part of its responsibility from recruitment, at admission, through the progression of courses and clinical experiences, and to decisions that completers are prepared to teach effectively and are recommended for certification. The provider demonstrates that development of candidate quality is the goal of educator preparation in all phases of the program. This process is ultimately determined by a program's meeting of standard 4
Program impact	The provider demonstrates the impact of its completers on P-12 student learning and development, classroom instruction, and schools, and the satisfaction of its completers with the relevance and effectiveness of their preparation
Provider quality assurance and continuous improvement	The provider maintains a quality assurance system comprised of valid data from multiple measures, including evidence of candidates' and completers' positive impact on P-12 student learning and development. The provider supports continuous improvement that is sustained and evidence-based, and that evaluates the effectiveness of its completers. The provider uses the results of inquiry and data collection to establish priorities, enhance program elements and capacity, and test innovations to improve completers' impact on P-12 student learning and development

Source: Adapted from http://caepnet.org/~/media/Files/caep/standards/caep-standards-one-pager-061716.pdf?la=en

harm or loss to your organization's future success if you do not explore them" (BPEP 2015a, p. 50). Thus, it is reasonable to argue, especially because of how quality standards are used as an instrument of coordination and regulation, that TEQSA is a next level form of QA based on what Williams et al. argued were the synergies between the two (cf. Timmermans and Epstein 2010). This view is also consistent with the Bradley Review that proposed TEQSA as an entity that performs both accreditation and quality assurance for the higher education sector (Bradley et al. 2008; Dow and Braithwaite 2013).[4]

Illustrating the connections with international organisations who pursue a TQM or TQM-related agenda as previously discussed, Australia's Schools Assistance Regulations 2009 made under the *Schools Assistance Act 2008* links the National Assessment Program –Literacy and Numeracy (NAPLAN) to the OECD's PISA assessments. And related to specific TQM practices for schools through the broader and overlapping that exists due to an inability to provide a single code for administrative practice (Aman and Mayton 2014), the *Queensland Public Service Act 2008* Chapter 8, §219A requires "Departments to have complaints management system for customer complaints… [that complies] with any Australian Standard about the handling of customer complaints that is in effect from time to time" (https://www.legislation.qld.gov.au/LEGISLTN/CURRENT/P/PublicServA08.pdf). The link is made through Queensland's Department of Education and Training Policy and Procedure Registry's complaints management policy for state schools (http://ppr.det.qld.gov.au/education/management/Pages/Complaints-Management---State-Schools.aspx). The Overview section states that "Complaints are responded to as a matter of priority and are used as a mechanism for improving services to students and parents/carers."

Staying in Queensland for consistency purposes, The Minister of Education is responsible for the *Jobs Queensland Act 2015* (https://www.legislation.qld.gov.au/view/pdf/inforce/current/act-2015-023), the body created to provide the State advice on skills needs, workforce development and planning and the

[4]To illustrate these points, per Part I, Division 2, Section 3, Number 3 of the TEQSA Act:

3 Objects

The objects of this Act are:

(a) to provide for national consistency in the regulation of higher education; and
(b) to regulate higher education using:
  (i) a standards-based quality framework; and
  (ii) principles relating to regulatory necessity, risk and proportionality; and
(c) to protect and enhance:
  (iii) Australia's reputation for quality higher education and training services; and
  (iv) Australia's international competitiveness in the higher education sector; and
  (v) excellence, diversity and innovation in higher education in Australia; and
(d) to encourage and promote a higher education system that is appropriate to **meet Australia's social and economic needs for a highly educated and skilled population**; and
(e) to protect students undertaking, or proposing to undertake, higher education in Australia by requiring the provision of quality higher education; and
(f) **to ensure students undertaking, or proposing to undertake, higher education, have access to information relating to higher education in Australia** (author's bold).

apprenticeship and traineeship in Queensland (Part 1, §3). The neoliberal perspective is palpable in its linkage of education to jobs. While it directly does not relate to TQM, the customer satisfaction and stakeholder focus of TQM is implicit.

A more direct connection between school regulations and TQM can be noticed in the *Education (General Provisions) Regulation 2017* undergirding the *Education (General Provisions) Act 2006* (https://www.legislation.qld.gov.au/view/pdf/inforce/current/sl-2017-0161). Part 2, Division 1, §4 asserts that principals must manage schools to "ensure effective, efficient and appropriate management of public resources" (§4(2)(a)) and "promote continuous evaluation and improvement of the institution's operations and delivery of services" (§4(3)(d)). The language in §4(2)(a) is pretty standard and on its own not directly connected to TQM. Likewise, for some, the language of §4(3)(d) is not directly linked to TQM either. However, when looking at how the language has been interpreted and the regulatory schemes enacted, §4(3)(d) is very much predicated on TQM thinking which also then impacts how §4(2)(a) is construed in action.

8.5 Concluding Discussion

> A state regulates relations to its citizens on two dimensions. One is the "input" side which relates to the access to public authority. The other is the "output" side and refers to the way in which that authority is exercised... This makes equality and impartiality partially overlapping concepts... based on the idea that democracy in the form of political equality on the input side must be complemented with impartiality on the output side of the political system, that is, in the *exercise* of public authority. (Rothstein and Teorell 2008, pp. 169–170, italics in original)

Bou-Llusar et al. (2009) indicate that TQM is an approach and that there are different models to apply it. Talking about TQM is not the same thing as talking about quality. Garvin (1984) suggested five approaches toward defining quality that are based on (1) a transcendent approach to philosophy; (2) product-based approach of economics; (3) user-based approach from economics, marketing and operations management; (4) manufacturing-based perspective; or (5) value-based approaches of operational management. The "eye of the beholder" becomes rather important in determining which perspective is used and it is often seen in the different application, viewpoints, results and purported impact of quality approaches, framework and models as applied by organisations, sectors and governments.

Navigating and reading through legislation, regulations and rules and figuring out the rule-making process often presents *decisional* and *action convergence* a juxtaposition between neoliberal viewpoints translated into action through the application of TQM principles, the deep-seated business and professional assumptions and beliefs and the resulting apparatus of government (cf. Homburg et al. 2007). This seems to be especially true in education where the reading of some of the above comments demonstrate either a direct contradiction or an uneasy accommodation. Where this is found in the chapter is up to the reader.

There would be less of a sense of a juxtaposed environment where Rothstein and Teorell's comment of complementarity between access and exercise of authority if a more "disinterested" if a more pragmatic or utilitarian philosophy prevailed in the creation of policy. Politics plays the wild card as the disparate beliefs vie for supremacy and imposition of a particular point-of-view (a strong term, but effectively reflects the end-game preference of people wanting to meet their desires). Thus, to understand rather than judge the current educational environment in order to accomplish the tasks of disseminating and, for the universities, creating knowledge it helps to use Bohr's *Theory of Complementarity*. Rather than focusing on the contradictions and juxtapositions as clashes, look at where the similarities lay to better understand and learn from the inherent contradiction and juxtapositions (Bohr 1963).

Similarly, both policymakers and educators need to be aware of the unintended consequences that regulatory actions bring. The issue is whether or not either side is willing to make the necessary adaptations/compromises. An example of this can be found in the article written by Hurley et al. (2013) on how the requirement of state report cards mandated under the USA's *No Child Left Behind Act of 2001* (Pub.L.107-110, 30 Stat. 750) (NCLB). Effectively, the idea of teaching mathematics and science in an integrated approach (Berlin and White 2009) was impaired because the report card only calls for reporting math results (along with literacy). Another effect was the almost complete elimination of integrated math-science teacher preparation courses in Education programs (Hurley et al. 2013).

Adoption of quality principles within the different education sectors has been slow and piecemeal (Kanji et al. 1999). Yet, the core concepts have become embedded into national and international educational frameworks over time (Chen et al. 2017) as exemplified by entrenchment into professional and program accreditation guidelines and standards (e.g., Australian Institute for Teaching and School Leadership [AITSL] 2015). TQM can be seen as part of Shapiro's (2005) identification of reforms made within the legal culture based on the capacity of economic analysts and risk assessors identification of public interest requirements. An intended effect is the shaping of social and student expectations regarding what education systems should be doing for the community, its economy and the students (Komulainen et al. 2011; Sahney et al. 2004).

For most, TQM has three primary principles: continuous improvement, customer focus and employee involvement. The first principle is something educators historically and presently try to do. The second principle is problematic because it is difficult to see students as customers. Like designers and engineers who complain that customers do not always know what their product is meant to do, how to use it or the full extent of its capacity, educators are concerned that students – and at times parents, other stakeholders, government officials and politicians – do not know what they do not know when it comes to learning and teaching. The third principle is full of contradiction and irony in that it seems that educators are the ones ignored in any discussion of quality and creation of schemes to improve learning. Yet, TQM approaches and principles in a broader sense can be beneficial to education, but these have to be adapted and modified to the sector.

This chapter began with a discussion of Birnbaum's (2000) view that TQM is a managerial fad. In some instances, the argument has some validity, but it is the validity that represents a pyrrhic victory because, as we have tried to illustrate, TQM has permeated the legal (law-making) and regulatory (rule-making) environments in all areas of government, including and especially education. This is the result of what Pollitt (2004) termed the buying and borrowing of public management reforms. Public oversight and regulatory review are now informed by TQM, although previous practices prevalent in public administration, particularly in the "New Public Management" approach are still present and at times makes for an interesting pairing of bedfellows. "Consequently, when applied within the context of the public sector, TQM views the public interest as representing the aggregation of individual interests and views public servants ultimately being responsive to these customer groups" (Maram 2008, p. 200).

As warned in the beginning, there is little in the literature regarding the nexus of administrative law (government policy and rule-making administration). This is one of the first traversals to find evidence of the connection. The importance of this exercise is to get educators at all levels – primary/secondary education, tertiary and higher education – and of all types – academic staff, administrators, professional staff – to consider that it is important to know how the quality movement has and makes a difference in day-to-day practice (Padró et al. 2016). The traversal has mainly focused on materials from Australia and the USA and it is deliberately not systematic. The randomness is a result of two rationales: [1] to demonstrate breadth, when it shows up where you most expect it and when it is found embedded or indirectly applied to educational practice (administrative or curricular) and [2] to acknowledge in doing a broad-based review. The scant literature on TQM and administrative law focuses on specific legal topics such as contracts, application to internal government regulatory agencies, employee-related torts and protections. These elements can be noted in many of the examples that have been provided.

In short, this chapter is an attempt to help educators, particularly those involved in administration, to make sense of an area that has no established conceptual framework and very little scholarly literature related specifically to the interstices among TQM, legislative and regulatory processes in education. It is, thus, an early exploration. As such, the intention is to discover areas, such as those found in NQAs, professional accreditation documents and standards frameworks, which may reveal tenets of TQM as they may pertain to education, even where these tenets are not made explicit. We hope that further exploration of these tenets, by us and by other authors, may lead ultimately to a clearly articulated framework. We also hope, in the current absence of such a framework, that the reader might benefit from being a partner in this explanation, and that, like us, she or he will learn to read the signs, and in so doing, extract elements of TQA from the sources that we have mentioned.

This book is dedicated primarily to school level administrators. For them the preponderance of examples from higher education may be unwelcome and possibly a turn-off. Why then the use of this material? It is because most of the statutory and regulatory material focuses on universities due to their more entrepreneurial relationship with their external environments. In countries such as Australia and the USA, much of the legal basis of administrative processes for primary and secondary schools are located at the state level legislative levels and these are fewer in number because of the more centrally regulated environment. Yet, we suggest that the language issues related to understanding TQM and the principles at play and their application are similar making this exercise worth their while. In effect, it is our hope that this chapter will be useful to educators in general and to others interested in looking at the broader impact TQM has had on government processes and national policy steering.

References

Aman, A. C., & Mayton. (2014). *Administrative law* (3rd ed.). St. Paul: West Academic Publishing.

Asif, M., Raouf, A., & Searcy, C. (2013). Developing measures for performance excellence: Is the Baldrige criteria sufficient for performance excellence in higher education? *Quality & Quantity, 47*, 3095–3111.

Australian Institute for Teaching and School Leadership (AITSL). (2015). *Accreditation of initial teacher education programs: Standards and procedures.* Melbourne: Education Services Australia.

Badri, M. A., Selim, H., Alshare, K., Grandon, E. E., Younis, H., & Abdulla, M. (2006). The Baldrige education criteria for performance excellence framework: Empirical test and validation. *International Journal of Quality & Reliability Management, 23*(9), 1118–1157.

Bae, S. H. (2007). The relationship between ISO 9000 participation and educational outcomes of schools. *Quality Assurance in Education, 15*(3), 251–270.

Baldrige Performance Excellence Program (BPEP). (2015). *2015–2016 Baldrige excellence framework: A systems approach to improving your organization's performance (Education).* Gaithersburg: U.S. Department of Commerce, National Institute of Standards and Technology.

Baldrige Performance Excellence Program (BPEP). (2015b). *2015–2016 Baldrige excellence framework: A systems approach to improving your organization's technology.* Gaithersburg: U.S. Department of Commerce, Technology, National Institute of Standards and Technology.

Berkes, F. (2007). Understanding uncertainty and reducing vulnerability: Lessons from resilience thinking. *Natural Hazards, 41*, 283–295.

Berlin, D. F., & White, A. L. (2009). Preservice mathematics and science teachers in an integrated teacher preparation program for grades 7–12: A 3-year study of attitudes and perceptions related to integration. *International Journal of Science and Mathematics Education, 8*, 97–115.

Berliner, D. C. (1982, March). *The executive function of teachers.* Paper presented at the Wingspread conference on relating reading research to classroom instruction, Racine, WI. pp. 12–16.

Bhat, V. N. (2006). TQM implementation: Does the legal system matter? *Total Quality Management & Business Excellence, 17*(6), 685–690.

Birnbaum, R. (2000). *Management fads in higher education: Where they come from, what they do, why they fail.* San Francisco: Jossey-Bass.

Bohr, N. (1963). *Essays 1958–1962 on atomic physics and human knowledge.* Bungay: Richard Clay and Company, Ltd.

Bou-Llusar, J. C., Escrig-Tena, A. B., Roca-Puig, V., & Beltrán-Martín, I. (2009). An empirical assessment of the EFQM model: Evaluation as a TQM framework relative to the MBQNA model. *Journal of Operations Management, 27*(1), 1–22.

Bradley, D., Noonan, P., Nugent, H., & Scales, B. (2008). *A review of Australian higher education: Final report*. Canberra: DEEWR.

Caraman, I., Lazar, G., Bucuroiu, R., Lungu, O., & Stamate, M. (2008). How IWA 2 helps to implement a quality management system in Bacau university. *International Journal for Quality Research, 2*(4), 305–308.

Chen, I.-S., Chen, J.-K., & Padró, F. F. (2017). Critical quality indicators of higher education. *Total Quality & Business Excellence, 28*(1–2), 130–146.

Cheng, Y.-Y., Lyu, J., & Lin, Y.-C. (2004). Education improvement through ISO 9000 implementation: Experiences in Taiwan. *International Journal of Engineering Education, 20*(1), 91–95.

Coaldrake, P., & Stedman, L. (2016). *Raising the stakes: Gambling with the future of universities* (2nd ed.). St. Lucia: University of Queensland Press.

Conti, T. A. (2007). A history and review of the European quality award model. *The TQM Magazine, 19*(2), 112–128.

Dow, K. L., & Braithwaite, V. (2013). *Review of higher education regulation report*. Canberra: Commonwealth of Australia. Retrieved from http://www.innovation.gov.au/highereducation/Policy/HEAssuringQuality/Documents/FinalReviewReport.pdf

Dworkin, R. (1986). *Law's empire*. Cambridge, MA: Belknap Press.

El Abbaddi, L., Bouayard, A., & Lamrini, M. (2013). ISO 9001 and the field of higher education: Proposal for an update of the IWA 2 guidelines. *Quality Approaches in Higher Education, 4*(2), 14–19.

Epstein, R. A. (2016). The role of guidance in modern administrative procedure: The case for *de novo* review. *Journal of Legal Analysis, 8*(1), 47–93.

Farazmand, A. (2005). Role of government in an era of Total Quality Management (TQM) and globalization: Challenges and opportunities. *Public Organization Review: A Global Journal, 5*, 201–217.

Federow, H. (1993). Total quality management: A survey of legal issues relating to implementation of TQM. *Commercial Law Journal, 98*, 96–116.

Folke, C., Colding, J., & Berkes, F. (2003). Building resilience and adaptive capacity in social–ecological systems. In F. Berkes, J. Colding, & C. Folke (Eds.), *Navigating social–ecological systems* (pp. 352–387). Cambridge: Cambridge University Press.

Fried, Y. (1995). TQM and the legal environment in the United States: A neglected issue in the TQM literature. *The Academy of Management Review, 20*(1), 15–17.

Garvin, D. A. (1984). What does "product quality" really mean? *Sloan Management Review, 25*(1), 25–43.

Godfrey, A. B. (1999). Total Quality Management. In J. M. Juran, A. B. Godfrey, R. E. Hoogstoel, & E. G. Schilling (Eds.), *Juran's quality handbook* (5th ed., pp. 14.1–14.35). New York: McGraw-Hill.

Hart, H. L. A. (1997). *The concept of law* (2nd ed.). Oxford: Oxford University Press.

Harvey, L. (2004). The power of accreditation: Views of academics. *Journal of Higher Education Policy and Management, 26*(2), 207–223.

Harvey, L., & Green, D. (1993). Defining quality. *Assessment & Evaluation in Higher Education, 18*(1), 9–34.

Hayek, F. A. (1998/1973). *Law, legislation and liberty: A new statement of the liberal principles of justice and political economy.* London: Routledge.

Homburg, V., Pollitt, C., & van Thiel, S. (2007). Introduction. In C. Pollitt, S. van Thiel, & V. Homburg (Eds.), *New public management in Europe: Adaptation and alternatives* (pp. 1–9). Hampshire: Palgrave Macmillan.

Houston, D. (2007). TQM and higher education: A critical systems perspective on fitness for purpose. *Quality in Higher Education, 13*(1), 3–17.

Hurley, M. M., Padró, F. F., & Hawke, M. F. (2013). Will race to the top have the same mixed results no child left behind had on student learning and preservice teacher preparation? *Quality Approaches in Higher Education, 4*(2), 20–29.

International Organization for Standardization (ISO). (2007). *IWA 2: 2007: Quality management systems – Guidelines for the application of ISO 9001:2000 in education.* Retrieved from: http://www.ips.pt/ips_si/web_gessi_docs.download_file?p_name=F799130955/IWA_2_2007.pdf

Japanese Union of Scientists and Engineers (JUSE). (2018). *The application guide for The Deming Prize/The Deming Grand Prize 2018: For companies and organizations overseas.* Retrieved from http://www.juse.or.jp/upload/files/en_oubo2018_3.pdf

Juran, J. M. (1989). *Juran on leadership for quality: An executive handbook.* New York: Free Press.

Kanji, G. K., & Asher, M. (1993). *Total quality management process: A systematic approach.* Oxford: Carfax.

Kanji, G. K., Tambi, B. A., & Wallace, W. (1999). A comparative study of quality practices in higher education institutions in the US and Malaysia. *Total Quality Management, 10*(3), 357–371.

Kelsen, H. (1952). *The principles of international law.* New York: Rinehart & Company, Inc.

Kelsen, H. (1982). The concept of the legal order. *The American Journal of Jurisprudence, 27*(1), 64–84.

Komulainen, K., Naskali, P., Korhonen, M., & Keskitalo-Foley, S. (2011). Internal entrepreneurship – A Trojan horse of the neoliberal governance of education? Finnish pre- and in-service teachers' implementation of and resistance towards entrepreneurship education. *Journal for Critical Education Policy Studies, 9*(1), 342–373.

Kontoghiorghes, C. (2003). Examining the association between quality and productivity performance in a service organization. *Quality Management Journal, 10*(1), 32–42.

Lindborg, H., & Spangehl, S. D. (2011). U.S. higher education and accreditation: A quality perspective. *ASQ Higher Education Brief December, 4*(6), 1–7.

Löffler, E. (2001). Defining and measuring quality in public administration. *Bristol Business School Teaching and Research Review, 5*(4), 15 pp.

Lowi, T. J. (1985). The state in politics: The relationship between policy and administration. In R. G. Noll (Ed.), *Regulatory policy and the social sciences* (pp. 67–104). Berkeley: University of California Press.

Maram, A. (2008). Reassessment of the application of TQM in the public sector. *International Public Management Review, 9*(2), 194–212.

Massachusetts Department of Elementary and Secondary Education (DESE). (2016). *Guidelines for program approval* (Revised ed.). Malden: Author. Retrieved from http://www.doe.mass.edu/edprep/ProgramApproval.pdf

McAdam, R., Reid, R., & Saulters, R. (2002). Sustaining quality in the UK public sector: Quality measurement frameworks. *International Journal of Public Sector Management, 22*(6), 478–498.

McAuslan, P. (1988). Public law and public choice. *The Modern Law Review, 51*(6), 681–705.

Metcalfe, A. (2010). Administrative law evolution: An administrator's point of view. *Admin Review, 59*, 59–69.

Organisation for Economic Cooperation and Development (OECD). (2017). *PISA for development assessment and analytical framework: Reading, mathematics and science. (Preliminary version)*. Paris: Author.

Padró, F. F. (1988). *Quality circles and their existence in present-day high schools.* Unpublished doctoral dissertation, University of Arizona, Tucson, AZ.

Padró, F. F. (2009). Deming's system of profound knowledge and its application to higher education institutions. *Journal for Quality Progress, 32*(1), 10–14.

Padró, F. F., Hawke, M. F., & Hawke, L. M. (2016). Assessment and quality: Policy-steering and the making of a *deus ex machina*. In Bower & P. L. Thomas (Eds.), *De-testing and de-grading schools: Authentic alternatives to accountability and standardization* (Revised ed., pp. 33–50). New York: Peter Lang.

Pierce, R. J. (1988). Two problems in administrative law: Political polarity on the district of Columbia circuit and judicial deterrence of agency rulemaking. *Duke Law Journal, 37*, 300–328.

Pollitt, C. (2004, November 3). *From there to here, from now till then: Buying and borrowing public management reforms.* Paper presented at CLAD ninth international conference, Madrid.

Popper, K. (2002/1959). *The logic of scientific discovery.* London: Routledge.

Radin, B. A., & Coffee, J. N. (1993). A critique of TQM: Problems of implementation in the public sector. *Public Administration Quarterly, 17*(1), 42–54.

Rothstein, B., & Teorell, J. (2008). What is quality of government? A theory of impartial government institutions. *Governance: An International Journal of Policy, Administration, and Institutions, 21*(2), 165–190.

Sahney, S. (2016). Use of multiple methodologies for developing a customer-oriented model of total quality management in higher education. *International Journal of Educational Management, 30*(3), 326–353.

Sahney, S., Banwet, D. K., & Karunes, S. (2004). A SERVQUAL and QFD approach to total quality education: A student perspective. *International Journal of Productivity and Performance Management, 53*(2), 143–166.

Sallis, E. (2002). *Total quality in education* (3rd ed.). London: Kogan Page.

Shapiro, S. A. (2005). *Pragmatic administrative law,* Wake forest legal studies research papers series. Research paper no, 05-02. Retrieved from http://ssrn.com/abstract=653784

Stewart, R. B. (2003). Administrative law in the twenty-first century. *New York University Law Review, 78*(2), 437–460.

Swift, J. A., Ross, J. E., & Omachonu, V. K. (1998). *Principles of total quality* (2nd ed.). Boca Raton: St. Lucie Press.

Swiss, J. E. (1992). Adapting Total Quality Management (TQM) to government. *Public Administration Review, 52*(4), 356–362.

Tabb, W. K. (1995). *The post-war Japanese system: Cultural economy and economic transformation.* New York: Oxford University Press.

Tague, N. R. (2005). *The quality toolbox* (2nd ed.). Milwaukee: American Society for Quality Press.

Thornhauser, T., & Passmore, D. L. (2006). ISO 9000 in education: A comparison between the United States and England. *Research in Comparative & International Education, 1*(2), 156–173.

Timmermans, S., & Epstein, S. (2010). A world of standards but not standards world: Towards a sociology of standards and standardization. *Annual Review of Sociology, 36,* 69–89.

Vlăsceanu, L., Grünberg, L., & Pârlea, D. (2007). *Quality assurance and accreditation: A glossary of basic terms and definitions* (Revised ed.). Paris: UNESCO.

Walton, M. (1986). *The Deming management method.* New York: Perigee Books.

Weick, K. E. (1993). The collapse of sensemaking in organizations: The Mann Gulch disaster. *Administrative Science Quarterly, 38*(4), 628–652.

Williams, R., Bertsch, B., Dale, B., van der Wiele, T., van Iwaarden, J., Smith, M., & Visser, R. (2006). Quality and risk management: What are the key issues? *The TQM Magazine, 18*(1), 67–86.

Winn, B. A., & Cameron, K. S. (1998). Organizational quality: An examination of the Malcolm Baldrige National Quality framework. *Research in Higher Education, 39*(5), 491–512.

9

Articulating the Idea of the Professional Teacher: Beyond Technocratic Compliance

Francine Rochford

9.1 Introduction

This chapter considers the idea of the contemporary teacher as a 'professional'. This is not a trivial discussion; professionalisation itself is a nuanced term, with positive connotations arising from the altruistic vocational ideal and negative connotations arising from the signification of power, privilege and status afforded to occupational groups.[1] In fact, the term 'professional' is not consistently applied in different countries and contexts. What is interesting about the term is, therefore, why it is used in conjunction with a particular vocational group at a particular time, and what meanings and practices are being imported by this use. In this account, the term becomes a lens through which to consider the changing nature of teaching training and practice and the external drivers to change. Using this device, this chapter will focus on the recent Australian experience of regulatory convergence creating a standardised framework for teacher training, however it will draw upon other jurisdictions to demonstrate common themes, and others to draw upon alternative conceptualisations of vocational excellence in teaching practice.

[1] Thomas S Popkewitz, 'Professionalisation in teaching and teacher education: some notes on its history, ideology, and potential' (1994) 10(1) 1–14, 2.

F. Rochford (✉)
School of Law, La Trobe University, Bundoora, Australia
e-mail: F.Rochford@latrobe.edu.au

K. Trimmer et al. (eds.), *The Palgrave Handbook of Education Law for Schools*,
https://doi.org/10.1007/978-3-319-77751-1_9

The most revealing aspect of the idea of the profession is the relationship between self-regulation and professional identity. The changing nature of university education and the relationship between universities and external accrediting bodies has required re-examination of the idea of self-regulation in all professions; but the centrality of education to productivity in national economies has resulted in an externally-steered bureaucratic approach to regulation through professional organisations. At the same time, the status of the teaching profession in many countries is challenged by criticism of standard of classroom teaching, measured by standardised testing of students, and techniques of accountability have converged across multiple jurisdictions. The narrative of 'crisis' deployed to describe student achievement in many countries, benchmarking against 'productivity' measures, justifies the incorporation of a whole suite of evaluative techniques. The challenge for the profession is to find space for discussion of governance, training and skill requirements outside this narrow economic evaluation.

This chapter considers the historic idea of the profession, using legal texts (in the form of case law) as illustrations of authoritative adjudication of both the characteristics of a professional and a source of commentary for the contemporary meaning. It considers the points at which the term was applied to teaching, and the external policy context in which that occurred. It then considers the 'lens' of professionalism to frame aspects of teaching, nominating five characteristics typically attributed to a profession, and the caveats and reservations surrounding those characteristics.

9.2 The Idea of the 'Professional'

The central aspect of the 'professional' as one who enters a vocation is the application of knowledge to work whilst exercising ethical duties arising from the knowledge or understanding of the field.[2] The term 'profession' is, in classical terms, distinguished from what is an 'art' or a 'science' – aligning it with the meaning of 'vocation' or 'calling'.[3] The four traditional professions of religion, medicine, law and the military were distinguished by a public declaration, promise or vow, consistent with the view that in entering a profession a

[2] Ludwig Edelstein, 'The Professional Ethics of the Greek Physician' (1956) 30 *Bulletin of the History of Medicine* 391, 410.

[3] Ludwig Edelstein, 'The Professional Ethics of the Greek Physician' (1956) 30 *Bulletin of the History of Medicine* 391, 410.

person answered a calling or vocation.[4] The dedication of the professional to societal good distinguished them from the Guilds, which were motivated by a desire to advance the position of their own members in society. The 'professionem', or public declaration,[5] is maintained in the traditional professions; lawyers, upon admission have to make an oath of allegiance and of office.[6] Similarly, medical practitioners swore the Hippocratic oath, later reformulated in the Declaration of Geneva[7] declared at the time of admission as a member of the medical profession. Similar oaths of allegiance are required in the Armed Forces and, of course, in taking a religious vocation.

Some have indicated that there should be a similar oath sworn by teachers.[8] For example, Whelan argues that '[a] pledge for educators could be made within schools and upon first employment. Its declaration could be made a requirement for all job applications, just like police checks. It would indicate a formal declaration to conduct oneself ethically in all educational contexts, regardless of whether or not some individuals ultimately fail to do so.'[9]

An avowal or public declaration in itself, of course, cannot be conclusive evidence of belonging to a 'profession' in the traditional (or Latin) sense of the word. It is also clear that the meaning of the term 'professional' is not fixed. Judicially, the term has been considered to take its ordinary meaning. Lord Justice Du Parcq asked 'would the ordinary man [sic], the ordinary reasonable man [sic] – the man [sic], if you like to refer to an old friend, on the Clapham omnibus – say now, in the time in which we live, of any particular occupation, that it is properly described as a profession?'[10] Lord Justice Scrutton, in an English context, acceded that the distinction between professional and non-professional work was not easy to make, and that 'the line of demarcation may vary from time to time.'[11] Intellectual qualification is not considered a sufficient requirement,[12] but in any case it is a matter of fact and degree.[13]

---

[4] Sharon Christensen and W D Duncan, *Professional Liability and Property Transactions*, Federation Press 2004, 3; John Southwick, 'Can the professions survive under a National Competition Policy?' *Competition Law and the Professions Conference,* Perth, 11 April 1997 online, available at http://ncp.ncc.gov.au/docs/NCP%20and%20the%20professions%20-%20the%20issues.pdf [accessed 20th January 2018].

[5] Ibid.

[6] Supreme Court Act 1986 (Vic).

[7] See https://www.wma.net/policies-post/wma-declaration-of-geneva/

[8] John Whelan, 'Doctors, lawyers and ministers all take a professional pledge: here's why teachers should too' *The Conversation* 31st August 2017 https://theconversation.com/doctors-lawyers-and-ministers-all-take-a-professional-pledge-heres-why-teachers-should-too-82909

[9] Ibid.

[10] Carr v Inland Revenue Commissioners (1944) All ER 163.

[11] Commissioner of Inland Revenue v Maxse (1919) KB 647, 657 (Scrutton LJ).

[12] Carr v Inland Revenue Commissioners (1944) All ER 163 (Scott LJ).

[13] *Currie v Commissioner of Inland Revenue* (1921) 2 KB 332, 336 (Lord Sterndale MR).

In this sense legal analysis acknowledges the sociological account: '[t]he concept of profession is a socially constructed word which changes in relationship to the social conditions in which people used it.'[14] Sociological literature identified professions as

> *occupations with special power and prestige, which were granted a privileged position because they fulfilled specific societal needs and maintained norms through the application of specialized bodies of knowledge and because they were "devoted to the service of the public, above and beyond material incentives".*[15]

The historical view of the teacher bears little resemblance to the professional in this limited sense of the term, and it may be the case that the ideal of the profession has never matched the reality. In fact, the term 'profession' incorporates an 'ideal type'[16] or aspiration towards the 'altruistic occupation'.[17] More cynical analysis considers the barriers to entry created by professional self-regulation as a mechanism to create scarcity and thus drive market prices.[18] Professions, according to Popkewitz, 'made their services a medium of exchange for the desirable resources of status, power, and compensation.'[19]

This may be a reasonable argument in relation to occupational groups whose status and privilege enables it to control entry to the profession and to demand greater financial compensation and occupational conditions. However, the occupational esteem afforded to teachers in many comparator economies does not reflect this thesis. Instead, the 'occupational hierarchy'[20] in education in the United States placed teachers at the bottom – beneath administrators and university professors developing university training. This could be reframed in a gendered analysis, since advancement paths in the growing field of analysing, supervising and administering the bureaucracy of

---

[14] Thomas S Popkewitz, 'Professionalization in teaching and teacher education: some notes on its history, ideology, and potential' (1994) 10(1) 1–14, 2.

[15] Michel W Lander, Bas AS Koene and Shelly N Linssen, 'Committed to professionalism: Organizational responses of mid-tier accounting firms to conflicting institutional logics' (2013) 38 *Accounting, Organizations and Society* 130–148, 131.

[16] Thomas S Popkewitz, 'Professionalization in teaching and teacher education: some notes on its history, ideology, and potential' (1994) 10(1) 1–14, 2.

[17] Thomas S Popkewitz, 'Professionalization in teaching and teacher education: some notes on its history, ideology, and potential' (1994) 10(1) 1–14, 2.

[18] A Abbott, The system of professions: An essay on the division of expert labor (1988) Chicago, IL: University of Chicago Press.

[19] Thomas S Popkewitz, 'Professionalization in teaching and teacher education: some notes on its history, ideology, and potential' (1994) 10(1) 1–14, 3.

[20] Thomas S Popkewitz, 'Professionalization in teaching and teacher education: some notes on its history, ideology, and potential' (1994) 10(1) 1–14, 4.

education tended to favour males and teachers were typically women.[21] The narrative of 'professionalisation' tended to be a disempowering one for those at the bottom of this occupational hierarchy, since it afforded autonomy and self-regulation to the apex of the occupational hierarchy, whilst teachers were 'ancillary', subject to the reforms introduced by school and classroom 'management' but not enjoying the capacity to influence those spheres. Teaching became a 'profession' when the word 'professional' became a synonym for 'managed', or 'regulated.'

Many economies have tracked this process, so there has been a convergence in meaning between, say, Australia, the United States and England. In countries in which the status of teaching has been, by whatever means, elevated, the comparative power of teachers is similarly escalated. It should not come as a surprise that the autonomy of the profession is similarly increased, and the capacity of the profession to resist efforts to regulate is increased. Thus, in Finland and Singapore, commentators note that the national governments have focused on the increase in the status of the profession through increased compensation and professional development, thus driving stronger academic ability amongst those training to teach. Instead of considering the profession as the defining feature of the occupation, it is useful, therefore, to consider it as an aspect of the relationship between the occupational category and the state. The higher the occupational status, the greater the capacity to resist threats to autonomy. 'Professionalism operates as an occupational strategy, defining entry and negotiating the power and rewards due to expertise, and as an organisational strategy, shaping the patterns of power, place and relationships around which organisations are coordinated.'[22]

Christensen and Duncan argue 'that the expansion of the concept of professionalism to include occupations not traditionally considered to be professional represents the professionalism of society, rather than confusion regarding the operational definition of 'profession'.'[23] It has been argued that 'many occupational groups are indeed assuming many of the characteristics of the traditional professions by establishing professional associations, introducing accreditation requirements and promulgating codes of ethics.'[24] The changing nature of 'work' in society has increased the range of occupations considered to have the characteristics of a 'profession', but at the same time a

[21] Thomas S Popkewitz, 'Professionalization in teaching and teacher education: some notes on its history, ideology, and potential' (1994) 10(1) 1–14, 4.

[22] J Clarke and N Newman, *The Managerial State* (1997) London: Sage Publications, 7.

[23] Sharon Christensen and W D Duncan, *Professional Liability and Property Transactions*, Federation Press 2004, 11.

[24] Ibid, citing Vollmer & Mills, *Professionalization* Prentice-Hall, Eaglewood Cliffs, NJ 1966, 2.

convergence of forces has tended to impose technocratic constraints on all professions – even the more venerable.

9.3 Features of a Profession

There would be little unanimity in any attempt to distinguish the key elements typical of a profession. However, to provide an organising tool for the various commentaries this chapter will adopt the following elements, which are largely derived from judicial pronouncements:

- organisational structure[25];
- self-regulation[26];
- education or skill requirements[27];
- public service[28];

It should be conceded that 'the characteristics commonly associated with [the professions] are myths which legitimate existing power and authority'.[29] However, like the term 'professional' they provide the interpretative lens through which the teacher and the profession negotiate their place in the modern context of education.

9.4 Organisational Structure

In defining key elements of a profession judicial statements are useful, both as authoritative sources and because they capture a contemporary meaning with the benefit of highly skilled advocacy and review of extant sources. Taking a judicial account of the definition, Lord Justice Scrutton stated:

---

[25] Currie v Inland Revenue Commission (1921) 2 KB 332, 343.

[26] F Raymond Marks and Darlene Cathcart, 'Discipline within the legal profession: is it self-regulation?' (1974) *University of Illinois Law Forum* 193–236.

[27] *Commissioner of Inland Revenue v Maxse* (1919) 1 KB 647, 657; F Raymond Marks and Darlene Cathcart, 'Discipline within the legal profession: is it self-regulation?' (1974) *University of Illinois Law Forum* 193–236.

[28] Michael S. Greco Remarks to the Connecticut Bar Association Westbrook Connecticut, September 25, 2009; John Southwick, 'Can the professions survive under a National Competition Policy?' Competition Law and the Professions Conference, Perth, 11 April 1997 online, available at http://ncp.ncc.gov.au/docs/NCP%20and%20the%20professions%20-%20the%20issues.pdf [accessed 20th January 2018].

[29] Thomas S Popkewitz, 'Professionalization in teaching and teacher education: some notes on its history, ideology, and potential' (1994) 10(1) 1–14, 2.

I myself am disposed to attach some importance in findings as to whether a profession is exercised or not to the fact that the particular man [sic] is a member of an organised professional body with a recognised standard of ability enforced before he [sic] can enter it and a recognised standard of conduct enforced while he [sic] is practicing it.[30]

The existence of a professional body regulating entry into a profession, and the conduct of those within the profession, is a long-standing indicator of the profession. Again, it is a necessary but not sufficient requirement. The organisational structure is, therefore, concomitant to the education and self-regulation requirements. The nature and role of the organisational structure is not fixed, and in particular the barriers to entry represented by some traditional professional groups presented a challenge to rules against anti-competitive collusion. For instance, the setting of prices by professional organisations for services is now highly circumscribed. Professions are not permitted to reserve to themselves the provision of certain types of work when others have the credentials to do that work, and restricting entry to a profession may constitute anti-competitive conduct in breach of the *Competition and Consumer Act 2010* (Cth). In the past thirty years in Australia, for instance, the roles and expectations of professional organisations have tended to converge as a consequence of compliance obligations and pressure to conform to social expectations. As Rowland notes,

[i]n common with the delineation of profession itself, the role and function of such organisations is itself in a state of flux, particularly in relation to the setting of standards governing the quality of professional work … which may need to be modified in response to societal and technological change.[31]

In Australia, regulation of professional bodies typically falls within the states' legislative competence. However, co-operative federalism has tended to result in convergence of legislative frameworks for those professions which have an economic impact. The National Competition Policy resulted in the revision of over 2000 pieces of legislation relating to Australian professionals to assess their anti-competitive impact.[32] Barriers to entry to any profession

[30] *Currie v Inland Revenue Commission* (1921) 2 KB 332, 343, Scrutton LJ.

[31] Diane Rowland, 'Negligence, professional competence and computer systems' (1999) (2) *Journal of Information Law and Technology* [available at http://www2.warwick.ac.uk/fac/soc/law/elj/jilt/1999_2/rowland/#fnb3].

[32] John Southwick, 'Can the professions survive under a National Competition Policy?' *Competition Law and the Professions Conference,* Perth, 11 April 1997 online, available at http://ncp.ncc.gov.au/docs/NCP%20and%20the%20professions%20-%20the%20issues.pdf [accessed 20th January 2018].

have to be justifiable. This convergence has been influenced by the competition principles.[33] In the Australian context, Fels notes that '[a]ssessing all regulations from an economy-wide perspective, as opposed to the perspective of only those being regulated, is important if the problem identified above are to be avoided.'[34] However, recognition of consumer interests including transparent market information, comparability, mediation of disputes, appeal from disciplinary proceedings and compliance with consumer protection laws has tended to create a tension between the independence of the professional organisation and the external regulatory framework. In the case of teaching organisations, additional regulatory impetus arises due to the strong public interest in education.[35]

The range and role of professional organisations in teaching is extensive; in some countries a strong distinction can be drawn between professional organisations with industrial relations orientation[36] and those with advocacy and regulatory orientation.[37] Taking the Australian situation as a case study, the integration of professional organisations with the legislative regulation of teaching is evident. Australia is a Federation, and legislative competence resides with the states. Each state has enacted regulations under the primary Act which reposes authority for teacher registration in the professional organisation. Despite the tendency for regulatory convergence, each Australian state retains its own Registration authority as indicated in Table 9.1:

The professional organisations are, accordingly, afforded particular status in the Australian states, acknowledged as sites of certification and regulation. Accountability to professional obligations represented by teacher organisations fixes those obligations within a convergent regulatory framework. The manner in which this presents in self-regulation and training requirements is considered below.

The organisational roles of teacher bodies in Britain and the United States arose, according to Popkewitz, as a 'by-product of a weak centralized state.'[38] In comparison, centralised and bureaucratic states such as those in Western

[33] See Allan Fels, 'Regulation, Competition and the Profession' *Industry Economics Conference* 2001, 13 July 2001 [available at https://www.accc.gov.au/system/files/Fels_Industry_Economics_14_7_01%5B1%5D.pdf].

[34] Ibid, 4.

[35] Senate, Employment and Training Reference Committee, 1998, Senate Inquiry into the Teaching Profession, *A Class Act* p. 12.

[36] For instance, in America the American Federation of Teachers, in Australia the Australian Education Union, and state equivalents, in England the National Education Union.

[37] For instance, in America the Association of American Educators.

[38] Thomas S Popkewitz, 'Professionalization in teaching and teacher education: some notes on its history, ideology, and potential' (1994) 10(1) 1–14, 3.

Table 9.1 Professional regulation by state

State	Registering body	Act	Regulations
Tasmania	Teachers Registration Board Tasmania	*Teachers Registration Act 2000*	Teachers Registration Regulations 2011
Victoria	Victorian Institute of Teaching	*Education and Training Reform Act* 2006	Education and Training Reform Regulations 2017
New South Wales	NSW Education Standards Authority	*Teacher Accreditation Act 2004* (NSW) *Education Standards Authority Act 2013* (NSW)	Teacher Accreditation Regulation 2015 (NSW)
ACT	ACT Teacher Quality Institute	*ACT Teacher Quality Institute Act (2010)*	ACT Teacher Quality Institute Regulation 2010
Queensland	Queensland College of Teachers	*Education (Queensland College of Teachers) Act 2005*	*Education (Queensland College of Teachers) Regulation* 2016
NT	Teacher Registration Board	Teacher Registration (Northern Territory) Act	Teacher Registration (Northern Territory) Regulations
Western Australia	Teacher Registration Board of Western Australia	Teacher Registration Act 2012 (Act)	Teacher Registration (General) Regulations 2012 Teacher Registration (Accreditation of Initial Teacher Education Programmes) Regulations 2012
South Australia	Teachers Registration Board of South Australia	*Teachers Registration and Standards Act 2004*	*Teachers Registration and Standards Regulations 2016*

Europe did not require professional groups to mediate social regulation. This thesis suggests that professional organisations, where they are sufficiently strong, will absolve the state of the need to exert regulatory power. Where political shifts advance the cause of decentralisation and local decision-making, the logical repository for regulatory power is the existing professional body.

The constitution of power in professional teacher organisations in Australian states, as indicated in Table 9.1, would appear to support this thesis, in the sense that education is within the legislative competence of the Australian states, and the comparatively weak position of the Federal Parliament thus could be seen to require a local repository of power. However, two arguments may be made to cast doubt on this proposition. In the first instance, state teaching organisations take their authority directly from State legislation. However, in teacher training and in some self-regulatory principles the States require compliance with Federal principles. The Federal parliament can assert power through influence other than legislative competence, namely in the provision of financial support. Secondly, the site of power in a decentralised school system is highly variable across comparator countries, regardless of whether the state is unitary or federal. The devolution of power to schools during the Kennett reforms of the 1990s in Victoria, Australia, for instance, still located schools within a public education 'system'.[39] Similar trends in the United Kingdom, New Zealand and Sweden showed a centralisation of matters which would be appropriately considered within the expertise of professional bodies, such as curriculum and accountability, and a decentralisation in matters such as financial accountability.[40] Similarly, England has centralised curriculum policy whilst devolving other forms of decision-making authority. Diversity of curricula in Finland is legislatively provided by the reformed National Curriculum.[41] 'School-based management' also characterised reform in most states in the United States and New Zealand.[42] The role of professionals in devolved decision-making could be enhanced in some forms of school- or site-based control, as practiced in some states in the United States, for instance. The power and autonomy of local authorities is also significant in the outcomes of each policy mix.[43] Theoretically, at least, a multitude of sites of negotiation place teacher organisations in a more difficult position in maintaining control over curriculum, teaching philosophy and advocacy of professional interests. Whether financing and financial accountability is devolved to a local authority, school council or principal, the overall transparency of decision-making is reduced. This compromises the leverage of a teacher organisation and dilutes the sense of a professional organisation.

---

[39] Brian Caldwell, 'Australian perspectives on leadership: the principal's role in radical decentralisation in Victoria's schools of the future' (1994) 21(2) *The Australian Educational Researcher* 45–62.

[40] Brian Caldwell, 'Australian perspectives on leadership: the principal's role in radical decentralisation in Victoria's schools of the future' (1994) 21(2) *The Australian Educational Researcher* 45–62, 46.

[41] Anne West & Annamari Ylönen (2010) Market-oriented school reform in England and Finland: school choice, finance and governance, Educational Studies, 36:1, 1–12, 7.

[42] Kenneth Leithwood and Teresa Menzies, 'Forms and effects of school-based management: a review' (1998) 12(3) *Educational Policy* 325–346.

[43] Anne West & Annamari Ylönen (2010) Market-oriented school reform in England and Finland: school choice, finance and governance, Educational Studies, 36:1, 1–12.

9.5 Self-regulation

One of the key traditional designators of professional organisations is the capacity for self-regulation.[44] Of course, there is no 'bright line' distinguishing self-regulation and public-regulation, 'but rather a spectrum containing different degrees of legislative constraints, outsider participation in relation to rule formulation or enforcement (or both), and external control and accountability.'[45] As national productivity becomes a key priority of government, there is a tension between self-regulation and other values, such as consumer protection and public accountability. Government economic priorities and electoral pressures give significant motivation for oversight of both certification and practise in professions with a significant economic influence. Education is central to government strategies for employability, and the public and private school systems are recipients of public funding.[46]

In the case of the teaching profession, regulation occurs throughout the professional life of a teacher, not just at the point of certification. Teachers remain subject to the disciplinary oversight of the relevant state body.[47] Thus, taking an Australian example, the Victorian Institute of Teaching approves and recognises the qualifications required for registration (creating an external accreditation requirement for providers of teaching education). Section 2.6.8(a)(i) of the *Education and Training Reform Act* 2006 (Vic) empowers the VIT (or the Minister) to ascertain whether the qualification is appropriate and that the applicant is suitable to be a teacher. Registration also requires a National Police History check[48] and the VIT is required to ensure checks are carried out every five years thereafter.[49] Initial Teacher Education registration requires a Literacy and Numeracy Test. The latter requirement is mandated by agreement between state and federal ministers. From January 1st, 2017 the accreditation requirements of Initial Teacher Education programs in Victoria included this test. Thus, although oversight of teacher registration remains with the professional body, the requirements of registration are steered by detailed government policy.

---

44 John Southwick, 'Can the professions survive under a National Competition Policy?' *Competition Law and the Professions Conference*, Perth, 11 April 1997 online, available at http://ncp.ncc.gov.au/docs/NCP%20and%20the%20professions%20-%20the%20issues.pdf [accessed 20th January 2018].

45 Anthony Ogus, 'Rethinking self-regulation' (1995) 15(1) *Oxford Journal of Legal Studies* 97–108, 100.

46 John Furlong (2013) Globalisation, Neoliberalism, and the Reform of Teacher Education in England, The Educational Forum, 77:1, 28–50.

47 See Table 9.1.

48 Section 2.6.12B Education and Training Reform Act 2006 (Vic).

49 Section 2.6.22A Education and Training Reform Act 2006 (Vic).

After registration professional bodies retain disciplinary oversight of registered teachers. The Victorian Institute of Teaching maintains a Register of Registered Teachers,[50] promulgates Codes of Ethics, and is empowered to investigate registered teachers in the case of complaints or concerns about the fitness of teachers.[51] Determinations may be reviewed by the Victorian Civil and Administrative Tribunal.[52] The mechanisms by which self-regulation occurs, therefore, are authorised by legislation even in relation to the powers able to be exercised by the regulatory body. A degree of 'self'-regulation is manifest in the utilisation of expertise from the profession,[53] but the oversight of the Minister is prioritised.[54] Section 2.6.6A requires the Minister to recommend persons to the VIT with expertise in management, finance, law and corporate governance, thus emphasising the financial, governance and process orientation of the organisation.

9.6 Education or Skill Requirements

Identification as a professional imports a concomitant legal duty to comply with the education standards of the professional.[55] Failure to do so can have legal consequences, such as liability in tort, contract or consumer protection statutes, and professional disciplinary consequences. Taking a judicial authority again, in *Commissioner of Inland Revenue v Maxse*[56] Scrutton LJ said:

> *A profession in the present use of the language involves the idea of an occupation requiring either purely intellectual skill, or of manual skill controlled, as in painting or sculpture, or surgery, by the intellectual skill of the operator, as distinguished from an occupation which is substantially the production or sale or arrangements for the production or sale of commodities. The line of demarcation may vary from time to time.*[57]

---

[50] Section 2.6.24 Education and Training Reform Act 2006 (Vic).

[51] Sections 2.6.30–2.6.52 Education and Training Reform Act 2006 (Vic).

[52] Section 2.6.55 Education and Training Reform Act 2006 (Vic).

[53] Section 2.6.6AB Education and Training Reform Act 2006 (Vic).

[54] Section 2.6.5 Education and Training Reform Act 2006 (Vic).

[55] *Eckersley v Binnie* (1988) 18 Con LR 1, 80 (Bingham LJ); John Southwick, 'Can the professions survive under a National Competition Policy?' *Competition Law and the Professions Conference,* Perth, 11 April 1997 online, available at http://ncp.ncc.gov.au/docs/NCP%20and%20the%20professions%20-%20 the%20issues.pdf [accessed 20th January 2018].

[56] [1919] 1 KB 647, 657.

[57] [1919] 1 KB 647, 657. *Robbins Herbal Institute v Federal Commissioner of Taxation* (1923) 32 CLR 457, 461 (Starke J), *GIO General Ltd. v Newcastle City Council* (1996) 38 NSWLR 558, 568 and *Weber v Land*

The current framework for teaching standards is heavily influenced by the Teacher Education Ministerial Advisory Group report *Action Now: Classroom Ready Teachers*.[58] This report made a number of key findings. These findings to a great extent reflect the political anxiety about education: it reported a 'need to lift public confidence in initial teacher education', citing the concern of 'Australians' that they are not confident in the capacity of all entrants to initial teacher education. The key directions included '[a]n overhauled national accreditation process for initial teacher education programs administered by a national regulator. Full program accreditation contingent upon robust evidence of successful graduate outcomes against the Professional Standards' and 'strengthened accreditation'.[59] The education and skills requirements of teachers are now generally nationally consistent (although full implementation will not occur until 2023) and based on an external accreditation process driving curriculum frameworks in universities as well as certification requirements. Thus, in the Australian context, the professional standards of teachers have been identified, systematised and promulgated at a national level, whilst their application remains devolved to the state and the profession.

Certification by the various state and territory teacher registration boards evidence achievement of that standard. Seven standards are to be met at various career stages and at different levels of experience. These standards are organised into three 'Domains' – Professional Knowledge, Professional Practice and Professional Engagement and are measured across four career stages (Graduate, Proficient, Highly Accomplished and Lead).

1. Know students and how they learn
2. Know the content and how to teach it
3. Plan for and implement effective teaching and learning
4. Create and maintain supportive and safe learning environments
5. Assess, provide feedback and report on student learning
6. Engage in professional learning
7. Engage professionally with colleagues, parents/carers and the community[60]

Agents Board (1986) 40 SASR 312, 317 (O'Loughlin J) contain similar pronouncements about the need for education, knowledge or skill.

[58] Teacher Education Ministerial Advisory Group, *Action Now: Classroom Ready Teachers* December 2014.

[59] Ibid, vii.

[60] Australian Institute for Teaching and School Leadership, *Australian Professional Standards for Teachers* February 2011.

The Australian Professional Standards for Teachers[61] finalised in 2010, were not exclusively driven or developed by the profession:

> *Work on the Australian Professional Standards for Teachers (the Standards) commenced under the auspices of the Ministerial Council for Education, Early Childhood Development and Youth Affairs (MCEECDYA) in 2009. Significant work was undertaken by the National Standards Sub-group of the Australian Education, Early Childhood Development and Youth Affairs Senior Officials Committee (AEEYSOC) during 2009–10.*[62]

That the standards to be met by teachers are not developed by the profession does not, in itself, indicate the elimination of the principle of self-regulation. Relatively uniform standards, developed by or with consultation with the profession, are common. In this case the standards are promulgated by the Australian Institute for Teaching and School Leadership Limited (AITSL) and although this body has significant teacher and teacher-educator input, in regulatory terms it is closely allied to government – it was formed to work with government and is funded by the Australian Government.

The trend towards standardisation of teacher education can be seen in other jurisdictions. England has seen a concentration of attention on teacher education with a series of political approaches to develop a prescriptive curriculum.[63] The significant reforms under New Labour, however, occurred outside the organisational structure of the profession: '[m]andatory national specifications were simultaneously imposed and inspected and educationalists (and the wider public) almost completely marginalised.'[64] The United States formed the National Board for Professional Teaching Standards in 1987, which 'articulated standards and developed assessments for evaluating accomplished teaching [and] led to revisions of standards for beginning teacher licensing'.[65]

Government actions (and reactions) on teaching standards are heavily influenced by social and economic policy, with the tendency to instrumentalise education as an ends-based enterprise rather than as having a process orientation. School performance anxiety at a national level motivates government

---

[61] Formerly the National Professional Standards for Teachers.

[62] Australian Institute for Teaching and School Leadership Limited, *Australian Professional Standards for Teachers* February 2011.

[63] John Furlong (2013) Globalisation, Neoliberalism, and the Reform of Teacher Education in England, The Educational Forum, 77:1, 28–50.

[64] Viv Ellis (2010) Impoverishing experience: the problem of teacher education in England, Journal of Education for Teaching, 36:1, 105–120, 105.

[65] Linda Darling-Hammond (2017) Teacher education around the world: What can we learn from international practice?, European Journal of Teacher Education, 40:3, 291–309, 295.

framing of teaching standards, because performance on international comparisons of scholastic performance are 'conceptualised as *the* proxy or predictor for innovation, economic development and achievement.'[66] The significant federal contribution to the education system allows leveraging of the state legislative competence, so that education is frequently highly politicised, and '[t]his is unfortunately complicated and exacerbated by the situation whereby education is constitutionally largely a state and territory responsibility yet funded substantially through the Commonwealth tax system.'[67]

As Sachs notes, 'the term 'professional teaching standards' is widely and uncritically used in educational policy documents and popular discourse.'[68] Sachs suggests that a critical analysis of the application of standards indicates that the development of standards is a manifestation of control of teachers and the profession itself, in which case it is the antithesis of self-regulation. She notes that 'the application of bureaucratic forces such as rules, mandates and requirements [are] a means to provide direct supervision, standardized work processes or standardized outcomes to control or regulate teaching.'[69] In the case of teaching standards, Sachs claims that 'because the standards have been set, in the main, by administrative agencies such as Departments of Education, they tacitly emphasise bureaucratic rather than professional controls over teaching.'[70] In Australia, as with other countries, the standards represent 'the construction of an imposing new apparatus of certification and regulation for teachers'.[71] As a result, it could be said that standards are not set by teacher professionals, but imposed upon them:

> *the role of professional standards for teachers has been twisted by some to be more about standardising, judging and dismissing teachers than developing and recognising them i.e., judgemental instead of developmental. Rather than being done with and for teachers, many measures advocated and being hastily and poorly implemented in the quest to improve teaching and learning are essentially being done to teachers and without their involvement, almost guaranteeing resistance, minimal compliance and inefficiency.*[72]

---

[66] Stephen Dinham, 'The quality teaching movement in Australia encounters difficult terrain: a personal perspective' (2013) 57(2) *Australian Journal of Education* 91–106, p. 97.

[67] Ibid, 102.

[68] Judyth Sachs (2003) Teacher Professional Standards: Controlling or developing teaching?, Teachers and Teaching, 9:2, 175–186, p. 176.

[69] Ibid, p. 177.

[70] Ibid, p. 179.

[71] Raewyn Connell (2009) Good teachers on dangerous ground: towards a new view of teacher quality and professionalism, Critical Studies in Education, 50:3, 213–229, 214.

[72] Ibid, 94.

In the European context Caena notes the centrality of education and training to driving policy in efficiency, equity, labour market needs and national targets on economic competitiveness. She attributes the alignment of policy discourse in these areas to the increasing convergence of reform in education systems across the world.[73] The pressure on the profession as a result of the overarching policy discourse is difficult to resist. Kohli et al. refer to the ongoing requirement of teacher professional development as 'antidialogical professional development', being 'increasingly technocratic [and] top-down'.[74] They note that '[u]nfortunately, with the rise of scripted PD and prescribed curriculum, teachers are increasingly the passive recipients of technical training.' It could be argued that this is the antithesis of professional education.

The technocratic mechanisms for certification, regulation and audit that characterise many of the advanced systems of education tend to convergence, with a suite of techniques adopted to measure the 'good teacher'. Whereas the teacher in an Australian colonial school acted as 'an obedient servant of the authorities'[75] instilling a basic curriculum and emphasising respectability and obedience, the idea of the 'good teacher' is in contemporary terms requires evidence of a capacity to produce in students a set of key competencies aligned to national economic interests.[76] The role of the professional teacher in the formulation and audit of the achievement of these economic outcomes appears quite limited. This is not surprising; the architecture of neo-liberalism is robust and self-serving, and the claims of a profession to manage education requirements are subject to claims of anti-competitive conduct.

9.7 Public Service

The final, and perhaps the true distinguishing feature a profession is the element of public service. The eminent American jurist Roscoe Pound is reported to have 'defined the essence of a profession',[77] saying that the term 'profession'

[73] Francesca Caena 'Teacher competence frameworks in Europe: policy-as-discourse and policy-as-practice' (2014) 49(3) *European Journal of Education* 311–331.

[74] Rita Kohli, Bree Picower, Antonio Nieves Martinez and Natalia Ortiz, 'Critical professional development: centering the social justice needs of teachers' (2015) 6(2) *The International Journal of Critical Pedagogy* 8–24.

[75] Raewyn Connell (2009) Good teachers on dangerous ground: towards a new view of teacher quality and professionalism, Critical Studies in Education, 50:3, 213–229, 215.

[76] Raewyn Connell (2009) Good teachers on dangerous ground: towards a new view of teacher quality and professionalism, Critical Studies in Education, 50:3, 213–229, 214.

[77] Michael S. Greco Remarks to the Connecticut Bar Association Westbrook Connecticut, September 25, 2009.

'refers to a group of persons pursuing a learned art as a common calling in the spirit of public service – no less a public service because it may incidentally be a means of livelihood. Pursuit of the learned art in the spirit of public service is the primary purpose. Gaining a livelihood is incidental.'[78] Indeed, as Chief Justice Murray Gleeson notes in the context of the legal profession, that '[l]awyers... originally regarded it as beneath their dignity to charge for their services ... the underlying idea, that they were officers of the court exercising a privilege of audience on behalf of litigants, is worth keeping.'[79] In the context of the medical profession, Chief Justice Gleeson, reflecting on the Hippocratic Oath, noted that there is, above all, 'a commitment to the idea of conduct governed by a sense of duty to help others.'[80]

The call to 'professionalism' imports the relatively uncontested rhetoric 'that teachers should participate in their work with autonomy, integrity and responsibility'.[81] As Popkewitz notes, however, the translation of this rhetoric into action at school level occurs not through the agency of teachers, but through the imposition of standards and the monitoring, measurement and certification of achievement of those standards.

The Australian Professional Standards for Teachers do not explicitly engage this requirement. However, each state professional body has an equivalent to a Code of Conduct and Code of Ethics. In Victoria the 'Codes of Conduct and Ethics' are described as public statements developed for and by the teaching profession to:

- reflect shared principles about practice, conduct and ethics to be applied to promote the highest standards of professional practice
- enable registered teachers to reflect on their ethical decisions
- inspire the quality of behaviour that reflects the expectations of the profession and the community
- provide a clear statement to the community about these expectations.[82]

In terms of the public service requirement inherent in the idea of the professional, the principle, for instance, that 'teachers provide opportunities for

[78] Ibid.

[79] Murray Gleeson, 'Are the Professions worth keeping?' (Speech) Greek-Australian International Legal and Medical Conference, 31 May 1999, available at http://www.hcourt.gov.au/assets/publications/speeches/former-justices/gleesoncj/cj_areprofe.htm

[80] Ibid.

[81] Thomas S Popkewitz, 'Professionalization in teaching and teacher education: some notes on its history, ideology, and potential' (1994) 10(1) 1–14, 3.

[82] Victorian Institute of Teaching, *Codes of Conduct and Ethics*, available at https://www.vit.vic.edu.au/professional-responsibilities/conduct-and-ethics

all learners to learn' describes a general obligation to society beyond the commitment required from the employment contract. The Code refers to the 'professional relationship' with learners, a 'collaborative relationship' with families and communities, and the principle of collegiality. These are explicit references to professional obligations. Breach of these Codes can result in disciplinary proceedings by the Victorian Institute of Teaching and potentially deregistration; however, they do not capture the public service ethos that distinguishes a profession. The 'public service' ethic in implementation thus is subject to measurement in the same way as education and skill requirements. In many ways this is the converse of autonomy.

9.8 Conclusion

'Professional' is a contested term, and the significance of the appellation in relation to an occupational group is more about *why* than *whether* – why use the term in relation to this group? Using the characteristics commonly attributed to the traditional designation as an analytical lens to assess the claim of teaching to professional status, it is evident that the framework of the professional construct can be used to create a reform agenda. Professionalism becomes the rhetorical device justifying the imposition of a wide-reaching bureaucracy armed with techniques of governance that reach into all aspects of a teacher's employment. This phenomenon is not limited to the teaching profession. The autonomy, or self-governance, of all professions has been eroded, not by explicit imposition of rules but by co-operative regulation. The professions have often acceded to external frameworks of control, whilst maintaining self-regulation within those frameworks.

It has been suggested that '*as a profession*, teaching is not accustomed or confident at evaluating its own practice and providing publicly convincing alternatives'.[83] This enables an uncontested discourse of external 'accountability' for a range of outcomes, nominally 'in return for the trust or privileges granted'.[84] However, this notional exchange of privilege for oversight is not readily apparent in the profession of teaching. The virtually uncontested subversion of education to national productivity goals is symptomatic of the lack of articulated alternatives to the superstructure surrounding teacher training and certification.

[83] Elizabeth Kleinhenz & Lawrence Ingvarson (2004) Teacher accountability in Australia: current policies and practices and their relation to the improvement of teaching and learning, Research Papers in Education, 19:1, 31–49 [emphasis in original].

[84] Senate, Employment and Training Reference Committee above n 35.

References

Abbott, A. (1988). *The system of professions: An essay on the division of expert labor.* Chicago: University of Chicago Press.

Australian Institute for Teaching and School Leadership (AITSL). (2011). *Australian professional standard for principals.* Education Services Australia, Carlton.

Caena, F. (2014). Teacher competence frameworks in Europe: Policy-as-discourse and policy-as-practice. *European Journal of Education, 49*(3), 311–331.

Caldwell, B. (1994). Australian perspectives on leadership: The principal's role in radical decentralisation in Victoria's schools of the future. *The Australian Educational Researcher, 21*(2), 45–62.

Carr v Inland Revenue Commissioners [1944] All ER 163.

Christensen, S., & Duncan, W. D. (2004). *Professional liability and property transactions.* Annandale: Federation Press.

Clarke, J., & Newman, N. (1997). *The managerial state.* London: Sage Publications.

Commissioner of Inland Revenue v Maxse [1919] KB 647.

Connell, R. (2009). Good teachers on dangerous ground: Towards a new view of teacher quality and professionalism. *Critical Studies in Education, 50*(3), 213–229.

Currie v Commissioner of Inland Revenue [1921] 2 KB 332.

Darling-Hammond, L. (2017). Teacher education around the world: What can we learn from international practice? *European Journal of Teacher Education, 40*(3), 291–309.

Dinham, S. (2013). The quality teaching movement in Australia encounters difficult terrain: A personal perspective. *Australian Journal of Education, 57*(2), 91–106.

Eckersley v Binnie. (1988). 18 Con LR 1, 80.

Edelstein, L. (1956). The professional ethics of the Greek Physician. *Bulletin of the History of Medicine, 30*, 391.

Education and Training Reform Act 2006 (Vic).

Ellis, V. (2010). Impoverishing experience: The problem of teacher education in England. *Journal of Education for Teaching, 36*(1), 105–120.

Fels, A. (2001, July). Regulation, competition and the profession. *Industry economics conference.* Available at https://www.accc.gov.au/system/files/Fels_Industry_Economics_14_7_01%5B1%5D.pdf

Furlong, J. (2013). Globalisation, neoliberalism, and the reform of teacher education in England. *The Educational Forum, 77*(1), 28–50.

GIO General Ltd v Newcastle City Council. (1996). 38 NSWLR 558.

Greco, M. (2009, September 25). Remarks to the Connecticut bar association Westbrook Connecticut.

Kleinhenz, E., & Ingvarson, L. (2004). Teacher accountability in Australia: Current policies and practices and their relation to the improvement of teaching and learning. *Research Papers in Education, 19*(1), 31–49.

Kohli, R., Picower, B., Martinez, A. N., & Ortiz, N. (2015). Critical professional development: Centering the social justice needs of teachers. *The International Journal of Critical Pedagogy, 6*(2), 8–24.

Lander, M., Koene, B., & Linssen, S. (2013). Committed to professionalism: Organizational responses of mid-tier accounting firms to conflicting institutional logics. *Accounting, Organizations and Society, 38*, 130–148.

Leithwood, K., & Menzies, T. (1998). Forms and effects of school-based management: A review. *Educational Policy, 12*(3), 325–346.

Marks, F. R., & Cathcart, D. (1974). Discipline within the legal profession: Is it self-regulation? *University of Illinois Law Forum, 2*(5), 193–236.

Popkewitz, T. (1994). Professionalization in teaching and teacher education: Some notes on its history, ideology, and potential. *Teaching and Teacher Education, 10*(1), 1–14.

Robbins Herbal Institute v Federal Commissioner of Taxation. (1923). 32 CLR 457.

Rowland, D. (1999). Negligence, professional competence and computer systems. *Journal of Information Law and Technology, 20.* Available at http://www2.warwick.ac.uk/fac/soc/law/elj/jilt/1999_2/rowland/#fnb3

Sachs, J. (2003). Teacher professional standards: Controlling or developing teaching? *Teachers and Teaching, 9*(2), 175–186.

Senate, Employment and Training Reference Committee. (1998). *A class act.* Senate Inquiry into the Teaching Profession.

Supreme Court Act 1986 (Vic).

Teacher Education Ministerial Advisory Group. (2014, December). *Action now: Classroom ready teachers.*

Vollmer, H., & Mills, D. (Eds.). (1966). *Professionalization.* Eaglewood Cliffs: Prentice-Hall.

Weber v Land Agents Board. (1986). 40 SASR 312.

West, A., & Ylönen, A. (2010). Market-oriented school reform in England and Finland: School choice, finance and governance. *Educational Studies, 36*(1), 1–12.

Whelan, J. (2017, August 31). Doctors, lawyers and ministers all take a professional pledge: Here's why teachers should too. *The Conversation.*

10

Meeting the Challenges Facing Religious Schools: An Australian Perspective

Jacquie Seemann

10.1 Introduction: Challenges and Competing Expectations

One of the great challenges facing religious schools is balancing the competing expectations and requirements that influence the running of the school. These include:

(a) priorities of the clergy and/or the school lay leadership to have the school community consist of a high level, or even exclusively, of students and teachers of that faith;
(b) the varying expectations of parents, who might place much or little importance on the role of religion in their children's education;
(c) educational authorities, particularly government, which generally prioritise academic results, enrolment numbers, compliance and funding;
(d) discrimination laws, which prohibit discrimination on the basis of religion or on other grounds which may conflict with the priorities of the school; and

I have presented versions of the material contained in this chapter at a number of education law conferences over the past few years. I would like to thank Bridget Nunn and David Chen, both of Thomson Geer, for their invaluable assistance at different times in preparing those papers and this chapter.

J. Seemann (✉)
Thomson Geer Lawyers, Sydney, NSW, Australia
e-mail: jseemann@tglaw.com.au

K. Trimmer et al. (eds.), *The Palgrave Handbook of Education Law for Schools*,
https://doi.org/10.1007/978-3-319-77751-1_10

(e) the duty of care of schools to students and staff to protect against harassment, vilification and bullying – both at common law and under safety and discrimination legislation.

How each school approaches this challenge will largely depend on what the school is seeking to achieve from both the religious perspective and the educational perspective. For example, is the school run strictly in accordance with the teachings and doctrines of the particular religion of the school, with all members of the school community expected to support those teachings in their lives and lifestyles, or is the school less concerned with a strict application of that religion and, instead, seeking to promote broader ethical values (including diversity and equality) within a general religious framework? Are parents sending their children to the school because they want them to learn about the religion and be able to practise their religious observances freely, and thus to maintain the same faith and practices as the parents, or because they want their children to identify and strengthen connections with a faith and/or ethnic-based community, or both?

In this context, this chapter explores the extent to which religious schools in Australia are able to give effect to their religious beliefs and practices in the way they manage enrolment, staffing, the general behaviour of both students and staff, and what they teach. The chapter addresses this question by considering the parameters placed on religious schools in Australia by relevant discrimination and other laws, and some of the specific issues that arise in seeking to balance all these competing expectations. As will be seen, the rights and responsibilities of these schools are set out in a complex and inconsistent mesh of laws at Commonwealth, State and Territory levels which have been enacted over time to protect different priorities.

It is useful to start by asking what rights Australians have to religious freedoms in the first place. How does the law seek to balance those rights against other rights, like the right to be free from unreasonable discrimination in work and employment contexts, and to be kept safe at work? And how can schools shape their thoughts about these issues in light of their own priorities?

After looking at that broad conceptual framework, the chapter examines the specific issues identified. There is a comparative aspect to the discussion: the chapter considers relevant cases and legislation from a number of jurisdictions – the UK, Europe, Canada and the USA. In some cases, those jurisdictions have considered issues not yet dealt with in the Australian context; in others, there are interesting contrasts between Australian approaches and approaches overseas. It is also instructive to look at cases in an employment context but outside the area of education, and some cases where public school systems have dealt with issues of religion.

10.2 Freedom of Religion in Australia

In considering the question of religious freedom in Australia, particularly in the context of schools, the work of Carolyn Evans and her colleagues is very significant (see Evans 2009, 2012; Evans and Ujvari 2009; Evans and Gaze 2010). In short, as explained by Evans (2009, 2012), there is no clear right to freedom of religion across all jurisdictions, and a number of different international and domestic law principles need to be considered to understand the state of play.

There are a number of aspects of this issue that must be considered. To summarise Evans' characterisation of the underlying framework (from Evans (2009), sections 1, 2, 3 and 5; and Evans (2012), especially Chapters 2 and 4):

(a) there is no clear common law right to freedom of religion, and to the extent there is one, it is susceptible to being overridden by statute;
(b) Australia has signed a number of international treaties that both protect the right to freedom of religion and prohibit discrimination on the basis of religion. In particular, Article 18 of the *International Covenant on Civil and Political Rights 1976* (which is based on but extends the *United Nations' Universal Declaration of Human Rights 1948* and came into effect in 1976) states:

   1. Everyone shall have the right to freedom of thought, conscience and religion. This right shall include freedom to have or to adopt a religion or belief of his choice, and freedom, either individually or in community with others and in public or private, to manifest his religion or belief in worship, observance, practice and teaching.
   2. No one shall be subject to coercion which would impair his freedom to have or to adopt a religion or belief of his choice.
   3. Freedom to manifest one's religion or beliefs may be subject only to such limitations as are prescribed by law and are necessary to protect public safety, order, health, or morals or the fundamental rights and freedoms of others.

4. The States Parties to the present Covenant undertake to have respect for the liberty of parents and, when applicable, legal guardians to ensure the religious and moral education of their children in conformity with their own convictions.

   The later, non-binding *Declaration on the Elimination of All Forms of Intolerance and of Discrimination Based on Religion or Belief 1981* adds, in Article 5(5), the limitation that '*practices of a religion or belief in which a child is brought up must not be injurious to his physical or mental health or to his full development*'. Australia is also signatory to other international conventions that include an obligation not to discriminate on the ground of religion in implementing measures to protect other rights – see for example Article 2 of the *International Covenant on Economic, Social and Cultural Rights 1976*, which provides: '*The States Parties to the present Covenant undertake to guarantee that the rights enunciated in the present Covenant will be exercised without discrimination of any kind as to race, colour, sex, language, religion, political or other opinion, national or social origin, property, birth or other status*';

(c) however, though international law does not become part of Australian law automatically, it does create obligations that can be enforced by international tribunals, and gives rights to Australian citizens to seek assistance – for example, non-enforceable opinions of the UN Human Rights Committee. International law also influences the interpretation of our legislation and the development of common law principles. There is a common law presumption that Parliament does not intend to breach international obligations entered into by the executive (per Mason CJ and Deane J in Minister for Immigration and Ethnic Affairs v Teoh (1995) 183 CLR 273), and while this presumption can be displaced by a clear statutory intention to the contrary (per McHugh J at [33], Hayne J at [241] and Callinan J at [297–298] in Al-Kateb v Godwin (2004) 219 CLR 562), it leaves room, for example, where two interpretations of a statute are possible, to choose the one that is consistent with Australia's international obligations to protect religious freedom, International law also enables the Commonwealth government to make laws to implement treaty obligations, while requiring that those laws be soundly based on the treaties that they seek to implement. However, as set out below, Australia has done very little to implement its treaty obligations to protect religious freedom through its laws; and

(d) the Commonwealth Constitution does include a provision (section 116) that the Commonwealth Parliament must not make laws that either prohibit the free exercise of religion or establish a religion. This provision does not restrict state governments (in fact, according to Professor George Williams (2017), it was intended to leave state governments free to regulate religious affairs if they so chose); and in the case of the Commonwealth, it only refers to legislation and actions taken under legislation. The few cases that have considered s 116 over time show the courts giving a narrow interpretation of the concepts. Thus the courts have held that, to show a prohibited restriction on 'free exercise of religion', the legislation must indicate, probably on its face, a purpose to restrict religious freedom. Thus, it was not a breach of the prohibition on restricting religious freedom to require a person to train for defence work despite a religious conscientious objection; nor was a legal requirement to reveal the contents of a religious confession in breach of the section.[1]

In challenges to the funding by the Commonwealth of non-government schools including religious schools in the early 1980s, the High Court held (*Attorney-General (Vic); Ex Rel Black v Commonwealth* (1981) 146 CLR 559 (***DOGS Case***)) that – unlike the position in the USA – the Commonwealth was not 'establishing a religion' when it funded such religious institutions. While the judgments of the majority in the *DOGS Case* differed, they all essentially held that 'establishment' required some form of identification of the religion with the state, with Gibbs, Stephen and Mason JJ referring to the creation of a 'state religion' or 'state church' at [567]–[630]. Further, Australia has no national bill of rights that would create a general protection beyond what is set out above – although Victoria and the ACT have human rights Acts that include protection of freedom of religion or belief.

The question is live in Australian discourse now – in November 2016 the Minister for Foreign Affairs, the Hon Julie Bishop MP, asked the Joint Standing Committee on Foreign Affairs, Defence and Trade to inquire into and report on the status of the human right to freedom of religion or belief. Submissions were originally to close in February 2017, then on 7 August 2017, but the Committee's website says that it is still accepting submissions

[1] See Krygger v Williams (1912) 15 CLR 366; SDW v Church of Jesus Christ of Latter-Day Saints (2008) 222 FLR 84 at 94–95, Adelaide Co of Jehovah's Witnesses Inc. v Commonwealth (1943) 67 CLR 116 and Church of the New Faith v Commissioner of Payroll Tax (1983) 154 CLR 120.

(it has already received 372, at the time of writing in December 2017). In his submission, Professor George Williams (2017) of UNSW notes:

> *Australia is exceptional. Indeed, we stand alone in being the only democracy without some form of national bill of rights incorporating protection of freedom of religion. The same problem applies to a number of other rights, including those that underpin our democracy, such as freedom of speech and association. Put simply, Australia does not protect freedom of religion and other rights as is thought appropriate in every other like nation.*

It follows that religious schools must look for protection of their rights to operate as they wish to either (where relevant) through the state-specific human rights Acts and otherwise through prohibitions of discrimination based on religion – as to which see below.

10.3 Discrimination Laws

The starting point in Australian discrimination law is, generally speaking, that the law prohibits (renders unlawful) certain types of discrimination based on specific 'grounds' (or 'reasons', or 'attributes') in certain areas of activity, including employment and education. The laws generally prohibit both 'direct' and 'indirect' discrimination. Speaking very broadly, direct discrimination occurs where one person is treated less favourably than another on prohibited ground (such as race) – for example, in employment, if an applicant is rejected because of race. Indirect discrimination occurs where the imposition of a facially neutral, but unreasonable, requirement or condition disadvantages a person because of a prohibited ground – for example, in employment, if an employee with a back injury is directed to stand all day at work when this is not necessary in order to perform the inherent requirements of the position.

For reasons of space, this chapter will not analyse the theoretical basis for or model of these anti-discrimination laws in any detail. Rather, it is important to note simply that these laws do exist in part, but somewhat theoretically, to protect rights to various freedoms; but in practice they are designed more directly to avoid harm to those who experience unfair and unlawful discrimination. Such harms might include, for example, economic harm such as the loss of job and/or income; denial of the opportunity to access educational services or benefits; damage to reputation; and/or emotional and psychological pain and suffering. It is against this avoidance of harm principle that the needs and desires of religious schools are measured under discrimination laws.

10.3.1 Discrimination on the Ground of Religion

In this context, with reference to religion specifically, all jurisdictions except New South Wales, South Australia and the Commonwealth expressly prohibit discrimination on the ground of religion.[2] In South Australia, section 21 of the *Equal Opportunity Act 1984* (SA) provides some limited protection, in that it prohibits discrimination on the ground of religious dress or appearance in employment or education.

In New South Wales, section 4(1) of the *Anti-Discrimination Act 1977* (NSW) prohibits discrimination on the ground of ethno-religious origin (as part of racial discrimination). These provisions are understood to prohibit discrimination against Sikhs and Jews, and it has been held that 'ethno-religious origin' also includes being of Middle Eastern Muslim origin, though not being Muslim generally (*Haider v Combined District Radio Cabs Pty Ltd. t/as Central Coast Taxis* [2008] NSWADT 123).

At the Commonwealth level, the Australian Human Rights Commission may inquire into discrimination on the basis of religion in employment or occupation under sections 3 and 31 of the *Australian Human Rights Commission Act 1986* (Cth). However, that inquiry cannot lead to a complaint that could ultimately result in an enforceable order.

Queensland, Tasmania and Victoria also have laws that prohibit vilification of a person or group based on religion, and the Commonwealth *Racial Discrimination Act 1975* and NSW *Anti-Discrimination Act 1977* both prohibit vilification based on race – which again includes ethnicity. There are of course interesting questions as to where genuine criticism of a religion stops and vilification, or incitement to hatred and violence, starts.[3]

10.3.2 Other Grounds

Other prohibited grounds of discrimination that are sometimes relevant to religious schools include:

(a) sex and gender identity/status;
(b) sexuality or sexual orientation; and
(c) marital or relationship status.

---

[2] See Discrimination Act 1991 (ACT) s 11 (in employment); Anti-Discrimination Act 1992 (NT) s 19(m); Anti-Discrimination Act 1991 (Qld) s7(i); Equal Opportunity Act 2010 (Vic) s 6(n); Equal Opportunity Act 1984 (WA) Part IV; Anti-Discrimination Act 1998 (Tas) ss 16(o) and (p).

[3] See Sutherland Shire Council v Folkes [2015] FCA 1288; Islamic Council of Victoria v Catch the Fire Ministries Inc. [2004] VCAT 2510 – discussed in more detail below.

Some religions have strong opinions about the way these issues should be treated – and those opinions do not always accord with the principle that Australian citizens should not be discriminated against on these grounds. Often, there are contrary opinions within religions or at least their denominations. All these issues play out in the way religious schools respond to these issues.

10.3.3 Workplace Laws

The *Fair Work Act 2009* (Cth) (**FW Act**), also prohibits an employer from taking 'adverse action' (including refusing to employ a person, or dismissing the person) against an employee or prospective employee because of the person's religion, sex, sexual orientation or marital status (s 351). This provision does not render unlawful any action that is not unlawful under anti-discrimination law in force in the place where action is taken (s 351(2)(a)). Accordingly, these provisions have the effect of generally mirroring anti-discrimination laws in the relevant jurisdiction, although the overlap between them can be complicated and the FW Act can provide additional remedies for people in those jurisdictions where discrimination on the ground of religion is prohibited.

10.3.4 Overview of Exemptions

All jurisdictions provide some exemptions that allow religious institutions to act in ways that would otherwise be unlawful discrimination.

There is a general exemption that appears in slightly different forms in all jurisdictions. For example, section 56 of the NSW *Anti-Discrimination Act 1977* provides:

Nothing in this Act affects:

(a) the ordination or appointment of priests, ministers of religion or members of any religious order,
(b) the training or education of persons seeking ordination or appointment as priests, ministers of religion or members of a religious order,
(c) the appointment of any other person in any capacity by a body established to propagate religion, or
(d) any other act or practice of a body established to propagate religion that conforms to the doctrines of that religion or is necessary to avoid injury to the religious susceptibilities of the adherents of that religion.

Other jurisdictions refer to 'religious bodies' and provide similar exemptions.[4]

This broad exemption may be relevant to schools run directly by churches but may not extend to incorporated organisations set up to run schools that are separate from those schools. However, to attract the exemption, the school would generally still need to show that it was set up to 'propagate religion'. It might be relevant, for this purpose, to check the objects of a school as set out in its Constitution – and these documents are often old and in need of reworking for a number of reasons, one of which may be that the Constitution might not refer to religion in a way consistent with the school's current operation.

However, a variety of additional exemptions exist in the various jurisdictions that are also of relevance to actions by religious schools. New South Wales has the broadest of these exemptions: it exempts all private educational authorities in relation to many grounds of discrimination. Other jurisdictions contain narrower exemptions for religious educational authorities engaging in discrimination on particular grounds where the discriminatory action, for example:

(a) conforms to the doctrines, tenets or beliefs of the religion of the school; or
(b) is necessary to avoid injury to the religious susceptibilities of adherents of that religion.

These exemptions are identified throughout the paper where relevant.[5]

The exemptions are frequently the subject of public debate, and there have been several parliamentary inquiries in various jurisdictions, and several proposals for their removal.[6] Clearly, Australians are not united in their views on how religious bodies should be allowed to conduct themselves as employers and educators, and the extent to which they should be permitted to discriminate on various grounds.

---

[4] See similar provisions in Sex Discrimination Act 1984 (Cth) ss 37(a)–(c); Discrimination Act 1991 (ACT) ss 32(a)–(c); Anti-Discrimination Act 1992 (NT) s 51(a)–(c); Anti-Discrimination Act 1977 (NSW) s 56(a) (c); Anti-Discrimination Act 1991 (Qld) ss 109(1)(a)–(c); Equal Opportunity Act 1984 (SA) ss 50(1)(a)–(ba); Equal Opportunity Act 2010 (Vic) s 82; Equal Opportunity Act 1984 (WA) s 72(a)–(c); Anti-Discrimination Act 1998 (Tas) s 52.

[5] For a detailed comparison of the exemptions across Australian jurisdictions see Walsh, G, 'The right to equality and the employment decisions of religious schools', (2014) 16 *The University of Notre Dame Australia Law Review,* 107–144.

[6] See most recently submissions to Conifer (2017); the Inquiry into the Status of the Human Right to Freedom of Religion or Belief (2017); Inquiry into the Commonwealth Government's exposure draft of the Marriage Amendment (Same-Sex Marriage) Bill (2017); and in years gone by proposals for reform advocated by the Greens, eg in 2016.

10.4 Other Relevant Laws

In navigating their religious way, schools also need to take into account various other sources of law and regulation.

10.4.1 Safety Legislation and Duty of Care

Work health and safety laws place a duty on schools to ensure, so far as is reasonably practicable, the health and safety of all persons who may be affected by the school's undertaking, including prospective and current staff and students.[7]

Schools also owe students and staff a duty of care at common law; that is, a duty to ensure that – if there is a significant risk of foreseeable injury to them – reasonable care is taken to avoid that injury. Because of the special nature of the school/student relationship, the duty in that case is similar, though not identical, to the duty that parents have to their children.

Both of these types of duties include an obligation to take reasonable steps to prevent students and staff from suffering physical or psychological harm as a result of unlawful discrimination, including harassment, or bullying.

The broader impact of failing to discharge this duty may be considerable – in the current climate, schools need to be concerned about the alienation of some students due to their sexuality, gender identity or mental health issues, for example. For a further exploration of this issue, see David Ford's paper, *Lesbian, Gay, Bisexual, Transgender and Intersex Students* (Ford 2016).

10.4.2 Educational Regulation

Education legislation in various states prescribes minimum curricula for all schools, and certain additional requirements for non-government schools that wish to be accredited for the purpose of academic achievements such as the Higher School Certificate (in NSW) and its various equivalents.[8] The requirements of these regulations may conflict with the religious aims of schools in terms of the amount of religious studies that they wish to provide and/or the

---

[7] See Work Health and Safety Act 2011 (ACT) s 19; Work Health and Safety Act 2011 (Cth) s 19; Work Health and Safety Act 2011 (Qld) s 19; Work Health and Safety Act 2011 (NSW) s 19; Work Health and Safety Act 2012 (SA) s 19; Work Health and Safety Act 2012 (Tas) s 19; Occupational Safety and Health Act 1984 (WA) ss 19 and 21(2); Occupational Health and Safety Act 2004 (Vic) ss 21 and 23.

[8] See for example Education Act 1990 (NSW) ss 8 and 10; Education and Training Reform Act 2006 (Vic) s 4.3.1(6)(b)(i) and Education and Training Reform Regulations 2007 (Vic) sch2 item 6.

way they wish certain subject areas to be taught. There is scope to seek exemptions from or modifications to minimum curriculum requirements[9] and in some cases the legislation specifically contemplates this occurring to make a syllabus compatible with a school's religious outlook.[10]

10.4.3 So How Does It All Work?

Perhaps not surprisingly, the variety of approaches at law and the interplay between laws leaves some of those charged with the responsibility of running religious schools somewhat confused. In research conducted by Evans and Gaze (2010), 19 out of 27 school principals interviewed said that they knew and understood their legal obligations, but their understanding was not always accurate; seven acknowledged some uncertainty or confusion about those obligations; and most generally approached the issues of religion, sexuality and marital status with caution.

In this context, the remainder of this paper considers how these principles and laws are enmeshed, and how they have played out – or might play out – in real situations faced by religious schools.

10.5 Religion and the Enrolment Process: Who Makes the Cut, and How May Different Students Be Treated?

As Evans and Gaze note (2010, p. 408), schools are seen by many not simply as a workplace or place of learning but also a community and, from this perspective, enrolment policies become important in deciding who makes up the community and the community's resulting values. The expectation of parents may be that their children will be attending a school with children from families of the same faith. Particularly for families of minority group religions, this may be important to enable children to experience some feeling of belonging, or of being part of a majority, which they do not experience in the wider world where they are a member of an identifiable minority. In this context, schools might choose to have an exclusive faith-based (or religious identity-based) enrolment policy, or a policy that prefers adherents of a particular religion.

---

[9] See for example Education and Training Reform Regulations 2007 (Vic) r 52.

[10] See for example, *Education Act 1990* (NSW) ss 8(3) and 10(3).

Other schools might choose an open enrolment policy which results in a religiously diverse student group. This brings its own challenges. For example, how does a school avoid segregation and exclusion of non-religious students or students of another religion – if for example the faith of the school strictly prohibits those students from participating in the religious activities of the school? Further, schools may find that lessons involving teachings of their faith are subject to greater scrutiny and resistance from students who do not adhere to that religion, which can create difficulty and disruption in the classroom.

In addition to balancing these challenges, schools must also ensure that their enrolment policies do not breach discrimination laws.

10.5.1 Relevant Exemptions

A number of jurisdictions contain specific exemptions for applications for admission to any school, college or institution under the direction or control of a religious body.[11]

This includes discrimination on the ground of religion and by providing for a single sex school.

10.5.2 Admission Based on Religion

For example, the *Discrimination Act 1991* (ACT) does not render unlawful the refusal by a religious educational institution of a person's application for admission as a student on the ground of religion, if that institution is conducted solely for students having a religious conviction other than that of the applicant (section 46).

Even where there is no specific exemption (such as in NSW), it is generally understood that discrimination on the ground of religion in terms of admission is permissible – in the case of NSW, because the State does not prohibit discriminating on the ground of religion in the first place.

However, as a case from the UK shows, there is an alternative argument that could apply in NSW – and potentially also in jurisdictions with a specific exemption.

[11] See Sex Discrimination Act 1984 (Cth) s 38(3); Anti-Discrimination Act 1992 (NT) s 30(2); Anti-Discrimination Act 1991 (Qld) s 41; Equal Opportunity Act 2010 (Vic) ss 82 and 83; Equal Opportunity Act 1984 (WA) s 73(3); Anti-Discrimination Act 1998 (Tas) s 51A; Discrimination Act 1991 (ACT) s 46.

In R (on the application of E) (Respondent) v The Governing Body of JFS and the Admissions Appeal Panel of JFS and others (Appellants) [2009] UKSC 15, the British Supreme Court ruled that a Jewish school discriminated unlawfully against a boy on the ground of race by denying him admission because his mother is Jewish by conversion, not by birth (i.e. he was not 'ethnically' Jewish). The Jews' Free School (**JFS**), a secondary school in London, is designated as a Jewish faith school. JFS gave precedence in admission to those children recognised as Jewish by the Office of the Chief Rabbi of the United Hebrew Congregation of the Commonwealth (**OCR**). The OCR only recognises a person as Jewish if that person is descended in the matrilineal line from a woman whom the OCR would recognise as Jewish or if he or she has undertaken a qualifying course of Orthodox conversion.

Both the father and his child in this case were practising Conservative (non-Orthodox) Jews. The mother was of Italian and Catholic origin and converted to Judaism under the auspices of a non-Orthodox synagogue – so her conversion was not recognised by the OCR. The child's application for admission to JFS was rejected as he did not satisfy the OCR requirement of matrilineal descent. The father challenged the admissions policy of JFS as directly discriminating against his child on grounds of his ethnic origins contrary to section 1(1)(a) of the *Race Relations Act 1976* (UK).

The majority found that the policy was unlawful direct discrimination, because the matrilineal test is a test of ethnic origin – and discrimination that is based upon that test is discrimination on racial grounds under the Act, rather than religion. The motive for the discrimination and/or the reason why the discriminator considered the victim's ethnic origins significant is irrelevant. Overall, this decision does not mean that no Jewish faith school can ever give preference to Jewish children. However, eligibility must depend on religion, not on ethnicity and while it may be arguable that an explicit exemption should be provided in order to allow Jewish faith schools to grant priority in admissions on the basis of matrilineal descent, formulating such an exemption is a matter for Parliament (paragraphs [69]–[70] in the *JFS Case* per Hale LJ).

By contrast, the minority held that there was no unlawful direct discrimination, but was divided on whether JFS had unlawfully discriminated against the applicant indirectly:

(a) in terms of direct discrimination, the minority said that to determine the ground on which JFS refused the child's admission, the Court should adopt a subjective approach which takes account of the motive and intention of JFS, the OCR and the Chief Rabbi; and those parties were subjectively concerned solely with the child's religious status, as determined by

Jewish religious law. In the minority's view, the availability of conversion demonstrates that the test applied is inherently of a religious rather than racial character; and

(b) on unlawful indirect discrimination:

   i. Lords Hope and Walker found that children who were not of Jewish ethnic origin in the matrilineal line were placed at a disadvantage by JFS's admission policy compared to those who did possess the requisite ethnic origins, but that this policy pursued the legitimate aim of educating those regarded as Jewish by the OCR within an educational environment espousing and practising the tenets of Orthodox Judaism. However, the failure of JFS to consider an alternative, potentially less discriminatory, admission policy means that the Court cannot find that the means which JFS employed were proportionate – i.e. there was unlawful indirect discrimination; however,
   ii. Lords Rodger and Brown found that the objective pursued by JFS's admission policy – educating children recognised by the OCR as Jewish – was irreconcilable with any approach that would give precedence to children not recognised as Jewish by the OCR in preference to children who were so recognised. The policy was a rational way of giving effect to the legitimate aim pursued and was not disproportionate – i.e. there was no unlawful indirect discrimination.

The case has been applied and referred to several times, but has never progressed the discussion on a relevant issue.[12]

By contrast, in Western Australia, in the earlier case *Goldberg v Korsunski Carmel School* [2000] EOC 93–074 found that a policy of the same kind was not unlawful discrimination on the ground of race. In that case, an Orthodox Jewish school was established to provide Orthodox education to Orthodox Jews (that is, those considered Jewish according to Halacha, the Orthodox Jewish law). Students who were not Halachic Jews were permitted to enrol subject to the approval of the Rabbi, on the basis that the family would support the school ethos and to the requirement that they could not participate in certain areas of school life.

---

[12] See Pothecary Witham Weld (A Firm) and Another v Bullimore [2010] UKEAT 0158_09_2903; HM Land Registry v Grant EAT [2010] UKEAT 0232_09_1504; Johns and Another, Regina (on The Application of) v Derby City Council and Another [2011] EWHC 375 (Admin); Bull and Another v Hall and Another [2013] UKSC 73; HM Chief Inspector of Education, Children's Services and Skills v The Interim Executive Board of Al-Hijrah School [2017] EWCA Civ 1426.

As in the *JFS Case*, the mother of the student in this case was not considered to be Halachically Jewish, which meant that the student was not Halachically Jewish. This meant that the student's enrolment would be subject to restrictions. The father argued that this was unlawful discrimination against non-Orthodox Jews on the grounds of religious conviction and race.

It was held that although the school had discriminated against the student on religious grounds, the discrimination was lawful because the school had acted in good faith 'in favour of the adherents of that religion or creed generally' and had not acted in a manner that discriminated against a particular class or group who were not adherents of that religion or creed (section 73(3) of the *Equal Opportunity Act 1984* (WA)). The claim regarding racial discrimination was also dismissed because the restrictions imposed on the student – including the activities in which he could participate at the school – were only due to theological, not racial, considerations.

Only one case, *Miller v Wertheim* [2001] FMCA 103, has applied *Goldberg*, and again this did not progress the discussion of relevant principles. The questions raised have since been only considered in the appeal decision *Miller v Wertheim* [2004] FCA 988, where Beaumont J upheld the first instance judgment and dismissed the appeal.

10.5.3 Treatment of Students Based on Sex

It is accepted in all Australian jurisdictions that some schools are set up only to educate students of one sex. However, how students are treated based on their sex/gender identity is potentially a controversial issue.

One UK case that cites the *JFS Case*, but makes points relevant to the issue of sex/gender rather than race in the context of religion, is *HM Chief Inspector of Education, Children's Services and Skills v The Interim Executive Board of Al-Hijrah School* [2017] EWCA Civ 1426, on appeal from a single judge of the High Court. The case concerned a report by the Chief Inspector of Education on an Islamic school, stating that the school was 'inadequate' and was discriminating unlawfully because, while it admitted both boys and girls, it had a policy (from the age of 9) of segregating them for all purposes within the school. Effectively, the school operated as if it were two single sex schools on one site – with both girls and boys being taught the same subjects and to the same standard. At issue was whether the students suffered educationally from the restriction on social interaction.

At first instance, the Court held that, while the denial of the opportunity to interact and socialise with the opposite sex might be seen as a 'detriment', it did not amount to 'less favourable treatment' under sections 13(1) and 23(1) of the *Equality Act 2010* (UK) (**EA**) because the treatment of both sexes was equivalent in nature and character, with equivalent consequences for both sexes. The Court of Appeal overturned this decision, the majority holding that:

(a) the school's policy of segregation was less favourable treatment for both male and female students by reason of their sex. It was incorrect to view each sex as a group, as section 13 of the EA specifies direct discrimination by reference to a 'person' and not to a 'group'. Each girl and boy is entitled, as an individual, to freedom from direct discrimination. Viewed from the perspective of an individual pupil, both the girl and the boy were treated less favourably than each other in being prevented from socialising with a student of the opposite sex – and the Inspector could reasonably take the view that this was a detriment, including because some of the students regarded it as such;
(b) the existence in the EA of a specific exception for single-sex schools but not for schools of this type indicates that Parliament did not intend to allow for segregation in notionally co-educational schools;
(c) the school's motivation for discrimination was also irrelevant, even though that motivation was adherence to what the school regarded as the applicable tenets of Islam;
(d) also irrelevant was parental choice of the school precisely because of the segregation policy: while the *Education Act 1996* required schools to have regard to the general principles that pupils are to be educated in accordance with their parents' wishes, this could not negate the statutory right of a child to be educated in a non-discriminatory manner; and
(e) insufficient evidence had been brought in the case to support the propositions that the segregation policy helped reinforce the power imbalance of women in society, or that the very fact of segregation could not be separated from deep-seated cultural and historical perspectives as to the inferiority of the female sex. Gloster LJ, dissenting, found that the evidence was sufficient to establish these propositions; she relied on evidence of school library books which were derogatory towards women; excerpts from work written by children at the school, and the fact that girls had to wait one hour longer than boys for their lunch break.

While there are no similar cases in Australia, the *Al-Hijrah School Case* prompts interesting consideration about how treatment of boys and girls, including in single-sex schools, and for that matter treatment of transgender students, by religious schools might fall foul of discrimination law prohibitions.

10.6 Staff and Their Faith: The Relevance of Religion in the Recruitment Process

Staff at any school are required to act as role models for their students. In religious schools, this often means modelling the religious values and beliefs of the school and the way of life that flows from those values and beliefs.

The position is put strongly by Kevin Donnelly (2013), director of the Melbourne-based Education Standards Institute, as follows:

> *Faith-based schools, by their very nature, are there to uphold and teach the spiritual values and morality embodied in their religion. If freedom of religion is to have any meaning, then it follows that schools should have the power to discriminate in relation to who they enrol and who they employ.*
>
> *… As publicly stated by the Catholic Education Commission of Victoria: 'Our schools promote a particular view of the person, the community, the nation and the world centred on the person and teachings of Jesus Christ, and they form an integral part of the church community in which all generations live, worship and grow together.'*
>
> *Those seeking to work or those seeking to enrol children in such schools can be in no doubt as to the religious nature of such schools and that there is a requirement, as members of the school community, to live according to the tenets on which the school is based.*
>
> *And it is wrong to argue that the freedom to discriminate should apply to only those teaching religious instruction in faith-based schools…*
>
> *All subjects, as well as what is known as the hidden curriculum involving a school's institutional practices and culture, contribute to … moral development. It is also true that teachers, regardless of their subject expertise, are role models and can have a significant and lasting impact on their students.*

Clearly, on a basis such as this, schools often prefer to employ staff of the same faith as the school; but sometimes this is simply not possible. As the Victorian Independent Education Union (2009, p. 3) reported to a parliamentary committee:

> *[c]lose to 29,000 teachers work in Victorian non-government schools, and some 13,000 are employed in various support roles. We are looking at a workforce of about 42,000. Due to the sheer amount of staff needed, it is simply not possible to employ those staff along denominational lines only … It is an undisputed fact that there is a diverse range of employees working in schools – staff in de facto relationships, non-Jewish staff working for Jewish school, non-Catholics working in Catholic schools, and non-Christians working in Christian schools.*

In other cases, schools do not wish to discriminate on the basis of either faith or lifestyle – particularly when staff are not engaged in teaching religious studies. Thus, in surveying the attitudes and practices of schools, Evans and Gaze (2010, p. 411) found that

> *[s]everal of the schools in the sample said that they celebrated diversity, including with respect to sexuality, and thus a staff member was welcome if they were the best qualified person for the job. There was no attempt by the school to hide the fact of that diversity. In one case this extended to a school chaplain who was gay, a fact which was known to the school community. While a couple of families left the school in protest at this development, the overwhelming majority of families were supportive — in part because they had chosen this school because of its liberal approach to religious issues.*

If their recruitment practices are more open or diverse, schools sometimes compensate for this by making staff not of the faith of the school conform to some of the school religion's practices. One example is Muslim schools requiring non-Muslim female teachers to wear a headscarf, in order to create 'an Islamic environment' which makes people 'feel comfortable' according to the President of the Council of Islamic Schools (Bachelard 2008).

10.6.1 Relevant Exemptions

A number of jurisdictions contain specific exemptions for employment of persons in any school, college or institution under the direction or control of a religious body.

For example, the *Discrimination Act 1991* (ACT) does not render unlawful discrimination on the ground of religious conviction by an educational authority in relation to employment or work in an educational institution conducted by the authority if the duties of the employment or work involve, or would involve, the participation by the employee or worker in the teaching, observance or practice of the relevant religion (section 44).[13] Also, the FW Act provisions, ss 351(2)(b)–(c), prohibiting adverse action on the basis of religion do not apply if the discrimination is:

[13] See similar provisions in Anti-Discrimination Act 1992 pari (NT) s 37A; Anti-Discrimination Act 1991 (Qld) ss 25(2) and 25(3); Anti-Discrimination Act 1998 (Tas) s 51(2); Equal Opportunity Act 2010 (Vic) ss 82 and 83; Equal Opportunity Act 1984 (WA) ss 73(1) and 73(2); Australian Human Rights Commission Act 1986 (Cth) s 3. There are no equivalent provisions in the other jurisdictions.

(b) taken because of the inherent requirements of the particular position concerned; or
(c) if the action is taken against a staff member of an institution conducted in accordance with the doctrines, tenets, beliefs or teachings of a particular religion or creed – taken:

 i. in good faith; and
 ii. to avoid injury to the religious susceptibilities of adherents of that religion or creed.

10.6.2 Cases

There are surprisingly few decided cases in this area, some under workplace laws and some under discrimination laws. The cases generally deal more with lifestyle issues, although there are at least some media reports of cases in which the issue is faith itself.

10.6.2.1 United Kingdom

In *Jones v Lee and Guilding* [1980] ICR 310, a principal was summarily dismissed from an English Catholic school for getting a divorce and remarrying an assistant teacher. The Court held that the summary dismissal was invalid.

In *De Groen v Gan Menachem Hendon Limited* 3347281/2016 (1 December 2017), a teacher was dismissed from a private ultra-Orthodox Jewish nursery school after concerned parents found out at a barbeque gathering that she was living with her boyfriend, and complained to the school. In this case, the nursery school said that premarital cohabitation was contrary to Jewish beliefs; the teacher considered herself a practising Jew but living with her boyfriend was not contrary to her belief system. The Employment Tribunal held that the teacher was directly discriminated against by reason of her sex and religion and/or beliefs, indirectly discriminated against on the ground of religion and/or beliefs and was also harassed on the grounds of sex and religious belief by the school. Notably, in relation to direct discrimination, it was suggested by the school that 'holding a religious belief but not adhering to a particular manifestation of it is not an absence of religion or belief within the meaning of the Act' – and accordingly that the teacher was not protected. The Tribunal disagreed:

> [D]iscrimination in relation to a manifestation of a belief (or lack of belief) will be direct discrimination where the detrimental treatment is done because of the manifestation of that belief (or lack of belief). (at [67])

The case was particularly interesting precisely because it illustrates the impact of differences of belief within religious denominations or groups – see commentary at [68]. Ultimately, the nursery school failed because it had not established, based on religious belief, that it was a genuine occupational requirement that the teacher comply with particular religious principles and not cohabit with her boyfriend – this had not been spelt out, and only a few parents (the parents themselves being from a variety of religious backgrounds) objected.

10.6.2.2 Australia

Similarly, in Australia, in *Thompson v Catholic College, Wodonga* [1988] EOC 92–217, a teacher was dismissed for being an unmarried mother living in a de facto relationship. On hearing her complaint under the *Sex Discrimination Act 1984* (Cth), the tribunal held that it was never made clear at the time of employment, nor would a reasonable person have been aware, that 'detailed conditions of lifestyle' would be demanded of the teacher. Hence, the religious exemption to the SDA did not apply. The teacher was awarded compensation for unfair dismissal, though not reinstatement.

In *Griffin v The Catholic Education Office* [1998] EOC 92–928, Ms. Griffin brought a complaint of homosexuality discrimination under relatively toothless provisions of the then *Human Rights and Equal Opportunity Commission Act 1986* (Cth). These provisions allow a declaration to be made that there has been discrimination, but there is no enforceable remedy. Presumably Ms. Griffin used the HREOC Act because (being in NSW) she could not complain of homosexuality discrimination by a private school under the *Anti-Discrimination Act 1977* (NSW). Ms. Griffin had applied to be a teacher in a Catholic school. Her application was refused by the Catholic Education Office (**CEO**) of the Archdiocese of Sydney and Ms. Griffin was unable to teach in any CEO schools in Sydney. The CEO's reasons for refusal were because of Ms. Griffin's 'high profile as a co-convenor of the Gay and Lesbian Teachers and Students Association (**GALTSA**) and her public statements on lesbian lifestyles', and that the discrimination was warranted due to the inherent requirements of the position: teachers were required not only to teach but to minister the Catholic faith, and even if Ms. Griffin supported Catholic principles in words, her conduct/lifestyle was inconsistent with it.

The Commission found that Ms. Griffin had suffered discrimination on the ground of sexuality. This hinged on the findings that there was no evidence that the CEO knew of Ms. Griffin's personal lifestyle or that Ms. Griffin acknowledged that she was a lesbian or advocated/engaged in homosexual activity. GALTSA did not promote homosexual activity – it only provided support for gay and lesbian teachers and students; Ms. Griffin did not advocate homosexual practices contrary to Catholic teachings, and Ms. Griffin only advocated against discrimination and violence against homosexuals, which is consistent with Catholic teachings. Religious institutions are also not entitled to and cannot legitimately seek exemption from the requirements of human rights law beyond that necessary to uphold the values and teachings of the particular religion. Where exemptions apply to religious institutions, the discrimination must be in good faith to avoid injury to the religious susceptibilities of members of that religion. While the private conduct of a teacher might attract disapproval, this is not necessarily injurious to religious susceptibilities.

Media reports have also referred to a number of Australian cases that have not reached hearing: for example, a primary school teacher at a Catholic school in Victoria was advised that her contract would not be renewed when she became pregnant from a non-marital relationship. The school did renew her contract after she complained under Victorian discrimination legislation, on condition that she sign an agreement not to promote her lifestyle (Fyfe 2009). Another primary school teacher at a Christian school was dismissed when she became pregnant from a non-marital relationship in violation of the school's lifestyle agreement (Jabour 2012). In another example, a Christian school refused to provide a Muslim woman training to be a teacher with a placement on the grounds that her religious beliefs were incompatible with the Christian commitments of the school – a result that was particularly disappointing to the applicant as the school was the closest to her home and taught subjects in which she had a particular interest (Tomazin 2009).

10.7 Navigating Religious Requirement and Custom Within the School Gates

Religion is inherently about action and custom as well as faith. Two areas in which this results in an interesting balancing process, navigating between religious freedom and other rights, are the type of dress and symbols that are worn, and the treatment of gay, lesbian and transgender students.

10.7.1 Religious Dress or Symbols: Staff

There are no relevant cases involving religious dress or symbols worn by staff of religious schools in Australia.

Looking abroad, two recent cases from the European Court of Justice, although they do not involve schools, give insight into how the issue of religious dress at work is currently being approached in Europe.

In *Achbita & Anor v G4S Secure Solutions NV* [2016] EUECJ C-157/15, Samira Achbita worked as a receptionist for the Belgian branch of G4S. She decided to start wearing a headscarf at work after three years. G4S advised her that she had broken unwritten policies prohibiting religious symbols. G4S then instated a written policy stating 'employees are prohibited in the workplace from wearing any visible signs of their political, philosophical or religious beliefs and/or from engaging in any observance of such beliefs.' When Ms. Achbita continued to insist on her wish to wear a headscarf her employment was terminated. The Court was only referred the question of whether G4S's policy directly discriminated against Ms. Achbita. On this question, the Court held G4S's policy was applied equally to all staff and therefore, did not directly discriminate against Ms. Achbita.

On the issue of indirect discrimination, the Court observed that it was open to find that the policy was capable of placing persons adhering to a particular religion or belief at a particular advantage, by comparison to other employees. However, this will not amount to unlawful indirect discrimination if the policy is objectively justified by a legitimate aim and if the means of achieving that aim are appropriate and necessary. The desire to display, in relations with both public and private sector customers, a policy of political, philosophical or religious neutrality must be considered legitimate, particularly if only applied to those workers who are required to come into contact with the employer's customers. The fact that workers are prohibited from visibly wearing signs of political, philosophical or religious beliefs is appropriate for the purpose of ensuring that a policy of neutrality is properly applied, provided that policy is genuinely pursued in a consistent and systematic manner. If the policy covered only G4S workers who interacted with customers, the prohibition must be considered strictly necessary for the purpose of achieving the aim pursued.

Similarly, but with a potentially different result, in *Bougnaoui v Micropole Univers SA* (2015) C-188/15, Asma Bougnaoui worked as a design engineer at IT consultancy firm, Micropole. Her employment was terminated after a customer complained that his staff had been 'embarrassed' by her headscarf while she was on their premises to give advice. She had been told before taking the job that wearing a headscarf might pose problems for the company's customers.

The Court was asked to determine whether the willingness of an employer to take account of the wishes of a customer not to have that employer's services provided by a worker wearing an Islamic headscarf constituted 'a genuine and determining occupational requirement' which would provide an exemption to relevant discrimination laws. The Court found that:

(a) it was necessary to ascertain whether Ms. Bougnaoui's dismissal was based on non-compliance with a rule in force that prohibited the wearing of any visible sign of political, philosophical or religious beliefs. If so, the findings and reasoning in the *Achbita Case* should be applied. If, however, the dismissal was not based on such an internal rule, then it was necessary to consider whether the willingness of an employer to take account of a customer's wish not to have services provided by a worker who, like Ms. Bougnaoui, has been assigned to that customer by the employer and who wears an Islamic headscarf constituted a genuine and determining occupational (and therefore fell within the relevant exemption);
(b) the *Achbita Case* is also relevant if a 'genuine and determining occupational requirement' refers to a requirement that is objectively dictated by the nature of the occupational activities concerned or of the context in which they are carried out. It cannot, however, cover subjective considerations, such as the willingness of the employer to take account of the particular wishes of the customer; and
(c) the willingness of an employer to take account of the wishes of a customer no longer to have the services of that employer provided by a worker wearing an Islamic headscarf cannot be considered a genuine and determining occupational requirement within the meaning of that provision.

The case was referred back to the French court for reconsideration based on these principles.

These rulings by the ECJ have been predicted to fundamentally change how some courts will assess similar cases, because since 2002 the assumption has been that religious symbols could only be barred from the workplace on safety grounds; and some experts have opined that the ruling seems to conflict with European Court of Human Rights rulings that allowed crosses to be worn at work, on the basis that sometimes wearing religious symbols is a manifestation of the right to freedom of religion. Note that the ECJ is the court of the European Union, while the ECHR is the high court of the 47-member Council of Europe. Not surprisingly, the rulings have been welcomed by the nationalist right across Europe, and lamented by religious bodies (Rankin and Oltermann 2017).

The reportage on the new European rulings does not seem to consider two important arguments:

(a) there is a fundamental difference between religious symbols that are worn as a matter of choice (such as crosses) and religious dress that religious adherents believe they are mandated to wear (such as some items of Islamic and Jewish Orthodox dress); and
(b) it may be reasonable to have policies that prohibit dress practices that are a matter of choice, but not those that are compulsory for the employee as a matter of religious faith or law;

and other than the type of non-political/secular image that the employer in these cases wished to project, the cases do not seem to consider the nature of the work being done by the employees, or the impact of the dress in question on that work.

By way of comparison, consider the approach taken in the earlier UK case of *Azmi v Kirklees Metropolitan Borough Council* [2007] UKEA/0009/07. Ms. Azmi was employed as a teaching assistant for children from minority ethnic backgrounds in a Church of England school 'controlled' by the Council. The school's population was 92% Muslim, most from minority ethnic backgrounds, and 25 out of 70 staff were Muslim, minority or both, and many wore hijab (traditional head coverings). Ms. Azmi, a devout Muslim aged 22, wanted to wear a veil – showing only her eyes – when in the presence of men, including male teachers whom she assisted. She was suspended for refusing an instruction not to wear her veil when in class. This direction was only given after much consultation, including observation of Ms. Azmi's teaching both with and without her veil.

The UK Employment Tribunal held that this was not direct discrimination on the grounds of religion or belief, but was indirect discrimination on that ground – because anyone who wished to cover their face while teaching would have been treated the same way, regardless of religion. However, the direction was held to be lawful as it was proportionate in support of a legitimate aim (as required by the relevant UK law). The UK Employment Appeal Tribunal upheld this finding. The legitimate aim was to raise the educational achievements of children in the school, in particular the support given to targeted pupils from minority ethnic backgrounds for whom English was a second or additional language. The instruction was regarded as proportionate because:

(a) Ms. Azmi was only required to be unveiled whilst she was teaching the children – she was free to wear the veil at all other times, and

(b) the head teacher and other teachers had observed her teaching with the veil and concluded that it impaired her communication with the children. The school, supported by the local education authority, gave the direction because it said she was far less effective teaching language while veiled, as (amongst other things) students needed to see her facial expression.

The decision did not criticise the school for also directing that, while Ms. Azmi could continue to wear hijab and a jabbah (long dress), she needed to ensure that the length of the jabbah did not compromise her safety – particularly when she was wearing heels under it.

The case is also interesting because of reference made to Ms. Azmi's particular belief that she must be veiled – which clearly was not a belief necessarily shared by all the Muslim women around her. This points to possible ethnic differentiation between Muslims, which creates interesting further legal questions.

10.7.2 Religious Dress or Symbols: Students

Similar ideas emerged in a different UK case, also in 2007: the *Denbigh High Case, R (SB) v Governors of Denbigh High School* [2007] 1 AC 100, in which the House of Lords upheld the uniform policy of a public school which had consulted widely with the local Muslim community, and had developed a version of the school uniform incorporating elements of Muslim clothing which satisfied most Muslims in the community: a shalwar kameeze, which is a combination of a long loose top and pants underneath. The complainant was a student who had accepted the policy for two years, but then refused to wear the uniform and began wearing a different type of clothing that she believed was religiously required of her: a jilbab – a long dress and coat combination. While the Court of Appeal found against the school, the House of Lords overturned the decision and found that the policy did not breach the *Human Rights Act 1998* (UK). Their Lordships noted that this was not a judgment about every restriction on religious clothing in schools but rather a case concerning 'a particular pupil and a particular school in a particular place at a particular time.' Relevant factors included that the student knew about the uniform when she joined the school; that she had other schools available to her where she could wear a jilbab; the trouble that the school had taken to consult about and develop a uniform that was respectful of Muslim requirements; the evidence that the uniform helped to promote cohesion and contributed to academic performance at the school, and the concerns that some students had expressed that they would be pressured into wearing a jilbab if the school permitted it to be worn as uniform.

The reasoning in the *Denbigh High Case* was subsequently applied in *R (on the application of Watkins-Singh) v Aberdare Girls' High School Governors* [2008] EWHC 1865, to disallow a school from prohibiting a Sikh student from wearing a kara (a small bangle that is religiously significant). By comparison, in *R (on the application of Playfoot) v Governing Body of Millais School* [2007] HRLR 34, a 'no jewellery rule' was permitted to be applied to a girl who wanted to wear a 'Silver Ring Thing purity ring' as a symbol of her decision to remain a virgin until marriage due to her Christian beliefs. These cases seem to acknowledge the significance of the religious obligation in each instance.

Using similar principles in a different context, in *Multani v Commission Scolaire Marguerite-Bourgeoys* [2006] 1 SCR 256, the Canadian Supreme Court found against a school that prohibited a Sikh schoolboy from attending school wearing a kirpan (a ceremonial dagger) which breached the policy against weapons and dangerous objects in schools. While the school and the student's parents agreed on an accommodation that would allow the boy to carry the kirpan if it was sealed and sewn up inside his clothes, this agreement was rejected by the school's governing board and, on appeal, by the relevant commission, which required him to wear a kirpan made of a substance other than metal. The boy refused to do so and eventually left the school. The Court found the policy to be an interference with religious liberty; and one that was not justified by the legitimate object of maintaining a reasonable standard of safety in schools, given that there was no evidence of a kirpan being used as a weapon in the 100 years that Sikh children had been attending schools in Canada, the likelihood of it being used as a weapon under the conditions agreed to were low, and there were all sorts of dangerous objects in schools (such as scissors, baseball bats and cafeteria knives) that were permitted while creating a higher risk to students.

The only Australian case on a student's religious dress, not surprisingly given the Australian legal framework, takes a far less rights-based approach but with similar results. In *Arora v Melton Christian College (Human Rights)* [2017] VCAT 1507, Melton Christian College (**MCC**) refused the enrolment application of five-year-old Sidhak Singh Arora because his long hair and patka, a head covering, both of which were required by his Sikh religious belief, violated MCC's uniform policy that boys must have short hair and may not wear any head coverings related to a non-Christian faith. The Victorian Civil and Administrative Tribunal held that MCC had indirectly discriminated against Sidhak under s 38(1) of the *Equal Opportunity Act 2010* (Vic). Because of his religious belief, MCC's uniform policy disadvantaged Sidhak by refusing him access to the emotional and social benefits associated with attending a school that his cousins also attended and practical advantages such as the proximity of the school to his home. The uniform policy was also unreasonable as:

(a) the disadvantages suffered by Sidhak were not proportionate to the results sought by MCC;
(b) a reasonable adjustment could have been made by allowing Sidhak to wear a patka in the colour of the school uniform;
(c) MCC should not have accepted enrolment applications from students of non-Christian faiths on the condition that they did not look like they practiced a non-Christian faith; and
(d) MCC could not exclude a potential student's enrolment application because he wore a patka as required by his religious belief or activity.

10.7.3 Sexuality/Sexual Orientation and Transgender Issues

New South Wales provides a broad exemption for private educational authorities from discrimination in education on the grounds of homosexuality (which includes both female and male homosexuality[14]) and transgender (ss 49ZO(3) and 38 K(3) of the *Anti-Discrimination Act 1977* (NSW)).

This quite broad reaching exemption is overridden by a more narrow exemption at federal level under the *Sex Discrimination Act 1984* (Cth) s 38(3), which prohibits discrimination in education on the ground of another person's gender identity or sexual orientation but provides an exemption in relation to education or training for 'an educational institution that is conducted in accordance with the doctrines, tenets, beliefs or teachings of a particular religion or creed,' where the discrimination occurs 'in good faith in order to avoid injury to the religious susceptibilities of adherents of that religion or creed'.

Other State and Territory jurisdictions except Tasmania provide a similarly qualified exemption as at federal level.[15] However, the Northern Territory, South Australia and Queensland provide an exemption only in relation to work[16] and not the provision of education to students.

[14] s 4(1) Anti-Discrimination Act 1977 (NSW).

[15] Discrimination Act 1991 (ACT) s 33(1) and (2); Equal Opportunity Act 2010 (Vic) s 83(2); Equal Opportunity Act 1984 (WA) s 73(1) and (3).

[16] Anti-Discrimination Act 1992 (NT) s 37A; Anti-Discrimination Act 1991 (Qld) ss 25(2) and 25(3); Equal Opportunity Act 1984 (SA) s 34.

We have not been able to identify cases decided in this area in Australia. We are aware of religious schools navigating carefully to accommodate students who 'come out' as homosexual or who have transitioned while at school – something that it is easier for some schools to do than others. The public debate about the 'Safe Schools' program indicates the level of controversy that these issues – and how to handle them at schools while keeping students safe from bullying and other risks – still generate. A recent example is contained in an ABC report (Haydar 2017) of former prime minister Tony Abbott commending the NSW Government's decision to 'ditch' the Safe Schools program.[17]

In the USA, there have been some celebrated public legal discussions of some of these issues – in particular the issue of the use of toilet facilities by transgender students, which has caused enormous controversy. In the landmark case *Coy Mathis v Fountain-Fort Carson School District 8* (2013) P20130034X, the Colorado Division of Civil Rights ruled in favour of a 6-year-old transgender girl, allowing her to use the girls' bathroom at her elementary school. In March 2016, the United States Department of Justice and the United States Department of Education released a joint guidance on the application of Title IX protections to transgender students, stating that, for the purpose of Title IX, the Department of Justice and the Department of Education treat a student's gender identity as their sex. In October 2016, the Supreme Court agreed to take up the case of Gavin Grimm, *G.G. [Gavin Grimm] v. Gloucester County School Board*, a transgender male student who was barred from using the boys' bathrooms at his high school in Gloucester County, Virginia. However, on 6 March 2017, as a result of the Trump Administration's rescission of the guidance of March 2016, the Supreme Court refused to hear the case and sent it back to the Fourth Circuit Court of Appeal.[18]

Public opinion regarding transgender bathroom rights in the U.S. is mixed. A Pew Research poll from October 2016 (Lipka 2016) found that about 51% of U.S. adults stated transgender individuals should be 'allowed

---

[17] Just one recent example of the significant press that the issue has received can be found in Haydar, N. (2017, April 16). Safe Schools program ditched in NSW, to be replaced by wider anti-bullying plan. *ABC News*. Retrieved from www.abc.net.au/news/2017-04-16/safe-schools-program-ditched-in-nsw/8446680, and the many links at the bottom of that article.

[18] See Hurley, L. (2017, March 7). U.S. top court throws out ruling favouring transgender student. *Reuters*. Retrieved from https://www.reuters.com/article/us-usa-court-transgender/u-s-top-court-throws-out-ruling-favoring-transgender-student-idUSKBN16D1OD and Turner, A. (2017, March 6). BREAKING: U.S. Supreme Court Remands and vacates Gavin Grimm Case. *Human Rights Campaign*. Retrieved from https://www.hrc.org/blog/breaking-united-states-supreme-court-remands-and-vacates-gavin-grimm-case

to use public restrooms that correspond with the gender they currently identify with', with nearly as many (46%) taking the opposite position. Younger people aged 18–29 were more likely to support transgender people's right to use the bathroom of the gender they identify with (67%). Research from YouGov in 2017 (McCarriston 2017) suggests that opinions on this issue have polarised along party lines. When asked whether they would favour or oppose a law that would require transgender people to use the bathroom corresponding to the gender of their birth, Americans were split 40% in favour and 40% opposing. Compared to 2016, an additional 12% of Democrats would now oppose such a law. The number of Republicans who said they would support it has increased 14%. The issue is an important one because of the apparent link between bathroom use issues and mental health for transgender people, for whom feelings of isolation and belonging are critical (Schuster et al. 2016).

10.8 Religion in the Classroom: What Can and Cannot Be Part of the Curriculum and the Teachings and Expressed Values of the School?

This section of the chapter admittedly overlaps with much of what has come before in principle – because it is at the heart of the activities of most religious schools that they be able to teach what they believe and act in accordance with those beliefs. When it comes to curriculum and values teaching, however, there is significant potential for conflict between the school and the public secular educational authorities with which it must coexist. Given this, the absence of specific guidelines and restrictions is stark.

As noted above, governments impose minimum curriculum requirements on schools, including non-government schools. For example, sections 8 and 10 of the *Education Act 1990* (NSW) provide for 'key learning areas'. However, non-government schools can apply to modify the NSW Education Standards Authority (NESA) (formerly BOSTES) syllabus to meet their religious requirements. As the NESA website states:

Where a school considers that one or more of the outcomes of a NESA syllabus are incompatible with the school's educational philosophy or religious outlook for part of the school's curriculum, the school may apply to NESA to use modified outcomes for that part of the syllabus.

A school may be granted approval for the use of modified outcomes for part of a syllabus if NESA is satisfied that:

- the identified NESA outcome(s) are incompatible with the educational philosophy and/or religious outlook of the school
- the proposed modified outcome(s) are compatible with the educational philosophy and/or religious outlook of the school
- the proposed modified outcome(s) comply with the curriculum guidelines developed by NESA.

Modifications approved under this provision of the Act are not permitted to the curriculum for the Record of School Achievement or Higher School Certificate.

The NESA website also provides some further information on how to do this, and the additional documentation required to show compliance. This is reiterated in the Registered and Accredited Individual Non-government Schools (NSW) Manual and also in the Registration Systems and Member Non-government Schools (NSW) Manual.

Within these types of guidelines, religious schools often teach general subjects from a religious perspective. This might be, for example, 'what do our faith's values say about the environment', or it might be teaching creationism rather than, or alongside, evolution. As Michael Bachelard reported in *The Age* in 2008:

> *Take the Accelerated Christian Education (or ACE) syllabus used by five Victorian schools and 41 Australia-wide. A sample page of the ACE curriculum shows that in primary school science class, students are confronted with this statement: 'God made many kinds of fish. He made them on day five.'*
>
> *The page accompanying the sheet gives a comprehension test, asking children on which day God made them.*
>
> *The Victorian curriculum asks schools to teach the theory of evolution, explaining the link between natural selection and evolution. But it is not compulsory for independent schools to teach the state curriculum.*
>
> *Victorian Registration and Qualifications Authority director Lynne Glover told The Age: 'Within the general provision of science, schools may choose to teach students about a range of theories related to science, including creationism and evolution.'*
>
> *The mix, she said, was 'up to schools to determine in consultation with their community'.*
>
> *The details vary but, in Christian schools, creationism is almost universal, and is taught not in religious education classes but in science….*

In a number of Christian schools, such as Chairo Christian College in Drouin, the science teacher talks about evolution and then moves on to suggest that the hand of God was the real creative force. The grade four class at Heatherton Christian College last year studied 'dinosaurs from a biblical perspective'.

Similarly, religious schools might teach sex education, gender issues and health from a faith-based perspective. Sometimes, this might bring the school into potential conflict with public policy – thus Bachelard notes that '*the Victorian curriculum expects students to deal with the issues of "sexual harassment, homophobia and/or discrimination", and issues such as "safe sex practices, sexual negotiation, same-sex attraction"...At religious schools, though, this is very tricky ground.*'

It seems that there is a lack of strict regulation governing the details of teaching of religion and religious views in non-government schools. Again, we need to consider the requirements of discrimination and safety laws. There is interesting potential for arguments that gay/lesbian/transgender students are being harassed at school by the teachings to which they are subjected; that harassment and/or bullying results; and that the school is being negligent in not considering their needs. The converse argument is that schools should be able to teach in accordance with their faith systems, and that if those systems do not suit particular students then they should choose other schools.

There are no Australian cases in which unlawful discrimination has been alleged based on what was being taught in a religious school. However, *A obo V and A v NSW Department of Education EOD* [2000] NSWADTAP 14, a case in the NSW public system, sheds some light on how religious schools might deal with students of a different faith or no faith in their community when it comes to religious teaching. In this case, the father of two Jewish pupils brought a claim under the *Anti-Discrimination Act 1977* (NSW) that the public school his children attended had discriminated against them on the ground of ethno-religious origin. The issues for the father were the practice of conducting school prayers at assembly, the school's activities focused on Christmas (in particular, the children's participation in the Christmas nativity scene at the school Christmas concerts and Christmas party, and the attendance of Santa Claus at one or both of those functions), and the exchange of Easter eggs and other events associated with the Easter story of the Christian faith. Once the father objected to his children participating in these activities, they were excused from further involvement and provided with alternative activities. The father also complained that this 'segregation' amounted to discrimination against his children.

The Tribunal found that the amendments to the definition of race to include the term 'ethno-religious' were not designed to allow members of such groups to lodge complaints in respect of discrimination on the basis of their religion. There was also no less favourable treatment of the father's children than the treatment accorded to every other child at the school in respect of the relevant activities. It was not sufficient to establish that the children were exposed to Christian teachings in the course of the Christmas and Easter activities at the school by virtue of their presence in the student body. Mere attendance at school cannot amount to the imposition of a requirement to participate in certain activities. What would have to be established is that the children's adherence to the Jewish faith was a factor in the respondent's decision to include them in the Christmas and Easter activities. In this case, the conduct in involving them in the Christian activities occurred in spite of their religion, not because of it. As for the 'segregation', that was an action taken by the school out of respect for the parents, not as a form of discrimination, and was required by section 33 of the *Education Act 1990*.

Some relevant examples about what might and might not be taught and done can be found in overseas case law. However, it should be noted that the cases that follow arise in jurisdictions where there is a clearer statement than is generally the case in Australia of what it is acceptable to teach, and where there are specific requirements to teach inclusivity and tolerance of lifestyles and structures that may be unacceptable to some religious groups.

In *E.T. v Hamilton-Wentworth District School Board* (2016) ONSC 7313, a Canadian case, a devout Greek Orthodox father whose children were in a public school was unsuccessful in his claim that the school Board should provide him with advance notice of specific curriculum areas being taught to his children. He also failed to obtain an order that he be permitted to withdraw the children from certain classes, lessons or activities that conflicted with his religious beliefs. The context was that the Ministry of Education had directed school boards to implement equity and inclusive education policies to help reduce racism, religious intolerance, homophobia and gender-based violence – while at the same time allowing for religious accommodation in accordance with the *Canadian Charter of Human Rights and Freedoms* (which provides for fundamental freedom of conscience and religion) and the *Ontario Human Rights Code*. Perhaps not surprisingly, the father's religious views clashed with many aspects of the inclusive education approach, including in particular classroom practices that were 'anti-homophobic and anti-heterosexist' and gave staff access to 'a wide variety of bias-free teaching and learning materials'. His faith compelled him to ensure that his children were taught about marriage and sexuality in accordance with a biblical perspective and the teachings of this church. He also objected to the Ministry's approach to a raft of issues including 'moral relativism', 'environmental worship', abortion and euthanasia. The Court found that he was sincere. It also found that the school Board acted reasonably when it refused to accommodate him – even though this infringed on his freedom of religion – because there was a limit to the accommodation that was possible. From the perspective of the Charter, the Board acted proportionately, balancing the relevant interests sensibly and practically. Important in this context was the Board's religious accommodation guideline, which provided that it could not 'accommodate religious values and beliefs that clearly conflict with mandated Ministry... policies'.

In terms of what may be taught in religious schools, an evangelical teachers' college in Canada successfully challenged the College of Teachers when it refused to approve the evangelical college for full teacher training on the basis that it listed homosexuality as a 'sexual sin' that was 'biblically condemned', and which its students were prohibited from committing. There was no evidence that teachers trained in the institution would not treat homosexual students equally and in accordance with the law, and the approval was therefore granted (*Trinity Western University v British Columbia College of Teachers* [2001] 1 SCR 772).

It seems likely that teachings that clearly contravene general societal norms and encourage the infringement of the rights of others, even if those teachings appear to have a religious basis, would be prohibited in Australia on the basis of either human rights or discrimination laws. Again, looking overseas for examples, the heads of a number of Christian private schools in the UK wished to use corporal punishment as a disciplinary device in their schools, and claimed that the prohibition of corporal punishment in the *Education Act 1996* s.548 was a breach of their freedom of religion under Article 9 *European Convention on Human Rights 2010*. The claim failed at first instance in the Administrative Court, in the Court of Appeal and also in the House of Lords (*R (Williamson) v Secretary of State for Education and Employment* [2005] 2 AC 246) – which held unanimously that there was a difference between freedom of religious belief and freedom to manifest that belief. The interference with the latter freedom was deemed justified in this case, as per Lord Nicholls at [18], 'necessary in a democratic society... for the protection of rights and freedoms for others'. While this reasoning might only apply directly in an Australian jurisdiction with a bill of rights, the balancing act is similar to that required under discrimination law, looking here at balancing gender-based rights and the need to ensure safety against the right to freedom of religion.

Very recently, schools in the UK that were teaching students that it is acceptable for a man to beat his wife, among other extreme views, have been forced to shut down. Again, however, the framework is different to that in Australia. Events in the UK over the past few years, including the 'Trojan Horse' controversy in which Islamic Boards of Governors of public schools were accused of introducing an Islamist, extremist ethos, have led to government guidelines about teaching 'British values' including 'mutual respect for and tolerance of those with different faiths and beliefs and for those without faith'.[19]

Beyond ordinary discrimination law, the prohibitions of racial and religious vilification in Australia impose some limits on religious schools.

One religious vilification case which did not involve a school but includes reasoning very relevant to schools is the *Catch the Fire Ministries Case* (*Islamic Council of Victoria v Catch the Fire Ministries Inc.* [2004] VCAT 2510), in which the Islamic Council of Victoria lodged a representative complaint against Catch the Fire Ministries, an evangelical Christian church. The church had conducted a seminar and published a newsletter and online material, that the Council claimed attacked the Islamic faith in breach of the Victorian provisions, under section 8 of the *Racial and Religious Tolerance Act 2001* (Vic). Catch the Fire defended the claim on the basis that its statements were accurate, and its actions were reasonable and undertaken in good faith, for a genuine religious purpose and in the public interest. The Victorian Civil and Administrative Tribunal upheld the complaint, finding that the cumulative effect of the statements and publications was hostile, demeaning and derogatory to Muslims and their faith, and that they were likely to incite others to religious hatred, contempt and ridicule. The Tribunal further found, under section 11 of the Act, that no legitimate defence could be sustained of engaging in such conduct reasonably and in good faith for any genuine religious purpose. However, the Victorian Court of Appeal set aside the Tribunal's orders (*Catch the Fire Ministries Inc. & Ors v Islamic Council of Victoria Inc.* [2006] VSCA 284), remitting the matter to be heard by a different Tribunal member, and the matter was settled confidentially – essentially leaving no clear public result. The principles outlined by the Court of Appeal included that, while breach of the legislation requires a definite link between religious beliefs and the hatred or other emotion incited, this was not necessarily of a causal nature as suggested in the Tribunal hearing. The matter for determination was rather whether Catch the Fire Ministries' audience was incited to

[19] See https://en.wikipedia.org/wiki/Operation_Trojan_Horse, which includes links to the relevant government report into the allegations, and to a very large number of media articles tracing the controversy and its aftermath.

hatred of Muslims because of their Islamic faith; and ultimately the legitimacy of the defence hinged on whether the conduct was engaged in 'reasonably' for a genuine religious purpose; and that this objective standard would naturally reflect the views of reasonable members of a tolerant, multicultural society.

10.9 Conclusion

The role that religious schools play in Australia's multi-faith, multicultural society is complex.

Returning to the questions with which this chapter began, as we have seen, Australian law does not include clear or well-defined rights to religious freedom, and our discrimination laws are inconsistent and not always helpful. Further, safety and negligence obligations do not always happily coexist with discrimination laws. This is combined with the relative lack of strict content requirements imposed by educational authorities. The case law to date is less than comprehensive – even while Australian schools can take some guidance from cases overseas, there is a long way to go in clarifying relevant law – and it is in any case an area where social opinion changes and laws can change as a consequence. In summary, the legal landscape that schools face is obscured by mist and includes some treacherous ground.

It follows that the answers to the choices – sometimes dilemmas – that Australian religious schools face in navigating their way through questions of faith and practice are often unclear. Religious schools are not always free to act as the doctrines to which they subscribe might ideally direct; and the issues arising in the context of enrolment, staffing behaviour and curriculum play out at school can therefore test relationships within school communities and between schools and regulators.

Luckily for the Australian community, most religious schools take their obligations seriously and seek to address these issues in good faith and with compassion.

References

Legislation

Anti-Discrimination Act 1977 (NSW).
Anti-Discrimination Act 1991 (Qld).
Anti-Discrimination Act 1992 (NT).

Anti-Discrimination Act 1998 (Tas).
Australian Human Rights Commission Act 1986 (Cth).
Discrimination Act 1991 (ACT).
Education Act 1990 (NSW).
Education and Training Reform Act 2006 (Vic).
Education and Training Reform Regulations 2007 (Vic).
Equal Opportunity Act 1984 (SA).
Equal Opportunity Act 1984 (WA).
Equal Opportunity Act 2010 (VIC).
Equality Act 2010 (UK).
Fair Work Act 2009 (Cth).
Occupational Health and Safety Act 2004 (Vic) ss 21 and 23.
Occupational Safety and Health Act 1984 (WA).
Racial and Religious Tolerance Act 2001 (UK).
Sex Discrimination Act 1984 (Cth).
Work Health and Safety Act 2011 (ACT).
Work Health and Safety Act 2011 (Cth).
Work Health and Safety Act 2011 (NSW).
Work Health and Safety Act 2011 (Qld).
Work Health and Safety Act 2012 (SA).
Work Health and Safety Act 2012 (Tas).

Cases

A obo V and A v NSW Department of Education EOD [2000] NSWADTAP 14.
Achbita & Anor v G4S Secure Solutions NV [2016] EUECJ C-157/15.
Adelaide Co of Jehovah's Witnesses Inc v Commonwealth (1943) 67 CLR 116.
Al-Kateb v Godwin (2004) 219 CLR 562.
Arora v Melton Christian College (Human Rights) [2017] VCAT 1507.
Attorney-General (Vic); Ex Rel Black v Commonwealth (1981) 146 CLR 559.
Azmi v Kirklees Metropolitan Borough Council [2007] UKEA/0009/07.
Bougnaoui v Micropole Univers SA (2015) C-188/15.
Bull and Another v Hall and Another [2013] UKSC 73.
Catch the Fire Ministries Inc & Ors v Islamic Council of Victoria Inc [2006] VSCA 284.
Church of the New Faith v Commissioner of Payroll Tax (1983) 154 CLR 120.
Coy Mathis v Fountain-Fort Carson School District 8 (2013) P20130034X.
De Groen v Gan Mecachem Hendon Limited 3347281/2016.
E.T. v Hamilton-Wentworth District School Board (2016) ONSC 7313.
G.G. [Gavin Grimm] v. Gloucester County School Board; see Shapiro, I, T Burrus and D McDonald. 'Gloucester County School Board v G.G', *Cato Institute*, 10 January 2017 accessed at https://www.cato.org/publications/legal-briefs/gloucester-county-school-board-v-gg-0

Goldberg v Korsunski Carmel School [2000] EOC 93-074.
Haider v Combined District Radio Cabs Pty Ltd t/as Central Coast Taxis [2008] NSWADT 123.
HM Chief Inspector of Education, Children's Services and Skills v The Interim Executive Board of Al-Hijrah School [2017] EWCA Civ 1426.
HM Land Registry v Grant EAT [2010] UKEAT 0232_09_1504.
Islamic Council of Victoria v Catch the Fire Ministries Inc [2004] VCAT 2510.
Johns and Another, Regina (on The Application of) v Derby City Council and Another [2011] EWHC 375 (Admin).
Jones v Lee and Guilding [1980] ICR 310.
Krygger v Williams (1912) 15 CLR 366.
Miller v Wertheim [2001] FMCA 103.
Miller v Wertheim [2004] FCA 988.
Minister for Immigration and Ethnic Affairs v Teoh (1995) 183 CLR 273.
Multani v Commission Scolaire Marguerite-Bourgeoys [2006] 1 SCR 256.
Pothecary Witham Weld (A Firm) and Another v Bullimore [2010] UKEAT 0158_09_2903.
R (on the application of E) (Respondent) v The Governing Body of JFS and the Admissions Appeal Panel of JFS and others (Appellants) [2009] UKSC 15.
R (on the application of Playfoot) v Governing Body of Millais School [2007] HRLR 34.
R (on the application of Watkins-Singh) v Aberdare Girls' High School Governors [2008] EWHC 1865.
R (SB) v Governors of Denbigh High School [2007] 1 AC 100.
R (Williamson) v Secretary of State for Education and Employment [2005] 2 AC 246.
SDW v Church of Jesus Christ of Latter-Day Saints (2008) 222 FLR 84.
Sutherland Shire Council v Folkes [2015] FCA 1288.
The Interim Executive Board of X School v. Her Majesty's Chief Inspector of Education, Children's Services and Skills [2016] EWHC 2813 (Admin).
Trinity Western University v British Columbia College of Teachers [2001] 1 SCR 772.

Books and Journal Articles

Evans, C. (2009). Legal aspects of the protection of religious freedom in Australia. *Melbourne Law School.*
Evans, C. (2012). *Legal protection of religious freedom in Australia*. Sydney: Federation Press.
Evans, C., & Gaze, B. (2010). Discrimination by religious schools: Views from the coal face. *Melbourne University Law Review, 34*, 392.
Evans, C., & Ujvari, L. (2009). Non-discrimination laws and religious schools in Australia. *Adelaide Law Review, 30*, 31.

Ford, D. (2016). *Lesbian, gay, transgender and intersex students*. Retrieved from www.emilford.com.au/imagesDB/wysiwyg/LGBTIStudentsandDutyofCare-November2016PaperbyDavidFord.pdf

Schuster, M., Reisner, S., & Onorato, S. (2016). Beyond bathrooms – Meeting the health needs of transgender people. *The New England Journal of Medicine, 375*, 101–103. https://doi.org/10.1056/NEJMp1605912.

Walsh, G. (2014). The right to equality and the employment decisions of religious schools. *The University of Notre Dame Australia Law Review, 16*, 107–144.

Media Reports

Bachelard, M. (2008, February 25). At the crossroads? *The Age*. Retrieved from www.theage.com.au/news/in-depth/at-the-crossroads/2008/02/24/1203788145887.html?page=5

Christodoulou, H. (2016, November 7). Four 'extremist' schools which teach 'men can beat their wives' fighting government orders to shut down. *The Sun*. Retrieved from www.thesun.co.uk/news/2130831/four-extremist-schools-which-teach-men-can-beat-their-wives-fighting-government-orders-to-shut-down/

Conifer, D. (2017, November 19). Ministers at odds over whether to include religious protections in same-sex marriage bill. *ABC News*. Retrieved from http://www.abc.net.au/news/2017-11-19/split-in-turnbull-government-over-religious-amendments-to-ssm-l/9166360

Donnelly, K. (2013, January 17). Schools practise what they preach. *The Sydney Morning Herald*. Retrieved from www.smh.com.au/federal-politics/political-opinion/schools-practise-what-they-preach-20130116-2ctpf.html

Fyfe, M. (2009, October 4). Teacher scorned for chosen lifestyle. *The Age*. Retrieved from www.theage.com.au/national/teacher-scorned-for-chosen-lifestyle-20091003-ghbl.html

Haydar, N. (2017, April 16). Safe schools program ditched in NSW, to be replaced by wider anti-bullying plan. *ABC News*. Retrieved from www.abc.net.au/news/2017-04-16/safe-schools-program-ditched-in-nsw/8446680

Human Rights Watch. (2016, September 13). Shut out: Restrictions of bathroom and locker room access for transgender youth in US schools'. *Human Rights Watch*. Retrieved from www.hrw.org/report/2016/09/13/shut-out/restrictions-bathroom-and-locker-room-access-transgender-youth-us-schools

Hurley, L. (2017, March 7). U.S top court throws out ruling favouring transgender student. *Reuters*. Retrieved from https://www.reuters.com/article/us-usa-court-transgender/u-s-top-court-throws-out-ruling-favoring-transgender-student-idUSKBN16D1OD

Jabour, B. (2012, May 1). Teacher sacked over pregnancy. *Brisbane Times*. Retrieved from www.brisbanetimes.com.au/queensland/teacher-sacked-over-pregnancy-20120501-1xw79.html

Lipka, M. (2016). Americans are divided over which public bathrooms transgender people should use. *Pew Research Center*. Retrieved from www.pewresearch.org/fact-tank/2016/10/03/americans-are-divided-over-which-public-bathrooms-transgender-people-should-use/

McCarriston, G. (2017, March 16). Partisan gap widens on transgender bathroom rights. *YouGov*. Retrieved from today.yougov.com/news/2017/03/16/partisan-lines-drawn-which-bathrooms-transgender-p/

Pells, R. (2016, October 14). Islamist girls' school that taught pupils gay people should be killed and men could beat their wives forced to close. *Independent*. Retrieved from www.independent.co.uk/news/education/education-news/islamist-girls-school-jamia-al-hudaa-taught-pupils-gay-people-should-be-killed-forced-closure-aliyah-a7361596.html

Rankin, J., & Oltermann, P. (2017, March 13). Europe's right hails EU court's workplace headscarf ban ruling. *The Guardian*. Retrieved from www.theguardian.com/law/2017/mar/14/employers-can-ban-staff-from-wearing-headscarves-european-court-rules

Tomazin, F. (2009, March 25). Christian school rejects teacher. *The Age*. Retrieved from www.theage.com.au/national/christian-school-rejects-teacher-20090324-98y0.html

Turner, A. (2017, March 6). BREAKING: U.S. Supreme Court remands and vacates Gavin Grimm case. *Human Rights Campaign*. Retrieved from https://www.hrc.org/blog/breaking-united-states-supreme-court-remands-and-vacates-gavin-grimm-case

Other

Human Rights and Equal Opportunity Commission Inquiry. (1998). HRC Report No 6.

James, D., & Clarke, T. (2009). Evidence to Scrutiny of Acts and Regulations Committee, Parliament of Victoria, Melbourne, *Inquiry into the exceptions and exemptions in the Equal Opportunity Act — Public hearing*. Victorian Independent Education Union, 3. Retrieved from www.parliament.vic.gov.au/images/stories/committees/sarc/EOV/transcripts/5_August__Victorian_Independent_Education_Union.pdf

NSW Education Standards Authority. (2017). *Modifications to a NESA syllabus*. Retrieved from http://rego.nesa.nsw.edu.au/registered-individual-non-government-schools/registration-requirements/curriculum/modifications-to-a-nesa-syllabus

NSW Education Standards Authority. (2017). *Registered and accredited individual non-government schools (NSW) manual*. Retrieved from http://educationstandards.nsw.edu.au/wps/wcm/connect/e9aad3a8-808b-468f-a8e1-92de94b10e31/reg-accred-individ-non-gov-manual.pdf?MOD=AJPERES&CVID

Victorian Independent Education Union. (2009). *Evidence to Scrutiny of Acts and Regulations Committee, Inquiry into the exceptions and exemptions in the Equal Opportunity Act — Public hearing*. Retrieved from http://www.parliament.vic.gov.au/images/stories/committees/sarc/EOV/transcripts/5_August_-_Victorian_Independent_Education_Union.pdf

Williams, G. (2017). *Submission to inquiry into the status of the human right to freedom of religion or belief.*

11

Translating Theory to Practice for Principals Working Within Inclusive Education Policy

Amanda A. Webster

11.1 Introduction

In the 21st century, inclusive education is considered not just good practice, but a right for all children, including students with disabilities (McLeskey et al. 2014; Peters 2007). As a reflection of this philosophy, many countries have passed legislation and policies establishing the right of children with disabilities to have the same educational opportunities as their peers (Artiles et al. 2011). Recent research (Graham and Spandagou 2011; Webster and Roberts 2015) suggests that although school leaders may believe in the theory of inclusive education, they often experience difficulties with the practical reality of addressing the diverse needs of students with disabilities within the mainstream curriculum and environment.

The belief of principals in the ability of students with disabilities to succeed in inclusive environments has been found to be the single most important factor in their decisions regarding placement and programs to support these students (Horrocks et al. 2008). Many principals report, however, that although they support the rights of students with disabilities as outlined in current policy, they do not feel they have been provided with adequate resources or training to actually meet the needs of these students within current school curriculum and environments (Angelle and Bilton 2009;

A. A. Webster (✉)
School of Education, University of Wollongong, Wollongong, NSW, Australia
e-mail: awebster@uow.edu.au

K. Trimmer et al. (eds.), *The Palgrave Handbook of Education Law for Schools*,
https://doi.org/10.1007/978-3-319-77751-1_11

Christensen et al. 2013). As a result, principals may make decisions and actions that could be constituted as either direct or indirect discrimination according to current legislation and policies. This chapter will overview the research on the factors that shape principal's attitudes and actions regarding current education policy. In addition, recommendations will be made for how principals can be supported to not just implement policy, but to envision and create effective inclusive school programs that translate inclusive policy into meaningful outcomes for all students.

11.2 Policy

In 1975, the United States of America passed PL 94–142, the Education for All Handicapped Children Act (EAHCA). This landmark legislation was one of the first in the world to establish the rights of individuals with disabilities to be provided with a quality education. Since that time many countries have come out with similar laws and policies (Artiles et al. 2011; Dempsey 2012), establishing the right of children with disabilities to be provided with supports and strategies and to be educated in inclusive environments. At the same time, parents and individuals with disabilities have advocated for more supportive school cultures and programs based on a human rights or social model of disability (Oliver and Barnes 2010).

Researchers have found that in the right contexts, inclusion leads to positive outcomes for many students with disabilities (Fredrickson et al. 2007; Hoppey and McLeskey 2013; Kurth 2009; Loreman 2014; Wehmeyer et al. 2012). As a result, inclusive education has become common policy for many countries and education departments. The international recognition of inclusive education was first reflected in the Salamanca Statement, which was developed in 1994 by representatives from 92 governments (Peters 2007). The Salamanca Statement confirms the right of all children to attend school in the general education environment unless there is a compelling reason not to do so, and promotes the development of positive school environments (Anderson and Boyle 2015).

In the years since the original EAHCA was first passed, the United States has extended their understanding and policy on inclusive practices in the Individuals with Disabilities Act (2004). In 2005, Australia passed the Disability Standards of Education. This established the right of students with disabilities to be provided with reasonable adjustments to participate and achieve on the same basis as their peers. Despite these policies, however, researchers suggest that the creation of inclusive policy does not equate to inclusive practice, and that currently a significant policy-to-practice gap exists (Dixon and Verenikina 2007). As a result, students with disabilities may still be stigmatised (Lilley 2012) and not provided with the same opportunities as their peers (Dempsey and Davies 2013).

The move towards inclusive school programs has placed additional pressure on school leaders to gain the knowledge and skills needed to make decisions and lead staff in creating school programs that support students with a range of needs. Although the general guidelines for inclusive education may be outlined in international resolutions or national policy, there is currently no mandate in countries such as Australia that requires schools to provide specific types of programs (Dickson 2008). Nor is there any stated requirement for children to receive their education in least restrictive environments such as general education classrooms. Additionally, there may be wide variance in countries like Australia (Boyle et al. 2011) as to how individual states interpret or implement national disability legislation and policies. This is illustrated in the differing state policies, which specify the types of students that are eligible for financial support or the criteria for accessing services and resources (Anderson and Boyle 2015). As Boyle and colleagues highlight (2011), making sense of inclusive practice requires school leaders to interpret both national and state level policy, before they can contextualise this information into a vision for their school and make decisions about how to best utilise organisational resources and instructional programs to support a diverse student population. This can be quite a challenge for school leaders who may have had little training on the needs of students with disabilities or the practices that will be most effective in supporting these students to achieve (Horrocks et al. 2008; Praisner 2003).

The lack of strong leadership for inclusive education has had a significant impact on the participation and outcomes of students with disabilities in schools. Recent data suggests that the number of students who are excluded from inclusive programs is increasing (Anderson and Boyle 2015) as more segregated programs are created (Graham and Jahnukainen 2011), and more students are suspended (Beauchamp 2012; Daly 2013). In addition, students are often left out of testing measures (Dempsey and Davies 2013), which means they are not counted in resourcing schemes that are derived from school data on student achievement. More importantly, their progress is often not systematically tracked and reported in a meaningful way.

Given the current focus on standardised measures to establish the success of school programs, the elimination of a significant group from data sets is particularly problematic as it may present a skewed picture of the school's success. Slee (2013) contends that high-stakes testing has led schools to engage in "educational triage" (p. 895) in which resources and energy are primarily focused on students who demonstrate the most potential, while those deemed as having limited potential are excluded or sacrificed. This is reflected in the experience of parents who report that their children with disabilities are often discounted during enrolment procedures (Lilley 2012) by school leaders who suggest they would be better served in other school settings. Thus, it is imperative that school leaders be given the knowledge and skills they need to interpret current policy and make complex decisions about the ways they will utilise resources to support all students at their school, including those with disability.

11.3 Leadership

School leaders play an essential role in creating, maintaining and improving inclusive education programs that are effective in supporting the achievement of all students at the school (Causton and Theoharis 2014). Researchers have found that the vision and support of the school's leaders are the most important predictors of a school's ability to implement a successful school program for students with differing backgrounds and needs (Villa et al. 1996). To be effective, school leaders must act in divergent roles, and must be able to act as moral leaders, instructional leaders, organisational leaders, and collaborative leaders (Crockett 2002). School principals and leaders must also be able to build consensus among the school community around school initiatives and priorities that incorporate inclusive practice (Causton and Theoharis 2014), and serve as drivers for systemic change at the whole school level (Agbenyega and Sharma 2014; Webster and Wilkinson 2015). Leaders must engage with school communities in specific ways if they are to implement school programs that not only comply with disability legislation and policy (Dempster 2009), but also enable all students, including those who are marginalised, to achieve (Hoppey and McLeskey 2013; Waldron et al. 2014; Webster 2016).

Researchers have consistently agreed that one of the primary roles of school leaders is to facilitate the development of a shared vision for the school community (Bays and Crockett 2007; Dempster 2009; Webster and Wilkinson 2015). Referred to as a moral purpose by Dempster, a shared vision has been found to be essential in creating a shared understanding between staff, parents and students about the primary aim of the school program, which then serves as the core driver for pedagogical decisions and practice. Essentially, the shared moral purpose of most schools focuses on enabling students to be active and lifelong learners who have the requisite skills and knowledge to succeed in different aspects of their life (Ministerial Council on Education, Employment, Training and Youth Affairs (MCEETYA) 2008). After establishing a shared vision, school leaders must engage staff to examine relevant data, evaluate their current practice, and determine what changes and actions are required to realise the vision. Dempster (2009) refers to this process of discussion, reflection, and planning as disciplined dialogue. Through this process, school leaders and staff collaboratively engage with data to ask what the data tells them about their current performance, what it means in relation to key priorities and outcomes, and how they will take action to address any issues. Dempster adds that in order to identify required actions for change, schools leaders must engage with relevant research to determine what strategies have an evidence-base for achieving the results they want. School leaders must also be able to contextualise this research knowledge and determine what specific evidence-based strategies will be most effective in their particular school community (Billingsley and McLeskey 2014; Boscardin 2005).

Researchers (Dempster 2009; Webster 2016) have found that to be effective in creating change that results in greater student outcomes, school leaders need to analyse their knowledge and practice in five key areas. These include: shared leadership, curriculum and teaching, conditions for learning, professional development, and parent and community support. Shared leadership entails creating school structures that support shared leadership and decision-making. This often involves elements of organisational leadership and the creation and implementation of policies and structures that will facilitate the desired outcomes (Crockett 2002; Waldron et al. 2011). It is also important that principals acknowledge the various roles that people can play in the decision-making process and ensure that all stakeholders feel they have a voice and role within the school community. This necessitates not just collaboration with staff, but also acknowledging and legitimising the value of parents and students as school leaders and decision-makers. Parent and community support is the area often indicated as the most problematic for principals (Webster and Roberts 2014; Webster and Wilkinson 2015). To be effective in this area, school leaders and staff must facilitate bi-directional communication between staff and parents about key learning goals and students' progress towards those goals (Auerbach 2010; Crockett et al. 2000). The goals of parents must also be acknowledged and their knowledge and ideas valued in problem solving and implementation processes.

Another important area that leaders and staff must consider is the conditions for learning at the school. To do this, school leaders and community members need to assess their current school environment to identify any barriers to student participation, engagement or learning. This could include things such as the playground environment, sufficient reading resources, ways that teacher aids are used, school signage, school layout, or any other aspect of the school environment that is pertinent to the performance of individuals within the school. In contrast, curriculum and teaching are those aspects of the school program that are directly related to the teaching process or learning of students. To assess their school's performance in this area, school leaders should engage staff in reviewing their current teaching practices as evidenced by student outcome measures. This includes examining data from assessments, research on effective strategies for groups of students, and the ways that staff plan and differentiate for the different needs of students in their school. By addressing each of these areas, school leaders will also determine the learning that is needed for staff to implement change, thereby establishing priorities for professional development. As Dempster (2009) highlights, it is not sufficient for leaders to merely identify the learning priorities for staff; they must also see themselves as active participants in the learning process. This establishes the priority of the learning for staff and enables staff to see the connections between professional learning and being able to achieve the shared vision and priorities of the school community.

Finally, research has consistently demonstrated that to be effective in bringing about change, leaders must be able to harness the human agency of the school in order to enable stakeholders to link their individual beliefs and goals with that of the group (Dempster 2009). In other words, school leaders need to be able to help staff, parents and students to see how the actions they take to achieve the shared vision will also help them to achieve personal goals they have set for themselves and for their students. As a key part of developing human agency in their school, leaders also have to maximise the use of the resources at the school in order to support everyone to achieve their goals (Masters 2009; Robinson et al. 2007). This includes working with staff to evaluate and determine how human, structural and physical resources will be organised and utilised for the maximum benefit of all students and staff. Similarly, school leaders must be able to help staff to develop a sense of shared responsibility for all students, including those with disabilities, and to create a flexible continuum of structures and programs that will support students with a variety of needs (Riehl 2000; Webster and Wilkinson 2015). This process often begins with facilitation of a collective understanding of what it means to be an "inclusive school".

11.4 Inclusion

Currently, there are a variety of definitions of "inclusion" and "inclusive schools". This is partially due to the way "inclusion" has been used by researchers and practitioners from a variety of disciplines to refer to schools, which support students with a range of needs. In describing inclusion in relationship to students with disabilities, McKleskey et al. (2014) define inclusive schools as "places where students with disabilities are valued and active participants and where they are provided with supports needed to succeed in the academic, social and extra-curricular activities of the school" (p. 4). Another common definition is the one used by Norman Kunc (1992).

In principle, inclusive education means: ... the valuing of diversity within the human community. When inclusive education is fully embraced, we abandon the idea that children have to become "normal" in order to contribute to the world....

In practice, inclusive education means: A classroom model in which students with and without disabilities are based in a regular structure and benefit from shared ownership of general and special educators. This includes: a student centred approach beginning with profiles, a schedule that accounts for the full range of needs in the class, a curriculum that is rich and accommodating for all students, a teaming process in which support staff work in flexible coordinated ways to strengthen collaborative relationships, a classroom climate that embraces diversity (pp. 38–39).

In general, all definitions concur that in inclusive schools, all students are viewed as competent learners who are integral members of the school community, and whose learning is the shared responsibility of all staff. Students are given the opportunity to engage with peers in general education classrooms, and are provided with the supports and resources needed to participate and achieve within the school program (McLeskey et al. 2014). Ainscow (2004) adds that inclusion is not just a philosophy, but a process, whereby the participation and achievement of all students is valued. As a part of this process, a particular emphasis is placed on those students who may be at risk of marginalisation, thereby enabling staff to identify and remove barriers that prevent students' full participation and success. If school leaders are to create inclusive school environments, they need to examine the beliefs, understandings and practices that promote exclusion and exclusionary practices (Slee 2011).

Since the initiation of inclusive school policy, researchers have consistently found that students achieve higher academic and social outcomes when they are included in programs with their peers, than if they are placed in segregated programs (Cole et al. 2004; Freeman and Alkin 2000; Loreman et al. 2011; Ruijs and Peetsma 2009). Despite these findings, exclusionary practices are still common (Graham and Jahnukainen 2011) with researchers citing numerous obstacles to truly inclusive practice. Common barriers include attitudes of staff and school leaders; poor resourcing; exclusionary policies; poor understanding and use of evaluation processes to measure student outcomes; limited knowledge and skills of school leaders and staff about students' needs or effective practices; and use of categorisation and labelling to drive programs (Anderson and Boyle 2015). The actions of schools are also influenced by competing policies and priorities within the system; the views and actions of members of the school community; and the criteria used by both the system and stakeholders to evaluate the performance of schools. Researchers highlight that although the development of a shared vision is an essential component of inclusive schools, it is not sufficient on its own to implement change processes for school improvement (Fisher et al. 2000; Hehir and Katzman 2012) or to create inclusive school environments where all students can succeed (Hoppey and McLeskey 2014). Lack of sustainability has also been cited as a key barrier to inclusion. Sustainability can be particularly affected by a change of leadership (Ryan 2010) or a shift in systems-level priorities (Hoppey and McLeskey 2014).

In order to maintain the momentum necessary to facilitate inclusive school programs, school leaders need to work with staff to evaluate the effectiveness of their actions and programs. Loreman (2014) outlines three outcome measures of inclusive school programs: student participation, student achievement and post-school outcomes. Kyriazopoulou and Weber (2009) also stress that evaluating inclusive programs entails examining these measures at three levels of school performance: inputs, processes and outcomes. Inputs are those elements, such as financial resources, policy, staffing, curriculum, and leadership that serve to create inclusive education programs. Processes are those practices in which schools engage to achieve outcomes. These include instructional practices and pedagogies, and the ways in which staff interact and collaborate. Finally, outcomes are the traditional measures of student achievement, but may also include non-traditional measures such as participation and engagement of students, and students' utilisation of social emotional and self-determination skills in settings outside the school grounds.

Researchers (Ainscow 2004) have also concluded that inclusive school practice involves the creation of social learning processes that engage staff in collaborative problem solving (Hoppey and McLeskey 2013). This requires stakeholders to find a common agenda and language to talk with each other in order to discover shared concerns and perspectives. As facilitators of collaborative processes, school leaders need to possess skills in leadership and relationship building, knowledge of effective practices and the needs of students in their school, as well as the ability to organise the school environment in a way that meets the needs of all stakeholders (Fixsen et al. 2013). They must be able to listen to and incorporate the feedback of different stakeholders in order to revise their practice as needed. This often requires school leaders to shift their thinking about the roles they play within the school community, shifting between acting as visionary leaders, instructional leaders, organisational leaders, and collaborative leaders (Bays and Crockett 2007) as needed. They must also examine their current beliefs, knowledge and skills in order to help staff to translate systems requirements into the "lifeworld" of their individual school context (Keeffe 2003). This enables school staff to see how these systems policies fit with the varying attitudes, goals and needs of staff, students and families within the school community. Unless they can work with staff to make this connection, school leaders will not be able to manage the competing priorities of systems and schools (Bays and Crockett 2007). Therefore, building the capacity of school principals to relate inclusion legislation and policy to the needs of their school community is paramount. In the next section, factors that influence the capacity of school principals to translate inclusive policy and legislation into practice will be discussed, and key actions of effective school leaders will be examined.

11.5 Moving from Policy to Practice

11.5.1 Attitudes

The attitudes and beliefs of school leaders have a significant influence on their actions. Graham and Spandagou (2011) suggest that principals' perceptions and subsequent actions in creating inclusive environments are shaped by their understanding and perception of inclusion, as well as by the individual characteristics of their school environment. In a survey of Australian principals, Graham and Spandagou found that principals recognised the important role they performed in helping staff to develop a shared understanding of how inclusion could be suited to their particular needs, as well as to the needs of their students and school community. In doing this, principals felt they often struggled to find a balance between legislation and policy guidelines and the reality of implementing inclusive practice in dynamic, complex school contexts in which needs of different groups of staff and students often conflicted with each other and with current policy. This resulted in principals' divergent perceptions of inclusion that Graham and Spandagou described as "being inclusive" versus "including them" (p. 226). In the "being inclusive" group, principals perceived that inclusive education meant creating cultures and pedagogies, which supported students and families with a wide variety of social, cultural and educational backgrounds and needs. For these principals, implementing inclusive policy for students with disabilities built on, rather than competed with current school priorities. In contrast, principals who spoke of "including them", clearly focused on the needs and deficits of students with disabilities and viewed support for these students as an additional issue the school had to address, which was predicated on available funding.

In an earlier study, Praisner (2003) found that only 20% of principals' expressed positive attitudes towards inclusion, while the majority were undecided and had a number of questions and concerns that remained unanswered. More importantly, principals with a positive attitude were more likely to include students with disabilities in mainstream programs. This was somewhat mitigated by the type of disability, as principals were more likely to place students with autism or emotional difficulties in segregated programs. Similarly Wood et al. (2014) found that principals are much less willing to include students with challenging behaviours, than they are for students with sensory, physical or intellectual disabilities. The findings of this study also suggest that principals remain conflicted in their beliefs about the benefits of inclusion, reporting that they although they feel inclusion might be beneficial for students with emotional needs, they do not feel it is helpful for their peers. In contrast, principals who did have a more positive attitude towards inclusion also tended to be more positive about the benefits of inclusion for their school, as well as the availability of resources and staff to create inclusive school environments.

Studies have also examined the training needs of school principals. Christensen et al. (2013) asked principals about the knowledge they needed to lead inclusive school programs and support students with disabilities. They reported needing information on how to meet legislation and policy requirements and how to build an inclusive school culture. Almost all of the principals (88%) felt they needed to increase their knowledge about how to modify curriculum and assessment for students with disabilities. A similar number (87%) had questions about the legal and policy requirements regarding disciplining students with disabilities, and most (81%) wanted more training to be included in professional preparation programs for principals.

Principals who have had special education training are more likely to have positive attitudes towards including students with disabilities (Horrocks et al. 2008). Unfortunately, many principals report having received little or no training related to either the needs of students with disabilities (Christensen et al. 2013; Crockett et al. 2000) or effective strategies for helping these students to access the curriculum (Horrocks et al. 2008). Positive experiences with students with disabilities, either in a professional or personal capacity, has also been found to positively impact principals' perceptions about the benefits of inclusion for all students (Horrocks et al. 2008; Praisner 2003; Sharma and Chow 2008). Past experience may also impact their confidence and ability to lead staff in creating inclusive school cultures and practices (Wood et al. 2014).

Interestingly the number of years that principals have been in schools is negatively correlated to their attitudes towards inclusion. Principals with less teaching experience tend to have a more positive attitude toward the inclusion of students with specific needs, whereas principals with more years of experience tend to have a more negative attitude (Horrocks et al. 2008; Sharma and Chow 2008). This finding may be due to several factors. These include: changing societal expectations, increasingly diverse student populations and the inclusion of diversity awareness content in teacher training programs in recent years. The experience that principals have had with different school cultures and populations is another influencing factor on principals' attitudes towards inclusion. Graham and Spandagou (2011) report that principals in schools with a more culturally diverse population had a more comprehensive view of inclusion, whereas principals in schools with homogenous populations tend to focus more on the integration of individual students rather than taking a whole-of-school approach to inclusive practice. They also found that principals with experience in a variety of settings had a more balanced and open view towards students with challenging behaviours or other needs. More significant than any of these factors, however, is the principal's belief that children with disabilities can be included and achieve in mainstream school programs (Horrocks et al. 2008). This requires principals to be able to see beyond inclusive policy, and view inclusive education as more than just a component of special education, but as essential for the achievement of all students (Graham and Spandagou 2011; Salisbury 2006).

11.5.2 Knowledge of Inclusive Legislation and Policy

As mentioned previously, the past 20 years has seen an increase in education legislation and policy establishing the requirements of schools and school leaders to support students with disabilities. As a result, school leaders have had to become familiar with these policies and interpret their meaning for their school community. Principals report having a mixed level of knowledge of relevant policy with some (52.5%) having a moderate level of knowledge, while others (47.5%) have only a limited understanding of disability legislation (Davidson and Algozzine 2002). Crockett et al. (2000) found that principals feel much of their work involving students with disabilities involves interpreting legal requirements or developing programs that comply with these requirements. Moreover, they are often required to communicate with parents about issues related to current policy. This places stress on school leaders to interpret current special education policy and understand its application within the context of their school environment.

Rather than help school leaders to implement inclusive practices, the increase in inclusion-related legislation and policy may have intensified the conflicting views of inclusion held by school principals. Christensen et al. (2013) argue that mandates for students with disabilities to access general education curriculum can be very daunting for school leaders who have little or no prior knowledge on how to adapt curriculum or instruction. Adding to this tension is the pressure on principals to demonstrate high levels of performance on school-wide measures (Slee 2013). Lack of knowledge and understanding about the implementation of inclusive education policy has led school leaders to develop different interpretations and implementation of these competing policies. Davidson and Algozzine (2002) argue that this variation in implementation can lead to a "ripple effect" (p. 48) in which principals become frustrated and avoid or relinquish their responsibility to others. They may also choose to focus on the policy that they view has been prioritised by the system (Keeffe 2004) or focus on specific groups of students that are more likely to be successful (Slee 2013).

Researchers have suggested that how principals access and use inclusive education policy on a day-to-day basis can be a barrier to the implementation of effective practice. Keeffe (2003) found that although principals in schools viewed the Australian "Disability Discrimination Act" (1992) (DDA) as extremely important, they rarely referred to the DDA guidelines when making decisions about students with disabilities. An analysis of disability discrimination legal cases reveals that principals' interpretations of this law are often inconsistent and unreliable (Keeffe 2003). Similarly, Graham and Spandagou (2011) suggest that the vision for inclusive education as communicated in current policy has had relatively little impact on school practice. These researchers argue that inclusion should not be a policy open to interpretation of principals, as the differing understanding and application of these policies by leaders at the school and systems level increases the gap between the intent of inclusive and the implementation in schools. This creates an inherent inconsistency in the ways that schools view the enactment of these policies and their responsibility regarding students with disability.

To explore the variations in principals' interpretation and implementation of inclusive education policy, Salisbury (2006) compared the practices of two groups of principals. The first group focused on implementing steps to create more inclusive school cultures. The second group employed a more traditionally integrated program, which focused primarily on accommodations and placements for individual students. Salisbury found that the two groups viewed their responsibility and tasks associated with inclusive practice very differently, which subsequently led to significant differences in the ways they implemented current systems-level policies. In the first group, the principals who were more inclusive were distinguished by their attitude to do whatever was necessary. They tended to use more inclusive language when working with school staff, and took a collaborative approach to decision-making. The principals in this "inclusive" group had a philosophical commitment to creating an inclusive culture and program at their school and spoke of the ways they worked to support students with disabilities through the general education program. In contrast, principals in the second group had a focus primarily on integration of students with disabilities. They were hesitant about the feasibility of inclusive practice and discussed their use of pull-out programs reporting that some students needed separate or specialised support.

Although principals were interviewed from three school districts, there was no association between the district and the attitude or practice of principals. Principals in both the inclusive and integrated groups were spread across each of the three districts. For these principals, the factor that most significantly shaped their implementation of inclusive education policy was their own attitudes and beliefs. Interestingly, few of the principals in either group saw a relationship between the implementation of inclusive programs and school improvement. Finding a "goodness of fit" between systems-level policies and the aims of school communities is a common theme reported by school leaders (Graham and Spandagou 2011, p. 6). Without this, tensions arise as to how to use resources, including staff time and energy, to enact competing policies. This also leads principals to include students with disabilities as a consequence of policies and legislation that reinforce "parent choice", rather than as the result of policy that supports the rights of and positive outcomes for all students.

Some principals also report that current legislation and policies do not reflect the complex decisions that are currently required in school settings (Keeffe 2004). These principals indicate that decision-making in school settings must consider a range of school factors and address a number of policies at school, state or national levels. They also stressed that leading inclusive school cultures involves solving problems and negotiating contexts that take precedence over the consequences they might experience due to their limited knowledge of disability policy. Trying to negotiate these conflicting guidelines results in a great deal of stress for school leaders and staff. This often leads them to engage in reactive decision-making particularly on issues involving students with disabilities or challenging behaviours. Moreover, principals indicate that system-level documents do not often place a high value on inclusive practice, and thus, are not seen as a priority by schools.

Keeffe (2004) suggests that school leaders who guide staff to create a shared understanding of inclusive practice are much more effective than those who impose requirements based on legislation. More importantly, effective leadership in inclusive schools is positively related to the principals' ability to respond to the needs of multiple stakeholders and necessitates a degree of uncertainty, flexibility and creativity that are not traditionally-defined roles of school leaders (Chrispeels and Martin 2002). Principals who develop school-based inclusive education policies through collaborative processes with staff, parents, and students, are more confident in the way they make decisions, and feel their philosophies fulfil the intent of the legislation in a manner that is relevant and meaningful to their school community (Waldron et al. 2014). To achieve this, school leaders must be able to balance management, administrative, and supervisory duties; monitor legal compliance; and ensure instructional quality (Bays and Crockett 2007; Hoppey and McLeskey 2013).

Keeffe (2003) describes this as the leaders' struggle to find an equilibrium between the systems world of policy and accountability and the lifeworld of the school, which includes the beliefs and skills of staff, resources available, and educational program being implemented. Maintaining this balance can result in an internal philosophical struggle (Wood et al. 2014) for school leaders. In order to facilitate inclusive school cultures, principals must guide staff in discussion, debate and clarification of different perspectives of systems policy until they can reach a shared understanding about the value and applicability of these policies in the context of their specific school culture. Throughout this process, stakeholders make validity claims in order to challenge the collective claims and knowledge of the group. This promotes discussion of the threats or barriers that may prevent them from connecting the systems world and lifeworld. Once they facilitate staff to make this link, principals can help them to collaboratively take action to reduce these barriers and implement proactive strategies for inclusive practice across the school.

11.5.3 Roles and Actions of Leaders

Researchers have consistently demonstrated that effective leaders take specific actions to implement inclusive school policy in real world contexts. In a review of the literature of outcomes of inclusive education, Loreman (2014) categorised the actions of school leaders across three levels: micro, meso, and macro. At the micro level, which involves individuals and classroom contexts, school leaders maintain positive attitudes towards inclusion. They put in place staff development programs and mentor new staff. They facilitate and support collaboration between stakeholders, are knowledgeable about different collaborative models and help to utilise collaborative processes to create inclusive curriculum, instruction and assessment practices. The meso level encompasses school level actions. At this level, school leaders accept responsibility for creating inclusive school programs. They build school teams and facilitate a shared leadership approach to developing strategies and taking action to build an inclusive school community. More importantly, principals identify key individuals to guide and build knowledge of effective practices among staff. Working with staff, school leaders use data to evaluate their practice and make decisions. At the macro or systems level, regional or district leaders create multi-year plans to develop the capacity of the region to implement inclusive school practice.

In a case study of an effective inclusive school, Waldron et al. (2011) revealed that leaders at the school were significantly involved with teachers, and led the staff in setting a direction for the school. They worked with staff to redesign the school organisation, improve working conditions for school staff, provide high-quality instruction in all settings and ensure data were used to drive decision-making. Waldron and McLeskey (2010) also stress that effective school leaders must ensure that they help staff to build coherence among school priorities, maintain their focus on improving teaching practice and student outcomes, and develop their staff's confidence and ability to implement these actions. In another study, Hoppey and McLeskey (2013) found that an essential part of the principal's success in leading his staff to transform their school was his ability to bring out the best in his staff by nurturing their strengths and providing professional development. He also served as a buffer from external systems-level pressures such as accountability measures and facilitated distributed leadership within the staff.

Distributed leadership has frequently been cited as a key action of school leaders in inclusive schools (Waldron and McLeskey 2010). This involves not only collaborative action planning, but also shared decision-making. This enables staff to come to a shared understanding of key school or student issues and priorities, and to align these with their own priorities. By engaging in this process, principals are able to facilitate a shared commitment of staff, thus establishing the foundation of an inclusive school culture. These actions also help to support sustainability of practice after the principal leaves. In addition to developing collaborations with school staff, effective school leaders also build connections with families and the greater community (Dempster 2009). This involves facilitating a bi-directional flow of communication in which both families and staff have a voice, develop trust, and feel they are contributors in development and implementation of meaningful programs for their children (Angell et al. 2009).

Although shared leadership is important, Causton and Theoharis (2014) outline three other essential actions of successful school leaders in inclusive schools. First, principals must lead staff in creating a vision for inclusive practice at the school (Bays and Crockett 2007; Causton and Theoharis 2014). This requires the leader to clearly articulate their own stance and willingness to be actively involved in this area. They must also help staff to explore new meanings of inclusion and diversity (Riehl 2000). This may involve creating a common definition of inclusive education and clarifying the commitment to outcomes for "all" students (Causton and Theoharis 2014). More essential though is the presumption of competence of all students, which requires principals and staff to ask "how can the student be successful?" rather than "can the student be successful" (Causton and Theoharis 2014, p. 35).

After establishing the vision, principals must provide leadership for inclusive instruction, by guiding staff to develop and implement a comprehensive and cohesive approach to flexible, creative, student-centred pedagogies and practices. To do this, principals need to identify key people that have knowledge in specific areas and position them as instructional leaders at the school. This does not, however, mean abdicating responsibility to this person. To give them authority, principals must be seen as actively working with these leaders to construct flexible curriculum, instruction and assessment, and to model the implementation of current policy within the school context and current student population (Causton and Theoharis 2014). Finally, principals need to act as administrative leaders, providing leadership and support for delivery of inclusive programs. This involves developing their knowledge and ability to contextualise inclusive legislation and policy, as well as manage resources (Riehl 2000), develop staff, and create supportive organisational structures and environments. School leaders must assess the human resources at the school and redesign current instructional delivery models when necessary so that general and special education staff have a shared responsibility for all students, including those with disabilities (Bays and Crockett 2007; Causton and Theoharis 2014). They may also need to provide differentiated support to teachers with differing levels of knowledge and experience.

Fixsen et al. (2013) describes the process of translating school policy into practice as a series of stages that incorporate common elements, or drivers. These drivers require leaders to have knowledge and skills in areas defined as: competency, organisation, and leadership. To enact inclusive education policy, school leaders must be able to utilise all three drivers if they are to guide staff through the implementation of inclusive practice. The competency driver the development of content-related knowledge and skills leaders need to undertake change processes. These include knowledge of effective practices for specific outcomes and current education policies and initiatives. Principals utilise organisation drivers by engaging in administrative tasks to support the staff and school to enact the work. For example, a principal would be using the organisation driver when they create schedules that enable special education and general education staff to plan together. Leadership drivers are those tasks that are related to facilitating a shared understanding and vision of inclusive practice at the school. Principals would be using this driver when they help staff to work through perceptions of conflicting priorities between staff and families. Only by utilising all three of these drivers can school leaders successfully support staff to successfully explore, install, implement and revise inclusive practice at the school.

Another critical part of this process is the continual use of communication and data in what Fixsen et al. (2013) describe as a practice-policy communication loop. Leaders communicate policies and priorities to the staff who will implement core actions. Subsequently, staff communicate and provide feedback to leaders about the issues involved in implementing these actions. This, in turn, informs the policy and the actions of leaders to build the capacity of the team and create the necessary environment to enact the policy. A final element of this process is the input of external experts or supports. As inclusion has been identified as a complex or "wicked" problem, (p. 218), it is essential that school leaders recognise that they cannot have all the competencies required for complex issues. Thus, successful leaders seek outside help to build their capability and the capability of their school in specific areas, such as dealing with children with challenging behaviours.

11.6 Recommendations: Creating Effective Leaders

Implementing inclusive school policy is a challenging process. It involves bringing together a number of people with conflicting backgrounds, needs, and priorities, and helping these individuals to co-construct a shared knowledge and belief in their ability to meet the needs of all students, including those with disabilities. Principals arguably play the most critical role in creating inclusive school programs (Riehl 2000; Webster and Roberts 2015). Researchers have outlined the factors that influence the attitudes and willingness of school leaders to implement inclusive policy, and the key actions leaders must take to realise these policies in the real world context of school environments. These studies have also highlighted areas that still pose a challenge for school leaders in bringing together the systems world of inclusive policy and the lifeworld of the school community to create inclusive school programs (Graham and Spandagou 2011; Keeffe 2003).

Chief among these challenges is the differing views of leaders about inclusive education, and the need to develop the ability of school leaders to see the feasibility and benefit of inclusive practice for all students. Principals need to be supported to see how implementing inclusive education policy is linked to school reform and increased outcomes for all students. Only then can principals lead staff in making the shift from asking "where should the student be educated?", "which program works?" or "does this student belong here?", to engaging in collaborative problem-solving processes that enable them to create relevant solutions and meaningful practice that meets the needs of all stakeholders (Riehl 2000). As Riehl states "real organizational change occurs not simply when technical changes in structure and process are undertaken, but when persons inside and outside of the school construct new understanding about what the change means" (Riehl 2000, p. 60).

Leadership for inclusion is not a straightforward process. Principals must first examine their own values and determine to what extent they have the knowledge and skills to lead change in this area. This may involve the input of outside experts or systems leaders who can build the capacity of school leaders to enact the key drivers of change (Fixsen et al. 2013). These external supports play a critical role in questioning the current processes and beliefs and thereby providing a foundation for change. Gaining the input of individuals who are external to the school, and even the school system, can help school leaders to overcome barriers related to the current culture and create a climate for change. More importantly, outside "experts" or systems leaders can build the knowledge of leaders in key content areas such as knowledge of needs of and effective practice for students with challenging behaviours. Systems leaders can also help school leaders to examine the underlying expectations of systems policy enabling them to address any concerns about those that seemingly conflict or pose a barrier to desired change for inclusive practice. This process is known as brokering and is a key aspect of helping principals to manage tensions between systems policy and the lifeworld of the school (Wenger 1998). Although research in this area is limited, Honig (2012) emphasises that systems leaders must engage in joint work with principals and must differentiate their support by using modeling and tools to help them to develop their capacity as instructional leaders at the school. This support must also be differentiated to the individual needs of different school leaders and school contexts.

Researchers have also learned that principals cannot mandate change but must develop trust with their staff (McLeskey and Waldron 2015). Trust is developed through bi-directional communication and is characterised by the extent to which individuals can depend on each other. For parents, bi-directional communication with schools means they have the opportunity to regularly ask questions and provide feedback and input about the school program including its organisational structures, policies and instructional processes. Too often school leaders communicate with parents, but do not facilitate or respond to parents in ongoing and meaningful ways. To facilitate trust in inclusion, principals must take an active role, not only as administrative leaders, but as instructional leaders and learners (Bays and Crockett 2007; Webster and Wilkinson 2015). Parents have indicated that they have a much higher trust in school leaders who are actively involved in IEP meetings or other decision making processes with parents (Shelden et al. 2010). School leaders must also be seen to actively participate in learning processes and to work with staff to implement differentiated instruction that is based on student needs rather than just current curriculum initiatives. To do this they need to work with staff to create processes and structures that support the inclusion of all students. For example, leaders and staff in a high school could create flexibility in homework policies to allow students to choose from a variety of options to work on specified learning objectives.

Leaders must also be able to recognise the systems world or lifeworld factors that pose a barrier or even oppress the implementation of inclusive school policy (Riehl 2000), and must utilise data to identify inequities in outcomes for marginalised groups such as students with challenging behaviours. Once they have identified these issues, school leaders and staff need to take action to adjust the environment and structures that are maintaining this gap. This may involve the creation of new forms of data and accountability to evaluate the outcomes of students with different needs and goals (McLeskey and Waldron 2015). For example, they may utilise videos to evaluate the ability of students to engage in social interactions and problem solving processes or develop alternative reporting formats for students with differing needs. By providing moral leadership (Crockett 2002), the principal can help the school community to not only address ethical issues involved in inclusive legislation and policy, but also to see how creating inclusive school cultures is linked to educational reform and better outcomes for all.

References

Agbenyega, J. S., & Sharma, U. (2014). *Leading inclusive education: Measuring 'effective' leadership for inclusive education through a Bourdieuian lens measuring inclusive education* (pp. 115–132). Bingley: Emerald Group Publishing Limited.

Ainscow, M. (2004). Developing inclusive education systems: What are the levers for change. *Journal of Educational Change, 6*, 109–124.

Anderson, J., & Boyle, C. (2015). Inclusive education in Australia: Rhetoric, reality and the road ahead. *Support for Learning, 30*(1), 4–22. https://doi.org/10.1111/1467-9604.12074.

Angell, M. E., Stoner, J. B., & Shelden, D. L. (2009). Trust in education professionals: Perspectives of mothers of children with disabilities. *Remedial and Special Education, 30*, 160–176.

Angelle, P., & Bilton, L. M. (2009). Confronting the unknown: Principal preparation training in issues related to special education. *AASA Journal of Scholarship & Practice, 5*(4), 5–9.

Artiles, A. J., Kozleski, E. B., & Waitoller, F. R. (2011). *Inclusive education: Examining equity on five continents*. Cambridge, MA: Harvard Education Press.

Auerbach, S. (2010). Beyond coffee with the principal: Toward leadership for authentic school-family partnerships. *Journal of School Leadership, 20*, 728–757.

Bays, D. A., & Crockett, J. B. (2007). Investigating instructional leadership for special education. *Exceptionality: A Special Education Journal, 15*, 143–161. https://doi.org/10.1080/09362830701503495.

Beauchamp, T. (2012). *Addressing high rates of school suspension*. Paramatta: UnitingCare Children, Young People and Families.

Billingsley, B. S., & McLeskey, J. (2014). Role of principals in inclusive schools. In J. McLeskey, N. L. Waldron, F. Spooner, & B. Algozzine (Eds.), *Handbook of effective inclusive schools, research and practice* (pp. 67–79). London: Routledge.

Boscardin, M. (2005). The administrative role in transforming secondary schools to support inclusive evidence-based practices. *American Secondary Education, 33*, 21–32.

Boyle, C., Scriven, B., Durning, S., & Downes, C. (2011). Facilitating the learning of all students: The 'professional positive' of inclusive practice in Australian primary schools. *Support for Learning, 26*(2), 72–78. https://doi.org/10.1111/j.1467-9604.2011.01480.x.

Causton, J., & Theoharis, G. (2014). How do schools become effective and inclusive. In J. McLeskey, N. L. Waldron, B. Algozzine, & F. Spooner (Eds.), *Handbook of effective inclusive schools, research and practice* (pp. 30–42). London: Routledge.

Chrispeels, J. H., & Martin, K. J. (2002). Four school leadership teams define their roles within organizational and political structures to improve student learning. *School Effectiveness and School Improvement, 13*(3), 327–365. https://doi.org/10.1076/sesi.13.3.327.3430.

Christensen, J., Robertson, J. S., Williamson, R., & Hunter, C. (2013). Preparing educational leaders for special education success: Principals' perspectives. *The Researcher, 25*(1), 94–107.

Cole, C. M., Waldron, N., Majd, M., & Hasazi, S. (2004). Academic progress of students across inclusive and traditional settings. *Mental Retardation, 42*(2), 136–144.

Crockett, J. B. (2002). Special education's role in preparing responsive leaders for inclusive schools. *Remedial and Special Education, 23*, 157–168. https://doi.org/10.1177/07419325020230030401.

Crockett, J. B., Neely, H., & Brown, K. G. (2000, February). *Administrating special education: Is it just a matter of discipline*. Paper presented at the Eastern Educational Research Association, Clearwater, FL.

Daly, E. (2013). *Student suspensions. A research review. Stage one. Commission for children Tasmania*. Retrieved January, 2, 2014 from http://www.childcomm.tas.gov.au/wp-content/uploads/2013/12/Student-Suspensions.A-Research-Review-Stage-One.-E.Daly-Nov-2013.pdf

Davidson, D. N., & Algozzine, B. (2002). Administrators' perceptions of special education law. *Journal of Special Education Leadership, 15*(2), 43–48.

Dempsey, I. (2012). The use of individual education programs for children in Australian schools. *Australasian Journal of Special Education, 36*, 21–31. https://doi.org/10.1017/jse.2012.5.

Dempsey, I., & Davies, M. (2013). National test performance of young Australian children with additional educational needs. *Australian Journal of Education, 57*(1), 5–18. https://doi.org/10.1177/0004944112468700.

Dempster, N. (2009). *Leadership for learning: A framework synthesising recent research. edVentures*. Canberra: The Australian College of Educators.

Dickson, E. (2008). The inclusion and exclusion of students with disability related problem behaviour: The contrasting approaches of Australia and the United States of America. *Australia & New Zealand Journal of Law and Education, 13*(2), 49–63.

Disability Discrimination Act. (1992). Retrieved from http://www.austlii.edu.au/au/legis/cth/consol_act/dda1992264/

Dixon, R. M., & Verenikina, I. (2007). Towards inclusive schools: An examination of socio-cultural theory and inclusive practices and policy in New South Wales DET schools. *Learning and Socio-cultural Theory: Exploring Modern Vygotskian Perspectives International Workshop 2007, 1*(1), 192–208.

Fisher, D., Sax, C., & Grove, K. A. (2000). The resilience of changes promoting inclusiveness in an urban elementary school. *The Elementary School Journal, 100*, 213–227.

Fixsen, D. L., Blase, K. A., Metz, A., & Van Dyke, M. (2013). Statewide implementation of evidence-based programs. *Exceptional Children, 79*, 243–230.

Fredrickson, N., Simmonds, E., Evans, L., & Soulsby, C. (2007). Assessing the social and affective outcomes of inclusion. *British Journal of Special Education, 34*, 105–115.

Freeman, S. F., & Alkin, M. C. (2000). Academic and social attainments of children with mental retardation in general education and special education settings. *Remedial and Special Education, 21*(1), 3–26.

Graham, L. J., & Jahnukainen, M. (2011). Wherefore art thou, inclusion? Analysing the development of inclusive education in New South Wales, Finland and Alberta. *Journal of Education Policy, 26*, 263–388. https://doi.org/10.1080/02680939.2010.493230.

Graham, L. J., & Spandagou, I. (2011). From vision to reality: Views of primary school principals on inclusive education in New South Wales, Australia. *Disability & Society, 26*(2), 223–237. https://doi.org/10.1080/09687599.2011.544062.

Hehir, T., & Katzman, L. I. (2012). *Effective inclusive schools: Designing successful schoolwide programs*. San Francisco: Jossey-Bass.

Honig, M. I. (2012). District central office leadership as teaching. *Educational Administration Quarterly, 48*(4), 733–774. https://doi.org/10.1177/0013161x12443258.

Hoppey, D., & McLeskey, J. (2013). A case study of principal leadership in an effective inclusive school. *The Journal of Special Education, 46*, 245–256. https://doi.org/10.1177/0022466910390507.

Hoppey, D., & McLeskey, J. (2014). What are qualities of effective inclusive schools? In J. McLeskey, N. L. Waldron, F. Spooner, & B. Algozzine (Eds.), *Handbook of effective inclusive schools* (pp. 17–29). London: Routledge.

Horrocks, J. L., White, G., & Roberts, L. (2008). Principals' attitudes regarding inclusion of children with autism in Pennsylvania public schools. *Journal of Autism and Developmental Disorders, 38*, 1462–1473. https://doi.org/10.1007/s10803-007-0522-x.

Individuals with Disabilities Education Act, 20 U.S.C. § 1400 (2004).

Keeffe, M. (2003). The principal's governance of inclusion and the requirements of the disability discrimination legislation: Are they words apart? (K. Lindsay, Ed.) *Australia and New Zealand Journal of Law and Education, 8*(1), 69–76.

Keeffe, M. (2004). Principal's stress: Tensions between the requirements of the disability discrimination legislation and the governance of inclusion in schools. In *Proceedings AARE annual conference*, Melbourne.

Kunc, N. (1992). The need to belong: Rediscovering Maslow's hierarchy of needs. In R. Villa, J. Thousand, W. Stainback, & S. Stainback (Eds.), *Restructuring for caring and effective education*. Baltimore: Paul Brookes.

Kurth, J. (2009). *Academic outcomes in inclusive and non-inclusive special education programs for adolescents with autism spectrum disorders*. Dissertation abstracts international Section A: Humanities and social sciences, *69*(11-A), 4291.

Kyriazopoulou, M., & Weber, H. (Eds.). (2009). *Development of a set of indicators for inclusive education in Europe*. Odense: European Agency for Development in Special Needs Education.

Lilley, R. (2012). It's an absolute nightmare: Maternal experiences of enrolling children diagnosed with autism in primary school in Sydney, Australia. *Disability and Society, 28*, 514–526. https://doi.org/10.1080/09687599.2012.717882.

Loreman, T. (2014). Measuring inclusive education outcomes in Alberta Canada. *International Journal of Inclusive Education, 18*, 459–483. https://doi.org/10.1080/13603116.2013.788223.
Loreman, T., Deppeler, J., & Harvey, D. (2011). *Inclusive education: Supporting diversity in the classroom.* Crows Nest: Allen and Unwin.
Masters, G. (2009). *A shared challenge improving literacy, numeracy and science learning in Queensland primary schools.* Camberwell: ACER.
McLeskey, J., & Waldron, N. L. (2015). Effective leadership makes schools truly inclusive. *Phi Delta Kappan, 96*(5), 68–73. https://doi.org/10.1177/0031721715569474.
McLeskey, J., Waldron, N. L., Spooner, F., & Algozzine, B. (2014). What are effective inclusive schools and why are they important? In J. McLeskey, N. L. Waldron, F. Spooner, & B. Algozzine (Eds.), *Handbook of effective inclusive schools, research and practice* (pp. 3–16). London: Routledge.
Ministerial Council on Education Employment Training and Youth Affairs. (2008). *Melbourne declaration on educational goals for young Australians.* Carlton South: MCEETYA.
Oliver, M., & Barnes, C. (2010). Disability studies, disabled people and the struggle for inclusion. *British Journal of Sociology of Education, 31*(5), 547–560. https://doi.org/10.1080/01425692.2010.500088.
Peters, S. J. (2007). 'Education for all?' A historical analysis of international inclusive education policy and individuals with disabilities. *Journal of Disability Policy Studies, 18*(2), 98–108.
Praisner, C. L. (2003). Attitudes of elementary school principals toward the inclusion of students with disabilities. *Exceptional Children, 69*, 135–145.
Riehl, C. J. (2000). The principal's role in creating inclusive schools for diverse students: A review of normative, empirical, and critical literature on the practice of educational administration. *Review of Educational Research, 70*(1), 55–81. https://doi.org/10.3102/00346543070001055.
Robinson, V., Hohepa, M., & Lloyd, C. (2007). *School leadership and student outcomes: Identifying what works and why.* Melbourne: Australian Council of Education Leaders.
Ruijs, N. M., & Peetsma, T. T. (2009). Effects of inclusion on students with and without special educational needs reviewed. *Educational Research Review, 4*(2), 67–79.
Ryan, J. (2010). Establishing inclusion in a new school: The role of principal leadership. *Exceptionality Education International, 20*(2), 6–24.
Salisbury, C. L. (2006). Principals' perspectives on inclusive elementary schools. *Research and Practice for Persons with Severe Disabilities, 31*, 70–82.
Sharma, U., & Chow, E. W. S. (2008). The attitudes of Hong Kong primary school principals towards integrated education. *Asia Pacific Education Review, 9*, 380–3781.
Shelden, D. L., Angell, M. E., Stoner, J. B., & Roseland, B. D. (2010). School principals' influence on trust: Perspectives of mothers of children with disabilities. *The Journal of Educational Research, 103*, 159–170. https://doi.org/10.1080/00220670903382921.

Slee, R. (2011). *The irregular school: Exclusion, schooling and inclusive education*. London: Routledge.

Slee, R. (2013). How do we make inclusive education happen when exclusion is a political predisposition? *International Journal of Inclusive Education, 17*(8), 895–907. https://doi.org/10.1080/13603116.2011.602534.

Villa, R. A., Thousand, J. S., Meyers, H., & Nevin, A. (1996). Teacher and administrator perceptions of heterogeneous education. *Exceptional Children, 63*(1), 29–45. https://doi.org/10.1177/001440299606300103.

Waldron, N. L., & McLeskey, J. (2010). Establishing a collaborative school culture through comprehensive school reform. *Journal of Educational and Psychological Consultation, 20*, 58–74. https://doi.org/10.1080/10474410903535364.

Waldron, N. L., McLeskey, J., & Redd, L. (2011). Setting the direction: The role of the principal in developing an effective, inclusive school. *Journal of Special Education Leadership, 24*(2), 51–60.

Waldron, N. L., McLeskey, J., & Redd, L. (2014). A case study of a highly effective, inclusive elementary school. *Journal of Special Education, 48*, 59–70. https://doi.org/10.1177/0022466912440455.

Webster, A. A. (2016). Utilising a leadership blueprint to build capacity of schools to achieve outcomes for students with autism spectrum disorder. In G. Johnson & N. Dempster (Eds.), *Leadership for learning and effective change* (pp. 109–128). Melbourne: Springer.

Webster, A. A., & Roberts, J. M. A. (2014). *Building the capacity of schools to achieve outcomes for students with autism spectrum disorders: A pilot project*. Cairns: Department of Education, Training & Employment, Far North Queensland.

Webster, A. A., & Roberts, J. M. A. (2015). *Developing a region-wide approach to supporting students with autism spectrum disorder in inclusive schools: Building autism friendly schools and communities*. Cairns: Department of Education, Training & Employment, Far North Queensland.

Webster, A. A., & Wilkinson, J. (2015). Leading school communities to implement a sustainable school-wide model leading to outcomes for students with ASD. *Special Education Perspectives, 24*, 27–37.

Wehmeyer, M. L., Davis, S., & Palmer, S. B. (2012). 10 steps to independence: Promoting self-determination in the home, *Research to practice in self-determination series*, (4), 5. Retrieved from National Gateway to Self-determination website http://ngsd.org/sites/default/files/research_to_practice_sd_-_issue_4.pdf

Wenger, E. (1998). *Communities of practice: Learning, meaning and identity*. Cambridge: Cambridge University Press.

Wood, P., Evans, D., & Spandagou, I. (2014). Attitudes of principals towards students with disruptive behaviour: An Australian perspective. *Australasian Journal of Special Education, 38*(01), 14–33. https://doi.org/10.1017/jse.2014.5.

Section II

Inclusive Schooling and the Impacts of Disability Discrimination Legislation

12

Towards Inclusive Schools: The Impact of the DDA and DSE on Inclusion Participation and Exclusion in Australia

Roselyn Dixon

Access to and participation in a quality education is seen as a basic human right for all children, including those with disabilities and is mandated by Commonwealth legislation in Australia. Internationally there is strong support for education being provided in regular classrooms in regular schools for students with diverse learning needs. This chapter aims to provide insights into the implementation of the two most significant pieces of legislation the Disability Discrimination Act (1992) (DDA) and the related Disability Standards for Education (2005) (DSE) in Australia. Firstly, it will outline the state of Inclusive Education in Australia. Then it will focus on the areas of access and participation in education settings. The discussion of this chapter reveals that despite operating under the same national legislative acts, school systems are enacting Inclusive education in different ways leading to inconsistent levels of access (enrolment) and participation (inclusion). The chapter will also highlight how governmental and particularly non-governmental systems of education are using legal and other means to deny students with disabilities these mandated rights. The chapter will conclude by discussing the need for a new approach to the DDA and the DSE to allow the goals of the legislation and the Inclusion philosophy to be realised.

R. Dixon (✉)
School of Education, University of Wollongong, Wollongong, NSW, Australia
e-mail: roselyn@uow.edu.au

K. Trimmer et al. (eds.), *The Palgrave Handbook of Education Law for Schools*,
https://doi.org/10.1007/978-3-319-77751-1_12

12.1 Introduction

In 1990, UNESCO challenged the exclusion of students with disabilities from high quality education. There was a call for allowing all students to successfully access education regardless of ethnicity, religion, gender, socio-economic standing or ability (UNESCO 1990). The UNESCO Salamanca Statement (UNESCO 1994) further expanded this idea and dictated that education in regular classes in regular schools should be available as a first option for 'all students' worldwide. Since then there has been a global movement supporting Inclusive Education (Graham and Jahnukainen 2011) (see Spandagou chapter for further UNESCO developments). However, there is still recognition that some educational systems are excluding students with diverse learning needs. In Australia this development has had an impact on access (which can be conceptualised as enrolment) and participation (which can be conceptualised as Inclusive Education), two key areas mandated by Commonwealth legislation for all students with diverse learning needs. Access and participation are one of Loreman's (2014) guides for the assessment of Inclusive School Environments.

Inclusive Education is a philosophy that is grounded in social justice and is a rights-based approach to the provision of education for students with disabilities (Dixon and Verenikina 2007). Guthrie and Waldeck have described inclusiveness in education as a rights-based approach to education, i.e. the right of a student to have equal access to education. In the context of disability discrimination, inclusiveness embraces the notion that 'separation of students by reason of differences arising out of their disability is detrimental not only to the student with a disability but also to all other participants in the education institution as well' (Guthrie and Waldeck 2008, p. 141).

Even though Inclusive Education was adopted over 20 years ago, it has not had an easy implementation in Australia (Forlin and Bamford 2005). Whilst there is no universally accepted definition for Inclusive Education (Graham and Slee 2008), it is internationally accepted that the meaning of Inclusive Education has shifted from being about students with a disability to an emphasis on diversity. However, in Australia, Inclusive Education is still largely seen through the lens of disability and special education. Shaddock et al. (2009), observe that the inclusion movement has primarily been a special education movement.

When the Australian Government developed the Disability Discrimination Act (1992) (DDA) its goal was to give students with disabilities, as far as is practicable, the same educational rights as all other students. The Disability Standards for Education (2005) (DSE) were developed to outline clearly the obligations of all education providers under the DDA (ComLaw 2016). The Disability Standards for Education (DSE 2005) (ComLaw 2016) came into effect in August 2005. The Standards are subordinate legislation under the Disability Discrimination Act (1992) and provide more detail about the rights of students with disability than the DDA does. The Standards are intended to clarify the rights of students with disability to access and participate in education and training, and to give education providers more guidance on how they can meet their obligations under the DDA. The DDA and the DSE apply to a very broad range of disabilities, and apply to all education settings ranging from early childhood to tertiary institutions. The DSE clearly outline that reasonable adjustments are required in every educational setting so that students with disabilities can experience inclusion. The DSE specify how education will be made accessible to students with disabilities by outlining key areas. These key areas are access (enrolment), participation (inclusion), curriculum development, accreditation and delivery, student support services and elimination of harassment and victimisation (Commonwealth of Australia 2011, p. 5). This chapter will be examining the relationship between the DDA and DSE and key areas of access and participation in the Australian Education system. There is a need to assess if the DDA and the DSE have had an impact on Inclusive Education particularly with regard to the education of students with a disability.

12.1.1 Limit of Rights Based Legislation

All education systems are governed by the legislative acts of the Australian Human Rights Commission Act (1986), DDA (1992) and DSE (2005), ComLaw (2016), Racial Discrimination Act (1975) and the Sex Discrimination Act (1984). However, the legislation does not mandate for Inclusive Education (Anderson and Boyle 2015) and does not stipulate that it is the right of students to receive their education in the least restrictive environment as does legislation in the UK and USA (Dickson 2008).

Even though it is more than ten years since the implementation of the DSE, many students are still denied access to an inclusive education (IE) (Cologon 2013). There is a need to assess if the DDA and the DSE have had an impact on IE particularly with regard to the education of students with a disability.

The focus of this chapter will be on how, in spite of it being unlawful under the DDA and the DSE, schools have been using the paucity of disability discrimination education case law, sophisticated litigation strategies under the complaints process, and minimal compliance to exclude students with disabilities across all sectors particularly in the areas of access and participation. The practice/policy divide identified by this author (Dixon and Verenikina 2007) and others (Graham and Spandagou 2011) is persisting in Australia.

12.2 Lack of Positive Precedents in Education Case Law

It has been postulated that the first step in understanding inclusion it to understand exclusion and exclusionary practices (Slee 2011). Anderson and Boyle (2015) suggest that the number of students who are excluded from inclusive programs is increasing and that even as Inclusive Education is the policy in all states of Australia and is being funded generously more segregated programs are being created (Graham and Jahnukainen 2011). Also, the rates of suspension for students with disabilities are increasing (Daly 2013). However, even though these practices seem to be in breach of the law there is a paucity of successful claims under the DDA. This has led to a lack of case law and positive precedent which is very important in the Australian legal system (O'Connell 2016). So given the breadth and depth of the Anti-Discrimination legislation related to education in Australian why are there so few complaints and even fewer cases taken to court?

This problem relates to the mechanism for dealing with breaches of the legislation. The complaints have to be made on an individual basis, usually by parents. The process involves extensive consultation before there can be access to the courts. Also complaint data is private so it is impossible to know the exact number of complaints and the issues that they relate to. Also data is destroyed after three years (O'Connell 2016).

Other reasons for the lack of complaints relate to fear of reprisals for students, advocacy fatigue for families and the negative impact of lack of case law. There have been a number of cases brought against the Education systems in Australia but most have not succeeded particularly, the ones that concern students with behavioural and emotional disabilities. The example of Walker v State of Victoria (2011) FCA, 258 is illustrative of many of the issues related to the failure of 'school' cases. Alex Walker had a diagnosis of dyslexia, attention deficit hyperactivity disorder and Asperger syndrome. These conditions led him to increasingly exhibit aggression, swearing, bullying of other students and occasional violence. As a result of these behaviours Alex was denied access to many areas of school such as lunch and recess and excursions. He was suspended many times and placed on part-time attendance by at least two state schools over a period of ten years. Alex was able to take his case to court because behaviour relating to a disability is protected under the DDA. The case was unsuccessful because of a technicality, however, it exemplifies features of most of the cases. All of which have been unsuccessful. The student concerned is male with a disability with Attention Deficit Hyperactivity Disorder and Asperger Syndrome being common and intellectual disability being occasionally a factor. Usually after an act of aggression, there is a pattern of increasing exclusion which parents then argue has led to less favourable treatment because of the student's disability. The lack of successful precedent is explained by O'Connell (2016) as the supposed impact of youth criminality overshadowing the protection offered by the DDA and that the courts are more likely to make judgements that support the safety needs of teachers and students and the maintenance of a positive learning environment. In other words the courts in Australia favour majority rights over protection for a student with disabilities if acts of aggression have been committed even if behavioural difficulties are part of the diagnosis. Obviously, the right to access and participation under the DSE is being overridden. This section of the DDA and the DSE needs greater clarification. Further explanation of significant landmark cases in Australian Disability Law are developed in the Dickson, the Dickson and Cumming, and the Poed chapters included in this section.

12.3 How America and Australia Differ in Enforcing Suspension and Expulsion

Dickson (2008) has outlined the differences for students facing suspension or expulsion between Australia and USA. In the United States, the issue of students with disability related problem behaviour is addressed in the context of the Individuals with Disabilities Education Act (IDEA 2004) which creates a positive right to inclusion for students with disabilities in 'the least restrictive environment'. The IDEA provides protection for students with disabilities who have displayed behaviour that might lead to a suspension and expulsion from their placement. There is an understanding that the school policy provisions for acceptable behaviour may not always apply to students with disabilities. Generally it is expected that a student with a disability can be suspended for a maximum of 10 days for discipline code violations. Dickson (2008) refers to these as 'Stay put' provisions where the first step in a process of meetings and consultation a 'manifestation determination' hearing, must be scheduled within 10 days of any attempt to exclude a child because of behaviour. Key concepts in the manifestation hearing are:

1. Was there a direct/ substantive link between the behaviour and the disability?
2. How aware was the individual of the nature and quality of their behaviour?
3. At the time of the behaviour, how able was the individual to control their behaviour?
4. If intervention strategies for managing behaviour have been identified, how effectively were these applied in this situation?
5. If the conduct in question was a direct result of the local educational agency's failure to implement the Individual Education Plan?

Whilst all of these questions will be discussed, if the behaviour is determined to be a result of either question 1 or 5 it will be held to be a manifestation of the child's disability. Where the behaviour is determined to be a 'manifestation' the general rule is that the student must be allowed to return to school and the onus is on the school to adjust the student's individual education program to address what can be done to mitigate the causes and effects of the behaviour.

The US position, slightly amended in 2004 to give schools more support to remove students who exhibit violence, is very different to the Australian position. These differences include a mandated provision of behavioural interventions, the opportunity for parents and teachers to make decisions based on evidence related to the incidents of students with disabilities, and an implied understanding that the school must take responsibility for implementing the Individual Education Plan. These mandated differences combined with a right to a least restrictive environment ensure that there is greater protection in the USA for students with behavioural problems.

By contrast in Australia, the areas of concern highlighted by the 'school' cases outlined above, there is:

1. *Limited acknowledgement of the relationship between the situation and the disability of the student.*
2. *Limited recognition of extenuating circumstances such as significant influence of cognitive development, confusion and stress at the time of many incidents.*
3. *Little significant evaluation of the established intervention strategies to determination the significance of the incident.*

4. *Little demand for more preventative strategies in the management of future incidents*
5. *Reliance on punishments that have been shown to have limited value as deterrents of future behaviours.*

12.4 Strategic Litigation Strategies

The second strategy that has enabled schools to avoid complaints being taken to court is that of strategic litigation strategies by all of the Education Systems. The complaints process relies on individuals, usually parents, to make complaints. These 'small complainants' are opposed by 'Big Responders' (i.e. the Education systems). Big Responders can significantly elongate legal proceedings often leading to advocacy fatigue in the parents. In addition, parents may be afraid of reprisals on their children if they win and having to pay exorbitant costs if they lose the case. If the education systems suspect that the complaint might have some validity, they offer confidential settlements. The only cases that are allowed go to court by the Education Systems are the ones that are assessed as being likely to fail in the legal process.

The decisions of the Australian courts which have led to no positive precedents in Case Law and the emphasis on confidential conciliated outcomes could be seen as support for exclusionary practices for students with problem behaviours. This support has also reduced the need for Australian school executive and staff to re-evaluate established intervention strategies to determine their significance to the incident or to apply more preventative strategies in the management of future incidents. Instead of implementing preventative strategies that might facilitate inclusion in the mainstream environment, they rely on punishments that have little significance as deterrents and also lead to exclusion. The USA model of 'manifestation determination' would ensure more inclusive outcomes for students with disability related problem behaviours.

Therefore, disciplinary action that does not use the DDA to protect the rights of the students with disabilities because of the conflict with the rights of the majority is one driver for the exclusion from access and participation of some students with disabilities. The other driver is the use of a mixture of formal and informal strategies to deny access and participation whilst maintaining the illusion of minimal compliance with the DDA and DSE. These strategies are particularly evident in the Independent School System in Australia.

12.5 The Illusion of Minimal Compliance with DDA and DSE

The Australian education system is complex (Dinham 2008). It is comprised of the public (state supported), Independent and Catholic systems, with responsibility for funding being shared between the Commonwealth and state/territory governments (Anderson and Boyle 2015). However, there is an over-representation of students with a disability in government schools, particularly in disadvantaged areas. This is because government schools receive extra funding from the state to support children with disabilities. Not all independent schools are entitled to this (Kenway 2013). It also follows logically that students with emotional and behavioural disabilities are overrepresented in government schools.

In theory, all education systems must conform to the provisions of the DDA and the DSE, however in reality non-government schools are able to employ exclusionary practices and deny enrolment to students with disabilities. This process is called gate-keeping, all school systems may be using some of these strategies but the extent of the gate-keeping problem is unknown because not all private schools, in all states, are required to be open about their enrolment processes, as they often feel their role is to provide "choice" for parents and not to have to provide for every student. As many private schools compete for enrolments and exam results, there is a disincentive for them to take students who may have a negative impact on their overall results.

Formal Processes which Schools may implement include:

1. *Citing 'unjustifiable hardship' in relation to having to provide facilities and resources for the student.*
2. *Asking parents to pay extra money so the school can employ support staff or purchase equipment.*
3. *Asking for NAPLAN (literacy and numeracy) results as part of their enrolment application process, citing they are needed for class placement. In reality there is also a high likelihood that a child with a poor NAPLAN record will not be offered a place.*
4. *Some Private schools may also employ a student interview process and some require children to sit academic entrance tests.*
5. *Making all student sign a behaviour contract that enforces Zero Tolerance for Behaviour.*
6. *In the government school sector, catchment boundaries are used (sometimes selectively) to deny enrolment to children with additional support needs* (Graham et al. 2016).

These are all formal processes, advertised on websites and school prospectuses. However, there are many more informal practices designed to present barriers to the enrolment of particular students.

12.6 Informal Processes

These informal practices are more insidious and involve:

1. *Advising parents to send their child to another school that could better support them*
2. *Limiting the time that the child spends in school, either through partial enrolment (only allowing the child to attend school on the days that funding is available) or*
3. *Informal suspension (regularly calling the parents to pick up the child during the day).*

12.7 A Way Forward

As the DDA and the DSE have been implemented for over a decade, it is timely to reevaluate their impact on Inclusive Education in Australia for students with disabilities. Although the Legislation and the Standards have been considered to be a strong framework, the implementation of the Standards into practice in school environments has been problematic, with the policy/practice divide showing few signs of abating. In fact, some educators feel that little has changed for many students with disabilities. Despite multiple inquiries, exclusion of students with disabilities has continued, which suggests that current protections are inadequate.

This chapter has highlighted three areas of concern that are impacting on access and participation in a quality education for students with disabilities in Australia. These are the lack of positive precedent in Case Law, the strategic litigation employed by the Education systems and the Illusion of Minimal Compliance, particularly by the Independent School sector which employ both formal and informal gate-keeping strategies.

The major conclusion of the first two areas of concern suggests that quite significant changes are needed to the complaints process. Future reform of the DDA and DSE requires a new approach. It has to move away from an individual complaints process driven by a deficit view of disability and advocacy fatigued parents to a strengths process which guarantees rights, such as the

USA model, and does not encourage recourse to the legal system which in the past has not supported the rights of students with disabilities particularly if they exhibit aggressive behaviour.

At the present time the lack of enforceable compliance, combined with the legal complexity of the complaints process decreases the effectiveness of the DDA and the DSE. Unless an individual makes a complaint, there is no consequence for the education providers so therefore there has been little incentive for systemic change. Systemic change might be brought about if the complaints focus is transformed to a compliance focus with improved monitoring and data collection.

The Illusion of Compliance which has been described in this chapter as gate-keeping can only occur in a system where the schools are reasonably confident they will not be penalised for it. The allocation of government funding to both private and independent schools may eliminate most of the gate-keeping strategies and encourage private schools to enrol students with a disability (Graham et al. 2016). Many of the strategies that are allowing schools to employ gate-keeping strategies could be overcome by allocating government funding to both private and public schools as an incentive to the private school system. In this way support can be provided to all students with a disability whichever school they attend.

12.8 Conclusion

Access to and participation in a quality education is seen as a basic human right for all children, including those with disabilities and is mandated by Commonwealth legislation in Australia. Internationally there is strong support for education being provided in regular classrooms in regular schools for students with diverse learning needs. This chapter has aimed to provide insights into the implementation of the two most significant pieces of legislation the Disability Discrimination Act (1992) (DDA) and the related Disability Standards for Education (2005) (DSE). It has revealed that even though all states operate under the same national legislative acts, school systems are enacting Inclusive education in different ways leading to inconsistent levels of access (enrolment) and participation (Inclusion). The chapter also highlighted how governmental and particularly non-governmental systems of education are using legal and other means to deny students with disabilities these mandated rights. The chapter concluded by discussing the need for a new national approach to the DDA and the DSE to allow the goals of the legislation and the Inclusion philosophy to be realised.

The chapters that follow expand more specifically on many of the themes outlined in this chapter and provide more specific evidence of the policy/practice gap. The Alvarado and Cathi Draper Rodriguez chapter reiterates the place of strong legislation in ensuring the rights of students with disabilities through a detailed discussion of how the legislation for people of Culturally and Linguistically Diverse set legal precedents that guaranteed the educational rights of students with disabilities, in the United States. This reinforces the negative impact of case law in Australia.

The call for stronger implementation outlined in this chapter is reiterated by Dickson and Cumming (in Chap. 14) who focus on the contentious area of adjustments in assessment under the DSE. Another area that is attracting attention from researchers and practitioners is the lack of participation in planning of educational programmes. Poed (in Chap. 15) uses the outcomes of two landmark cases to point out the different perspective and implications of ignoring or recognising student voice. She goes on to discuss the lack of student voice, the need for consultation and how this right has informed case law. The next chapter by Dickson (Chap. 16) and the following one by Cumming, O'Neill and Strnadova (Chap. 17) also pick up on one of the themes emphasised in this chapter, the difficulties encountered by students with problem behaviour under Australian Law and how they will be included in the school system after they have been in a juvenile justice placement. Dickson concentrates on the issue of problem behaviour through a detailed analysis of the notorious Purvis case of its impact on subsequent Case Law in Australia. Morgan, Murphy, Yeagar and Spies' chapter on the impact of assistive technology on the learning of students with disabilities, also considers the importance of school leaders being aware of the legal and ethical requirements for technology use for students with a range of diverse needs. They address the implications for school leaders, outline a conceptual framework and end with implications for practice. A bridge to the third section on International Law is provided by Spandagou's (Chap. 19) which emphasises Article 24 from the CRPD and the difficulties with implementation, recording and reporting of Inclusive Education. Finally, Felder (Chap. 20) discusses the Duty of Care which schools need to provide to students with complex medical needs.

References

Anderson, J., & Boyle, C. (2015). Inclusive education in Australia: Rhetoric, reality and the road ahead. *Support for Learning, 30*(1), 4–22. https://doi.org/10.1111/1467-9604.12074.

Australian Human Rights Commission Act 1986 – AustLII. www.austlii.edu.au/au/legis/cth/consol_act/ahrca1986373/

Cologon, K. (2013). *Inclusion in education: Towards equality for students with disability*. Issues paper, Children and Families Research Centre, Macquarie University.

ComLaw. (2016). *Disability standards for education 2005 [Cth] (DSE)*. Retrieved from http://www.comlaw.gov.au/Details/F2005L00767

Commonwealth of Australia (Attorney – General's Department). (2011). Disability standards for education. http://www.ag.gov.au/Humanrightandantidiscrimination

Daly, E. (2013). *Student suspensions. A research review. Stage one. Commission for children Tasmania*. Retrieved January, 2, 2014 from http://www.childcomm.tas.gov.au/wp-content/uploads/2013/12/Student-Suspensions.A-Research-Review-Stage-One.-E.Daly-Nov-2013.pdf

Dinham, G. (2008). Mandatory reporting of child abuse requirements for medical imaging professionals throughout Australia. *The Radiographer, 55*(3), 9–12.

Dickson, E. (2008). The inclusion and exclusion of students with disability related problem behaviour: The contrasting approaches of Australia and the United States of America. *Australia & New Zealand Journal of Law and Education, 13*(2), 49–63.

Disability Discrimination Act. (1992). Retrieved from http://www.austlii.edu.au/au/legis/cth/consol_act/dda1992264/

Dixon, R. M., & Verenikina, I. (2007). Towards inclusive schools: An examination of socio-cultural theory and inclusive practices and policy in New South Wales DET schools. *Learning and Socio-cultural Theory: Exploring Modern Vygotskian Perspectives International Workshop 2007, 1*(1), 192–208.

Forlin, C., & Bamford, G. (2005). Sustaining an inclusive approach to schooling in a middleschool location. *Australasian Journal of Special Education, 29*(2), 172–181.

Graham, L. J., & Jahnukainen, M. (2011). Wherefore art thou, inclusion? Analysing the development of inclusive education in New South Wales, Finland and Alberta. *Journal of Education Policy, 26*, 263–388. https://doi.org/10.1080/02680939.2010.493230.

Graham, L., & Slee, R. (2008). An illusionary interiority: Interrogating the discourse/s of inclusion. *Educational Philosophy and Theory, 40*(2), 277–293.

Graham, L. J., & Spandagou, I. (2011). From vision to reality: Views of primary school principals on inclusive education in New South Wales, Australia. *Disability & Society, 26*(2), 223–237. https://doi.org/10.1080/09687599.2011.544062.

Graham, L., Proctor, H., & Dixon, R. M. (2016). *How schools are avoiding enrolling students with disabilities in the conversation yearbook 2016: 50 outstanding chapters from Australia's greatest thinkers*. Melbourne: Melbourne University Press.

Guthrie, R., & Waldeck, E. (2008). Disability standards and inclusiveness in education: A review of the Australian landscape. *International Journal of Discrimination and the Law, 9*(3), 133–162.

Individuals with Disabilities Education Act (IDEA). (2004). U.S. Department of Education.

Kenway, J. (2013). Challenging inequality in Australian schools: Gonski and beyond. *Discourse: Studies in the Cultural Politics of Education, 34*(2), 286–308.

Loreman, T. (2014). Measuring inclusive education outcomes in Alberta Canada. *International Journal of Inclusive Education, 18*, 459–483. https://doi.org/10.1080/13603116.2013.788223.

O'Connell, K. (2016, May 5–6). *How the DDA and the DSE have been implemented in NSW for students with challenging behaviours.* Paper presented at the Aspect Autism in Education Conference, Melbourne.

Shaddock, A., MacDonald, N., Hook, J., Giorcelli, L., & Arthur-Kelly, M. (2009). *Disability, diversity and tides that lift all boats: Review of special education in the ACT.* Chiswick: Services Initiative.

Slee, R. (2011). *The irregular school: Exclusion, schooling and inclusive education.* Abingdon: Routledge.

UNESCO. (1990). *World declaration on education for all.* Online at http://www.unesco.org/education/efa/ed_for_all/background/jomtien_declaration.shtml. Accessed 28 July 2014.

UNESCO. (1994). *The Salamanca statement and framework for action on special needs education.* Paris: UNESCO.

13

Education of Students with Disabilities as a Result of Equal Opportunity Legislation

Jose Luis Alvarado and Cathi Draper Rodriguez

13.1 Introduction

Students with disabilities have many legal protections in the United States. Many of these protections can be traced back to lawsuits which were fought to better the education of students from culturally and linguistically diverse populations (Yell 2016). Because of these early and historic efforts by parents and advocates for fairness and equality, approximately, 6.5 million students with disabilities now have a right to a free and appropriate public education in the United States.

This chapter explores how seminal court cases that advocated for the rights for Culturally and Linguistically Diverse (CLD) students led to federal equal rights legislation for students with disabilities. The iterative process of litigation that leads to legislation makes clear how early district, state and federal court cases in the 1930s, 1940s, and 1950s set legal precedent that led to the historic Supreme Court ruling in Brown v. The Board of Education (1954). It was the Brown ruling that laid the foundation for Federal Legislation that

J. L. Alvarado (✉)
College of Education, California State University Monterey Bay, Seaside, CA, USA
e-mail: alvarado@csumb.edu

C. D. Rodriguez
Department of Education and Leadership, California State University Monterey Bay, Seaside, CA, USA
e-mail: cdraperrodriguez@csumb.edu

K. Trimmer et al. (eds.), *The Palgrave Handbook of Education Law for Schools*,
https://doi.org/10.1007/978-3-319-77751-1_13

guaranteed the educational rights of students with disabilities (Sauer and Jorgenson 2016). This chapter will present several cases, chronologically ordered, in order for educators to understand the education of students with disabilities has been shaped by legislation and court cases related to civil rights.

13.1.1 Dred Scott v. Sanford (1857)

Dred Scott v. Sanford (1857) involved the plaintiff, Dred Scott, who was born a slave in Virginia and sold to a military surgeon stationed in Missouri, where slavery was legal. In the course of service to the military surgeon, Scott frequently traveled to U.S. territories where slavery had been abolished. After the surgeon's death, the surgeon's widow "rented out" Scott and his family for domestic work on St. Louis homes. In 1846, Scott filed a suit in St. Louis circuit court claiming that since he had traveled to areas in which slavery was abolished, he should be granted freedom. The case eventually reached the U.S. Supreme Court and the decision was issued in 1857 remanding Scott to slavery. In essence, the Supreme Court determined that race, not slave status, defined a person's legal status, thus, blacks regardless of the fact that they were free or slaves, had no legal rights (Ehlrich 1974). This case is relevant in that it established the legal thinking at the time that race was the primary factor that determined the legal rights, or lack thereof, of black citizens.

13.1.2 Plessy v. Ferguson (1896)

This case involved a 34 year old African American who purchased a train ticket from New Orleans to Covington, Louisiana and attempted to board a whites-only rail car. Mr. Plessy's arrest and subsequent court case worked its way through the court system and it reached the U.S. Supreme in 1896. The U.S. Supreme court ruled that Louisiana's Separate Car Act of 1890 that called for separate accommodations based on race, was constitutional (Horton and Moresi 2001). This case set the constitutional foundation for the principle that separate facilities for blacks were constitutional as long as they were equal, or what came to be known as the *separate but equal* doctrine.

13.1.3 Robert Alvarez v. The Board of Trustees of the Lemon Grove School District (1931)

This was the first successful school desegregation court decision in the history of the United States (Alvarez 1986). The case is important because it established the rights to an equal education for children of Mexican immigrants despite the existing local, regional, and national attitudes of the time. Just as importantly, it punctuated the notion that the struggle to ensure an equal education for all had a much broader scope, one that was more than one being fought only in the deep south between African Americans and Anglo Americans.

The historic court-ordered desegregation case occurred in Lemon Grove, California in *Roberto Alvarez vs. the Board of Trustees of the Lemon Grove School District (1931)*. On July 23, 1930, the Lemon Grove school board started discussions on what to do with the more than 75 Mexican students who were attending the local grammar school. At the time, Latino and White students attended the Lemon Grove elementary school in nearly equal numbers, with a total enrollment of 169. Because of concerns over what Sanchez (2004) notes, the situation in the school, "had reached emergency conditions," which according to the school board included overcrowding as well as purported "sanitary and moral" disorders that were engendered by Mexican children. Thus, the School Board decided to build a separate "Americanization" school for them but no notice was given to the parents of the Mexican students (Alvarez 1986).

On January 5, 1931, the principal of the Lemon Grove Grammar School refused entry to Mexican students and directed them to go to the new school building, a wooden structure that came to be known as the stable or barn ("caballeriza"). Rather than following the Principal's directive, the students returned home and thereafter the parents boycotted the new "Americanization" school refusing to send their children to the separate school (Madrid 2008). Several Mexican parents sought assistance from the Mexican consul, and these parents, in turn, were put in contact with two lawyers who had worked for the consul in the past. These two lawyers filed a writ of mandate to prevent the school board from forcing their children to attend the segregated school (Alvarez 1986). The lawyers chose a student, Roberto Alvarez, to be the plaintiff in the class action suit. It is Important to note that most of the students had been born in the United States and spoke English. At least one student spoke no Spanish at all.

According to Alvarez (1986), on February 24, 1931, Judge Claude Chambers began hearing the case. In the progression of the case, Judge Chambers revealed the injustice of the differential treatment of Mexican students. In a telling exchange between the defendants and Judge Chambers, the Judge asked district representatives what they did when American children were behind academically. Specifically, the district representative noted that these students were kept in a lower grade. The Judge asked rhetorically if the district segregated these students. No response was given by the district and Judge Chambers noted why the district would do the same for Latino children. He further noted the benefits of the association of American and Mexican children in learning English.

The state municipal court judge ruled that the Lemon Grove segregated school was not educationally justified or supported by state law. The judge ordered the Mexican-American children to attend school on an equal basis with the others in the community (Bowman 2001). As cited in Bowman, the remedial order followed two days later and made clear that "the laws of the State of California do not authorize or permit the establishment or maintenance of separate schools for the instruction of pupils of Mexican parentage, nationality, and/or descent (p. 1771)." This was a bittersweet victory in that the court considered the state law permitting the segregation of African and Indian students and concluded that because Latinos were not African or Indian, their segregation was not defensible under state law (Alvarez 1986; Bowman 2001; Madrid 2008). Given that this was a municipal state court, the decision only applied to Lemon Grove.

To add context to the Alvarez case, it is important to recognize that historically in the United States, Latinos' classification as White rather than as African American. According to Bowman (2001), this justified the admission of Mexicans as United States citizens after the Mexican–American War. The Treaty of Guadalupe Hidalgo ended the Mexican–American War in 1848 and stipulated that former Mexican citizens were to be given all the rights of citizens of the United States. As Bowman notes, despite the clear language of the treaty,

> *Latinos in these areas struggled for American citizenship and when California gained statehood in 1850, its constitution allowed Latinos to become citizens by virtue of their whiteness. California courts followed their state constitution's lead, granting some Latinos the benefits of American citizenship, but, only because of their classification as White males. Unfortunately, courts that assigned Latinos a White racial identity for purposes of determining citizenship failed to recognize that Latinos did not have the social privileges that came with being White. Latino children often attended segregated schools; Latino neighborhoods were segregated from White neighborhoods; and Latinos suffered from employment discrimination. This characterization of Latinos as White is an outgrowth of the legacy of slavery. African Americans were not guaranteed United States citizenship until the passage of the Fourteenth Amendment in 1868, yet to have classified Latinos as African American would have been difficult for nineteenth century courts, given the clarity of the two groups' different geographical origins.* (pp. 1763–1764)

As historic as the Alvarez case was, it was limited in its impact on segregation practices in schools within the state of California and the nation.

13.1.4 Mendez et al. v. Westminster School District of Orange County et al. (1946)

This court case challenged racial segregation of students from Mexican heritage in California public schools. By 1945, protests against school segregation by Mexican-American parents had worked with the Ontario school board to consider integrating the previously all-Mexican Grove School. Similar protests were taking place in numerous Southern California districts. In Westminster, Gonzalo Mendez and several other Mexican American parents persuaded the Westminster School board to approve a bond issue to construct a new integrated school. But when voters turned down the bond, the board refused to take further action (Bowman 2001). In a neighboring Southern California district, Santa Ana, William Guzman was one of several parents protesting segregation practices within their school district. The parents asked that all children of Mexican descent who desired to transfer out of the "Mexican" schools be allowed to do so. The board refused the request, and further cut back the small number of symbolic transfers that it traditionally granted. Mendez and Guzman were among the five plaintiffs in the *Mendez v. Westminster* case. These parents decided to take legal action only after receiving no remedy from their respective school boards (Wollenberg 1974).

The Fourteenth Amendment to the United States Constitution was the basis for the Mendez suit filed in a California federal district court in 1945 (Wollenberg 1974). While the school districts claimed to segregate students for the purpose of language instruction, the district court concluded that the student assignment process was sometimes arbitrary with no knowledge of the student's English language proficiency. It is important to note that Latino students in California never were segregated at the demand of a state statute, but the district court concluded in Mendez that because the practice of segregating Latinos in public schools was a de facto practice, it violated the state and federal constitutions. It was therefore determined that the plaintiffs were entitled to injunctive relief so the defendant school districts could no longer segregate Latino students. The court's ruling noted, as cited in Bowman, that a "paramount prerequisite in the American system of public education is social equality" and as such, it must be "open to all children unified school association regardless of lineage" (pp. 1773–1774).

Important historical facts regarding this case were that the *National Association for the Advancement of Colored People (*NAACP) filed an amicus brief in Mendez at the appellate level. An amicus brief is a legal document filed in appellate court cases by non-litigants with an interest in the subject matter. The briefs advise the court of relevant, additional information or arguments that the court might wish to consider. This brief submitted by the NAACP introduced social science evidence about the general harm of segregation and the Ninth Circuit Court of Appeals affirmed the district court's decision, but the social science evidence was not part of its reported decision. As Wollenberg (1974) noted on the historical impact of the Mendez case: this case "was part of a process which stripped away the formal structure of legalized segregation and exposed the underlying conditions of racism and reaction that divide the American people and plague their consciences (p. 330)."

13.1.5 Hernandez v. Texas (1954)

This case involved a Latino man who was found guilty of murder by an all-white jury. Mr. Hernandez appealed the decision based on the fact that the state of Texas systematically excluded persons of Mexican heritage from jury duty. Attorneys for Mr. Hernandez argued that the Fourteenth amendment guaranteed protection on the basis of race and class. The decision extended constitutional protection for Mexican Americans and prohibited group-based discrimination. This was not an education-related case but the decision handed down by the U.S. Supreme Court, but, it set precedent for court challenges that followed addressing issues such as education, housing, school segregation, and voting rights (Cobb 2017).

13.1.6 Brown v. The Board of Education (1954)

In 1954, a ruling was made that would change the education of students with disabilities in the United States. In Brown v. The Board of Education (1954), it was argued that having separate schools for African American students was not an equal means of providing public education. It was the Brown ruling that laid the foundation for Federal Legislation that guaranteed the educational rights of students with disabilities (Sauer and Jorgenson 2016). Though the Brown decision was directly related to African American students, lawyers in later years successfully used the Brown decision as precedent for allowing women and children with disabilities to have more rights in public education (Chinn 2004).

The lawyers were able to show that 'separate but equal' was not appropriate for students with disabilities as well. The Brown decision meant that if a state decided to provide free, public education to its citizens then this opportunity must be afforded to all of the citizens. Until this argument was made for students with disabilities, many students with disabilities were still excluded from the public education setting (Chinn 2004).

13.1.7 Civil Rights Act of 1964

This landmark piece of legislation is considered the bedrock upon which all other civil rights legislation was built upon (Middleton et al. 1999). The Civil Rights act established the three foundational provisions of affirmative action, antidiscrimination, and equal opportunities found in subsequent civil rights legislation. President John F. Kennedy's focus, prior to his assassination was the civil rights bill. Upon his succession to the position of President of the U.S., President Lyndon B. Johnson forged a partnership with civil rights organizations in efforts to establish mutual support to pass civil rights legislation. Within three months of taking office, President Johnson saw the Civil Rights Bill pass the House and the Senate (Karatzas 2016). On June 2, 1964, President Johnson signed the civil rights bill into law which prohibited "the exclusion from participation in, or denial of benefits of, and the discrimination under Federally assisted programs on ground of race, color or national origin (p. 31)."

13.1.8 Wolf v. State of Utah (1969)

According to Crockett and Kauffman (1999), the repudiation of racial segregation in prevailing national views were applied to the notion that offering an education in separate environments would reinforce stigma. According to Burgdof, as cited in Crockett and Kauffman, these prevailing views held that by separating children and labeling them "exceptional" or "special" had a stigmatizing effect on these children. One of the first U.S. right to education cases that espoused this view was litigated in Utah. The *Wolf v. State of Utah* (1969) case involved two students, Richard Paulsen who was 18 years old, and 12-year old Joan Wolf (Crockett and Kauffman 1999). Both students were described in terms we would use today as having moderate cognitive disabilities and both had been denied admission to a public school system in the state of Utah. Because of this denial, parents had to pay for private daycare. The ruling in this case relied heavily on *Brown* and made the case that it would be difficult for children to succeed if they were denied the right and opportunity to an education. The ruling, just as in Brown, was grounded on the Fourteenth Amendment principle of equal protection under the law. The court further noted that segregating students had a negative impact on students' educational, emotional, and mental development.

Important to note that cases involving students with disabilities, as compared to Latino or African American students, were more than just about segregation, and in fact, these cases often dealt with the basic denial of access to an education. Whereas students of color were often educated in public facilities that were inferior to those of white children, students with disabilities were sometimes segregated, but often these children were denied a free and appropriate public education.

13.1.9 Diana v. Board of Education (1970)

In the Diana case, the misuse of standardized assessments with children from diverse populations was brought to light. This case centered around 9 Spanish-Speaking Mexican American children in Central California. Based on data received from intelligence assessments given only in English, the children had been placed in classrooms for students with intellectual disabilities. Further investigations indicated that the norming sample of the assessments did not match the backgrounds of the students and that items on the assessments were found to be culturally biased. It was determined that the use of these assessment instruments was inappropriate.

It was found that the Fourteenth Amendment rights of the students had been violated because the students were unable to understand the testing materials. When the students were allowed to take a cognitive assessment without the language impact, they scored an average of one standard deviation higher. This case was settled by consent decree, which is an agreement or settlement that resolves a dispute between two parties without admission of guilt or liability. The decree has several stipulations. Mexican American and Chinese American students needed to be reassessed. The students must be assessed again using their primary language. Local school districts had to develop plans to reintegrate the inappropriately placed children into general education. School districts became responsible for explaining any disproportionality in special education. This case led to the determination and subsequent legal changes that assessments must be conducted in the child's primary language. The state of California was required to develop assessments for use with non-English speaking students as well as nonverbal measures.

13.1.10 PARC v. The Commonwealth of Pennsylvania (1972)

The equal protection of children with intellectual disability was protected through the class action suit Pennsylvania Association for Retarded Children (PARC) v. the Commonwealth of Pennsylvania in Federal District Court. This was the first court case brought that considered the exclusion of children due to their disability. The plaintiffs in this case believed that the rights of children with intellectual disabilities had been violated through their exclusion from public school. The plaintiffs in this case established four points: (1) all children identified with intellectual disability will benefit from an individualized education, (2) public education does not consist only of academic instruction and experiences for students, (3) the state could not deny education to students with identified disabilities, and (4) the earlier intervention is provided to students with intellectual disabilities, the larger impact on their learning. This case was decided through consent decree in a Federal District Court where both sides of the case consent to the above. In addition, it was determined that all students with disabilities from 6 to 22 had the right to a free and appropriate public education and this education should be predominantly with their typical peers. Once again the solution in this case was largely based on the children's Fourteenth Amendment rights. It is important to note that this decree and resulting educational improvements took 11 years.

13.1.11 Mills v Board of Education of the District of Columbia (1972)

Another case which dealt with the exclusion of student with disabilities from public school was Mills v Board of Education of the District of Columbia. This class action suit was brought by the parents of children who had several different disability areas (e.g., intellectual disability, emotional disturbance, health impairment). This case was also based on the Fourteenth Amendment rights of the students. The students in this case had been removed from school in a variety of ways (e.g., expulsion, suspension, reassignment) without a due process. This resulted in the students being denied their right to an education. This case was also settled in a consent decree and it expanded upon the decree from PARC. The result was a specific set of processes related to the assessment, identification and placement of students with disabilities. This case along with PARC provided the foundation for the federal legislation which would be passed a few years after this case.

13.1.12 Section 504 of the Rehabilitation Act of 1973

In 1973 Congress passed The Rehabilitation Act of 1973, Section 504 was a short provision that was the first federal civil rights law to protect the rights of persons with disabilities. The law states:

> *No otherwise qualified individual with a disability in the United States, as defined in* section 705 (20) *of this title, shall, solely by reason of his or her disability, be excluded from the participation in, be denied the benefits of, or be subjected to discrimination under any program or activity receiving Federal financial assistance.* (U.S. Department of Labor 1973)

The significance of this law was that it mirrored other federal civil rights laws that prohibited discrimination by agencies that receive federal funds on the basis of race. Important to note that the law cited above has been updated to reflect changes in reference to individuals with disabilities as opposed to handicapped persons. This anti-discrimination law did not include funding for implementation and offered a broader definition of a person with a disability than the special education laws that followed. Under Section 504, the definition of a person with disability is functional and lists two broad categories of impairments (physical and mental) that impact major life functions.

13.1.13 Larry P. v. Riles (1972, 1979, 1984)

The Larry P v. Wilson Riles is another case that had a large impact on how students with disabilities are assessed in the United States, particularly, in California where students who are African American cannot be assessed using cognitive assessment. The plaintiffs in this case filed suit against the San Francisco Unified School District stating that the intelligence assessments being used to determine special education decisions were biased. However, unlike Diana, the assessments in this case were not believed to be biased due to language but rather culture. The students in this court case were African American and the impact of the biased assessments was a disproportionate number of African American students in special education.

It was found that in relation to the number of African American children in the district there were a larger number than should be expected in classes for children with intellectual disabilities. The court found for the plaintiffs in this case and stated that students from diverse populations could not be placed in special education until a non-biased identification process was identified. It was also decided that African American children in classrooms for students with intellectual disabilities should be reassessed using other approaches.

13.1.14 Education for All Handicapped Children Act: PL 94-142 (1975)

This landmark piece of Federal legislation came about because of parents of children with disabilities who exercised their civil rights (Itkonen 2007). This was the 142nd Public Law (PL) passed by the 94th session of the U.S. Congress, known as The Education for All Handicapped Children Act (EAHCA). This legislation assured access to public education for all children ages 3 to 21 with disabilities. Prior to PL 94-142, children who did not "fit" schools were often excluded from public schools (Keogh 2007). Because of the systematic exclusion of children with disabilities from access to a public education, the U.S. Congress was compelled to pass the EAHCA that established an educational bill of rights for students with disabilities with the promise of federal financial incentives for states to adopt policies that assure all qualified students with disabilities receive a free and appropriate public education. The Act, signed by President Gerald Ford on November 29, 1975, established a key set of principles: A free and appropriate public education, due process, non-discriminatory assessment, and an Individual Education Plan (IEP) for every student with a disability who qualified for special education (Yell 2016).

13.1.15 Smith v. Robinson (1984)

The case involved the Cumberland, Rhode Island, school district's refusal to fund a student's placement in a special education program. The parents filed a lawsuit against the school district seeking to overturn the decision to deny their child an education. The Federal District court ruled in favor of the parents and the court held that the child was entitled to a free and appropriate public education paid for by the school district. Parents sought reimbursement for attorney fees and through a series of appeals the case was heard by the U.S. Supreme Court. On July 5, 1984, the Supreme Court ruled that though parents won their case against the school district, the EAHCA was sole source of relief in cases brought under law. The law did not explicitly grant parents the right to a reimbursement of attorney fees and thus the parent's claim for the reimbursement of attorney fees was denied (Justia ND).

13.1.16 Handicapped Children's Protection Act (1986)

Congress recognized the importance of early intervention for young children and consequently passed this Federal law that expanded the ages of eligibility from 3 to 21 years to birth to 21 years. The law additionally addressed what many in Congress viewed was an injustice for parents who won their cases against school districts yet were unable to be reimbursed for attorney fees. The *Smith* ruling essentially created a system in which only those with sufficient resources could afford to advocate and challenge school districts. Thus, another important change in Federal disability law was the clarification that parents who were successful in challenging school districts in court were entitled to be reimbursed for attorney fees (Yell 2016).

13.1.17 Honig v. Doe (1988)

Though PARC and Mills both attended to the inclusion of students with disabilities in schools, there was still the question of removing students with disabilities from school as a disciplinary action. In 1988, the Supreme Court heard *Honig v. Doe* to determine the appropriate procedures for applying these disciplinary actions to students with disabilities. In this case, two students with emotional disturbance were expelled from school and it was maintained that this was a violation of their Individuals with Disabilities Education Act (IDEA). However, the court determined that in situations where the student is a danger to themselves or others, schools may remove them from the educational setting.

The court did adopt several guidelines that have since managed how school districts may impose disciplinary actions which involve the removal from their placement or school are to be determined. These guidelines are: (1) students with disabilities may not be removed from the educational setting for more than 10 days without the team considering a new Individualized

Education Plan (IEP), (2) the stay-put provision, which states that until determination regarding change in placement or setting is made, the child stays in their current placement, and (3) allows for the normal usage of discipline; however, provides guidelines for implementation.

13.1.18 Timothy W. v. Rochester School District (1989)

The Rochester school district refused to offer an education based on the argument that the student was not educable and that the services that he needed were medical rather than educational (Hentoff 1990). The parents filed a lawsuit against the school district and the Federal District Court ruled in favor of the school district noting that for a student with disability to qualify for special education, there had to be evidence that the child could benefit from such an education. The parents filed an appeal and on May 24, 1989, the First Circuit Court of Appeals ruled that under the Education for All Handicapped Children Act (EAHCA), schools were required to provide special education services to all students with disabilities regardless of severity of disabilities. On November 27, 1989, the U.S. Supreme Court declined to hear the Rochester, N.H., school district appeal of a court's decision thus affirming the First Circuit Appeals Court's findings that point to the fact that federal law made it abundantly clear that all handicapped children between the ages of three and twenty one have the right to a free and appropriate education, thus affirming the "zero reject" principle of the EAHCA. As Samuels (2014) quotes the First Circuit Court of Appeals,

> *...public education is to be provided to all handicapped children, unconditionally and without exception. It encompasses a universal right, and is not predicated upon any type of guarantees that the child will benefit from the special education and related services before he or she is considered eligible to receive such education.*
>
> *Congress explicitly recognized the particular plight and special needs of the severely handicapped, and rather than excluding from the Act's coverage, gave them priority status. The district court's holding is directly contradicted by the Act's legislative history, as well as statutory language.*

As Samuels points out, the case technically only applied to the jurisdictions under the First Circuit Court, however, the significance of the case was the fact that this was the first time that a district challenged the EAHCA on the grounds that a child was not educable.

13.1.19 Individuals with Disabilities Education Act (1997, 2004)

Amendments to the Education for All Handicapped Children Act (1975) were made in 1990. One of the changes was a change in the title of the legislation; the more person-first name of the Individuals with Disabilities Education Act (IDEA) was chosen. This change was made throughout the legislation. All references to the 'handicapped child' were changed to 'child with a disability' thus promoting the importance of the child over the disability. This reauthorization also extended the child's right to the Least Restrictive Environment (LRE) to ensure that the child spent the most amount of time feasible with students without disabilities. Other changes to the law were to include two new disability areas such as Traumatic Brain Injury and Autism (Yell 2016). Transition planning for students with disabilities, additional clarification of what related services students could receive, and meeting students' needs through assistive technology were also added.

The 1997 amendments of IDEA furthered the rights of students with disabilities (Yell 2016). This reauthorization included language which limited the amount of time a student with a disability could be out of school without a review of the impact of their disability on the problem behavior (e.g., manifestation determination). It also listed certain behaviors that would allow students with disabilities to be out of school for up to 45 days. During this revision, the legislation was reframed to encourage dispute resolution as opposed to litigation. A large focus of this revision was to continue improvements in the educational gains of students with disabilities. In order to ensure that schools districts were focusing on the educational growth of students with disabilities, students with disabilities must be included in any statewide assessment taken by all typically developing students. Districts must provide accommodations that meet the student's Individualized Education Plan during the assessments.

IDEA was once again reauthorized in 2004. While the rights of students with disabilities largely remained the same, some changes to these rights were made with this revision. One big change was a reversal of previous procedures based on the *Honig vs. Doe* decision. This reauthorization changed the previous 'stay-put' provision from the student having the right to stay in their current setting to the student having the right to an interim alternative education setting. Other rights that were changed in the 2004 revision were the parental right to request a due process hearing was limited to 2 years from the date of the issues being adjudicated. The 2004 reauthorization added language which allows school districts to use a Response to Intervention model during the identification of Learning Disabilities. This change may alleviate some of the difficulties with assessment that were raised in early court cases. It is likely that IDEA will be reauthorized again in the near future to continue to meet the needs of students with disabilities in the United States.

13.1.20 Every Student Succeeds Act (ESSA) (2015)

The seminal legislation regarding the education of students in the United States, the Elementary and Secondary Education Act (1965), was reauthorized in 2015 (ESSA 2015). There were few changes in this legislation which impacts the education of students with disabilities. Many believe the largest benefit for students with disabilities was the maintenance of the 1% ratio of alternative assessments (Darrow 2016). This allows for up to 1% of students identified with significant cognitive impairment to take an alternative assessment to determine their progress. Since IDEA (2004), there have not been substantive changes in how students with disabilities are educated in the United States. It will be important for a thorough review of rights, processes and procedures when Congress undertakes the reauthorization of the Individuals with Disabilities Education Improvement Act (IDEA 2004).

The Every Student Succeeds Act maintains rights for students with disabilities. Students with disabilities continue to have the right to access the general education curriculum. School districts must offer accommodations to students with disabilities during assessments. The revision of the legislation includes language related to Universal Design for Learning and the requirement that school districts are utilizing evidence-based practices.

13.2 Conclusion

Educational rights in the United States have been a common struggle for students from minority groups, those who speak languages other than English, and for students with disabilities. In discussing the details of each of the landmark court cases, it is clear to see the pattern of advocacy on the part of parents and civil rights organizations that leads to litigation. As the legislation is implemented, clarity on the limitations, or sometimes interpretation of said legislation then results in additional litigation that further refines future legislation. It is important to note that the U.S. system is designed with the principle of advocacy at its core and therein lies a limitation of this system as it relates to immigrants, minority students, and their families. The system fails to work as it should when parents come into the U.S. system holding a different set of values that are not based on the notion that parents are first and foremost advocates for their children's education. In many parts of the world, parents view educators and educational systems with the utmost respect and to question the decisions of an educator or an educational system would be considered disrespectful. Thus, for parents who espouse such values and yet have children receiving a public education in the U.S., it is clear to see that without the parent's advocacy, their children may not receive an appropriate education. It behooves educational systems and advocates to equip all parents whose children are educated in public schools in the U.S. with the necessary tools to be the best advocates for their children.

References

Alvarez, R. R., Jr. (1986). The lemon grove incident. *The Journal of San Diego History, 32*(2), 116–135.

Bowman, K. L. (2001). The new face of school desegregation. *Duke Law Journal, 50*, 1751–1808.

Brown v. Board of Education of Topeka, 347 U.S. 483 (1954).

Chinn, P. (2004). Brown's far reaching impact. *Multicultural Perspectives, 6*(4), 9–11.

Cobb, J. (2017). Hernandez v. Texas: A class apart. *Bullock Museum Online*. Retrieved May 2, 2017, from http://www.thestoryoftexas.com/discover/artifacts/hernandez-v-texas-spotlight-050115

Crockett, J. B., & Kauffman, J. M. (1999). *The least restrictive environment: Its origins and interpretations in special education, The LEA series on special education and disability*. New York: Routledge.

Darrow, A. A. (2016). The every student succeeds act (ESSA): What it means for students with disabilities and music educators. *General Music Today, 30*, 41–44. https://doi.org/10.1177/1048371316658327.

Diana v. California State Board of Education, No. C-70, RFT, (N. D. Cal. 1970).

Dred Scott v. Sandford, 60 U.S. 393 (1857).

Ehrlich, W. (1974). The origins of the Dred Scott case. *The Journal of Negro History, 59*(2), 132–142.

Every Student Succeeds Act of 2015, Pub. L. No. 114–95 § 114 Stat. 1177 (2015).

Handicapped Children's Protection Act of 1986, Public Law 99–372, 20 U.S.C. [section] 1415 (1986).

Hentoff, N. (1990). How Timothy W. got into school. *The Washington Post*. Published January 2, 1990. Retrieved May 1, 2017, from https://www.washingtonpost.com/archive/opinions/1990/01/02/how-timothy-w-got-into-school/c1b83691-a1b4-4a59-98f5-6976b5aebc3a/?utm_term=.24e2a0f46fd4

Honig v. Doe, 485 U.S. 305, 108 S.Ct. 592, 98 L.Ed, 2d 686 (1988).

Horton, J. O., & Moresi, M. G. (2001). Roberts, Plessy, and Brown: The long, hard struggle against segregation. *OAH Magazine of History, 15*(2), 14–16.

Individuals with Disabilities Education Act, 20 U.S.C. § 1400 (2004).

Individuals With Disabilities Education Act Amendments of 1997, 20 U.S.C. § 1415 et seq. (1997).

Individuals With Disabilities Education Improvement Act of 2004, 20 U.S.C. § 1400 et seq. (2004).

Individuals with Disabilities Improvement Education ACT (IDEA). (2004). Available from http://idea.ed.gov

Itkonen, T. (2007). PL 94-142: Policy, evolution, and landscape shift. *Issues in Teacher Education, 16*(2), 7–17.

Karatzas, K. D. (2016). Lyndon B. Johnson and the civil rights act of 1964. *Science Journal of History, Area Studies, International Relations, 21*(3), 25–33.

Keogh, B. K. (2007). Celebrating PL 94–142: The education of all handicapped children act of 1975. *Issues in Teacher Education, 16*(2), 65–69.

Larry P. v. Riles. 343 F. Supp 401 (N.D. CA., 1972).

Larry P. v. Riles, 495 F. Supp. 926 (N.D. Cal. 1979).

Larry P. v. Riles. United States Court of Appeals. Ninth Circuit. No. 80–427. January 23, 1984. Trial Court Decision Affirmed.

Madrid, E. M. (2008). The unheralded history of the lemon grove desegregation case. *Multicultural Education, 15*(3), 15–19.

Mendez et al. v. Westminister School District of Orange County, 64 F. Supp. 544 (1946).

Middleton, R. A., Harley, D. A., & Rollins, C. W. (1999). The historical and political context of the civil rights of persons with disabilities: A multicultural perspective for counselors. *Journal of Multicultural Counseling and Development, 27*(2), 105–120.

Mills v. Board of Education of District of Columbia, 348 F. Supp. 866 (D.D.C. 1972).

Plessy v. Ferguson, 163 U.S. 537 (1896).

Samuels, C. (2014). Landmark special ed. case confirming 'zero reject' rule marks 25 years. *Education Week Blog*, Published December 8, 2014. Retrieved April 29, 2017, from http://blogs.edweek.org/edweek/speced/2014/12/landmark_special_ed_case_confi.html

Sanchez, L. (2004, May 18). Before Brown. *The San Diego Union-Tribune* [Electronic version]. Retrieved April 28, 2017, from http://signonsandiego.com/uniontrib/20050518news_1n18grove.html

Sauer, J. S., & Jorgenson, C. M. (2016). Still caught in the continuum: A critical analysis of least restrictive environment and its effect on placement of students with intellectual disability. *Inclusion, 4*(2), 56–74.

Smith v. Robinson, 104 S. Ct. 3457 (1984).

Timothy W. v. Rochester School District, 875F.2d954 (1st Cir. 1989).

U.S. Department of Labor. (1973). *National rehabilitation act of 1973 § 504*. Retrieved May 1, 2017, from https://www.dol.gov/oasam/regs/statutes/sec504.htm

Wolf v. State of Utah, Civ. No. 182646 (Utah Dist. Ct. 1969).

Wollenberg, C. (1974). Mendez v. Westminster: Race, nationality and segregation in California schools. *California Historical Quarterly, 53*(4), 317–332.

Yell, M. L. (2016). *The law and special education* (4th ed.). Upper Saddle River: Pearson.

14

Reasonable Adjustment in Assessment: The Australian Experience

Elizabeth Dickson and Joy Cumming

14.1 Introduction

This chapter will explain the legislation, which underpins the right to reasonable adjustment in education in Australian schools. It will give examples of the kinds of adjustment which may be made to promote equality of opportunity in the area of assessment. It will also consider some of the controversies which have confronted, or which, it may be speculated, are likely to confront Australian education institutions as they work towards compliance with laws which impose the obligation to make reasonable adjustment to assessment policies and practices.

14.2 The Role of Assessment in Education

The process of school engagement has many elements: teachers prepare curriculum and work programs to target student learning; provide instruction and activities to promote student learning in these targets; and engage in

E. Dickson (✉)
School of Law, Queensland University of Technology, Brisbane, QLD, Australia
e-mail: e.dickson@qut.edu.au

J. Cumming
Learning Sciences Institute Australia, Australian Catholic University, Brisbane, QLD, Australia
e-mail: Joy.Cumming@acu.edu.au

K. Trimmer et al. (eds.), *The Palgrave Handbook of Education Law for Schools*, https://doi.org/10.1007/978-3-319-77751-1_14

assessments to make judgments about whether students have achieved the intended learning. Most systems of education also engage in external assessments of students, for certification or educational accountability purposes.

Increasingly, researchers, policy makers and practitioners have recognised the significant role that assessment plays in quality education. The nature and focus of assessment can be the drivers of student learning, a backwash effect that can be both negative and positive for learning. Assessment outcomes are used to indicate the academic standing of a student and can serve as gatekeepers to future work and study opportunities. They are, then, high stakes for all students, and especially for students with disability. In Australia, it is known that students with disability are less likely to complete secondary school and to transition to post school training and employment than peers without disabilities (Australian Bureau of Statistics 2011). The majority of students with disability, however, should be able to achieve similar education pathways and standards as students without disability (Australian Curriculum Assessment & Reporting Authority 2013).

Accessibility of assessment is identified by students and parents as a barrier for many students with disability (ACT Government Education & Training 2013; NSW Ombudsman 2013; Victorian Equal Opportunity & Human Rights Commission 2012). Even without a knowledge of law, it is apparent that many students with disability will not be able to complete assessments in the same form as other students and may be disadvantaged in demonstrating what they do know and can do (Cumming and Dickson 2013; Cumming et al. 2013). Assessments may need adjustments to address the circumstances of students with disability. The right to such adjustments is established in Australian law.

14.3 The Right to Reasonable Adjustment in Assessment

Before considering specific issues relevant to adjustment of assessment for students with disability, it is necessary to examine the legislative scheme, which operates generally to protect the interests of students with disability. Australia has a two-tiered system of anti-discrimination laws. At the Commonwealth level, there is a series of attribute specific anti-discrimination acts, including, relevantly, the *Disability Discrimination Act* 1992 (Cth) (DDA). Each state and territory has a generic anti-discrimination or equal opportunity act, prohibiting discrimination on the basis of a range of protected attributes, including impairment or disability, across a range of areas of public life, including education. The definition of disability (or 'impairment' in some Acts), the tests for discrimination and many of the exemptions which render discrimination lawful, as set out in the DDA, are mirrored in the state and territory Acts (See, e.g., *Discrimination Act 1991* (ACT) ss 7(j), 18; *Anti-Discrimination Act 1977* (NSW) s 49 L; *Anti-Discrimination Act* (NT) ss 19(j), 29; *Anti-Discrimination Act 1991* (Qld) ss 7(h), 38, 39; *Equal Opportunity Act 1984* (SA) s 74; *Anti-Discrimination Act 1988* (Tas) ss 16(k), 22(1)(b); *Equal Opportunity Act 2010* (Vic) ss 6E, 38, 40; *Equal Opportunity Act 1984* (WA) ss 66A, 66I).

While the Commonwealth could seek, perhaps, to oust the states and territories from this jurisdiction, relying on s. 109 of the *Australian Constitution* and its obligations under international human rights treaties, it explicitly tolerates duplication of protection (DDA s 13(3)). However, in respect of disability discrimination in education, the DDA sets the benchmark for what is required by schools if they are to avoid disability discrimination and minimise the potential for litigation. The DDA explicitly requires the making of 'reasonable adjustments' for students with disability so as to support their inclusion[1] in and achievement at school (ss. 5, 6, 22). Moreover, the *Disability Standards for Education 2005* (Cth) ('DSE'), passed under the authority of DDA s. 31, have been implemented to give guidance to education institutions as to the making of those reasonable adjustments. The DSE specify that reasonable adjustment is required in the areas of enrolment (Part 1), participation (Part 2), curriculum development, accreditation, and delivery (Part 3), and student support services (Part 4). Education institutions must also take 'reasonable steps' to prevent the harassment of students with disability (5). Moreover, in respect of the DSE, the Commonwealth does seek to prevail over state laws, indicating in DDA s 13(3A) that the terms of the DSE will override any inconsistency that may arise under a state or territory act. For this reason, the policies and procedures of education institutions in respect of the education of students with disabilities should be informed principally by the DDA and the DSE and those pieces of Commonwealth legislation will be the principal focus of this chapter.

The way legislation works, however, is demonstrated in the related case law. As well as cases which interpret and apply the DDA and DSE, this chapter shall refer, where relevant, to cases decided by state and territory tribunals and

[1] It is acknowledged that 'inclusion' is a contested term in the context of the education of students with disability. Analysis of the meaning of the term is beyond the scope of this chapter. For the purpose of this chapter, 'inclusion' is used by the authors to mean enrolment at a mainstream school which also enrols students without disability. It is also acknowledged that the *Disability Standards for Education 2005* (Cth) use the word 'participation' rather than inclusion in this context.

courts applying state and territory legislation. To date, there is only a handful of education cases, which interpret and apply the DDA and DSE, so state and territory case law assists in filling gaps in our understanding of the way the Commonwealth law protects students with disability. It should be noted, too, that because of the high stakes ramifications of assessment decisions for students in the tertiary sector, many of the cases, to date, concern those students. The way the law has been applied in these cases, however, is instructive for those working with students in the compulsory sector.

The DSE are particularly important for schools in that the effect of DDA s 34 is that compliance with the DSE protects against any liability for breach of the DDA. Conversely, however, failure to comply with the DSE may amount to either direct or indirect discrimination in breach of the DDA. Over the course of the decade since they were implemented, it has become apparent that complainants plead both breach of the DSE and breach of the DDA in the same action. There is no remedy, however, for breach of the DSE. Rather, it enlivens the opportunity to seek a remedy for breach of the DDA.

14.3.1 Definitions: 'Disability' and 'Education'

The DDA and DSE protect people with a wide range of disabilities and apply to a wide range of education settings. Relevant DDA definitions are adopted by DSE (s. 1.4). DDA s 4 defines disability to cover physical, psychiatric, behavioural and sensory disabilities. It is particularly relevant for this chapter, that the definition explicitly includes 'a disorder or malfunction that results in the person learning differently from a person without the disorder or malfunction' (para. (f)). It shall be seen, below, that the assessment of students with learning disorders is a controversial issue for educators.

The legislation (DDA s. 4; DSE ss. 1.2, 2.1) applies to any educational authority, 'a body or person administering an educational institution', any educational institution, which 'means a school, college, university or other institution at which education or training is provided', and education providers, 'an organisation whose purpose is to develop or accredit curricula or training courses' used by educational authorities or institutions. The broad scope of these definitions indicates that education bodies who accredit the curriculum, implement it, and assess it are all caught by the legislation.

14.3.2 Direct and Indirect Discrimination

The DDA seeks to protect 'formal equality', equality of treatment, by prohibiting direct discrimination. To give an example from the assessment context, direct discrimination might occur if a student is denied the opportunity to participate in an assessment process because of his or her disability. See *TT v Lutheran Education Queensland*, for example, where a student complained that he had not been allowed to complete an assessment item he had missed when absent from school.

The DDA also seeks to protect against 'systemic discrimination', by prohibiting indirect discrimination, the imposition of unreasonable policies and conditions that disadvantage a person because of his or her disability (DDA S 6). Assessment items inevitably involve the imposition of conditions upon students, both implicit and explicit. In *Bishop v Sports Massage Training School*, for example, the complainant, who had dyslexia, narrowly failed a written examination causing him 'a delay in his career and a significant loss of self-esteem' (at para. [1]). The Human Rights and Equal Opportunity Commission (HREOC), which at that time was the relevant hearing tribunal, found (at para [1]) that the respondent 'required [Bishop] to complete the examination in the same two-hour period as the other, able-bodied students'.

14.3.3 Disability Standards for Education and 'Reasonable Adjustment'

The key obligation placed upon schools by the DSE is to make 'reasonable adjustment' to the education environment to support the full inclusion of students with disabilities (Part 3; s. 3.4 note). A failure to make reasonable adjustment may result in direct or indirect discrimination (DDA ss, 5(2), 6(2)). As such, the legislation shifts, from the student to the school, the burden of ensuring the removal of barriers to equal opportunity in education. Guidance about how this is to be achieved is provided by the DSE in relation to a number of key aspects of the delivery of education services: enrolment (Part 4); participation (Part 5); curriculum development, accreditation and delivery (Part 6); student support services (Part 7); and the elimination of harassment and victimization (Part 8). It is also interesting to note that in relation to each of these aspects, the DSE set out not only the legal obligations of education providers but also student rights, 'consistent with the rights of the rest of the community' (Introduction). The DSE also set out 'measures of compliance' in relation to each aspect and these are of particular importance as they act as benchmarks against which an education institutions performance may be assessed.

As only 'reasonable' adjustments are required by the DSE, 'reasonableness' is, by implication, a limit on any adjustment required. The DSE provide for the further limit, however, that a *reasonable* adjustment may be avoided if it would create unjustifiable hardship (s 10.2). Proof of reasonableness and unjustifiable hardship will engage similar arguments relating to cost, effect, inconvenience, benefit and detriment to those involved. It is not clear, however, how the two limits of reasonableness and unjustifiable hardship will, in practice, interact as both cover similar territory. That both limits are contemplated by the legislation, however, suggests a fairly thick protection is provided to schools to resist requests for expensive, difficult or disruptive adjustments (Dickson 2014).

14.4 Reasonable Adjustment in Assessment: What Does This Entail in Practice?[2]

The relevant terms of the DSE impose an obligation to make reasonable adjustment to 'curriculum development, accreditation and delivery' (Part 6) so as 'to give students with disabilities the right to participate in educational courses or programs that are designed to develop their skills, knowledge and understanding, including relevant supplementary programs, on the same basis as students without disabilities' (s 6.1). Guidance about how reasonable adjustment in assessment is to be achieved is provided as follows (s 6.3(f)):

> the assessment and certification requirements for the course or program are appropriate to the needs of the student and accessible to him or her; and…
>
> the assessment procedures and methodologies for the course or program are adapted to enable the student to demonstrate the knowledge, skills or competencies being assessed.

It is clear, then, that the DSE contemplate that reasonable adjustment may require changes to assessment requirements, assessment instruments and assessment conditions. A student with a disability, along with his or her parents or guardians, if appropriate, will have a say on the kinds of adjustments they would prefer. The DSE mandate consultation between the education institution and student (s 3.5) but acknowledge that the school may suggest alternatives, which are less 'disruptive' (s 3.6). A series of poisonous discrimination cases in Australia where schools, and sometimes parents, have been criticised by courts and tribunals for intransigent resistance to reasonable cooperation, has left the clear message that it is imperative for school staff and

[2] This section of the chapter is informed by commentary in Dickson (2012). That article provides more detailed analysis of the academic integrity issue.

students and their families to keep in regular, respectful communication about the impact of the relevant disability and its management (see, e.g., *Murphy and Grahl*, *Minns* and *TT*).

The variety of individual disabilities, assessment circumstances and school subjects makes it difficult to state that any one variety of adjustment will always be reasonable. Many different adjustments have been considered 'reasonable' in Australian education cases. Against the background of those cases, the following kinds of adjustments have been addressed as part of the suite of adjustments available in Australian schools:

Extra time to finish an exam or assignment (*BI*, *Bishop*, *Beanland*, *Brackenreg*, *W*)

Completing a course over a longer than usual time (*Beanland*)

Supervised rest, food and medication breaks in examinations (*BI*)

Adjustment to the format of an exam paper – font, paper colour and size, paper 'masks' (*Hinchliffe*)

Separate venues to minimize distraction or to accommodate assistance animals

Alternatives to writing – viva voce, examination, scribe, assistive technology (*Beanland*)

Alternatives to reading – brailed and/or taped materials, assistive technology (*Beanland*, *Hincliffe*)

Alternatives to hearing – written stimulus materials, translators, assistive technology (*Hurst*)

Alternatives to speaking – written rather than spoken responses allowed

Adjusted scheduling of assessment (*Brackenreg*, *W*)

Adjusted level of achievement thresholds where performance on a particular item has been compromised by disability ('special consideration') (*Brackenreg*, *W*)

Adjusted weighting of assessment for students who have missed an assessment item because of disability (*Brackenreg*, *W*)

Excusal from an assessment item (*TT*)

14.5 Australian Controversies in Reasonable Adjustment

While the adjustments listed above should be available, they will not automatically be reasonable in every case. Schools are entitled, for example, to refuse an adjustment, which is not reasonable because it would erode the academic integrity of a piece of assessment. There is evidence, though, that sometimes schools have resisted adjustments which should be made because of a misguided concern that they should not be seen to be 'benefitting' students with disability, or because of a misguided belief that a student is already achieving at a high level, or is able to 'cope' without adjustments. While schools are unlikely to be held accountable for failure to make reasonable adjustment for a student whose disability has not been disclosed, the longer they delay the making of adjustments for a student with a known disability, the higher the risk of breaching their obligations under the law.

14.5.1 Reasonable Adjustment and Integrity of Assessment

The Australian law is clear that there is no requirement that an education institution take steps to pass a student who is failing a course simply because he or she has a disability. This remains the case even when the disability is clearly causally related to the failure. A distinction must be drawn between adjustments to the way a piece of assessment is structured, formatted, delivered and to be completed, and adjustments to the scope or standard of essential skills or knowledge to be demonstrated in order to complete the piece of assessment. It may be speculated that the former kind of adjustments will almost always be required, the latter kind almost never.

The DSE explicitly recognise a limit to the notion of 'reasonable adjustment' in respect of students who cannot meet 'inherent' or 'essential' course requirements (s. 3.4(3)):

> *In assessing whether an adjustment to the course of the course or program [sic] in which the student is enrolled, or proposes to be enrolled, is reasonable, the provider is entitled to maintain the academic requirements of the course or program, and other requirements or components that are inherent in or essential to its nature.*
>
> *Note In providing for students with disabilities, a provider may continue to ensure the integrity of its courses or programs and assessment requirements and processes, so that those on whom it confers an award can present themselves as having the appropriate knowledge, experience and expertise implicit in the holding of that particular award.*

Aside from the express terms of the DSE, a long list of decided cases, including *Brackenreg*, *W*, *Chung* and *Reyes-Gonzalez* demonstrates that tertiary institutions will not be required to continue to accommodate those students whose impairments mean that they do not have the capacity to 'pass' their course. In *Brackenreg* for example, the Queensland Anti-Discrimination Tribunal made the clear finding (para. [4.2.2.4 iv]) that '[t]here is no obligation on the respondent to pass a student just because they have a disability'.

In that case, a law student had disclosed a spinal disorder, cervical cancer and, particularly relevant to her studies, Attention Deficit Hyperactivity Disorder (ADHD). She was excluded from the degree course when she breached progression rules, including the 'double fail rule'. It was held (para. [4.2.1.3]) that there were 'multiple causes' for her assessment difficulties and ultimate exclusion – 'her disabilities…circumstances in her personal life, and studying as an external student' – but none of them was any failure to adjust by her university, Queensland University of Technology (QUT):

> *…even when consideration was given to the complainant by the respondent for her disabilities, such as giving her extra time to complete exams, extensions of times in handing in assignments, and by giving her conceded passes on numerous occasions after considering her circumstances, she still demonstrated an inability to satisfactorily complete a law degree to the standard required by the respondent.* (para. 2.2.4(iv))

Although the decided academic integrity cases involve tertiary students, where passing or failing has an obvious impact on future employment prospects, the reasoning process informing the cases is clearly relevant to the certification processes at the compulsory levels of education too. Competition for university places has already prompted complaints that tertiary entrance scores have been compromised by failure to make reasonable adjustment to assessment. See, for example, the cases *Wong* and *BI*, discussed below.

14.5.2 Determining 'Inherent' Course Requirements

There has been significant activity across the Australian tertiary sector towards articulating the 'inherent requirements' of tertiary courses (Brett et al. 2016). While inherent requirements statements have been prompted by legal obligations under the DDA and the DSE, it is argued that they are potentially helpful not only for staff adjusting assessment for a course, but also for students enrolling in a course in that they render transparent the knowledge and skills essential to a course (Brett et al. 2016, p. 4). Inherent requirements statements may work as a tool towards inclusion if they inform the reasonable adjustment process by allowing assessors to determine against explicit benchmarks whether and what changes can be made to an assessment regime without undermining its integrity. There is some concern, however, that statements may also be abused as tools for exclusion, with assessors using them to 'protect' entry to a course or unit without explicit consideration of whether adjustment is possible. McNaught (2013, p. 28) reports that it is 'increasingly common for universities to make explicit the inherent requirements to students prior to entry, and in many cases, for students to sign [disability] disclosure statements and attest to the ability to meet inherent requirements'. Such a strategy, absent any rigorous enquiry into the availability of reasonable adjustment to support the inclusion of a potential student with disability, suggests an avoidance of the obligation to make reasonable adjustment.

Unlike universities, schools have long worked with documents which purport to set out the inherent or essential aspects of a course of study – subject syllabuses and curriculums. It is nevertheless important to be alert to the issues of whether a skill assumed to be essential is essential, and to what extent its achievement needs to be assessed. If spelling is claimed as an 'essential' skill, for example, can an adjustment of allowing access to a computer with spell check in an examination ever be 'reasonable'? While spelling may be an essential element of communication in English, it may not be for Maths. Moreover, even if it is an essential skill for the English curriculum, it may not be necessary or appropriate for it to be assessed in every assessment item.

The case illustrates the further point that school authorities must be careful in how they identify and explain the mandatory aspects of the courses they offer. *Beanland* addressed the following conundrum: If a mandated skill for the school subject 'German' is the ability to 'read' the German language, can an adjustment of allowing a vision impaired student to 'listen' to someone else reading German text aloud be reasonable? Does 'reading' then become another, different, mandated skill, 'listening'? That the Queensland German Syllabus was amended in 2009 to mandate not 'reading' and 'listening' but 'comprehension (receptive communication)' suggests a recognition that what we sometimes hold onto, or hold out, as 'essential' may not be so. The new terminology recognises that 'reading' and 'listening' are merely varieties of the genuinely essential skill of 'comprehension'. The problem of assessing the German language comprehension skills of a vision impaired student, like Beanland, now disappears – he or she may demonstrate comprehension through reporting on what he or she has listened to, if not through what he or she has read.

14.5.3 Reasonable Adjustment and Learning Disorders

Learning disorders are expressly covered in the DDA (s 4) and most state acts. What little case law there is in this area suggests that adjustments to assessment will, prima facie, be required for students with learning disorders. In *Bishop* the complainant, who had dyslexia, narrowly failed a written examination causing him 'a delay in his career and a significant loss of self-esteem'

(p. 1). The HREOC found that the respondent 'required [Bishop] to complete the examination in the same two-hour period as the other, able-bodied students' and that '[t]here [was] a real chance that had [the complainant] been given an extra half-hour, or had the examination been conducted orally in his case, he would have passed' (p. 1). The complainant was awarded $3000 damages to compensate him for losses including the cost of relocating to another massage school where his disability was properly accommodated.

Despite the clear example of the *Bishop* case, however, the accommodation of learning disorders, such as dyslexia, has been resisted by some Australian education institutions. The Australian National Assessment Program (NAPLAN) illustrates this resistance. While each application for adjustment is assessed on its merits, NAPLAN *Disability Adjustment Scenarios* (Australian Curriculum, Assessment & Reporting Authority N.D.) suggest, for example, that neither readers nor scribes will be available for students with learning disorders, impairing their ability to comprehend stimulus materials and to communicate that comprehension. Moreover, the use of word prediction and spelling and grammar correction software during the tests is 'unacceptable' (p. 23). The clear implication is that it is illegitimate to adjust for a disability that manifests as an inability to perform an essential skill unaided, even if an adjustment would allow performance of that skill. It could be argued that an intransigent refusal to adjust unreasonably and unnecessarily consigns students to failure.

Despite the best attempts of disability advocates to defeat such misconceptions, another rationale underpinning the reluctance to adjust for learning and behavioural disorders may be inferred as a reluctance to 'advantage' students with a disability. This was the rationale advanced in the NSW assessment case *BI v Board of Studies* where a student with Attention Deficit Disorder (ADD) was granted rest breaks but not extra time for his Higher School Certificate examinations (Year 12 certification) (paras. [28], [42], [52]). The special provisions policy did not authorise extra time for students with ADHD. BI's case failed because the New Wales Supreme Court accepted that, despite the mandatory nature of the policy under consideration, there was discretion to vary the policy upon proof of need, and that BI had not proved such a need. A future complainant, drawing on the experience of BI, may have more success in pleading his or her case.

14.5.4 Reasonable Adjustment When a Student Can 'Cope' with an Assessment Task as Designed

Another problematic response to disability is to assume that an adjustment to assessment is not necessary because the student can 'cope' with it unadjusted.

The DDA case, *Hurst v State of Queensland*, is not explicitly about assessment but it demonstrates a hardy approach to class room practice which may unwittingly result in unlawful discrimination, including in assessment. In *Hurst*, the complainant alleged discrimination in that she was not provided with an Auslan interpreter to assist her in class. Tiahna Hurst was profoundly deaf and grew up using Auslan, the Australian indigenous sign language, to communicate. When she enrolled at primary school, she was told that an Auslan interpreter would not be provided because Education Queensland used signed English interpreters instead to support its students with hearing impairments. The case was constructed as an indirect discrimination case – a condition was imposed on Tiahna that she receives her education without the support of an Auslan interpreter. At first instance, it was held that Tiahna could comply with this condition and that, therefore, she could not prove the elements of indirect discrimination. Tiahna was a clever child and had been well supported by therapists arranged privately by her family and the evidence was that she could 'cope' with a signed English interpreter.

On appeal, however, the Full Court of the Federal Court of Australia held that even if a student could 'cope' with the way their education was delivered, this did not amount to their compliance with a condition that it be delivered in that way. Tiahna could technically 'cope' with a signed English interpreter, but to expect her to do so would compromise her educational opportunities and prospects for achievement. The assessment ramification for schools of this decision is that assumptions should not be made about what a student can 'manage' in terms of assessment conditions – adjustments should be made to remove barriers to optimum performance which are related to a student's disability.

14.5.5 Reasonable Adjustment and Students Who Are Apparently Succeeding in Their Studies

It should not be assumed that assessment discrimination claims will be made only by students who fail. Students may allege discrimination if they believe they could have done better had certain adjustments been made. They may initiate legal action if their poorer than anticipated performance excludes them from future opportunities, or even if their pride is hurt. In *Hinchliffe v University of Sydney*, a student with a visual impairment claimed that she had been the victim of discrimination in that the University of Sydney had failed to provide course materials to her in an accessible form. The case is interesting because, unlike other Australian university cases, the complainant was not failing subjects. On the contrary, she achieved a distinction, two credits and four passes in her first semester of studies in Occupational Therapy at the University of Sydney and a high distinction, three distinctions, a credit and four passes in the second semester. By her own admission her results would 'probably not be perceived as being poor' (para. [25]). Her claim was, nevertheless, that her academic future had been compromised by what she presented as the University's failure to provide her with course materials in an acceptable format which accommodated her disability. She was not successful, however, in proving her case of indirect discrimination, with the Federal Magistrates Court finding that the actions of University disability support staff were 'sufficient and adequate' (para. [121]).

In the more recent case, *Wong*, a New South Wales student achieved a Tertiary Entrance score of 99.95, and won a place studying medicine at the University of New South Wales. She claimed, however, that she would have performed even better if the joint hyper mobility of her hand had been accommodated by the granting of extra time and access to a computer in her Higher School Certificate (HSC) English and Modern History exams. She had been granted rest breaks and rejected the offer of a scribe. The NSW Administrative Appeals tribunal was not satisfied that her performance had been compromised by the failure to make the requested adjustments. To adopt the language of the DSE, the adjustments sought were not 'reasonable'. Wong's explanation for her complaint (Hall and Patty 2012), however, indicates the rationale for the adjustments sought and highlights the potential for a failure to accommodate disability to impact even upon high performing students:

> *"The point isn't that I was doing badly. I did do well, what a normal person would consider well," she said. "But you want your disability to be sufficiently addressed with special examination provisions so that everyone has a capability to communicate what they know in the HSC examinations, otherwise it is not a fair test of your knowledge."*

14.5.6 Reasonable Adjustment and Unknown Disability

In the United Kingdom, the relevant legislation explicitly provides that there can be no discrimination on the basis of an 'unknown' disability (*Equality Act 2010* (UK), ch 15, s 15(2)). Australian legislation is silent on the point but case law suggests that it will be difficult to prove a causal link between a disability and treatment if the disability is not known to the potential discriminator. The case of *Sluggett v Flinders University* is one of a number of cases where students have failed to prove discrimination because they have failed to reveal their disability until after they have suffered some harm on its account. Sluggett, who had mobility impairments alleged discrimination in that she had been allocated class rooms and a work placement which were not accessible to her because her disability. Sluggett did not inform the respondent university of her impairment until after she experienced difficulties getting to classes on the hilly campus of Flinders University and climbing a spiral staircase while on work experience. It was held that the University had not failed to make adjustments to her disability – Sluggett herself had been at fault in not alerting the university to her condition and accessing available support.

If some responsible staff member knows of the disability, however, it seems that the school administration responsible for ensuring adjustments are made will be deemed to know. This point is clear from the facts of *Bishop*, discussed above. While the Sports Massage School administration argued that Bishop had 'had not done enough to bring his disability to its attention prior to the examination', HREOC held that it was sufficient that he had told his lecturer (p. 2).

There is a potential problem for schools relating to unknown disabilities, and particularly unknown learning disorders, in that teachers are, notionally, trained to suspect and detect potential learning disorders from the behaviour of their students. This point was made by the New South Wales Administrative Appeals Tribunal in *Chinchen v NSW Department of Education and Training*. Rhys Chinchen had been classified as 'gifted' but, nevertheless, failed to thrive in his primary school extension classes. When he did not perform as expected, he was regarded as 'lazy and unmotivated' (para. [29]) and relocated to a regular class. At first instance, the school was found to have discriminated against Rhys in its failure to refer Rhys for assessment by a school counselor equipped to diagnose learning disorders (para. [303]). The case ultimately failed on appeal for technical reasons relating to the way it had been pleaded, but the point made by the tribunal is still valid. A school cannot claim that it did not know of a disability if its staff should have recognized the signs:

> *… [it] is clear that teachers do not have the expertise and training to diagnose motor dyspraxia. Nonetheless, in accordance with the Respondent's policies, they have a responsibility to ensure that students are educated to their full potential and to be alert to any learning difficulties which might inhibit this… We are satisfied that in 1999 the characteristics of Rhys's disability . . . were evident to [teaching staff] Ms Hawkes and Mr Ogilvie. The characteristic, difficulty completing tasks under a time constraint, is of particular significance. It was clear to the School that although Rhys was experiencing difficulty completing tasks in class, none of the strategies introduced*

by Ms Hawkes had proved effective. In these circumstances, the School had a responsibility to investigate the matter further by seeking the intervention of the school counsellor. (paras. [193]–[194])

14.5.7 Reasonable Adjustments and Timing Issues

As noted earlier, the *Disability* DSE impose an obligation on education institutions to consult with students and, if appropriate, their parents or guardians, as to adjustments which should be made. The DSE s 3.6(b) also requires education institutions to 'assess whether the adjustment may need to be changed over the period of a student's education or training'. A couple of cases indicate the problems that can flow from communication problems between school and student, from situations when the school has not been kept informed of the student's circumstances, or the student has not been kept informed of the school's plans.

The Hinchliffe case, discussed above, illustrates problems that can flow for a student who fails to keep his or her school informed about changed preferences in terms of adjustments to be made. Upon enrolment, Hinchliffe had provided the university with very clear details as to the format in which she would require course materials to be made available to her. Specifically, it was her preference that material be provided in an enlarged font on light green paper. It is significant, however, that during the course of her studies Hinchliffe discovered that she preferred materials to be provided, where possible, in an audio format. While the court accepted Hinchliffe's allegations that there were delays in the provision of materials, it attributed these delays, in large part, to the fact that the university was initially unaware of the changed preference and to the fact that it was more time consuming to produce audio than paper based materials.

In the Beanland case, discussed above, the respondent school won the case because Beanland could not prove that it had actually refused to adjust assessment requirements to allow him to study his preferred subjects before he left to attend a more accommodating school. The respondent was criticized, however, for its slow processing of Beanland's requests and the clear implication of the decision is that education institutions must manage adjustment processes promptly and efficiently in order to avoid causing detriment to affected students:

It is understandable the complainant and his parents felt frustration and anxiety with the approach that had been adopted, particularly as the matter was flagged at

> *an early stage by the parents... It is fundamentally important... [that school staff] are fully aware of the precise measures that may be undertaken by way of special consideration to assist those students with impairments to satisfy the requirements of the syllabus for each subject. No student should be left to commence senior studies without knowing precisely what special considerations will be afforded to the student in respect of the subjects chosen by that student, whatever year that subject may be being undertaken by the student.* (Beanland, para. 72)

14.6 Conclusion

This discussion has shown that, in recognition of the barriers educational assessment, as with other aspects of education, can create for students with disability, the right of students with disability to adjustments to assessment, to address such barriers, have been legislated. As with all law, such rights are not unfettered. The intention is that assessment does not create artificial barriers that prevent students from demonstrating their learning. The effects of a disability on a student's participation in assessment are also to be recognised.

The legislative principles and cases we have cited demonstrate that the matter of adjustments to assessment from both legal and practical perspectives is demanding for principals and teachers. Major constraints in how assessment adjustments will be approached are concerns of fairness, advantage/disadvantage and, from an educational assessment perspective, the validity of what is being assessed (Cumming 2012).

From an assessment perspective, equitable assessment requires that students are neither advantaged nor disadvantaged over others in demonstrating their knowledge; assessments do not need to be the same (Camilli 2013; Victorian Certification and Assessment Authority 2012). Most adjustments that teachers consider in adjustments to assessment centre on 'accommodations' in assessment discussed in US literature, predominantly focused on external standardised testing and frequently multiple choice test forms. While many of these adjustments, such as up to 25 per cent extra time, are implemented in Australian education, it is important to note that there is very little empirical validation of their appropriateness for demonstration of achievement by students with disability.

Concerns with fairness and equity are also voiced by students with disability (NSW Ombudsman 2013). While disability discrimination legislation is intended to empower students with disability, these students may well want to be treated the same as their peers without disability, and will not accept or seek adjustments if they identify negative social consequences (Ofsted 2010;

O'Rourke and Houghton 2008). The challenge for principals and teachers will be to work within the legal requirements to provide appropriate assessment adjustments for students.

The final challenge for educators is the issue that we alluded to in discussion of the Australian case *Hurst* – educational adjustments to enable optimum demonstration of achievement by students with disability, as opposed to sufficiency of achievement. 'Reasonable adjustment' is an ill-defined phrase for practical implementation. The extent to which 'reasonable' may be considered to be optimum in Australian law is still to be addressed. In England, advice to parents is that school authorities are only required by law to provide "an 'adequate' education for your child … [not] the best education" (The National Autistic Society 2015). At the time of writing, a legal challenge is under consideration in the US on whether the education provided for students with disability through the Individuals with Disabilities Education Act is to provide "some educational benefit" or a "meaningful benefit", interpreted to be a higher standard (Beitsch 2016). The Australian standard may still be to emerge.

The legal expectations for principals and teachers to address assessment for students with disability are high and an area where teachers report low confidence, insufficient preparation, expertise, and overall support in working with diverse learners (Forlin et al. 2008). We hope that this chapter provides some insights for principals and teachers into the legal framework for assessment adjustments for students with disability, the parameters that have been considered and the issues that are still unresolved.

References

ACT Government Education & Training (ACTGET). (2013). *Taskforce on students with learning difficulties*. Canberra: ACT.

Australian Bureau of Statistics. (2011, March). 4102.0 – Australian social trends. 'Year 12 attainment'. Canberra: ACT.

Australian Curriculum Assessment & Reporting Authority. (2013). *Student diversity and the Australian curriculum. Advice for principals, schools and teachers*. Sydney: ACARA.

Beitsch, R. (2016, December). Special education case at Supreme court could prove costly for schools. *Stateline*. Retrieved from http://www.pewtrusts.org/en/research-and-analysis/blogs/stateline/2016/12/08/special-education-case-at-supreme-court-could-prove-costly-for-schools

Brett, M., Harvey, A., Funston, A., Spicer, R., & Wood, A. (2016). The role of inherent requirement statements in Australian universities. Report for the National Centre for Student Equity in Higher Education (NCSEHE), Curtin University.

Camilli, G. (2013). Ongoing issues in test fairness. *Educational Research and Evaluation: An International Journal on Theory and Practice, 19*(2–3), 104–120.

Cumming, J. J. (2012). *Valuing students with impairments: International comparisons of practice in educational accountability*. Dordrecht: Springer.

Cumming, J., & Dickson, E. (2013). Educational accountability tests, social and legal inclusion approaches to discrimination for students with disability: A national case study from Australia. *Assessment in Education Principles, Policy & Practice, 20*(2), 221–239. https://doi.org/10.1080/0969594X.2012.730499.

Cumming, J., Dickson, E., & Webster, A. (2013). Reasonable adjustments in assessment: Putting law and policy into practice. *International Journal of Disability, Development, & Education, 60*(4), 295–311. https://doi.org/10.1080/1034912X.2013.846467.

Dickson, E. (2012). The assessment of students with disabilities: The Australian law as to reasonable adjustment and academic integrity. *International Journal of Law and Education, 17*(2), 49–62.

Dickson, E. (2014). Disability standards for education 2005 (Cth): Sword or shield for Australian students with disability. *International Journal of Law and Education, 19*(1), 5–20.

Disability Discrimination Act. (1992). Retrieved from http://www.austlii.edu.au/au/legis/cth/consol_act/dda1992264/

Forlin, C., Keen, M., & Barrett, E. (2008). The concerns of mainstream teachers: Coping with inclusivity in an Australian context. *International Journal of Disability, Development and Education, 55*(3), 251–264.

Hall, L., & Patty, A. (2012, 4 July). Student loses appeal over 99.95 HSC mark. *Sydney Morning Herald.* Retrieved from http://www.smh.com.au/national/education/student-loses-appeal-over-9995-hsc-mark-20120703-21flw.html

McNaught, K. (2013). The potential impacts of 'inherent requirements' and 'mandatory professional reporting' on students, particularly those with mental health concerns, registering with university disability/support services. *Journal of the Australian and New Zealand Student Services Association, 42*, 25–30.

NSW Ombudsman (NSW O). (2013). *A level playing field? HSC disability provisions.* Sydney: NSW O.

O'Rourke, J., & Houghton, S. (2008). Perceptions of secondary school students with mild disabilities to the academic and social support mechanisms implemented in regular classrooms. *International Journal of Disability, Development and Education, 55*(3), 227–237.

Ofsted. (2010). *The special educational needs and disability review. A statement is not enough*. Manchester: Ofsted.

The National Autistic Society. (2015). *Choosing a school in England*. Retrieved from http://www.autism.org.uk/about/in-education/choosing-school/england.aspx

Victorian Certification and Assessment Authority. (2012). *VCE chemistry assessment handbook 2010–2015*. Melbourne: VCAA.

Victorian Equal Opportunity & Human Rights Commission (VEOHRC). (2012). *Held back: The experiences of students with disabilities in Victorian schools*. Carlton: VEOHRC.

15

Student Voice and Educational Adjustments

Shiralee Poed

15.1 Introduction

When we examine the history of education opportunities afforded to children with disabilities, the voice frequently unheard is that of the child (Byrnes and Rickards 2011; Slee 2011; Whitburn 2016). Children with disabilities were viewed as 'objects of concern rather than as persons with voice' (Prout and Hallett 2003, p. 1). Instead, their history was recorded by academics, teachers, parents, public policy makers, or medical or allied health professionals. As society's views about the abilities of those with disabilities have changed, so too has the expectation that people with disabilities are entitled to agency over their lives (Aldred 2013; Arnstein-Kerslake and Flynn 2017; Norwich 2014; Rioux 2013).

15.2 The Importance of Consultation

It is critical that students are consulted in relation to the impact of their disability on their learning (and the impact of the teaching, curriculum, resources, environment and relationships on their disability) as it enables educators to make adjustments to reduce these impacts. Even more critically, it provides

S. Poed (✉)
Melbourne Graduate School of Education, The University of Melbourne,
Parkville, VIC, Australia
e-mail: spoed@unimelb.edu.au

K. Trimmer et al. (eds.), *The Palgrave Handbook of Education Law for Schools*,
https://doi.org/10.1007/978-3-319-77751-1_15

young people with the skills necessary to become adults who have agency over their lives. The opportunity to meaningfully participate in decision-making is not only an important step for the student, but also strengthens the relationship between the family and the school (Lai and Vadeboncoeur 2013; Williams-Lewis 2014).

Consultation should commence from the point of enrolment (or at the point of diagnosis if that occurs post-enrolment), and continue both informally and at any ongoing planning meetings, such as those where an Individual Education Plan (IEP) is being developed. Consultation is only effective, however, when educators believe that the student (and their family) can make a meaningful contribution to educational decisions, and then facilitate this by providing the supports required and taking the time to really listen to any concerns (Ashby 2011; Miller et al. 2014).

15.3 Legal Obligation to Consult Students

Today, student voice in educational decisions is an enshrined human right. Under the United Nations *Convention on the Rights of the Child* (2000, Article 12), children who are capable of articulating their views are entitled to have those views considered. Article 7.3 of the United Nations *Conventions on the Rights of Persons with Disabilities* (2006) extends that provision stating 'that children with disabilities have the right to express their views freely on all matters affecting them, their views being given due weight in accordance with their age and maturity, on an equal basis with other children, and to be provided with disability and age-appropriate assistance to realize that right'. These enshrined rights have been extended into a body of literature that supports the rights of persons with disabilities to have a say in decisions that affect them (Aldred 2013; Al Zidjaly 2015; Lindström 2011; Shoemaker 2010; Stolz 2010; Weber 2013).

In Australia, drafting of Federal disability discrimination legislation was first proposed in 1990. While the initial focus was to address discrimination in employment, the issue of discrimination in education was continually mentioned during public hearings and written submissions into the proposed legislation (Shelley 1991). From the assent of the Australian *Disability Discrimination Act* 1992, section 22 has called for the elimination of discrimination in education. The Act makes it unlawful for an educational authority to directly or indirectly treat a student with a disability less favourably than a student who does not have a disability (s3). It lists that the goal, "as far as practicable", is for students with disabilities to have the same educational rights as their peers. Until cognitively able, both Conventions and Australian disability discrimination legislation recognise it is the responsibility of an *associate* to best represent a child's needs. An associate may be a spouse, domestic partner, relative, carer, or business, sporting or recreational partner. In education settings, associates are typically a child's parent or carer.

In 2003, in accordance with the *Commonwealth Government's Legislation Review Schedule*, the Act was referred to the *Australian Productivity Commission* to consider, among other things, the social impact of the legislation, including costs and benefits to the community as a whole and to people with a disability (Australian Government [Productivity Commission] 2004). The *Productivity Commission's* inquiry found that the Act had been relatively successful in reducing physical barriers to inclusion, particularly in relation to education, but highlighted the need for additional work to redress attitudinal barriers, especially where race, language, socioeconomic background and remoteness were additional variables that impacted on the voice of the person with a disability from being heard. A set of Disability Standards were promulgated for the purpose of clarifying the obligations of education providers.

Having ratified the *Convention on the Rights of the Child*, Australia legislated the right to participate in educational decision-making in the *Disability Standards for Education 2005* (ComLaw 2016). The Standards require that schools consult students with disabilities, or their associate, when making adjustments. This obligation to consult provides students a voice in their education, where they can report on how their disability impacts on their learning as well as how the learning environment could be better altered to *reasonably* accommodate their needs.

15.4 What Is Reasonable?

Section 3.4.2 of the Disability Standards for Education 2005 (ComLaw 2016) outlines the considerations taken into account by judges and commissioners when determining whether a school has taken reasonable steps to provide adjustments (Fig. 15.1). In sum, when considering whether an adjustment is reasonable, the following questions are asked:

As one of the four factors considered by judges when determining the reasonableness of adjustments, 'student voice' is a cornerstone of the *Disability Standards for Education 2005* (ComLaw 2016). The term 'student voice' is broadly defined as having agency over educational decisions, regardless of the communication system used by the student with a disability. While some students with disabilities are able to communicate their needs and preferences

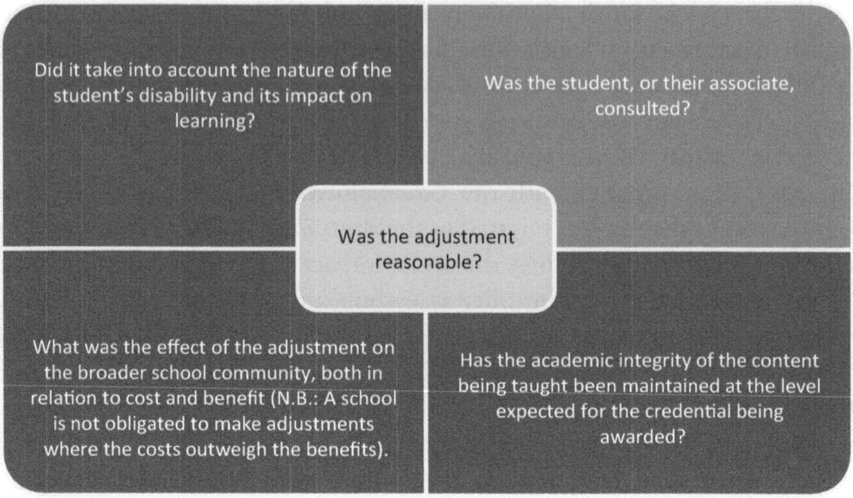

Fig. 15.1 Questions considered when determining the reasonableness of adjustments for students with disabilities

using spoken work, "student voice" also assumes gestures, facial expressions, body language and movements, silence, vocalisations, signed communication, communication through symbols, and communication aided by assistive technology as forms of communication. Consultation that includes student voice is essential if schools are to provide reasonable adjustments to accommodate the needs and preferences of students with disabilities.

15.5 Limits of Legislation

Unfortunately, in Australian legislation, these right-based approaches offer little advice to students, their families, or educators on the specifics of consultation (Lewis 2008). Unlike the United States, where the structural arrangements mandate the involvement of students with disabilities in the individual planning process, there is evidence to suggest that Australian students with disabilities, or their families, are not consulted when schools plan and make adjustments (Dixon and Tanner 2013; Victorian Equal Opportunity and Human Rights Commission 2012; Wilson et al. 2015). For students, Jackson and Varnham (2007) contend that the obligation to consult was diminished by the legislative inclusion of consulting with parents. This perpetuates the historical practice of adults making decisions for students with a disability.

Despite the Australian government's ratification of United Nations conventions, and enshrining the obligation to consult in law, tensions continue to arise between students, families and schools over the *reasonableness* of adjustments to curriculum. At times, these escalate into a bitter legal proceeding where, even though both Conventions recognize that the student has a right to participate in legal proceedings, the voice of the child is usually lost amidst the voices of the parents and educators (Jackson and Varnham 2007).

15.6 Australian Disability Discrimination Claims in Education

From the introduction of Federal disability discrimination legislation in 1992 until 30 September 2014, 134 judicial decisions have been published from actions taken by 84 families of school-aged students with a disability. Copies of the published judicial decisions were retrieved from searching the *Australasian Legal Information Institutes* [AustLII] database and then cross-checked against reported decisions available on Australian Federal, State and Territory anti-discrimination tribunal and court websites. These low rates of litigation may surprise some readers, but these figures are believed to represent only 7% of the total number of complaints made by families to the courts, with the remaining 93% conciliated without necessitating a trial (Australian Government [Department of Education Employment and Workforce Relations] 2012). Conciliated cases in Australia are confidential, so it is not possible to access the decisions from these matters.

An examination of these 134 judicial decisions revealed that 92 decisions involving 54 families discussed tensions around the reasonableness of adjustments to curriculum. Other cases examined issues related to access to services such as transportation; bullying, harassment or victimisation; denied enrolment or forced enrolment in a non-preferred location; and responses to complex behaviour.

15.7 Student Voice During Litigation

While both UN Conventions state that children have a right to be heard in any legal proceedings that affect them, the analysis of these judicial decisions revealed very few students took part. Goldfarb et al. (2015) contend that it is important for the voices of children to be heard in litigation so that they are not misrepresented. There are significant issues related to the direct examination of children in court cases. Notably, children may be incompetent based on age (Robinson 2015); find the questions too difficult (O'Neill and Zajac 2013); they may become anxious, emotional, withdrawn or distressed (Castelli and Goodman 2014; Thoman 2013); or they may have poor recall of events (Knutsson and Allwood 2014). The complexities are exacerbated by disability, where questions of competence abound (Brown and Lewis 2013; Watkins 2014). In the cases examined, the issue of student voice was raised in judicial decisions involving only 4 of the 54 children.

15.7.1 Case 1: Purvis v. The State of New South Wales (Human Rights & Equal Opportunity Commission 2000)

In this case, the complainant alleged that his son's suspension, and later expulsion, from a Government high school was discriminatory as the school had failed to train teachers to accommodate his individual needs, and failed to seek advice from specialist staff in relation to the impact of his disability on his behaviour. There was no discussion in any of the judicial decisions relating to this matter of whether the student was consulted in relation to adjustments made for him. Further, the student did not give evidence during the hearing. In making his determination, Commissioner Innes cited Article 12.1 of the *Convention on the Rights of the Child*, that 'children be given appropriate involvement in decisions and actions affecting them' (HREOC 2000, s.1).

The Commissioner expressed a desire to meet the complainant so that he would 'gain a better understanding of the person to whom the complaint refers' (HREOC 2000, s.1) but the complainant declined this invitation. The Commissioner would have been entitled, under various Australian legislative provisions to summon the complainant (an older adolescent at the time of the hearings) to appear, but instead extended the Convention to mean a child is also entitled to decline the opportunity to take part in decisions involving them.

15.7.2 Case 2: Finney v. Hills Grammar School (HREOC 1999)

In contrast, in the case of Finney, the complainant's parents alleged the respondent discriminated against their daughter by refusing to accept her enrolment at a non-Government, non-denominational private school. Noting on her enrolment application that the complainant had spina bifida and would require extensive modifications to the physical school environment, including wheelchair accessibility, the school undertook an extensive investigation into whether they would be able to meet the student's needs across the planned 13 years of schooling, and ultimately decided the costs to do so would have caused unjustifiable hardship. Despite the complainant being aged six, her legal counsel made application for her to give evidence, particularly in relation to how she felt upon learning her enrolment had been rejected. The complainant stated, 'I felt a bit disappointed that I could not go to that school – I wanted to go to that school. They wrote a book that they do take people with disabilities' (HREOC 1999, p. 4, s.4.1.1).

The same Commissioner who heard the earlier-mentioned Purvis case resided over this matter, and in this case, he noted,

> *The opinion of the person with the disability should not be accepted without question because this could place respondents in very invidious positions. But the person's views should be given weight, alongside the views of experts in the field who have had a chance to assess the individual in question and form an opinion. The greatest barriers which people with disabilities face in our community are the negative assumptions made about them by other members of the community.* (HREOC 1999, p. 43, s.6.14)

In making this claim, the Commissioner upheld the intent of the Disability Standards for Education 2005 and the Convention on the Rights of the Child.

15.7.3 Case 3: JC on Behalf of BC v. The State of Queensland (Anti-Discrimination Tribunal of Queensland 2006)

In this matter, JC had lodged a complaint of discrimination stating that her son's high school had failed to provide the necessary adjustments to accommodate his disabilities, which had caused him distress, and he had taken leave from school. She further claimed that the school had stated her son would not be able to return to school without a psychological assessment, and that this requirement was also discriminatory. During proceedings, JC indicated she did not wish for her son to take part in the litigation, as it would cause him further trauma. The President of the anti-discrimination commission indicated while it was BC's right to be heard, his mother was not obligated to call him as a witness. BC had provided a written statement which was disregarded by the Commissioner, as the respondent was unable to cross-examine written claims. Of the cases examined, this was the only Australian discrimination claim where a parent had actively sought for their child to not give evidence, although it may have been possible that the parent was acting on the advice of her son.

15.7.4 Case 4: Mrs. Robyn Beasley (on Behalf of Dylan Beasley) v. The State of Victoria (Department of Education and Training) (Victorian Civil & Administrative Tribunal 2006)

In the final case of note, the complainant, Dylan, was a young Deaf student who used Auslan, the native sign language of the Australian Deaf community. He alleged that during his primary education in a mainstream school, his school had failed to use the best communication method, Auslan, instead instructing him using a combination of spoken English, fingerspelling and Signed English, a sign language dialect that matches signs to spoken English. Dylan took part in the litigation process, claiming that he was unable to understand staff 100% of the time, an argument countered by the respondent who argued that Dylan was able to understand, and that neither he, nor his parents, had complained during the five years he attended the school. In her findings, the Deputy President of the Tribunal noted that Dylan was the best person to judge whether he could understand the method of communication, although did conclude he was likely to have understood more than that which he indicated.

15.8 Student Voice in Educational Planning

There has been worldwide advocacy for the active involvement of students with disabilities in determining the necessary supports to ensure their participation in their education (Cambra 2016; Cavendish and Connor 2017; Jubran 2015; Nolan-Spohn 2016; Pagliano and Gillies 2015; Palmer et al. 2017; Seong et al. 2015). Student involvement in educational planning has been linked to:

- Better post-school outcomes (Cobb et al. 2009; Wehmeyer et al. 2015);
- Higher rates of graduation (Cavendish 2013);
- Improved ability to communicate with adults (Nolan-Spohn 2016);
- Improved understanding of how their disability impacts their learning (Cambra 2016); and

- Improved understanding of their strengths, needs, interests and preferences leading to increased motivation and independence (Collier et al. 2016; Jubran 2015).

In the 134 discrimination cases examined, no case mentioned that the student was consulted in relation to the adjustments made to their curriculum. Where minutes of meetings about adjustments were discussed during litigation, these only ever mentioned adults being present. This may reinforce the position of Jackson and Varnham (2007) who argued that the obligation to consult students was diminished by the inclusion of the obligation to consult with an associate. Alternatively, it may simply be that given the age of the students, or the nature of their disabilities, parents were acting on behalf of their children, as supported UN Conventions. Whatever the reason, not engaging students with disabilities in meaningful conversations about their perspectives on the structures and supports needed to allow them to participate fully in their education poses an increased risk of student disengagement and heightens the risk for them leaving school early (Gordon 2010).

15.9 Guidance for Improving Meaningful Participation

While collaboration is a key to improving meaningful participation, it would appear that students, parents, and teachers would benefit from more concrete advice on how students could be assisted in making a meaningful contribution to educational decision-making in relation to curriculum adjustments.

15.9.1 Whose Voice?

The report on the Nationally Consistent Collection of Data on Disability (Education Council 2016) showed over 18% of Australian students receive educational adjustments. Schools receive additional resourcing to support only 5.7% of these students, but continue to provide adjustments for a further 12.4% of students despite no additional resourcing. At present in Australia, only children who meet the criteria for additional resourcing are mandated to have an IEP. Therefore, the 12.4% of students who have a disability that does not entitle them to additional resourcing (such as those with foetal alcohol syndrome, mental health conditions, learning disabilities, mild communication impairments) may have no official forum through which they can meaningfully participate in educational decisions. As these students meet the criteria for disability outlined in the federal legislation, urgent attention must be given by policy makers on how to ensure schools can meaningfully capture the voices of these students.

15.9.2 Meaningful Participation of Students

If attendance of all students with disabilities at IEP meetings were mandated (in addition to, rather than by their families), it is not enough to then assume students with disabilities would have the skills to actively participate in a meaningful way (Griffin et al. 2014; Pawley and Tennant 2008). Attendance, but then playing a passive role, will perpetuate a model of services being provided to, rather than designed with, the student (Kaczkowski 2012). The keys to improve involvement of students in educational decision-making include:

- Training students to take a meaningful role during their IEP meeting (Meadan et al. 2010; Wilson et al. 2015);
- Focusing on student strengths as a pathway for determining adjustments (Cavendish and Connor 2017); and
- Considering ways in which technology could be used to allow students to have a voice (see the work of Van Laarhoven-Myers et al. 2016).

15.9.3 Meaningful Participation of Families

There is a moderate effect size that comes from families who take an active role in their child's education, especially families of children with a disability (Hattie 2009; Mitchell 2014). In addition to the earlier noted benefits of involving students in educational decision-making, the involvement of parents has also led to:

- Higher rates of student attendance at school (Landmark et al. 2007);
- Increased parental expectations for their child, especially in relation to post-school career options (Smith 2016);
- Improved academic outcomes (de Apodaca et al. 2015; Mitchell 2014) and
- Opportunities for home-based concerns to be addressed (Chua 2015).

However, key barriers to family involvement include:

- Feeling alienated by the school (Valle 2009)
- Feeling coerced into signing IEPs with which they disagree (Valle and Aponte 2002)

- Cultural differences and possible feelings of intimidation (Landmark et al. 2013), and
- Time, lack of confidence, lack of information, hostile staff attitudes, personal crises, or needs of other family members (Chua 2015).

While not all families wish to be actively involved in the educational decisions made for their child, it is critical that schools minimise potential barriers so that families have the opportunity to be active partners. It is indeed critical for the small number of students, particularly those with severe to profound disabilities, for whom autonomous decision-making poses significant challenges (Watson 2016).

15.10 Final Word

An analysis of judicial decisions has revealed that the voices of students with disabilities are silent, both during decision-making at school, and throughout the litigation process. This must prompt educators to consider whether the silence is related to issues of power, or structural barriers (Lewis 2008). Finding opportunities for students with disability to have agency over educational decisions allows their voice to be turned into classroom practice (Vlachou and Papananou 2015). Parent involvement is a mechanism for supported decision-making (Watson 2016), but must not come at the exclusion of the person for whom the decision has the most profound effect.

References

Al Zidjaly, N. (2015). *Disability, discourse and technology: Agency and inclusion in (inter) action.* Hampshire: Palgrave Macmillan.

Aldred, R. (2013). *Broadening the boundaries of agency: Cognitive disability, agency, and autonomy.* Doctoral dissertation, University of Calgary. Retrieved from http://theses.ucalgary.ca/jspui/bitstream/11023/822/2/ucalgary_2013_aldred_raymond.pdf

Anti-Discrimination Tribunal of Queensland. (2006, July 11). *JC on behalf of BC v State of Queensland (ADTQ).* Retrieved from http://www.austlii.edu.au/cgi-bin/sinodisp/au/cases/qld/QADT/2006/27.html?stem=0&synonyms=0&query=JC%20on%20behalf%20of%20BC

Arnstein-Kerslake, A., & Flynn, E. (2017). The right to legal agency: Domination, disability and the protections of article 12 of the convention on the rights of persons with disabilities. *International Journal of Law in Context, 13*(1), 22–38. https://doi.org/10.1017/S1744552316000458.

Ashby, C. (2011). Whose "voice" is it anyway? Giving voice and qualitative research involving individuals that type to communicate. *Disability Studies Quarterly, 31*(4), 26. Retrieved from http://dsq-sds.org/article/view/1723/1771

Australian Government [Department of Education Employment and Workforce Relations]. (2012). *Report on the review of the disability standards for education 2005*. Canberra: Author.

Australian Government [Productivity Commission]. (2004). *Review of the disability discrimination act 1992: Productivity commission inquiry report* (Vol. 1). Melbourne: Author.

Brown, D. A., & Lewis, C. N. (2013). Competence is in the eye of the beholder: Perceptions of intellectually disabled child witnesses. *International Journal of Disability, Development and Education, 60*(1), 3–17. https://doi.org/10.1080/1034912X.2013.757132.

Byrnes, L. J., & Rickards, F. W. (2011). Listening to the voices of students with disabilities: Can such voices inform practice? *Australasian Journal of Special Education, 35*(1), 25–34. https://doi.org/10.1375/ajse.35.1.25.

Cambra, J. E. (2016). *Preparing for student led IEPs*. Masters dissertation. Retrieved from http://csusm-dspace.calstate.edu/bitstream/handle/10211.3/174686/CambaJordan_Summer2016.pdf?sequence=1

Castelli, P., & Goodman, G. S. (2014). Children's perceived emotional behavior at disclosure and prosecutors' evaluations. *Child Abuse & Neglect, 38*(9), 1521–1532. Retrieved from https://www.researchgate.net/profile/Paola_Castelli3/publication/261102978_Children's_perceived_emotional_behavior_at_disclosure_and_prosecutors'_evaluations/links/5751b41f08ae17e65ec33f20.pdf

Cavendish, W. (2013). Student perceptions of school efforts to facilitate student involvement, school commitment, self-determination and graduation track. *Social Psychology of Education, 16*, 257–275. https://doi.org/10.1007/s11218-013-9212-z.

Cavendish, W., & Connor, D. (2017). Toward authentic IEPs and transition plans: Student, parent, and teacher perspectives. *Learning Disability Quarterly*. Advance online publication. doi: https://doi.org/10.1177/0731948716684680.

Chua, A. C. K. (2015). A triple-E framework on parental involvement of children with autism spectrum disorder in early intervention. *International Journal of Multidisciplinary Research and Development, 30*, 579–586. Retrieved from https://www.researchgate.net/profile/Arnold_Chua3/publication/283150879_A_Triple-E_Framework_on_Parental_Involvement_of_Children_with_Autism_Spectrum_Disorder_in_Early_Intervention/links/562cd92208ae518e348244f9.pdf

Cobb, B., Lehmann, J., Newman-Gonchar, R., & Alwell, M. (2009). Self-determination for students with disabilities: A narrative metasynthesis. *Career Development for Exceptional Individuals, 32*, 108–114. https://doi.org/10.1177/0885728809336654.

Collier, M. L., Griffin, M. M., & Wei, Y. (2016). Facilitating student involvement in transition assessment: A pilot study of the student transition questionnaire. *Career Development and Transition for Exceptional Individuals, 39*(3), 175–184. https://doi.org/10.1177/2165143414556746.

ComLaw. (2016). *Disability standards for education 2005 [Cth] (DSE).* Retrieved from http://www.comlaw.gov.au/Details/F2005L00767

de Apodaca, R. F., Gentling, D. G., Steinhaus, J. K., & Rosenberg, E. A. (2015). Parental involvement as a mediator of academic performance among special education middle school students. *School Community Journal, 25*(2), 35–54. Retrieved from http://files.eric.ed.gov/fulltext/EJ1085649.pdf

Disability Discrimination Act. (1992). Retrieved from http://www.austlii.edu.au/au/legis/cth/consol_act/dda1992264/

Dixon, R. M., & Tanner, K. (2013). The experience of transitioning two adolescents with Asperger syndrome in academically focused high schools. *Australasian Journal of Special Education, 37*(1), 28–48. https://doi.org/10.1017/jse.2013.5.

Education Council. (2016). *Nationally consistent collection of data – School students with a disability: 2016 emergent data on students in Australian schools receiving adjustments for disability.* Retrieved from http://www.educationcouncil.edu.au/site/DefaultSite/filesystem/documents/Reports%20and%20publications/ED17-0046%20SCH%20NCCD%20Report%202017_ACC.PDF

Goldfarb, D., Goodman, G. S., & Lawler, M. (2015). Children's evidence and the convention on the rights of the child: Improving the legal system for children. In S. Mahmoudi, P. Leviner, A. Kaldal, & K. Lainpelto (Eds.), *Child-friendly justice: A quarter of a century of the UN convention on the rights of the child* (pp. 85–109). Leiden/Stockholm: Brill Nijhoff.

Gordon, M. (2010). Student voice key to unlocking inclusive educational practices. *Canadian Journal of New Scholars in Education, 3*(2), 1–11. Retrieved from https://journalhosting.ucalgary.ca/index.php/cjnse/article/viewFile/30480/24877

Griffin, M. M., Lounds Taylor, J., Urbano, R. C., & Hodapp, R. M. (2014). Involvement in transition planning meetings among high school students with autism spectrum disorders. *The Journal of Special Education, 47*(4), 256–264. https://doi.org/10.1177/0022466913475668.

Hattie, J. (2009). *Visible learning: A synthesis of over 800 meta-analyses relating to achievement.* Milton Park: Routledge.

Human Rights & Equal Opportunity Commission. (1999, July 20). *Finney v the Hills grammar school (HREOC).* Retrieved from http://www.austlii.edu.au/cgi-bin/sinodisp/au/cases/cth/HREOCA/1999/14.html?stem=0&synonyms=0&query=Finney

Human Rights & Equal Opportunity Commission. (2000, November 13). *Purvis v state of New South Wales (Department of education) (HREOC).* Retrieved from http://www.austlii.edu.au/cgi-bin/sinodisp/au/cases/cth/HREOCA/2000/47.html?stem=0&synonyms=0&query=Purvis

Jackson, J., & Varnham, S. (2007). *Law for educators: School and university law in Australia*. Chatswood: LexisNexis.

Jubran, L. N. (2015). *Student voice for enhancing the quality of inclusive education*. Doctoral dissertation. Retrieved from https://bspace.buid.ac.ae/bitstream/1234/778/1/120043.pdf

Kaczkowski, M. (2012). *A qualitative case study: Student perceptions of "voice" in the IEP process*. Doctoral dissertation. Retrieved from http://search.proquest.com/openview/c5dee189df2175348be5364e362a8488/1?pq-origsite=gscholar&cbl=18750&diss=y

Knutsson, J., & Allwood, C. M. (2014). Opinions of legal professionals: Comparing child and adult witnesses' memory report capabilities. *The European Journal of Psychology Applied to Legal Context, 6*(2), 79–89. Retrieved from https://doi.org/10.1016/j.ejpal.2014.06.001.

Lai, Y., & Vadeboncoeur, J. A. (2013). The discourse of parent involvement in special education: A critical analysis linking policy documents to the experiences of mothers. *Educational Policy, 27*(6), 867–897. https://doi.org/10.1177/0895904812440501.

Landmark, L., Zhang, D., & Montoya, L. (2007). Culturally diverse parents' experiences in their children's transition: Knowledge and involvement. *Career Development and Transition for Exceptional Individuals, 30*, 68–79. https://doi.org/10.1177/08857288070300020401.

Landmark, L., Roberts, E., & Zhang, D. (2013). Educators' beliefs and practices about parent involvement in transition planning. *Career Development and Transition for Exceptional Individuals, 36*, 114–123. https://doi.org/10.1177/2165143412463047.

Lewis, A. (2008). Silence in the context of 'child voice'. *Child & Society, 24*, 14–23. https://doi.org/10.1111/j.1099-0860.2008.00200.x.

Lindström, M. (2011). *Promoting agency among people with severe psychiatric disability: Occupation-oriented interventions in home and community settings*. Retrieved from https://www.diva-portal.org/smash/get/diva2:458648/FULLTEXT01.pdf

Meadan, H., Shelden, D., Appel, K., & DeGrazia, R. (2010). Developing a long-term vision: A road map for students' futures. *Teaching Exceptional Children, 43*, 8–14. https://doi.org/10.1177/004005991004300201.

Miller, G. E., Colebrook, J., & Ellis, B. R. (2014). Advocating for the rights of the child through family–school collaboration. *Journal of Educational and Psychological Consultation, 24*(1), 10–27. https://doi.org/10.1080/10474412.2014.870483.

Mitchell, D. (2014). *What really works in special and inclusive education: Using evidence-based teaching strategies* (2nd ed.). Milton Park: Routledge.

Nolan-Spohn, H. (2016). Increasing student involvement in IEPs. *Mid-Western Educational Researcher, 28*(3), 300–308. Retrieved from http://www.mwera.org/MWER/volumes/v28/issue3/v28n3-Nolan-VOICES-FROM-THE-CLASSROOM.pdf

Norwich, B. (2014). How does the capability approach address current issues in special educational needs, disability and inclusive education field? *Journal of Research in Special Educational Needs, 14*(1), 16–21. https://doi.org/10.1111/1471-3802.12012.

O'Neill, S., & Zajac, R. (2013). Preparing children for cross-examination: How does intervention timing influence efficacy? *Psychology, Public Policy, and Law, 19*(3), 307–320. https://doi.org/10.1037/a0031538.

Pagliano, P., & Gillies, R. M. (2015). Inclusive practices. In A. Ashman (Ed.), *Education for inclusion and diversity* (5th ed., pp. 131–161). Melbourne: Pearson.

Palmer, S. B., Wehmeyer, M. L., & Shogren, K. A. (2017). The development of self-determination during childhood. In M. L. Wehmeyer, K. A. Shogren, T. D. Little, & S. J. Lopez (Eds.), *Development of self-determination through the life-course* (Ch. 6, pp. 71–88). Dordrecht: Springer.

Pawley, H., & Tennant, G. (2008). Student perceptions of their IEP targets. *Support for Learning, 23*(4), 183–186. https://doi.org/10.1111/j.1467-9604.2008.00392.x.

Peter, S. J. (2010). The heterodoxy of student voice: Challenges to identity in the sociology of disability and education. *British Journal of Sociology of Education, 31*(5), 591–602.

Prout, A., & Hallett, C. (2003). Introduction. In C. Hallett & A. Prout (Eds.), *Hearing the voices of children: Social policy for a new century* (pp. 1–8). London: Routledge Falmer.

Rioux, M. (2013). Disability rights in education. In L. Florian (Ed.), *The Sage handbook of special education: Volume 1* (2nd ed., pp. 131–147). London: Sage.

Robinson, J. (2015). The experience of the child witness: Legal and psychological issues. *International Journal of Law and Psychiatry, 42*, 168–176. Retrieved from https://doi.org/10.1016/j.ijlp.2015.08.022

Seong, Y., Wehmeyer, M. L., Palmer, S. B., & Little, T. D. (2015). Effects of the self-directed individualized education program on self-determination and transition of adolescents with disabilities. *Career Development and Transition for Exceptional Individuals, 38*(3), 132–141. https://doi.org/10.1177/2165143414544359.

Shelley, M. (1991). Report on the national consultations with people with a disability. In *Disability advisory council of Australia*. Canberra: Australian Government Printing Service.

Shoemaker, D. (2010). Responsibility, agency, and cognitive disability. In E. Feder Kittay & L. Carlson (Eds.), *Cognitive disability and its challenge to moral philosophy* (Ch. 12, pp. 201–224). West Sussex: Wiley.

Slee, R. (2011). *The irregular school: Exclusion, schooling and inclusive education.* Abingdon: Routledge.

Smith, K. M. (2016). *Investigating transition processes for students with special needs.* Masters dissertation. Retrieved from http://opus.ipfw.edu/cgi/viewcontent.cgi?article=1037&context=grad_research

Stolz, S. M. (2010). *Disability trajectories: Disabled youths' identity development, negotiation of experience and expectation, and sense of agency during transition*. Doctoral dissertation. Retrieved from https://escholarship.org/uc/item/7zg9w5ht

Thoman, D. H. (2013). Testifying minors: Pre-trial strategies to reduce anxiety in child witnesses. *Nevada Law Journal, 14*, 236–267. Retrieved from http://scholars.law.unlv.edu/cgi/viewcontent.cgi?article=1532&context=nlj&sei-redir=1&referer=https%3A%2F%2Fscholar.google.com.au%2Fscholar%3Fstart%3D10%26q%3Dcourt%2B%2522children%2Bas%2Bwitnesses%2522%26hl%3Den%26as_sdt%3D0%2C5%26as_ylo%3D2013%26as_yhi%3D2017#search=%22court%20children%20as%20witnesses%22

United Nations. (2000). Conventions on the Rights of the Child (CROC). Retrieved from http://www.ohchr.org/en/professionalinterest/pages/crc.aspx

United Nations. (2006). Conventions on the Rights of Persons with Disabilities (CRPD). Retrieved from http://www.un.org/disabilities/convention/conventionfull.shtml

Valle, J. W. (2009). *What mothers say about special education: From the 1960s to the present*. London: Palgrave Macmillan.

Valle, J. W., & Aponte, E. (2002). IDEA and collaboration: A Bakhtinian perspective on parent and professional discourse. *Journal of Learning Disabilities, 35*, 469–479. https://doi.org/10.1177/00222194020350050701.

Van Laarhoven-Myers, T. E., Van Laarhoven, T. R., Smith, T. J., Johnson, H., & Olson, J. (2016). Promoting self-determination and transition planning using technology: Student and parent perspectives. *Career Development and Transition for Exceptional Individuals, 39*(2), 99–110. https://doi.org/10.1177/2165143414552518.

Victorian Civil & Administrative Tribunal. (2006, June 6). *Beasley v State of Victoria Department of Education & Training* (VCAT). Retrieved from http://www.austlii.edu.au/cgi-bin/sinodisp/au/cases/vic/VCAT/2006/1050.html?stem=0&synonyms=0&query=Beasley

Victorian Equal Opportunity & Human Rights Commission (VEOHRC). (2012). *Held back: The experiences of students with disabilities in Victorian schools*. Retrieved from http://www.humanrightscommission.vic.gov.au/media/k2/attachments/1404-VEOHRC_HeldBack_-_StudentwithDisabilityReportW3.pdf

Vlachou, A., & Papananou, I. (2015). Disabled students' narratives about their schooling experiences. *Disability & Society, 30*(1), 73–86. https://doi.org/10.1080/09687599.2014.982787.

Watkins, B. T. (2014). *Reducing court-related stress through court education: Examining child witnesses, attorneys and parents*. Doctoral dissertation. Retrieved from http://digitalscholarship.unlv.edu/thesesdissertations/2228/

Watson, J. (2016). *The right to supported decision-making for people rarely heard*. Doctoral dissertation. Retrieved from https://www.researchgate.net/profile/Joanne_Watson/publication/258997358_Thesis_The_right_to_supported_decision-making_for_people_rarely_heard/links/5751420a08ae17e65ec149cf.pdf

Weber, M. (2013). Children with disabilities, parents without disabilities, and lawyers: Issues of life experience, affinity, and agency. In B. A. Ferri & A. Kanter (Eds.), *Righting educational wrongs: Disability studies in law and education*. Syracuse: Syracuse University Press.

Wehmeyer, M. L., Shogren, K. A., & Seo, H. (2015). Promoting the self-determination and goal attainment of youth with learning disabilities and behavioral disorders. In B. G. Cook, M. Tankersley, & T. J. Landrum (Eds.), *Transition of youth and young adults* (pp. 173–196). Bingley: Emerald Group.

Whitburn, B. (2016). Voice, post-structural representation and the subjectivity of 'included' students. *International Journal of Research & Method in Education, 39*(2), 117–130. https://doi.org/10.1080/1743727X.2014.946497.

Williams-Lewis, Y. R. (2014). *Principal leadership that creates a school culture supportive of inclusive education for students on the autism spectrum*. Doctoral dissertation. Retrieved from https://sdsu-dspace.calstate.edu/bitstream/handle/10211.3/138246/WilliamsLewis_sdsu_0220D_10674.pdf?sequence=1

Wilson, A., Poed, S., & Byrnes, L. (2015). Full steam ahead: Facilitating the involvement of Australian students with impairments in individual planning processes through student-led program support group meetings. *Special Education Perspectives, 24*(1), 15–25. Retrieved from http://aase.edu.au/wordpress/wp-content/uploads/documents/SEP-Contents-Vol24-No1-18Jun15-.pdf.

16

The Inclusion and Exclusion of Students with Disability Related Problem Behaviour in Mainstream Australian Schools

Elizabeth Dickson

16.1 Introduction

The enrolment of students with disabilities in mainstream schools, rather than 'special' schools, has been aspired to in Australia for at least two decades. The 2002 report of a Senate enquiry into the education of students with disabilities concluded that 'inclusive practices' had become the 'prevailing orthodoxy' in Australian schools (Senate Employment, Workplace Relations and Education Committee 2002, p. 29). More recently, the National Disability Strategy 2010–2020 (Council of Australian Governments 2011, p. 49) committed Australia to the goal of inclusion of students with disability in a 'high quality education system that is responsive to their needs'. Underpinning any 'right' to 'inclusion'[1] is the *Disability Discrimination Act 1992* (Cth) ('DDA') which has the object of ensuring 'as far as practicable, that persons with disabilities have the same rights to equality before the law as the rest of the community' (s. 3). The DDA is informed and enlivened by Australia's ratification of an array international rights instruments (s. 12(8)). It was amended in 2009 to acknowledge the newly ratified Convention on the Rights of People

[1] It is acknowledged that 'inclusion' is a contested term in the context of the education of students with disability. Analysis of the meaning of the term is beyond the scope of this chapter. For the purpose of this chapter, 'inclusion' is used by the author to mean full time enrolment at a mainstream school which also enrols students without disability.

E. Dickson (✉)
School of Law, Queensland University of Technology, Brisbane, QLD, Australia
e-mail: e.dickson@qut.edu.au

K. Trimmer et al. (eds.), *The Palgrave Handbook of Education Law for Schools*,
https://doi.org/10.1007/978-3-319-77751-1_16

with Disabilities which explicitly stipulates in Article 24 that states parties shall 'ensure' that '[p]ersons with disabilities are not excluded from the general education system on the basis of disability'.

Australia's achievement of the goal of inclusion has proved difficult, however, in respect of people with disability related problem behaviour. Most disability discrimination in education cases which end up in court involve problem behaviour flowing from intellectual, psychiatric or behavioural disability. Such behaviour may be disruptive, stressful or even dangerous. It might be the impulsiveness of a person with Down's syndrome (See, e.g., *P*[2]) or Attention Deficit Hyperactivity Disorder (ADHD) (see, e.g., *Walker, Abela*), the problems with bowel control and regurgitation of a person with a developmental disorder (See, e.g., *L*), or most problematically, the unwilled violence of a person with brain damage (See, e.g., *Purvis*). In Australian anti-discrimination legislation, the protected attribute of disability (or, for some Acts, impairment) typically extends to disturbed or disturbing behaviour. For example, the DDA definition of disability covers 'a disorder, illness or disease that affects a person's thought processes, perception of reality, emotions or judgment or that results in disturbed behaviour' (DDA s 4). Moreover, since 2009, the DDA definition has made it plain in s. 4 what the Courts had acknowledged (See, e.g., *Purvis*) that a disability 'includes behaviour that is a symptom or manifestation of the disability'.

It is indicative, perhaps, of the controversy that has historically attended the inclusion of students with problem behaviour, that the first disability discrimination in education case to be litigated in Australia, brought under the *Anti-Discrimination Act 1991* (Qld), *L*, involved a student excluded from her mainstream school because of her disability related behaviour. The complainant failed to prove unlawful discrimination, but the case excited extensive media coverage and polarised public opinion on the issue of inclusion (see, e.g., Atkins 1995; Butler 1995, 1996; Oberhardt 1995; Atkins 1996). Two similar Queensland 'behaviour' cases, *P* and *K*, heard shortly after *L*, were also decided against the complainants. Recent disability discrimination in education cases, including *Walker* and *Abela*, has also concerned students excluded for problem behaviour. The issue still troubles school communities: teachers and administrators, parents of students with and without disability, and students.

---

[2] Cases are referred to by their abbreviated names throughout this chapter. For the full citation of the case "*P*", and the full citations other cases referred to by their abbreviated names in the chapter, please see the case list at the end of the chapter.

A student who is refused enrolment at a mainstream school, or excluded from a mainstream school, may claim direct discrimination, 'less favourable treatment' (See, e.g., DDA s. 5). A student may also claim indirect discrimination if an unreasonable condition is imposed, with which he or she cannot comply and which has the effect of disadvantaging him or her (See, e.g., DDA s 6). Claims of indirect discrimination have been extrapolated, for example, from the blanket imposition of school codes of conduct. Proof of either direct or indirect discrimination has been difficult for students with disabilities manifesting as problem behaviour.

This chapter will consider the strategies for exclusion which the relevant case law reveals may be relied upon by schools when problem behaviour poses a health and safety risk or disrupts the learning of others. It will consider how the courts have narrowed the scope of any obligation to include students with disability related problem behaviour, through the manner in which they have interpreted and applied various aspects of anti-discrimination law: direct and indirect discrimination, the unjustifiable hardship exemption to unlawful discrimination, and the obligation upon education providers to make reasonable adjustment for students with disability.

The benchmark case in this area, and a primary focus of the chapter, is *Purvis*. In that case, the High Court of Australia controversially determined that a school could lawfully exclude a student with disability related problem behaviour, and to achieve that result, construed the test for direct discrimination in a manner which has subsequently undermined the utility of an action for direct discrimination across the areas and attributes protected in Australian anti-discrimination law (Thornton 2009). School 'code of conduct' indirect discrimination cases have also been defeated on the basis that the imposition of such a code is 'reasonable' (See, e.g., *M & C, Minns*). Further, in the event that a complainant should succeed in proving a prima facie case of direct or indirect discrimination, the unjustifiable hardship exemption will likely render such discrimination lawful (See, e.g., *L, K, P*).

The implementation of the *Disability Standards for Education 2005* (Cth) (DSE), a year after the decision in *Purvis*, was an opportunity for both schools and courts to revisit the issue of the accommodation of problem behaviour. The DSE impose on education providers, including schools, the obligation to make reasonable adjustment for students with disabilities. Reasonable adjustment, however, is also excused where a school can prove that it would cause unjustifiable hardship. Cases decided since the introduction of the DSE have not delivered any greater prospects of inclusion for students with problem behaviour (See, e.g., *Walker* and Abela).

Both Commonwealth and state laws prohibit discrimination on the basis of disability (or impairment) in the protected area of education. There is significant overlap between Commonwealth and State laws in respect of proof of discrimination and the exemptions which will render a prima facie case of discrimination lawful. Since the DDA was amended in 2009 to impose an institutional obligation to make reasonable adjustment for students with disability, the DDA, and the associated DSE, arguably offer superior protection to students with disability. Moreover, the effect of DDA s. 13(3A) is that the DSE, and its obligation to make reasonable adjustment, will override any inconsistent state law. As such, the law as stated in and applied under the DDA and the DSE will be the primary focus of this chapter. Discrimination complaints may still be brought under state legislation, however, and relevant case law from the state courts will also be addressed.

16.2 *Purvis v. New South Wales*: Direct Discrimination and Problem Behaviour

The *Purvis* case, as the only directly relevant High Court case, is a logical place to begin an explanation of the complexities of the relevant law. It represents the most complete examination of the inclusion issue by an Australian court to date. The complainant in *Purvis,* Daniel Hoggan, was excluded from Year 7 at South Grafton High School, in New South Wales, because of what a witness neurologist described as his 'difficult' behaviour, 'disinhibited and uninhibited' behaviour (paras. [29], [182]). Daniel's behaviour was caused by and a consequence of brain damage sustained during infancy as a result of an infection with encephalitis. Over the course of his enrolment in Year 7, Daniel was suspended several times and ultimately excluded for repeated verbal abuse and violence which included kicking not only furniture and school bags but also other children and teaching staff. A majority of the High Court held that Daniel's exclusion did not offend the DDA.

16.3 *Purvis* and the 'Right' to Inclusion

Four of the Justices on the Court, Chief Justice Gleeson CJ (para [6]), Justices McHugh and Kirby (para. [123]) and Justice Callinan (para. [238]), made some explicit comment on whether and to what extent there is a right to a 'mainstream' education available to students with disabilities. There is a measure of overlap in the analyses of these four judges, despite the fact that

Justices McHugh and Kirby ultimately found, in a minority judgment, that Daniel Hoggan had been the subject of unlawful discrimination. All four implied that the source of any right to inclusion could be traced to the international rights treaties behind the DDA. All four agreed that a mainstream education may not be available where the inclusion of a student impinged on the safety of other students and staff. Three implied that a further limit may arise when educational opportunities of other students are adversely affected.

Chief Justice Gleeson made the clear point that the *Purvis* case concerned a clash between competing rights: 'The present case illustrates that rights, recognised by international norms, or by domestic law, may conflict. In construing the Act, there is no warrant for an assumption that, in seeking to protect the rights of disabled pupils, Parliament intended to disregard Australia's obligations to protect the rights of other pupils' (para. [6]). Chief Justice Gleeson implied that school students – and, indeed, staff – have a right to safety which school administrators have a duty to protect. He questioned whether Parliament is constitutionally entitled to enact legislation which does not allow competing rights to be reconciled:

> *...a contention that the legislative power of the Commonwealth Parliament extends to obliging State educational authorities to accept, or continue to accommodate, pupils whose conduct is a serious threat to the safety of other pupils, or staff, or school property, would require careful scrutiny.* (para. [6])

Justices McHugh and Kirby, like Chief Justice Gleeson, found that 'the Act provides for a balance to be struck between the rights of the disabled child and those of other pupils and, for that matter, teaching staff' (para. [123]). Like Chief Justice Gleeson, they found that a limit on the right to inclusion of students with disabilities would arise when the safety of others was put at risk: 'The nature of the detriment likely to be suffered by *any persons concerned*, if the student was admitted, would comprehend consideration of threats to the safety and welfare of other pupils, teachers and aides' (para. [123]). Arguably, however, they implied a further limit by stating that 'any negative impact that may be caused by the presence of a student with disability in a mainstream class is a proper matter to be considered when making a decision on whether that individual student can be admitted' (para. [123]). The vague phrase 'any negative impact' may be broad enough, for example, to encompass an adverse impact on the educational opportunities of others in a classroom.

Justice Callinan was prepared to make explicit the limit implied by Justices McHugh and Kirby. Citing the *International Covenant on Economic, Social and Cultural Rights*, he found that any right to inclusion of students with a disability must be weighed against the 'the right of everyone to education' (para. [238]). That universal right, he found, 'could be adversely affected by an insistence that the education to which a disabled person is equally entitled should be provided in circumstances which cause disruption to the education of others' (para. [238]). Justice Callinan was also concerned that the right to safety of others must be paramount. Emphasising the 'quasi-criminal' nature of Daniel Hoggan's behaviour, he, like Chief Justice Gleeson, cast doubt on the constitutional validity of legislation which would compel States to ignore State criminal laws by excusing or allowing violent behaviour, even when caused by disability, to continue to pose a threat to others (paras. [266], [271]).

16.4 *Purvis* and Strategies for Exclusion

To support their dismissal of Daniel Hoggan's claim of direct discrimination flowing from his exclusion, the majority judges developed controversial tests for proof of less favourable treatment and causation which allow the impact of disability related problem behaviour to be considered. There is little doubt that they were influenced in their reasoning by the absence in the DDA, as it then was drafted, of the availability of the unjustifiable hardship exemption post enrolment (Dickson 2005; Edwards 2004; Rattigan 2004). In earlier cases, such as *L*, *K* and *P*, the unjustifiable hardship exemption had been relied on to render prima facie direct discrimination lawful (Dickson 2004).

The majority judges were also, clearly, influenced by a perceived need to construe the Act to deliver an interpretation which allowed for 'a proper intersection between the operation of the Act [*DDA*] and the operation of State and Federal criminal law' (para. [227] per Justices Gummow, Hayne and Heydon.):

> *Daniel's actions constituted assaults. It is neither necessary nor appropriate to decide whether he could or would have been held criminally responsible for them. It is enough to recognise that there will be cases where criminal conduct for which the perpetrator would be held criminally responsible could be seen to have occurred as a result of some disorder, illness or disease. It follows that there can be cases in which the perpetrator could be said to suffer a disability within the meaning of the Act.* (para. [227] per Justices Gummow, Hayne and Heydon)

It would be a startling result if the Act, on its proper construction, did not permit an employer, educational authority, or other person subject to the Act to require, as a universal rule, that employees and pupils comply with the criminal law. (para. [228] per Justices Gummow, Hayne and Heydon)

16.5 Purvis and the 'Comparator'

Proof of direct discrimination requires a comparison between the treatment of the complainant with disability and the treatment of a 'comparator' person without the disability in order to determine whether the complainant has been treated 'less favourably' (DDA s. 5). Complainants and respondents have argued diametrically opposed interpretations of the 'identity' of the notional comparator. In the context of impairments which cause problem behaviours which impact on others, the question is not only poignant but crucial to the outcome of the case. In *Purvis*, as well as in earlier cases such as *L*, *P* and *K*, the complainants argued that the appropriate comparator is a person without the impairment and without the impairment induced behaviour. If the comparison is between the treatment of the person with the problem behaviour and the treatment of a person without it then it is obviously easier to prove 'less favourable treatment' because it could only rarely be proved that a person without the behaviour would have been disciplined or excluded in the same manner as the complainant. Respondents in those cases argued that the appropriate comparator is a person without the impairment but with the behaviour. When the behaviour is common to complainant and comparator it is obviously easier to rebut any allegation of discrimination as it could only rarely be proved that the comparator would *not* have been disciplined or excluded in the same manner as the complainant. The decision of the High Court in *Purvis* appears to have settled the answer to the comparator question: the appropriate comparator is a person *without* the complainant's impairment but *with* the complainant's behaviour, even though the complainant's behaviour is a manifestation of and caused by disability. Because the 'normal' comparator who 'misbehaves' would be sanctioned, it is appropriate that the complainant be sanctioned, and, as such, there is no less favourable treatment (para. [12] per Chief Justice Gleeson, per Justices Gummow, Hayne and Heydon, para. [222]). The majority approach in *Purvis* at the time was directly at odds with the view taken by the minority, by earlier benches of the High Court (see, for example, *IW*, p. 33 per Justice Toohey, pp. 40–1 per Justice Gummow, p. 67 per Justice Kirby), and by assorted anti-discrimination tribunals (See, e.g., *L*, *K* and *P*). Moreover, allowing the unwilled acts of the complainant to be compared with the willed violence of a person without disability must understandably be offensive to those with disabilities and their supporters. The *Purvis* approach to the comparator issue remains the law, however, and, as discussed, below, has been readily applied in later cases involving disability related problem behaviour.

16.6 Purvis and Causation

Discrimination must be causally related to a protected attribute before it will be unlawful. The DDA prohibits, for example, discrimination 'because of' disability (ss. 5, 6). In *Purvis*, each of the judgments identified causation as an issue relevant to liability (paras. [12]–[13] per Chief Justice Gleeson, para. [166] per Justices McHugh and Kirby, para. [236] per Justices Gummow, Hayne and Heydon, paras. [267]–[270] per Justice Callinan). Justices across the minority and the majority accepted that it was necessary to look at 'why' or the 'real reason' the relevant treatment had occurred. Even though there was significant agreement between the judges as to the relevant test, the minority and majority could reach different conclusions because of the different way they read 'disability'. The minority justices would not have authorised a separation of the behavioural manifestations from the underpinning disability, and exclusion because of Daniel's behaviour, they found, was exclusion because of his disability. As with their treatment of the comparator issue, however, the majority justices could comfortably separate the behavioural manifestations of the disability for the purpose of working out the cause of the treatment. In their view, the legitimate answer to the question, 'why was Daniel Hoggan expelled?', would have been a 'lawful' reason: 'because of his behaviour'.

The judgment of Chief Justice Gleeson exemplifies the majority conclusion: "The expressed and genuine basis of the principal's decision [to exclude Daniel] was the danger to other pupils and staff constituted by the pupil's violent conduct, and the principal's responsibilities towards those people' (para. [13]). His Honour's judgment, however, arguably goes further than any of the other judgments in *Purvis* in its potential to protect a school seeking to exclude a student with disability related problem behaviour. While his 'true basis' test for causation is superficially similar to that expounded by other members of the Court, upon closer reading Chief Justice Gleeson places much more emphasis on a subjective enquiry into the thought processes of the alleged discriminator and, particularly, into the express reasons for the treatment offered by the alleged discriminator. It is true that the analyses offered by Justices Gummow, Hayne, Heydon, McHugh and Kirby suggest that there is an element of subjectivity involved in the causation enquiry, to the extent, at least, that the reason for the treatment is a question of fact. Chief Justice Gleeson, however, went further in his analysis implying that there is no room, on the particular facts of *Purvis* at least, for any objective analysis of the motivation of the alleged discriminator: 'There is no reason for rejecting the principal's statement of the basis of his decision as being the violent conduct of the pupil, and his concern for the safety of other pupils and staff members' (para. [14]).

The judgment of Chief Justice Gleeson suggests that the explanation offered by the alleged discriminator is simply to be accepted as the reason for his actions. Indeed, his Honour says that it would be 'unfair' to the principal of South Grafton State High School to find a discriminatory 'basis' for his decision: 'It is not incompatible with the legislative scheme to identify the basis of the principal's decision as that which he expressed. On the contrary, to identify the pupil's disability as the basis of the decision would be unfair to the principal and to the first respondent [the State of New South Wales]' (para. [14]). While Chief Justice Gleeson concedes that from the point of view of Daniel Hoggan it may be reasonable to believe that he was expelled 'because of' his disability, his Honour stresses that, as it was the lawfulness of the *principal's* actions that was in question, it was *his* point of view which was relevant to the enquiry (para. [13]).

Allowing an exclusively subjective enquiry such as this into the reasons advanced by the alleged discriminator is potentially dangerous in that it encourages the unscrupulous invention of 'authorised' reasons for acting. As such, Chief Justice Gleeson's reading of causation would inevitably mean less pressure on institutions and individuals to accommodate people with disabilities. The unscrupulous school administration, for example, could escape liability simply by asserting that it was a student's 'truancy', not his or her impairment, that was the 'basis' of a decision to exclude (See, e.g., *BI* for a case concerning disability related non-attendance). Upon the analysis of Chief Justice Gleeson there is no need to evaluate, objectively, the reasons advanced for the 'truancy', no need, even, to enquire whether the 'truancy' was an incidence of the student's impairment. Further, the unscrupulous school could be encouraged to manufacture a misleading document trail which supported the stated reason for exclusion.

16.7 *Purvis* Applied

Later courts and tribunals considering disability discrimination in education cases were quick to adopt the majority approach in *Purvis* to both the comparator issue and causation. In *Tyler*, a 2006 DDA case, Federal Magistrate Driver, of the then Federal Magistrates Court (since 2014, the Federal Circuit Court), found that the temporary exclusion of a student with Down's syndrome, who had, allegedly, thrown an object from a balcony which hit a teacher, was not discriminatory. There were problems with proof of a link between the disability of the complainant and his behaviour with Federal Magistrate Driver noting that, 'while there is clearly evidence that Joseph presented with behavioural difficulties, I have no medical evidence at all that these were a consequence of his Down's syndrome' (para. [105]). Nevertheless, the decision arguably extends the scope of *Purvis* beyond the context of students proved to be violent to apply to students who simply stand accused of being violent. Although Federal Magistrate Driver refused to find that the complainant had thrown the object or even that he was 'involved' in the throwing incident (para. [105]), he found that a comparator without the complainant's disability but similarly standing accused of throwing would also have been temporarily excluded (para. [107]). The subjective approach of Chief Justice Gleeson to causation was also influential in this case. Federal Magistrate Driver simply accepted the reason advanced by the principal of the school as the operative reason for the suspension:

> *...it is clear from the evidence of Rabbi Spielman [the principal], which I accept, that he took his action not because of any concern about a behavioural consequence of Joseph's disability, but rather because of his concern about the College's duty of care to its teachers and its students (including Joseph). Rabbi Spielman was seriously concerned, after the alleged throwing incident, that the College might breach its duty of care if it did not take immediate action.* (para. [105])

His honour, like the majority of the High Court, was impressed by duty of care issues and found that '[i]t would have been irresponsible for Rabbi Spielman [the principal] to have taken no action as that would have exposed the College to substantial risk' (para. [105]).

The majority approach in *Purvis* was also quickly applied in an education case beyond the context of the *DDA*. In 2004, the Victorian Civil and Administrative Tribunal relied on it to defeat a claim of discrimination made under the *Equal Opportunity Act 1995* (Vic) by a student with problem behaviour linked to his disabilities. In *Zygorodimos* the plaintiff student had been shifted to a different class in response to his behaviour problems and the stress they caused his teacher. He had not exhibited 'violence' of the kind complained of in *Purvis* but had nevertheless been 'difficult' (para. [49]). He had, among other misdemeanours, thrown tantrums, been inattentive, put 'inappropriate objects' in his mouth, and run from the classroom. This case demonstrates not only a willingness to apply the majority approach in a less 'dangerous' context than that postulated in *Purvis*, but also in the context of state legislation where the availability of other exemptions (In *Zygorodimos*, relevantly, *Equal Opportunity Act 1995* (Vic) s 39, special services or facilities exception) would have already, perhaps, allowed an 'out' to a court keen to authorize the apparently 'less favourable' treatment of a 'problem' complainant. It is of further interest that the Tribunal refused to consider evidence of other 'circumstances' asserted by the complainant to be relevant to his treatment. This evidence may have brought into issue the appropriateness of the school's response to the complainant's behaviour:

> *Before leaving this claim I should add that Mr Gray, counsel for Ben, relied on various matters which he said I should take into account to formulate the proper comparator. These included provisions concerning disciplinary policies of state schools in the Education Regulations 2000, the absence of a provision for the transfer of a child from one class to another in VCD's code of student conduct, and views expressed by some of the witnesses, such as the education expert Professor Branson, about when it would be appropriate to transfer a child for behavioural reasons from one class to another. While this evidence may be appropriate in general terms in dealing with the challenging behaviour of children, the only evidence which, in my view, is relevant to the proper comparator here, is how Dr Pearce would have treated a child other than Ben without epilepsy, but with similar behaviour.* (para. [100])

16.8 Law Reform After *Purvis*

The DDA was amended, after and in response to *Purvis*, in 2009, to make it plain that a disability included its manifestations (DDA s. 4) (See *Disability Discrimination and Other Human Rights Legislation Amendment Act 2009* (Cth)). This amendment, however, delivers little practical benefit in respect of the application of the DDA because of the way the comparator and causation tests were settled in *Purvis*. While the problematic manifestations of the disability are allowed to be separated from the underlying disability, direct discrimination will remain difficult, if not impossible, to prove. In the same suite of amendments, the unjustifiable hardship exemption was made available post-enrolment. While this amendment was too late to counter the impact of the High Court's construction of the comparator and causation tests in *Purvis*, its impact on proof of unlawful discrimination is addressed, below.

The 2009 amendments also imposed an express obligation to make reasonable adjustment (DDA ss. 5 and 6) in response to the finding of the High Court in *Purvis* that an implied obligation could not be drawn from the text of the DDA (See *Disability Discrimination and Other Human Rights Legislation Amendment Act 2009* (Cth) ss 13–17). That obligation, in the education context, is now enshrined in the DSE which were implemented in 2005 and which are also considered below.

16.9 Indirect Discrimination

Indirect discrimination (DDA s. 6) potentially occurs if a condition, often implied but sometimes express, is imposed on a group. It may be discriminatory if a person with disability is unable to 'comply' with that condition, and the effect is that the condition causes disadvantage to him or her. It will be discriminatory, if the condition is then not proven to be reasonable. It was suggested by Chief Justice Gleeson in *Purvis* that Daniel Hoggan's case was not framed as one of indirect discrimination in order to avoid the reasonableness enquiry (para. [3]). It is instructive to compare how the reasonableness issue has been dealt with in cases similar to that of Daniel Hoggan, but formulated as indirect discrimination claims. The New South Wales Administrative Decisions Tribunal (NSWADT) case of *M&C*, and the *DDA* case, *Minns*, both involved allegations of indirect discrimination against students with Attention Deficit Hyperactivity Disorder (ADHD).

Both M, of *M&C*, and Ryan Minns were frequently disciplined for breaches of the school rules. In *Minns*, Federal Magistrate Raphael explicitly drew attention to the similarities between that case and the *Purvis* case commenting that the consequence of Daniel Hoggan's disability was 'violent and anti-social behaviour very similar to that exhibited by Ryan Minns' (para. [191]).

Both the NSWADT and Federal Magistrate Raphael emphasised that it was reasonable that schools have and enforce codes of conduct. Indeed, the NSWADT found the point so 'trite' that it required 'no further discussion' (para. [123]). Federal Magistrate Raphael determined that such codes were necessary to enable 'all students to benefit from the educational opportunities offered and the requirement to allow this to happen in a safe environment' (para. [247]).

The issue in both cases, however, was not the reasonableness of the *code*, per se, but the reasonableness of the required *compliance* with the code imposed on the complainants who alleged that their impairment prevented such compliance. The evidence of M's mother, in *M&C*, was that M 'simply was not capable of controlling her behaviour' (para. [117]). The complainant's case in *Minns*, disputed by the respondent, was that Ryan's impairment made it 'impossible for him to behave in a manner compliant with the discipline policy' (para. [250]).

The NSWADT found against M on a technical issue and her case failed (See Dickson (2004) for further detail). The Tribunal was nevertheless critical of the inflexible administration of discipline policy at both schools which M attended. Whilst there was considerable discretion as to which penalty was meted out, there was no discretion to give no penalty at all. The Tribunal characterised the slavish adherence to the discipline policy as 'unreasonable':

> *While such behaviour [physical aggression] is clearly unacceptable, and it is reasonable to require that such children [children with ADHD] respect others and their property, it seems to us that it is unreasonable to apply a disciplinary regime in blanket fashion to all children regardless of their subjective features.* (para. [131])

The Tribunal compared the inflexible application of the discipline code with a mandatory sentencing regime, 'a form of punishment and social control, which has been shown to be largely ineffective in modifying the conduct of people with significant psychiatric or psychological difficulties' (para. [135]).

The Tribunal also emphasised that it was not reasonable to expect a child such as M to comply with the policy unless she had 'special support to enable…her to do so' (para. [131]). The facts here, were that M did not have this 'special support'. Thus, the Tribunal found a clear causal link between the lack of support and M's failure to comply with the discipline code:

> *Not only was M an ADD sufferer, she was well behind her colleagues academically…In those circumstances, it was unreasonable to expect that she could significantly modify her behaviour as a result of being frequently disciplined in the absence of that attention, support and special care. It was in our view therefore unreasonable to punish her in the same fashion as any other member of the student body if she failed to comply with the requirements of the Code.* (para. [133])

The Tribunal's reasoning here is similar to the reasoning of Commissioner Innes at first instance in the HREOC hearing of the *Purvis* case. Commissioner

Innes found that the South Grafton High School had not taken reasonable steps to accommodate Daniel Hoggan's impairment and that this failure had contributed to his behaviour problems. Ultimately this analysis of the evidence was rejected by the majority in *Purvis*. The cynical view, however, is that the Tribunal only made its pointed criticism of the respondent because having already found against M, it could safely admonish the respondent without actually having to enforce, controversially, any improvement in the respondent's treatment of its students.

The facts of the *Minns* case differed from the facts of *M&C* in that there was not the same weight of evidence of lack of specialist support for Ryan. In addition, there was evidence that the school had administered the discipline policy flexibly to accommodate Ryan's impairment. It should also be noted that Ryan and his mother objected to Ryan's taking prescribed medication which may have modified his behaviour. Nevertheless, the complainant argued, along the lines of *M&C* that the respondent had failed to take reasonable steps to deal with Ryan. The complainant suggested alternative methods of management of Ryan's behaviour. The Court was not convinced, however, that this line of argument was relevant (para. [256]) and found that the complainant had not proved that the requirement that Ryan comply with the code was 'not reasonable':

> *I am of the view that the requirement that was placed upon Ryan to comply with each of the school's disciplinary policies as modified was reasonable in all the circumstances. The classes in which Ryan was placed would be unable to function if he could not be removed for disruptive behaviour. The students could not achieve their potential if most of the teachers' time was taken up with handling Ryan. The playgrounds would not be safe if Ryan was allowed free rein for his aggressive actions. Therefore the claim for indirect discrimination must fail in the manner in which it is put.* (para. [263])

Thus, in determining the reasonableness issue against Ryan Minns, Federal Magistrate Raphael balanced the benefit to Ryan in allowing him 'free rein' against the potential detriment to others in the school community and Ryan's interests yielded to the interests of the majority. His language is clearly reminiscent of the language of Chief Justice Gleeson (paras. [11]–[14]) and Justice Callinan (para. [266]) in the High Court in *Purvis* who were so concerned about the detriment to others in the South Grafton State High School community should Daniel Hoggan's enrolment be maintained. There seems little doubt that, had the *Purvis* claim been framed as one of indirect discrimination, alleging that Daniel could not comply with a condition that he comply with the school's discipline code, it would have stumbled upon proof that the condition was not reasonable.

16.10 The Unjustifiable Hardship Exemption

Proof that avoiding discrimination of a student with disability related problem behaviour would cause unjustifiable hardship to the discriminator will render a prima facie case of discrimination lawful (see, e.g. DDA s 29A). In the DDA, pursuant to s. 11, the hardship enquiry will consider the 'effect' of the disability, and the impact of inclusion for 'any person concerned', balancing the 'benefit' that flows from inclusion against the 'detriment' – the education and social benefits for all students, for example, of an inclusive school against the risk of danger or disruption that the inclusion causes. The cost of avoiding the discrimination and the financial resources of the discriminator – the education institution – are also relevant.

As noted above, when Daniel Hoggan was excluded from his mainstream school, the unjustifiable hardship exemption was not available to schools after the point of enrolment. As such, there was no sign-posted legislative method of authorising Daniel's exclusion. When the comparator question had arisen in the context of other anti-discrimination legislation, most notably in the ADAQ cases, *L*, *P* and *K*, tribunals could allow a reading which accorded respect to prevailing disability theory, and, arguably, to the object of the anti-discrimination legislation of protecting against 'unfair' discrimination (See, e.g., DDA s 3, ADAQ long title), because they could rely on the unjustifiable hardship exemption to legitimise the removal of the problem student. In the ADAQ cases there was no pressure on the QADT to separate behaviour from impairment for the purpose of making a comparison, as a more direct route to finding no compensable discrimination was available. The QADT could accommodate the arguments of both complainant and respondent in that they could find both that discrimination had occurred and that it was not unlawful. The Queensland legislation, as interpreted by the QADT, allowed the Tribunal to make at least a 'show' of understanding the discrimination suffered by the complainant. While it must be conceded that it is doubtful that this 'show' delivered any more comfort to the complainants in *L*, *K* and *P*, than the outright denial of discrimination delivered by the High Court to Daniel Hoggan, it can be concluded that the ADAQ, as interpreted by the QADT, allowed, then, a more honest weighing of competing considerations than the DDA as manipulated by the majority in *Purvis*, while still balancing minority and majority rights and delivering a 'fair' decision.

16.11 Unjustifiable Hardship and 'Cost'

It can be argued that if enough support – support which may well be expensive – were made available many more students could be placed in mainstream schools. In the *Purvis* case, for example, the minority justices found that more could have been done to support the inclusion of Daniel Hoggan (paras. [106]–[107]). In cases such as *L* (p. 17) and *P* (p. 787) it was also clear from the facts that more teacher aide and specialist teacher support would have reduced both the stress to staff and the disruption to the learning environment which accompanied the inclusion of the complainants.

The link between the spending of money on resources, on the one hand, and the avoidance of threats to safety and of disruption of the learning environment, on the other, was made plain, however, in the case of *K*. In that case the Tribunal conceded that K 'could be properly educated in a regular classroom setting' (p. 623) but that the provision of resources by the school needed to facilitate her inclusion at the respondent independent school would have caused unjustifiable financial hardship (p. 623). More recent cases have indicated that the cost of supporting a student with disability, and particularly of the one-on-one support that may mitigate the impact of problem behaviour on other students and on staff, may amount to unjustifiable hardship even for state run schools. In *Sievwright*, for example, Justice Marshall cited Chief Justice Gleeson in *Purvis* (para. [7]) in making the point that, '[t]he obligations of the State in respect of individual children must be considered alongside the wider legal responsibilities which teachers and administrators owe to all students' (para. [207]). Allocation of one on one support to students such as Sievwright would have required a doubling of the disability support budget for the state of Victoria and, by implication, directed already scarce resources away from other priorities (para. [109]).

16.12 Disability Standards for Education 2005 (Cth)

The High Court in *Purvis*, both minority and majority justices, rejected the complainant's contention that the DDA imposed upon institutions such as schools an implied duty to make 'reasonable accommodation' for people with disabilities. Before *Purvis*, it had been generally accepted that there was such a duty (see Dickson 2006). The minority justices found on the facts that the school had failed to do enough to support Daniel and that as a result he was treated less favourably. The majority justices, of course, focussed on Daniel's behaviour rather than on the way the school supported, or failed to support him.

When the DSE came into force in 2005, they fixed the 'problem' of the missing obligation under the DDA to the extent that they do impose on education institutions an obligation to make 'reasonable adjustment' for students with disability across a range of aspects of school life: enrolment, participation, curriculum and student support. As noted, above, the DDA was then amended in 2009 to impose an obligation to make reasonable adjustment across a range of protected areas, including education. This was done both to remove any doubt about the legality of the obligation in the DSE, absent authority in the DDA (see DSE s 1.6; Dickson 2014), and to shift the burden of compliance with the DDA away from a complaints based mechanism driven by disaffected students, towards a positive institutional obligation to take action to remove discriminatory policies and practices (Dickson 2006).

A clear benefit of the DSE for all students with disability is that they mandate consultation with the student and, where appropriate, the student's parents or guardians, about the support they see as necessary to effect inclusion at a mainstream school. Consultation must occur at the point of enrolment (s. 4.2(3)), and during enrolment at a school (ss. 5.2(3), 6.2(3), 7.2(7)). To discharge its obligations under the DDA, a school must consider what adjustments may be necessary to support a student's enrolment as an integral part of working out whether those adjustments are reasonable. Rejecting an enrolment without first considering reasonable adjustment exposes a school to allegations both of breach of the DSE (DDA s. 32) and of direct discrimination under the DDA (s. 5).

There are immediately apparent problems with the DSE, however, as they apply to students with disability related problem behaviour. First, it is implicit in the obligation to make reasonable adjustments, that 'unreasonable' adjustments will not be required. Adjustments are obliged only if 'reasonable'. The same sorts of matters as are relevant here as to proof of reasonableness in respect of indirect discrimination. Further, the unjustifiable hardship exemption will excuse a school from making even a reasonable adjustment (DSE s.10). The same sorts of considerations relevant to proof of unjustifiable hardship in the DDA will apply in respect of the subordinate DSE as the DSE imports the definition of unjustifiable hardship from the DDA (s.10 note). This scheme sets up a very thick set of limits on any adjustments which may support inclusion (Dickson 2014). The effect of including a disruptive or dangerous student on others in the school community and the cost of supporting his or her enrolment will be relevant to both reasonableness (s. 3.4(2)) and hardship (DDA s 11). The capacity to pay for expensive adjustments is relevant to hardship (DDA s 11).

Two of the few Federal Court cases to date which have interpreted and applied the DSE, *Walker* and *Abela*, concerned students with problem behaviour. In both cases, a *Purvis* style analysis of proof of less favourable treatment and causation was applied: there was no less favourable treatment of the complainant because a student without his disability, but with his problem behaviour would also have been excluded; there was no causal link between the disability and the treatment because its 'true basis' was concerns about safety concern not the student's disability. Further, in both cases there was no reasonable adjustment identified which may have mitigated the behaviour and contained its impact on the school community and which had not been made available. Since the *DSE* were introduced, it may be incumbent upon education providers to demonstrate attempts to accommodate problem behaviour via adjustments such as individual aide support and withdrawal from settings which may stimulate or aggravate the problem behaviour. However, the facts of *Walker* and *Abela* suggest that there may be situations where adjustments cannot remove, or even reduce to an acceptable level, the risk of harm posed by the enrolment of the student with the disability related problem behaviour.

16.13 Conclusion

It is clear from the decided cases that many students with behavioural and intellectual impairments are guaranteed fewer educational opportunities than students with other impairments or without impairments. These students have fewer opportunities principally because their inclusion in the mainstream class room is perceived to interfere with majority rights. Some commentators have suggested that the problem is community 'intolerance' rather than individual 'interference' and that all that is required to effect full inclusion of students with impairments is a change of 'attitude' on the part of staff and students (Christensen 1996; Slee 2008). The courts, however, have been concerned by what they regard as tangible threats to community safety and to the viability of the learning environment posed by students who cannot, because of impairment, conform to school rules and standards of behaviour.

It is to be hoped, however, that the regime of limitations acknowledged and constructed by Australian courts and tribunals does not permit education institutions in Australia to avoid making adjustments that would allow schools to operate more inclusively. While uncontrollable violence cannot be neutralised, that situation should be distinguished from the situation where a student reacts 'violently' to an inflexible and unsympathetic environment. Anti-discrimination legislation, such as the DDA, aims to eliminate discrimination 'as far as possible' (DDA s. 3) acknowledging that sometimes discrimination will be lawful where it is fair to allow it. Care must be taken, however, that discrimination which is not 'fair', but which is simply 'convenient' or 'expedient' or 'cost effective', is not allowed to flourish under an inflexible and unsympathetic regime which accords more respect to the letter of the law than to the interests of people with impairments.

References

Atkins, D. (1995, December 15). A question of hardship. *The Courier Mail*, p. 6.

Atkins, D. (1996, January 19). Commonsense win or rights setback? *The Courier Mail*, p. 2.

Butler, G. (1995, December 16). QC defends all pupils' rights. *The Courier Mail*, p. 6.

Butler, G. (1996, January 23). Row over disabled students. *The Courier Mail*, p. 3.

Christensen, C. (1996). Disabled, handicapped or disordered: "What's in a name?". In C. Christensen & F. Rizvi (Eds.), *Disability and the dilemmas of justice and education* (pp. 63–78). Buckingham: Open University Press.

Council of Australian Governments. (2011). *National disability strategy 2010–2020*. Retrieved from https://www.dss.gov.au/sites/default/files/documents/05_2012/national_disability_strategy_2010_2020.pdf

Dickson, E. (2004). Disability discrimination, unjustifiable hardship and students with disability-induced problem behaviour. (K. Lindsay, Ed.) *Australia and New Zealand Journal of Law and Education, 9*(2), 37–52.

Dickson, E. (2005). Disability discrimination in education: Purvis v. New South Wales (Department of education and training), amendment of the education provisions of the disability discrimination act 1992 (CTH) and the formulation of disability standards for education. *University of Queensland Law Journal, 24*(1), 213.

Dickson, E. (2006). Disability standards for education and the obligations of reasonable adjustment. (J. Cumming, & E. Dickson, Eds.) *Australia and New Zealand Journal of Law and Education, 11*(2), 23–42.

Dickson, E. (2014). Disability standards for education 2005 (Cth): Sword or shield for Australian students with disability. *International Journal of Law and Education, 19*(1), 5–20.

Edwards, S. (2004). Purvis in the high court behaviour, disability and the meaning of direct discrimination. *Sydney Law Review, 26*(4), 639–652.

Mark Oberhardt, M. (1995, December 15). School integration policy under fire. *The Courier Mail*, p. 5.
Rattigan, K. (2004). The Purvis decision: A case for amending the disability discrimination act 1992. *Melbourne University Law Review, 28*(2), 532–563.
Senate Employment, Workplace Relations and Education Committee, Parliament of Australia, Education of students with disabilities (2002).
Slee, R. (2008). Beyond special and regular schooling? An inclusive education reform agenda. *International Studies in Sociology and Education, 18*(2), 99–116.
Thornton, M. (2009). Disabling discrimination legislation: The High court and judicial activism. *Australian Journal of Human Rights, 15*(1), 1–28.

17

Youth Transitioning from Juvenile Justice Settings Back into School: Leadership Perspectives

Therese M. Cumming, Sue O'Neill, and Iva Strnadová

17.1 Introduction

People first enter the justice system when they have contact with police for an alleged offence. They may then have legal action initiated against them that may or may not involve the courts. If the courts are involved, then there are charges against the person that must be answered in court, while non-court actions include cautions, conferences, counselling or infringement notices (Australian Institute of Health and Welfare (AIHW) 2015a). Young people in Australia comprise 8–21% of all persons arrested (Richards 2011). According to the Australian Institute of Health and Welfare (AIHW 2016), the justice system for young people in Australia can be described as follows:

> *The youth justice system is the set of processes and practices for managing children and young people who have committed, or allegedly committed, an offence. In Australia, it deals primarily with young people aged 10–17 at the time of the offence, although there are some variations among the states and territories.* (http://www.aihw.gov.au/youth-justice/)

T. M. Cumming (✉) • S. O'Neill • I. Strnadová
School of Education, University of New South Wales, Sydney, NSW, Australia
e-mail: t.cumming@unsw.edu.au; sue.oneill@unsw.edu.au; i.strnadova@unsw.edu.au

K. Trimmer et al. (eds.), *The Palgrave Handbook of Education Law for Schools*,
https://doi.org/10.1007/978-3-319-77751-1_17

The youth justice system serves youth that are under community-based and detention orders. Young people may be supervised under one or more types of orders. Unsentenced orders take place while the young person is waiting for the outcome of a court case or sentencing and include detention and supervised or conditional bail. Detention is defined here as removal from the community to a juvenile justice facility or the like for the safety of the young person or community (Austin et al. 2005). In NSW, supervised bail involves a young person who has entered a guilty plea to an offence meeting weekly with juvenile justice personnel (Australian Institute of Criminology 2015). Conditional bail is when the court grants bail but with requirements in areas such as conduct (e.g., curfew), security (e.g., money to be paid for failing to attend court), character acknowledgements (e.g., person of good character vouches for the young person), or enforcement conditions (e.g., comply to drug testing) (Legal Aid NSW 2015). Sentenced orders occur after the youth is proven guilty in court, and include detention, probation, suspended detention and parole, or supervised release (AIHW 2015b). Young people may be supervised under multiple types of orders at the same time, and some orders may be interrupted by detention or ended if the youth violates the conditions of the order, or if the order is cancelled.

Due to their age, incarcerated youth have a more complex set of circumstances than their adult counterparts, and are likely to have more stakeholder, such as school personnel, employers, and parents, involved in their transition out of the juvenile justice system back into the community (Chuang and Wells 2010). This is especially true in the education sector, where school principals, counsellors, and support teachers are often involved in the transition process (Mathur and Griller Clark 2013). Difficulties in moving from the juvenile justice system back to traditional school settings are well documented, particularly for students with complex needs (Lanskey 2015; Unruh et al. 2010).

Communication and collaboration amongst or between the student, family, justice system, the education system provided in a juvenile justice setting, and the leadership team of the receiving school is crucial to successful reintegration (Hirschfield 2014). This chapter explores both the challenges and solutions involved with this difficult transition, via the lens of school leadership teams. The authors interviewed six principals and three assistant principals of schools located in juvenile justice centres in New South Wales Australia. The interviews were analysed using content analysis (Elo and Kyngäs 2008). The citations from these interviews are used in the chapter to illustrate the main issues.

17.2 Who Are Juvenile Offenders with Complex Needs?

The most recent Australian statistics are from 2015, and state that 23 young people per 10,000 were under youth justice supervision on an average day (AIHW 2016). Out of these youth, 85% of them were supervised in the community, with 2 in 5 young people in detention at some point during the year. Demographically, most (80%) were males between 14 and 17 years old, and 2 out of 5 were Indigenous. The average amount of time spent under supervision was six months (AIHW 2016). The rate of recidivism in Australian studies ranges from 57% to 71% within two years of release (Kasinathan 2016).

Young people are more likely than adults to have contact with the justice system (Fagan and Western 2005). Fagan and Western (2005) surmise that this is due to the fact that criminal involvement seems to peak in adolescence and diminish as young people enter adulthood. Richards (2011) adds that youth tend to commit crimes in groups, in public areas close to where they live, and are inexperienced at committing offences, thereby increasing the chances that the police will identify and proceed against them. The crimes most frequently committed by young people also differ from those committed by adults, with theft (32%), acts intended to cause injury (16%), and public order offences (11%) being the most common to youth, and public order offences (19%), illicit drug offences (19%), and acts intended to cause injury (18%) being most prevalent to adults. Young people are also more likely to have charges of unlawful entry and property damage than adults (AIHW 2015a).

The majority of this population experiences multiple forms of complex social disadvantage, which may or may not include uncertainty about housing, family dysfunction, an incarcerated parent, being in out of home care, and drug or alcohol use (Cumming et al. 2014). Further research indicates that for many young people these issues may be multiple and co-occur in the context of complex social disadvantage (Hamilton 2010). Another characteristic of juvenile offenders that must be addressed is a higher than expected rate of disability among this population. Although juvenile offenders with disabilities are not always identified or formally diagnosed, Cumming et al. (2014) point out that research has emerged showing a higher than expected prevalence of cognitive disability, mental health disorder, speech, language and communication difficulties, specific learning difficulties, and social, emotional and behavioural difficulties among young offenders. Overall, mental illness (or emotional disturbance), learning disabilities, and borderline intellectual disabilities have been identified as the most prevalent disabilities found in juvenile correction facility populations (Gagnon and Richards 2008). Having a serious mental health issue, such as schizophrenia, bipolar disorder, a family history of mental illness, and temporary accommodation on release, are predictive of rapid reincarceration (Kasinathan 2016). There also appears to be high comorbidity between having a mental health disorder and having a borderline to low range IQ score, particularly so for young people from an Aboriginal background (Haysom et al. 2014).

These characteristics indicate that in order to cater for and hopefully moderate the complex disadvantages experienced by the majority of this population of young people, that current systems and policies may require revisions in order to adequately serve these young people. The next section examines current International, Federal, and State legislation and policy and how it relates to this vulnerable group of young people.

17.3 Legislation and Policy

The overall goal should be to minimise young people's contact with detention (Robinson 2014). This is a principle that is echoed in a number of international frameworks that Australia has signed on to (Richards and Lee 2013). An examination of international agreements and national laws in Australia state that a young person who is serving a custodial sentence has a right to an education. Australia is signatory to several international conventions that assert the rights of young people to an education. Under the *United Nations Convention for the Rights of the Child* (UNCRC: United Nations 1989a, b, c), the Australian government is obligated to provide education for all children. Under this convention, a central aim of education is to prepare the young person for a "responsible life in a free society" (Article 29.1). It should be noted that although under the UNCRC secondary education is not mandatory, in other covenants such as the *International Covenant on Economic, Social and Cultural Rights* (United Nations Human Rights 1976), "secondary education, shall be made generally available and accessible to all by every appropriate means" (Article 13.4.b). Further, if the young person has a disability, as is the case of many young people in the juvenile justice system (Indig et al. 2011), the *United Nations Convention for Rights of Persons with Disabilities* (UNCRPD: United Nations 2006) asserts that, "Persons with disabilities can access an inclusive, quality and free primary education and secondary education on an equal basis with others in the communities in which they live" (Article 24.b). This is to facilitate an effective education (Article 24.d), through the provision of individualised support measures within general education (Article 24.e). It should be noted, however, that signing such covenants does not legally bind a nation to enact the articles.

So what binding laws exist? Young Australians are required by Australian law, under the *Compact with Young Australians* (Australian Government Department of Education and Training 2009), and in New South Wales under the *Education Act 1990 No. 8* (section 21b: NSW Government 2012), to compulsorily attend school until they complete Year 10, or reach the age of 17. If below age 17 at the completion of Year 10, the young person is required to participate in ongoing education or training until they reach 17. This education or training can take place at secondary schools, via home schooling, technical colleges, via an apprenticeship, or training through a private training organisation. Based on the national compact and state law, it can be assumed a young person under the age of 17 both while detained and at the time of release from custody, should legally be provided with an education. Although the right to an education exists, where that education takes place can be affected by whether the young person has previously committed violent crime. The following is an overview of legislation from New South Wales' government, and Department of Education policies relating to the rights of students returning to school from custody, along with the responsibilities of the leadership team of the receiving school.

17.3.1 State Legislation

A young person's right to privacy regarding their criminal history is protected by the *Privacy and Personal Information Protection Act 1998 No 133* (New South Wales Government 2016a). There are, however, limitations to this law, ergo under Division 1, Section 19.2.h where, "the disclosure is permitted or required by an Act (including an Act of the Commonwealth) or any other law". School principals are bound by three state laws to protect staff and students at their school sites: the *Work Health and Safety Act 2011 No 10* (New South Wales Government 2016b), the *Children and Young Persons (Care and Protection) Act 1998 No 157* (New South Wales Government 1998), and the *Education Act 1990 No 8* (New South Wales Government 2012). This necessitates principals requesting information from the Department of Juvenile Justice, and that Department in supplying the information.

Under the *Work Health and Safety Act 2011 No 10* (New South Wales Government 2016b), Division 1, Section 17 (a), the person is required to, "to eliminate risks to health and safety, so far as is reasonably practicable". In order to comply with this law, the school principal must assess all the potential risks to their staff. Likewise, the principal must also ensure the school environment is free from violence for their students. Section 8b of the *Children and Young Persons (Care and Protection) Act 1998 No 157* (New South Wales Government 1998) states, "that all institutions, services and facilities responsible for the care and protection of children and young persons provide an environment for them that is free of violence and exploitation …" (p. 5).

The *Education Act 1990 No 8* (New South Wales Government 2012) enables the school principal, or a higher authority, to request information about any student they perceive may pose a risk due to behaviour, in this case, from the Department of Juvenile Justice as a 'relevant agency' (Division 2, Section 26C). Under Part 5A of the *Education Act 1990 No 8*, it is stated that:

> *Information may be obtained under this Division solely for the purposes of assisting the Secretary or schools: (a) to assess whether the enrolment of a particular student at a school is likely to constitute a risk (because of the behaviour of the student) to the health or safety of any person (including the student), and (b) to develop and maintain strategies to eliminate or minimise any such risk.* (Division 2, section 26B.1, p. 27)

Under Section 26D.5, the information they obtain from the Department of Juvenile Justice may also be passed to another school that may be considering enrolling the student. If the young person has had a history of violence, the principal may assess the risk to staff as too high given the resources available at that site. This may delay enrolment whilst a behaviour management plan is formulated and/or resources obtained to minimize potential risks. The risk level may prevent enrolment altogether.

17.3.2 Department of Education Policies

The Department of Education has a number of policies and memorandums that may impede the transition of young people who have a history of violence back to mainstream education. These policies and memorandums uphold the NSW legislation outlined previously, and provide guidance to school principals on how to meet the legislative requirements.

In deciding whether to accept the enrolment of a student returning to community, principals can consult the *Enrolment of students in government schools: A summary and consolidation of policy* (New South Wales Department of Education and Training 1998). Guidance is offered on enrolling students with disabilities based on "the capacity of the system to provide the level of support services required..." (p. 13). Having requested information from the Department of Juvenile Justice under Part 5A of the *Education Act 1990 No 8*, if there is a documented history of violent behaviour, a principal can refuse student enrolment on the basis of perceived risks to staff and students. Enrolment can be refused if there is evidence that the young person has not developed self-management skills. This policy also provides guidance on enrolment into distance education. This option could be offered for students "whose special circumstances prevent them from attending school on a regular basis (p. 17)". Providing the student with the option of distance education would meet the *Education Act 1990 No. 8*, if the young person was under 17 years of age.

If the principal does decide to enrol the young person, they must adhere to the requirements of the Prevention of Violence in Schools and TAFE NSW Colleges: Provision of Information to Staff on Students with a History of Violence (DN/03/00589) memorandum (New South Wales Department of Education and Training 2006). Here, relevant information must be made available to staff who could be affected, but they should only be given as much information as is deemed necessary to protect themselves or their students from psychological or physical harm. This memorandum balances the requirements of the Privacy and Personal Information Protection Act 1998 No 157 and the Work Health and Safety Act 2011 No 10. Enrolment can only proceed if the young person's school records have been received, and issues surrounding safety have been addressed. This memorandum recommends that school executives provide staff with a behaviour management plan, to reduce prejudice towards the student.

If a serious violent incident occurred after enrolment, then principals must adhere to the *Suspension and expulsion of school students procedures – 2011* (New South Wales Department of Education 2015). In making a decision as to whether to suspend or expel the student, under Section 4.6 of the policy, if the young person has a disability, the principal must have considered the requirements of the Disability Discrimination Act (1992), and Disability Standards for Education (2005). They must have ensured that reasonable adjustments had been made to permit participation in education on the same basis as other students without disabilities. If a decision to suspend is made, under Section 5.10, a risk assessment of the student's behaviour must be undertaken and strategies to manage the risk upon the student's return must developed whilst the young person is suspended. The principal may also decide that expulsion is appropriate. Enrolment at an alternate education setting or distance education may be offered by the Executive Director, Public Schools, where enrolment at another local mainstream school has been denied.

In addition to explaining the policies that outline the rights of the transitioning student as well as the staff and students at the school, the preceding overview illuminates the tension between a young person's right to education and privacy, and the receiving school principal's obligations to ensure a safe work and learning environment. The disconnect between the policies may impede the student's successful transition from custody to school and leave the school leadership team in a difficult position.

17.4 Issues and Challenges from a School Leadership Perspective

School leaders can potentially experience challenges during the transitions of incarcerated youth back to mainstream schools. Leaders of juvenile justice schools, cite challenges that include: (a) youth returning to the same environment; (b) prejudice among mainstream school teachers and the local community; (c) a lack of clarity about the roles and responsibilities of people involved in transition planning; (d) a lack of funding affecting transition planning; and (e) a lack of stable community workers.

A recent study conducted by the authors (O'Neill et al. 2017) examined the challenges experienced by the principals and assistant principals of juvenile justice schools. The participants agreed that one of the substantial challenges when it comes to the successful return and inclusion of incarcerated youth back to the community is that they return to the same (often problematic and/or dysfunctional) environment. Furthermore, the juvenile justice setting is often the best setting these young people have experienced in their lives. As one assistant principal said:

> *They get everything in here. (…) They get their health; they get everything looked after. They've got Maslow's hierarchy of needs met. They're safe, secure, they get an education… (…) … they get out of here, and they go back go nothing. The dysfunction that they come from. (…) It's just…set up to fail.* (Alice)

Even more concerning is that some incarcerated youth perceive juvenile justice setting as a welcome respite time in their challenging life circumstances. This was well explained by one of the participants:

> *Some of the boys come here just for respite, because they're looking after their siblings, or they've got someone, a parent, who's sick at home, or have their own issues that they're dealing with.* (Emma)

The participants also discussed the prevailing prejudice of mainstream schools towards discharged youth: "... *the biggest issue seems to be the schools taking them back...*" (Sonia). The research literature supports this finding, as principals in receiving schools often view a young person returning to community from juvenile justice school as 'risky', in that their presence may disrupt the learning of others or mar the school's performance (Lanskey 2015).

The participants also empathised with incarcerated young people returning back to mainstream schools: "... for the boys to get their head around walking back inside that front gate, and to face up to the people in that school, whether it be staff or students and the things that they've done, is massive" (Emma).

The prejudice towards the incarcerated youth was also shared by the wider community, which made social inclusion even harder for the incarcerated youth upon their discharge.

> *... They might have done a lot of damage and a lot of heartbreak in that community, and obviously communities are wary of taking a person like that back in, and giving them another chance. They might have had several chances already, and a lot of them have, so it can be very difficult at times finding a solution and gaining people's trust again, and then taking a risk, and it is a risk, because a lot of these young people have actually damaged things and hurt people physically, so it can be very dramatic, like, for schools or for communities to take a lot of these boys back in..* (Alan)

Youths' reputation of being involved in juvenile justice system was even more influential in rural areas, and affected their training and job opportunities. As one of the participants summarised:

> *So, training opportunities in the western area are nearly zero. Job opportunities within the western area and outlying area is zero. Because it's a small town, everybody knows, and an employer is not going to employ somebody who's robbed their shop three times before.* (Alice)

The principals also shared the ways they attempted to change prevailing negative attitude towards these young people in communities, such as excursions to the community. In this context they highlighted the need for a mentor for discharged youth, who would provide these young people with support and guidance:

> *I think mainly what it is, in terms of if you want young people to be successful in the community, they ... (...) need a mentor in the community that can keep an eye on them, and give them advice, and be there for them in the initial stages, because otherwise you're just pulling the mat from underneath them....* (Mark)

The (assistant) principals were also concerned about the lack of clarity about roles and responsibilities of people involved in transition planning. As one of the participants commented:

> I'd just like to know what we are supposed to do, what we're allowed to do, and whose job it is to do it. So who has that main responsibility? Is it Juvenile Justice? Is it their direct carers? Is it education that has to communicate with schools? And work experience, should that be a school thing? I just want to know what my role should be, and when I should be doing these things. (Jennifer)

Another challenge was the lack of funding provided to juvenile justice schools, which affected transition planning: "… we're not funded on a secondary school budget. We're funded as a primary school, so we don't have that relief staff to be able to put that time in to transition." (Jennifer) Another principal elaborated further on this issue, stating: "… a transition adviser costs the school 0.4 of a position, so actually the school is actually paying for the privilege of having a transition adviser, so we're losing face to face teaching because of that, and I think that needs to be addressed." (Alan).

Funding was however not perceived as the only barrier to transition planning. Another issue was a lack of formal transition training, which was much called for by the participating school leaders. As one of the school leaders elaborated: "*I've had none. I've had no transition planning training at all... Again, like I said, I haven't received that formal training, so I'm just getting word of mouth from colleagues.*" (Jennifer).

The role of stable community worker was seen as essential for successful transition back to mainstream school, and more widely, back to community:

> *I think if they had stable key workers. Not such a change of people looking after their case. Someone that they can see in here, and that face is still out there for them as well, to support them. That seems to work well....* (Jennifer)

The role of juvenile justice officers (JJOs) was especially highlighted in this context. Their role was perceived as essential in supporting discharged youth in returning to mainstream school: "*...and also the JJO who's really important in terms of getting them back to school, because someone needs to physically take them. Otherwise it just won't happen.*" (Mark).

In addition to the challenges experienced by juvenile justice school leaders, the literature in the field cites additional challenges from the perspectives of receiving school leaders, including a lack of timely information about the juvenile offender who is transitioning to a mainstream school; prejudice among mainstream school teachers, and a lack of shared information about the juvenile offender from relevant stakeholders (Gagnon and Barber 2010; Mathur and Schoenfeld 2010). It is clear from the literature and the accounts above that there is room for improvement in the transition planning and processes for this vulnerable population, particularly in the area of stakeholder collaboration.

17.5 The Role of Schools

Schools have the potential to significantly influence a young person's trajectory. Engagement in full-time education is seen as a protective factor in reducing recidivism (Lanskey 2015; Unruh et al. 2009). Leone et al. (2003) point out ways that schools contribute to the misconduct and delinquency of youth, through overcrowding and the absence of clear rules and policies, and ineffective follow-through when rules are broken. Punitive responses to student misbehaviour in the form of suspensions or exclusion can alienate and disenfranchise students, and seldom address underlying behavioural or learning problems (McGregor et al. 2015). However, Becroft (2006) believes that schools fail youth through their inability to keep all students engaged, as it is estimated that 80% of incarcerated youth are not engaged with the school system at the time of arrest. The ability of schools to engage school-aged young people on return to community in full time education is likewise dismal (Lanskey 2015). Reasons for this lack of engagement vary, but zero-tolerance exclusionary practices such as suspension and expulsion are believed to be main factors (Daly 2013), as is truancy (Becroft 2006). This becomes a "chicken-egg" situation, where many times educational systems punish truancy with suspension and expulsion.

Conversely, many students with complex needs do not ever come in contact with the juvenile justice system, and looking at what makes them successful is useful when planning intervention. Research suggests that having parents who are affectionate, firm but fair, encouraging, and involved in their children's education may negate the negative factors associated with having complex needs (McLaren 2000). Educational systems can play a positive role here also, as students who are positively engaged with school are less likely to form bonds with antisocial peers (McLaren 2000). Students who feel connected to their school, that is they believe that teachers and school leaders care about their learning and their overall well-being, are less likely to engage in misconduct, therefore avoiding exclusionary practices such as suspension and expulsion (Blum and Libbey 2004). This underscores the importance of practices that have a strong research base to support their effectiveness of keeping students with complex needs connected to their schools.

17.5.1 Promising Practices for Leadership Teams to Intervene with School to Prison Pipeline

There are several evidence-based practices and others that show great promise that can be implemented within a school to improve school connectedness and reduce problem behaviour. Leadership teams can assist by having knowledge in the area of what works and supporting the introduction and implementation of these. Cregor and Hewitt (2011) describe efforts on the state and local levels in the US that are being made to combat the rising disciplinary rates. School districts in many states are implementing School-Wide Positive Behaviour Interventions and Supports (SWPBIS), an evidence-based approach to improving school discipline that has been shown to reduce disciplinary incidents, increase academic achievement, and improve staff morale and perceptions of school safety (www.pbis.org). Positive Behavioural Interventions and Supports (PBIS) is defined by Sugai and Simonsen (2012, p. 1) as: "an implementation framework that is designed to enhance academic and social behaviour outcomes for all students by (a) emphasising the use of data for informing decisions about the selection, implementation, and progress monitoring of evidence-based behavioural practices; and (b) organising resources and systems to improve durable implementation fidelity." PBIS has been widely implemented in the US, the UK, and Australia. School principals are crucial to the implementation of this approach, as it must be implemented throughout the school in order to be effective. When implemented with fidelity, SWPBIS has been found to reduce suspensions (Cregor and Hewitt 2011). Increased structure helps keep students with behavioural challenges out of trouble and achieving success (Marshall et al. 2012). The following evidence-based practices, taken from Kohler's Taxonomy for Transition Programming (Kohler 1996) can be successfully integrated into the PBIS framework in the classroom and school to improve student connectedness to their schools and prevent behavioural problems.

Individual Education Plans (IEPs)/Transition Plans Test et al. (2009) found a moderate level of evidence to support student participation in IEP meetings, self-advocacy strategy, and self-directed IEPs as a part of the student-focused planning suggested by Kohler's Taxonomy for Transition Programming

(Kohler 1996). Martin et al. (2006) discovered that the Self-Directed IEP intervention resulted in greater student participation in IEP meetings, particularly in leadership roles, and transition plans at these meetings included more comprehensive post-school transition statements, as students were able to express their interests, skills, and limits across transition areas. The Self-Directed IEP, originally designed by Martin et al. (1997), uses video modeling, students activities, and role-playing to teach students the goal setting, self-advocacy, public speaking and planning skills needed to lead their IEP meetings. Ideally, teachers would use the multimedia lesson package to teach the 11 steps of the Self-Directed IEP process to groups of students a few weeks before their IEP meetings, and then review the steps with each student prior to his or her meeting.

Skaff et al. (2016) cite the low rates of employment and engagement in higher education of people with disabilities in their call for a strengthening of transition efforts for these students. The results of their study found that both parents and teachers believed that well written transition plans provided students with disabilities with important tools and activities to support their post-school success.

Nellis and Hooks Wayman (2009) advocate the use of transition plans for students with disabilities transitioning from juvenile justice settings back into the community. They stress the importance of transferring the educational, vocational, medical, and social services records from the juvenile justice facility to the relevant community stakeholders. This is particularly important in the case of receiving schools, who will be tasked with writing and implementing the student's IEP and transition plan, to tailor the plans for to the student's unique needs and abilities. Without records, some schools may delay the student's enrolment, which may be detrimental to the student's re-engagement with education (Mathur and Schoenfeld 2010).

Teaching Employment and Life Skills There is strong evidence to support the use of functional and life skills curricular interventions across educational environments, disability types, ages and gender to improve positive transition-related outcomes in students with disabilities (Alwell and Cobb 2006). These interventions included directly teaching and using community-based instruction to support students in acquiring functional skills in the areas of: (a) money and purchasing, (b) self-protection, (c) leisure, (d) housekeeping, and (e) personal self-care. One of the challenges posed involved the setting in which the skills should be taught and whether or not it would be appropriate or feasible to teach these skills in general education environments. These are skills that all students require for successful transition to post-school environments and could be integrated into general education. The suggested skills naturally lend themselves to particular general education subject areas; money and purchasing skills are typically taught in mathematics classes, self-protection and leisure skills could be taught in physical education, and personal self-care would fit in well in the health studies curriculum. However, some students and teachers may find that these skills are better taught in a special education setting via a pull-out model. Regardless of the setting chosen, in order for the implementation of these curricular interventions to be successful, the school's leadership team would have to be supportive of their inclusion into the curriculum.

Employment skills are critical for students with disabilities returning to school and the community from juvenile justice settings (Risler and O'Rourke 2009). The risk of reoffending is significantly lower when a student is still gainfully employed six months after release from the juvenile justice facility (Bullis et al. 2004). Other skills that are important for successful attainment and maintenance of employment include working with others, accepting criticism, and following directions (Slaughter 2010).

Check-In/Check-Out Programs As stated previously, school engagement and drop out can be significant problems for this population of young people, so attention should be focused on the factors involved in these problems that are responsive to school intervention. These factors include: (a) attendance; (b) appropriate behavior; (c) assignment completion; (d) class preparation; and (e) supervision and monitoring of academic progression (Cheney et al. 2013). Check-in/check-out (CICO) programs are evidence-based student support systems designed to increase engagement and prevent dropout of at risk students and students with disabilities (Sinclair et al. 1998). CICO consists of mentoring, monitoring of school performance, case management, and other supports depending on the student's individual needs (Cheney et al. 2013).

A designated adult checks in with the students in the morning to review behavioural goals for the day and discuss any issues the student is having. The student receives feedback from adults throughout the day via a daily progress report, then checks out with the designated adult at the end of the day to discuss whether the day's goals were met. The report is taken home to be reviewed and signed by parents, then returned to school the next day. Data from the reports are used by the behavioural support team for data-based decision making (Crone et al. 2010). Although originally designed for use with middle school students, the program has been adapted and shown promise for use in high school settings. By combining academic and social supports, the program addresses the relationship between academic failure and problem behaviour.

Cross Sector Collaboration Griller Clark and Unruh (2010) discuss the importance of engaging the student in the community immediately upon release. For many young people, school is the best way to do this. This underscores once again the importance of timely sharing of records. The student's transition back to school, home, and the community will be smoother and more successful if there is collaboration and shared accountability amongst the correctional, educational, familial, and community systems (Marshall et al. 2012; Nellis and Hooks Wayman 2009). Along with record sharing, coordinated pre-release planning is crucial (Hirschfield 2014). Brock et al. (2008) recommend that a team consisting of the student, family members, and representatives from juvenile justice and the receiving school collaborate to plan the transition out of the juvenile justice centre. The team can then coordinate transition activities such as a pre-release visit to the receiving school together. Such a visit would be beneficial in assisting the student in adjusting to his or her new environment by meeting the principals and teachers, and learning the school's expectations and discipline procedures. This can be a good opportunity for the student to demonstrate growth and improve poor relations, if the school was the one he or she last attended.

The school leadership team can also assist by offering to assist in the coordination of other services. These are commonly called wraparound services and are simply a set of services based on the student's needs and strengths (Brock et al. 2008). These services vary based on the individual student, but can include (in addition to education) medical and mental health care, substance abuse treatment, housing, employment assistance, probation, and recreation. Some students with disabilities who have been incarcerated access several of these services, and coordinating them improves access.

Many successful wraparound programs are coordinated by school personnel, such as a transition or wraparound coordinator (Bruns and Suter 2010). Bruns and Suter (2010) conducted an exploration of the wraparound evidence base and found that when wraparound is collaborative, team based with a student and family focus, uses natural supports, community-based, individualised, and strengths-based that there are significant positive outcomes in the following areas: (a) reduced aggression, (b) reduced exclusionary discipline incidents, (c) reduced likelihood of arrests and recidivism, (d) reduced transiency, (e) less restrictive educational placements, (f) improved moods, and (g) improved academic performance. In Australia, some alternative schools, such as those discussed in McGregor et al. (2015), offer wraparound services in caring, supportive, and relational education environments. These schools could provide young people returning to community with a viable option to achieving a meaningful education through personalised learning and flexible approaches (Hirschfield 2014).

Collaboration with Family The need for family involvement in transition planning is well acknowledged in the research literature (Kohler 1996). This is also the case when it comes to incarcerated youth, as the majority of evidence-based practices for this population are family-based programs, such as the above-mentioned wraparound services, Functional Family Therapy, and Functional Family Probation/Parole Services (Arya 2014). There are a number of strategies and practices that can be effectively used to engage and collaborate with families of incarcerated youth. Among these belong opportunities for frequent communication between juvenile justice staff and families, in an atmosphere where families do not feel blamed for their offspring's involvement in the juvenile justice system (Walker et al. 2015). Also, holding exit conferences at juvenile justice settings at times and places suitable for families can assist in promoting successful collaboration. If families live in remote areas, it is important to provide opportunities for transport, or to ensure that families can attend exit conference via phone, Skype, or other means. Informing families of a release date well ahead of time would provide opportunities for families to prepare for their discharged offspring. This is, however, often beyond control of juvenile justice settings, as they often do not get much advance notice themselves.

Families often do not have the skills to advocate for their children, and may require guidance in this area (Garfinkel 2010). The family is instrumental in helping the young person develop a "non-offender identity" (McAra and McVie 2010). This involves advocating for the youth and supporting him in goal setting and realising the person he wants to become. Typically, this is accomplished via a close one-to-one relationship with a key worker at the juvenile justice centre, but in order to be effective, it must also be undertaken within the contexts of home and community (McAra and McVie 2010). Communication between the family and the police and justice system is crucial to the success of this endeavour (Garfinkel 2010). Brock et al. (2008)

advocate for the use of culturally and linguistically sensitive practices to promote good communication with families. They also suggest the use of parent advocates within the juvenile justice system to assist families in navigating police and court processes and in encouraging family-friendly sentencing options, such as graduated release programs.

17.6 Future Directions

High school completion is a strong predictor of positive outcomes (Gagnon and Richards 2008). Education should be flexible and meaningful (McGregor et al. 2015), especially for those young people who were disengaged with school before they were incarcerated. If they were unsuccessful with traditional schooling models, then alternative schools (Hirschfield 2014), distance education, or night classes may support their success.

Planning for Exit on Entry Several authors have asserted that principals of juvenile justice schools must ensure that planning for post-school transition must begin on entry to the school and in a timely manner (see for examples, Hirschfield 2014; Marshall et al. 2012). Exiting with a transition plan and portfolio can assist in reducing recidivism in young people with disabilities by 64% in the first month post release (Griller Clark et al. 2011).

Transfer of Records Online student records can speed up the process of obtaining necessary student information for students arriving in juvenile justice schools and in returning to schools in community. Including IEPs in such online records could provide smoother transitions between sites, and minimise the duplication of academic and behavioural assessments (Marshall et al. 2012). To overcome unexpected exits, these records would need to be kept up-to-date. Detailed educational plan sent to receiving school no later than 5 days prior to re enrolment (Hirschfield 2014).

Taking a Positive, Strength-Based View of Young People School principals' and staff attitudes to young people transitioning back to community from juvenile justice can be poor, leading to little tolerance in problem behaviour, and suspension and expulsion (Cole and Cohen 2013; Marshall et al. 2012). School leaders are well placed to communicate unconditional regard and respect to the young person and school staff. This can be achieved by giving students a chance, focusing on strengths, and well-designed behaviour management plans (Cole and Cohen 2013). Catch them being good rather than watching their every move waiting for a mistake to justify suspension or exclusion (Cole and Cohen 2013).

Mentors Assigning a school-based mentor to a young person returning to school can assist in develop school connectedness. Programs such as Check-In Check-Out have growing research evidence of effectiveness, and can provide young people with daily, positive interactions with school staff (ref). Using other community members to act as mentors (Hirschfield 2014).

Transition Coordinators or Specialists Employing staff specifically to assist the smooth transition between facility and community, including receiving schools has shown great promise in studies conducted in the US. Such personnel can assist with information sharing, addressing receiving school concerns, and service coordination (Cole and Cohen 2013), and the creation of transition plans and portfolios (Griller Clark et al. 2011). This person could also coordinate training for school and juvenile justice staff, as it is paramount to the effective transition planning of young people from juvenile justice to mainstream schools.

Resource Allocation Although not an evidence-based practice, resource allocation is crucial to the effective implementation of the practices discussed above. Federal funds are available in the U.S. via *Race to the Top,* to fund the implementation of SWPBIS, in the UK via *Skills for Care,* and in Australia as part of the *Safe Schools* program (pbis.org; skillsforcare.org.uk; safeschoolshub.edu.au). Schools may want to allocate a teaching position or other funding for a transition or wraparound specialist to support students with disabilities through educational transitions. Using part of funding to have a transition specialist should however not affect face-to-face teaching, which was an issue raised by one of the participants. Systemic solutions, rather than solutions on a level of individual juvenile justice schools are needed.

17.7 Conclusion

Young people with disabilities are at a higher risk of offending and being incarcerated when compared to those without disabilities. They also typically have a more difficult time reintegrating back into educational settings (Cumming et al. 2014; Lanskey 2015). While literature exists that presents evidence-based practices identified as effective for this population, a significant gap between theory and practice remains. To address this systemic changes are needed.

School leadership teams can maximise student engagement and ease the re-entry of adjudicated youth by implementing school wide positive behaviour interventions and supports, and the evidence-based transition practices found within the SWPBIS system.

Acknowledgements The authors would like to express their sincere gratitude to the participating school leaders of juvenile justice schools in New South Wales, Australia, for taking time to participate in interviews. They would also like to extend their gratitude to the NSW Department of Education, and NSW Department of Juvenile Justice, for funding and supporting this important study.

References

Alwell, M., & Cobb, B. (2006). *A systematic review of the effects of curricular interventions on the acquisition of functional life skills by youth with disabilities*. Kalamazoo: National Secondary Transition Technical Assistance Center.

Arya, N. (2014). Family-driven justice. *Arizona Law Review, 56*(3), 623–706.

Austin, J., Johnson, K. D., & Weitzer, R. (2005). *Alternatives to the secure detention and confinement of juvenile offenders*. OJJDP Juvenile Justice Practice Series. Retrieved from https://www.ncjrs.gov/App/Publications/abstract.aspx?ID=208804

Australian Government Department of Education and Training. (2005). Disability standards for education. Canberra: Attorney-General's Department, Department of Education, Science and Training. Retrieved from https://education.gov.au/disability-standards-education

Australian Government Department of Education and Training. (2009). *Compact with young Australians*. Canberra: Australian Government. Retrieved from https://www.education.gov.au/compact-young-australians

Australian Institute of Criminology. (2015). Annual report 2014–2015. Canberra: Australian Institute of Criminology. Retrieved from https://aic.gov.au/publications/annualreport/2015

Australian Institute of Health and Welfare (AIHW). (2015a). *Youth justice fact sheet no. 54. Comparisons between the youth and adult justice systems: 2013–14*. Cat. no. JUV 73. Canberra: AIHW.

Australian Institute of Health and Welfare (AIHW). (2015b). *Youth justice fact sheet no. 47. Types of community-based youth justice supervision: 2013–14*. Cat. no. JUV 66. Canberra: AIHW.

Australian Institute of Health and Welfare (AIHW). (2016). *Youth justice*. Retrieved from http://www.aihw.gov.au/youth-justice/

Becroft, A. J. (2006). *Youth offending: Factors that contribute and how the system responds*. Symposium child and youth offenders: What works, Te Kooti Taiohi o Aotearoa. Retrieved from http://www.justice.govt.nz/courts/youth/publications-and-media/speeches/youthoffending-factors-that-contribute-and-how-the-system-responds

Blum, R. W., & Libbey, H. P. (2004). Executive summary. *Journal of School Health, 74*, 231–232.

Brock, L., O'Cummings, M., & Milligan, D. (2008). *Transition toolkit 2.0: Meeting the educational needs of youth exposed to the juvenile justice system*. Washington, DC: National Evaluation and Technical Assistance Center for the Education of Children and Youth Who Are Neglected, Delinquent, or At Risk (NDTAC). Retrieved from http://www.neglecteddelinquent.org/nd/resources/toolkits/transition_200808.asp

Bruns, E. J., & Suter, J. C. (2010). Summary of the wraparound evidence base. In E. J. Bruns & J. S. Walker (Eds.), *The resource guide to wraparound*. Portland: National Wraparound Initiative.

Bullis, M., Yovanoff, P., & Havel, E. (2004). The importance of getting started right: A further examination of the facility-to-community transition of formerly incarcerated youth. *The Journal of Special Education, 38*, 80–94.

Cheney, D., Cumming, T., & Slemrod, T. (2013). Issues and approaches in accommodating adolescent EBD students at the secondary level. In H. Walker & F. Gresham (Eds.), *Evidence-based practices for addressing school-related behaviour problems and disorders* (pp. 344–360). New York: Guilford Press.

Chuang, E., & Wells, R. (2010). The role of inter-agency collaboration in facilitating receipt of behavioural health services for youth involved with child welfare and juvenile justice. *Children and Youth Services Review, 32*, 1814–1822. https://doi.org/10.1016/j.childyouth.2010.08.002.

Cole, H., & Cohen, R. (2013). Breaking down the barriers: A case study of juvenile justice personnel perspectives on school reentry. *The Journal of Correctional Education, 64*, 13–35.

Cregor, M., & Hewitt, D. (2011). Dismantling the school-to-prison pipeline: A survey from the field. *Poverty and Race, 20*(1), 5–7.

Crone, D. A., Hawken, L. S., & Horner, R. H. (2010). *Responding to problem behavior in schools: The behavior education program* (2nd ed.). New York: Guilford Press.

Cumming, T., Strnadová, I., & Dowse, L. (2014). At-risk youth in Australian schools and promising models of intervention. *International Journal of Special Education, 29*(3), 16–25.

Daly, E. (2013). *Student suspensions. A research review. Stage one. Commission for children Tasmania*. Retrieved January, 2, 2014 from http://www.childcomm.tas.gov.au/wp-content/uploads/2013/12/Student-Suspensions.A-Research-Review-Stage-One.-E.Daly-Nov-2013.pdf

Disability Discrimination Act. (1992). Retrieved from http://www.austlii.edu.au/au/legis/cth/consol_act/dda1992264/

Elo, S., & Kyngäs, H. (2008). The qualitative content analysis process. *Journal of Advanced Nursing, 62*(1), 107–115.

Fagan, A., & Western, J. (2005). Escalation and deceleration of offending behaviours from adolescence to early adulthood. *Australian and New Zealand Journal of Criminology, 38*, 59–76.

Gagnon, J., & Barber, B. (2010). Characteristics of and services provided to youth in secure care facilities. *Behavioral Disorders, 36*(1), 7–19.

Gagnon, J. C., & Richards, C. (2008). *Making the right turn: A guide about improving transition outcomes of youth involved in the juvenile corrections system*. Washington, DC: National Collaborative on Workforce and Disability for Youth, Institute for Educational Leadership.

Garfinkel, L. (2010). Improving family involvement for juvenile offenders with emotional/behavioural disorders and related disabilities. *Behavior Disorders, 36*(1), 52–60.

Griller Clark, H., & Unruh, D. (2010). Transition practices for adjudicated youth with E/BDs and related disabilities. *Behavioral Disorders, 36*(1), 43–51.

Griller Clark, H., Mathur, S. R., & Helding, B. (2011). Transition services for juvenile detainees with disabilities: Findings on recidivism. *Education and Treatment of Children, 34*(4), 511–529.

Hamilton, M. (2010). People with complex needs and the criminal justice system. *Current Issues in Criminal Justice, 22*(2), 307–324.

Haysom, L., Indig, D., Moore, E., & Gaskin, C. (2014). Intellectual disability in young people in custody in New South Wales, Australia – Prevalence and markers. *Journal of Intellectual Disability Research, 58*, 1004–1014. https://doi.org/10.1111/jir.12109.

Hirschfield, P. J. (2014). Effective and promising practices in transitional planning and school re-entry. *The Journal of Correctional Education, 65*, 84–96.

Indig, D., Vecchiato, C., Haysom, L., Beilby, R., Carter, J., Champion, U., et al. (2011). *2009 NSW young people in custody health survey: Full report*. Sydney: Justice Health and Juvenile Justice.

Kasinathan, J. (2016). Predictors of rapid reincarceration in mentally ill young offenders. *Australian Psychiatry, 23*, 550–555. https://doi.org/10.1177/1039856215597532.

Kohler, P. D. (1996). *A taxonomy for transition programming: Linking research and practice*. Champaign: Transition Research Institute, University of Illinois.

Lanskey, C. (2015). Up or down and out? A systematic analysis of young people's educational pathways in the youth justice system in England and Wales. *International Journal of Inclusive Education, 16*, 568–582. https://doi.org/10.1080/13603116.2014.961675.

Legal Aid NSW. (2015). *A guide to bail*. Retrieved from http://www.legalaid.nsw.gov.au/publications/factsheets-and-resources/guide-to-bail

Leone, P. E., Christle, C. A., Nelson, C. M., Skiba, R., Frey, A., & Jolivette, K. (2003, October). *School failure, race, and disability: Promoting positive outcomes, decreasing vulnerability for involvement with the juvenile delinquency system*. College Park: The National Center on Education, Disability, and Juvenile Justice.

Marshall, A., Powell, N., Pierce, D., Nolan, E., & Fehringer, E. (2012). Youth and administrator perspectives on transition in Kentucky's state agency schools. *Child Welfare, 91*, 97–118.

Martin, J. E., Marshall, L. H., Maxson, L. M., & Jerman, P. L. (1997). *The self-directed IEP*. Longmont: Sopris West.

Martin, J. E., Van Dycke, J. L., Christensen, W. R., Greene, B. A., Gardner, J. E., & Lovett, D. (2006). Increasing student participation in IEP meetings: Establishing the self-directed IEP as an evidenced-based practice. *Exceptional Children, 72*(3), 299–316.

Mathur, S. R., & Griller Clark, H. (2013). Prerelease planning and practices for youth with disabilities in juvenile detention. *Journal of Special Education Leadership, 26*, 82–92.

Mathur, S., & Schoenfeld, N. (2010). Effective instructional practices in juvenile justice facilities. *Behavioral Disorders, 36*(1), 20–27.

McAra, L., & McVie, S. (2010). Youth crime and justice: Key messages from the Edinburgh study of youth transitions and crime. *Criminology and Criminal Justice, 10*(2), 179–209.

McGregor, G., Mills, M., te Riele, K., & Hayes, D. (2015). Excluded from school: Getting a second chance as a 'meaningful' education. *International Journal of Inclusive Education, 16*, 608–625. https://doi.org/10.1080/13603116.2014.961684.

McLaren, K. (2000). *Tough is not enough – Getting smart about youth crime*. Wellington: Ministry of Youth affairs.

Nellis, A., & Hooks Wayman, R. (2009). *Back on track: Supporting youth reentry from out-of-home placement to the community*. Washington, DC: Juvenile Justice and Delinquency Prevention Taskforce, Youth Reentry Task Force.

New South Wales Department of Education and Communities. (2015). *Suspension and expulsion of school students procedures – 2011*. Sydney: New South Wales Department of Education and Communities. Retrieved from https://education.nsw.gov.au/policy-library/associated-documents/suspol_07.pdf.

New South Wales Department of Education and Training. (1997). *Enrolment of students in government schools: A summary and consolidation of policy*. Sydney: New South Wales Department of Education and Training. Retrieved from https://www.det.nsw.edu.au/policies/student_admin/enrolment/enrolpol/pd02_06_enrolment_of_students.pdf

New South Wales Department of Education and Training. (2006). *Collection, use and disclosure of information about students with a history of violence,* Legal issues bulletin no. 40. Sydney: Legal Services Directorate, New South Wales Department of Education and Training. Retrieved from https://www.nswtf.org.au/files/legal_issues_bulletin_no.40.pdf

New South Wales Government. (1998). *Children and young persons (care and protection) act 1998 no 157*. Sydney: NSW Government. Retrieved from http://www.legislation.nsw.gov.au/acts/1998-157.pdf

New South Wales Government. (2012). *Education act 1990 no 8*. Sydney: NSW Government. Retrieved from http://www.legislation.nsw.gov.au/inforce/fc4bcf6a-d005-68af-fa91-fd9a7d10cd09/1990-8.pdf

New South Wales Government. (2016a). *Privacy and personal information protection act 1998 no 133*. Sydney: NSW Government. Retrieved from http://www.legislation.nsw.gov.au/#/view/act/1998/133

New South Wales Government. (2016b). *Work health and safety act 2011 no 10*. Sydney: NSW Government. Retrieved from http://www.legislation.nsw.gov.au/#/view/act/2011/10/full

O'Neill, S. C., Cumming, T. M., & Strnadová, I. (2017). *How juvenile justice and education support the transition of school-aged youth from within a custodial environment to the community: Lessons to be learned and celebrations to share*. Sydney: UNSW Sydney School of Education.

Richards, K. (2011). What makes juvenile offenders different from adult offenders? *Trends and Issues in Crime and Criminal Justice, 409*, 1–8.

Richards, K., & Lee, M. (2013). Beyond the 'three dogmas of juvenile justice': A response to Skaff, Kemp, Sternesky McGovern, and Fantacone (2016). Educator and parent views of the effectiveness of individualized learning plans for students with disabilities. *Career Development and Transition for Exceptional Individuals, 39*(2), 28–38.

Risler, E., & O'Rourke, T. (2009). Thinking exit and entry: Exploring outcomes of Georgia's juvenile justice educational programs. *The Journal of Correctional Education, 60*, 225–239.

Robinson, A. (2014). *Foundations for youth justice: Positive approaches to practice*. Bristol: Policy Press.

Sinclair, M. F., Christenson, S. L., Evelo, D. L., & Hurley, C. M. (1998). Dropout prevention for high-risk youth with disabilities: Efficacy of a sustained school engagement procedure. *Exceptional Children, 65*(1), 7–21.

Skaff, L. F., Kemp, J. N., Sternesky McGovern, L. A., & Fantacone, J. M. (2016). Educator and parent views of the effectiveness of individualized learning plans for students with disabilities. *Career Development and Transition for Exceptional Individuals, 39*(2), 68–78.

Slaughter, D. (2010). *Improving transition outcomes for youth involved in the juvenile justice system: Practical considerations*. Info Brief, 25, 1–12. Washington, DC: National Collaborative on Workforce and Disability for Youth.

Sugai, G., & Simonsen, B. (2012). *Positive behavioural interventions and supports: History, defining features, and misconceptions*. Center for PBIS & Center for Positive Behavioral Interventions and Supports, University of Connecticut. Retrieved from: http://www.pbis.org/common/pbisresources/publications/PBIS_revisited_June19r_2012.pdf

Test, D. W., Fowler, C. H., Richter, S. M., White, J., Mazzotti, V., Walker, A. R., Kohler, P., & Kortering, L. (2009). Evidence-based practices in secondary transition. *Career Development for Exceptional Individuals, 32*(2), 115–128.

United Nations. (1989a). *Convention on the rights of the child*. Online. www.unicef.org.uk/Documents/Publication-pdfs/UNCRC_PRESS200910web.pdf. Accessed 07 Mar 2017.

United Nations. (1989b). *Convention on the rights of the child*. General assembly resolution 44/25, 20 November 1989. UN Doc. A/RES/44/25.

United Nations. (1989c). *Convention on the rights of the child*. New York: United Nations. Retrieved from http://www.ohchr.org/EN/ProfessionalInterest/Pages/CRC.aspx.

United Nations. (2006). *Convention on the rights of persons with disabilities and optional protocol*. New York: United Nations. Retrieved from http://www.un.org/disabilities/convention/conventionfull.shtml

United Nations Human Rights. (1976). *International covenant on economic, social and cultural rights*. New York: Office of the High Commissioner Human Rights. Retrieved from http://www.ohchr.org/EN/ProfessionalInterest/Pages/CESCR.aspx

Unruh, D., Gau, J., & Waintrup, M. (2009). An exploration of factors reducing recidivism rates of formerly incarcerated youth with disabilities participating in a re-entry intervention. *Journal of Child & Family Studies, 18*, 284–293.

Unruh, D., Waintrup, M., & Canter, T. (2010). Project STAYOUT: A facility-to-community transition intervention targeting incarcerated adolescent offenders. In D. Cheney (Ed.), *Transition of secondary students with emotional or behavioural disorders. Current approaches for positive outcomes* (2nd ed., pp. 347–374). Champaign: Research Press.

Walker, S. C., Bishop, A. S., Pullmann, M. D., & Bauer, G. (2015). A research framework for understanding the practical impact of family involvement in the juvenile justice system: The juvenile justice family involvement model. *American Journal of Community Psychology, 56*(3–4), 408–421.

18

Legal and Ethical Considerations Regarding the Integration of Assistive and Educational Technology for Students with Disabilities: Perspectives from the United States of America

Joseph John Morgan, Kristopher H. Yeager, Sarah J. Murphy, and Tracy Griffin Spies

The access to technology for students enrolled in public schools throughout the United States of America continues to increase, as availability of these technologies becomes more and more common (Nelson et al. 2016). In 2008, according to the National Center for Education Statistics (NCES) in the United States Department of Education (USDOE 2016), 98% of all students enrolled in U.S. public schools had access to computers connected to the Internet during their school day, with a ratio of computers to students of 3:1. This percentage represented an increase of 21% between the years of 2000 and 2008 (USDOE 2016). In 2013, approximately 72% of the U.S. population reported being users of the Internet and of that population 91.5% used the Internet from their home environment using a high-speed connection (USDOE 2016). Since access to technology has become more readily available for students and teachers to use in their learning and has fundamentally changed the way learning occurs (Mishra and Mehta 2017), it is important for educational professionals to have a strong understanding of how to appropriately integrate technology to support these student outcomes. However, these technologies are being fundamentally underutilized in the educational programming of students with disabilities (Smith and Okolo 2010).

J. J. Morgan (✉) • K. H. Yeager • S. J. Murphy • T. G. Spies
University of Nevada, Las Vegas, NV, USA
e-mail: joseph.morgan@unlv.edu

K. Trimmer et al. (eds.), *The Palgrave Handbook of Education Law for Schools*,
https://doi.org/10.1007/978-3-319-77751-1_18

In 2014, the National Assessment of Educational Progress (NAEP) introduced a new assessment focused on measuring student academic performance related to technology and engineering (Technology and Engineering Literacy; TEL) to begin understanding students' abilities regarding the use of technology for learning. Overall, 43% of eighth grade students in the U.S. performed at the Proficiency level or above on this assessment. However, only 13% of students with disabilities were proficient in this measure of technology (NAEP 2014). This indicates that there is a significant gap in the technology performance of students with disabilities when compared to their typical peers. Since there are several legal and policy requirements governing the use of technology by students with disabilities and their access to a college- and career-ready curricula in the public-school environment, it is important that educational leaders understand and consider the legal, policy, and ethical issues that govern the integration of assistive and educational technology (A/ET) into the educational programming of students with disabilities. While these two types of technology serve different purposes in the education of students with disabilities (i.e., assistive technology provides access, educational technology supports learning), the intersection of them in the education of students with disabilities is important for the academic, behavioural, and social-emotional outcomes of this population of students.

18.1 Overview of the Individuals with Disabilities Education Act

Any conversation of the legal, policy, and ethical requirements of A/ET must be contextualized within the lens of the Individuals with Disabilities Education Act (IDEA 2004), the federal law governing the provision of special education to students with disabilities in U.S. public schools. The central focus of IDEA (2004) is to provide a free and appropriate public education (FAPE) to all students with disabilities, wherein students with disabilities are provided access to the general education environment to the maximum extent possible (Pazey et al. 2016; Yell et al. 2006, 2008).

While education provided to students with disabilities in their Individualized Education Program (IEP) should be appropriate for their academic, behavioural, social-emotional, and transition needs, the reauthorization of IDEA (2004) required that schools set rigorous and challenging goals so that students could be successful after they graduate from high school (Pazey et al. 2016; Yell et al. 2006, 2008). A continuum of alternative placements best suited to the needs of a student with disabilities is provided for in IDEA (2004); however, all students with disabilities should be working towards mastery of academic content standards or alternative achievement standards set by the IEP team (Yell et al. 2006).

Whatever access and programming is provided in the general education environment should be provided to students with disabilities, with a focus on providing educational benefit for students in their IEP program (Pazey et al. 2016; Yell et al. 2006, 2008). Assistive and educational technology are both important to consider within the context of IDEA, as one provides increased access to the general education curriculum and one is often used within the general education curriculum as the metric for providing core instruction. Legal and policy considerations for A/ET are discussed below.

18.2 Legal Requirements for Assistive Technology Integration for Students with Disabilities

Legal requirements for the use of assistive technology (AT) to support the educational outcomes of students with disabilities are extensive (Bouck 2016; Dalsen 2017; Etscheidt 2016). The first piece of legislation requiring the consideration of AT in the individualized education of students with disabilities was passed in 1988, and a variety of other legislative acts and judicial findings have expanded and enhanced these considerations (Dalsen 2017). Since AT has the potential to provide access to educational environments for students with disabilities and is required as a component of the Individualized Education Program (IEP), it is important for school leaders to have a thorough and complete understanding of the legal requirements for the consideration and selection of AT devices (Etscheidt 2016).

18.3 Defining Assistive Technology and Assistive Technology Services

In U.S. law, both assistive technology and assistive technology services are required in the IEP process. Assistive technology (AT) is defined as:

> *Any item, piece of equipment or product system, whether acquired commercially or off the shelf, modified, or customized, that is used to increase, maintain, or improve*

the functional capabilities of a child with a disability. Exception. – The term does not include a medical device that is surgically implanted, or the replacement of such device. (Individuals with Disabilities Education Act 2004)

Assistive technology varies greatly. Devices can be low-tech, including communication boards or pencil grips, to high-tech, including adapted computers and communication devices (Etscheidt 2016). Assistive technology has been linked to a variety of positive outcomes for students with disabilities, including increased academic skills, communication skills, daily living skills, and behavioural skills (Etscheidt 2016). The key with AT integration is the provision of access to general education and natural environments for students with disabilities (Bouck 2016; Dalsen 2017; Etscheidt 2016).

Along with the definition of AT, U.S. law also defines the provision of AT services to support students in using the device chosen for his or her educational access. Assistive technology services are defined as:

Any service that directly assists a child with a disability in the selection, acquisition, or use of an assistive technology device. Such term includes:

(A) the evaluation of needs including a functional evaluation, in the child's customary environment;
(B) purchasing, leasing, or otherwise providing for the acquisition of assistive technology devices;
(C) selecting, designing, fitting, customizing, adapting, applying, maintaining, repairing, or replacing of assistive technology devices;
(D) coordinating and using other therapies, interventions, or services with assistive technology devices, such as those associated with existing education and rehabilitation plans and programs;
(E) training or technical assistance for a child with disabilities, or where appropriate that child's family; and
(F) training or technical assistance for professionals (including individuals providing education and rehabilitation services), employers or other(s) who provide services to employ, or are otherwise, substantially involved in the major life functions of that child (20 U.S.C. 1401(2)).

Based on these two definitions, it is apparent that the legal requirements for AT include both the technology itself and the pairing of the technology with the needs of the student, as well as the training and integration of that technology into the individualized education of students (Dalsen 2017). Educational professionals and leaders should have a working knowledge of the evaluation procedures for AT devices and how to best integrate these into the education of students with disabilities to provide access and educational benefit (Bouck 2016; Dalsen 2017; Etscheidt 2016).

18.4 Legal History of Assistive Technology in Special Education

The consideration of AT in the education of students with disabilities was first introduced in the Technology-Related Assistance for Individuals with Disabilities Act (1988) (Dalsen 2017). This law provided federal funding to local state education agencies to purchase AT devices for students with disabilities to provide access to a Free and Appropriate Public Education (FAPE) (Bouck 2016; Etscheidt 2016). The IDEA first incorporated language related to AT in the reauthorization that occurred in 1990 (Bouck 2016), requiring IEP teams to consider AT in the provision of access to the general education environment. These initial laws were important in introducing AT to the education of students with disabilities, but did not require that schools and districts assess students and their potential need for AT nor did it require that AT be considered for every student (Dalsen 2017). Due to this, it was inconsistent how AT provisions were applied in special education.

In 1997, the IDEA was reauthorized and required the consideration of AT for *all* students with disabilities; this was important, because prior to this reauthorization AT was primarily considered for students with more severe and profound disabilities (Bouck 2016). The 1997 reauthorization of IDEA made AT a consideration for any student who may benefit from the integration of AT supports in their educational environments. For students with disabilities who would potentially benefit from AT supports, the IEP team was required to evaluate his or her need for AT and choose a device that provided access to the general education environment (Bouck 2016; Dalsen 2017; Etscheidt 2016). The 2004 reauthorization of IDEA upheld this standard for AT, and clarified that needed AT must be provided regardless of cost except for in the case of surgical implants (Etscheidt 2016).

18.5 Current Legal and Ethical Issues Related to Assistive Technology Integration

While the legislative mandate for the consideration of AT in the individualized education of students with disabilities in U.S. public schools is clear, there are several current issues that educational leaders should be aware of in the provision of these services (Bouck 2016). These issues are important to consider, as the rates of AT use and research relative to AT integration in the education of students with disabilities is not always commensurate with the legal requirements delineated above (Okolo and Diedrich 2014).

Consideration of Assistive Technology for All Students One major issue relative to the use of AT devices in the education of students with disabilities is the consideration of AT services for all students (Bouck 2016; Etscheidt 2016; Okolo and Diedrich 2014). Bouck (2016) found that students with high incidence disabilities were less likely to use AT devices in secondary schools and less likely to report having been evaluated for potential need for AT devices within the IEP. Additionally, there have been several due process cases that challenged school districts' effective evaluation for the need for AT devices for all students (Dalsen 2017; Etscheidt 2016). There has been a trend in legal proceedings that suggests school districts may not be considering AT needs nor evaluating these needs effectively for all students with disabilities (Bouck 2016; Dalsen 2017; Etscheidt 2016). It is important that educational leaders be aware of the procedures for evaluating the need for AT devices in individualized education to ensure that all students have access to this legal requirement.

Appropriateness of Assistive Technology Evaluation and Device Selection Another issue that has arisen in legal proceedings related to the integration of AT in the education of students with disabilities is the appropriateness of the evaluation for AT, as well as the selection process for determining appropriate AT devices (Dalsen 2017; Etscheidt 2016). Due process cases have overwhelmingly found that the AT evaluation process must be comprehensive and use appropriate measures for determining the specific AT needs of students (Etscheidt 2016). These assessments must be conducted in a timely manner after a potential AT need has been determined (Dalsen 2017). Assessments of need should be conducted in all settings the student engages to receive their individualized instruction to ensure that chosen AT is appropriate for the specific needs of the student throughout their learning experience (Etscheidt 2016).

Once an evaluation has been conducted, it is important that educational leaders be aware of the selection of appropriate devices (Dalsen 2017; Etscheidt 2016). There have been several due process actions relative to the appropriateness of the AT in providing educational benefit to students with disabilities. Often, parents and families of children with disabilities desire the highest quality AT devices for their child's individualized education and challenge districts when this technology is not provided (Etscheidt 2016). However, legal precedent has suggested that the AT device chosen must result in educational benefit for the child being assessed; there is no requirement for the quality of the device (Dalsen 2017; Etscheidt 2016). Educational leaders should be aware of the assessment of students using the AT device to ensure that maximum benefit is being received through the integration of the AT device.

Training and Support for Educators and Parents in the Use of Assistive Technology A final legal issue that is of important consideration in the integration of AT devices for students with disabilities is the training and support provided to educators and parents once an AT device has been chosen (Dalsen 2017; Etscheidt 2016; Okolo and Diedrich 2014). It is imperative that professional development and support be provided to educators and parents working with the student who has a specific AT device so that they can support the student in accessing the general education and natural environments. Courts have found that a failure to provide training to adults working with the child denies access to FAPE (Etscheidt 2016) and educational leaders are responsible for ensuring that the AT is being maximized in the education of students with disabilities. Therefore, it is important that once an AT device is chosen that professional development is provided to maximize its impact.

Overall, legal requirements for AT are focused primarily on providing access to the general education and natural environment for students with disabilities (Dalsen 2017; Bouck 2016). Assistive technology devices and services both have the potential to augment the method through which a student with a disability interacts with the general education and natural environment (i.e., using an AT device for communication to access social networks, using an AT device for writing in an academic setting). Since the focus of IDEA is on the provision of access, it is essential that educational leaders have an awareness and understanding of the legal requirements and processes governing the selection and integration of AT devices in the individualized education of students with disabilities.

18.6 Current Educational Policy in the United States Focused on Educational Technology

While not legislatively governed in the same way as AT, there are several current U.S. educational policies focused on the integration of educational technology into the education of students – including those with disabilities. The

Association for Educational Communications and Technology defines ET as "the study and ethical practice of facilitating learning and improving performance by creating, using, and managing appropriate technological processes and resources" (Robinson et al. 2008). The integration of ET has become even more important as U.S. educational policy has begun to focus more and more on college- and career-readiness and twenty-first-century learning skills, both of which require proficiency in the use of ET for furthering learning outcomes (Bromberg and Theokas 2016; Darrow 2016; Morgan et al. 2014; Rothman 2011). Two of these main shifts that have required educators to begin thinking about the integration of ET in classroom environments are (1) the passage of the Every Student Succeeds Act, and (2) the integration of the National Education Technology Plan.

18.6.1 The Every Student Succeeds Act (P.L. 114-95)

In 2015, President Obama signed into law the reauthorization of the Elementary and Secondary Education Act (ESEA) which is the federal law that guides federal policy and spending related to public education in the United States, the Every Student Succeeds Act (ESSA) (Darrow 2016). The ESEA was signed in the 1960s and focused on providing equity for all students enrolled in U. S. public schools (Darrow 2016; McLeskey et al. 2010). Prior to ESSA, the most recent reauthorization of the ESEA was coined No Child Left Behind (NCLB) (Darrow 2016). Unlike prior authorizations of ESEA, NCLB for the first time held schools accountable for ensuring that all students showed mastery of grade level content, particularly those from historically underperforming groups (Darrow 2016). This accountability took the form of annual standardized assessments that were tied to federal funding mechanisms. There was much disdain for NCLB provisions, as the U. S. federal government defined what was an appropriate level of mastery; many states felt that this represented too much federal involvement in local education (Darrow 2016).

The enactment of ESSA made several changes to the ESEA under NCLB. First, while testing and accountability are still central metrics used to determine growth and mastery of students, each state determines its own definition of appropriate progress using multiple metrics (Darrow 2016; Murphy and Warren 2015; Skinner and Kuenzi 2015). Additionally, schools that were not making appropriate progress as defined by these accountability indicators became able under ESSA to use federal funding to develop intervention programs to support students who were struggling towards mastery (Darrow

2016; Murphy and Warren 2015). States were also required to adopt rigorous, college- and career-ready standards that aligned directly to entry level coursework within the states' public higher education institutions (Skinner and Kuenzi 2015). With these major changes, the focus of ESSA became not on accountability alone year-over-year but on preparing all students to graduate from high school with the ET and twenty-first-century skills needed to be college- and career-ready (Bromberg and Theokas 2016; Darrow 2016; Skinner and Kuenzi 2015). There is a focus in ESSA that states provide instruction and intervention to ensure that all students attending schools in the United States have access to college- and career-ready curricula (e.g., counseling for career trajectories, advanced placement courses, education focused on ET skills).

18.6.2 National Education Technology Plan

In 2017, the Office of Educational Technology in the U.S. Department of Education released the National Education Technology Plan (NETP) which provided a framework for educational professionals to consider the integration of technology into teaching and learning in U.S. public schools. The NETP is the guiding document for educational policy related to the integration of ET in public school environments, and provides funding to schools and districts for integrating ET into public school settings. The goal of the NETP was to provide guidance to educational professionals on engaging students in public school settings in learning experiences that teach them how to be active members of a globalized society (OET 2017). The focus of the NETP was on providing personalized learning experiences to students, with a primary objective of increasing student mastery of twenty-first-century skills (i.e., critical thinking, complex problem solving, collaboration, multimedia communication) through integration of these skills using technology-based teaching approaches. In addition to these critical learning skills, the NETP maintained a focus on supporting students in the development of non-cognitive skills (i.e., developing relationships, working cooperatively, interacting with others, maintaining perseverance) while using technology as a critical part of the learning experience. Overall, the NETP sought to prepare students to have control over their own learning in a technology-rich environment and to ensure that students leave public school with the skills to utilize technology to drive their own learning experiences (OET 2017).

The NETP provided guidance for both teachers and school leaders in considering critical technology skills that could be integrated across content areas

(OET 2017). This included recommended skills to be included in preservice and inservice teacher preparation and development programs, as well as leadership infrastructures to be considered when determining how and when to integrate technology (i.e., costs, infrastructure, training). Additionally, the NETP suggested that technology be used to drive assessment procedures and protocols to empower school professionals to make data-based decisions regarding personalized learning to ensure that students are mastering critical and important educational constructs (OET 2017). However, little attention was paid throughout the NETP to the adaptation of instruction to support students with disabilities nor to the skills necessary to teach these populations of students to better access and master twenty-first-century skills.

18.7 Considerations for Integrating Educational Technology for Students with Disabilities

Research indicates that students with disabilities show educational benefit from the use of educational technology during their specially designed instruction and individualized programming (Hwang and Riccomini 2014; Kennedy et al. 2014). However, as indicated, there is an underutilization of technologies in their education (Smith and Okolo 2010). While IDEA (2004) does not specifically address the use of educational technology for students with disabilities, it does require that students with disabilities be provided access to the general education curriculum (Darrow 2016; Pazey et al. 2016). Current educational policy dictates that this general education curriculum is focused on college- and career-ready skills that integrate ET and legal precedence suggests that the expectation is that students with disabilities garner the same access to ET opportunities as their typical peers.

Smith and Okolo (2010) posit several reasons why technology is not used more frequently with students with disabilities, including a lack of teacher training for the integration of ET, a lack of understanding for how to connect technology to key instructional components, and a limited understanding of how to integrate technology into special education. It should be noted that these concerns are like the issues addressed above related to AT usage by special education professionals. Additionally, Dalsen (2017) indicated that technology has become more and more sophisticated in the recent past making AT and ET interconnected. For example, an iPad may be used to provide instruction but also may have accessibility features that provide a student access to a specific environment. Since the issues related to A/ET are alike, and both are important for the educational outcomes of students with disabilities in today's U.S. educational context, it is apparent that educational leaders need to ensure that teachers are well-versed in both legal and policy requirements for the use of A/ET in the education of students with disabilities to support their academic, behavioural, and social-emotional outcomes.

18.8 Connecting Assistive and Educational Technologies to the Education of Students with Disabilities: Recommendations

To better provide students with disabilities the access to A/ET required by law and policy in the U.S., the following guidelines are recommended for educational leaders to support their teachers and other staff members in using technology in the education of this population of students (see Fig. 18.1).

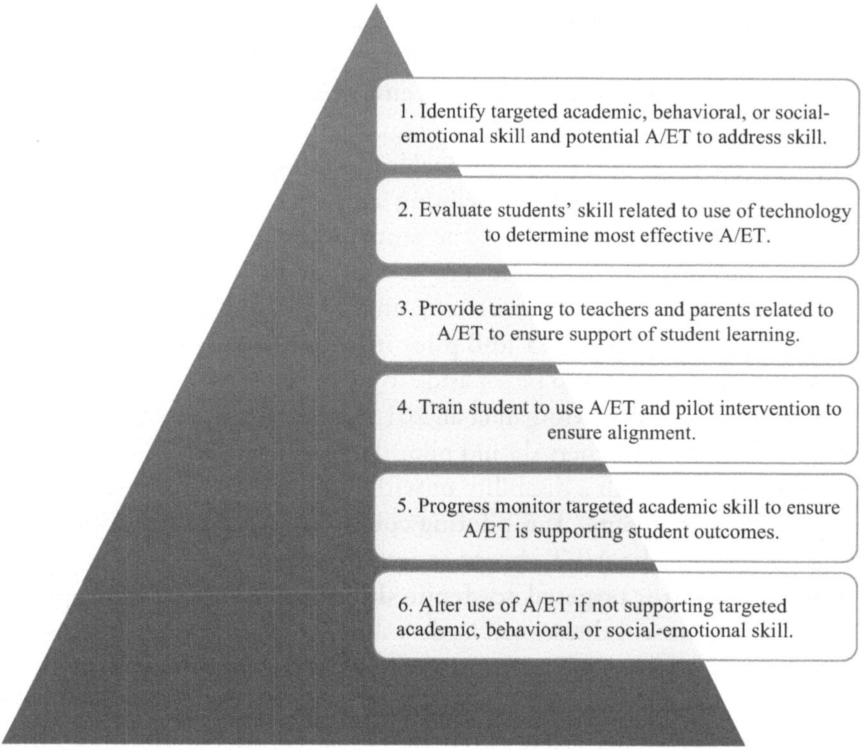

Fig. 18.1 Decision making process for educational leaders regarding the integration of AT/ET in the education of students with disabilities

1. **Identify targeted academic, behavioural, or social-emotional skills and potential A/ET to address that skill**. Educational leaders should ensure that teachers are prepared to assess the specific needs of students with disabilities and to be able to connect A/ET that could be used to support that identified skill. Educational leaders should focus on providing teachers with a variety of assessment metrics to identify student needs, as well as professional development on a variety of A/ET that may be available to provide access and learning for students with disabilities (Boone and Higgins 2007). A/ET considered should be accessible and appropriate for students with disabilities, and resources may need to be expended to ensure that these technologies are available.
2. **Evaluate students' skill related to use of technology to determine most effective A/ET**. Educational leaders should also ensure that methods are in place to pre-test students' ability to use A/ET. It is often assumed that students are masters of technology because they have grown up with it, but research indicates that students are often not adept at using technology to drive their learning (Morgan et al. 2013). This is particularly true for students with disabilities. Once A/ET is determined, assessment of student skills should be completed.
3. **Provide training to teacher and parents related to A/ET to ensure support of student learning**. When integrating A/ET into the education of students with disabilities, educational leaders should ensure that consistent professional development and training support is provided for adults that are supporting the learning of the student using the technology. If the teacher and/or parents are not sure how to use the technology, its impact will be limited at addressing the outcomes of the student.
4. **Train students to use A/ET and pilot intervention to ensure alignment**. Training time should also be set aside to teach the student with a disability how to use the A/ET (Morgan et al. 2013; Nelson et al. 2016). Once training is completed, teachers should pilot the use of the A/ET either with the targeted student with a disability or with a similar student to ensure it has the intended outcome. This piloting could save schools and districts time and resources if the A/ET chosen is not effective.
5. **Progress monitor targeted academic skill to ensure A/ET is supporting student outcome**. Educational leaders should ensure that teachers are provided with, and are using, consistent progress monitoring metrics that determine whether the A/ET being used is having the intended outcome on student academic, behavioural, and social-emotional outcomes. If it is not, then adjustments to its use need to be made.

6. **Alter use of A/ET if not supporting targeted skill**. Related to progress monitoring, educational leaders and teachers should be making data-based decisions regarding the impact of A/ET. If the technology is not having the intended outcome, then other types of A/ET or intervention should be used to provide maximum educational benefit.

18.9 Conclusion

Education law and policy in the United States has focused on the integration of A/ET in the educational of students with disabilities, as these technologies have a positive impact on the learning outcomes of this population of students. Additionally, these skills are essential for students to be college- and career-ready and to engage in a globalized, technology-connected society. While requirements of the provision of AT for this population of students are very clear (Bouck 2016; Dalsen 2017), policies related to ET are not as clear on how the needs of students with disabilities should be met (Darrow 2016; Pazey et al. 2016). Additionally, the needs of teachers related to the integration of technology are quite similar across both AT and ET. Therefore, it is important for educational leaders to be well-versed on these legal aspects of technology integration to best prepare students with disabilities for today's modern society.

References

Boone, R., & Higgins, K. (2007). The software checklist: Evaluating educational software for use by students with disabilities. *Technology in Action, 3*(1), 1–16.

Bouck, E. C. (2016). A national snapshot of assistive technology for students with disabilities. *Journal of Special Education Technology, 31*, 4–13. https://doi.org/10.1177/0162643416633330.

Bromberg, M., & Theokas, C. (2016). *Meandering toward graduation: Transcript outcome of high school graduates*. Washington, DC: Education Trust.

Dalsen, J. (2017). Technology, disability, and law: Then and now. *Journal of Special Education Technology, 32*, 102–108. https://doi.org/10.1177/0162643417704438.

Darrow, A. A. (2016). The every student succeeds act (ESSA): What it means for students with disabilities and music educators. *General Music Today, 30*, 41–44. https://doi.org/10.1177/10483713166658327.

Etscheidt, S. L. (2016). Assistive technology for students with disabilities: A legal analysis of issues. *Journal of Special Education Technology, 31*, 183–194. https://doi.org/10.1177/01626434116673912.

Hwang, J., & Riccomini, P. J. (2014). Enhancing mathematical problem solving for secondary students with or at risk of learning disabilities: A literature review. *Learning Disabilities Research and Practice, 31*, 169–181. https://doi.org/10.1111/ldrp.12105.

Individuals with Disabilities Education Act, 20 U.S.C. § 1400 (2004).

Individuals with Disabilities Improvement Education ACT (IDEA). (2004). Available from http://idea.ed.gov

Kennedy, M. J., Thomas, C. N., Meyer, P., Alves, K. D., & Lloyd, J. W. (2014). Using evidence-based multimedia to improve vocabulary performance of adolescents with LD: A UDL approach. *Learning Disability Quarterly, 37*, 71–85. https://doi.org/10.1177/0731948713507262.

McLeskey, J., Landers, E., Williamson, P., & Hoppey, D. (2010). Are we moving toward educating students with disabilities in less restrictive settings? *Journal of Special Education, 46*, 131–140.

Mishra, P., & Mehta, R. (2017). What we educators get wrong about 21st-century learning: Results of a survey. *Journal of Digital Learning in Teacher Education, 33*, 6–19. https://doi.org/10.1080/21532974.2016.1242392.

Morgan, J. J., Boone, R., & Higgins, K. (2013). Integrating technology in content area classrooms to support reading comprehension. In R. T. Boon & V. G. Spencer (Eds.), *Adolescent literacy: Strategies for content comprehension in inclusive classrooms* (pp. 157–169). Baltimore: Brookes Publishing.

Morgan, J. J., Brown, N. B., Hsiao, Y. J., Howerter, C., Juniel, P., Sedano, L., & Castillo, W. L. (2014). Unwrapping academic standards to increase the achievement of students with disabilities. *Intervention in School and Clinic, 49*, 131–141. https://doi.org/10.1177/1053451213496156.

Murphy, P., & Warren, P. (2015, December 11). Good timing for new federal education law. *Viewpoints: PPIC Blog*. Retrieved from http://ppic.org/main/blog_detail.asp?i=1923

National Assessment of Educational Progress (NAEP, 2014). *The nation's report card 2014: Technology and engineering literacy*. Retrieved from https://www.nationsreportcard.gov/tel_2014/#

Nelson, N. J., Fien, H., Doabler, C. T., & Clarke, B. (2016). Considerations for realizing the promise of educational gaming technology. *Teaching Exceptional Children, 48*, 293–300. https://doi.org/10.1177/0040059916650639.

Office of Educational Technology (OET, 2017). *National education technology plan*. Retrieved from https://tech.ed.gov/netp/

Okolo, C. M., & Diedrich, J. (2014). Twenty-five years later: How is technology used in the education of students with disabilities? Results of a statewide study. *Journal of Special Education Technology, 29*, 1–20. https://doi.org/10.1177/016264341402900101.

Pazey, B. L., Schalock, R. L., Schaller, J., & Burkett, J. (2016). Incorporating quality of life concepts into educational reform: Creating real opportunities for students with disabilities in the 21st century. *Journal of Disability Policy Studies, 27*(2), 96–105. https://doi.org/10.1177/1044207315604364.

Robinson, R., Molenda, M., & Rezabek, L. (2008). Facilitating learning. In A. Januszewski & M. Molenda (Eds.), *Educational technology: A definition with commentary* (pp. 15–48). New York: Lawrence Erlbaum Associates.

Rothman, R. (2011). *Something in common: The common core standards and the next chapter in American education.* Cambridge, MA: Harvard Education Press.

Skinner, R. R., & Kuenzi, J. J. (2015). *Reauthorization of the elementary and secondary education act: Highlights of the every student succeeds act* (Report no. R44297). Washington, DC: Congressional Research Service.

Smith, S. J., & Okolo, C. (2010). Response to intervention and evidence-based practices: Where does technology fit? *Learning Disability Quarterly, 33*, 257–272.

U.S. Department of Education, National Center for Education Statistics. (2016). *Internet access in U.S. public schools and classrooms: 1994–2005 and educational technology in U.S. public schools: Fall 2008.* Retrieved from https://nces.ed.gov/programs/digest/d15/tables/dt15_218.10.asp?current=yes

Yell, M. L., Shriner, J. G., & Katsiyannis, A. (2006). Individuals with disabilities education improvement act of 2004 and IDEA regulations of 2006: Implications for educators, administrators, and teacher trainers. *Focus on Exceptional Children, 39*, 1–24.

Yell, M. L., Katsiyannis, A., Ryan, J. B., McDuffie, K. A., & Mattocks, L. (2008). Twenty ways to ensure compliance with the individuals with disabilities education improvement act of 2004. *Intervention in School and Clinic, 44*, 45–51. https://doi.org/10.1177/1053451208318875.

19

A Long Journey: Disability and Inclusive Education in International Law

Ilektra Spandagou

19.1 Introduction

This chapter discusses the development of understandings of inclusive education in international policy. It begins with an overview of how disability and the education of students with disability have been addressed in United Nations' (UN) treaties and related documents. This is followed by a discussion of the Article 24: Education of the UN Convention on the Rights of Persons with Disabilities, which provides the normative content for States Parties to implement inclusive education. The third part of the chapter illustrates the complexities around the implementation of inclusive education with examples from key documents in the Convention's reporting process. In the concluding section, the recent General Comment 4 is presented to demonstrate the practice implications for educational systems and schools.

19.2 Disability: From Invisibility to Visibility

The journey of disability in international policy and law is one from invisibility to visibility defined with a long period of 'struggle in the darkness' (Kayess and French 2008). Degener and Begg (2017) provide a chronology of United

I. Spandagou (✉)
Sydney School of Education and Social Work, The University of Sydney, Camperdown, NSW, Australia
e-mail: ilektra.spandagou@sydney.edu.au

K. Trimmer et al. (eds.), *The Palgrave Handbook of Education Law for Schools*,
https://doi.org/10.1007/978-3-319-77751-1_19

Nations' (UN) disability policy with four distinct periods in how people with disabilities were perceived: invisible citizens (1945–1970), subjects of rehabilitation (1970–1980), objects of human rights (1980–2000), and agents of human rights from 2000 onward.

The Convention on the Rights of Persons with Disabilities (CRPD) was developed and negotiated with unprecedented participation by civic society. The working group responsible with developing the Convention's draft text included 12 organisations of people with disability (Degener and Begg 2017). Thus CRPD sealed the transition to visibility and its adoption day on the 13th of December 2006, was called a 'dawn of a new era' by the then Secretary-General of the United Nations (Kanter 2015). This chapter discusses this journey from the perspective of education. Consideration of how disability and equality have been constructed at different points of this journey is essential in understanding the current debates around inclusive education.

19.3 Disability Models

The CRPD can be seen as both as the inevitable historical development of the UN work on disability and a clear departure from a large part of this work. It was preceded by a number of non-binding policies which were introduced in the hope that they would have an influence on national legislation, policies and practices. While influential in providing a space for recognising disability as a policy issue, they had limited success in making a difference in the systemic disadvantage that people with disability have historically experienced and thus a binding instrument become the inevitable next step. On the other hand, the CRPD is a clear deviation from previous international policy insofar as disability is presented for the first time from a social model perspective rather than a medical one.

The medical model has been the dominant model of conceptualising disability in international policy. The medical model perceives disability as a personal problem residing within the individual and requiring a personal response. A social construction of disability sees disability as a social problem and as Oliver (1996) has argued the social model of disability "does not deny the problem of disability but locates it squarely within society" (p. 32). The way that social institutions, environment, and societal norms and attitudes are organised result in the exclusion and discrimination of people with disability.

As the Preamble of the CRPD states, "disability is an evolving concept" that "results from the interaction between persons with impairments and attitudinal and environmental barriers that hinders their full and effective participation in society on an equal basis with others". Impairment in itself is not seen as an exceptional state but rather as part of the diversity of the human condition, which again is a departure from previous conceptualisations in UN policy documents. This paradigm shift from a personal tragedy or medical problem understanding of disability to a socially constructed one impacts on how equality is conceptualised.

19.4 Conceptions of Equality

Promoting equality is a key principle of the CRPD. Conceptualisations of equality relate to how individuals are perceived in terms of their attributes, in this case disability, as well as the role of the state and of social systems, in this case education and schools, in responding to these attributes. Discrimination due to an individual attribute is the opposite of equality and therefore non-discrimination goes hand in hand with equality. Understandings of equality in international law have evolved following a similar pattern to the increased visibility of disability discussed earlier.

Arnardottir (2009) identifies three periods of understandings of equality in UN policy. In the 1950–1970 period, named universal sameness, formal equality was the dominant approach treating difference as sameness perceiving that "neutrality in the application of the law and the absence of different treatment are presumed to result in equality" (Rioux and Riddle 2011, p. 42). Simply put, formal equality recognises direct discrimination but not indirect discrimination. This approach doesn't account for the disadvantage of the social construction of an individual characteristic. In the case of disability for example, the expectation that people with disability conform to existing norms "simply reinforces a particular norm and perpetuates disadvantage" (Fredman 2005, p. 203).

The period 1970–1990, called specific difference, moved to a substantive difference model (Arnardottir 2009). In this model individual attributes are recognised as potentially resulting in disadvantage and for this to be corrected reasonable accommodations or affirmative action is utilised. Despite the expansion of the remits of equality, Arnardottir (2009) argues that this model in addition of not acknowledging the structural nature of disadvantage, it was limited in what types of differences it could address. The difference of disability was "perceived as so profoundly incomparable to the prevailing standard, that under international law it remained largely unnoticed as an equality issue" (Arnardottir 2009, p. 54).

The next development from the mid-1990s is multidimensional disadvantage, which recognises that individual attributes are not mere deviations from the norm and that they are not in themselves the causes of disadvantage. The recognition of the structural nature of social disadvantage identifies a positive obligation for states to take action to change the underpinning structures that perpetuate it.

The CRPD, according to Degener (2016), represents all three concepts of equality. This means that in addition of prohibiting direct and indirect discrimination and providing reasonable accommodations, states have the responsibility to "enable meaningful participation for organizations of disabled persons in the implementation and monitoring of the Convention" (p. 19).

19.5 Disability and Education in International Law: From Exclusion to Inclusion

This section presents how disability and education are discussed historically in UN policy. As it is expected there are clear parallels with Degener and Begg's (2017) chronology. The 1948 Declaration of Human Rights (DHR) is the seminal starting point and framework of action of the newly established United Nations and its organisations involved in education projects, namely United Nations Educational, Scientific and Cultural Organisation (UNESCO), United Nations Development Programme (UNDP), United Nations Children's Fund (UNICEF), World Bank Group (WBG), and World Health Organisation (WHO).

Universality is a cornerstone principle of human rights as proclaimed in DHR's Article 2: "*All* human beings are born free and equal in dignity and rights. They are endowed *with reason and conscience*" (emphasis added). This is asserted also in Article 26 on education: "everyone has the right to education". Due to dominant views about disability at that time, assumed lack of or diminished 'reason and conscience' were common and acceptable justifications for exclusion, segregation and institutionalisation of people with disability. Even though the popularity of the Eugenics movement decreased after the atrocities of World War II, a long history of perceiving people with disabilities as 'less than human' prevailed in attitudes and practices. So for those reading the DHR at the time, 'all' didn't necessarily include (all) people with disabilities.

Such a perception was reinforced by the fact that the DHR doesn't refer to disability as a personal attribute in Article 2: "Everyone is entitled to all the rights and freedoms set forth in this Declaration, without distinction of any kind, such as race, colour, sex, language, religion, political or other opinion, national or social origin, property, birth or other status". There is only reference to disability, in Article 25, and it refers to it as an unfortunate circumstance: "Everyone has the right to a standard of living adequate for the health and well-being of himself and of his family, including food, clothing, housing and medical care and necessary social services, and the right to security in the event of unemployment, sickness, *disability*, widowhood, old age or other lack of livelihood in circumstances beyond his control" (emphasis added). This is the only reference to disability in the three instruments that constitute the International Bill of Rights (DHR 1948; International Covenant on Economic, Social and Cultural Rights (ICESCR) 1966a; International Covenant on Civil and Political Rights (ICCPR) 1966b).

In the following 30 years, disability and education of children with disability are mentioned mainly in the 'soft law' of non-binding declarations. These declarations take a deficit, medical approach to disability and consequently qualify the extent of provision of rights. Education is seen as an element of rehabilitation. For example in the 1968 Declaration on Social Progress and Development, Article 19, point (d), "treatment and technical appliances, education, vocational and social guidance, training and selective placement, and other assistance" are presented together in order to enable people with disability "to the fullest possible extent to be useful members of society".

The two disability specific Declarations of the 1970s also follow a medical/personal model of disability but there is a slight shift between them, more likely because the second one refers to all people with disabilities while the first one is only to 'mentally retarded people', a group of people whose 'reason and conscience' were historically questioned. In the 1971 Declaration on the Rights of Mentally Retarded Persons, rights are seen as conditional as it is stated in paragraph 1 "The mentally retarded person has, *to the maximum degree of feasibility*, the same rights as other human beings" (emphasis added). While the 1975 Declaration on the Rights of Disabled Persons paragraph 3 gives a less qualified version: "Disabled persons, whatever the origin, nature and seriousness of their handicaps and disabilities, have the same fundamental rights as their fellow-citizens of the same age." The CRPD Preamble doesn't mention these two declarations as "these instruments tend to be paternalistic, and legitimise segregation through specialised services and institutions" (Kayess and French 2008, p. 15).

In 1976 the year 1981 was proclaimed as the International Year of Disabled Persons (IYDP) with the theme of 'full participation and equality'. Activities took place at international, national and local level. They included public campaigns to raise awareness as well as the establishment of organisations by people with disability. A major outcome of the IYDP was the adoption in 1983 by the UN General Assembly of the World Programme of Action concerning Disabled Persons (WPA). The WPA utilises the WHO's (1980) classification that distinguishes between impairment, disability, and handicap. The latter accounts for the 'cultural, physical or social barriers' that deny or limit the opportunity for equal participation. Despite of this acknowledgment of the discrimination experienced by people with disability, there is a firm focus on impairment as defining people's potential. The WPA's section on education refers to the right of education but mostly in terms of providing special education support. It concludes by commenting on advances related to the education of children with disability stating that "the advances concern early detection, assessment and intervention, special education programmes in a variety of settings, *with many disabled children able to participate in a regular school setting, while others require very intensive programmes*" (emphasis added). To promote WPA, the decade 1983–1992 was named the UN decade for Disabled Persons and from 1992 onwards the 3rd of December has been the International Day of Persons with Disabilities (originally International Day of Disabled Persons). Towards the end of that decade there was increased focus on disability that intensified in the 1990s.

In 1989, the Convention on the Rights of the Child (CRC) was adopted. CRC is a thematic convention, focusing on a specific group. It is the first convention that refers to disability as a personal attribute: "States Parties shall respect and ensure the rights set forth in the present Convention to each child within their jurisdiction without discrimination of any kind, irrespective of the child's or his or her parent's or legal guardian's race, colour, sex, language, religion, political or other opinion, national, ethnic or social origin, property, *disability*, birth or other status" (Article 2, emphasis added). Comparing with Article 2 of the DHR cited above, ethnic (origin) and disability are the only two additional attributes in CRC. Article 23 of the CRC refers specifically to children with disability and their requirements for 'special care' to receive "*education*, training, health care services, rehabilitation services, preparation for employment and recreation opportunities in a manner conducive to the child's achieving *the fullest possible social integration and individual development*, including his or her cultural and spiritual development" (emphasis added). Education is now top of the list as the emphasis on 'rehabilitation' lessens. However, there is still a qualification of potential outcomes.

On the 20th of December 1993, the UN General Assembly adopted The Standard Rules on Equalization of Opportunities for Persons with Disabilities. The Standard Rules are not legally binding and as with the previous declarations, they do not include reporting mechanisms of progress. They were a response to failed attempts for a Convention on disability. The 22 Rules were presented as "a strong moral and political commitment of Governments to take action to attain equalization of opportunities for persons with disabilities" (n.p.). While the Standard Rules refer to the WHO (1980) definition of disability, there is mention of the increased critique raised about the medical emphasis of the term 'handicap'. In terms of education, the Standard Rules refer to 'integrated education' as the objective of education, perceiving special education as the place to prepare students with disability for the general school systems when the general school system is not yet in a position to meet their needs. This means that students with disability need to demonstrate their 'fitness' for general education before accessing it. Thus, the Standard Rules outline a process of "gradual integration of special education services into mainstream education".

Without minimising the importance of the Standard Rules, the following year a document introduced into policy a new term, this of inclusive education. UNESCO's Salamanca Statement and Framework for Action on Special Needs Education was the outcome of a conference in Salamanca, Spain attended by more than 300 delegates including representatives from 92 countries and 25 international organisations in 1994. This conference was organised in the context of the Education for All (EFA) movement, which aimed to meet the basic learning needs of all by 2000. The Preface to the Salamanca Statement by Frederico Mayor, the then director-general of UNESCO, notes the conference's aims to consider "the fundamental policy shifts required to promote the approach of inclusive education, namely enabling schools to serve all children, particularly those with special educational needs" (p. iii). The Salamanca Statement doesn't define disability but it puts forward an understanding of disadvantage based on one or more personal attributes. In addition, the Statement brings the education of students with disability within a development discourse that has been developing mostly in parallel up to this stage. More importantly, the Salamanca Statement requires schools in principle to be 'fit' for all students, rather than the other way round. This is the first time the structural nature of social disadvantage in terms of equality (Arnardottir 2009) is evident in a policy for students with disability. However, the Salamanca Statement still considers that 'all' doesn't mean 'all'. It states that segregated education should be exceptional "in those infrequent cases where it is clearly demonstrated that education in regular classrooms is incapable of meeting a child's educational or social needs or when it is required for the welfare of the child or that of other children" (p. 12). Moreover, the Salamanca Statement is evidence of the ongoing separation of thinking between disability and development policy, and its influence was mostly contained within the field of inclusive education (Miles and Singal 2010).

At the beginning of the century, the commitment to Education for All was reaffirmed at a Conference in Dakar, Senegal which adopted the Dakar Framework for Action: Education for All: Meeting our Collective Commitments (2000). This framework sets six key education goals. The Dakar framework refers to children with special learning needs or special needs but it doesn't use the term disability. In the same year, the United Nations adopted the Millennium Development Goals (MDGs). These were broader development goals but all of them require sustained investment in education. Goal 2 was specific to education aiming to "achieve universal primary education" by 2015. This increased emphasis on children with disabilities in EFA, was accompanied with a recognition that children with disabilities were left increasingly behind in the implementation of the EFA agenda.

However, the spirit of the Salamanca Statement was not always at the foreground of debates around inclusive education. Medical and deficit models of disability have remained influential. An example is the discussion about the choice between 'inclusion or special classes/schools' in the Conceptual Paper: The Right to Education for Persons with Disabilities: Towards Inclusion put forward by UNESCO's EFA Flagship in 2004. When referring to the dual-track approach to the education of students with disability in the countries of the North, it states: "*Those who can thrive* in general education programs are encouraged to do so. *Those who are unable* to be in general education have the option to choose specially designed instruction or other assisted learning programs and an array of related services" (emphasis added, p. 16). This statement's deficit approach negate any reason for reforming educational systems as the success or not of participation in general education relates to the individual's level of ability. While the debate on defining inclusive education is still very much alive, the binding nature of the CRPD will add another dimension to it.

19.6 Inclusive Education in the Convention of the Rights of Persons with Disabilities

The CRPD was adopted by the UN General Assembly on 13 December 2006, opened for signature on 30 March 2007 and came into force on 3 May 2008. In April 2018, there were 188 signatories and 177 parties (including the European Union).

Article 24 is the current culmination of a long journey of disability advocacy and international policy to expand the educational opportunities of people with disabilities. It is also a deviation from more prudent and compromised understandings of inclusive education presented in the previous section. While Article 24 is called Education, it actually refers to the right to inclusive education. This wasn't the initial intention but rather the result of the negotiation process. The role of the facilitator, Rosemary Kayess, is acknowledged as instrumental in providing a consolidated draft upon which the final version is based (Degener 2017; Della Fina 2017). The involvement of people with disability and their organisations in the negotiations was crucial for Article's 24 development.

Article 24 makes a very clear proclamation for inclusive education. The justification of requiring an inclusive education system is to realise "this right without discrimination and on the basis of equal opportunity". A clear outline of inclusive education is presented where exclusion from the general education system on the basis of disability should not take place. Reasonable accommodations are provided within the general education system and "effective individualized support measures are provided in environments that maximize academic and social development, consistent with the goal of full inclusion" (par. 2, point 3).

On the other hand, Article 24 recognises concerns of some specific groups of people with disabilities and debates around their education. In particular Paragraph 3, point (c) states that "ensuring that the education of persons, and in particular children, who are blind, deaf or deafblind, is delivered in the most appropriate languages and modes and means of communication for the individual, and in environments which maximize academic and social development." The repetition between par. 2 point 3 above sets the expectation of the right but in the latter instance avoids referring to inclusion. The word environments, on the other hand, appears deliberate in its use to avoid introducing a 'special education' language.

However, what is implicit in Article 24 but not spelled out, is inclusive education as a reform project. This project requires educational system to implement structural changes to ensure 'full inclusion'. While Article 24 sets out in particular the positive requirements of equality in terms of reasonable accommodations, and individualized support measures, it doesn't – and to some extent couldn't within the constraints of a thematic convention- outline the grand project of reform that is required to ensure inclusive education for all students. Nevertheless, Article 24 elegantly expresses inclusive education using a human rights language and therefore avoids the common pitfalls of the educational debate on inclusive education.

19.7 Interpretations of Article 24

Despite the debate during the negotiations, Article 24 appeared initially to be accepted will less reservation than other CRPD articles (United Nations Treaty Collection https://treaties.un.org/Pages/ViewDetails.aspx?src=IND&mtdsg_no=IV-15&chapter=4&clang=_en). For example, nine declarations/reservations were made by state parties in relation to Article 12 Equal recognition before the law and eight about Article 25 Health, while only three about Article 24. The Republic of Suriname's (2007) reservation was on its inability to guarantee the implementation of 24 paragraph 2(b) due to "the educational system is still far from inclusive education". Mauritius' (2007) reservation on the same paragraph was due to having "a policy of inclusive education which is being implemented incrementally alongside special education". United Kingdom's (UK) (2007) reservation on paragraph 24 2(a) was due to reserving the right to educating children away from their local community "where more appropriate education provision is available elsewhere", and on paragraph 24 2(b) expressed a more fundamental opposition to CRPD's inclusive education. While the UK declared commitment "to continuing to develop an inclusive system where parents of disabled children have increasing access to mainstream schools and staff, which have the capacity to meet the needs of disabled children", it also stated that "the General Education System in the United Kingdom includes mainstream, and special schools, which the UK Government understands is allowed under the Convention". Rieser (2012) has commented that this reservation indicates that it wasn't about the progressive realisation of inclusive education, but rather that the UK government "was not prepared to envisage a fully inclusive education system at any point in the future" (p. 192).

The CRPD is the first disability specific instrument that includes a reporting process. State Parties that have ratified the CRPD are required to regularly report on compliance with their obligations and the Committee on the Convention on the Rights of Persons with Disabilities role is to provide recommendations for future direction. The process of reporting is described in Article 35. The initial comprehensive report is to be submitted to the Committee within two years from CRPD entering into force for the State Party. Consequent reports should be submitted at least every four years. As per point 4 of Article 35, States Parties are 'invited' to prepare reports in an 'open and transparent process' with due consideration of the provision of point 3 in Article 4 – General obligations, which states that in decision-making processes States Parties "shall closely consult and with actively involve persons with disabilities, including children with disabilities, through their representative organizations". The process of reporting involves the following stages: (a) Initial support submitted by State Party, (b)

List of Issues identified by the Committee. These issues are areas that the Committee requires clarifications, and/or additional information or statistics, (c) Reply by the State Party to the List of Issues, (d) Discussion of the reports in a Committee's meeting, (e) Concluding Observations by the Committee, and (f) Follow-up in a set timeframe if required in the Concluding Observations. All the documents are publically available at the Committee's website.

The rest of this section presents an analysis of the reporting documents for States Parties covering the period 2010-August 2016. One of these States Parties in the European Union. Another one is China whose report includes separate sections on Hong Kong and Macau. For the purpose of the analysis, China, Hong Kong and Macau were analysed as separate cases, resulting in 42 cases. The dataset isn't complete. Documents are missing (Replies of Australia, Austria, European Union and Hungary to the List of Issues), or are available in other official UN languages but not in English (e.g. the Initial Report of Ecuador and the Replies of Argentina, Costa-Rica, Ecuador, El Salvador, Paraguay, Peru, and Spain that are available in Spanish), and one link didn't work when accessed (Reply of Czech Republic). The analysis focuses on Article 24 and only the related section of the relevant documents were analysed. The cases are: Argentina, Australia, Austria, Azerbaijan, Belgium, Brazil, Chile, China including the reports of Hong Kong and Macau, Cook Islands, Costa Rica, Croatia, Czech Republic, Denmark, Dominican Republic, Ecuador, El Salvador, European Union, Gabon, Germany, Hungary, Kenya, Lithuania, Mauritius, Mexico, Mongolia, New Zealand, Paraguay, Peru, Portugal, Qatar, Korea, Serbia, Slovakia, Spain, Sweden, Thailand, Tunisia, Turkmenistan, Uganda, Ukraine.

Table 19.1 presents a comparison of how often the terms inclusive, mainstream, general and special are used to qualify education in the four sets of

Table 19.1 Comparison of the number and % of use of inclusive, mainstream, general and special qualifiers for inclusion in the four types of documents

	Initial reports	List of issues	Replied	Concluding observations
	(86,500 words)	(35,466 words)	(35,697 words)	(7,890 words)
Education	2,700	120	1,052	287
Inclusive	184 (6.81%)	41 (34.16%)	102 (9.69%)	85 (29.61%)
Mainstream	20 (0.74%)	9 (7.50%)	18 (1.71%)	14 (4.87%)
General	40 (1.48%)	1 (0.83%)	12 (1.14%)	2 (0.69%)
Special	441 (16.33%)	11 (9.16%)	203 (19.29%)	18 (4.18%)

Notes: The total number of words for the Initial Reports and Replies are approximations as different counties follow different formatting (e.g., use of footnotes)

documents. This comparison is based on a simple count of the instances that each qualifier appears and it doesn't take into account the positive, negative or otherwise meaning of each reference. However, as CRPD asserts inclusive education to become the driver of policy development and practice, it could be expected that a substantial number of references to inclusive education are to be found in the documents. This is not the case in the documents produced by the countries, i.e., initial reports and replies. For example in the more than 86,500 words of the initial reports, there are more than 2700 uses of the word education (or educational). From these references, 441 are qualified with 'special' and 184 with 'inclusive'. Twenty-four reports refer to both terms. Five do not refer to special education, eight do not refer to inclusive education, and four to neither term.

For the documents produced by the Committee of the CRPD, the list of issues and concluding observations, the opposite is evident. For example, in the list of issues, more than one third of the references to education is qualified with 'inclusive'. Many of the issues raised from the Committee are about exploring the inclusive education direction of education systems. Indicative examples are "What measures have been taken to implement inclusive education and to adopt regulations on reasonable accommodations?" (Belgium – United Nations Committee on the Rights of Persons with Disabilities 2014a) and "Please indicate the State's strategy for establishing an inclusive education system for person with disabilities" (Ecuador – United Nations Committee on the Rights of Persons with Disabilities 2014b). Information about the specific 'measures' taken and statistical data are the most common requests. Despite the Committee's effort to direct the information received towards inclusive education, the state's replies tend to parallel the initial reports with the emphasis on special education.

This results in very disappointed concluding observations by the Committee. Seventy-two uses of 'concern/ed' are identified, four of 'regret' and one of 'disappointed'. On the other hand, there are only five uses of commend/ing and two of 'note with appreciation'. All countries have at least one mention of 'concern/ed', while only six of them have a commendation. Despite Article 24 providing a framework for the implementation of inclusive education, this framework is largely ignored in the States Parties' reports. The predominant discourse identified is that of special education – with implicit deficit assumptions. This is a discourse where provision for students with disability is an add-on to the regular education system, an add-on that is mostly located at the periphery of the educational system through a parallel system of classes and schools.

Even when States Parties are called to explicitly comment on inclusive education, there is resistance to do so. Of course this hasn't escaped the attention of the Committee. Degener (2017), who is a member of the Committee, comments that "the majority of States Parties' reports to the CRPD reveal an understanding of disability that follows the traditional medical model of disability" (p. 42). This isn't restricted to Article 24 but it is clearly illustrated in the understandings of the right to participating into the mainstream as conditional to be 'fit' to be integrated. As mentioned, Article 24 outlines inclusive education but it doesn't define what an inclusive education system should look like. This has been the focus of the most recent developments in international policy.

19.8 The Journey Continues

The CRPD establishes the right to inclusive education. The justification for this, as it is stated in the report of the Office of the United Nations' High Commissioner for Human Rights on the Thematic Study on the Right of Persons with Disabilities in Education, is that "inclusive education has been acknowledged as the most appropriate modality for States to guarantee universality and non-discrimination in the right to education" (UN 2013, p. 3).

It is a common assertion that inclusive education is difficult to define and it can mean different things to different people (Armstrong et al. 2010). Part of the challenge of defining inclusive education is based on its diverse origins as a project of change. Inclusive education as increasing participation for students with disability in the general education system is different from inclusive education as a critique to special education provision, as an education development project, or as education system reform project. Thus the purpose of inclusive education defines who is inclusive education is relevant for and of course what is seen as an inclusive educational system. The necessary focus of inclusive education in the CRPD on people with disability could be seen as limiting its construction as an educational system reform.

The conceptual difficulty is that when inclusive education is seen solely through a disability lens, its universality is limited as the focus tends to be on the particular needs for reasonable accommodations, supports, training and budget resources. All these are essential, but they don't respond to the question of why systems with substantial investment in providing reasonable accommodations, specialists, training to teachers and so forth, still have educational systems that are far from providing inclusive quality education to all their students. An examination of the systemic exclusionary practices of educational systems requires both to be able to keep the attention to all students, and acknowledge at the same time the interplay of disadvantage for individuals and groups. Such an understanding of inclusive education isn't popular.

As discussed, international policy on disability developed parallel to development policy in education (Armstrong et al. 2011). There have been convergences between the two but also differences (Winzer and Mazurek 2014). In recent years the convergences have increased. As the EFA goals weren't met by 2015, the international community set new goals. In May 2015, at the World Education Forum at Incheon, Republic of Korea the Incheon Declaration for Education 2030: Towards inclusive and equitable quality education and lifelong learning for all. In November of the same year, the UN 17 Sustainable Development Goals (SDG) (2015) were also adopted with Goal 4 being to "ensure inclusive and quality education for all and promote lifelong learning":

> *Inclusion and equity* in and through education is the cornerstone of a *transformative education agenda*, and we therefore commit to addressing *all forms of exclusion and marginalization, disparities and inequalities in access, participation and learning outcomes. No education target should be considered met unless met by all.* (p. 7, emphasis added)

This is the point of fully 'mainstreaming' inclusive education within the development agenda. A year later, the General Comment No 4 (UN 2016) on the Right to Inclusive Education was finalised. The comment makes a very strong case for inclusive education but in a broader context than Article 24. It also refers to 'transformation' as "inclusive education entails a transformation in culture, policy and practice in all formal and informal educational environments to accommodate the differing requirements and identities of individual students, together with a commitment to removing the barriers that impede that possibility" (p. 2). The General Comment 4 in its interpretation of Article 24 locates the development of inclusive education squarely within a universal educational system.

The CRPD hasn't been without criticism. For instance, Kayess and French (2008) argued that it was informed by an understanding of the social model that tends to ignore the underlying reality of impairment and they urged for the CRPD interpretations to be informed by more sophisticated explanations of impairment and disability within the social context. Meekosha and Soldatic (2011), on the other hand, questioned the dualistic distinction of impairment and disability and the notion that impairment is 'natural' as impairment in the global South is often connected to processes of colonisation and imperialism (p. 1390). The analysis above also questioned whether the Article 24 presents a framework of inclusive education that is more detailed when it comes to individualised accommodations and supports and sketchy when it refers to an inclusive, quality educational system for all. Nevertheless, the CRPD is an negotiated text of its time with practical implications. In that sense, it has challenged long-held understandings of disability and equality in education.

This chapter presented an overview of the development of understandings of disability and education in international law. It presented a discussion of how Article 24 of the CRPD is interpreted based on documents available as part of the reporting process. The Initial Reports provide many examples where segregation and integration are presented as inclusive education practices. While the Concluding Observations identify and comment on these contradictions, there is strong evidence that the definition of inclusive education in Article 24 is far from universally accepted. In some cases it appears that CRPD and Article 24 becomes the justification for the establishment and/or expansion of segregation in education. The contested nature of inclusive education as an international construct needs to be recognised in policy and relevant debates but shouldn't be an excuse for watering down the ultimate goal of inclusive education. It remains to be seen whether the recent developments in this area will be fruitful.

References

Armstrong, A. C., Armstrong, D., & Spandagou, I. (2010). *Inclusive education: International policy & practice*. London: Sage.

Armstrong, D., Armstrong, A. C., & Spandagou, I. (2011). Inclusion: By choice or by chance. *International Journal of Inclusive Education, 15*(1), 29–39.

Arnardottir, O. M. (2009). A future of multidimensional disadvantage equality? In O. M. Arnardottir & G. Quinn (Eds.), *The UN convention on the rights of persons with disabilities: European and Scandinavian perspectives* (pp. 41–66). Lieden: Martinus Nijhoff Publishers.

Degener, T. (2016). Disability in a human rights context. *Laws, 5*(35), 1–24. https://doi.org/10.3390/Lwas5030035.

Degener, T. (2017). A new human rights model of disability. In V. Della Fina, R. Cera, & G. Palmisano (Eds.), *The United Nations convention on the rights of persons with disabilities; a commentary* (pp. 41–59). Cham: Springer.

Degener, T., & Begg, A. (2017). From invisible citizens to agents of change: A short history of the struggle for the recognition of the rights of persons with disabilities at the United Nations. In V. Della Fina, R. Cera, & G. Palmisano (Eds.), *The*

United Nations convention on the rights of persons with disabilities; a commentary (pp. 1–39). Cham: Springer.

Della Fina, V. (2017). Article 24 [Education]. In V. Della Fina, R. Cera, & G. Palmisano (Eds.), *The United Nations convention on the rights of persons with disabilities; a commentary* (pp. 439–470). Cham: Springer.

Fredman, S. (2005). Disability equality; a challenge to the existing anti-discrimination paradigm? In A. Lawson & C. Gooding (Eds.), *Disability rights in Europe: From theory to practice* (pp. 199–218). Oxford: Oxford University Press.

Kanter, A. S. (2015). *The development of disability rights under international law*. Oxon: Routledge.

Kayess, R., & French, P. (2008). Out of darkness into light? Introducing the convention on the rights of persons with disabilities. *Human Rights Law Review, 1*(8), 1–34.

Meekosha, H., & Soldatic, K. (2011). Human rights and the global South: The case of disability. *Third World Quarterly, 32*(8), 1383–1397.

Miles, S., & Singal, N. (2010). The education for all and inclusive education debate: Conflict, contradiction or opportunity? *International Journal of Inclusive Education, 14*(1), 1–15.

Oliver, M. (1996). *Understanding disability: From theory to practice*. London: Macmillan Press.

Rieser, R. (2012). Inclusive education: A human right. In M. Cole (Ed.), *Education, equality and human rights; issues of gender, 'race', sexuality, disability and social class* (3rd ed., pp. 190–216). Oxon: Routledge.

Rioux, M. H., & Riddle, C. A. (2011). Values in disability policy and law: Equality. In M. H. Rioux, L. A. Basser, & M. Jones (Eds.), *Critical perspectives on human rights and disability law* (pp. 37–55). Lieden: Martinus Nijhoff Publishers.

United Nations. (2013). *Report of the office of the United Nations high commissioner for human rights: Thematic study on the right of persons with disabilities*. New York: United Nations.

United Nations. (2016). *General comment no. 4 (2016) on the right to inclusive education*. New York: United Nations.

United Nations Committee on the Rights of Persons with Disabilities. (2014a). *Concluding observations on the initial report of Belgium*. Geneva: United Nations.

United Nations Committee on the Rights of Persons with Disabilities. (2014b). *Concluding observations on the initial report of Ecuador*. Geneva: United Nations.

Winzer, M., & Mazurek, K. (2014). The convention on the rights of persons with disabilities: Notes on genealogy and prospects. *International Journal of Special Needs Education, 17*(1), 3–12. https://doi.org/10.9782/2159-4341-17.1.3.

World Health Organization. (1980). *International classification of impairment, disability and handicap (ICIDH)*. Geneva: World Health Organization.

20

Changing Nappies: A Duty for Teachers in Inclusive Classrooms?

Franziska Felder

20.1 Introduction

The numbers of students in schools who have complex medical needs has grown in the last 10 years. This is due to the fact that more premature babies with serious medical conditions survive and also conditions such as Type 1 diabetes can be diagnosed earlier in children's lives. Many of these students now learn in the regular education setting. Often, these pupils require a broad spectrum of interventions, ranging from minimal to intense (Pufpaff et al. 2015). As physical care for students with health care needs does not only extend to physical safety, but can be seen as a requirement for education and learning itself, the role of the teacher and other professionals such as school nurses and teacher aides has become of utmost importance.

Traditionally, teachers as well as other professionals in schools are expected to act in loco parentis (Conte 2000), or as having the same responsibilities to students as sensible and careful parents would have. This includes, at a minimum, caring for the safety and wellbeing of the pupils. This is just one obligation among the wide range of responsibilities, all of which have different legal sources. They include international human rights law, federal, state, and local laws as well as different regulations. The latter, including codes of professional responsibility, bind teachers and professionals to ethical standards and codes

F. Felder (✉)
University of Birmingham, Birmingham, UK
e-mail: ffelder@bham.ac.uk

K. Trimmer et al. (eds.), *The Palgrave Handbook of Education Law for Schools*,
https://doi.org/10.1007/978-3-319-77751-1_20

of practice and are most often adopted by local school districts, teachers' associations, state education departments or other federations.

The UN Convention for the Rights of Persons with Disabilities (UNCRPD), often seen as a major improvement in the social view of disability and people with disabilities, stipulates a right to inclusive education (Article 24). It requires States Parties to ensure that

> (a) Persons with disabilities are not excluded from the general education system on the basis of disability, and that children with disabilities are not excluded from free and compulsory primary education, or from secondary education, on the basis of disability;
> (b) Persons with disabilities can access an inclusive, quality and free primary education and secondary education on an equal basis with others in the communities in which they live;
> (c) Reasonable accommodation of the individual's requirements is provided;
> (d) Persons with disabilities receive the support required, within the general education system, to facilitate their effective education; and
> (e) Effective individualized support measures are provided in environments that maximize academic and social development, consistent with the goal of full inclusion. (United Nations 2006)

The stress on "reasonable accommodations" being provided for all means that students should receive the support that makes full inclusion possible and education effective. This should include health and medical care.

With the increase in children with complex health care and medical needs in inclusive classrooms and the overall pressure towards inclusive education of all children, the principle of in loco parentis may be challenged. Important questions arise, among them: Does the requirement of inclusive schooling also cover medical or health care needs of individual children with special health care requirements? Is it within the duty of a regular school, or are these children obliged to go to a special school with designated health care professionals? If regular schools do have a duty of care and these children are allowed to be educated in regular schools, who is responsible for delivering the services needed to address their health care needs? Is it the teacher or is it the support staff?

The primary role of the teacher of students with or without disabilities is to provide a quality education. Both in the UK and the USA, the role of meeting health care and complex medical needs rests with school nurses. In the USA, the National Association of School Nurses defines their profession as follows: "School nursing, a specialized practice of nursing, protects and promotes student health, facilitates optimal development, and advances academic success.

School nurses, grounded in ethical and evidence-based practice, are the leaders who bridge health care and education, provide care coordination, advocate for quality student-centred care, and collaborate to design systems that allow individuals and communities to develop their full potential" (National Association of School Nurses 2017).

However, in reality it is often teachers who are the primary medical care provider in the classroom, even performing specialized health care procedures – for instance catheterization – that they have not been trained for. The American Federation of Teachers (AFT) defends the position that nursing services "must be provided by the school nurse, licensed practical nurse, or well-trained and competent health aide working under the direction of the school nurse" (2009, p. 31). Legally, most of the health care procedures needed to be done during school days must be supervised or performed by a state-licensed health personnel such as a registered nurse. While non-licensed personnel may be trained to perform some of the not so demanding tasks, the school nurse has both the deeper medical knowledge as well as – legally – the ultimate responsibility for deciding which tasks can be delegated and to whom, and for ensuring that the procedures are being done correctly (ibid., p. 5). Additionally, the school nurse is responsible for developing and regularly updating the student's individualized health care plan, providing general health care training to those who have regular contact with the student, for instance classmates, bus drivers or people working in the school canteen.

School nurses, however, are not common or available in all countries. Also, the legal situation in different countries is quite diverse. Some countries do not even have a legal framework that would allow these questions to be addressed. In Switzerland, for instance, no comprehensive uniform constitutional approach in planning decisions concerning the proper educational resources for students with special health care requirements is yet in place. Also, there is neither federal, nor state (cantonal) nor local law that determines the content, the amount and the degree of the responsibilities concerning special health care needs of students with disabilities among different partners. There is not even a debate about those questions within important organisations or the wider public.

The Swiss Teachers Association, the national confederation for teachers, only mentions children with special health care needs briefly in a statement on the felicity conditions for inclusive education of all students (Swiss Teachers Association 2008). The Association claims that therapeutic professionals such as physiotherapists should receive the necessary education that enables them to conceive adequate therapeutic and health care support in inclusive classrooms (in contrast to their work in special classes and special schools) and furthermore enables them to work collaboratively with regular school teachers. There is no mention, however, of the specific roles and obligations of teachers and other staff working in inclusive classrooms.

Also, because there is no comprehensive national data available, it might be assumed that students with health care or more complex needs are simply not included (or at least not in great numbers) in mainstream classes in Switzerland. Observation and exchanges with professionals in the field suggests that such children are more likely to be educated in special schools or even in schools attached to hospitals who provide care for children with very complex health care needs or after recovery from accidents and severe illnesses.

Also, Switzerland is not the only country with a lack of legislation and public debate about the care needs of those being educated in inclusive classrooms. On the contrary, very few countries have specific laws and regulations. Two countries which have specific laws and regulations are the United Kingdom (UK) and the United States of America (USA), both with a long history in inclusive education.

Therefore, this chapter takes these two countries as examples and reflects on their current legal policy, and how they are dealing with the challenges of inclusion of students with medical conditions. The aim is to shed light on the necessary conditions to make an inclusive school possible, for those students who have more complex medical and health care needs. The chapter demonstrates that dealing with these dilemmas requires a strong focus on participation of the student with disabilities and an equally committed focus on collaboration and partnership between the different stakeholders in the student's environment. This includes, among other things, a shared language concerning both the educational and medical needs of the students.

20.2 Current Legal Policy in the UK and the USA

20.2.1 The UK

In the UK, discrimination law is mainly contained in the Equality Act of 2010. This law prohibits direct and indirect discrimination against a pupil on grounds of disability, race, religion or belief, pregnancy, sex, sexual orientation and trans status. These characteristics are called "protected characteristics". The Equality Act states that schools and colleges have a duty to treat pupils with disabilities with equal consideration as those without disabilities. They must furthermore take reasonable steps to ensure that students with disabilities do not suffer a substantial disadvantage, if compared with students without disabilities. Thirdly, the Act requires local authorities, schools and colleges to plan to increase access to educational services for students with disabilities.

A substantial disadvantage must originate from one of these three sources:

1. A PCP – an acronym for provision, criterion or practice – which occurs, for instance, when a student with disabilities needs medication related to their condition but there is a school policy which states that no drugs are allowed in the school.
2. A physical feature, for instance, where access to important facilities in the school, such as toilets for people with disabilities, is not accessible to wheelchair using students.
3. The lack of an auxiliary aid, such as providing information in an accessible format for blind children, an induction loop for students with hearing aids, special computer software or additional personal help.

The Children and Families Act (2014) is also relevant to inclusive education for children with disabilities. Section 100 of this Act puts a statutory duty on governing bodies of schools and academies to arrange the support of their students with medical conditions and health care needs. It states that a pupil's health should be sufficiently supported in school so that the student can play an active and engaging role in school life, while at the same time achieving their academic potential and remaining healthy. When carrying out their statutory duties under the Children and Families Act 2014, Section 25 of the Act stresses that local authorities must do so with a view to making sure that services work together and aim at promoting children and young people's wellbeing. Furthermore, Sections 26–28 state that local authorities must work collaboratively to assess local needs. Concretely, local authorities and health bodies must have arrangements in place to plan and commission education, health and social care services jointly for children and young people with disabilities.

Individual healthcare plans usually specify the type and level of support required to meet the medical and health care needs of such students. If they also have so called "special educational needs" (SEN), coordination between the two is required. In England, schools are obliged to take account of the statutory guidance "Supporting Pupils at School with Medical Conditions" (2014). Statutory guidance means that bodies and professionals must have regard to the guidance and comply with it unless there is a good reason not to. Published by the Department of Education, this statutory guidance is accompanied by other non-statutory advice on how to support students with medical conditions and health care needs.

The responsibility in meeting medical and health care needs is shared by health bodies and local school authorities. The expectation that school nurses, teachers aids and teachers as well as the corresponding administrative bodies work together mainly originates from the National Health Service (NHS) Act 2006, Section 82, as well as from the Children Act 2004, Section 10. The latter requires local authorities to co-operate with their relevant partners, including health bodies, to safeguard and promote the welfare of children in their local area.

In practice, "key workers" or "care co-ordinators" – many of them registered nurses – are seen as essential for collaboration as a multidisciplinary approach requires co-ordinated assessment, planning and commission. In England, the guidance publication "Healthy Lives, Brighter Futures: The Strategy for Children and Young People's Health", (2009), describes and advises collaboration between agencies and reinforces Standard 8 of the National Service Framework for Children, Young Children and Maternity Services, (Children's NFS) which was published in 2004. This lays down the national standards and shows best practice guidance for children's health and social care. It also acts as a benchmark to which those working in practice and their governing boards should aspire.

Finally, the English Joint Planning and Commissioning Framework for Children, Young People and Maternity Services (2006) presents a structure to help local commissioners to strategically plan a unified system in each local area to achieve an overall picture of the needs of children and collaboration between different professionals.

20.2.2 The USA

In the USA, at the Federal level, there are three important acts in the area of inclusive education: the Individuals with Disabilities Education Act (IDEA) of 2004, Section 504 of the Rehabilitation Act of 1973, and the Americans with Disabilities Act of 1990. Since the passage of the Education for All Handicapped Children Act (EAHCA) (1975), now slightly modified, elaborated and referred to as the Individuals with Disabilities Education Act (IDEA), a free appropriate public education has been available to all children with disabilities. These acts provide the legal framework under which children with disabilities receive special education and related services. The major device for implementing the IDEA is through the use of an Individualized Education Program (IEP). This is a written statement for a child or young person with a disability that is developed, reviewed and revised and outlines educational programming.

The second important act is Section 504 of the Rehabilitation Act of 1973. This Section 504 requires the provision of "Free Appropriate Public Education" in a "Least Restrictive Environment" for all children with disabilities attending public school. Third, there is the Americans with Disabilities Act Amendments Act of 2008 (Amendments Act), which amended the Americans with Disabilities Act of 1990 (ADA).

Children in need of educational support services, such as special education or speech-language therapy, typically fall within IDEA. Examples include children whose learning achievements are below the expectation for their age, children who cannot follow classroom instructions or who show disorderly or disruptive behaviour. In contrast, children with diabetes who need school nursing assistance for the administration of medication fall under Section 504. Section 504 defines a person with a disability as "any person who has a physical or mental impairment that substantially limits one or more of that person's major life activities, or a person who has a record of such impairment or a person who is regarded as having such impairment" (Section 504 Regulations, 29 U.S.C., Art. 794). Section 504's reference to major life activities includes functions such as caring for one's self, performing manual tasks, walking, seeing, hearing, speaking, breathing, learning and working. The determination of the extent of the limitation of a major life activity due to an impairment is based on individual assessments.

Section 504's mandate is much broader than IDEA because it covers students who may not be classified under the thirteen specific disability labels covered by IDEA (Schraven and Jolly 2010). In other words: The relation between IDEA and Section 504 is that all children covered by IDEA are also covered by Section 504. However, some students covered by Section 504 may not be covered by IDEA. This includes cases such as of children with diabetes, or asthma.

Another difference between IDEA and Section 504 is the source of the funding. While IDEA is a federal law that supports special education services in public schools, Section 504 is a civil rights statute (Schraven and Jolly 2010). Thus, for example, while IDEA's focus is on access to a Free Appropriate Public Education (FAPE), Section 504 emphasizes equal treatment for children with disabilities participating in federally funded programs. Unlike IDEA, Section 504 and the ADA Amendments Act (2008) are antidiscrimination laws and unfunded mandates, which means there are no monetary compensations to ensure that their mandate is carried out (Zirkel and Weathers 2015). As a result, the burden rests with the states to determine how to provide for students who require more extensive support.

IDEA requires public schools to develop an Individualised Education Program or IEP for every student with a disability who meets the federal and state requirements for special education. This eligibility is bound to 14 categories outlined in IDEA. These include: autism, deaf-blindness, deafness, developmental delay, emotional and behavioural disorders, hearing impairment, intellectual disability, multiple disability, orthopedic impairment, other health impairment, specific learning disability, speech and language impairment, traumatic brain injury and visual impairment, including blindness. The IEP must be designed so that it provides the student with a free appropriate public education, or FAPE. The IDEA requires that an IEP is written with respect to the needs of each student who is eligible under the IDEA. An IEP must also meet state regulations. Individualized Education Programs (IEP) and 504 Plans are federal regulations put in place to guarantee an education for children with special needs.

IEP and 504 Plans are two separate plans with distinct requirements although there can be some overlap between the two. Each plan creates a legal document which outlines the child's individual needs and accommodations while at school. Parents and schools generally work together to create a plan for the child. Some state laws require a specific health care plan to be in place for all students who require medication and/or treatment while attending school. This could be a 504 Plan, IEP, or another document called an Individualized Health Care Plan (IHCP or IHP). IHCP's or IHP's give detailed information about the medical services the child needs at school. Very broadly, the question of whether a child needs an IEP or 504 Plan is that of how special the accommodation needs to be. If the child needs something different than what is already available at the school, in other words a special or individual accommodation, then an IEP or a 504 Plan will be put in place. If there are already systems in place to meet the child's medical and health care needs, then only an IHCP may be needed. For most schools, this includes systems as to how to deal with taking pills, food allergies, asthma and other quite common health issues.

IDEA considers a medical service to be a related service if it is limited to diagnostic and evaluation purposes. For instance, the Supreme Court case Irving Independent School District vs Tatro (1984) stipulated that medical services should be provided by the school if the child has a disability that requires special education, the service is needed to help a child with a disability benefit from special education, and a nurse or other qualified person who is not a physician can provide the service. The case concerned a child named Amber Tatro, who was born with spina bifida. Amber had various health issues, including a bladder condition that required her to be catheterized several times during the day. The procedure called clean intermittent catheterization (CIC) was relatively simple and could be learnt by a nonprofessional in a few hours. In 1979, when Amber was three, the Irving Independent School District in Texas formed a special education program for her, which did not include CIC. Her parents requested this provision from the school, but it refused. The Tatros subsequently filed suit and claimed that this was a violation of the Education for All Handicapped Children Act or Public Law (PL) 94–142 because this law would require schools that receive federal funding to provide "related services". Related services would include school health services, so that a child with disability can benefit from special education. The Tatros also cited the Rehabilitation Act of 1973, which bars a child with disability from being excluded from or denied the benefits of a program that received federal funds. The U.S. Supreme Court held that under those definitions, CIC in fact was a school health service. Further, it noted that without CIC, Amber would be unable to attend school in general and thus would not benefit from special education in particular.

In a subsequent Supreme Court case, Cedar Rapids Community School District v Garret F (1999), the court continued to state that services by physicians or hospitals are not allowable in IEPs but indicated that nursing services, such as clean intermittent catheterization and full-time nursing can be related services if the child requires them to attend school. The case concerned Garret F., a student in Cedar Rapids, Iowa, who was badly hurt in a motorcycle accident when he was four years old. It left him quadriplegic and in need of a ventilator. During the day, he needed constant personal supervision and an attendant to care for his health need. The attendant needed, for instance, to do the urinary catheterization, suctioning of his tracheostomy tube, and observing of any possible respiratory distress. From the age of kindergarten through to the fourth grade, his family provided this personal care and attendance during the school day. When he was in the fifth grade, however, his mother asked the school board to supply the needed health care services, but the board rejected it. His family took the case to the Supreme Court. In their decision, the justices of the Supreme Court ruled that a school board was obliged to fund such related services to help guarantee that students such as Garret were included in public schools.

Both Supreme Court cases clearly show the legal pressure towards the inclusion of children with severe medical needs in regular classrooms in the

USA. However, even countries with a long tradition in inclusive education, such as the UK or the USA are facing challenges on different levels.

20.3 Problems and Challenges

The inclusion of many children with a wide range of disabilities in regular classrooms is making the provision of health care and medical services outside of special educational settings a larger and more complex issue. Adequate classroom and school modifications (e.g. ramps and accessible sinks and toilets) and support personnel (e.g. instructional assistants, school nurses, or special education teachers) are needed in more classrooms and schools in all those countries that have adopted the UNCRPD.

Challenges include, but are not limited to, confusion about the scope of different services, the responsibilities of professionals providing it and the collaboration between different groups of professionals, including teachers. These are reflected in difficulties in understanding eligibility for, as well as implementation and provision of health care services to students with medical and health care needs.

In the USA, for instance, the legal justification for the provision of related services without qualifying for special education placement can be found in Section 504 of the Rehabilitation Act of 1973. This prohibits discrimination based on disability within federal and federally assisted programs. Unfortunately, in practice, there are schools that still provide few services. Children with chronic health issues such as asthma or diabetes, who usually function well in the regular classroom, still need consideration for related services or special services such as access to medication (for children with asthma) or no pets in the classroom (for children with severe allergies). Some of the provisions needed do not fit well in the established laws and regulations, even if they are well developed and already addressing important issues, as in the USA or the UK.

There has also been reported uncertainty about the responsibility for, and the administration of, complex nursing treatment and therapy in schools (Sneed et al. 2004). State and local guidelines have inconsistencies about which health care professionals should prescribe the type and amount of physical, occupational or speech therapy. There is also a frequent lack of provision of related services for children who may not qualify for special education but who have chronic diseases and disabling conditions that impair their ability to attend and participate in school. This may reflect back to the supposedly unclear distinction between educationally related service and rehabilitation services. Not surprisingly, therefore, the lack of co-operation between different government departments and services is often cited as a major barrier to inclusion (O'Hanlon 2017).

In practice, these inconsistencies often lead to confusion about responsibilities as well as to difficulties in collaboration between different groups of professionals. In the UK, for instance, there is no explicit statutory obligation on the NHS or the local authority to act as the lead agency. This can lead to a child "drifting" between those agencies while each authority blames the other for service failures. Within a school setting, numerous service providers participate in their care. Collaboration and partnership among different stakeholders – which also include the child and the parents – is important, so that the student with medical and health care needs is not only safe at school, but also able to learn and make progress. However, delivery of this care is often fractured. When supports are compartmentalized in that the teacher only attends to academic learning and progress and the school nurse addresses solely the health care needs, problems may emerge.

However, an overlap in roles, can be seen as problematic. For instance, in the USA, the school nurse and the special education teacher share the majority of service implementation responsibility in the school setting. Due to an overlap in roles, coupled with the increasing issue of limited staff support due to austerity measures, questions about the scope and exact content of professional responsibilities relative to care for these students often exist. It is important that there is both a clear definition of the distinct roles of school nurse and special education teacher but they must work together in a highly collaborative environment.

20.4 Focus on Participation and the Need for Continuity and Cooperation Among Different Professionals

Both the clarification of the responsibilities of different professionals as well as overlap in collaboration can be seen as very important, not only generally for the success of inclusive education, but also more specifically for the meeting of medical and health care needs of children who require special assistance in schools.

This includes and maybe starts with funding cycles that determine the amount of aid and support a pupil will get, and for what reasons. Funding of special education is being identified as a key factor in the success of inclusion. In countries like Denmark, Finland or New Zealand, funds follow students and not schools and, and this opens the way to more inclusive practices. This would lead, at least ideally, to continuity and cooperation among different professionals rather than separate and perhaps conflicting domains (Sneed et al. 2004).

According to Norwich and Eaton (2015), the conditions for successful multidisciplinary cooperation include strong leadership and a clear vision of what is to be achieved and how, conflict management that includes a no blame culture, time for reflective learning and opportunities for joint training. The last two conditions highlight the need for exchange and collaboration apart or distinct from the daily struggle in the field where time for reflection is often lacking and where there is pressure for instant solutions and actions.

Aligned to these challenges and problems is also a considerable lack of common language that bridges education and medical or health care issues. The final question in this chapter is therefore not concerned with who provides the service, or on what legal bases are these decisions being made. Instead, the question is more fundamental: What model could provide for a common language that would be able to bridge professions and their aims as well as being clear enough to make potentially inform the legal framework of laws and regulations?

There is reason to think, especially if we think in global dimensions, that the World Health Organization's International Classification of Functioning, Disability and Health (ICF) could provide for such a framework of common language (World Health Organization 2001). The ICF model itself represents a bio-psychological-social model and aims at integrating the medial and social model of disability. Based on the critique of its predecessor ICIDH for being too deficit oriented, static and medical, the ICF took one central insight of the progressive disabilities community into account: the fact that disability is influenced by social and cultural norms and the environment where people live in. Disability in the ICF is thus seen as a phenomenon that stems both from individual and environmental factors that interrelate and influence each other. Participation and activities are seen as including health, relationships, competencies and development (Simeonsson et al. 2003).

Judith Hollenweger (2011) is one of a group of researchers who have expanded the model to include the educational vision. In her view, this implies that educational provision has to be seen as a key environmental influence on functioning, and that educational and developmental goals are linked to the participation aspect of disability. In the ICF approach, assessment is personalised. Hollenweger (2011) suggests that educational systems that respect the idea of a continuum of functioning should also offer a continuum of services based on the idea of personalising education. Her approach distinguishes three different information types. Information of the type 1 contains information that is independent of contexts and can be generated by a specialist in a clinical setting, e.g. diagnosis of a disease and establishment of an impairment (ICD-10, body functions). This information is context-free, which means it is valid independent of the family situation or the current life situation of the child. Information of the type 2 can hypothetically be generated by one person, but is dependent on temporal and spatial dimensions of specific life situations. The ability to learn, for instance, can only be observed in a situation where learning occurs. Such context-specific information, e.g. on activities and participation or on environmental factors, can only be validly assessed if a variety of data from different occurrences or specific settings is compared and validated. While information types 1 and 2 can be objectively assessed (both used in basic assessment module of the procedure), some information of type 3 depends on contextual factors, such as the availability of resources, cultural values, perceived treatment priorities or prognosis on future functioning of the child, and so on.

The reported lack of collaboration obviously has different sources. One of them is the lack of resources, in particular the low numbers of available school nurses. In the UK, for instance, due to austerity measures, there is a severe lack of available school nurses, putting children with chronic health conditions, such as asthma, epilepsy or diabetes, at risk (Connett 2017). A second lack of collaboration is due to the complexity of the different legal sources concerning the responsibilities – and even their acknowledgment – for care of children with medical and health care needs. In the USA, for instance, with the complex relationship between federal law and civil rights law, it is very difficult for parents, carers but also professionals to determine the source for funding for necessary health care. Without legal advice it is very likely that some children with chronical health care issues end up with no legal decision concerning their case, or with a decision that acknowledges their need under Section 504 of the Rehabilitation which includes no funding.

A third source, finally, can be seen in the lack of language, apart from legal considerations, that establishes and yet makes collaboration possible in the first place. With a coherent and overarching language that – for instance – the ICF provides, it is possible to determine, both in medical and educational terms, the needs of a child in focus. It thus not only provides new grounds to determine eligibility criteria in practice (Hollenweger and Moretti 2012). It can be suspected, that, with coherent eligibility processes in place, the way legal procedures and professional regulations are drafted can become more coherent, both on national and international level. This would help children with disabilities in need for covering both their physical and academic needs in regular classrooms around the world.

Reference

American Federation of Teachers. (2009). *The medically fragile child in the school setting: Caring for children with special healthcare needs in the school setting*. Washington, DC: American Federation of Teachers.

Connett, D. (2017, August 25). School nurse shortage "Putting children's lives at risk". *The Guardian*.

Conte, A. E. (2000). In loco parentis: Alive and well. *Jurisprudence, 121*(1), 195.

Department of Education. (2014). *Supporting pupils with medical conditions at school*. [online]. Available at: https://www.gov.uk/government/publications/supporting-pupils-at-school-with-medical-conditions—3. Accessed 31 Oct 2017.

Department of Health. (2004). *National service framework for children, young children and maternity services*. [online]. Available at: https://www.gov.uk/government/publications/national-service-framework-children-young-people-and-maternity-services. Accessed 31 Oct 2017.

Department of Health. (2009). *Healthy lives, brighter futures: The strategy for children and young people's health*. [online]. Available at: http://webarchive.nationalarchives.gov.uk/+/http://www.dh.gov.uk/en/Publicationsandstatistics/Publications/PublicationsPolicyAndGuidance/DH_094400. Accessed 31 Oct 2017.

HM Government. (2006). *English joint planning and commissioning framework for children, young people and maternity services*. [online]. Available at: http://www.regionalcommissioning.co.uk/resources/A9%20DfES%20Joint%20Planning%20and%20Commissioning.pdf. Accessed 31 Oct 2017.

Hollenweger, J. (2011). Development of an ICF-based eligibility procedure for education in Switzerland. *BMC Public Health, 11*(Suppl 4), S7.

Hollenweger, J., & Moretti, M. (2012). Using the international classification of functioning, disability and health children and youth version in education systems: A new approach to eligibility. *American Journal of Physical Medicine & Rehabilitation, 91*(13 Suppl 1), 97–102.

Legislation.gov.uk. (2014). *Children and Families Act from 2014*. [online]. Available at: http://www.legislation.gov.uk/ukpga/2014/6/contents/enacted. Accessed 31 Oct 2017.

Legislation.gov.uk. (2016). *Equality Act 2010*. [online]. Available at: http://www.legislation.gov.uk/ukpga/2010/15/contents. Accessed 31 Oct 2017.

National Association of School Nurses. (2011, revised 2017). *Position statement: Role of the school nurse*. [online]. Available at: https://schoolnursenet.nasn.org/blogs/

nasn-profile/2017/07/28/chronic-health-conditions-students-with-the-role-of-the-school-nurse. Accessed 31 Oct 2017.
National Association of School Nurses. (2017). *Definition of school nursing*. [online]. Available at: https://www.nasn.org/home. Accessed 31 Oct 2017.
Norwich, B., & Eaton, A. (2015). The new special education needs (SEN) legislation in England and implications for services for children and young people with social, emotional and behavioural difficulties. *Emotional and Behavioural Difficulties, 20*(2), 117–132.
O'Hanlon, C. (Ed.). (2017). *Inclusive education in Europe*. London: Routledge.
Pufpaff, L. A., McIntosh, C. E., Thomas, C., Elam, M., & Irwin, M. K. (2015). Meeting the health care needs of students with severe disabilities in the school setting: Collaboration between school nurses and special education teachers. *Psychology in the Schools, 52*(7), 683–701.
Schraven, J., & Jolly, J. L. (2010). Section 504 in American public schools: An ongoing response to change. *American Educational History Journal, 37*(1/2), 419–436.
Simeonsson, R. J., Leonardi, M., Lollar, D., Bjorck-Akesson, E., Hollenweger, J., & Martinuzzi, A. (2003). Applying the International Classification of Functioning, Disability and Health (ICF) to measure childhood disability. *Disability and Rehabilitation, 25*(11–12), 602–610.
Sneed, R., May, W., & Stencel, C. (2004). Policy versus practice: Comparison of prescriping therapy and durable medical equipment in medical and educational settings. *Pediatrics, 114*(5), 612–625.
Swiss Teachers Association (Dachverband Lehrerinnen und Lehrer Schweiz). (2008). *Gelingensbedingungen für eine integrierte Förderung aller*. https://www.lch.ch/publikationen/stellungnahmen/dokument/gelingensbedingungen_fuer_eine_integrierte_foerderung_fuer_alle/
United Nations. (1999). *Convention on the rights of the child*. Geneva: United Nations.
United Nations. (2006). *Convention on the rights of persons with disabilities*. Geneva: United Nations.
World Health Organization. (1990). *International classification of diseases and related health problems (ICD-10)*. Geneva: World Health Organization.
World Health Organization. (2001). *International classification of functioning, disability and health*. Geneva: World Health Organization.
Zirkel, P. A., & Weathers, J. M. (2015). Section 504-only students: National incidence data. *Journal of Disability Policy Studies, 26*(3), 184–193.

US Laws

Americans with Disabilities Act of 1990, 42 U.S.C. § 12101.
Americans with Disabilities Act Amendments Act of 2008, Pub. L. No. 110-325.
Education for All Handicapped Children Act from 1975, Pub. L. No. 94-142.

Individuals with Disabilities Act from 1997, Pub. L. No. 105-17.
Section 504 of the Rehabilitation Act of 1973, Pub. L. No. 93-112.

US Supreme Court Cases

Irving Independent School District vs Tatro, 468 U.S. 833 (1984).
Cedar Rapids Community School District v Garret F, 526 U.S. 66 (1999).

Section III

International Context and Rights of the Child

21

The Rights of the Child: Are We Creating a World in Which All Children Are Enabled to Reach Their Full Potential?

Yvonne S. Findlay

The last twelve months has brought into living rooms, in safe and secure countries, images that should cause governments to question their responsibility towards the world's children. A battered, bruised and bewildered child sitting in an ambulance after yet another shelling of his home town in Syria; schoolgirls kidnapped in Africa; lifeless little bodies washed up on Europe's shores; children wandering across the European continent looking for a place to stop, rest and be fed. It is estimated that there are about 25,000 displaced children in Europe alone, with about 10,000 of them with no adult to care for them. What should the response of educators be in the face of the conflicting challenges posed by vast numbers of dispossessed people and the underlying current of suspicion which travels with them?

This chapter will consider five international statements: The United Nations Convention on the Rights of the Child (UNCRC); A world fit for children; The Universal Declaration of Human Rights; The United Nations Millennium Declaration; The state of the world's children. From these five statements, three imperatives for action are suggested – economic, educational and moral – and challenges posed regarding legislation, finance and acceptance to meet the imperatives.

Y. S. Findlay (✉)
University of Southern Queensland, Toowoomba, QLD, Australia
e-mail: Yvonne.Findlay@usq.edu.au

K. Trimmer et al. (eds.), *The Palgrave Handbook of Education Law for Schools*,
https://doi.org/10.1007/978-3-319-77751-1_21

21.1 The UNCRC (United Nations Convention on the Rights of the Child)

The UNCRC (United Nations Convention on the Rights of the Child) provides a base from which to build a response. The convention clearly sets out responsibilities in regards to the children trapped in adult created circumstances. All young people under the age of 18 are considered to come under the protection of the convention – unless a specific country has set the age of majority earlier.

Article 4 of the UNCRC states: States Parties shall undertake all appropriate legislative, administrative, and other measures for the implementation of the rights recognized in the present Convention. With regard to economic, social and cultural rights, States Parties shall undertake such measures to the maximum extent of their available resources and, where needed, within the framework of international co-operation.

Articles 28 and 29 of the UN Convention on the Rights of the Child (UNCRC) have particular significance for education authorities and educators.

21.2 Article 28

1. States Parties recognize the right of the child to an education and with a view to achieving this right progressively and on the basis of equal opportunity, they shall, in particular:

    (a) Make primary education compulsory and available free to all;
    (b) Encourage the development of different forms of secondary education, including general and vocational education, make them available and accessible to every child, and take appropriate measures such as the introduction of free education and offering financial assistance in case of need;
    (c) Make higher education accessible to all on the basis of capacity by every appropriate means;
    (d) Make educational and vocational information and guidance available and accessible to all children;
    (e) Take measures to encourage regular attendance at schools and the reduction of drop-out rates.

2. States Parties shall take all appropriate measures to ensure that school discipline is administered in a manner consistent with the child's human dignity and in conformity with the present Convention.

3. States Parties shall promote and encourage international cooperation in matters relating to education, in particular with a view to contributing to the elimination of ignorance and illiteracy throughout the world and facilitating access to scientific and technical knowledge and modern teaching methods. In this regard, particular account shall be taken of the needs of developing countries.

21.3 Article 29

1. States Parties agree that the education of the child shall be directed to:
    (a) The development of the child's personality, talents and mental and physical abilities to their fullest potential;
    (b) The development of respect for human rights and fundamental freedoms, and for the principles enshrined in the Charter of the United Nations;
    (c) The development of respect for the child's parents, his or her own cultural identity, language and values, for the national values of the country in which the child is living, the country from which he or she may originate, and for civilizations different from his or her own;
    (d) The preparation of the child for responsible life in a free society, in the spirit of understanding, peace, tolerance, equality of sexes, and friendship among all peoples, ethnic, national and religious groups and persons of indigenous origin;
    (e) The development of respect for the natural environment.
2. No part of the present article or article 28 shall be construed so as to interfere with the liberty of individuals and bodies to establish and direct educational institutions, subject always to the observance of the principle set forth in paragraph 1 of the present article and to the requirements that the education given in such institutions shall conform to such minimum standards as may be laid down by the State.

Both articles could provide a global education foundation of rights, responsibilities and core curriculum. A knowledge and understanding of the UNCRC provisions becomes essential for educators if the global challenge of educating the world's children is to be met. The concept of "think global, act local" should be applied as school educators adopt and adapt the UNCRC provisions to meet the needs of all children in their care, whether permanent resident, citizen or refugee seeking shelter.

An integral part of the Rights of the Child is that "State Parties recognise the right of the child to an education…" (Article 28.1). This right is mere words on paper for so many children in today's conflict stricken world. An ABC news report of 15 February, 2017, ran the headline "Refugee camp teachers struggle to teach displaced Syrian children". The report included the words of the Director of the Wisdom School at the Atmeh camp in Syria, "There is no future for these children, no schools or university for them because of war" (Ahmed Ibrahim).

21.4 The Universal Declaration of Human Rights

As well as the rights set out in the UNCRC, there are parallel rights set out in the "Universal Declaration of Human Rights" (1948). Article 26 states:

1. Everyone has the right to education. Education shall be free, at least in the elementary and fundamental stages. Elementary education shall be compulsory. Technical and professional education shall be made generally available and higher education shall be equally accessible to all on the basis of merit.
2. Education shall be directed to the full development of the human personality and to the strengthening of respect for human rights and fundamental freedoms. It shall promote understanding, tolerance and friendship among all nations, racial or religious groups, and shall further the activities of the United Nations for the maintenance of peace.
3. Parents have a prior right to choose the kind of education that shall be given to their children.

21.5 The United Nations Millennium Declaration

The "United Nations Millennium Declaration" (UN 2000) set out to reaffirm the work of the organisation as a force for unifying countries towards creating a world in which peace, prosperity and justice were pre-eminent. Included in the Declaration is paragraph 19 which states the resolve: "To ensure that, by the same date (2015), children everywhere, boys and girls alike, will be able to complete a full course of primary schooling and that girls and boys will have equal access to all levels of education" (p. 5). To meet the targets set by the

UN, eight Millennium Development Goals (MDGs) were set to be reached by 2015. The eight goals are:

1. Eradicate extreme poverty and hunger
2. Achieve universal primary education
3. Promote gender equality and empower women
4. Reduce child mortality
5. Improve maternal health
6. Combat HIV/AIDS, malaria and other diseases
7. Ensure environmental sustainability
8. Develop a global partnership for development

Goal 2 of the MDGs reflected directly the statement from the Millennium Declaration by aiming to provide primary education for every child.

A report on how these goals were being met was drafted by the UN in 2015. The data provided for Goal 2 indicated that considerable progress had been made in the provision of primary schooling for the world's children. The enrolment rate for primary aged children has risen from around 83% in 2000 to about 90% in 2015. However, there are two distinct issues to consider. Firstly, an enrolment rate of at least 97% is used as the benchmark figure for universal enrolment to have been achieved. Secondly, the aggregated data does not reflect the differences found in various parts of the world. For example, in sub-Saharan Africa, despite the difficulties of high levels of poverty, armed conflicts and other emergencies, the enrolment numbers has more than doubled from 62 to 149 million children. The numbers in other parts of the globe such as Syria indicate a worrying trend of falling enrolments as a consequence of continued conflict. It is estimated that only 12% of Syrian refugee children in Lebanon are enrolled in a school setting.

21.6 A World Fit for Children

A "World fit for Children" was adopted by the United Nations General Assembly on 10 May, 2002. Ten principles and objectives were stated in this document as a sound basis for creating a world fit for children. Educators across the world have the opportunity to make a difference to the lives of children in many ways. One such way is embracing the "Ten Pillars of a Good Childhood" in this Decade for Childhood (2012–2022), an initiative led by The Association for Childhood Education International (ACEI n.d.) and the Alliance for Childhood. The "Ten Pillars of a Good Childhood" mirror the provisions in the United Nations (UN) document and provide a check list against which can be measured the effectiveness of strategies towards creating a world fit for children. The Ten Pillars are:

1. Safe & secure places for living & learning & access to health care, clothing, shelter, & nutritious food
2. Strong families & loving, consistent caregivers
3. Social interactions & friendship
4. Creative play & physical activity
5. Appreciation & stewardship of the natural environment
6. Creative expression through music, dance, drama, and the other arts
7. Education that develops the full capacities of the child – cognitive, physical, social, emotional, & ethical
8. Supportive, nurturing, child-friendly communities
9. Growing independence & decision making
10. Children & youth participating in community life

International educators share a responsibility to know about and give serious consideration as to how these principles are enacted in education systems.

21.7 The State of the World's Children

The UNICEF report, "The State of the World's Children 2016; A fair chance for every child" reminds us that:

> "If the soul of a society can be judged by the way it treats its most vulnerable members, then by a similar measure, a society's future – its long term prospects for sustainable growth, stability and shared prosperity – can be predicted by the degree to which it provides every child with a fair chance in life" (p. 1) The report authors contend that unless inequity is tackled today, in 2030 60 million children of primary school age will be out of school.

National obligations under international law are clear, therefore. The implications are of paramount importance to the legislators of signatory countries. It is in the implementation that the words come off the page and begin to take shape in providing a society that cares for its children. As Alderson (2016) questions, "How can we be sure international rights are realities, not merely passing ideologies?" (p. 1). The first step is for governments who have adopted the UNCRC to enshrine the provisions into domestic law thus protecting children's rights. The UN Committee on the Rights of the Child (2003) contended that such a move "should mean that the provisions of the Convention can be directly invoked before the courts and applied by national authorities…economic, social and cultural rights, as well as civil and political rights, must be regarded as justiciable."

Arising from all of the sources mentioned in this chapter thus far, there are three imperatives to consider. Firstly the word "development" in the MDGs implies a link to the economic health of a nation state; that every child having a sound, basic education will provide an economic boost for a country. Secondly, there is the imperative to have an education infrastructure to provide schools and teachers to provide the education. Thirdly, there is a moral imperative that we all share to ensure that the UNCRC provisions are met in our own national and cultural context.

21.8 Economic Imperative

"Up to half of the world's jobs – around 2 billion – are at high risk of disappearing due to automation in the coming decades……Only quality education for all children can generate the needed skills, prevent worsening inequality and provide a prosperous future for all" (ICFGEO 2016, p. 12). The International Commission on Financing Global Education Opportunity (ICFGEO) noted that globally there is a turn from high employment in manual labour type jobs to automation. The high employment areas of the industrial age are making way for jobs requiring particular skills in technology and critical thinking. In countries where the skill gap is not closed, economic growth will be stunted. The result of an economic is slump is a rise in unemployment numbers. The cumulative effect is significant because as under and unemployment grows then wages are less and, consequently, spending is less. The spiral effect is of an economic slump and national budgets less able to support those who need financial help the most. Of particular concern is the evidence that global and domestic spending in education is not a priority in many countries. Delors (1996) presaged in his report, "Learning: the treasure within", the necessity of appropriate education for all children to meet the needs of the 21st century. He stated that "…education is at the heart of both personal and community development" (p. 17). The report proposed four pillars as the foundation for learning in the 21st century: *learning to live together; learning to know; learning to do; learning to be.* The concepts behind each pillar go beyond the traditional curriculum of content silos and encourage skills such as team work, creativity, problem solving and critical thinking as well as numeracy and literacy. The development of these skills enables future generations to work in the increased globalised information and knowledge economy.

The economic imperative to provide a quality education for all children is clear. To enable this to happen, governments need to enact budget policies to meet the educational demands of employers and the cognitive developmental needs of its children. Legislation for education should reflect these needs and ensure that, as far as is possible, the provisions of both the Universal Declaration of Human Rights and UNCRC for free and compulsory primary education for all children, are met. Unless children are prepared for entering the globalised and digitised work place, then a country's economy will suffer and the standard of living gaps, evident across all regions of the world, will widen. The 21st century learner will be able to capitalise on global earning opportunities while those ill prepared will fall further behind economically.

21.9 Education Imperative

The multiple UN declarations and resolutions noted above all include a clear statement that there should be universal free primary education for all children. MDG 2 is clear about that expectation. How can this be achieved? The scale of the challenge is beyond the means of the poorest countries and therefore requires a global response. The ICFGEO envisions the setting up of Multilateral Development Banks (MDBs) to raise finance for global funding for education thus enabling free primary education worldwide. The vision for this investment is that "...all classrooms – from the remotest village and the most desolate refugee camp to the most crowded city – will be online with a scalable digital infrastructure" (p. 4). The implications for learning and teaching are the need to have teachers with the confidence to work in online environments and who can adapt their practice to meet the needs of their students rather than the needs of a set curriculum. In turn, then, there is a need for teacher educators who can equip teachers with the skills to meet the challenges of the refugee camp as well as the inner-city school. This demands of the teacher educator a global perspective to education and an understanding of the provisions of the UNCRC. If governments take their responsibilities under the UN conventions and resolutions, which they have signed and agreed to implement, then Standards for Teachers prevalent in a number of countries should reflect this global concern. A good example of this inclusion in standards for teachers can be found in the General Teaching Council

Scotland (GTCS) "Code of Professionalism and Conduct" (2012). In the statement on the purpose of the code, the GTCS states that it is based on the general principles of the UNCRC. Section 2.7 states that teachers should "... be aware of the general principles of the UN Convention on the Rights of the Child..." At the time of writing, the author is not aware of this specific inclusion in any other nation's standards for teacher registration.

The provision of teachers in remote and troubled parts of the world should be of concern to the international community. There is the well-established "Médecins sans Frontièrs". Perhaps it is now the time to consider a task force of "Teachers without Borders" who can travel to the areas of most need and provide basic education to children trapped in refugee camps, for example, as a result war and/or terrorism. If governments who have endorsed international conventions such as the UNCRC take their responsibilities as members of the global community then the outworking of that responsibility may be to provide a funding and legislative framework to allow for teachers to be where they are most needed in times of crisis. The MDBs, supported by finance from the developed countries of the world, would be an appropriate funding body for this task force. Having online classrooms / learning and teaching spaces is one aspect of universal education provision, but those spaces require appropriate adult mediation for the children to be able to access appropriate learning resources and make sense of them. It may be that both teachers and teacher educators have a role in training some of the adult residents of the camps to be the mediators. A body such as a possible "Teachers without borders" could be a major force in bringing diverse international communities together through children being able to communicate and learn about each other's lives.

21.10 Moral Imperative

What exactly is the role of school and teachers in 21st Century schools? The neo-liberal zeitgeist of standardisation would dictate that schools are about attainment targets for students and the nation state's place in the PISA rankings in literacy, numeracy and science. Standardised testing such as NAPLAN (National Assessment Programme Language and Numeracy) in Australia has evolved into high stakes measurements of education performance for schools and classroom teachers. Evidence points to the narrowing of the curriculum when classroom practice is judged by national standardised tests. (Au 2007; Black and Wiliam 1998; James and Tanner 1993) The curriculum designed and the teaching strategies for meeting national test outcomes reflect too closely what Freire (1972) designated the "banking system" (p. 46) in which the teacher deposits information in to the student's mind and this information is then withdrawn in a test situation. The test then measures memory rather than knowledge and understanding. Freire considers this a form of oppression because the content of the curriculum is decided by an outside body – usually the government of the day – and transmitted to the students. The students have no say in what they learn and are passive recipients of the curriculum content. In this model, there is no place for the development of critical thinking skills, nor of deep inquiry strategies.

In contrast, Rennie et al. (2012) regard schools as having the "social role of preparing our youth to be responsible adults and sensible citizens" (p. viii). The authors see the starting point of this approach is the "proposition that we live in a global community" (p. viii). The concept of community suggests a "sense of fellowship, affinity, identity of character and joint ownership" (p. viii). In this digitalised and connected world, the community is global and the attributes of community membership identified are equally applicable. If students are to be "responsible adults and sensible citizens" of this global community, then the school curriculum needs to reflect a global perspective on knowledge and understanding of what matters in the connected world community.

Article 29 of the UNCRC sets out 5 guiding principles on which school education should be developed.

In Scotland, the General Teaching Council Standards for Leadership and Management requires, "Embracing locally and globally the educational and social values of sustainability, equality and justice and recognising the rights and responsibilities of future as well as current generations" (Personal Values and Commitment GTCS 2012). Building such expectations into teacher standards will raise the bar as far as the requirement for teachers to be globally aware as well as knowledgeable about the UNCRC provisions. But what of the children to whom these provisions apply? How can they or their family's judge whether their rights are being met? There is a moral responsibility to include teaching about the Declaration of Human Rights and the UNCRC as a first step towards creating a world in which children know that they have a place and that they are respected and safeguarded. Alderson (2016), in discussing citizenship education and its possible dilemmas, asserts that knowledge about rights should be a crucial inclusion in school curricula. She comments that "…rights serve as powerful structures that can help to prevent and remedy wrongs, and they work as enduring high standards and aspirations" (p. 1). However, if human rights and children's rights are not enshrined within the domestic laws of individual countries then they are toothless tigers without impact on real lives. There are those who see children as "persons in the making" (Brighouse 2000, p. 11) rather than as individuals who are living full lives in the present. The opening statement of Governance fit for Children reminds us that "... the Convention confirmed the status of the child, who has to be considered as a person, not as an object of adults' benevolence, entitled with dignity and rights" (2014, p. 1).

It is easy for children to become "invisible" when they are considered unable to speak for themselves. Article 12 of the UNCRC states:

> States Parties shall assure to the child who is capable of forming his or her own views the right to express those views freely in all matters affecting the child, the views of the child being given due weight in accordance with the age and maturity of the child.

This concept is further developed in the "Ten Pillars of a Good Childhood" numbers 9 and 10 which infers that children are capable in being involved in decision making about their lives.

Pillar 9: Growing independence and decision making.
Pillar 10: Children and young people participating in community life.

The outworking of these two pillars in society is commented on by Pulkkinen (2012). She comments in regards to Pillar 9 that parents should be offered support to understand their child's cognitive development and the factors that impact on the development. In regards to Pillar 10, there needs to be recognition that "Childhood is a unique stage of its own in human development, as is old age" (p. 167). Pulkkinen's views on these two pillars reinforce the understanding that children are real people at a specific point in their development and not people in the making simply waiting in the wings of life's stage until they reach a certain age.

21.11 Challenges

> *We reaffirm our obligation to take action to promote and protect the rights of each child – every human being below the age of 18 years, including adolescents. We are determined to respect the dignity and to secure the well-being of all children. We acknowledge that the Convention on the Rights of the Child, the most universally embraced human rights treaty in history, and the Optional Protocols thereto, contain a comprehensive set of international legal standards for the protection and well-being*

> *of children. We also recognize the importance of other international instruments relevant for children.* (United Nations General Assembly, 11 October 2002)

Three particular challenges arise from all of the above. They are those of legislation, finance and acceptance.

The challenge of *legislation* lies in the need for countries to not only sign the UNCRC but to embrace and enact the provisions of the Declaration into domestic law. Signatories to the act are but paying lip service to its provisions if the core tenets of the Declaration are not made visible in law and in practice. For example, the treatment of refugee children can fall short of the provisions under Article 22 of the Convention:

> States Parties shall take appropriate measures to ensure that a child who is seeking refugee status or who is considered a refugee in accordance with applicable international or domestic law and procedures shall, whether unaccompanied or accompanied by his or her parents or by any other person, receive appropriate protection and humanitarian assistance in the enjoyment of applicable rights set forth in the present Convention and in other international human rights or humanitarian instruments to which the said States are Parties.

In other words, nation states who are signatories to the Convention have at the very least a moral obligation to protect refugee children through the enactment of appropriate legislation into domestic law. Subsumed within Article 22 is the right of the child to free education provision wherever they are resident. The challenge is to legislators to enshrine these rights within domestic law so that lip service becomes practical service.

The challenge of *finance* lies within the purview of governments to include the needs and rights of children in their national budgets. Internationally there are a variety of responses to the specific inclusion of a "children's budget" in national budgeting plans. For example, in Lithuania civil servants considered it too problematic to analyse indirect and direct funding for matters relating to children to be quantified within their national budget. Wales, on the other hand, has initiated a budget analysis to indicate funding for children every year from the 2014–2015 budget. The Swedish government includes a section on "Childs Rights Policy" in their budget (HRC 2014). Citizens and tax payers have a crucial role in challenging governments on their spending priorities regarding the rights and welfare of all children within our national borders.

The challenge of *acceptance* is recognition that children are not adults in the making but people in their own right at whatever age and stage of development.

One challenge could be for schools to have a student council if one does not already exist. This would allow children to have a voice in an environment which they inhabit for many years of their lives.

There are those, however, who do not have the opportunity to be represented by a student council or any other student body. These are the refugee children who arrive at a national border, unaccompanied and with no documentation to indicate who they are, where they have come from or their date of birth. A report by the UK Refugee Council (2012) discusses the dichotomy faced by immigration at the front line of determining the status of people wishing to enter the country. On the one hand, national security and unauthorised entry to the country is of high importance. On the other hand, however, is the need to fulfil obligations under the UNCRC to care for refugee children and allow them sanctuary from conflict in their homeland. Specific issues arise when the age of the young person cannot be established because they have no identification and their appearance suggests that they are possibly over the age of 18 years. The report cites five stories of "age disputed" (p. 5) young people who were initially assessed as being over 18 years of age but later found to be between the ages of 14 and 16 years. Without the intervention of a body such as the Refugee Council, these young people would have been sent back to war torn areas of the world such as Afghanistan, Iran and Eritrea.

21.12 Next Steps? Over to You: The Reader!

The European Union Human Rights and Democracy action plan (2012) has the potential to provide an impetus for member states to work together to create an environment in which the challenges set out above might be met. The final statement in the document encompasses that ideal: "While respecting their distinct institutional roles, it is important that the European Parliament, the Council, the Member States, the European Commission and the EEAS commit themselves to working together ever more closely to realise their common goal of improving respect for human rights" (p. 9).

The introductory statement to the challenges section applies to all children and young people. How do we as individuals respond to the challenges inherent within that statement? How do we encourage our legislators to enshrine the provisions of the UNCRC into domestic law? Are we playing our role in creating a world in which all children can be enabled to reach their full potential?

> *The true measure of a nation's standing is how well it attends to its children – their health and safety, their material security, their education and socialization, and their sense of being loved, valued, and included in the families and societies into which they are born.* (UNICEF 2007)

21.13 Overview of Succeeding Chapters

Continuing the theme of this chapter, the remaining contributions deal with the specifics of the application of both international and domestic legislation to education systems in different parts of the world: Australia; UK; Europe; and, Canada. While some of the views presented may seem country specific, the underlying issues regarding children's rights are universal in application.

Meehan (Chap. 22) reviews the relationship between education and the law as experienced in England and Wale. Consideration is given to the way in which this relationship may or may not lead children and young people to become active and responsible citizens.

Shanks and Peter (Chap. 23) raise the positive and negative aspects of the proposed national Named Person Service in Scotland. The service aims to provide a comprehensive approach to the care of all children and young people. The authors recognise that should the service prove to be a success, it could provide a benchmark in this area of care which could be replicated internationally.

The question of citizenship within the broader European context is raised by Nyúl (Chap. 24). The European Union, while forming a strong economic union across, currently, 28 nation states, creates a dilemma in the political sense in that each state has its own sense of citizenship. How, then, to create a union of diverse cultures and languages into a union of European citizens with a common understanding of the term "citizenship"?

Violence against children is a topic found across all countries and cultures. Biffi (Chap. 25) explores this difficult topic through the lens of UNCRC and WHO reports on the state of the world's children. The UNICEF report "*Hidden in Plain Sight*" is accessed to provide disturbing statistics from all corners of the globe.

Restrictive practices are considered by Steele (Chap. 26) to be a form of violence against children with disabilities. The chapter reviews the United Nations Convention on the Rights of Persons with Disabilities (CRPD) and recent Australian government inquiries, which provide a strong policy basis for viewing restrictive practices as violence, which should be prohibited.

Revell, Bryant and Elton-Challcraft (Chap. 27) challenge the requirement for teachers to be front-line personnel in the prevention of terrorism in the UK. A new role for teachers is to be on the alert for possible radicalised pupils in their schools. In this way, their professional identity is compromised as their involvement as part of a counter terrorist strategy is normalised. This chapter examines how student teachers regard this new aspect of their role as educators.

Battiste and Henderson (Chap. 28) tackle the problem of educating the children of native peoples in a system grounded in western cultural norms. The chapter deals with this issue within the context of Indigenous children in Canada.

References

ACEI. (n.d.). *The ten pillars of a good childhood.* http://www.acei.org/decade-for-childhood/. Accessed 07 Mar 2017.

Alderson, P. (2016). International human rights, citizenship education, and critical realism. *London Review of Education, 14*(3), 1–12. https://doi.org/10.18546/LRE.14.3.01.

Au, W. (2007). High-stakes testing and curricular control: A qualitative metasynthesis. *Educational Researcher, 36*(5), 258–267.

Black, P., & Wiliam, D. (1998). *Inside the black box: Raising standards through classroom assessment.* Retrieved from http://www.pdkintl.org/kappan/kbla9810.htm website.

Brighouse, H. (2000). *School choice and social justice.* Oxford: Oxford University Press.

British Refugee Council. (2012). *Not a minor offence: Unaccompanied children locked up as part of the asylum system.* Retrieved from London www.refugeecouncil.org.uk

Delors, J. (1996). *Learning: The treasure within.* Paris: United Nations Educational Scientific and Cultural Organization.

Freire, P. (1972). *Pedagogy of the oppressed.* Middlesex: Penguin.

General Teaching Council Scotland. (2012). *Standards for leadership and management. http://www.gtcs.org.uk/web/FILES/the-standards/standards-for-leadership-and-management-1212.pdf (accessed 07 March, 2017).*

General Secretariat. (2012). 2012 strategic framework on human rights and democracy. Retrieved from https://europa.eu/european-union/topics/human-rights_en

ICFGEO. (2016). The international commission for global education opportunity. The learning generation: Investing in education for a changing world. p. 12. Retrieved from http://educationcommission.org/about/

James, J. C., & Tanner, C. K. (1993). Standardized testing of young children. *Journal of Research and Development in Education, 26*(3), 143–152.

Pulkkinen, L. (2012). *Goals for the decade of childhood based on ten pillars of a good childhood: A Finnish perspective.* http://www.allianceforchildhood.eu/files/Book2013/QOC13-Chapter5-Pulkinnen.pdf. Accessed 07 Mar 2017.

Rennie, L., Venville, G., & Wallace, J. (2012). *Knowledge that counts in a global community*. Abingdon: Routledge.

UNICEF. (2007). *Child poverty in perspective: An overview of child well-being in rich countries, Innocenti report card*. 7, 2007 UNICEF Innocenti Research Centre, Florence.

UNICEF. (2016). The State of the World's Children 2016: A fair chance for every child. https://www.unicef.org/sowc2016/. Accessed 07 Mar 2017.

United Nations. (1948). Universal Declaration of Human Rights. www.un.org/en/universal-declaration-human-rights/. Accessed 07 Mar 2017.

United Nations. (1989). Convention on the Rights of the Child. www.unicef.org.uk/Documents/Publication-pdfs/UNCRC_PRESS200910web.pdf. Accessed 07 March 2017.

United Nations. (2000) United Nations Millennium Declaration. http://www.un.org/millennium/declaration/ares552e.htm. Accessed 07 Mar 2017.

United Nations. (2002). A world fit for children. https://www.unicef.org/specialsession/wffc/. Accessed 07 Mar 2017.

United Nations. (2015). The Millennium Development Goals Report 2015. https://www.unicef.org/sowc2016/. Accessed 07 Mar 2017.

United Nations General Assembly on the Rights of the Child. (2002). *Resolution 56/138* (A/RES/56/138).

22

Considering the Relationship Between the Education of Children and the Application of the Law: A Brief Global View

Patrick Meehan

22.1 Introduction

This chapter will examine some views on what it is that we (adults in western liberal democratic nation states), think education, (by which is meant formal schooling), does for us as a society. It will consider how the design and delivery of mass compulsory public education has created a situation wherein 'childhood' is a form of public property, Heywood (2004) and Cunningham (2005, 2006). It will consider the interaction between law and education in terms of both expected and actual outcomes with respect to the evolution of the child into a citizen of such a society. It will do these things in the context of the United Kingdom.

Prior to the late 18th century debates over what constitutes 'appropriate' education and to whom it is delivered, when and by whom, were essentially of two kinds. The first kind was the province of families when speaking of individual children and the education they were to receive to fit them for some sort of life course preferred by their adult relatives.

The second kind was the province of either organised religion or private philanthropy when speaking of children as a societal sub-group, Cunningham (2005).

P. Meehan (✉)
School of Childhood and Education Sciences, Canterbury Christ Church University, Canterbury, UK
e-mail: patrick.meehan@canterbury.ac.uk

K. Trimmer et al. (eds.), *The Palgrave Handbook of Education Law for Schools*,
https://doi.org/10.1007/978-3-319-77751-1_22

Government at a national level was not particularly concerned with the life course of individuals provided taxes were paid and neither blasphemy nor sedition were uttered openly (Parsons 1962; Hobsbawm 1962; Kennedy 1989).

22.2 The Rise of the 'Average Man'

During the period 1750–1850 however, two things happened which began to stir national governments from their ancient indifference toward the ways in which the ordinary citizen raised their children. Firstly, the massive expansion of overseas territories and trade, (especially British trade after their victory over France in 1759) created a similar sized increase in the need for a literate clerical and administrative workforce in both civilian and military fields, Hobsbawm (1962, 1975, 1991) and Kennedy (1989). Whether it was being able to accurately compile the monthly accounts at a trading post in India or concisely report on the activities of local tribes in Africa, the need for literate middle level workers (subalterns) grew rapidly.

Secondly, the explosive growth of scientific knowledge from 1750 to 1850 required these literate managers (and their underlings) to become conversant with new machines, chemicals, processes and understandings of the world. (Hobsbawm 1962, 1975, 1991; Kennedy 1989; Rodger 1988; Uglow 2002; Holmes 2009).

This chapter considers the interaction of law and public education by examining the contribution of a theory of rationalist utilitarianism set within a paradigm, namely Modernism, in the field of Public Education especially in the United Kingdom. Rationalist Utilitarianism has arguably made three main contributions to how law and public education applies to children in the UK. Firstly, it led the late Enlightenment thinkers to create an epistemology of reason as the sole basis of public policy wherein public education was to be a tool for promoting both social and personal improvement. This epistemology was transformed and strengthened some decades later in the work of Comte (1848).

Secondly, it led to a belief that public education can, and perhaps even should, be applied as an industrial process which is mostly divorced from social context. Thirdly, it supports the Utilitarian view of how law operates in society in an allegedly neutral manner amongst free individuals who allegedly share equal ability to behave as a result of rational choices between clearly understood alternatives.

This suggests a situation in which education becomes a reproductive rather than transformative activity Friere (1970) because any attempt to define normality necessarily constructs everything outside it as pathology, Hacking (1990). The Rationalist Utilitarians sought to apply what would later be called 'scientific management' Taylor (1911), to a process which is actually an evolving conversation unique to each group of learners and their teacher Gadamer (1976).

That statement however is itself a reflection of a conception of education which draws heavily on the work of Kuhn (1962) and which follows a constructivist path like Dewey (1915), Wong (2007), rather than a behaviourist one like Skinner (1974). That is to say, it conceives of the learner as an active autonomous agent committed to participation in their learning rather than a mere passive receptacle into which knowledge is deposited by the teacher against future need (Freire 1970).

In that sense the ontological approach of this work reflects Pfeiffer and Jones (1975) Five Stage model which begins with the learner noticing a phenomenon and proceeding through an investigation of causation and replication into an examination of the future utility of the phenomenon.

Such an approach contrasts sharply with the Rationalist Utilitarian attempts to derive fixed principles through a reasoning process somewhat divorced from actual experience. My ontological approach conceives of knowledge itself as a more finite and contingent entity than the Rationalist Utilitarian thinkers would allow and accepts Kant's (1781) view that while experience is useful for gaining information, reason is required to structure that information into knowledge.

The attempt by Taylor (1911) to use 'scientific management' to identify the single 'best' way to run a machinery shop is a reflection of the late 18th and early 19th century Rationalist Utilitarian's attempt to devise a single 'best' way for a society to be managed and governed.

In like manner, they both overlook humans as individuals who sometimes (arguably often) act in irrational ways. It was argued by Satir (1994) that people, families and especially children, will usually behave in a way which may be coherent to them for dealing with issues but which may appear irrational to outsiders. Families are therefore important as primary locations of education as they are where children learn how you can or 'should' deal with other people whom they encounter in the wider world.

Scientific Management (which continues today by other names), deliberately seeks to eliminate the action of chance and thereby creates education as a rationalist utilitarian process that can be uniformly applied, Dwork (1987), and which can guarantee outcomes for students and society as discussed by

Cravens (1985), Hacking (1990) and Turmel (1998). Such a construction of education however runs the risk of striking from the hand of each generation their own chance at refashioning the world, (Arendt 1954) and thereby alienating those whom it was intended to socialise. Of interest to this work, is that traditional versions of how law works to regulate society make similar claims about impersonal and 'predictable' uniformity of both process and outcome. Radical, Realist, Marxist, Feminist and Critical scholars of law all produce considerable argument suggesting that chance is being deliberately eliminated in order to advantage some people and to disadvantage others. Those arguments are valid but not central to this work.

22.3 What Is It That Education Is Meant to Do?

According to Arendt (1954) who by her own admission was not an educationalist, education is meant to do two things for its society. Firstly and most obviously it is supposed to make every person who passes through it technically literate and numerate to an agreed standard of competence. Secondly though, it is the process by which the coming generation of children absorbs not only all the propositional knowledge, but also all the social norms and mores which the adult members of its society deem appropriate. In such a view of the intended goals of education, Arendt is in accord with Dewey (1915), Lawrence (1952) and Plowden (1967).

However, Holt (1964), Tough (2012) and Moylett (2013) take a view similar to Hume (1739) in that since the future is always dynamic then education should be about equipping children with skills as learners rather than focusing on retention of propositional knowledge.

22.4 What Is It That Education Does Do?

When most people, especially in Western countries use the term 'education' what they mean is roughly thirteen years of formal academic studies delivered indoors by a paid stranger to groups of children arranged by year of birth. This process relies heavily on the transmission of a specified curriculum comprised of propositional knowledge e.g. London is the capital of the UK and the performance of repetitive examples of application of the knowledge by the children. The success of this transmission is tested by assessing through formal academic tasks, how much of such knowledge has been retained and assimilated by those children.

> *A curriculum embodies distinct beliefs about the type of knowledge that should be taught in schools, the inherent nature of children, what school learning consists of, how teachers instruct children and how children should be assessed.* (Schiro 2013 p. 2)

It is asserted by Sampson (1921), Harber (2004) and Pring (2004) that any such mainstream curriculum necessarily marginalises some children due to class, gender, ethnicity etc. and consequently their ability, and willingness to engage with, and succeed through it is sharply reduced. Such arguments revisit the debates which preceded the passage of the Elementary Education Act (England and Wales) 1870 and remain relevant in 2017.

22.5 What Is Law and What Is It Meant to Do?

Broadly speaking law can be considered to be a set of written rules about how people will deal with each other and how government will deal with them. It is a way of managing potentially violent disagreements between individuals and groups about how to do things, or for determining what should be done in a given situation.

The famous legal scholar Dicey (1885) defined law as being way of settling disputes in a way which is fair to everyone because the substance of a complaint or offence, the process for hearing it and the process for redress or punishment are matters of ordinary law known by and applying equally to, everyone within a given society. He further argued that law was derived from the natural rights of every person rather than being a privilege bestowed by government. Such a construction of law is echoed by Parsons (1978) who argued that *law* serves to mitigate conflict by establishing norms for social interaction between individuals and government. He further asserted that only adherence to a pre-existing system of rules permits routine social interactions from breaking down into overt, chronic conflict.

If we accept this logical premise that law is a necessary part of any complicated society wherein strangers must be able to interact routinely and peacefully, then we must accept that what we mean by the term law, will amount to some sort of process for formalizing how these interactions take place.

This means, that by its very nature, law must be impersonal and necessarily strict about how it uses words and meanings. It will be a process of putting ideas in conveniently labelled boxes, and putting people into categories of relationship (parent/child, spouse, partner, business partner, tenant, patient etc.). As can therefore be seen, such a process can be either inclusive or exclusionary of some types of people depending on the views of a particular society and its elites.

In this chapter then, unless otherwise specified, the term law will be referring to a concept known as a *'General Legal System'*. The development of this is a crucial societal evolution, Braudel (1993) and Diamond (1998), and broadly speaking it can be described as:

> *an integrated system of universalistic norms which is applicable to a society as a whole rather than to a few functional or segmental sectors. It will be highly generalised in terms of principles and standards and relatively independent of both the religious agencies that legitimize the normative order of the society and the vested interest groups in the operative sector, particularly the government.* (Parsons 1964)

In order to function effectively in regulating social interactions within a given society the general legal system must possess a basis of *Legitimation* in order to obtain compliance and conformity. That is to say, the overwhelming majority of the people in that society must accept that the particular system of laws is fair and that it is being established and maintained by a government which those people also support.

The system must possess some means to solve the problem of *Interpretation* regarding which abstract legal rules will govern particular situations and define specific rights. That means there must be some person or persons empowered to interpret the meaning of statutes on behalf of the particular society.

The general legal system must logically also provide *Sanctions* for non-conformity with the provisions of the particular statutes. It must also specify by whom these sanctions may be applied and under what circumstances. These sanctions may range from positive inducements such as payments to parents for raising their children in particular ways to coercive (including lethal), force against individuals who engage in interpersonal violence. Lastly, the system must establish *Jurisdiction* to determine the specific circumstances under which a particular rule or set of rules actually applies (Parsons 1976; Slapper 2011).

22.6 What Is It That Law Does Do?

Writing in 1944 in reaction to the rise of Fascism in Germany & Stalinism in Russia Friedrich von Hayek argued that law exists to limit government power and to protect individual liberty and private property. He argued that law is not however a means to redress social inequality, especially via compulsory redistribution of wealth.

This conception considers law as being a stable set of minimum rules which are applied universally in a non-discretionary manner. Such a conception is based upon Immanuel Kant's (1781) *Ethical Formalism* (That the action in a particular case ought to be the action in every similar case), and rests upon a construction of society comprised of rational equals who broadly accept the Rule of Law as defined by Dicey (1885).

The growth of the welfare state in the western world during the period 1946–1978 arguably rejected von Hayek's (1944) construction of society as politicians on all sides sought to use law to rectify social inequalities of gender, class and race.

Indeed, writing in 1979 Joseph Raz criticises Von Hayek's theory as too simplistic and he argues that law in fact functions as a formal procedural device for ordering and controlling society. As such Raz argues, the western concept called the *Rule of Law* says nothing about how a particular law is made; e.g. by tyrants, democratic majorities or any other way. It says nothing about fundamental rights, about equality or justice.

According to Raz (1979) what matters then, is how laws are made and by whom as these things largely determine their objective fairness. Hence the Rule of law is merely a political ideal which the legal system of a particular society may objectively possess to a greater or a lesser degree.

22.7 What Does Law Do in Respect of Children and Education?

The previous historical overview illustrates that since the French Revolution there has been a policy direction pursued by the established interests both secular and religious to control and channel the coming generations of children in industrial urban societies. Beginning with the formalisation and standardisation of orphanages, hospitals, schools, workhouses and prisons there has been a use of legislation to construct particular forms of childhood as normal. In the UK arguably much of the initial impetus for this policy trajectory came from the views of human nature and the concerns about popular unrest that were held by religious, political and economic elites (Bentham 1776, 1789; Mill 1825a, b; Quetelet 1835; Hilton 1988a, b; Langford 1989). These concerns led to particular forms of citizenship and childhood being defined as abnormal (Hacking 1983, 1990; Turmel 1998). Over the next

200 years education and law would both be deployed to shape the normal and to exclude the pathological forms of childhood. Such an exclusionary process naturally affects both public constructions of childhood and the life-course of children (Mayer and Tuma 1990).

Life-course is defined as the actual and potential paths taken, or which are open to be taken, across the lifetime of a particular individual. Across the latter part of the nineteenth and early twentieth century the life-course of individuals in urban industrialised societies increasingly became standardised into four phases. The first two were childhood, wherein people were too young to work, and youth, where people began some form of paid work outside the home. The second two were adulthood, where people's lives revolved around full-time paid work, and retirement, where people were too old for work and were supported either by their families or, increasingly, by the State (Mayer and Tuma 1990). It was found by Kohli (1986, 1987) and Mayer (2000) that in all European countries these four phases showed clear and strong differences of experience due to social class.

The impacts on families of urbanising industrialisation such as concentration of production and populations centres meant that there were progressively smaller amounts of space available per family/family member in an average home. When combined with the daily demands of industrial and urban life the amount and types of social relationships became standardised due to the need to ensure the routine peaceful interaction with large numbers of strangers. Families came to regard life as binary in nature with the factory as a place of work/earning of money to pay for goods to satisfy basic and other needs (Maslow 1943), and the home as a place of refuge from the demands, hardships and hierarchies of work and society (Rothenbacher 2002).

Work became standardised across the 19th century due to influence of prevalence of factory-based production model and became divided between 'blue-collar' (both skilled and unskilled), and 'white-collar' (both skilled and unskilled). Life in general for the average person became less uncertain, but more standardised and class-differentiated, due to the introduction of guaranteed regular income in exchange for standardised labour during standardised hours (e.g. 5 × 8 hr. work days + 2 × rest days = 1 week) (Hareven 1982; Kocha 2010).

The passage of the *Elementary Education Act 1870* and the *Prevention of Cruelty to, and Protection of, Children Act 1899* began a process whereby the form and substance of childhood itself became a national concern. It should be noted that these Acts relate only to England and Wales. Over the next century national government became increasingly concerned not only with the care, control and education of children as a societal sub-group, but also with the lives of children as individuals. The continued raising of the school leaving age (coincidentally usually occurring during years of sharp economic downturn), and the increased provision of additional services such as Free School

Meals led to the creation of an increasingly rigid construction of a 'normal' childhood centred on completion of formal schooling.

Certainly the ratification of the *United Nations Convention on the Rights of the Child* (UNCRC) 1989 and the passage of the *Children's Act 1989* strengthened the public view that the State had not only the right but the duty to intervene in childhoods deemed to be sub-standard. This Act again relates only to England and Wales, but it explicitly defined which children could be said to be 'in need' of the assistance of their local government in order to achieve and maintain an expected standard of life. It even defined the parameters of what was mean by 'in need' and as the years 1997–2010 showed there was always a tendency to broaden that definition in accord with contemporary political agendas. Such expansion naturally increased the legitimacy of State intervention in families and also the financial burden to tax-payers.

Concerns about the need to improve the economy by returning mothers to the workforce were deliberately entangled with child protection concerns by the Blair government through the Every Child Matters 2003 agenda and the enactment of the Children's Act 2004. This was followed by the Childcare Act 2006 which imposed a duty on all UK local authorities to provide childcare for every child residing within their municipal boundary. It should be noted that this policy and these Acts relate to England and Wales but not to Scotland and Northern Ireland.

It is therefore interesting to note that this increased level of responsibility placed on local government in England and Wales in 1989, 2004 and 2006 was not accompanied by increased budget allocations. Indeed since 2009 the general trend has been significant funding reductions which have led to reductions of service provision for children. Arguably some such reductions such as the closure and/or sale of public parks and libraries may actually breach UK obligations under the UNCRC 1989 but thus far this appears not to be an issue of either official or public concern.

22.8 Some Concrete Ways that the Law Affects Children and their Education

It is again noted that the following discussion relates only to England and Wales as both Scotland and Northern Ireland have their own regulatory regimes for education which different in important ways from England and Wales. With the rise of compulsory mass education (roughly 1870–1880) there came a need to apply coercive sanctions for non-compliance with the process as parents reliant upon children's wage resisted the loss of those wages due to school attendance, Heywood (2004), Cunningham (2005) and

Gillard (2011). As Harber and Mncube (2012) argues, the differences of opinion between parents and the State about whether forcing children to undergo a single form of formal education is beneficial or not remains problematic and parents remain liable to fines and even imprisonment for failing to ensure school attendance by their children.

As mentioned at the outset debates in England and Wales about who should be taught what, by whom and in what ways have been constantly reviewed in the Hadow reports between 1923 and 1933, Plowden Report (1967), Warnock (1978), Swann (1985), DFS (1992), DfEE (1997), DCSF (2009) and DfE (2010) and they show no sign of diminishing in intensity. It is therefore worthy of note that the Hadow reports were the result of national consultation within England and Wales, and both Plowden and Warnock constitute expert opinion while the reports since the 1980s have arguably been ideological rather than pedagogic in origin as they are policy documents without public consultation or neutral expertise (Gillard 2011).

In terms of daily effects on children's lives, there are two further areas where law impacts in concrete ways. These are, the construction of the child in England and Wales via the Children's Act 1989 as capable of expressing views in the manner envisaged by the UNCRC 1989 and the continued permissibility of corporal punishment within UK families. Both of these appear likely to remain problematic due to BREXIT and the possibility of reducing or removing the application of the European Convention on Human Rights 1950 to the UK context.

22.9 Children Being Capable of Expressing Views About Their Life (and Being Heeded)

22.9.1 UNCRC 1989

The United Nations Convention on the Rights of the Child (1989) or UNCRC (1989) is a landmark document in terms of how children are seen around the world. It represents more than a decade of negotiations and it has served as a basis for the development of substantive policy agendas such as the Millennium Development Goals (MDGs). It is not however an uncontroversial document for several reasons, none of which involve children directly. One of the main criticisms of it centres on the fact that its constructions of children and childhood originate as products of Western, liberal urban and industrialised views. Unsurprisingly then it is criticised for being a document which contains, but does not sufficiently address, the numerous socio-economic and political disparities and cultural differences between the Global North and South.

In its defence, it has now been ratified by 196 out of 197 nations on Earth (the USA continues to decline Congressional approval), and it has served as both a model for subsequent supranational documents such as the African Charter on the Rights and Welfare of the Child 1999, or ACRWC (1999) and also for improved domestic legislation and policy around the world. The fact that all Islamic nations and several secular ones have placed reservations on the nature and degree of their adherence to it remains problematic and the UNCRC (1989) is most often heard of in terms of breaches of its provisions in many countries.

Inequalities of wealth continue to reduce the ability of Global South nations to adhere to the goals and the UK continues to fail in State obligations regarding poverty reduction, paying heed to their views, provision of basic services and media treatment of children, Payne (2009) and Children's Rights Director for England (2014).

22.9.2 Children's Act 1989

The Children Act 1989 was a response of the Conservative Government, in England and Wales, to four things. Firstly there was a need to align UK legislation with the soon to be signed UN Convention on the Rights of the Child (UNCRC 1989). Secondly, there was a desire to simplify the work environment around children by consolidating the powers, roles, offences and duties from 21 older Acts regarding the education and care of children in England and Wales. Thirdly, there was a need to formally (and effectively) respond to the findings from the Cleveland Inquiry 1988 where a single Social Worker and a sympathetic Doctor misdiagnosed sexual abuse of children and wrongly took over 100 children away from their families. Lastly, as Conservatives part of their response to Cleveland was a desire to restrict the degree to which government intervenes in the lives of ordinary families. The potential savings to the public budget from tightening the parameters for State intervention were of course an additional bonus.

The Children's Act 1989 is underpinned by four principles which are that the welfare of the child is paramount in all matters affecting their life, Sect 1 (1), that there should be no delay in making decisions about matters affecting the child (and the voice of the child should be heard Sect 1 (2)). In 2017 it remains an under debated issue in the UK whether being heard is the same as having your views acted upon.

The third principle is that no coercive court order should be sought by professionals unless the welfare of the child cannot be supported in other ways, Sect 1 (5). Such ways should ideally include detailed discussion with parents about courses of action and their consequences.

Lastly, Sect (2) of the Children's Act 1989 seeks to establish which persons hold *Parental Responsibility* responsible for feeding clothing, housing and caring for the child until they turn 18 years of age. Under this section numerous sub-sections set out who can and cannot hold this Parental Responsibility for a child or children. If no 'good enough' parent/carer can be found then the State must step in and have Local Authorities act as parent/carer.

In the event that such State intervention is determined to be necessary *Children's Act 1989 Section 8 (1)* permits courts to make four kinds of orders with respect to children. Firstly there are *Contact Orders*, which require the person with whom a child lives, or is to live, to allow the child to visit or stay with the person named in the order, or for that person and the child otherwise to have contact with each other.

Alternatively the court may make a *Prohibited Steps Order* which means that no step which could be taken by a parent in meeting his parental responsibility for a child, and which is of a kind specified in the order, shall be taken by any person without the consent of the court.

To resolve issues involving where the child or children lives the court may make a *Residence Order* which determines the arrangements to be made regarding the person with whom a child is to live. Finally the court may make a *Specific Issue Order* to give directions for the purpose of determining a specific question which has arisen, or which may arise, in connection with any aspect of parental responsibility for a child.

Children's Act 1989 Sections (9) & (10) place restrictions on when, how and with whom Courts may make and use such orders regarding the lives of children so as to ensure that any such orders are consistent with the four principles of the Act.

Early in their second term the Labour government of Tony Blair introduced an additional piece of legislation, *Children's Act 2004* which expanded but did not replace the Children's Act 1989 in England and Wales. The main features of the newer legislation are the expansion of definitions of which children need State intervention in their family life and the creation of a senior bureaucratic apparatus (and position) called the *Office of The Children's Commissioner*.

The remit of this official is to actively seek the views of children in England and Wales regarding matters affecting them such as health and educational provision and several important but not necessarily influential reports have been produced as a result. Increasingly this organisation is functioning as a kind of observational ombudsman for children and families to express broad concerns about public and private sector provision of services and in this role it has at least managed to bring some issues of inadequate resourcing and poor practice to public attention.

22.10 Children Expressing Views About Actions Affecting Their Lives

The main case on the right of children in England and Wales to express their views on matters related to their lives is Gillick vs. West Norfolk and Wisbech Area Health Authority and DHSS [1986]AC 112 House of Lords (Lords Fraser, Scarman, Bridge, Brandon and Templeman). This case gave rise to a decision-making process called Gillick Competence which was originally for medical staff but by extension could apply to any professional who deals with children.

This case involved the right of a girl who was almost 16 years of age to doctor-patient confidentiality from her mother in respect to the provision of contraception or abortion advice. In this case the issue was that the mother held strong religious views prohibiting use of contraception and when she learned that a local doctor had provided advice and the contraceptive pill to her daughter (who was legally still below the age of consent), without consulting her as the parent/guardian she sued both the doctor and the local NHS Trust.

The local NHS Trust counter-sued arguing that the doctors' actions were consistent with their policies of harm-minimisation through patients making informed decisions about their own behaviour. The doctor had attempted to have the girl bring her mother to a consultation and had requested her consent to discuss the issues with the mother but the girl had feared her mother's anger and declined to include her in the process.

Accordingly the doctor took the view that the girl was within six months of the age of consent and that it was likely she was going to engage in sexual activity with or without the medical advice or assistance. Further the girl had confidentially approached the medical practice seeking to avoid either pregnancy or Sexually Transmitted Infections (STI) and she was clearly trying to be responsible in her conduct. So, in pursuit of minimising potential harms the doctor provided the contraceptive pill and condoms to the girl.

Gillick Competence holds that if a child under 16 is able to satisfy the court (or the professional) that they possess a reasonable level of general intelligence, sufficient understanding of relevant facts about their situation and sufficient understanding of the implications of any proposed actions, then the court (or professional) should allow the child to exercise their ability to make informed decision regarding the proposed action.

In delivering the verdict in this case, the presiding Judge Lord Fraser expressed the courts' view that the girl obtaining contraceptive advice in this matter was akin to a child consenting in the absence of a parent to having a doctor repair a broken limb after a school sporting mishap.

Their Lordships felt that parental involvement was always to be desired in any serious matters involving the health education and care of children as they were after all the ones with primary responsibility to care for the child. They recognised though that some matters involving children could have serious and permanent consequences if not dealt with effectively and rapidly. Therefore they reasoned that the absence of explicit parental consent was not automatically grounds for inaction, because children below 16 years had long been held legally capable of entering into limited contracts, being sued and giving evidence under oath in courts.

In summation of the verdict Lord Fraser said:

> *It is in my view, contrary to the ordinary experience of mankind, at least in Western Europe in the present century, to say that a child or young person remains in fact under the complete control of his parents until he attains a definite age of majority, now until 18 in the United Kingdom, and that on attaining that age he suddenly acquires independence. In practice most wise parents relax their control gradually as the child develops and encourage him or her to become increasingly independent. Moreover, the degree of parental control actually exercised over a particular child does in practice vary considerably according to his understanding and intelligence and it would, in my opinion, be unrealistic for the courts not to recognise these facts. Social customs change, and the law ought to, and does in fact, have regard to such changes when they are of major importance.*

In ruling as they did the court was entirely consistent with the previous decision of *Hewer v Bryant [1969] 3 All ER 578* where the court had held that:

> *The legal right of a parent is a dwindling right which the court will hesitate to enforce against the wishes of the child, the older he is. It starts with right of control and it ends with little more than advice.*

That case marked the end of the existing legal position that children were the property of their parents until they attained the age of majority and the decision was echoed in the *Children's Act 1989 Section 2 (4)* which ended the presumption that children in England and Wales should always go to their father in the event of divorce.

However, the verdict in the Gillick case to allow children under the age of consent to make serious decisions needs to be set against the case of *W (A Minor) (Medical Treatment), RE [1992] 3 WLR 758 4 All ER 627 Court of Appeal (Lord Donaldson of Lymington MR, Balcombe and Nolan LJJ)* where the court held that even persons over 16 years of age may not be held legally competent by virtue of the nature of a medical condition or mental state. In this case the court held that a girl of 16 years could not refuse treatment for the eating disorder Anorexia Nervosa because the nature of that disorder impeded her *Gillick Competence* to understand the severity of her actual situation and the potentially fatal consequences of refusing the treatment.

22.10.1 Physical Punishment of Children

In 2017 England and Wales remain some of the last countries in the developed world to permit parents to physically punish children and this appears unlikely to change given the strong views usually advanced by tabloid media whenever rational discussion is attempted, Hume (2003), Mason and Fattore (2005), Levy (2008), and Saunders and Goddard (2009). Unfortunately the literature review on parental -child homicide by Wilczynski (1995) suggested that when physical violence in the name of child discipline is tolerated then it is merely a question of degree between a crying child and a dead one.

That research by Wilczynski (1995) also suggested that many instances of excessive force derive from a lack of understanding of by parents or carers of actual rather than assumed levels of child development which causes the adult to ascribe deliberate intent to children's actions where none exists. Currently the situation in England and Wales is that parents may *reasonably chastise* their child provided they remain within the bounds of force outlined in the following cases.

In the case of *Costello-Roberts vs. United Kingdom (1995) EHRR 112* it was held that three smacks on buttocks with soft sole of shoe was not a violation of Article 3 European Convention on Human Rights (1950) as long as it, is not done routinely, does not amount to physical injury, is not done to embarrass the child publicly and does not leave lasting injury or trauma.

In the case of *A v United Kingdom [1998] 2FLR 959 European Court of Human Rights* the court was asked to determine whether the right of a child not to be subjected to inhuman and degrading treatment under Article 3, EUCHR (1950) was adequately protected by the UK government.

This case involved a child (A) who was severely & regularly beaten by his stepfather with a garden stake. Initially the Stepfather was charged with causing *Actual Bodily Harm* to the boy but the UK jury acquitted him on grounds of *'reasonable chastisement'*.

Child A then lodged an appeal with the European Court of Human Rights asserting that UK had failed to protect him as required under Article 3 EUCHR (1950). The court decided that as the original intent of that Article was to protect persons from State sanctioned torture and enslavement, the ill-treatment would need to attain a minimum level of severity before it could be applied.

On that occasion the European Court of Human Rights decided that such matters must be decided on a case-by-case basis with regard to:

- Age and sex of child, and health of child
- Relationship between child and the adult
- Nature and context of the treatment
- Period of time over which it occurs
- Number of times it occurs
- Physical or mental effects upon child

In this particular case it was held by the court that severe physical assaults on a 9 year old boy on more than one occasion probably meets these standards. In their summation of this matter the court took the progressive view that the prosecution does not have to prove *'beyond reasonable doubt'* that the chastisement was *'unreasonable'*.

In order for *'Reasonable Chastisement'* to remain a defence to allegations of violation a child's rights under Article 3 EUCHR (1950), the European Court of Human Rights has ruled that the injuries inflicted CANNOT amount to more than those used in offences defined as *'Common Assault'*

> *That is, where injuries amount to no more than grazes, scratches, abrasions, minor bruising, swellings, reddening of the skin, superficial cuts or a "black eye". An undisplaced broken nose is to be regarded as a borderline case.* (*Charging Standard for Offences Against the Person 2005*)

If the injuries exceed this level then the ECHR and the Crown Prosecution Service in England and Wales agree that *'Reasonable Chastisement'* no longer applies and the perpetrator should be charged with *'Assault Occasioning Actual Bodily Harm'*.

However, since 2001 any jury in such cases must be specifically instructed by the presiding Judge to consider total circumstances of case, especially any reason given by perpetrator for inflicting such punishment and effects upon a child.

There has however been some progress, with Section 58 Children's Act 2004 which removes *'Reasonable Chastisement'* as a defence for use of force against a child in both criminal and civil cases at any time where the level of force rises above the threshold of *'Common Assault'*. This Section also requires the court to consider whether the use of force was intended by the perpetrator to harm the child as opposed to merely punishing them.

22.11 Some Conclusions from International Research and Some Intriguing Directions for Society

All societies expect that their education system will turn raw children into finished adults. Frequently today though there is a tendency, especially for politicians and media to equate education with formal schooling and to assume that the difficult and complex activity of educating a child is able to operate as a predictable, linear production process. Arguably this is exacerbated by the current global political obsession with 3–5 year electoral cycles which require each government, and each minister to 'make their mark' by tinkering with functioning systems. Equally arguable is the attribution of blame for the creation of such an instrumental and reductive view of education solely to the late Baroness Thatcher. This however is to ignore objective views of history. All societies have had differences of opinion about design and delivery of education and these invariably reflect similar debates about the nature of those societies.

The modern versions of such debates over what constitutes 'appropriate' education and to whom it is delivered, when and by whom, date from at least the late 18th century. Unfortunately, as Alexander et al. (2010) point out, the terms of the debate remain depressingly similar and the construction of schooling as a factory-like activity with quality-assured processes leading to guaranteed performance outcomes continues as the mainstream view.

In 1970 Paolo Freire argued that *education is either a means of reproducing society or of transforming it.* He asserted that the degree of equality and potential for individual growth in an education system will necessarily reflect these things within that society.

The experience of public education in the UK and Brazil since 1990 seems to illustrate the influence of the two positions fairly accurately. The UK (at least in England and Wales), has pursued a construction of education which distrusts teachers and sees learning as the pouring of propositional information into children and increasingly frequent standardised high stakes tests.

It still insists that more of the same will lead to changes and yet demonstrably continues to fall behind similar advanced nations in PISA results for literacy, numeracy and basic sciences. Brazil took a conscious decision to reorganise its educational provision around the ideas of Freire and it now leads the England and Wales on many diverse indicia of educational, social and economic success.

22.12 Your Children, Your Schools, Our Future

Again it is noted that the following discussion relates to England and Wales but not to Scotland and Northern Ireland. It has been argued that New Labour had a penchant for reducing complex policy to titles just six words long and comprising three sets of two word phrases, Fairclough (2000), which no 'reasonable person' could find surface fault with. It is also arguable that they made a practice of telling awful truths quickly and then moving swiftly on before allowing examination of questionable decisions. The title of this section echoes the title of the last major policy document on education which the Orwellian sounding Department for Children, Schools and Families produced before the 2010 general election. The choice to do so is an expression of my view that New Labour's education policy was driven more by the Fabian socialist views of Friedrich Engels (1884) than by any sound pedagogic models.

My assertion is that schools were deliberately utilised by New Labour as a means of replacing children's familial concerns and loyalties with those of the nation/corporate state, Garan (2004) and Saltmann (2007).

Since their return to government in 2010, the Conservatives have continued their 1988 policy trajectory of asserting the primacy of national curriculum standards and central government oversight of how schools operate. What has changed though is their willingness to continue the New Labour trajectory of seeking to maintain control of curriculum content without having to assume financial responsibility for delivery of public education. We see this through the process by which publicly funded schools being forced to become private for-profit academies after being judged as 'failing'.

The fact that these schools are given a *'change or close'* choice by either government assessors or their private sub-contractors (often working for large companies which coincidentally operate academies) is deeply concerning for the ownership of public school assets and public education, Beckett (2007) and Barker (2010).

22.13 Old Arguments and New Dilemmas

In the 18th-century Enclosure laws in England and Wales deprived the British public of the use of land which had been previously held in trust for common usage for centuries. This was done through the ability of the rich to use parliament to grant them exclusive use for private profit of what was until then a public asset used as a form of social welfare, Cain and Hunt (1979). Arguably in the 21st century other rich people have been able to use parliament to grant themselves exclusive rights for private profit over public assets and services in education, prisons and health. In this as in the earlier cases, it appears such actions inevitably amplify social inequalities and create stratified systems of provision for crucial services, which in turn, solidify class distinctions based on money.

The Government in England and Wales in the 21st century currently appears (through the expansion of the Grammar school system and forced academisation of all other schools), to be committed to a system of education which is increasingly standardised and stratified and this is problematic for an advance nation purporting to be a democracy. In this context I consider standardisation of education to mean:

> *The degree of institutional uniformity of funding, curriculum, pedagogic practice and assessment within an educational system or between comparable systems.* (*Mau and Verweibe* 2010)

In the same context stratification is taken to mean:

> *The degree of selectivity in the transitions to higher educational levels. That is, how many children out of each age cohort actually reach the highest levels of formal education.* (*Mau and Verweibe* 2010)

Standardisation and stratification within an educational system have been consistently found to exert strong direct influence, upon both individual labour-market opportunities and actual occupational trajectories over the life-course (Allmendinger 1989; Allmendinger and Hinz 2009). This returns us to Arendt's (1954) argument that in addition to making you literate and numerate your formal school also teaches you what it is realistic for a person of your gender, class, ethnicity, physical abilities and religion to expect from your life in that particular society.

Therefore in closing this chapter I would like to pose three questions for consideration which derive from Sallust (66 BCE) Mandeville (1714) and Sampson (1921).

1. Is the provision of advanced education to more people than there are jobs requiring such education for, an intolerably socially destabilising force?
2. If as predicted, advances in Artificial Intelligence (AI) do lead to the replacement of 70% of current jobs by 2030, how can we realign education to enable the potential for human creativity able to be unleashed?
3. Is the proposed provision of Universal Basic Income (if combined with limitless and free WiFi), an enabling thing or simply – Panem et circenses?

References

Alexander, R. (Ed.). (2010). *Children, their world, their education: Final report and recommendations of the Cambridge primary review*. London: Routledge.

Allmendinger, J. (1989). *Career mobility dynamics: A comparative analysis of the United States, Norway and West Germany*. Berlin: Edition Sigma.

Allmendinger, J., & Hinz, T. (2009). Occupational careers under different welfare regimes: West Germany, Great Britain and Sweden. In W. Heinz et al. (Eds.), *The life-course reader; individuals and societies across time* (pp. 63–84). Frankfurt: Main Campus.

Arendt, H. (1954). The crisis in education. In Arendt, H. (1958). *Between past and future: Eight exercises in political thought*. London: Penguin.

Barker, B. (2010). *The pendulum swings: Transforming school reform*. Stoke-on-Trent: Trentham Books.

Beckett, F. (2007). *The great city academy fraud*. London: Continuum.

Bentham, J. (1776). A fragment on government. Current edition (1988) Harrison, R. (Ed.), *Cambridge texts in the history of political thought*. Cambridge: Cambridge University Press.

Bentham, J. (1789). *An introduction to the principles of morals and legislation*. London. Current edition (1907). Oxford: Clarendon Press. http://oll.libertyfund.org/?option=com_staticxt&staticfile=show.php%3Ftitle=278&Itemid=27. Accessed 12 May 2013

Braudel, F. (1993). *A history of civilisations*. London: Penguin.

Cain, M., & Hunt, A. (1979). *Marx and Engels on law*. London: Academic.

Children's Rights Director for England. (2014). *The united nations convention on the rights of the child: How children say the UK is doing*. London: OFSTED.

Comte, A. (1848). Trans. Bridges, J. H. (1865); *A general view of positivism*. Trubner and Co. (Reissued by Cambridge University Press, 2009).

Council of Europe. (1950). European convention for the protection of human rights and fundamental freedoms as amended by protocol no. 11, Nov. 4, 1950, 213 U.N.T.S. 221.
Cravens, H. (1985). Child-saving in the age of professionalism, 1915–1930. In J. Hawes & R. Hiner (Eds.), *American childhood* (pp. 415–488). Westport: Greenwood Press.
Cunningham, H. (2005). *Children and childhood in Western society since 1500*. Abingdon/Oxford: Routledge.
Cunningham, H. (2006). *The invention of childhood*. London: BBC Books.
DCSF. (2009). *Independent review of the primary curriculum: Final report*. Nottingham: DCSF.
DES. (1992). *Curriculum organisation and classroom practice in primary schools: A discussion paper*. London: HMSO.
DFS. (1992). *Curriculum organisation and classroom practice in primary schools: A discussion paper*. London: HMSO.
Dewey, J. (1915). *The school and society and the child and the curriculum*. Chicago: University of Chicago Press.
DfE. (2010). *White paper: The importance of teaching*. CM 7980. London: HMSO.
DfEE. (1997). *White paper: Excellence in schools*. Cmnd 3681. London: HMSO.
Diamond, J. (1998). *Guns, germs and steel: A short history of everybody for the last 30,000 years*. New York: Vintage books.
Dicey, A. V. (1885). *Introduction to the study of law of the constitution*. London: Macmillan.
Dwork, D. (1987). *What is good for babies and other young children: A history of the infant and child welfare movement in England. 1818–1918*. London: Tavistock Publications.
Engels, F. (1884). *The origins of the family, private property and the state* (trans: West, A.). (1942). London: Penguin Classics.
Fairclough, N. (2000). *New labour, new language?* London: Routledge.
Freire, P. (1970). *Pedagogy of the oppressed* (Current Edition 2007). London: Continuum.
Gadamer, H. G. (1976). Man and language. In E. David (Ed. and trans.), *Philosophical hermeneutics*. Berkeley: University of California Press.
Garan, E. M. (2004). *In defense of our children: When politics, profit and education collide*. Portsmouth: Heinemann.
Gillard, D. (2011). *Education in England: A brief history*. http://www.educationengland.org.uk/history/index.html. Accessed Apr 2017.
Hacking, I. (1983). *Representing and intervening: Introductory topics in the philosophy of natural science*. Cambridge: Cambridge University Press.
Hacking, I. (1990). *The taming of chance*. New York: Cambridge University Press.
Harber, C. (2004). *Schooling as violence; how schools harm pupils and societies*. London: Routledge.

Harber, C., & Mncube, V. (2012). *Education, democracy and development: Does education contribute to democratisation in developing countries?* Oxford: Symposium.
Hareven, M. (1982). *Family time and industrial time.* New York: Cambridge University Press.
Heywood, C. (2004). *A history of childhood.* Cambridge: Polity Press.
Hilton, A. J. B. (1988a). *The age of atonement; the influence of evangelicalism on social and economic thought 1795–1865.* Oxford: Oxford University Press.
Hilton, A. J. B. (1988b). *A mad bad dangerous people? England 1783–1846.* Oxford: Oxford University Press.
Hobsbawm, E. (1962). *The age of revolution 1789–1848.* London: Abacus.
Hobsbawm, E. (1975). *The age of capital 1848–1875.* London: Abacus.
Hobsbawm, E. (1991). *The age of empire 1875–1914.* London: Abacus.
Holmes, R. (2009). *The age of wonder: How the romantic generation discovered the beauty and terror of science.* London: Harper.
Holt, J. (1964). *How children fail.* London: Penguin.
Hume, D. (1739). *Treatise of human nature: Being an attempt to introduce the experimental method of reasoning into moral subjects.* London, John Noon. Current edition (1985) London: Penguin Classics.
Hume, M. (2003, May 5). Give the NSPCC a clip around the ear, somebody. *The Times.*
Kant, I. (1781). *Groundwork for the metaphysics of morals.* (2002, trans/Ed. Wood, A. W.). New Haven: Yale University Press.
Kennedy, P. (1989). *The rise and fall of great powers; economic change and military conflict from 1500–2000.* London: Fontana.
Kocha, J. (Ed.). (2010). *Work in a modern society. The German historical experience in a comparative perspective.* Oxford: Berghahn Books.
Kohli, M. (1986). The world that we forgot: A historical review of life course. In V. W. Marshall (Ed.), *Later life: The social psychology of aging* (pp. 271–303). London: Sage.
Kohli, M. (1987). Retirement and the moral economy: A historical interpretation of the German case. *Journal of Aging Studies, 1*(2), 125–144.
Kuhn, T. S. (1962). *The structure of scientific revolutions.* Chicago/USA: University of Chicago Press.
Langford, P. (1989). *A polite and commercial people. England 1727–1783.* Oxford: Oxford University Press.
Lawrence, E. (Ed.). (1952). *Friedrich Froebel and English education.* London: University of London Press.
Levy, A. (2008, November). Police chief calls to bring back a clip round the ear for naughty children. *The Daily Mail.* Accessed 3 May 2017.
Mandeville, B. (1714). *The Fable of the bees and other writings.* (1997 ed.). Abridged and Ed. Hunert, E. J. Indianapolis: Hackett Publishing.
Maslow, A. (1943). A theory of human motivation. *Psychological Review, 50*(4), 370–396.

Mason, J., & Fattore, T. (Eds.). (2005). *Children taken seriously: In theory, policy and practice*. London: Jessica Kingsley Publishers.
Mau, S., & Verweibe, R. (2010). *European societies; mapping structure and change*. Bristol: The Policy Press.
Mayer, K. U. (2000). Promises fulfilled? A review of 20 years of life course research. *Archives Europeennes de Sociologie, XLI*(2), 259–282.
Mayer, K. U., & Tuma, N. B. (Eds.). (1990). *Event history analysis in life course research*. Madison: University of Wisconsin Press.
Mill, J. (1825a). *Education*. London. Encyclopedia Britannica. http://oll.libertyfund.org/index.php?option=com_staticxt&staticfile=show.php%3Ftitle=1764&Itemid=99999999. Accessed 13 May 2013.
Mill, J. (1825b). *Prisons and prison discipline*. London. Encyclopedia Britannica. http://oll.libertyfund.org/index.php?option=com_staticxt&staticfile=show.php%3Ftitle=1766&Itemid=99999999. Accessed 13 May 2013.
Moylett, H. (Ed.). (2013). *Characteristics of effective early learning; helping young children become learners for life*. Berkshire: Open University/McGraw-Hill.
Organization of African Unity (OAU), African Charter on the Rights and Welfare of the Child, 11 July 1990, CAB/LEG/24.9/49 (1990). Available at http://www.refworld.org/docid/3ae6b38c18.html. Accessed 4 Apr 2018.
Parsons, T. (1962). The law and social control. In W. M. Evan (Ed.), *Law and Sociology*. New York: Free Press.
Parsons, T. (1964). *Sociological theory and modern society*. New York: Free Press.
Parsons, T. (1976). Social structure and the symbolic media of interchange. In P. M. Blau (Ed.), *Approaches to the study of social structure*. London: Open Books.
Parsons, T. (1978). Law as an intellectual stepchild. In H. M. Johnson (Ed.), *Social system and legal process*. San Francisco: Jossey-Bass.
Payne, L. (2009). Twenty years on: The implementation of the UN convention on the rights of the child in the United Kingdom. *Children & Society, 23*, 149–155.
Pfeiffer, W., & Jones, J. E. (1975). *A handbook of structured experiences for human relations training*. La Jolla: University Associates.
Plowden. (1967). *Children and their primary schools Report of the central advisory council for education (England)*. London: HMSO.
Pring, R. (2004). The aim of education: Liberal or vocational? In R. Pring (Ed.), *Philosophy of education: Aims, theory, common sense, and research*. London: Continuum.
Quetelet, A. (1835). Sur l homme et le developpement de ses facultes ou essai de physique sociale, 2 vol., Paris, Bachelier (Republished Paris, Fayard, 1991); translated as A treatise on man and the development of his faculties, London, 1842.
Raz, J. (1979). *The authority of law*. Oxford: Clarendon Press.
Rodger, N. A. M. (1988). *The wooden world: An anatomy of the Georgian navy*. London: Harper Collins.
Rothenbacher, F. (2002). *The European population 1850–1945*. London: Palgrave Macmillan.

Saltmann, K. J. (2007). *Capitalizing on disaster: Taking and breaking public schools.* London: Paradigm Publishers.
Sampson, G. (1921). *English for the English: A chapter on national education* (Current Edition 1952). Cambridge: Cambridge University Press.
Satir, V. (1994). *Peoplemaking.* London: Souvenir Press.
Saunders, B. J., & Goddard, C. (Eds.). (2009). *Physical punishment in childhood: The rights of the child.* London: Wiley-Blackwell.
Schiro, M. S. (2013). *Curriculum theory: Conflicting visions and enduring concerns.* London: Sage.
Skinner, B. F. (1974). *About behaviourism.* New York: Alfred A. Knopf.
Slapper, G. (2011). *How the law works* (2nd ed.). Abingdon/Oxfordshire: Routledge.
Swann. (1985). *Education for all report of the committee of enquiry.* Cmnd 9453. London: HMSO.
Taylor, F. W. (1911). *The principles of scientific management.* Mineola: Dover Publications.
Tough, P. (2012). *How children succeed: Grit curiosity and the hidden power of character.* New York: Random House.
Turmel, A. (1998). Childhood and normalcy: Classification, numerical regularities and tabulations. *International Journal of Educational Research, 27*(8), 661–672.
Uglow, J. (2002). *The lunar men: The friends who made the future.* London: Faber and Faber.
United Nations Convention on the Rights of the Child (UNCRC). (1989). United Nations, New York.
Von Hayek, F. (1944). *The road to serfdom.* Abingdon: Routledge.
Warnock. (1978). *Special educational needs report of the committee of enquiry into the education of handicapped children and young people.* Cmnd. 7212. London: HMSO.
Wilczynski, A. (1995). Child killing by parents: A motivational model. *Child Abuse Review, 4*, 365–370.
Wong, D. (2007). Beyond control and rationality; Dewey, aesthetics, motivation and educative experiences. *Teachers College Record, 109*(1), 192–220.

23

Issues and Impact of the Named Person Legislation in Scotland

Rachel Shanks and Scott Peter

23.1 Introduction

This chapter concerns the proposed national Named Person Service in Scotland and the issues it creates for school principals. These will be of interest for those in other countries where greater inter-agency working between education, health, social care services and the police may be proposed. The Named Person Service provides an example, for other countries with well-developed state welfare systems, of the Getting it Right for Every Child approach that has 'the potential to be world-leading in its national, strategic approach to enhancing the well-being of all children via universal public services' (Coles et al. 2016, p. 335).

The Named Person Service creates a new role to carry out three functions related to the well-being of children: firstly, to advise, inform and support children and young people and parents; secondly, to help them access services or support; and, thirdly, to discuss or raise a matter about a child or young person with other agencies as appropriate. The scheme raises several issues at a system, school and individual level. There are issues related to increased

R. Shanks (✉)
School of Education, University of Aberdeen, Aberdeen, UK
e-mail: r.k.shanks@abdn.ac.uk

S. Peter
School of Education, University of Aberdeen, Aberdeen, UK

Wallacestone Primary School, Falkirk, UK
e-mail: scott.peter.09@aberdeen.ac.uk

K. Trimmer et al. (eds.), *The Palgrave Handbook of Education Law for Schools*,
https://doi.org/10.1007/978-3-319-77751-1_23

surveillance of children, information-sharing and confidentiality; the potential for interference with the right to private and family life, and with parents' rights; leadership and management in schools; inter-agency working; increased workloads without increased resources; training and skills required to act as a Named Person; schools' relationships with parents; the involvement of children and young people in decisions that affect them; and the definition of well-being. It is also an example of a universal, as opposed to a targeted approach, to public service working for the safeguarding of children's well-being.

When a child is of school age a member of school staff will provide the Named Person Service. In primary schools this is likely to be the principal or their deputy and in secondary schools it is likely to be a guidance teacher overseeing pupils' overall well-being throughout their time at that school. Thus, the Named Person Service adds extra obligations onto school principals as they must ensure that they, or a member of their staff, are the Named Person for each of the pupils at their school. This member of staff will have responsibility for being the contact point for anyone who wishes to raise a concern about a particular pupil's well-being. The Named Person will have overall responsibility for liaising with other agencies, co-ordinating meetings and actions by other agencies and including the parents or carers and, if appropriate, the young person themselves. It has been suggested that calling the Named Person the 'first point of contact' would have been less challenging than a 'Named Person for every child' (Coles et al. 2016, p. 351).

Not everyone has been happy with the development of the Named Person Service. Several charities and parents brought a case against the Scottish Government. In The Christian Institute case (2016) the UK Supreme Court upheld some parts of the Named Person Service but ruled that changes had to be made to the information-sharing provisions of the enabling legislation, the Children and Young Person (Scotland) Act 2014. The Supreme Court ruled that the legislation contained too low a threshold for disclosure of confidential information for children and young people and this amounted to an infringement of Article 8 of the European Convention on Human Rights (ECHR) which protects the right to private and family life. The Convention is incorporated into UK law through the Human Rights Act 1998.

After the Supreme Court judgement the Scottish Government conducted an engagement process on how to adapt the legislation so that it would comply with the European Convention on Human Rights. The engagement process was meant to gather opinions from people who supported the policy and those with concerns, including practitioners who would deliver the Named Person Service, parents, young people, third sector organisations, the

Children's Commissioner and the Information Commissioner (Scottish Government 2016). At the time of writing (June 2017) it is envisaged that new legislation will be laid before the Scottish Parliament providing new provisions to ensure that the Supreme Court's judgment is addressed with children and young people's rights to private and family life fully respected. The aim is to have the Named Person Service in place in 2018 (Sutherland 2016).

After briefly describing what the legislation entails and its aims, the issues these new duties raise for principals will be addressed. These issues include general leadership and management matters in terms of ensuring that: staff members are fully trained; information sharing and data storage are fully compliant with relevant legal requirements; any extra workload is monitored; relationships with other agencies are supported; relationships with parents and families are cultivated; and children and young people are heard. The chapter will conclude with reflections on the Named Person role, the controversy surrounding it and how this role may develop.

23.2 What Is the Named Person Service?

Under the 2014 Act every child and young person in Scotland will have a nominated 'Named Person' or, in some cases, a 'Lead Professional'. It is the Named Person's duty to promote, support or safeguard the well-being of the child or young person by:

> S.19 Named Person Service
>
> (5) (a) (i) advising, informing or supporting the child or young person, or a parent of the child or young person,
>
> (ii) helping the child or young person, or a parent of the child or young person, to access a service or support, or
>
> (iii) discussing, or raising, a matter about the child or young person with a service provider or relevant authority, and
>
> (b) such other functions as are specified by this Act or any other enactment as being functions of a Named Person in relation to a child or young person.

Examples of services a Named Person may signpost or refer children, young people or families to, include bereavement counsellors, mental health services and speech and language therapy.

Five questions have been provided as a framework to help those with the Named Person role:

1. What is getting in the way of this child or young person' wellbeing?
2. Do I have all the information I need to help this child or young person?
3. What can I do now to help this child or young person?
4. What can my agency do to help this child or young person?
5. What additional help, if any, may be needed from others? (Health and Social Care Alliance 2016, p. 7).

However, these are vague questions and do not provide thresholds for when to perform certain actions. Stoddart (2015) has stated that these thresholds are highly important for when a Named Person decides a number of pieces of information or jigsaw pieces point to possible harm to a child's well-being.

A strong case can be made that many principals and classroom teachers were already carrying out the role of the Named Person without the mandate or backing of legislation. Several local authorities had been using a Named Person scheme before the introduction of the legislation and to the authors' knowledge these schemes continue despite the delay in the introduction of the relevant parts of the 2014 Act. There are currently no reported cases of parents bringing an action against a local authority in the exercise of the Named Person scheme.

The local authority is responsible for delivering the Named Person Service for those children who are school-age up to the age of 18. The local authority where a child or young person lives is not responsible if they attend a school managed by a different local authority, or attend a grant aided school, an independent school, are in secure accommodation, in legal custody or in the armed forces. The Named Person Service does, however, continue for those still at school after attaining the age of 18 years. While at school, therefore, the efficient and effective operation of the Named Person Service will fall on the shoulders of the principal. It is worth considering why the Scottish Government decided this legislation was needed when there was already the Getting It Right For Every Child (GIRFEC) policy framework.

23.3 Aims of the Legislation

There are several stated aims for the Named Person Service, with the paramount aim being to enhance the well-being of all children and young people in Scotland. Part of this is to prevent children and young people from slipping between different agencies with an emphasis on early intervention rather than waiting for later signs of welfare risks. The service is designed to promote inter-agency working so that public services work together to support children's well-being rather than perform the separate functions of their individual services. By having one single person as the point of contact for all agencies, professionals will know who to go to with concerns about the well-being of any child or young person. This one Named Person, or Lead Professional in certain circumstances (such as inter-agency involvement, complex or specialist support required and/or when child protection concerns raised), is then in charge of organising meetings and ensuring that action points are carried out. Burns (2015) summarises the purpose as being 'about children, young people and parents getting the help they need, when they need it' (p. 65) rather than every child being appointed a social worker.

The Named Person Service can also be seen as a result of several reviews into cases where children have not been safeguarded, for example the Victoria Climbié case (Lamming 2003). While the Named Person Service does not guarantee the safety of all children and young people it helps to make sure that professionals and others who have any concerns will know who to contact. It could be argued the 2014 Act is an admission that certain aspects of the Scottish GIRFEC policy have not succeeded and thus require statutory force to be complied with (Coles et al. 2016). There is also a case for arguing that the Named Person duties do not add any new responsibilities to principals in Scotland. Professional Standard 4.4.4 of the Standards for Leadership and Management (General Teaching Council for Scotland 2012a) states (Table 23.1):

Table 23.1 Standards for Leadership and Management (GTCS 2012a) Professional Standard 4.4.4

The Professional Standard	Professional Actions
4.4.4 Head teachers build, maintain and review partnerships with other professions and agencies to support the learning, pastoral and emotional needs of learners	• adhere to and implement child protection policies and procedures to ensure the care and welfare of all learners; • understand the National Practice Model within GIRFEC, and develop this understanding in colleagues; • recognise and encourage the wide and diverse range of partnerships which contribute to the well-being of all learners; • ensure that systems are in place which enable all partners to contribute to, and support the diverse needs of all learners in line with local and national policy and legislation.

The legal duty being placed on principals as Named Persons through the 2014 Act thus echoes the existing professional obligation from the General Teaching Council for Scotland (GTCS). To understand the Named Person Service it is necessary to understand the GIRFEC policy framework and that GIRFEC is the most important Scottish policy related to children's welfare in the last 20 years. The policy aims to improve children's lives through early intervention and co-ordination across relevant agencies and universal services. Put simply, it is about joined-up working between agencies and professionals at a local level putting the child's welfare and well-being at the centre of decision-making. GIRFEC marks the change from prioritising children's welfare to focusing on children's well-being. As Coles et al. (2016) state 'GIRFEC represents an aspirational and transformational change agenda in terms of promoting well-being and embodying new working practice, and as such, it plays a crucial part in the future direction of child welfare and family policy in Scotland' (p. 335). Burns (2015) argues that the preventive part of the Named Person Service is about early identification and most importantly, early engagement with families so that acute services are not needed later on.

A distinctive part of Scottish policy-making, in comparison to the rest of the UK but not elsewhere, is that broad policy frameworks at a national level are then interpreted and administered at the local level. This local discretion in the 32 local authority areas in Scotland presents challenges for practitioners, such as school principals, on the ground. Local discretion means practitioners must decide how to interpret and implement GIRFEC policy, and, if enacted, its, legislative provisions. Above all the GIRFEC approach is meant to shift practitioners from working with a 'silo' mentality and move agencies away from working independently of one another and only focussing on the one aspect of a child's life that they had responsibility for. Instead the focus is to be on the whole child and their well-being through the prism of the SHANARRI indicators (Safe, Healthy, Achieving, Nurtured, Active, Respected, Responsible, Included) and Curriculum for Excellence (four capacities of Confident Individuals, Effective Contributors, Responsible Citizens and Successful Learners) (Health and Social Care Alliance 2016, p. 10). Thus, there is a focus on outcomes rather than procedures and outputs, inter-professional working rather than turf wars.

The Named Person Service could lead to schools and mental health services working more closely thus leading to an improvement in mental health outcomes for children (Chadwick 2016). For example, the Named Person Service could make a difference is in assisting in the diagnosis of mental health problems experienced by children who have suffered neglect or abuse (ibid).

One difference between the legislative provisions and the previous policy framework is that there is a duty on local authorities and health boards to provide the Named Person Service and there is an obligation on other agencies to comply with requests for information. We will now turn to the detail of what the Named Person Service entails.

23.4 Issues for School Principals

Several criticisms have been made of the Named Person Service and some of these have a direct bearing on school principals' duties in relation to the scheme. There have been concerns raised about information-sharing, confidentiality of information, the state's interference in family and private life, the state becoming a 'third parent' and infringing parents' rights and diluting parents' role (Waiton 2016; Jackson 2016; Peterkin 2016). Concerns have been raised about the increasing surveillance culture and an ever-extending collection, analysis and storage of data on children (Stoddart 2015). There has also been criticism that the focus on well-being diminishes the scope for children's rights. It has even been alleged that the scheme 'bears the hallmarks of a totalitarian approach' (Jackson 2016, p. 28). While the Supreme Court ruled that the principle of having a Named Person for every child in Scotland was 'unquestionably legitimate and benign', certain provisions related to information-sharing in the 2014 Act were held to be incompatible with Article 8 of the European Convention on Human Rights.

For school principals there are several issues to consider regarding the introduction of the Named Person Service: issues related to leadership and management in schools, interagency working and increased workloads; the new role's effect on relationships with parents and carers; and how the voice of children and young people is included. These issues are due to the change from a general professional duty to legal obligations to advise, inform and support children and young people and their parent/s, to help them to access services or support, and to discuss matters with them.

For principals who are the Named Person or who have staff who are the Named Person there are a number of issues to be addressed. For example, what does the concept of 'well-being' actually mean; what does being a Named Person mean; what is their role as a named person; what are their responsibilities as a named person; how should the assessment tools be used. While school principals may feel that as the Named Person there is increased responsibility placed on them, in fact the legislation stipulates a 'Named Person Service', thus, in the public sector, the duty is placed firmly on local authorities and health authorities. The authorities are responsible for ensuring the service is provided rather than the individual practitioner. These authorities must provide training about Named Person duties and procedures and support their staff in their role as a Named Person. Chadwick (2016) states that 'adequate training of named persons and articulation of a solid framework for intervention will be essential for successful implementation of the role' (p. 6).The costs of implementing the Named Person Service across Scotland have been commented on in relation to the training of staff in the first year only (Hudson 2013). After the first year it is assumed that training will be subsumed within other training for school and other staff.

Concerns raised by members of the trade union Unison in a survey of health visitors (cited in Jackson 2016, p. 21) included the worry of 'scapegoating' of professionals if a child is harmed, the possibility of facing legal action and being sued by parents, information overload and damage to relationships with parents. Stoddart (2015) states it is 'arguably beyond the competence of even an experienced guidance or pastoral care teacher' to determine whether other agencies should be involved (p. 108). However, this seems to denigrate teachers' professional skills, abilities and judgement but the Supreme Court found the provisions on information-sharing had to be more precise.

Several issues of particular importance for principals are now considered: general leadership issues relating to information; workload; inter-agency working; relationships with parents; and the rights of children and young people.

(a) General leadership and management issues

A distinction can be made between issues related to leading people and those involving the management of resources and processes. While there is currently no specific literature on leadership and management issues related to the Named Person Service in Scotland it is possible to consider work on the previous Every Child Matters scheme in England which was similar to the GIRFEC policy in Scotland. Dudau (2009) has queried whether responsibility rested with individuals or organisations. Traditional leadership literature focuses on individuals within organisations, Dudau (2009) suggests that different models of leadership may be required. The Named Person, as an individual, will have access to support and help at other levels and from different agencies. Dudau (2009) suggests that 'leadership is located within people, organizations and processes in partnerships' (p. 403) and this would seem to mirror the type of working that will be required under the Named Person Scheme.

A balance will have to be struck by school principals and other professionals between need and risk. Through the GIRFEC framework the intention is to meet the well-being needs of all children, the universal part of the policy, and thus, reduce the potential risks of later harm to some children, the child welfare part. This tension, balancing need and risk, has to be handled by practitioners in the field with three separate, and potentially competing, discourses around need, risk and well-being (Coles et al. 2016).

Coles et al. (2016) detail several challenges in the Named Person Service: the absence of a definition of 'well-being'; the lack of thresholds for intervention; alongside the implications of lowering information-sharing thresholds; the tensions between supporting and protecting children; privacy and intrusion issues; how professional roles and practices will accommodate the service; and how the necessary change management process will develop (p. 356). Many of these issues relate to the information that a Named Person will receive and have to store while that child or young person is at their school.

23.4.1 Information-Sharing and Data Storage Issues

In the Christian Institute case (2016) the Supreme Court summarised the challenges in relation to information-sharing into four questions:

(i) 'what are the interests which article 8 of ECHR protects in this context,
(ii) whether and in what respects the operation of the Act interferes with the article 8 rights of parents or of children and young people,
(iii) whether that interference is in accordance with the law, and
(iv) whether that interference is proportionate, having regard to the legitimate aim pursued'. (paragraph 70)

In answer to the first question the Supreme Court held that the processing of information about an individual's private life, including information related to their health, came within the scope of article 8 (paragraphs 71–77). It then went on to answer question (ii) above and decided the sharing of personal data between public authorities would interfere with the Article 8 rights of the people whose personal data was shared, in particular, sections 23, 26 and 27 (paragraph 78). The Court then went on to consider whether that interference was permissible under the exceptions contained in Article 8(2) with the measure not only having some basis in domestic law, which the obviously 2014 Act meets, but be accessible to the person affected and its effects being foreseeable. The Supreme Court held there was not enough precision to protect people against arbitrariness in the exercise of the Named Person role. The Supreme Court ruled that the lack of safeguards in the legislation meant that it would not be possible to examine the proportionality of any interference with a person's Article 8 rights. Therefore, the information-sharing sections of Part 4 did not satisfy the requirement of being 'in accordance with the law'.

When new legislation is put forward and is implemented school principals will have to ensure that they and/or other staff members who carry out the function of the Named Person perform their information-sharing and data storage in line with Article 8 of the ECHR, the Data Protection Act 1998, new Statutory Guidance for the 2014 Act and, for the time being, the Council Directive 95/46/EC on the protection of individuals with regard to the processing of personal data and on the free movement of such data.

While school principals in Scotland, may, in appropriate circumstances, receive police reports and information from various other agencies such as health services and social work with the Named Person Service the school staff member, whether it is the principal, deputy principal or guidance teacher, may receive more information relating to a child or young person than before. School principals will require guidance on how long information should be held and how to ensure the material is destroyed when necessary (Jackson 2016). Today, there is perhaps more disquiet about different state agencies holding data on families than in previous generations, and parents are able to request copies of the information held on their child/ren through their right to request information under the Freedom of Information Act 2000.

The sharing of information was a major concern of those opposed to the Named Person Service (Stoddart 2015; Waiton 2016) and the new legislation and Statutory Guidance is eagerly awaited to see how the Scottish Government will adhere to the Supreme Court's 2016 judgement on this issue.

23.4.2 Increased Workload

While the Getting to Know GIRFEC Parent and Carer Information (2016) states that 'in most cases, the Named Person will not have to do anything more than they normally do in the course of their day to day work' (p. 6) it could be argued that extra legal obligations are placed onto school principals as they must ensure that they, or a member of their staff, is the Named Person for each of the pupils of their school. This member of staff will have responsibility for being the contact point for all the different agencies that might be involved with the well-being of a child or young person such as health services, social work, and the police. The person carrying out the duties of the Named Person Service (the Named Person) can be regarded as the main point of contact for that child or young person. They must take overall responsibility for the child or young person's well-being, co-ordinate meetings and actions between multiple agencies which may include the parents or carers and, if appropriate, the young person themselves.

From the legislation itself it is not possible to say if the introduction of the Named Person Service will increase principals' workloads. As stated above it could be argued that schools and principals were already performing the role of a Named Person without the statutory footing now available through the 2014 Act. Principals have always had a role in promoting, supporting and safeguarding the well-being of children and young people in their care.

Part of the duties from the 2014 Act can be described as simply 'signposting' or 'referring' and so, are clearly what teachers, principals and health visitors would have been doing already (Kidner 2013). This has also been referred to as the Named Person being a 'gatekeeper to services' (Coles et al. 2016, p. 345). However, the 2014 Act also places further duties on the Named Person and while the legislation was being drafted, there were concerns about workload and whether professionals would have the ability to carry out these functions (Kidner 2013).

Additional workload may arise in relation to conducting background research on a child or young person, completing paper work, formal scheduled and informal unscheduled meetings with external agencies and/or parents and carers, telephone calls, emails, follow-up actions arising from meetings etc. and the possibility of being called upon during school holidays. It is likely that local authorities will make alternative arrangements over the longer summer holidays. This extra workload would be difficult to keep track of as it would likely to be an hour here or there rather than a regular whole or half day in the diary. However, it has also been suggested that the new service might reduce the time spent by school staff on child protection case conference meetings and in children's hearings (Kidner 2013). One saving of time for principals may come from more meetings taking place at the school site rather than at other agencies' offices thus saving the principal or other Named Person teacher the travelling time to and from meetings.

Concerns have been raised about the lack of capacity to implement the policy and gaps in certain services which may undermine the new approach in parts of the country (Coles et al. 2016). At present it is not known what workload issues, if any, will arise as a result of full-scale implementation of the Named Person Service. Bureaucracy and workload are currently high on the agenda for teachers and principals in Scotland and these issues are unlikely to disappear soon. Large scale research studies would be necessary to ascertain how the Named Person Service affects workload for school staff. The size of the school may affect the impact of these new duties as some primary schools can have as many as 800 pupils while others have as few as 10. In larger primary schools the principal will need other staff to take on the role of the Named Person.

23.4.3 Relationships with Other Agencies

As Connelly (2012) puts it 'the GIRFEC approach intends to encourage professionals to view the child as part of a wider system comprising family and community, to be vigilant towards the child's broader developmental needs and to avoid a child at risk of neglect or abuse disappearing from the professional "radar"' (p. 842). This requires inter-agency working at closer level than previously achieved. The overarching aim of both the wider GIRFEC policy framework and the 2014 Act is to transform the way agencies and practitioners work together to protect the well-being of every child in Scotland but there are still tensions in inter-agency working. This new model requires transformational change at the level of culture and day-to-day working practices. Some agencies and some practitioners are going to be happier at adapting previous practices and adopting new practices than others. The Named Person Service may challenge some people's perceptions about their and others' professional roles and it may bring to light certain underlying values within agency or professional cultures (Coles et al. 2016). Many public services are set up to respond to specific problems or targets rather than to deal with the whole child and their family by providing universal support and preventative action as required. While there is a universal education service and a national health system the two have worked more separately in the past with the addition of social services as and when required in particular circumstances for child protection.

Principals may be interested in the 12 conditions for effective inter-agency working created from two separate studies (Cassidy 2008 and Statham 2011 as cited by Connelly 2012, p. 844), in particular 'having a commitment to joint working among managers and practitioners; … making efforts to develop strong personal relationships and trust between partners; … putting efforts into maintaining good communication; … having clear procedures for information sharing, including databases.'

For guidance teachers who perform the role of Named Person it will be important to have opportunities to engage with professionals from other agencies in order to learn and understand more about their jobs, their professional learning and their professional cultures (Connelly 2012).

(b) Relationships with parents and families

One argument made against the Named Person Service was that it introduced the concept of 'a State Guardian' thus undermining the role of parents (Peterkin 2016). The Named Person has been defined as 'a state named professional "guardian" who will oversee the interests of every child in Scotland from birth' (Waiton 2016, p. 1). Those opposed to the Named Person Service have argued it is the 'Trojan Horse' of child protection that is allowing whole scale changes to the state's relationship with families (Jackson 2016; Stoddart 2015). For NO2NP (No to Named Person) campaigners the loss of parental rights and issues related to privacy were of paramount concern (Stoddart 2015). It has been reported that at NO2NP road shows parents were worried about 'children coming home and telling their parents that they do not have to go to bed, or that they do not have to do French at school, because they have got rights' (Stoddart 2015, p. 7). Campaigners imagine the Named Person Service as practitioners overseeing the well-being of all children in a more active sense than it would appear the role will function in practice. An opposing view is that put forward by Burns (2015) who argues that rather than diminishing parents' role the Named Person Service is part of how the government can enable parents 'to be empowered to fulfil their own lives and make their own choices' (p. 65).

Kay, Tisdall and Davis (2015) criticise the lack of a solid definition of well-being in the 2014 Act. They point out that the SHANARRI indicators suggest part of the concept but do not provide a tangible whole meaning. It has been argued that the lack of definition means the assessment of a child's well-being could be subjective and different professionals may vary in their perceived thresholds for intervention (Stoddart 2015). There are concerns that 'too low a threshold might be set, requiring intervention into family life that would be considered highly intrusive and counter to parental rights to make decisions based on their own values, perhaps including some religious beliefs' (Stoddart 2015, p. 107).

Principals may find that their relationships with parents and carers have not been improved by the controversy surrounding the introduction of the Named Person Service. In one interpretation of the act it is parenting rather than children's well-being that will be assessed by the Named Person and other practitioners. When new legislative provisions are drafted and, assuming these are passed by the Scottish Parliament, principals across Scotland will have to communicate the role of school staff in performing their duties under the Named Person Service. This could prove difficult with some parents or carers raising concerns about the sharing of information between agencies. School principals' first role may be to allay parents' concerns that the Named Person Service does not mean that parents and families are being minutely scrutinised and assessed as to whether they are good parents or not. If some teachers and/or school principals are over-zealous in their referrals to other agencies, in particular social services, there is the possibility that the Named Person Service will be viewed with suspicion and it could damage schools' relationships with parents and pupils. Adequate training and good inter-agency working is necessary to prevent situations like this. Stoddart (2015) points out the 'extent to which a family has the social/ cultural capital to negotiate between the expectations of the Named Person Service and their own, perhaps but not necessarily, idiosyncratic approach to parenting is worthy of future discussion' (p. 114).

Cunningham notes 'a shift in the balance of power between adults and children' in the twentieth century (p. 191) and the Named Person Service could be seen as putting school principals and teachers in-between parents and children. In the late nineteenth and early twentieth centuries children's rights meant an increased role for the state in their lives with the state intervening in relation to child employment, home and school situations and 'the interests of the child and the interests of the state were one and the same' (Cunningham 2005, p. 163). It could be argued this is the case with the Named Person Service and that parents are being squeezed out further. Cleland and Sutherland (2009), on the other hand, see that the right to respect for privacy and family life under Article 8 can be 'interpreted in an adult-centric way, making the European Convention on Human Rights a virus waiting to attack children's rights' (p. 2).

(c) Children's rights

The United Nations Convention on the Rights of the Child (UNICEF 1989) recognises children as rights' holders (article 40) and also affirms that parents have rights, responsibilities and duties, as their child matures (articles 5 and 14). The UK Government ratified the UNCRC in 1991 and under the Scotland Act 1998 the Scottish Government must observe and implement international obligations (Kay et al. 2015). However, this does not produce any specific rights that can be argued for in court if they are not complied with and so the UNCRC has moral rather than legal force in Scotland (ibid). There are exceptions to this and gradually the Scottish Parliament is laying down rights from the UNCRC into national legislation, for example children have the right to have their views considered in decisions about their schooling that significantly affect them under s.2(2) of the Standards in Scotland's Schools Act 2000. It is not entirely clear what relationship the Scottish Government sees between GIRFEC and the UNCRC as there are conflicting texts on this (Kay et al. 2015), however, in the GIRFEC Parent and Carer Information Pack (Health and Social Care Alliance Scotland 2016) it is stated that the UNCRC is "the foundation of GIRFEC" (p. 16).

Well-being appears to have trumped children's rights meaning there is a looser, more diluted obligation on the part of public authorities and less ability for children, and others, to argue the state has not upheld or enforced their rights.

Alderson (1999) (cited in Quennerstedt and Quennerstedt 2014, p. 119) argues that if children are to be regarded and accepted as holding rights then the concept of childhood and of the child have to be reassessed. One way to encapsulate the issue of children's participation or voice in the decisions which affect them, thus accepting that children have rights and legal status as rights' holders in their present rather than only their future lives, is to accept them as human beings, thus diminishing the impact of the 'human becoming' approach (Invernizzi and Williams 2008, p. 6). Children, then, should be recognised as an active participant in the here and now (Quennerstedt and Quennerstedt 2014). By recognising children as rights' holders school could provide children with opportunities not only to learn about human rights but also to practise their human rights and thus learn about rights and enhance their self-confidence (ibid). Cleland and Sutherland (2009) state that 'despite some recent legislative improvements, the child's voice is something of a whisper, since there is no principle of allowing children to be heard in education decisions affecting them' (p. 10). In relation to protecting children from risk there is a tension as a more risk-free environment means their lives are 'highly governed and means their activities/ participation is controlled' (James, Curtis and Birch in Invernizzi and Williams 2008, p. 89).

There is perhaps also a tension for school pupils aged between 16 and 18 years old. In Scottish elections those aged 16 years and above are eligible to vote but under the 2014 Act 16 and 17 year olds require a Named Person to assist and support them (Stoddart 2015). The 2014 Act does not specify who will be the Named Person for those aged between 16 and 18 who have left school. At a national GIRFEC training event in January 2017 the trainer suggested a senior youth worker at the local authority would take on this role.

23.5 Conclusion

The Named Person Service is still uncertain as new legislation is required for compliance with the European Convention on Human Rights (ECHR). The information sharing provisions must be appropriate and proportionate to the well-being concerns that will operate.

At the current time teachers may be more trusted than social workers for the most part and teachers are in regular contact with families, thus enabling better communication and service provision to families through signposting, support and referring on to other agencies. One benefit of the Named Person Service and its universal coverage rather than a targeted approach is that stigma is removed and families will hopefully feel less different or isolated than before. Depending on the operation of the service this relationship between families and schools may be tested. Over time it will be discovered if the Named Person Service reduces trust in teachers and school principals and thus undermines the Named Person Service. The service may make parents view educators in the same way that social workers in Scotland are currently viewed, namely as professionals who may take their children away.

Although the Named Person Service has moved attention to well-being, going beyond welfare and child protection issues, it is important to remember the lessons highlighted in the Victoria Climbié Death Inquiry. Lamming (2003) recommended that health and education professionals worked together and shared information on an inter-agency basis. The Climbié case is particularly pertinent as a teacher suspected Victoria was being physical abused but did not alert medical staff as she thought hospital staff would make sure she was protected. This and similar cases are strong arguments in favour of the Named Person Service and GIRFEC approach. However, it could be argued this is all a sticking-plaster approach. More responsibility is being laid at professionals' doors while wider socio-economic and structural problems such as poverty and other fundamental causes of inequality are not addressed (see for example, Kay et al. 2015). Tan (2011) posits that policy preoccupations across the UK focusing on outcomes rather than addressing issues of social justice and children's rights are for political convenience. However, Burns (2015) argues that the Named Person Service presents 'a critical opportunity to "break the cycle" of poverty, disadvantage and poor life chances which characterise the lives of thousands of people in our society' (p. 64). It is not clear how a signposting and referral system can achieve all that.

Future research is needed in this key policy area, for example investigating the views of principals and local authority officers involved in the Named Person scheme and longitudinal studies to determine whether it has improved the well-being of children and young people in Scotland. Another possible focus for future research is the impact the legal duty has on the dynamics and practicalities of inter-agency working. An examination of individual leadership in and between organisations such as health, social work and the police would be useful to understand how the duty works in practice.

The arguments against the Named Person Service in relation to privacy breaches and third way parenting may be missing the point of the legislation, namely that for the majority of children and young people and their families the new duty will be irrelevant as it will not be exercised but the provisions need to comply with the European Convention on Human Rights. The view conveyed at training events held over the last three years attended by the authors is as Waiton (2016) suggests:

> *[t]eachers will not be interested in minor issues and will only get involved, as a Named Person, in more serious cases. To some extent this may be the practical reality, although it also goes against the very idea of the Named Person as someone who is overseeing the well-being of the whole child in all aspects of their life and development.* (p. 7)

Burns (2015) argues that the Named Person Service is part of a shift to making childhood in Scotland better with a change in culture and 'a shared public service agenda which is focused around prevention, parenting and family support' (p. 67) while Jackson (2016) contends that the Named Person Service is 'a huge mallet to crack a small nut' (p. 3).

An equally damning view, albeit from a very different perspective, is provided by Kay et al. (2015) who state that GIRFEC policy and the 2014 Act do not ensure that children's rights are upheld, do not ensure that 'outcomes are meaningful to children and their families or that practice avoids discrimination or services are based on children's and their family members' views' (p. 226). Early information-sharing was a requisite for the system to work as planned. To prevent future risk of harm, the threshold for information sharing was lowered at the same time as 'the grounds for sharing information … broadened' (Coles et al. 2016, p. 352). Burns (2015) argued that this early identification, intervention, engagement, prevention and support, with the Named Person Service as an extra conduit to facilitate and provide assistance, would mean that problems were nipped in the bud but the Supreme Court ruled that the information-sharing provisions were incompatible with Article 8 of the ECHR.

Some issues related to the implementation of the Named Person Service operate at the school and so are specific to each school and principal, there are also system-wide issues which need to be addressed, such as relations with families, interagency working, information-sharing and weighing up need and risk.

If the Scottish Named Person Service is deemed a success nationally and internationally, it may become one of the borrowed policies. The same issues and concerns will need to be addressed in other jurisdictions, in particular confidentiality, responsibility, relationships with other agencies, with parents and above all, with children and young people.

When new provisions are enacted, school principals in Scotland will have to walk a multi-layered tightrope: protecting children's welfare and well-being; (trans)forming ever closer working relationships with other agencies and practitioners; keeping parents and families informed about the Named Person Service; adhering to information-sharing legislation and guidance; and involving children in decisions that significantly affect their lives.

References

Burns, M. (2015). The 'Named Person' debate: The case for. *Scottish Journal of Residential Child Care, 14*(3), 64–68.

Chadwick, G. (2016). Could the named person scheme have a role in addressing mental health problems in vulnerable children? *International Journal of Culture and Mental Health, 10*(1), 1–6. https://doi.org/10.1080/17542863.2016.1250798.

Cleland, A., & Sutherland, E. E. (2009). *Children's rights in Scotland* (3rd ed.). Edinburgh: W. Green.

Coles, E., Cheyne, H., Rankin, J., & Daniel, B. (2016). Getting It Right For Every Child: A national policy framework to promote children's well-being in Scotland, UK. *The Millbank Quarterly, 95*(2), 334–365.

Connelly, G. (2012). Multi-agency working. In T. G. K. Bryce, W. M. Humes, D. Gillies & A. Kennedy. (Eds.), *Scottish education* (4th ed.). (pp. 840–849). Edinburgh: Edinburgh University Press.

Cunningham, H. (2005). *Children and childhood in western society since 1500* (2nd ed.). Harlow: Pearson Longman.

Data Protection Act 1998, ch.29.

Dudau, A. (2009). Leadership in public sector partnerships: A case study of local safeguarding children boards. *Public Policy and Administration, 24*(4), 399–415.

Freedom of Information Act 2000, ch.36.

General Teaching Council for Scotland. (2012a). *The standards for leadership and management: supporting leadership and management development.* Retrieved from http://www.gtcs.org.uk/web/FILES/the-standards/standards-for-leadership-and-management-1212.pdf.

Health and Social Care Alliance Scotland. (2016). *Getting It Right For Every Child: Parent and information pack*. Edinburgh: The Alliance Scotland.

Hudson, N. (2013). *Children and young people (Scotland) bill SB 13/59*. Edinburgh: Scottish Parliament. Retrieved from http://www.scottish.parliament.uk/ResearchBriefingsAndFactsheets/S4/SB_13-59.pdf

Invernizzi, A., & Williams, J. (Eds.). (2008). *Children and citizenship*. London: Sage.

Jackson, R. (2016). *State guardian or head gardener? The imposition of state guardianship by the Scottish Government*. A discussion paper. Sheffield: Centre for Welfare Reform.

Kay, E., Tisdall, M., & David, J. (2015). Children's rights and well-being: Tensions within the children and young people (Scotland) act 2014. In A. B. Smith (Ed.), *Enhancing children's rights* (pp. 214–227). London: Palgrave Macmillan.

Kidner, C. (2013). *Children and young people (Scotland) bill SB 13/38*. Edinburgh: Scottish Parliament. Retrieved from http://www.scottish.parliament.uk/ResearchBriefingsAndFactsheets/S4/SB_13-38.pdf

Lamming, W. H. (2003). The Victoria Climbié death enquiry, presented to Parliament by the Secretary of State for Health and the Secretary of State for the Home Department (CM 5730).

Peterkin, T. (2016, April 2). Revealed: What can happen when a named person reports on your children. *The Scotsman* [Online]. Retrieved from http://www.scotsman.com/news/revealed-what-can-happen-when-a-named-person-reports-on-your-children-1-4089077

Quennerstedt, A., & Quennerstedt, M. (2014). Researching children's rights in education: Sociology of childhood encountering educational theory. *British Journal of Sociology of Education, 35*(1), 115–132.

Scottish Government. (2016). *Engagement to implement named person*. Retrieved from http://news.gov.scot/news/engagement-to-implement-named-person

Stoddart, E. (2015). The named person: Surveillance and the well-being of children and young people in Scotland. *Surveillance and Society, 13*(1), 102–116.

Sutherland, E. E. (2016, September 19). Beyond the named person service. *The Journal of the Law Society of Scotland*. Retrieved from http://www.journalonline.co.uk/Magazine/61-9/1022210.aspx

Tan, J. (2011). Education and children's rights. In P. Jones & G. Walker (Eds.), *Children's rights in practice* (pp. 109–123). London: Sage.

The Christian Institute and others (Appellants) v The Lord Advocate (Respondent) (Scotland) [2016] UKSC 51. Retrieved from https://www.supremecourt.uk/cases/uksc-2015-0216.html

Waiton, S. (2016). Third way parenting and the creation of the "named person" in Scotland. The end of family privacy and autonomy? *SAGE Open, 6*(1), 1–13. https://doi.org/10.1177/2158244016629525.

24

Difficulties of Comprehension in the Citizenship Education in Europe

Eszter Anna Nyúl

24.1 Introduction

Democratic social-political systems expect children to grow up to be adults making decisions in common affairs or to shape decisions with their opinions. While this is indeed a great opportunity to change the circumstances, it is also a heavy burden in terms of responsibility and preparation. Individuals, as citizens, receive this right; and the European Union firmly supports its member states in active and democratic citizenship education. Though democratic citizenship education is a common issue of the member states of the European Union, reflections on it show essential interpretational differences that must be kept in mind to really understand each other.

What is "citizenship education"? Firstly, guiding on behalf of adults and the embedding of school into reality. It could be compared to 3D glasses: the two different colour lenses represent two disciplines each – education and law. At the first glance the different lenses are odd but they are just necessary to enliven the desired picture. Similarly, citizenship education will show a more precise image if we do not forget that it stands in the intersection of law and education.

In the case of citizenship education, we must start out from Seneca's critical thought, non scholæ, sed vitæ discimus – we do not learn for life, but for school. (Seneca). This is amended by Dewey's idea: "*I believe that education,*

E. A. Nyúl (✉)
Doctoral School of Education, Faculty of Humanities, University of Pécs, Pécs, Hungary

K. Trimmer et al. (eds.), *The Palgrave Handbook of Education Law for Schools*,
https://doi.org/10.1007/978-3-319-77751-1_24

therefore, is a process of living and not a preparation for future living (…) I believe, finally, that the teacher is engaged, not simply in the training of individuals, but in the formation of the proper social life" (Dewey 1897: 77–80).

Decades ago, when frontal education was the almost exclusive method of education, citizenship education was considered to necessitate educational methods different from other curricula. This was recognized in both the Western part of Europe and its state socialist countries as well. But while on one side of Europe the democratic citizenship education, on the other side the idea of the socialist citizen was pronounced (Berzsnyánszky 1981).

Amongst all knowledge taught at school, citizenship education is the most dependent on the social-political system of a given state. It is an intersection closely connected to both national and international social and legal norms. In this theme precise definitions are more necessary than generally expected in educational matters. Besides different languages, cultures and historical paths, even legal history derived from national and international politics will have a strong influence on the content behind these words.

A serious problem nowadays in the subject of citizenship education is the international discourse, when partners do not understand each other's notion of citizen. Citizenship refers to different identities in Western Europe, North America, Central or Eastern Europe.

This study intends to call attention to the importance of precise definitions of expressions in this topic, as different languages allow misunderstanding which may result in talking about purposes instead of dialogues. The basis of this mistake originates from the different roots which nurture our ideas.

24.2 The International Discourses in the European Union

The European Union is a political and economic partnership that is unique in international law, presently still uniting 28 member states. This latter expression initiates debates among member states at the same time: yes, we are united, but how closely? Its member countries, which continue to be independent and sovereign states, constantly keep forming their own attitudes towards the Union, meanwhile making common decisions in common institutions.

It is not easy to operate a mechanism which has 24 official and working languages, and its functionaries will use 2 or 3 languages during their daily work (mainly English, French and German). Although it operates one of the largest translating services in the world, the question still remains whether politicians and European citizens speak the same language on the level of understanding and interpretation. Regions of the EU do not differ in their material potentials only, but also in their ideas of state and their political socialization are highly different.

The motto of the EU must remain living in citizenship education, too. "United in diversity" refers to a European Union established towards peace and well-being, and a cultural, linguistic and traditional diversity, which enriches our continent. These all are essential to live democratic citizenship in its entirety in any of the member states.

Democratic citizenship education wishes to develop three fields: knowledge, skills and behaviour. These are of equal value and if one is damaged, they will not function effectively. Even goodwill may be dangerous without knowledge; without skills there will be no effectivity; findings will only seem as circularities without acting. Civics of a given state, as primus inter pares, will give the extra emphasis needed because we can talk about citizenship education and not only community organization.

Currently in Europe the aim of citizenship education is considered to be the acquisition of critical thinking and analytical skills, and the enhancement of active participation in school and social life.

According to the Citizenship Education in Europe Eurodyce report of 2012, citizenship education is realized in ISCED1, ISCED2 and ISCED3 circles (ISCED 1997, International Standard Classification of Education, UNESCO 1997) in the majority of the member states of the European Union; and examined the presence of 10 themes in the European national curricula: 1. socio-political system of the country, 2. human rights, 3. democratic values, 4. equity and justice, 5. cultural diversity, 6. tolerance and discrimination, 7. sustainable development, 8. national identity and belonging, 9. European identity and belonging, 10. European history, culture and literature.

These themes are all important for the interpretation of the concept of citizenship. An example for this is the theme of European culture and identity in the U.K. The Eurodyce report of 2012 demonstrates that common European conscience is not at all part of the English Citizenship Education; however it is part of the Scottish one in all the studied age groups. On 23 June 2016, in the question of Brexit 62% of the Scottish votes were for remaining in the EU, while England voted for the exit. The thinking about the public affairs had affected the curriculum, or perhaps the different curriculum had an effect on public affairs. Whatever the order was, the relation of education and politics will sooner or later materialize in law.

Another example of the importance of the themes is the lack of education of the social and political system in Hungary. With the change of regime in 1989 Hungarian society got an opportunity to define itself as living in a democratic country, and as such, adopt those attitudes which are typical with active citizens and which have deeper roots in Western societies and have become better realized and treasured values.

Current Hungarian opinions are reflected by Márton Gerő and Andrea Szabó's research, which was published under the title "Report on the political way of thinking, political integrity and participation of the Hungarian society, 2015". In the topic of "Democracy versus dictatorship" they came to the following conclusion: *"On the whole, based on the positions in the social hierarchy, the ethos of democracy is the most interpretable for the middle class and the upper middle class. In the spring of 2015 members of the lower class and the working class do not feel the substantive difference 'between democracy and dictatorship, since according to six tenth of the former and 45% of the latter, "for people like me, one system is just like the other". Finally it seems that the lower middle class which beware wash-out and has existential worries – which is the most endangered class – under certain circumstances they are the most disposed to accept the seemingly easy set of devices of dictatorship*" (Gerő – Szabó 2015: 58).

It can be seen from the example that living in democracy needs to be learned too, and this change is a slow process because it is driven forward by intellectual and emotional revelations, for which knowledge, experience and naturally, time are necessary. This learning lasts from early childhood to elderly age and different age-groups are receptive in different ways.

24.3 What Is a Citizen of a State Like?

Citizenship education is present in the core curricula for primary and secondary schools in each member state, though it is hardly manifested in teacher training. Member states are autonomous in education; there are recommendations and voluntary commissions on behalf of the member states. This knowledge is typically passed on thorough History and Geography lessons at school.

After the terror attack of 7 January 2015 in Paris, at French initiation, politicians of the European Union started to deal with citizenship education on both member state and union levels; since the role of education has become obvious in the fight against acts of terrorism and in the acquisition of basic democratic values.

In March 2015, Paris, the "Declaration on Promoting citizenship and the common values of freedom, tolerance and non-discrimination through education" (the Declaration of Paris) was passed by the Education Ministers. According to this Declaration, education has an essential role in forming basic social values, promoting social inclusion, decreasing discrimination and geographical and social differences, and furthermore, in strengthening tolerance and solidarity. The European Commission pronounced in an official statement that "*Education is important to prevent and tackle marginalisation and radicalisation*" (COM (2015) 408 final: 5). After such utterances one expects that the presence of intention, experience and necessary resources will result in perceptible changes.

Citizens must be aware of their citizenship and it is in their individual and collective interest to be citizens.

We need prepared, conscious and active citizens, says the EU; but whose interest is it to have these "good citizens"? For example, the individuals, who have been more and more in focus since the end of the twentieth century, due to the change of paradigm resulting from the emphasis on human rights, which enables the recognition of the rights of citizens, even ones confronting their own countries. (Kopper 2010) Furthermore, it is the interest of the station where the citizen lives, because it is necessary for the functioning of the local government. For their own functioning, the countries also need citizens, who know their rights and obligations. The European Union also needs citizens who have both national and European identities.

"No one is born a good citizen; no nation is born a democracy. Rather, both are processes that continue to evolve over a lifetime. A society that cuts off from its youth severs its lifeline." The thought above was pronounced by UN Secretary General Kofi Annan (1997–2006) in his address to the World Conference of Ministers Responsible for Youth, Lisbon 8 August 1998.

We might get stuck with the statement that "one has to become a citizen" if we only consider that the lucky majority of people who are not fugitives, from the legally acknowledged start of their lives – be it conception or live birth –, are provided with the chance of belonging to one or more countries and to be granted citizenship status.

This is obviously an exclusively legal interpretation of the meaning of the expression "citizen". From the word Hungarien "állampolgár" (loan translation: citizen of the state), it is easy to associate to the relationship between the state and the citizen – to the legal system of the state in which the citizens have their own places. This is regulated by the citizenship law, which is no other than "*the mapping of a given state's idea of nation*", its "*translation to the language of law*" (Kisteleki 2011: 9). If we give further considerations to

Kisteleki's interpretation, the purely legal definition of the word "citizenship" no longer seems narrow; it would not require wider interpretation.

We can talk about citizenship from the formation of states in their modern sense, when a new system of relations was shaped, dominated by the idea of state sovereignty and the principle of territoriality. The self-definition of the state was formed along the set borders and it shaped its internal legal system while the states developed together the international law for their external relations. According to Foucault, the states can only be interpreted in the plural form in this new system (Foucault 2004: 7). The well separated countries that aim for a balance of power are not empires but states; its dwellers are not simply subjects or inhabitants but the citizens of a particular state.

The citizens are part of the population forming the state; they are objects of rights and obligations. Citizenship is a legal institution, in which both legal regulations and, beyond them, moral contents are present. The former must be taught to young people; the latter is essential to the recent generations for the proper functioning of the society. What is "desirable" in different countries of a given era may be highly variable, as this is not only a matter of culture but of politics as well.

According to Habermas, citizenship is not connected to national identity but to a certain political culture which is essential for the citizen to become part of the community (Habermas 1994). The European Union needs citizens with European identity but it can only be achieved along the conscience of citizenship of the peoples of a territorially divided Europe. In Europe, ethnic, cultural and national conscience was connected to civic identity in different ways.

"Nation-state and democracy are the twin born of the French Revolution" (Habermas 1994: 22), where "nation" establishes the political identity of the citizens of a democratic community. During the formation of national states, the territory was given in Northern Europe; civic conscience developed separately from local people's ethnic conscience, along a common political aim. It was civic conscience that united locals into a political community, into a nation. In contrast, Eastern European national conscience had identified with ethnic conscience earlier, thus belonging to a nation and citizenship do not mean the same. After the peace treaties of Versailles following World War I, Eastern and Central European states had to form political nations from their citizens, while their minorities already had a strong sense of national conscience by then. These minorities as citizens are aboriginal state-forming factors in the different countries. Meanwhile, they have such a national conscience in our days, too, that it makes the concepts of citizenship and nation incompatible in this region. There is a difference between East and West on the level of words: which identity is related to which word.

This may be the reason why József Antall, the first freely elected Hungarian Prime Minister of the change of regime's sentence caused incomprehension in June 1990: "*In a legal meaning, based on the Hungarian public law, as the Head of Government of all Hungarian citizens, of this country of 10 million people – in my soul, in my feelings I wish to be the Prime Minister of 15 million Hungarians*" (Debreczeni 1998: 137). It was a hard diplomatic job to clarify that this did not mean territorial demands but the undertaking of the reborn Hungary towards the Hungarian communities annexed to neighbouring countries by the peace treaty of Trianon, as "*it is a special responsibility of the Hungarian Government to support the subsistence of the Hungarian nation as a cultural and ethnic community*" (Government programme presented to the Parliament on 22 May 1990) (Jeszenszky 2010: 63).

In our study we may not ignore the distortion caused by the Hungarian translation of the Kofi Annan-citation. The Hungarian text is the following:

> Senki sem születik jó állampolgárnak, ahogy egyetlen államban sincs magától értetődő demokrácia. Sokkal inkább igaz, hogy mind a kettő egy folyamat, amely egy életen át tart és fejlődik. A fiatalokat születésüktől kezdve be kell vonni ebbe a folyamatba.

We can see that "citizen" is not quite the same as "állampolgár", neither is "nation" the equivalent of the word "állam" (state). The intention of the translator is understandable, as they tried to reflect the past UN Secretary General's message in the clearest way possible.

Since the lack of a definition was perceptible, as our conceptual images behind the words and highly different, Recommendation No. 1735 of the Council of Europe in 2006 aimed to clarify the idea of "nation". In their study about the idea of nation, which was compiled, based on forms filled by 35 national parliamentary delegations and the opinions of legal and political experts, the Council of Europe came to the conclusion that it is hard, almost impossible to give a common definition to the concept of "nation". The recommendation even went as far as stating that the words used in national languages have no acceptable equals in English or French.

Though, as international discourses are held mainly in these two languages and the results of discussions are translated back and forth from these languages, it is worth having a look at Kofi Annan's sentence about citizenship education in French as well: "*On ne naît pas bon citoyen et il n'existe pas de nation démocratique par essence. Ces deux états sont en fait des processus perpétuellement en marche. Les jeunes doivent y participer dès la naissance.*"

The English and French sentences are much more similar to each other, the Hungarian one obviously differs from them. In the citation meant as example, the English "citizen", the French "citoyen" and the Hungarian "állampolgár" expressions seem to be becoming constant in citizenship education, while they have diverse meanings.

Hungarian word "polgár" may mean an inhabitant of a royal free city, a member of "polgárság" as a social class, and more rarely, a (state) citizen. Nowadays, it appears with this content in the phrase "európai polgár" (citizen of Europe), because the word (state) citizen would be questionable in this form. Hungarian legal terminology makes an express difference between the expressions "polgár" ("citizen") and "állampolgár" ("state citizen"), while English and French will not. According to Gábor Pap, this differentiation requires great precaution, as "*English and French authors will not always define what they mean by citizen or citoyen*" (Pap 2013: 94). Is it possible that the analysis of the meanings of these words is not so important for them, or have they not yet realized the importance of this? Member states of the EU need a lookout and comparison, since these may lead to the communal thought of "these are us" and may realize European multiplicity. As we are talking about sovereign states, we cannot expect them to line up behind the citizenship concept of a different country just because communication happens in that language.

Catherine Neveu studied the anthropology of citizenship in particular; and contrasted that between Great-Britain and France. She also detected the difference between "citizen" and "citoyen" (Neveu et al. 1998). She claims that the anthropological view of citizenship tries to grab both the vertical dimension, which is the relationship between individuals and the state in a broader meaning, and the horizontal dimension at the same time, which is the relationship among citizens. According to her, the essence of citizenship is the set of values which are associated to it, the cultural and political capital which are invested into it by the society.

The question for us is whether a discourse in a foreign language can embrace these values and represent them in decision-making.

If we looked only at its legal interpretation, even that would involve several aspects: "Citizenship did not appear on its own in the era of civil revolutions. Revolutionary metamorphosis, together with the birth of a civil state and its legal institutions, closely linked to them or embedded into them. (State) citizenship is related to people's representation, people's sovereignty, nation, individual rights and the constitution itself. All these together have remained the basic institutions of the civil state to this day" (Pap 2013: 94).

While interpreting the English and French "citizen" expression within Europe, it is worth remembering that until the British National Act of 1948 (British Nationality Act 1948 (11 & 12 Geo. 6), Chapter 56) the expression "citizen" was not present in the legal regulations. Subjects were mentioned in all cases, even if the content of this latter was converted to a democratic political system.

Jean-Jacques Rousseau was the first to write about the (state) citizen in its current sense in his treatise "The Social Contract", seeing that in his work, *"citizenship is entwined with equality, state and sovereignty"* (Pap 2013: 96). The French expression "citoyenneté" is the first station of our present modern concept of citizenship; this legal institution is rooted in France.

According to Rousseau, "This character beyond individuals, deriving from the union of all individuals (…) has the name of republic or political society, and its members call it state. (…) As for the members of the consociation, they together have the name of people, individually, they are called citizens, if they have a share of the main power, and subjects, if they are subjected to the laws of the state" (Rousseau 1762: VI).

In chronological order, in 1753 Diderot writes in his Encyclopaedia about the "citoyen", but this is yet to be interpreted in the context of people and individuals. The first law about citizenship was the 1787 Constitution of the United States of America. This was followed by the 1789 French Declaration of the Rights of Man and of the Citizen. The events of America were regarded by the philosophers of the Enlightenment as echoes of their own views. As Alexis Tocqueville wrote:

> The American Revolution, no doubt, exercised considerable influence over ours, but that influence was less a consequence of the deeds done in America than an inference from the prevailing ideas in France. In other European countries the American Revolution was nothing more than a strange and new fact; in France it seemed a striking confirmation of principles known before. It surprised them, it convinced us. The Americans seemed merely to have carried out what our writers had conceived; they had realized what we were musing. (Toqueville 1994: 176–177)

The legal institution of citizenship was first determined by the Code Napoleon in 1804. Its influence can be detected in several countries, due to the considerable conquests of the French Empery. Its language was aimed at the French citoyens, aided by its consciously clearly written common language.

"Napoleon considers Code Civil the real constitution of France. In fact: systems and constitutions have come and gone in the past nearly two centuries – Code Civil has remained" (Ruszoly 1997: 145). And if we accept the concept that sooner or later we will start to think the way we live, we can deduct in a rational way that adopting the French legal regulation abroad was able to affect the way of thinking among broader levels of society. Due to the widespread views of the enlightenment, we presume to know the French citoyen.

The situation is further complicated by the recent rather popular usage of "citoyen" as an attributive in France. This is happening because in today's France, taking from the culture of enlightenment, this has become the main point of reference in immanence. A constant central topic of public thinking and politics is "citoyenneté", involving amongst others the power of sensibility, science and reflexion, autonomy of the individual and acknowledgement of human rights. (Sami-Nair 2013).

Those who had hoped for justification and support from this word initiated a change of concept which even though has not emptied the previous content of the word, it still may cause a difference between its national and international usage. We think that in the citizenship education we should "*cast a watchful eye on Paris*" (Batsányi 1790), but it is the safest for the discourse partners to clarify at the start of international discussions, which concept a given country's expressions for citizenship education are derived from, and what expectations and social attitudes are associated with them.

24.4 Conclusion

Presently, the most frequently used languages at international discussions, conferences and meetings in Europe are English and French. The latter, however, only holds its position due to the capital status of Brussels, while the ideology of a modern state is derived much from this language. We can only hope that partners dealing with citizenship education, speaking different languages, know precisely what they mean by the expressions "nation" and "citizen" that they use; and they intend to get to know each other.

Meanings should be constantly clarified and checked in international discourses because due to different languages and different past, discourse partners may mean different things (i.e. processes) or place main emphasis elsewhere. They do so in an international environment where common thinking and mutual understanding is essential. We think it is best during discussions to add automatically which meaning of citizen is being used (which country's idea of citizen, in what depth of meaning). Only in this way can discussion partners understand each other's concerns, aims and proposals. Otherwise no results can be expected from common reflection on citizenship education. This also projects the question of the existence of European identity and ultimately, the matter of keeping the EU together.

References

Batsányi, J. (1790). A franciaországi változásokra 1789 Magyar Museum II. évad I.kötet http://mek.oszk.hu/00600/00611/00611.htm#14

Berzsnyánszky, L. (1981). Hagyományok és útkeresések az állampolgári nevelésben. Acta Paedagogica Debrecina. N 82. Debrecen.

British Nationality Act, 1948 (11 & 12 Geo. 6.) Chapter 56.

Citizenship Education in Europe Eurodyce Report. (2012). Education, Audiovisual and Culture Executive Agency (EACEA P9 Eurydice and Policy Support). Brussels. http://eacea.ec.europa.eu/education/eurydice/documents/thematic_reports/139EN.pdf

COM. (2015). 408 final. 26.8.2015, Brussels. https://ec.europa.eu/transparency/regdoc/rep/1/2015/EN/1-2015-408-EN-F1-1.PDF

de Tocqueville, A. (1994). A régi rend és a forradalom (The Old Regime and the Revolution). Translated, preface, notes, and bibliography by Hahner Péter ed. Kontler László. Circus Maximus. Atlantisz Könyvkiadó. Budapest.

Debreczeni, J. (1998). A Miniszterelnök. Antall József és a rendszerváltozás. Osiris. Budapest.

Déclaration de Paris (2015). http://cache.media.education.gouv.fr/file/03_-_mars/66/9/2015_mobilisation_declaration_FR_401669.pdf

Dewey, J. (1897, January). My pedagogic creed. *School Journal*, *54*, 77–80p. http://dewey.pragmatism.org/creed.htm

European Commission Press release, Brussels. 31 May 2012: Citizenship education now taught in all European countries but specialist training for teachers lacking. http://europa.eu/rapid/press-release_IP-12-514_en.htm

Foucault, M. (2004). Naissance de la biopolitique Cours au College de France 1978–1979. Hautes Études. Gallimard Seuil.

Gerő, M., & Szabó, A. (2015). Politikai Tükör. Jelentés a magyar társadalom politikai gondolkodásmódjáról, politikai integráltságáról és részvételéről (Report on the political way of thinking, political integrity and participation of the Hungarian society). MTA Társadalomtudományi Kutatóközpont. Budapest. http://www.socio.mta.hu/uploads/files/2015/poltukor_online.pdf

Habermas, J. (1994). Citizenship and national identity. In B. van Steenbergen (Ed.), *The condition of citizenship* (pp. 20–36). London: Sage.

Jeszenszky, G. (2010). Antall József, a nemzetpolitikus. Sóvidék 2. évf. 2. sz. (2010, november) 62–65 p.

Kisteleki, K. (2011). Az állampolgárság fogalmának és jogi szabályozásának történeti fejlődése: koncepciók és alapmodellek Európában és Magyarországon. Opitz. Budapest.

Kopper, Á. (2010). Állampolgárság határon innen és túl. Beszélő Folyóirat. *15*, 5 (May–June).

Neveu, C., Bier, B., & Roudet, B. (1998). Pour une anthropologie de la citoyenneté, une approche comparative France/Grande-Bretagne. In: Agora débats/jeunesses.1998/12. Jeunes en Europe: politique et citoyenneté. 43–51p. https://www.persee.fr/doc/agora_1268-5666_1998_num_12_1_1605

Pap, G. (2013). Az állampolgárság intézményének eredetéről. Publicationes Universitatis Miskolcinensis. Sectio Juridica et Politica. *Tomus*, *XXXI*, 93–101.p.

Rousseau, J.-J. (1762). Du contrat social ou Principes du droit politique. Paris. http://classiques.uqac.ca/classiques/Rousseau_jj/contrat_social/Contrat_social.pdf

Ruszoly, J. (1997). Európa Jogtörténete (History of European Law). Püski Kiadó Kft. Budapest.

Sami-Nair. (2013). Pour une herméneutique de la Charia (For the hermeneutics of the Saría), the introduction by the member of the scientific council of the Res Publica Foundation, which was presented at the seminar "What does it mean to us: Sária?" on 15 April 2013. http://www.fondation-res-publica.org/Pour-une-hermeneutique-de-la-Charia_a723.html

Seneca Lucius Annaeus: Epistulae morales ad Lucilium, Libri XVII-XVIII Epistula CVI. http://www.intratext.com/IXT/LAT0230/_P2Y.HTM

The text of Secretary-General Kofi Annan's statement to the opening of the World Conference of Ministers Responsible for Youth, in Lisbon, on 8 August http://www.un.org/press/en/1998/19980810.sgsm6670.html

UNESCO International Standard Classification of Education I S C E D. (1997). http://www.unesco.org/education/information/nfsunesco/doc/isced_1997.htm

25

Training Teachers to Prevent Violence Against Children: The First Line Against Family Violence

Elisabetta Biffi

25.1 Introduction

It is not easy to pin down the meaning of 'violence against children', given that it is a complex, multifactorial and multidimensional phenomenon that is difficult to circumscribe within a definition. The United Nations Committee on the Rights of the Child, in its General Comment No. 13 (2011), affirmed the right of the child to freedom from all forms of violence, defined as physical violence, sexual violence, mental violence and neglect or negligent treatment. These are macro-categories that cover a wide range of violent actions, from corporal punishment to assisted violence to abandonment. Also of note is the definition provided by the *World Report on Violence and Health* (2002), issued by WHO (World Health Organization), in which violence is described as "the intentional use of physical force or power, threatened or actual, against oneself, another person or against a group or community, that either results in or has a high likelihood of resulting in injury, death, psychological harm, maldevelopment or deprivation" (Krug et al. 2002, p. 5). This definition in turn informed the *UN Study on Violence Against Children*, 2006, which states that "violence against children takes a variety of forms and is influenced by a wide range of factors, from the personal characteristics of the victim and

E. Biffi (✉)
University of Milano-Bicocca, Milan, Italy
e-mail: elisabetta.biffi@unimib.it

K. Trimmer et al. (eds.), *The Palgrave Handbook of Education Law for Schools*,
https://doi.org/10.1007/978-3-319-77751-1_25

perpetrator to their cultural and physical environments" (United Nations General Assembly On The Rights Of The Child, 2006[1]).

Numerous studies have drawn attention to how extensive and widespread violence against children actually is – the most recent report by UNICEF, *Hidden in Plain Sight. A statistical analysis of violence against children* (2014a, b) provides disturbing data on the phenomenon. As commented by J. O'Malley in his foreword to the report, "the first step in curbing all forms of violence against children is bringing the issue to light" (UNICEF 2014, p.1). This means, at the macro level, increasing research and studies on the phenomenon and, at the micro level, bringing violence out into the open, and helping victims to tell their stories.

In sum, violence is a serious contemporary issue, with repercussions at both the individual and social levels (in terms of social costs as well, as specified in: Krug et al. 2002). Models of violence experienced in the home/family may be reproduced for generations, especially when children are physically abused (Rosewater and Goodmark 2007; Edleson et al. 2004). This in turn has a knock-on effect on society, which is becoming increasingly violent.

In Western countries, child protection is based on multi-professional systems that draw together different fields of competence, health, welfare, law as well as education. Indeed, several studies have underlined the role of schools (Baginsky 2003, 2007), and different authors have demonstrated that, if child protection is to be effective, it is crucial for teachers and educators "to be clear and confident about their own pastoral role with regard to sensitive issues of child protection, especially when collaborating in multidisciplinary child protection work" (McKee and Dillenburger 2009, p. 3). The first requirement is for teachers to be aware of the regulatory measures that define the role of the teacher in addressing violence against children. While it is necessary to be familiar with specific national provisions, it is of the utmost importance to identify the transnational documents that lay down the general regulatory framework for the signatory countries.

Given this background, this chapter first discusses the international strategies underpinning the battle against violence towards children as a necessary prerequisite to defining the key part to be played by teachers.

The second section of the chapter then focuses on the specific role of schools in promoting children's rights and preventing violence against children, in keeping with international policy.

---

[1] Available at: http://srsg.violenceagainstchildren.org/sites/default/files/documents/a_61_299_un_study_on_violence_against_children.pdf (last accessed: 26 May 2016).

In light of the general guidelines discussed in the first two sections, the third section examines the role of teachers in addressing specific forms of violence, such as family violence. Teachers need to be familiar with both the regulations/laws and risk factors related to violence: lack of knowledge, in these areas, can contribute to a lack of appropriate reporting and risk identification. Teachers are well-positioned to prevent and fight violence, given that they spend long periods of time with children and their families, who generally recognise them as playing an institutional role.

More specifically, teachers and educators have a crucial role to play in the battle against violence:

- because they spend whole days with children, and so have the opportunity to observe them and note significant changes, or signs that something is wrong;
- because they can help parents to develop non-violent parental practices and, at an earlier stage, to ask for help in critical situations, before developing forms of violence;
- because they can provide expert opinions to child protection specialists, given that their relationship with the children and their families predates the involvement of the social services.

Finally, the fourth section of the paper looks at the specific training required by teachers if they are to effectively contribute to the battle against violence, with reference to the specific case of family violence. Teachers need to develop specific professional competencies (informed by pedagogical, psychosocial as well as legal knowledge) for recognizing and addressing violence against children. More specifically, they must receive training in:

- the relevant norms and procedures;
- listening to and receiving stories from children;
- developing the inner emotional competence required to fearlessly deal with the violence emerging from victims' stories.

Indeed, it is crucial for training to focus on teachers' own professional competence and wellbeing, if they are to effectively facilitate early recognition of the risk of family violence, within the earlier-mentioned framework laid down by the 1989 United Nations Convention on the Rights of the Child for the respect and fulfilment of children's right to be free from all forms of violence.

25.1.1 International Strategies for Fighting Violence Against Children

The first key document guiding the definition of international strategies for fighting violence against children is, as stated above, the United Nations Convention on the Rights of the Child, adopted via General Assembly Resolution n. 44/25 of 20 November 1989.

The Convention binds the signatory states to actively promote and defend the rights of the child, viewed as the responsibility of the international community. Hence, under Article 44 of the Convention, the signatory states undertake to submit regular reports to the United Nations on the measures they have adopted to give effect to the rights recognized in the treaty and on the progress they have made in ensuring that children benefit from these rights. In 1991, in keeping with the Convention's spirit of international cooperation, the UN set up the *Committee on the Rights of the Child,*[2] composed of 18 independent experts. The Commission's work is not only to monitor the progress of individual countries, but also to provide the signatory states with the support that they need, especially in terms of encouraging governments and populations to maintain a strong focus on human rights. To this end, the Commission organizes, for example, *Days of General Discussion*, at which delegates debate specific articles of the UNCRC or other themes of strategic importance for the Commission.

Historically, the Commission has displayed strong commitment to fighting violence against children (organizing discussion days on related themes such as: the role of children in armed conflict scenarios, in 1992; the role and protection of the girl child, in 1995; the administration of juvenile justice, in 1995). More specifically, at the 23rd session of the Days of General Discussion, in January 2000, the Commission decided to devote the following two annual editions (September 2000 and September 2001) to two different aspects of "violence against children". In 2000, the focus was on state violence suffered by children, either while in the care of the State, or in the context of "law and public order" enforcement. In 2001, the focus was on violence suffered by children in schools and within the family. These dedicated discussions led the Committee on the Rights of the Child to call for more in-depth study of the theme of violence against children.

Other initiatives from the same period include the report published in 2001 by WHO - World Health Organization, on violence and public health,

[2] See: http://www.ohchr.org/EN/HRBodies/CRC/Pages/CRCIndex.aspx (last accessed: 26 November 2016).

one section of which specifically focused on children (Krug et al. 2002). Also in 2002, the declaration "A World Fit for Children",[3] was issued following a special session on children held by the United Nations' General Assembly, at which the participating heads of state undertook to promote the rights of the child at the world level and to implement the agreed strategies and pursue the agreed objectives.

As a result, the United Nations, via General Assembly Resolution 56/138, called for an international study to be conducted on the question of violence against children, with the aim of advancing understanding of the phenomenon and developing recommendations for the member states in terms of strategic actions to be implemented. This study was commissioned to Paulo Sérgio Pinherio in 2003, and was carried out with the cooperation of: the Office of the High Commissioner for Human Rights (OHCHR), United Nations Children's Fund (UNICEF), World Health Organization (WHO) and International Labour Organization (ILO), following a participatory research design that involved regional and country-level consultations, meetings and visits. Participants in the regional consultations included children themselves, a key feature of the study that allowed children's own perspectives and experiences as well as their ideas about how to fight violence to be taken into account. The output of this research was the *United Nations Study on Violence Against Children,*[4] which was presented to the General Assembly in 2006, and which on the one hand showed that violence was a widespread phenomenon across the member countries, and on the other provided a series of operational recommendations. These included the proposal to appoint a special representative with the role of addressing violence against children. To this end, in 2008, via GA Resolution A/RES/62/141, the United Nations created the role of Special Representative of the Secretary-General on Violence against Children.[5]

Again over the past decade, the United Nations has maintained a strong focus on the issue of violence against children, asking member states to modify their existing national legislative frameworks to adopt specific provisions for protecting children from violence. Furthermore, the United Nation has

[3] Main source: https://www.unicef.org/specialsession/wffc/ (last accessed: November 2016).

[4] See: Pinheiro, Independent Expert for the United Nations Secretary-General's *Study on Violence against children*, 2006. Available at: http://www.unviolencestudy.org (last accessed: November 2016).

[5] This office was created to supplement other key existing figures, such as the Special Representative of the Secretary-General for children and armed conflict, the Special Rapporteur on the sale of children, child prostitution and child pornography, the Special Rapporteur on violence against women, the Special Rapporteur on trafficking in persons, especially women and children, and of course, the Committee on the rights of the child itself. For further information, see: http://srsg.violenceagainstchildren.org (last accessed: 26 November 2016).

played a key role by reiterating and emphasizing in all official documents and contexts that violence against children is never acceptable and may never be justified. As recently affirmed once again in General Comment No. 13 of the Committee on the Rights of the Child: Freedom, "The right of the child to freedom from all forms of violence"[6] applies to all the world's children.

The United Nations has not implemented its international strategy alone, but in collaboration with OHCHR, UNICEF and WHO, all of which work together and with NGOs to enhance the protection of children and promote their rights.

This work is reflected in the recent report, published on November 2016 by the International NGO Council on Violence Against Children, entitled *10 Years on: Global Progress & Delay in Ending Violence Against Children – the Rhetoric & the Reality*. This document may be viewed as the most recent step in the battle against violence towards children originally launched by the UNCRC. The report outlines the key actions that have been taken and the key results that have been achieved: for example, the number of states that have adopted a total ban on the corporal punishment of children (in all contexts, including home and school) has tripled since the publication of the first *UN Study*.

Nonetheless, it should be pointed out that the results achieved have mainly been at the formal, legal level, while much remains to be done, especially at the socio-cultural level. The *UN Study on Violence against Children* identified 2009 as the target date for reaching a total global ban on violence against children, a goal that has not yet been achieved. On the positive side, however, the battle continues. The *Sustainable Development Goals* identified in the UN's 2030 Agenda include SDG 16.2: *End abuse, exploitation, trafficking and all forms of violence against and torture of children*, an aim that reflects international efforts to stop violence against children, specifying that it is referred "all forms of violence against children". A Global Partnership[7] has been set up to support all those working to meet this goal across the world, giving substance to what has become an international strategy. More specifically, the main UN recommendations that are salient to this chapter include: strengthening national and local commitment and action; prohibiting all forms of violence while actively promoting the prevention of violence and a culture of peace and non-violence; developing the capacity to address violence of all who work with and for children (including teachers); ensuring that children have the

[6] Full text available at: http://www2.ohchr.org/english/bodies/crc/docs/CRC.C.GC.13_en.pdf (last accessed: 26 November 2016).

[7] Source: www.end-violence.org (last accessed: December 2016).

opportunity to participate in the life of their communities. Schools can play a key role in the pursuit of all these goals by developing strategies for enhancing children's awareness of their own rights and their level of participation in school life, as well as by working with families to prevent violence and promote awareness and non-violent values.

25.1.2 The Role of Schools in Promoting a Culture That Opposes Violence Against Children

There are several reasons why schools play a key part in the battle against violence, especially from a human rights perspective.

First, the international strategy outlined above has included a specific focus on fighting violence in schools, a topic that was addressed by an *ad hoc* working group of the Committee on the Rights of the Child at the 23rd session of the Days of General Discussion. The group concluded that all violent methods of 'discipline' (such as corporal punishment and other degrading, humiliating and cruel practices) fail to meet the requirement of respect for the child's dignity (CRC, art. 28.2) (CRC/C/111, 28th Session, 28 September 2001).

Second, schools play a role in implementing children's rights strategies, in the broad sense. When school managers and head teachers are familiar with children's rights, and when teachers are appropriately trained, schools can bring the international strategies described above to the local level, offering local arenas in which adults and children can encounter a children's rights perspective, discovering that we are all – whether adults or children – citizens of one wider community. This implies actively working to increase children's participation in community life: children's time at school should foster learning about how to be members of a community, and how to engage in active citizenship, by allowing children to participate in decision-making processes in line with their current resources. Thus, child advocacy and agency, which are key aspects of overall children's rights strategy, can feasibly begin within schools.

Third, schools are directly involved in addressing violence among children, by dealing with bullying and violence inflicted on students by other students. In these situations, schools have the specific duty to protect children from violence, given that children have the right to receive education in a safe context, as set out in Art. 28 and Art. 9 of the CRC. Bullying is, in our contemporary era, a worldwide problem. It may be defined as actions, physical or verbal, that have a hostile intent and are repeated over time, cause distress to the victim, and involve a power imbalance between the perpetrator and victim (Olweus 1991; Pepler and Craig 1995). The recent UNICEF study, *Hidden in Plain Sight*, published in 2014 and mentioned above, presents a statistical analysis of violence against children in 62 countries. Data collected from 106 countries through the HBSC and GSHS show "that the proportions of adolescents aged 13 to 15 who say they have recently experienced bullying ranges from 7 per cent in Tajikistan to 74 per cent in Samoa" (UNICEF 2014, p. 120). In relation to bullying, it is important to flag the issue of cyberbullying (or online bullying), which has been defined by the Cyberbullying Research Center in the United States as "wilful and repeated harm inflicted through the use of computers, cell phones, and other electronic devices".[8] Within this overall scenario, schools are often the material and/or virtual context in which bullying takes place, in that even in cyberbullying schoolmates tend to be the bully's main victims.

In addition, schools play an official role within the child protection system: lack of knowledge, in these areas, can contribute to a lack of appropriate reporting and failure to identify risk scenarios. The active contribution of schools to the child protection system is a specific component of their institutional role and is related to the need for social awareness that violence prevention is a key health priority for our societies (Corso et al. 2008).

Although legal reforms are crucial to winning the battle against violence, they are not enough. Complex and participatory discussion in local cultural contexts is also needed if we are to build a shared awareness of the rights of the child and of the negative effects of violence in all its possible forms. For example, cultural debate can usefully challenge the use of violence as a method of discipline. This point will be more fully developed in the next section.

Finally, schools are the main actors in formal education and the institutional voice of social communities. This means that they have a crucial part to play in building a culture of peace for the future of the world. This is closely related to the previously discussed institutional role of schools in children's rights strategies, and is a mission that pervades all aspects of school life. From the layout of the educational setting, to the specific educational activities offered, to the 'mood' characterizing daily community life, schools are places in which peace may be experienced, and not merely learned.

25.1.3 The Case of Family Violence: Identifying the Teacher's Role

Numerous studies have demonstrated that child abuse and neglect have a major impact on children's development, with consequences that vary as a function of the duration and extent of the abuse or neglect suffered, the relationship

[8] Cyberbullying Research Center, http://cyberbullying.us/about-us/ (last accessed: 26 November 2016).

between child and perpetrator, the age of the child, the timing and structure of intervention (see, for example: Veltman and Browne 2001).

In general, it has been reported that children who have experienced violence display difficulties at school, in terms of deficits or delays in their skills development and knowledge acquisition (McKee and Dillenburger 2009). Parental violence against children is, at the time of writing, the most common form of violence experienced by children. This holds true for both 'corporal punishment' and 'abuse'. The above-mentioned UNICEF study, *Hidden in Plain Sight*, found that 70 percent of children globally reported having experienced some form of psychological violence, while 60 percent reported having received physical punishment, especially in the home (UNICEF 2014).

Many other researchers have pointed out that teachers and educators – including those operating in early childhood education services (McKee and Dillenburger 2012) – are in a position to contribute to the early identification of maltreatment and family violence in general, although it is a complex task (Walsh et al. 2008). At the same time, teachers and educators enjoy a professional relationship with families that allows them to support parents and offer them 'positive parental education'. In brief, there are two different ways for schools to support the development of a non-violent culture towards children:

- **via the early identification of family violence**
- First, schools and educational services play a privileged role in the process of early identification of the risk of family violence, which is based specifically on:
    - listening competence: teachers and educators should be able to listen empathically to children, so that they will feel free to ask for their help if necessary. For teachers and educators, this implies developing advanced competence in non-directive listening;
    - observational competence: signs of maltreatment and family violence are often implicit in minor changes in a child's behaviour, which in turn are only visible to those paying close attention. Hence, teachers and educators require competence in the area of attentive observation as one of their leading childhood protection resources;
    - knowledge of procedures: when risk factors have been identified in a specific situation, it is necessary for teachers and educators to exactly know what steps to follow. This means that they must be familiar with the official procedures for situations in which the risk of family violence has been identified.

- **by promoting a 'positive parental attitude'**

Secondly, teachers can play a key role in training families in positive parental attitudes. This also means encouraging families who are in a critical situation to ask for help, or to deal with their situation by developing parental strategies that are positive for their children and do not rely on violent actions. It has been shown that parenting programs may be an effective means of reducing violence within families (Fraser et al. 2013; Knerr et al. 2013; Lundahl et al. 2006). However, it has also been pointed out that programs focused on maltreatment may be insufficient, and that a more integrated approach is required to ensure adequate conditions for healthy development (Lannen and Ziswiler 2014). This is particularly true of early childhood, but applies to the entire span of children's development. Schools can contribute to promoting nonviolent attitudes, first by providing a model of community life in which conflicts and issues may be addressed without recourse to violence, and second by directly supporting parents, and offering opportunities and venues for counselling in parenting skills, given that parental education is among the teacher's responsibilities (Ulivieri Stiozzi 2013, 2008; Riva 2014; Iori 2012).

25.1.4 Defining Teacher Training for Preventing and Dealing with Family Violence

As stated above, if they are to address violence against children, teachers require appropriate training, both in identifying risks and preventing them.

This training should be initiated at the pre-service stage, for example, detailed knowledge and awareness of the main rules, regulations and procedures may be imparted early in the teacher training process and kept up to date throughout teachers' careers via in-service training. It has been observed, on the contrary, that in high-income countries, teacher training programmes have not focused sufficiently child abuse and neglect (Sinclair Taylor and Hodgkinson 2001; Baginsky and Macpherson 2005) and violence in general. In this direction, few studies have explored the experience-based knowledge drawn on by teachers in their daily work with children with histories of violence (Walsh and Farrell 2004). Walsh and Farrell's qualitative study on early childhood teachers' knowledge of child abuse and neglect offers some useful guidelines. For example, teachers require clear knowledge of the phenomenon, in terms of risk factors and procedures, an understanding of the specific needs of learners who have experienced violence, and the required level of competence for working with families. In addition, the authors emphasize that it is important for teachers to be aware of their own personal limits, including in terms of being able to seek help when necessary (Walsh and Farrell 2004, p. 595). This last point is crucial to our conclusions here: violence is an 'object' that is not always clearly defined, requiring methods that work jointly at the individual and cultural levels.

However, the main component of teacher training in addressing violence should take the form of in-service training, based on the real-life experience of teaching in schools. Violence, as stated at the outset, is a complex, multidimensional concept that appears to elude precise definition, and is closely related to social, cultural and personal dimensions. Alice Miller (1997, 2002) argued that addressing issues of violence against children evokes inner involvement on the part of adults, obliging them to go beneath the surface, beyond the 'declared level', in order to construct a personal understanding of their own experience of violence. In other words, teachers must develop the capability to relate empathically to their pupils, but also to recognise their own vulnerability when addressing topics such as violence that run deep and are related to other complex dimensions of education, such as the role of power, the boundaries between permission and control, and the potential for education itself to become a form of abuse (Biffi 2013; Riva 1993; Iori 2012).

Within this complex framework, in order to effectively contribute to the childhood protection system and to the promotion of a children's rights culture, teachers must not only receive ad hoc pre-service training, but also need to be supported throughout their professional development, via in-service training and supervision programmes. Such training will help teachers to enhance their daily practices and to move on from their personal stories to construct their professional identities.

25.2 Conclusion

In conclusion, while the international children's rights strategy provides the necessary framework for halting violence against children, the first line in this battle is made up of all the individual adults composing our society: teachers, educators, parents, politicians, and ordinary people. Building a world without violence against children represents both a dream and a long-term project.

A dream, because history – most recently the last century and its world wars – teaches us about the limits of human civilization, and the banality of the evil (Arendt 2006). Consequently, humanity must bear in mind its own limitations, its own vulnerability, in order to defend itself. This said, human rights – from which children's rights derive – may be viewed as humankind's most recent, albeit relative, strategy for defining the ideal human beings of the future.

An ongoing project, because it must be built day by day, via a never-ending strategic endeavour that is concurrently cultural, political, social and economic. But which is, first and foremost, based on our personal, individual efforts to embrace our own life stories, take care of the needs of our inner child, and seek healing for the hurt we have been caused through our family history, from a trans-generational perspective that, ultimately, connects the individual with the whole of humanity. A 'good enough' (Winnicott 1953) adult will raise another 'good enough' adult, a child who will be a future parent, teacher, politician, man and woman. On the one hand, therefore, it is critical that each of us take individual responsibility for our specific adult role within our community. On the other hand, it is critical for the community to develop shared approaches that individuals can look to for guidance. Against this general backdrop, schools can and must model a society in which respect for the individual can feasibly go hand in hand with an emphasis on collective wellbeing, in a drawing together of the micro-personal and the macro-public that is crucial to the battle against violence towards children.

References

Arendt, H. (2006). *Eichmann in Jerusalem: A report on the banality of evil.* Paperback.

Baginsky, M. (2003). Newly qualified teachers and child protection. *Child Abuse Review, 12*, 119–127.

Baginsky, M. (2007). *Schools, social services and safeguarding children.* Leicester: NSPCC.

Baginsky, M., & Macpherson, P. (2005). Training teachers to safeguard children: Developing a consistent approach. *Child Abuse Review, 14*(5), 317–330.

Biffi, E. (2013). Tutela. *Pedagogia Oggi, 2*, 243–261.

Corse, P. S., Edwards, V. J., Fang, X., & Mercy, J. A. (2008). Health-related quality of life among adults who experienced maltreatment during childhood. *American Journal of Public Health, 98*(6), 1094–1100.

Edleson, J., Daro, D., & Pinderhughes, H. (2004). Finding common ground in the study of child maltreatment, youth violence, and adult domestic violence. *Journal of Interpersonal Violence, 19*(3), 282–298.

Fraser, J. G., Lloyd, S., Murphy, R., Crowson, M., Zolotor, A. J., Coker-Schwimmer, E., & Viswanathan, M. (2013). A comparative effectiveness review of parenting and trauma-focused interventions for children exposed to maltreatment. *Journal of Developmental & Behavioral Pediatrics, 34*(5), 353–368.

Iori, V. (2012). Diventare genitori nella società dell'incertezza. In G.B. La Sala & C. Rinaldi, (Eds.), *La "normale" complessità del diventare genitori*. Reggio Children. Reggio Emilia.

Knerr, W., Gardner, F., & Cluver, L. (2013). Improving positive parenting skills and reducing harsh and abusive parenting in low-and middle-income countries: A systematic review. *Prevention Science, 14*(4), 352–363.

Krug, E. G., Dahlberg, L. L., Mercy, J. A., Zwi, A. B., & Lozano, R. (Eds.). (2002). *World report on violence and health*. Geneva: World Heath Organization.

Lannen, P., & Ziswiler, M. (2014). Potential and perils of the early years: The need to integrate violence prevention and early childhood development (ECD +). *Aggression and Violent Behaviour, 19*(6), 625–628.

Lundahl, B., Nimer, J., & Parsons, B. (2006). Preventing child abuse: A meta-analysis of parent training programs. *Research on Social Work Practice, 16*(3), 251–262.

McKee, B. E., & Dillenburger, K. (2009). Child abuse and neglect: Training needs of student teachers. *International Journal of Educational Research, 48*(5), 320–330.

McKee, B. E., & Dillenburger, K. (2012). Effectiveness in child protection training for pre-service early childhood educators. *International Journal of Educational Research, 53*, 348–359.

Miller, A. (1997). *The drama of the gifted child: The search for the true self.* New York: Basic Books.

Miller, A. (2002). *For your own good: Hidden cruelty in child-rearing and the roots of violence*. London: Macmillan.

Olweus, D. (1991). Bully/victim problems among school children: Some basic facts and effects of a school-based intervention program. In D. Pepler & K. H. Rubin (Eds.), *The development and treatment of childhood aggression*. Hillsdale: Erlbaum.

Pepler, D. J., & Craig, W. M. (1995). A peek behind the fence: Naturalistic observations of aggressive children with remote audiovisual recording. *Developmental Psychology, 31*(4), 548–553.

Riva, M. G. (1993). *L'abuso educativo. Teoria del trauma e pedagogia*. Milano: Unicopli.

Riva, M. G. (2014). Violence interrogates adult education today. A radical and critical reflection. In B. Käpplinger, N. Lichte, E. Haberzeth, & C. Kulmus (Eds.), *Changing configurations of adult education in transitional times* (pp. 642–653). Berlin: ESREA - European Society for Research on the Education of Adults.

Rosewater, A., & Goodmark, L. S. (2007). *Steps toward safety: Improving systemic and community responses for families experiencing domestic violence*. Book Gallery. Book.

Taylor, A. S., & Hodgkinson, K. (2001). Subjecting the initial teacher training curriculum for England and Wales to the test of child protection. *Teacher Development, 5*(1), 75–86.

Ulivieri Stiozzi, S. (2008). Pensarsi padre. La paternità come esperienza autoformativa. Milano. CUEM.

Ulivieri Stiozzi, S. (2013). Paper school or flesh and blood school? Pedagogic analysis of some symptoms of suffering in contemporary schools. *Society, Integration, Education. Proceedings of the International Scientifical Conference, 1*, 310–319.

UNICEF. (2014). *Hidden in plain sight. A statistical analysis of violence against children*. New York: United Nations.

United Nations Committee on the Rights of Persons with Disabilities. (2014a). *Concluding observations on the initial report of Belgium*. Geneva: United Nations.

United Nations Committee on the Rights of Persons with Disabilities. (2014b). *Concluding observations on the initial report of Ecuador*. Geneva: United Nations.

United Nations General Assembly on the Rights of the Child. (2006). Report of the independent expert for the United Nations study on violence against children (A/61/299).

Veltman, M. W., & Browne, K. D. (2001). Three decades of child maltreatment research implications for the school years. *Trauma, Violence, & Abuse, 2*(3), 215–239.

Walsh, K., & Farrel, A. (2004). Identifying and evaluating teacher's knowledge in relation to child abuse and neglect: A qualitative study with Australian early childhood teachers. *Teaching and Teachers Education, 24*, 585–600.

Walsh, K., Bridgstock, R., Farrel, A., Rassafiani, M., & Schweitzer, R. (2008). Case, teacher and school characteristics influencing teachers' detection and reporting of child physical abuse and neglect: Results from an Australian survey. *Child Abuse & Neglect, 32*(10), 983–993.

Winnicott, D. (1953). Transitional objects and transitional phenomena. *International Journal of Psychoanalysis, 34*, 89–97.

26

Restrictive Practice in Education Settings: Institutional Violence, Disability and Law

Linda Steele

26.1 Introduction

All children with disabilities enjoy the fundamental right to inclusive education (CRPD 2008, Article 24; Committee on the Rights of Persons with Disabilities 2016, p. 3). One of the core features of 'inclusive education' is '[i]nclusive learning environments [which create] an accessible environment where everyone feels safe, supported, stimulated and able to express themselves' (Committee on the Rights of Persons with Disabilities 2016, p. 5). Despite this right and a broader shift in Australia towards desegregation of special education, children with disabilities are subjected to exclusion, segregation and violence within purportedly 'inclusive' mainstream settings (Poed et al. 2017; Senate Community Affairs Reference Committee 2015, pp. 57–58).

Violence against children with disabilities in schools takes many forms (Children with Disability Australia 2015). This chapter focuses on one specific category of violence: use of restrictive practices. Restrictive practices are non-consensual interventions directed towards restricting the movement of students with disabilities purportedly for their protection, and/or the protection of their peers and teachers (National Framework for Reducing and Eliminating the Use of Restrictive Practices cited in Senate Community Affairs Reference Committee 2015, p. 91). Restrictive practices can take the

L. Steele (✉)
University of Technology Sydney, Sydney, NSW, Australia
e-mail: Linda.Steele@uts.edu.au

K. Trimmer et al. (eds.), *The Palgrave Handbook of Education Law for Schools*,
https://doi.org/10.1007/978-3-319-77751-1_26

form of restraint (mechanical, physical or chemical) or seclusion (Senate Community Affairs Reference Committee 2015, pp. 91–92).

Recent media coverage and government inquiries have documented the extent of the widespread use of restrictive practices in schools (Senate Community Affairs Reference Committee 2015, pp. 101–114) and highlighted the harmful impacts of these practices (see e.g., Glanville 2017; Senate Community Affairs Reference Committee 2015). Restrictive practices in schools takes many forms including locking a child in a storage room, cupboard or cage, confining a child in a small fenced area within the playground, strapping a child to a chair or a pillow, and holding down a child (Children with Disability Australia 2015, pp. 11–14; Senate Community Affairs Reference Committee 2015, p. 103, see also p. 105). One particularly high profile example widely reported in the Australian media was of a ten year old boy diagnosed with autism being locked in a cage in a classroom in the Australian Capital Territory (Senate Community Affairs Reference Committee 2015, pp. 101–102; Macdonald 2016).

Restrictive practices in schools 'are often downplayed and justified as "behaviour management" and/or "behaviour modification" practices' (Disability Alliance in Senate Community Affairs Reference Committee 2015, p. 58). Yet, these practices are inherently harmful, posing risks of physical injury, trauma, death and suicide (Lyons 2015, pp. 202–203; see also Kaplan 2010, pp. 581–82). Indeed, in the context of the United States of America, it is estimated 'that there are eight to ten restraint-related deaths of children annually in the US' (Lyons 2015, p. 201). While there is no data on deaths from the use of restrictive practices in Australian school settings, the potential deadliness of their use in school settings is implicitly acknowledged in state and territory government documentation regulating their use (see e.g., the requirement to actively monitor children's breathing when using physical restraint (State of Victoria Department of Education and Training 2017a, p. 17)), and deaths have occurred from the use of restrictive practices in Australian mental health settings (McSherry 2016).

Recently, a series of Australian government inquiries have recommended a 'zero tolerance' approach involving the elimination of restrictive practices in schools (Senate Community Affairs Reference Committee 2015, p.xxi; Senate Education and Employment References Committee 2016, p. 72). While this chapter focuses on Australia, it is important to note that other countries are grappling with the use of restrictive practices in school settings (see e.g., in the US context National Disability Rights Network 2012; in the Canadian context Inclusion BC and Family Support Institute of BC 2013).

The current legal framework governing restrictive practices in schools is one of regulation as opposed to prohibition by reason of a combination of policies and guidelines, work health and safety laws, negligence law and the doctrine of necessity. Law is central to the enactment (rather than the prevention or prosecution of) this violence against students with disabilities. Importantly, while use of restrictive practices in schools remains lawful in many countries, New Zealand recently 'banned the use of seclusion in its schools, and issued guidance on behaviour management to minimise physical restraint' (NSW Ombudsman 2017, p. 26). This suggests that it is not absolute and natural that restrictive practices should remain lawful – other legal futures are possible. As such, the central aim of this chapter is twofold: (i) to provide an overview of the legal framework of the use of restrictive practices in schools, and (ii) to identify some critical entry points into questioning the self-evidence of this legal framework. Ultimately, it is hoped this chapter will encourage readers to engage with the broader debate around the prohibition of restrictive practices as violence.

In doing so, the chapter draws on critical disability scholarship on children with disabilities and education. Critical disability studies scholars have argued that a medical model of disability pervades legal, social welfare, educational and health service responses to disability. Instead critical disability studies scholars approach disability as socially constructed by reference to norms of ability reflecting what is socially, politically, and economically valued. Individuals are disabled when they do not meet these norms, a status which is determined through disciplinary processes of observation, testing, measurement and treatment (Goodley and Runswick-Cole 2012, p. 54). Some critical disability scholars have developed these ideas of disability and normalcy specifically in relation to children with disability (see, e.g., Chapman 2014; Cooper 2013; Erevelles 2000; Goodley and Runswick-Cole 2012, 2011a, b; Goodley et al. 2016; Kafer 2013; Karmiris 2016, 2017). For example, Karmiris argues that 'educational practices and policies ... only include disability by conditional degrees and [in ways] that serve to safeguard normalcy. Normalcy as able-bodied, heteronormative, middle class, white, and male, remains the measure of conditional inclusion for other versions of being and becoming human' (2017, p. 107).

The chapter begins by introducing restrictive practices in schools and then provides an overview of the current legal framework that regulates the use of restrictive practices, and ultimately positions these practices beyond legal definitions of unlawful violence and hence beyond legal liability. The chapter then discusses the United Nations Convention on the Rights of Persons with Disabilities (CRPD) and recent Australian government inquiries which provide a strong policy basis for viewing restrictive practices as violence in need of prohibition.

26.2 Regulation of Restrictive Practices

The use of restrictive practices in schools is currently legally sanctioned through a combination of a variety of different laws: education guidelines and policies, the doctrine of necessity, work health and safety law ('WHS') and law of negligence. The current framework is one of regulation as opposed to prohibition, despite the non-consensual and harmful nature of restrictive practices. Ultimately, this framework of regulation has the effect of locating restrictive practices outside of the limits of unlawful violence in criminal and civil law. The use of restrictive practices is incapable of being viewed as an injustice, and hence victims of these practices have no access to legal redress.

26.2.1 Guidelines and Policies

In Australia's federal system, each state and territory has legislative responsibility for regulating restrictive practices in schools. There is no uniform, national approach to this regulation. This can be contrasted with the disability service sector where governments have recently developed national standards (Senate Community Affairs Reference Committee 2015, p. 93; see similar disparity in the United States of America: Weissbrodt et al. 2012, p. 287). In the education context there is variation between each state and territory jurisdiction, notably in relation to the scope of what kinds of practices are regulated. For example, Victoria provides explicit guidance on physical and mechanical restraint and seclusion, but none on chemical restraint (McSherry 2016). Regulation 25 of the Education and Training Reform Regulations 2017 (Vic) provides that: 'A member of staff of a Government school may take any reasonable action that is immediately required to restrain a student of the school from acts or behaviour that is dangerous to the member of staff, the student, or any other person.' The Victorian Department of Education and Training's policy 'Restraint of Students' emphasizes the extreme and narrow circumstances in which restrictive practices should be used, stating that: 'Physical restraint and seclusion should not be used unless immediately required to protect the safety of the student or any other person' and must not be 'used as a routine behaviour management technique, to punish or discipline a student' (State of Victoria Department of Education and Training 2017b). The Department's guidelines on restrictive practices go on to state that:

> *Physical restraint or seclusion must not be used except in situations where the student's behaviour poses an imminent threat of physical harm or danger to self or others; where such action (i.e. to physically restrain or seclude) would be considered reasonable in all the circumstances; and where there is no less restrictive means of responding in the circumstances.* (State of Victoria Department of Education and Training 2017a, p. 5)

In contrast, in New South Wales 'there is no specific legislative framework regulating the use of restrictive practices, such as physical restraint or seclusion, in schools in NSW' (NSW Ombudsman 2017, p. 26). Instead, in New South Wales there is a collection of policies and guidelines that regulate various aspects of restrictive practices. For example, Guidelines for the Use of Time-out Strategies Including Dedicated Time-out Rooms provide that 'time-out strategies', which 'include isolation in the student's classroom, another teacher's room or with an executive member of staff, or the use of a dedicated time-out room', 'should be used only for the minimum period of time necessary for the student to regain enough composure to be able to return safely to class' (NSW Government Education and Communities 2011, pp. 3, 4). A bulletin issued by the Legal Services Directorate of the NSW Department provides that physical restraint may be required for school staff to meet their 'duty of care to students to take reasonable care to protect them against risks of not insignificant injury which are reasonably foreseeable', a duty that 'extends to taking reasonable care to prevent a student from injuring him or herself, injuring others or damaging property'. However, the Legal Services Directorate notes: 'Any decision taken by staff to physically restrain a student should be exercised only in those circumstances where there is a real and immediate threat of injury to a person or serious damage to property and there is no other practical way of preventing the likely injury or damage' (NSW Government Education and Communities 2012, p. 1).

There are four significant observations to be made of these guidelines and policies. The first is that ultimately, these state and territory policies and guidelines permit rather than prohibit the use of restrictive practices. As such, these policies and guidelines have the dual purpose of setting standards and safeguards for the enactment of restrictive practices which purportedly protect those subjected to them and protecting practitioners from criminal and civil liability for the use of these restrictive practices (Chandler et al. 2014, p. 97; see further Senate Community Affairs Reference Committee 2015, pp. 94–98). This means that a child with disabilities who is subjected to restrictive practices which are compliant with these policies and guidelines cannot seek criminal or civil legal recourse for unlawful violence.

The second observation is that while the state and territory policies and guidelines differ in relation to their precise form, wording and scope, ultimately they all share an approach to regulation that is focused on what is 'necessary' and 'reasonable' (McSherry 2016). I will return to this point below in my discussion of the doctrine of necessity.

The third observation is that the application of these policies and guidelines intersects with problematic ideas about children with disabilities' 'challenging behaviour'. For example, the Senate Inquiry noted 'Evidence to the committee indicates the conflation of disability and behaviour management within the school environment' (Senate Community Affairs Reference Committee 2015, p. 101). Some critical disability scholars have problematised the concept of 'challenging behaviour' on the basis that it pathologises individuals' legitimate resistance to authority and abuse and shifts attention away from problems and failures of institutions and the illegitimacy of their authority and practices (see e.g., Beaupert 2017; Dowse 2017; Goodley and Runswick-Cole 2011b; Nunkoosing and Haydon-Laurelut 2012; O'Connell K 2017, forthcoming; Spivakovsky 2017). Erevelles has argued that 'the disabled student invokes the "unruly" subject whose physiological excesses are seen as disrupting the disciplined control of schooling' (Erevelles 2000, p. 34, p. 42; see also Erevelles 2011; Watts and Erevelles 2004). Goodley, Runswick-Cole and Liddiard propose that in school settings children with disabilities are positioned as inherently deviant because they do not follow normative developmental progression and hence remain 'leaky, who fail to contain and control their unpredictable bodies and, who deviate from the normative trajectory, will remain monstrous, a ghostly spectre of the human' (Goodley et al. 2016, p. 776). Ultimately, restrictive practices can be more easily viewed as necessary and reasonable because of the pathologization and individualization of children with disabilities' behaviour which invokes the inevitably of their bodies as sites of intervention (Dowse 2017).

A fourth observation is that in policies focusing on the harms to be avoided through intervention in the bodies of children with disabilities, the harms to the bodies themselves shift from being part of the harms to be avoided to being merely harms to be managed. This shift is strikingly demonstrated by the Victorian principles which acknowledge the dangerousness of physical restraint and direct teachers to 'ensure the child is breathing and has not come to any harm' (State of Victoria Department of Education and Training 2017a, p. 17) – the child's safety is of concern only once the decision has been made to enact the restraint.

26.2.2 Necessity

Additional to any specific policies and guidelines, the use of restrictive practices in schools are also regulated by reason of the effect of the common law doctrine of necessity. Broadly speaking, the doctrine of necessity operates as a defence in relation to civil and criminal wrongs related to non-consensual interventions, where that conduct has occurred 'in urgent situations of imminent peril' to an individual or property (Southwark London Borough Council v Williams 1971). It is available where an individual's acts 'are reasonably necessary to protect life or property', notably overcoming the need to obtain an individual's consent to intervene in their bodies when this consent cannot be immediately obtained and there is an urgent need to act (e.g. medical surgery, personal care) (see e.g., Secretary, Department of Health and Community Services v JWB 1992, p. 310; Re F (Mental Patient Sterilisation) 1990, p. 75).

This doctrine does not provide a specific framework detailing when restrictive practices can occur (cf the policies and guidelines discussed above). Rather if a criminal or civil legal action is brought retrospectively against a teacher who has used restrictive practices, the doctrine can be relied upon in court as a defence to criminal and civil liability for assault, battery and false imprisonment. However, it has been noted that there is systemic reliance by medical and care workers on vague approximations of the doctrine of necessity to inform the use of non-consensual interventions in their service provision to people with disabilities. For example, Carter (2006) in his review of the use of restrictive practices in the Queensland disability service sector noted that there is a routine reliance on

> *irrelevant but nonetheless palatable legal clichés such as "the doctrine of necessity". Because it was necessary to protect others from the challenging behaviour of the disabled person, it was acceptable to restrain or detain, not only in the best interests of the person with intellectual disability but also of the community.* (p. 161, see also p. 83, p. 147)

Carter's observations suggest that the doctrine of necessity has taken on its own normative meaning amongst health care workers in such a way that justifies a broader range of interventions than what a court might interpret as technically fitting within the doctrine. A similar observation about more expansive interpretations of 'necessity' was made by the NSW Ombudsman in the school context: 'our work has identified matters in which physical restraint has been used at times when there was not a "real and immediate threat" to the student or others, but was part of a broader response to the student's behaviours of concern' (NSW Ombudsman 2017, p. 32).

It is interesting to note that the concept of 'necessary' is present in various dimensions of the legal framework regulating restrictive practices. Elsewhere, the author has argued that while the concept of what is 'necessary', particularly at a time of acute crisis or emergency, might seem self-evident, an analysis of the leading decision on medical necessity (In re F) illustrates that there are different understandings based on dis/ability both of what constitutes an acute crisis and what is a legitimate response to this crisis (Steele 2016, 2017). On another level, reliance upon what is 'necessary' is problematic because this reliance involves a value judgement following the weighing of relative harms of intervening or not intervening. It follows that embedded within this reliance upon what is necessary is recognition that harm might occur but that this harm is of lesser significance than that which is avoided through the intervention. Thus, there is an implicit hierarchical valuing of bodies who might be justifiably harmed and it is proposed that hierarchy intersects with the broader sociocultural devaluation of the bodies of children with disabilities which has been explored by critical disability studies scholars.

26.2.3 Duty of Care and WHS Law

Restrictive practices might also be legally 'permissible' because of the effect of legal obligations on teachers to protect other students. Teachers owe a duty (and school authorities a non-delegable duty) to students to ensure their safety (Commonwealth v Introvigne 1982). Teachers and schools also have obligations under work health and safety law to ensure students are safe on school premises and that reasonable care is taken of them while they are attending school. Restrictive practices can be legal when done to protect the student or their peers pursuant to these obligations. (see e.g., WorkSafe Victoria undated; see also in the ACT context Shaddock et al. 2015, p. 49, p. 155, p. 156). While safety might seem to be self-evidentially of benefit to all students, children with disabilities are themselves positioned in the application of these laws as the site of risk and harm.

As alluded to above in my discussion of challenging behaviour, it is important to note that achieving school safety through restrictive practices involves identifying the source of the safety risk and the site of risk prevention as the body of a child with disabilities (see also Spivakovsky's nuanced exploration of the use of WHS to legitimate restrictive practices in the context of disability group homes: 2017, pp. 377–379). This is noted by the Victorian Human rights and Equal Opportunity Commission in relation to the Victorian WHS 'conceptuali[sing] students with disability as a risk or hazard. It does not talk about the risks to the student if restraint or seclusion is used' (Victorian Equal Opportunity and Human Rights Commission (VEOHRC) 2012, p. 118; see acknowledgement that risks to child through restrictive practices should also be taken into account in Shaddock et al. 2015, pp. 155–156). This has the effect of reducing the child to a threat to the system (here the safety of the school) and in turn negates the violence done to that child via restrictive practices through framing the use of restrictive practices as a means of restoring the order (or safety) of the system (Goodley and Runswick-Cole 2011b, p. 610). Moreover, the application of WHS and duty of care implicitly segregates the child with disabilities within the space of the school because they are positioned as a risk to that space and legitimate expressions of 'resistance or protest to maladaptive environments' which could prompt '[c]hanging services, systems and environments' (Frohmader and Sands 2015, p. 46) instead further embed them within these environments.

26.2.4 Discrimination and Human Rights Protections

Technically, the use of restrictive practices might be limited by domestic anti-discrimination legislation and (in the two jurisdictions with such legislation: ACT and Victoria) contrary to human rights legislation (Shaddock et al. 2015, pp. 153–154). This is on the basis that students with disabilities are being treated less favourably because of behaviour associated with their disabilities.

Unfortunately, this is not the case. One reason is that the use of restrictive practices can be framed as related to the student's behaviour as opposed to their disability (Purvis v New South Wales (Department of Education and Training) 2003; O'Connell 2017). This signals a problematic (yet ultimately legally productive) contradiction where challenging behaviour is associated with a child's disabilities in order to necessitate restrictive practices which target the individualised and pathologised child's body at the same time that challenging behaviour is separated from disability in order to remove the ground for rights or legal protections on the basis of disability.

Another reason is that the use of restrictive practices is subject to various legislative exceptions to non-discrimination such as the balancing requirement in reasonable adjustments, the need to protect safety and the need to comply with work health and safety laws or other legal obligations (Shaddock et al. 2015, pp. 47–48, pp. 154–155; Victorian Human Rights and Equal Opportunity Commission 2012, p. 108; McSherry 2016). To the extent that these draw on the very concepts of necessity and safety and the very legislation that permits restrictive practices, these more progressive promises of human rights and anti-discrimination can fold back into the permissibility of restrictive practices.

A further reason why the use of restrictive practices is not limited by anti-discrimination law is that specific policies and guidelines on restrictive practices (discussed above) do not generally identify human rights as relevant considerations in assessing what is 'necessary' and 'reasonable' in the circumstances, such that any consideration of human rights is external to the core assessment of whether to use restrictive practices. Even the recently revised Victorian guidelines that contain references to human rights legislation do not provide any explicit guidance as to how these human rights are relevant to restrictive practices, notably whether human rights actually provide a basis for the absolute impermissibility of restrictive practices (Victorian Human Rights and Equal Opportunity Commission 2012).

26.3 Restrictive Practices as Disability-Specific Lawful Violence

The above overview of the legal framework regulating the use of restrictive practices in relation to students with disabilities highlights that restrictive practices are permitted rather than prohibited. This suggests that the use of restrictive practices in schools is a form of 'disability-specific lawful violence' (Steele 2014, 2015; Steele and Dowse 2016; see also consideration in law reform context in Senate Community Affairs Reference Committee 2015, pp. 71–115). 'Disability-specific lawful violence' are interventions (including sterilisation, mental health treatment and detention, and restrictive practices) that are not consented to by the individuals subjected to them but are nevertheless lawful because other individuals (e.g. courts, doctors, parents, guardians) have the legal authority to decide when these interventions should occur and they are 'disability-specific' because the legitimacy of granting this authority to third parties is by reason of medicalised assumptions about the lack of capacity and rationality of persons with disabilities to themselves make these choices coupled with their innate needs for protection, treatment and/or control.

In legal terms, disability-specific lawful violence is possible by reason of how criminal and civil law defines unlawful violence. For example, absence of consent is typically a defining element of unlawful violence (e.g. criminal offences of assault, or torts of battery and false imprisonment). In very general terms, criminal law defines assault and civil law defines battery in terms of non-consensual interpersonal physical contact or the non-consensual threat of such contact (R v Brown 1994, p. 231, see also pp. 244–245), (although consent does not always negate assault where the contact occasions actual bodily harm or greater (R v Brown 1994, pp. 231–234)). Despite these legal principles, certain defences to criminal responsibility and tortious liability operate to exclude certain conduct from liability, including the doctrine of necessity (discussed earlier), consent including third party consent for an individual lacking mental capacity (Secretary, Department of Health and Community Services v JWB 1992) and lawful authority (see e.g., Coco v R 1994; Cowell v Corrective Services Commission of New South Wales 1988). The legal framework for the regulation of restrictive practices in education settings, discussed above, inserts restrictive practices in this gap of exclusions to liability. And it does so in a way that is 'disability-specific' because of the associations between disability, risk and harm that simultaneously position children with disabilities as more violent and harmful and less worthy of protection from violence and harm (Dowse 2017).

In sitting outside of legal categories of unlawful violence, restrictive practices do not attract liability under civil or criminal law: there is no access to remedies under tort law, no possibility of perpetrators being punished under criminal law and no possibility of accessing victims compensation statutory schemes because these define violence by reference to criminal law. While there might be scope for imposing liability where the restrictive practices are enacted negligently or contrary to law, this does not unsettle the fundamental legality of these interventions per se. Moreover, there is a large grey zone between lawful and unlawful interventions which serves to further expand the legality of this violence. There is a lack of knowledge of teachers on the ground as to what is permissible in part because of the lack of legal guidance and the lack of senior training and advice (NSW Ombudsman 2017, p. 32; Shaddock et al. 2015, pp. 46 & 170; see in the context of restrictive practices more broadly, Australian Law Reform Commission 2014, p. 249). There is a lack of external oversight and accountability by reason of a lack of reporting and independent monitoring (NSW Ombudsman 2017, p. xi, p. 32; Victoria Human Rights and Equal Opportunity Commission 2012, 105) and complaints mechanisms (NSW Ombudsman 2017, pp. xii–xiii, 64–86).Thus, any limitations on the use of restrictive practices and any associated opportunities for recognition and redress when teachers act beyond these limitations is largely ineffectual due to the lack of practical application of and oversight of the regulatory framework.

In building on the idea of disability-specific lawful violence, this chapter proposes that because the violence of restrictive practices in sitting at a very specific intersection of the institution and 'challenging behaviour' the use of restrictive practices might also be understood as 'systemic violence'. In their research on violence against children with disabilities, Goodley & Runswick-Cole draw on Žižek's notion of 'systemic violence' to argue that violence against children with disabilities is enabled and negated by reason of its assumed necessity for the functioning and preservation of a system of order that is threatened by 'disabled, disruptive, unruly and different children' (Goodley and Runswick-Cole 2011b, p. 611). Goodley and Runswick-Cole argue that the categorisation of children with disabilities' behaviour as 'challenging behaviour' and the related interventions this permits can be viewed as 'systemic violence' because these interventions constitute 'violence as part of the maintenance of the system' (Goodley and Runswick-Cole 2011b, p. 610).

26.4 Momentum Towards Prohibition?: International Human Rights and Domestic Law Reform

Some recent developments in international human rights law and domestic law reform signal greater recognition of the violent and discriminatory status of the use of restrictive practices, and provide a basis for working towards prohibition.

26.4.1 Convention on the Rights of Persons with Disabilities

The United Nations Convention on the Rights of Persons with Disabilities 2515 UNTS 3 ('UNCRPD') was opened for signature on 13 December 2006 and came into force in 2008. UNCRPD's approach to disability indicates a shift from a medicalised approach to disability as an internal, individual pathology epitomized by diagnostic definitions of particular impairments. Instead disability is viewed as a form of social and political difference, and there is an appreciation of the role of stigma and social barriers in the inequality experienced by people with disabilities.

Article 24 of the UNCRPD provides the right to inclusive education and that '[e]ffective individualised support measures are provided in environments that maximise academic and social development, consistent with the goal of full inclusion'. Article 24 should be read in the context of the UNCRPD's approach to violence, notably obligations on states parties to protect people with disability from violence (Article 16). In its recent General Comment on Article 24, the Committee states:

> *Persons with disabilities, particularly women and girls, can be disproportionately affected by violence and abuse, including physical and humiliating punishments by educational personnel, for example, the use of restraints and seclusion … . Article 16 requires that States parties take all appropriate measures to protect from and prevent all forms of violence and abuse towards persons with disabilities, including sexual violence. Such measures must be age, gender and disability sensitive. The Committee strongly endorses the recommendations of the CRC, the Human Rights Committee and CESCR that States parties must prohibit all forms of corporal punishment, and cruel, inhuman and degrading treatment in all settings, including schools, and ensure effective sanctions against perpetrators.* (Committee on the Rights of Persons with Disabilities 2016, p. 17)

The Committee has also expressed concern about Australia's use of restrictive practices in schools (Committee on the Rights of Persons with Disabilities 2013, para. 35). It is important to note that the CRPD marks a significant shift from the earlier Convention on the Rights of Children which was more ambivalent about restrictive practices (Lyons 2015).

26.4.2 Government Inquiries

In 2015 the Senate Community Affairs Reference Committee ('the Committee') conducted an inquiry into institutional violence against people with disabilities. Its inquiry considered 'disability-specific interventions', including restrictive practices in schools. The Committee was particularly concerned with the lower safeguards available to people with disabilities in prisons and schools, as compared to disability service settings (Senate Community Affairs Reference Committee 2015, pp. 100–114). It concluded that: 'The committee is highly disturbed at the evidence presented of restrictive practice. Clearly, in many cases what is deemed to be a necessary therapeutic or personal safety intervention is in fact, assault and unlawful deprivation of liberty' (Senate Community Affairs Reference Committee 2015, p. 115). The Committee also stated that: 'Many of the systemic problems that lead to the use of restrictive practices actually reinforce an attitude that facilitates the mistreatment of children with disability because they are viewed as different' (Senate Community Affairs Reference Committee 2015, p. 114).

Ultimately the Committee recommended that Commonwealth and state governments 'implement a national zero-tolerance approach to eliminate restrictive practice in all service delivery contexts', and recommended that 'the use of restrictive practice against children must be eliminated as a national priority' (Senate Community Affairs Reference Committee 2015, p. xxi). The Committee also urged 'a national approach with regard to regulation' and that 'states and territories need to establish and implement enforceable policies and guidance for school teachers and principals that eliminates the use of 'restrictive practices'' (Senate Community Affairs Reference Committee 2015, p. 114). The Committee also made some headline recommendations, including 'a Royal Commission into violence, abuse and neglect of people with disability be called, with terms of reference to be determined in consultation with people with disability, their families and supporters, and disability organisations' (Senate Community Affairs Reference Committee 2015, p. xv, pp. 267–268).

The Committee reiterated its approach to restrictive practices and institutional violence in its subsequent report on its inquiry into indefinite detention of people with cognitive and psychiatric impairment (Senate Community Affairs Reference Committee 2016), although it did not explicitly address education settings (Senate Community Affairs Reference Committee 2016, pp. 162–169). Also in 2016, the Senate Education and Employment References Committee's report on its inquiry into access to education for students with disability recommended: 'the government works with states and territories to end restrictive practices in schools, consistent with the recommendations of the 2015 [Senate institutional violence inquiry]' (Senate Education and Employment References Committee 2016, p. 72).

This momentum towards elimination of restrictive practices has not trickled through to state and territory education inquiries, which is unfortunate given that these jurisdictions are ultimately responsible for legislative reform in this area (Deloitte Access Economics 2017; NSW Ombudsman 2017; NSW Parliament Legislative Council 2017; Shaddock et al. 2015, Victoria Ombudsman 2017, Victorian Human Rights and Equal Opportunity Commission 2012). One notable exception is a Victorian Human Rights and Equal Opportunity Commission recommendation to prohibit seclusion (Victorian Human Rights and Equal Opportunity Commission 2012, p. 14). Rather, the state and territory inquiries focus on improving the regulation of restrictive practices through better on the ground support and training, greater transparency and accountability in relation to the use of restrictive practices by teaching staff, introduction of senior figures (e.g. Senior Practitioner) to lead oversight and training in relation to restrictive practices, and a greater focus on positive approaches to student behaviour and individualised behaviour support planning. There is a notable absence of discussion of restrictive practices in terms of violence, crime, liability and police, and the absence of considerations of justice, compensation and reparations. Indeed, quite disturbingly, the report which was prompted by the ACT caging incident makes no mention of this specific example nor does it refer to seclusion in terms of 'caging' or by reference to the aforementioned terms. These reports continue to rely on notions of 'necessary' and 'reasonable' as the central factor (see e.g., Deloitte Access Economics 2017, p. xiii; Shaddock et al. 2015, p. 168). Also, in Australian state and territory reports published after the Commonwealth Senate inquiries it is notable that there is no adoption of the Committee's recommendation for a 'zero tolerance' approach to restrictive practices.

26.5 Conclusion

This chapter began by identifying a fundamental 'tension' in contemporary school settings – children with disabilities have been included in mainstream schooling at the same time that they are subjected to disproportionate rates of violence. The discussion of the legality of one form of violence – restrictive practices – suggests that violence against children with disabilities has been accepted as a 'necessary' and 'reasonable' means of inclusion (Steele 2016). As such, the current use of (and legal support for) restrictive practices might reflect critical disability scholars Snyder and Mitchell's notion of 'inclusionism', a government rights rhetoric that prioritises 'inclusion' of people with disabilities in ways that ultimately continues to exclude and degrade. They state: '[i]nclusionism requires that disability be tolerated as long as it does not demand an excessive degree of change from relatively inflexible institutions, environments, and norms of belonging' (Mitchell and Snyder 1997, p. 14; see also Karmiris 2017, pp. 107–108).

International human rights law and recent government inquiries signal a greater willingness to engage with restrictive practices as forms of violence and to recognise and address law's complicity in these practices. However, in ultimately achieving the 'zero tolerance' elimination of these practices, we must tackle the concepts of 'necessary', 'reasonable', and 'safety' that pervade the current legal framework in order to make apparent the extent to which they are implicitly informed by hierarchies of ability and problematic assumptions about disability that simultaneously position children with disabilities as more violent and harmful and less worthy of protection from violence and harm. We must 'deconstruct[ ] and reform[ ] the very cultural [and legal] norms that legitimise violence against disabled people in the first place' (Goodley and

Runswick-Cole 2011b, p. 614). Once we do this we might move closer towards realising what Karmiris refers to as the 'hopeful possibility that teaching and learning might be otherwise than the continued perpetuation of hierarchies of exclusion' (2017, p. 102).

Acknowledgements Thank you to Claire Spivakovsky for referring the author to some useful references on restrictive practices in schools. Thank you to the editors and anonymous reviewers for their feedback.

References

Beaupert, F. (2017). *Freedom of opinion and expression: From the perspective of psychosocial disability and madness*. (Unpublished paper).

Carter, W. J. (2006). *Challenging behaviour and disability: A targeted response*. Report to Honourable Warren Pitt MP, Minister for Communities, Disability Services and Seniors. https://www.communities.qld.gov.au/resources/disability/centre-of-excellence/carter-report-full.pdf

Chandler, K., Willmott, L., & White, B. (2014). Rethinking restrictive practices: A comparative analysis. *QUT Law Review, 4*(2), 90–122. https://doi.org/10.5204/qutlr.v14i2.568.

Chapman, C. (2014). Becoming perpetrator: How I came to accept restraining and confining disabled Aboriginal children. In B. Burstow, B. A. LeFrancois, & S. Diamond (Eds.), *Psychiatry disrupted: Theorizing resistance and crafting the (r) evolution* (pp. 16–33). Montreal/Kingston: McGill-Queen's University Press.

Children with Disability Australia. (2015). *Submission to inquiry into violence, abuse and neglect against people with disability in institutional and residential settings*. Collingwood: Children with Disability Australia. http://www.cyda.org.au/cdasubmissions#section5

Coco v R 1994 179 CLR 427 (Austl.).

Committee on the Rights of Persons with Disabilities. (2013, October 21). *Concluding observations on the initial report of Australia*, 10th session. CRPD/C/AUS/CO/1. http://docstore.ohchr.org/SelfServices/FilesHandler.ashx?enc=6QkG1d%2FPPRiCAqhKb7yhsnzSGolKOaUX8SsM2PfxU7tjZ6g%2FxLBVYsYEv6iDyTXyNk%2BsAB%2FHgrVpAKHcEYTB%2B1t%2FH3HX1F%2F%2Bo%2Bk3O4KhxfhPoTQZ3LeS75n8PHidYHE3

Committee on the Rights of Persons with Disabilities. (2016, September 2). *General comment no 4 (2016): Article 24: Right to inclusive education*. CRPD/C/GC/4. http://www.ohchr.org/EN/HRBodies/CRPD/Pages/GC.aspx

Commonwealth v Introvigne. (1982). 150 CLR 258.

Cooper, H. (2013). The oppressive power of normalcy in the lives of disabled children: Deploying history to denaturalize the notion of the 'normal child'. In

T. Curran (Ed.), *Disabled children's childhood studies* (pp. 136–151). Houndmills/New York: Palgrave Macmillan.
Cowell v Corrective Services Commission of New South Wales 1988 13 NSWLR 714 (Austl.).
Deloitte Access Economics. (2017). *Review of education for students with disability in Queensland state schools.* Brisbane: Department of Education and Training (Queensland). http://education.qld.gov.au/schools/disability/docs/disability-review-report.pdf
Dowse, L. (2017). Disruptive, dangerous and disturbing: The "challenge" of behaviour in the construction of normalcy and vulnerability. *Continuum, 31*(3), 447–457. https://doi.org/10.1080/10304312.2016.1275148.
Erevelles, N. (2000). Educating unruly bodies: Critical pedagogy, disability studies, and the politics of schooling. *Educational Theory, 50*(1), 25–47. https://doi.org/10.1111/j.1741-5446.2000.00025.x.
Erevelles, N. (2011). *Disability and difference in global contexts: Enabling a transformative body politic.* New York: Palgrave Macmillan.
Frohmader, C., & Sands, T. (2015). *Australian Cross Disability Alliance (ACDA) submission to the Senate inquiry into violence, abuse and neglect against people with disability in institutional and residential settings.* Sydney: Australian Cross Disability Alliance. http://www.pwd.org.au/issues/violence-inquiry.html
Glanville, B. (Reporter). (2017, October 9). Hundreds of complaints of abuse of disabled children. In *7.30 Report.* [Television broadcast]. Sydney: Australian Broadcasting Corporation.
Goodley, D., & Runswick-Cole, K. (2011a). Problematising policy: Conceptions of 'child', 'disabled' and 'parents' in social policy in England. *International Journal of Inclusive Education, 15*(1), 71–85. https://doi.org/10.1080/13603116.2010.496197.
Goodley, D., & Runswick-Cole, K. (2011b). The violence of disablism. *Sociology of Health & Illness, 33*(4), 602–617. https://doi.org/10.1111/j.1467-9566.2010.01302.x.
Goodley, D., & Runswick-Cole, K. (2012). Reading Rosie: The postmodern disabled child. *Educational & Child Psychology, 29*(2), 53–66.
Goodley, D., Runswick-Cole, K., & Liddiard, K. (2016). The DisHuman child. *Discourse: Studies in the Cultural Politics of Education, 37*(5), 770–784. https://doi.org/10.1080/01596306.2015.1075731.
Lyons, D. (2015). Restraint and seclusion of students with disabilities: A child rights perspective from Victoria, Australia. *International Journal of Children's Rights, 23,* 189–239. https://doi.org/10.1163/15718182-02301009.
Kafer, A. (2013). *Feminist, queer, crip.* Bloomington: Indiana University Press.
Kaplan, A. (2010). Harm without recourse: The need for a private right of action in federal restraint and seclusion legislation. *Cardozo Law Review, 32*(2), 581–614.
Karmiris, M. (2016). Breaks and ruptures: Cripping the reading of resistance. *Canadian Journal of Disability Studies, 5*(4), 205–222. http://cjds.uwaterloo.ca/index.php/cjds/article/view/319

Karmiris, M. (2017). De-centering the myth of normalcy in education: A critique of inclusionary policies in education through disability studies. *Critical Disability Discourses, 8*, 99–199. https://cdd.journals.yorku.ca/index.php/cdd/article/view/39722

Macdonald, E. (Reporter). (2016, August 11). Autism cage timeline: From Canberra classroom to the United Nations. *Canberra Times*. http://www.canberratimes.com.au/act-news/autism-cage-timeline-from-canberra-classroom-to-the-united-nations-20160811-gqqnjm.html

McSherry, B. (2016, November 29). Breaking bad: Regulating the responses of teachers to students' 'behaviours of concern', paper delivered at *Dean's Lecture Series*. Melbourne. http://education.unimelb.edu.au/news_and_activities/events/event/2016/breaking-bad-regulating-the-responses-of-teachers-to-students-behaviours-of-concern

Mitchell, D. T., & Snyder, S. L. (1997). Introduction: Disability studies and the double bind of representation. In D. T. Mitchell & S. L. Snyder (Eds.), *The body and physical difference: Discourses of disability* (pp. 1–31). Ann Arbor: University of Michigan Press.

National Disability Rights Network. (2012). *School is not supposed to hurt: The U.S. Department of Education must do more to protect school children from restraint and seclusion*. Washington, DC: Author. http://www.ndrn.org/images/Documents/Resources/Publications/Reports/School_is_Not_Supposed_to_Hurt_3_v7.pdf

New South Wales Government Education & Communities. (2011). *Guidelines for the use of time-out strategies including dedicated time-out rooms*. https://education.nsw.gov.au/policy-library/associated-documents/timeout_gui.pdf

New South Wales Government Education & Communities. (2012). Physical restraint of students. *Legal Services Bulletin, 9*. Reviewed June 2012. https://www.det.nsw.edu.au/media/downloads/about-us/how-we-operate/legal-issues-bulletins/number_09.pdf

New South Wales Parliament Legislative Council. (2017). *Education of students with a disability or special needs in New South Wales*, Report no. 37, Portfolio Committee No. 3 – Education. Sydney: Author. https://www.parliament.nsw.gov.au/committees/DBAssets/InquiryReport/ReportAcrobat/6114/170921%20-%20Final%20report.pdf

NSW Ombudsman. (2017). *NSW Ombudsman inquiry into behaviour management in schools*. Sydney: Author. https://www.ombo.nsw.gov.au/news-and-publications/publications/reports/community-and-disability-services/nsw-ombudsman-inquiry-into-behaviour-management-in-schools-august-2017

Nunkoosing, K., & Haydon-Laurelut, M. (2012). Intellectual disability trouble: Foucault and Goffman on 'challenging behaviour'. In D. Goodley, B. Hughes, & L. Davis (Eds.), *Disability and social theory: New developments and directions* (pp. 195–211). Basingstoke: Palgrave Macmillan.

O'Connell, K. (2017). Should we take the 'disability' out of discrimination laws? Students with challenging behaviour and the definition of disability. *Law in Context, 35*(2), 108–128.

Poed, S., Cologon, K., & Jackson, R. (2017, October). Gatekeeping and restrictive practices with students with disability: Results of an Australian survey, paper delivered at *Inclusive Education Summit.* Adelaide. http://allmeansall.org.au/wp-content/uploads/2017/10/TIES-4.0-20172.pdf

Purvis v New South Wales (Department of Education and Training) 2003 217 CLR 92 (Austl.).

R v Brown 1994 1 AC 212 (United Kingdom).

Re F (Mental Patient Sterilisation) 1990 2 AC 1 (United Kingdom).

Shaddock, A., Packer, P., & Roy, A. (2015). *Report of the expert panel on students with complex needs and challenging behaviour.* Canberra: Authors. https://www.education.act.gov.au/__data/assets/pdf_file/0003/856254/Attach-4-Expert-Panel-Report-Web.pdf

Southwark London Borough Council v Williams 1971 Ch 734 (United Kingdom).

Spivakovsky, C. (2017). Governing freedom through risk: Locating the group home in the archipelago of confinement and control. *Punishment & Society, 19*(3), 366–383. https://doi.org/10.1177/1462474517703968.

State of Victoria (Department of Education and Training). (2017a). *The principles for reduction and elimination of restraint and seclusion in Victorian government schools.* East Melbourne: Author. http://www.education.vic.gov.au/Documents/school/principals/participation/15Principals.pdf

State of Victoria (Department of Education and Training). (2017b). *Restraint of students policy.* East Melbourne: Author. http://www.education.vic.gov.au/school/principals/spag/governance/Pages/restraint.aspx

Steele, L. (2015). *Submission to Senate Community Affairs References Committee Inquiry into violence, abuse and neglect against people with disability in institutional and residential settings, including the gender and age related dimensions, and the particular situation of Aboriginal and Torres Strait Islander people with disability, and culturally and linguistically diverse people with disability*, submission no. 94. https://www.aph.gov.au/Parliamentary_Business/Committees/Senate/Community_Affairs/Violence_abuse_neglect/Submissions

Steele, L. (2016). Court-authorised sterilisation and human rights: Inequality, discrimination and violence against women and girls with disability? *UNSW Law Journal, 39*(3), 1002–1037. http://www.unswlawjournal.unsw.edu.au/sites/default/files/393-4.pdf

Steele, L. (2017). Temporality, disability and institutional violence: Revisiting In re F. *Griffith Law Review, 26*(3), 378–400. https://doi.org/10.1080/10383441.2017.1436368.

Steele, L., & Dowse, L. (2016). Gender, disability rights and violence against medical bodies. *Australian Feminist Studies, 31*(88), 117–124. https://doi.org/10.1080/08164649.2016.1224054.

Victorian Equal Opportunity & Human Rights Commission (VEOHRC). (2012). *Held back: The experiences of students with disabilities in Victorian schools*. Retrieved from http://www.humanrightscommission.vic.gov.au/media/k2/attachments/1404-VEOHRC_HeldBack_-_StudentwithDisabilityReportW3.pdf

Victorian Equal Opportunity and Human Rights Commission. (2017). *Held back: The experiences of students with disabilities in Victorian schools: Analysis paper*. Carlton: Victorian Equal Opportunity and Human Rights Commission. https://www.humanrightscommission.vic.gov.au/home/our-resources-and-publications/reports/item/1602-held-back-the-experiences-of-students-with-disabilities-in-victorian-schools-analysis-paper

Victorian Ombudsman. (2017). *Investigation into Victorian government school expulsions*. Melbourne: Author. https://www.ombudsman.vic.gov.au/Publications/Parliamentary-Reports/Investigation-into-vic-gov-school-expulsions

Watts, I. E., & Erevelles, N. (2004). These deadly times: Reconceptualizing school violence by using critical race theory and disability studies. *American Educational Research Journal, 41*(2), 271–299.

Weissbrodt, D., Maderia, W., Stewart, D., & Dikel, W. (2012). Applying international human rights standards to the restraint and seclusion of students with disabilities. *Law and Inequality, 30*, 287–307. http://scholarship.law.umn.edu/faculty_articles/365?utm_source=scholarship.law.umn.edu%2Ffaculty_articles%2F365&utm_medium=PDF&utm_campaign=PDFCoverPages

27

Counter Terrorism Law and Education: Student Teachers' Induction into UK Prevent Duty Through the Lens of Bauman's Liquid Modernity

Lynn Revell, Hazel Bryan, and Sally Elton-Chalcraft

27.1 Introduction

This chapter is derived from research prompted by the development of counter terrorist legislation in the UK designed to prevent radicalisation and extremism that requires teachers and schools to act in new and different ways. The data discussed in this chapter is part of a larger research project that is exploring the ways schools are responding to the duties placed upon them by the Counter Terrorism and Security Act 2015 (HMO 2015). Data generated through the research suggests that student teachers' induction experiences are highly varied in relation to the Prevent Duty. This has significant implications for the ways in which student teachers conceptualise their role in relation to their students, and the ways in which student teachers conceptualise their relationship with subject knowledge relating to radicalisation and extremism. It also has significant implications for student teachers' opportunity to observe,

L. Revell (✉)
Canterbury Christ Church University, Canterbury, UK
e-mail: lynn.revell@canterbury.ac.uk

H. Bryan
University of Gloucestershire, Cheltenham, UK
e-mail: hbryan@glos.ac.uk

S. Elton-Chalcraft
University of Cumbria, Carlisle, UK
e-mail: sally.elton-chalcraft@cumbria.ac.uk

K. Trimmer et al. (eds.), *The Palgrave Handbook of Education Law for Schools*,
https://doi.org/10.1007/978-3-319-77751-1_27

learn about and develop pedagogical practices most appropriate for this new statutory dimension to teacher work.

We use Bauman's (2012) concept of Liquid Modernity as the conceptual framework in this research to cast light upon issues of change in relation to policy initiatives, in order to understand why teachers and student teachers are acting, practicing and developing in certain ways. Bauman's thesis is helpful to this research as it addresses the consequences of shifting social norms and power relationships in contemporary society.

27.2 Context/Background

In 2003 the UK Home Office published the first iteration of CONTEST, its counter-terrorism and anti-extremism strategy. Developed in response to the attacks in America in 2001 (referred to as the 9/11 attacks), CONTEST was modified in 2006 following the attacks on the London transport network in 2005 (known as the 7/7 attacks). CONTEST comprises four strands, namely:

- Pursue: directly disrupting and preventing terrorist attacks;
- Prevent: stopping people becoming terrorists or from supporting terrorism;
- Protect: strengthening the UK's protection against a terrorist attack;
- Prepare: mitigating the effects of a terrorist attack when it cannot be prevented. (Home Office 2003)

Of these four strands, the second, Prevent, relates directly to education, where education professionals working in schools, colleges and early years childcare settings are required to enact a 'Prevent Duty'. Launched on 1st July 2015, the Prevent Duty is set out in the 'Revised Prevent Duty Guidance for England and Wales' (2015) in which statutory guidance is articulated under section 29 of the Counter-Terrorism and Security Act 2015. The Prevent Duty expects that "schools should be safe spaces in which children and young people can understand and discuss sensitive topics, including terrorism and the extremist ideas that are part of terrorist ideology, and learn how to challenge these ideas. The Prevent Duty is not intended to limit discussion of these issues" (DfE 2015, p. 11). Schools are required to demonstrate their Prevent Duty through risk assessment (where they should be able to identify pupils at risk of radicalization and have in place 'robust safeguarding policies'), working with other agencies, the training of staff and IT policies and practices (DfE 2015, p. 11).

The Prevent Strategy has also, uniquely, informed the development of the most recent set of Teachers' Standards in England. The Teachers' Standards (DfE 2012) draw upon the Prevent Strategy in requiring teachers to promote 'fundamental British values'. Originally articulated as 'not undermining' fundamental British values, teachers should:

> '...uphold public trust in the profession and maintain high standards of ethics and behaviour, within and outside school by:
>
> - not undermining fundamental British values, including democracy, the rule of law, individual liberty and mutual respect, and tolerance of those with different faiths and beliefs
> - ensuring that personal beliefs are not expressed in ways which exploit pupils' vulnerability or might lead them to break the law'. (DfE 2012)

That a counter terrorism strategy should inform a set of teachers' standards makes clear the degree to which UK government positions teachers as key players in counter-terrorism. This is strengthened by the requirement for teachers to promote fundamental British values both within and outside of school, that is, within the public and private spheres.

It is within this relatively new policy backdrop that this research has taken place. We were interested to know what the experiences of student teachers were in relation to Prevent whilst on school placement. The research is intended to provide insight into the students' perceptions of what schools are doing in terms of risk assessment, the identification of pupils at risk, working with other agencies and IT policies and practices.

27.3 Conceptual Framework

In his thesis on Liquid Modernity, Bauman (2012) argues that contemporary society can be characterised as in a state of transition – a constant state of transition. Modernity, Bauman suggests, represents a solid state that has little resonance in contemporary times, where change is the only permanence. Such a state of flux and fluidity has consequences, and Bauman (2012) notes the fragility that characterises all strata of society, from changing geographical boundaries of nation states to the freedom to determine one's own gender. Bauman argues that within such a state of liquidity, power is manipulated in ways that differ from the way power is channelled in times of Modernity. In a state of Modernity, power is exercised by constraint, whereas, Bauman argues, in times of Liquid Modernity, power is wielded through uncertainty (Bauman and Haugaard 2008).

Liquidity also permeates social norms; Modernity celebrated cultural capital and all that this represents in the form of narratives of stability, artefacts, possession and icons. In times of Liquid Modernity, however, investment in such representations of culture are losing their monopoly, as different narratives of consumption, transition and mobility emerge. A consequence of permanent fluidity is the weakening of social norms, which arguably melt faster that new norms emerge. This in turn results in a society with decreasing frames of reference for actions (Bauman 2005) and, in such a state of liquefaction, the exercise of human agency is necessarily inhibited. This may at first appear contradictory, but Bauman's thesis highlights the way in which post-modern societies, in exchanging the notion of collective security for maximum individual freedom, arrive at a state of uncertainty and anxiety (Bauman 2005): there is a particular irony in the way in which increased personal freedom gives rise to a state of heightened anxiety.

27.4 Method and Methodology

The project began with one hundred and fifty post graduate student teachers from one University in the South of England engaged in a survey that captured their experiences of the ways in which schools are engaging with this new legislation. The student teachers, from a predominantly white background were invited to reflect on their understanding of the role of teachers in relation to the new duties. The questions asked the students to gather information about the execution of aspects of Prevent in their practicum schools, including; the approach to the promotion of fundamental British values, visible signs of Prevent and fundamental British values, the way Prevent and issues relating to radicalisation and extremism were dealt with as part of their induction into the life of the school and the way the school framed the role of the teacher in relation to the radicalisation process.

In the second year of the study fifteen students from a specialised cohort of Citizenship Education students were interviewed and the data analysed using a framework developed from Bauman's (2012) theory of Liquid Modernity. The interviews took the form of dialogic spaces where both the interviewee and the interviewer were involved in the production of knowledge (Holstein and Gubrium 1995). This approach meant that the interview was not envisioned as an 'interpersonal drama' but as an interpretative praxis whereby understanding and meaning are crafted as part of the interview process (Holstein and Gubrium 1995, p. 16). This type of interview was selected because of the focus of the research and because of the use of Bauman's notion of Liquid Modernity (Bauman 2012). Within Liquid Modernity the individual is adrift in multiple changing narratives and the fluidity of their professional environment means they struggle to make sense of the world in which they live, and their place within it. In a climate where the Prevent Duty and requirement to promote fundamental British values are relatively new, it would have been naïve on our part to undertake interviews which assumed that participants had already developed coherent responses to complex political and professional issues. Our choice of interview type was also influenced by our understanding of the way the professional identity of teachers develops (Day et al. 2006).

27.5 Data

27.5.1 Approaches to the Promotion of Fundamental British Values

Data from the questionnaires suggests that all schools were aware of their duties under the Counter Terrorism and Security Act 2015, Prevent and the Teacher's Standards (DfE 2012) in the two academic years that the data was collected (2015–2106 and 2016–2017). This finding confirmed conclusions from the small number of other projects that have examined the impact of Prevent in education (Bryan 2012; Revell and Bryan 2016; Farrell 2016; Panjwani 2016; Elton-Chalcraft et al. 2017; Bryan 2017). However, the nature of that engagement differed between schools. A minority of schools did not address any aspect of Prevent in lessons or whole school activities but in those that did the most common strategy was through PSHE, Citizenship lessons and assemblies. The approach taken by schools was varied and ranged from dedicating a term within Citizenship Education for issues relating to extremism and radicalisation to using existing schemes within the school. One school integrated their approach to radicalisation through its Growth Mind-set Education programme and another located it with their Behaviour Watch initiative.

27.5.2 Visible Signs of Fundamental British Values and the Prevent Duty

In response to the question 'Did you identify any visual evidence of Prevent in your school?' ninety two per cent of students reported that their schools displayed visual signs of compliance with the law, and these included posters about extremism, the promotion of fundamental British values, displays of pupil work and lessons on aspects of extremism, fundamental British values and radicalisation. A minority of students reported that the visual presence of Prevent was minimal. One student commented that there 'was one small poster in a school of 2, 300' and another that there were 'a few posters on fundamental British values but very little else'. Primary schools were more likely to display posters on aspects of Britishness, and these were often accompanied by artefacts relating to popular British icons (bunting, flags, scones).

27.5.3 Induction and Prevent

Student experience of induction into their role in executing Prevent was mixed. Sixty per cent of all students said that at no point in their practicum did their mentors or other teachers explain how the school was responding to Prevent – this did not feature in their induction programme. Neither did these schools indicate how the student teachers would be expected to address relevant issues or questions in any part of the curriculum. Of the forty per cent that did receive some input this was part of their general induction to the life of the school or as part of a series of introductory sessions about aspects of the professional responsibility of the teacher. The most common approach to fulfilling the Prevent Duty appeared to be through the promotion fundamental British values with only twenty seven per cent of schools directly addressing the issues of radicalisation or extremism.

27.5.4 Framing the Role of the Teacher in Relation to Radicalisation; the View from the Student Teacher Perspective

When asked to describe what other teachers thought about the Prevent Duty eighty per cent (120) said 'Most teachers thought that it was a good idea' and in answer to the question about how they understood the role of the teacher in relation to Prevent eighty eight per cent agreed that 'Teachers should do everything they can to support government initiatives in relation to countering radicalisation and promoting fundamental British values'. Students were also asked to give two examples of what they thought might constitute active or vocal opposition to fundamental British values in the context of schools. Most respondents described incidents or views that could be categorised as 'intolerance of those of other cultures and religions' or of showing lack of respect to 'minority groups and those of other faiths or no faith'. A minority of students gave examples that related to 'the rule of law' or 'democracy'. Examples included 'acting as though the law didn't apply to them and thinking they had a right to impose their views on others' and 'believing that other people's views weren't important even when they were in the minority'.

It was in this section of the questionnaire that students were more likely to express some criticism of aspects of Prevent in the form of comments about the nature of fundamental British values. Just under a quarter of students included comments about the scope and nature of the values:

> *'It's ridiculous that they're called British, why not human values?'*
>
> *'Calling them British is just short sighted, anyone that isn't British is going to feel excluded, it tells them that their values aren't as important.'*
>
> *'What does calling them British even mean, every single thing is covered by the ethos of the school anyway'.*
>
> *'In my experience it's the British who don't have these values, they're an insult to everyone else in the world who has had these values for a lot longer!'*

During their interviews the Citizenship Education students confirmed that they were aware of Prevent and that the purpose of legislation and policy was to stop radicalisation. All students knew that they were now expected to identify pupils at risk from radicalisation and that even where they did not know the details they knew that in schools there would be protocols about how their suspicions should be dealt with. All students were certain about how they would identify pupils at risk from radicalisation and most were able to cite the markers given in Prevent.

Where students were less certain was how they would distinguish between pupils who legitimately displayed signs of alienation, changed behaviour and students who were genuinely at risk from radicalisation. Only two of the fifteen students thought that 'there might be issues' caused by their lack of expertise in areas to do with radicalisation and extremism. The thirteen students who thought that there were no significant issues in relation to identifying pupils at risk from radicalisation gave similar reasons for their confidence in this area, including:

- They were aware, or assumed that there were, senior members of staff in the school who would take responsibility for the process of monitoring at risk pupils and coordinating with Channel (reporting procedure for potentially radicalised).

- They considered pupils who might be at risk from radicalisation to be similar to other at risk pupils. This meant that even though pupils displayed warning signs that might not mean they were at risk from radicalisation – they were probably still vulnerable and therefore in need of observation.
- They were aware that mistakes could be made (and that mistakes had been made) but that it was safer to be too vigilant than to be negligent.

Students were asked about their political views at the start of the interview. They all identified as individuals to whom politics was interesting and of personal importance. They were able to talk about their political beliefs eloquently and many said that one of the attractions of training to be a teacher of Citizenship Education was the expectation that the discussion of political issues would be a routine part of the curriculum. Students were then asked whether they thought it was, or ever would be appropriate for them to talk about their own political views in the classroom and whether they thought it would be appropriate for them as teachers to try to influence the views of pupils. All students thought it would be inappropriate for a teacher to deliberately attempt to influence the views of pupils even when they thought that pupils' views were unacceptable. While they were all shocked at the idea that it would ever be acceptable for them to bring their own views into the classroom they all believed that it was a legitimate part of their professional role to encourage debate where pupils could 'come to understand' or 'realise that there are other ways of seeing the world'.

27.5.5 Discussion

Our findings are taken from 150 questionnaires and interviews with 15 students from a predominantly white background, and as such it would be illegitimate to make generalisations from such a small number. However the data from the questionnaires did confirm some findings that are emerging from the growing literature on Prevent in schools. Most schools are engaged in some way with the Prevent agenda. Our findings indicate that schools are displaying concepts, artefacts and icons of Britishness: primary schools in particular have engaged in notably elaborate displays. All student teachers in the study were aware of the new legal duties placed upon them and were familiar with the narrative of fundamental British values that underpins counter terrorism legislation. The data presented by the National Police Chiefs' Council showing that since 2012 there have been 2422 referrals to Channel from schools alone, demonstrates the rapidity with which new social forms – in this case a Prevent Duty – are introduced. The notion of transition from a solid to a liquid form of modernity is expressed here in relation to the rapidity of change (Bauman 2005). The number of referrals is also a reflection of the impact Prevent is having on teacher work, where teachers know that there are serious consequences if Prevent is not enacted in school, and where all teachers in our research assumed their Duty without question. The idea that teachers are referring pupils to Channel to be 'on the safe side' is in itself an expression of insecurity.

The speed with which forms change in society results in a state of constant anxiety (Bauman 2012). Indeed, the various iterations of Prevent reflect this very process, where subsequent alterations in terms of the nature of the Prevent document can be read as an exercise in uncertainty.

Similarly, student teachers reported that all teachers with whom they came into contact during their practicum believed it was appropriate for them to have a Prevent Duty; this was not questioned. The students reported that teachers however, did not have a depth of knowledge of the processes of radicalisation that would enable them to prevent their pupils from becoming radicalised, and no student teacher heard a teacher expressing concern about their lack of subject knowledge in this area. There are a number of reasons why this may be the case, and Bauman's notion of constant transition (2008) is helpful here in terms of understanding the continuous shifts in policy that shape education. Teachers are enacting their statutory Duty with no frame of reference for this work (Bauman 2005); as professionals they would normally attend subject knowledge enhancement courses, training days and join Subject Associations to ensure their subject knowledge is secure. In the case of Prevent, teachers are unquestioningly engaging in new territory but with no 'muscle memory'. It is here that the consequences of liquidity can be understood; whilst teachers have no subject knowledge to bring to the classroom in relation to radicalisation, and in spite of the fact that they are statutorily required to prevent radicalisation, they do not complain because they practice in a state of liquidity; liquidity is their norm. There should be tension here but it is not apparent – we had fully expected teachers to challenge the Prevent Duty in terms of their preparation and expertise to enact this Duty but it has not materialised. And it is here that liquidity is situated, in the space where tension should be located. This indifference, this absence, is the essence of Liquid Modernity, where fluidity and uncertainty are the norms.

Student teachers also reported that, in their experience, all schools were aware of their Prevent Duty but that not all schools enacted the Prevent Duty through lessons or whole school activities. Analysis of the questionnaires and interviews shows that the Prevent Duty was enacted largely by foregrounding narratives and icons of Britishness. These were apparent in the posters displayed around schools on values, and in displays of British artefacts, famous British people, well-known landmarks and monuments. Student teachers also reflected that The Rule of Law and Democracy were less obviously addressed through displays or posters and posters and/or displays on radicalisation and extremism were not evident. The aspect of the Prevent Duty that requires teachers to prevent pupils from becoming radicalised was less apparent in schools. Interestingly, the student teachers were untroubled by this discrepancy, oblivious to the fault line running through the enactment of the Prevent Duty. Teachers too were untroubled by this discrepancy. Our student teachers' experiences suggested that they had little sense of who was taking overall responsibility for ensuring Prevent was enacted appropriately by each teacher, and that teachers were working collectively on some aspects of Prevent but that not all teachers were au fait with all aspects of Prevent. Significantly, this did not cause them concern. In a sense, they did not assume agency over their work in this area. Bauman suggests that liquefaction results in restricted human agency (Bauman 2012; Best 2017), and this is helpful in understanding why the teachers in this study did not appear to take individual responsibility for this area of work –the restriction of agency in professional practice has been brought about by waves of change and Prevent, it seems, is the latest.

In relation to countering terrorism, all student teachers said they felt that teachers should do all they can to counter terrorism, and yet no student reflected that their teacher training did not include this, or that their induction programme did not cover this aspect of the Prevent Duty. There is a sense here of the student as consumer, rather than seeking a solid understanding of the subject matter in hand. Bauman's notion of consumption (2008) as a feature of Liquid Modernity, and of the subsequent fragile nature of this consumption is apparent in this data, where the students had no sense of, or concern about, the fragility of their knowledge. And it is here again that Bauman's (2012) thesis on liquidity highlights a new aspect of professional practice where the student teachers were untroubled by flux, by the changing nature of practice in schools, by competing demands upon their professional knowledge and skills, because this is what it is to be a professional educator in times of Liquid Modernity.

In a similar vein, all students agreed that they should do all they can to promote fundamental British values, although some then reflected that, in their view, the concept of fundamental British values is problematic – too limited, too inward looking. This though was a dilemma that once expressed, abated, and students carried on with their Prevent Duty. The shadow of lack of professional agency fell over the data once again, as we considered how comfortable students were practicing in this contested field.

Whilst student teachers were confident that their future schools would have protocols to address Prevent, this was viewed in two ways; firstly, in terms of offering a counter narrative to terrorism through the promotion of fundamental British values, through posters, displays and artefacts and secondly, through the curriculum where radicalisation and terrorism would be explored. However, none of the participating student teachers received induction into the processes of radicalisation – this was not part of the induction programme, although they as teachers are required to prevent pupils from becoming radicalised. It is significant that an introduction to the processes of radicalisation was not part of induction, although of greater significance is the fact that student teachers had not raised this as an issue. Some 60% of students had no discussion about or introduction to the Prevent Duty from their Mentor, despite the statutory nature of the Prevent Duty within both the Teachers' Standards (DfE 2012) and the OfSTED inspection framework for ITT providers; Mentors will have been acutely aware of both frameworks and would have understood the significance of this from both perspectives. It was also clear that the way schools fulfilled their legal duties in relation to Prevent varied, so that while some schools embedded the obligation to promote fundamental British values in and across the curriculum and inducted student teachers into the protocols for reporting potential radicalisation in the school, for other schools the engagement with Prevent was largely invisible.

Bauman (2012) argues that in liquid times power is wielded through uncertainty, and this is apparent in the ways in which teachers and student teachers are engaging with the Prevent Duty. The education professionals in this research accepted their Duty without question. They did not query the nature of the latest iteration of Prevent and articulated complete compliance with Government requirements. Government then, has assumed a position of power in relation to teachers in spite of the fact that this is an inchoate field.

There are two observations to make on the data. Firstly, the data demonstrated many discrepancies (for example, schools understood the statutory nature of the Prevent Duty and yet students received variable induction in this; teachers had limited expertise in the processes of radicalisation and yet no teacher expressed concern about this – and so on). These discrepancies highlighted where one might expect to find tensions, and yet no tensions were articulated. There was a sense of absence when we listened to the students describe their practice or that of their teachers – and the space between the discrepancies became a place of focus for us. The student teachers seemed to feel little agency in relation to this work, and a sense of indifference in relation to the discrepancies. This sense of indifference, the space between the issues, expresses a central dimension of Liquid Modernity.

The second observation is the ease with which the student teachers handled the state of flux they found themselves in. In the past, flux would have been an interruption, whereas these student teachers regarded flux and uncertainty as part of the educational landscape, and are a defining feature.

27.6 Conclusion

This research indicates that there are implications for the ways in which student teachers, through their experiences in schools, are conceptualising their Prevent Duty. In a sense this is unsurprising because the Prevent Duty offers an incomplete narrative of fundamental British values as a counter narrative to radicalisation and extremism. Bauman's (2012) thesis has enabled us to interpret this data from the perspective of liquidity and change, and it is here that our most valuable insights lie. It seems from the research that students are enacting what we would wish to identify as a new form of professionalism – liquid professionalism – where some of the grand narratives of 'Teacher Professionalism', namely subject knowledge and professional autonomy, are recast in liquid times; none of our participants expressed concern about their lack of subject knowledge of radicalisation or extremism and none of our participants expressed a concern that they had been bestowed with a Prevent Duty, despite the fact that this is beyond what teachers have traditionally been required to do as teacher work. While Bauman (2012) offers the notion of boundaries melting away, which is helpful when conceptualising the notion that teachers should promote fundamental British values within and outside of school; the private and public spheres are without boundaries in this policy space – and student teachers and teachers have not expressed concern in this regard. It could even be suggested that these student teachers' lack of concern towards the imposition of Prevent duties might characterise a teacher/pupil relationship which is fluid, exemplifying restricted human agency (Bauman 2012) and indifference towards radicalisation and extremism. While not all student teachers adopted an uncritical and compliant attitude, it is concerning that that the majority did.

References

Bauman, Z. (2005). Education in liquid modernity. *Review of Education, Pedagogy and Cultural Studies, 27*(4), 303–317.

Bauman, Z. (2012). *Liquid modernity*. Cambridge: Polity.

Bauman, Z., & Haugaard, M. (2008). Culture, modernity and revolution. *Journal of Power, 1*(2), 111–130.
Best, S. (2017). Education in the interregnum: An evaluation of Zygmund Bauman's liquid turn in education. *British Journal of Sociology of Education, 38*(2), 203–220.
Bryan, H. (2012, August). Reconstructing the teacher as post-secular pedagogue: A consideration of the new teachers' standards. *Journal of Values and Beliefs, 33*(2), 217–228.
Bryan, H. (2017, in press). Developing the political citizen: How teachers are navigating the statutory demands of the counter-terrorism and Security Act 205 and the prevent duty. *Journal of Education, Citizenship and Social Justice.* Available at http://journals.sagepub.com/doi/abs/10.1177/1746197917717841 accessed on 12.05 .18
Day, C., Kington, A., Stobart, G., & Sammons, P. (2006). The personal and professional selves of teachers: Stable and unstable identities. *British Educational Research Journal, 32*(4), 601–616.
Elton-Chalcraft, S., Lander V., Revell, L., Warner, D., & Whitworth, L. (2017, February). To promote, or not to promote fundamental British values? Teachers' standards, diversity and teacher education. *British Educational Research Journal, 43*(1). Available at http://onlinelibrary.wiley.com/doi/10.1111/berj.2017.43.issue-1/issuetoc
Farrell, F. (2016). Why all of a sudden do we need to teach fundamental British values? A critical investigation of religious education student teacher positioning within a policy discourse of discipline and control. *Journal of Education for teaching, 42*(3), 280–297. Special issue: Fundamental British Values.
Holstein, J., & Gubrium, J. (1995). *The active interview.* London: Sage.
Panjwani, F. (2016). Towards an overlapping consensus: Muslim teachers' views on fundamental British values. *Journal of Education for Teaching, 42*(3), 329–340. Special issue: Fundamental British Values.
Revell, L., & Bryan, H. (2016). Calibrating fundamental British values: How head teachers are approaching appraisal in the light of the Teachers' Standards 2012, Prevent and the Counter-Terrorism and Security Act, 2015. *Journal of Education for Teaching: International Research and Pedagogy, 42*(3), 341–353.

28

Compulsory Schooling and Cognitive Imperialism: A Case for Cognitive Justice and Reconciliation with Indigenous Peoples

Marie Battiste
and James [Sa'ke'j] Youngblood Henderson

28.1 Introduction

Marie Battiste is a Mi'kmaw scholar and educator from Potlotek First Nations, Nova Scotia, full professor in the Department of Educational Foundations at the University of Saskatchewan and fellow of the Royal Society of Canada. With degrees from Harvard and Stanford Universities, she is widely published and recognized for initiating institutional change in the decolonization of education, Indigenizing of the academy and activating social justice and post-colonial educational approaches that recognize and affirm the political and cultural diversity of Canada.

J. Youngblood (Sa'ke'j) Henderson, JD, IPC, FRSC, is a member of Chickasaw Nation. He is Research Fellow at the Native Law Centre of Canada, College of Law at the University of Saskatchewan and a fellow of the Royal Society of Canada. He created litigation strategies to restore Aboriginal knowledge, heritage, culture, institutions, self-determination and rights in North America and the United Nations. During the constitutional process (1978–1993) in Canada, he served as a constitutional advisor for the Mi'kmaw nation and the National Indian Brotherhood-Assembly of First Nations. He has continued to develop the concepts of Aboriginal and treaty rights in constitutional law.

M. Battiste (✉) • J. [Sa'ke'j]. Y. Henderson
University of Saskatchewan, Saskatoon, SK, Canada
e-mail: marie.battiste@usask.ca; sakej.henderson@usask.ca

K. Trimmer et al. (eds.), *The Palgrave Handbook of Education Law for Schools*,
https://doi.org/10.1007/978-3-319-77751-1_28

28.2 Introduction

Compulsory schooling law for Aboriginal children in Canada has created a crisis both in their education and in their social and economic well-being. Learning before compulsory schooling was a process that involved relational, communal, contextualized, purposeful activities that supported the ages and stages of life, and was transmitted through a language that was known and used throughout the Indigenous community. Indigenous learning for generations was responsive to their needs within an ecology and the communities, cultivated in holistic lifelong learning processes that were the foundations of Indigenous knowledge systems (IKS). These processes created vast learning civilizations built on multiple skills and competencies that have been transmitted to succeeding generations through Indigenous languages, oral traditions and community socialization, cultural and spiritual ceremonies and traditions, and extended relationships with large Indigenous confederacies and alliances. The success of these holistic processes for lifelong learning created a collective sustainable lifestyle that contributed sufficiently to the needs of the present and took into consideration the needs of the future seven generations (Bouvier et al. 2016).

The Aztec Triple Alliance in North America, which governed modern-day central Mexico in the 15th and early 16th centuries, is said to be the first Indigenous nation to make education mandatory for all children (Soustelle 2002, p. 173), well before the development of compulsory education laws in North America that required children to attend a public or state-accredited private schools for a certain period of time. Little is known about those schools but much has since been written about the colonial schools and their purposes and the largely negative outcomes they generated among Indigenous children, their families and their collective cultural communities. The literature and the testimonies of Indigenous peoples across Canada have revealed the traumatic and devastating consequences to Indigenous peoples, their languages, cultures and psyches of not just the children who attended the schools but also the generations that followed.

How current compulsory education, schools and teaching can begin to reconcile the traumatic Indigenous education of the past with the future around the urgent calls for action from the Truth and Reconciliation Commission Canada around reconciliation is the current quest and mandates taken up at all levels of Canadian government, education, health, legal and media and other areas that have been most implicated in the last two hundred years of denigration of Indigenous peoples. In s. 93 of the Canadian

Constitution Act, 1867 (UK 1867), the Queen in Parliament formalized jurisdiction over public funding of education in the confederating provinces, but signalled a distinctive category for Indians whose education would be given to the federal government. However, in the attempt to implement the treaty obligations to education (Henderson 1995), Canadian administrators and educators did not implement either the Indigenous vision of lifelong learning and invigorating collective well-being or the treaty commitments. Instead, in regards to the education of the Indians, the federal Indian Act established an administrative authority for withdrawing the children from their parents and community to forcibly assimilate them by compulsory education in Indian residential schools and days school which were required to use solely British values and beliefs (Canada 1883, pp. 1107–08). Starting in 1870, three years after Confederation, the federal government established funding for the compulsory federal Indian Residential School system to be delivered by various denominations of Catholic and Protestant churches (Truth and Reconciliation Commission, Canada (TRC) 2015c). The federal government and churches chose to use compulsory education as a tool of cognitive imperialism (Battiste 1986). Compulsory school law enacted in 1876 and revised in 1920 became a deep betrayal of broken promises regarding the education provisions in the Georgian and Victorian treaties, radically eroding or destroying much of Aboriginal knowledge systems, traditions and languages of the peoples. It was based on the false premises concerning the assumed inferiority of Aboriginal knowledge systems, languages, cultures, and livelihood that have generated a legacy of systemic racism in residential and provincial schools. These compulsory federal schools established a long and tragic history of an intergenerational failure (Royal Commission on Aboriginal People (RCAP) 1996, vol. 3: 433–34; TRC 2015b) as survivors of that system testified as generating enduring trauma, nihilism, confusion, despair, rejection, poverty, and multilayered abuses that have reverberated in all forms of negative outcomes and cycling of tragedies in their families. The current astonishing numbers of children in both the child welfare and criminal justice system are a testament to that era and its reverberating effects through the generations. While most residential school began closing in the 1970s, the last one did not close until 1996, after increasingly criminal and civil suits against the school were launched by Indian Residential School survivors.

In 2008, the then Canadian Prime Minister Stephen Harper apologized to Aboriginal survivors of Canada's Indian residential schools not only for the destruction of their lives by the federal residential school system, but also for the creation of the system that he acknowledged was meant to "kill the Indian in the child" (Canada 2008). Thereafter, Harper declared Canada's commitment would be to "forg[e] a new relationship… based on the knowledge of our shared history, a respect for each other and a desire to move forward together with a renewed understanding that strong families, strong communities and vibrant cultures and traditions will contribute to a stronger Canada for all of us (np)." While the apology was viewed among many as a welcomed first step, the apology, however, did not translate into correcting the funding structures of the schools that left First Nations schools underfunded compared to provincial schools nor address the underfunding of care for children pulled from their families and homes from social services during the years following the residential schools. It also did not address the shortages that would build the needed schools, correct the structures that failed so many Aboriginal children, or build a system that fit the treaty and Aboriginal rights that were promised them.

Under the Indian Residential Schools Settlement Agreement (2007), the court-mandated Truth and Reconciliation Commission Canada (TRC 2015c) set out to study the oppressive history, purpose, operation, and supervision of the Indian Residential school system and collect testimonies from those associated with those schools. After eight years of laborious and painful testimonials largely if not solely from the survivors and research in truth finding, the TRC determined:

> Canada's residential school system for Aboriginal children was an education system in name only for much of its existence. These residential schools were created for the purpose of separating Aboriginal children from their families, in order to minimize and weaken family ties and cultural linkages, and to indoctrinate children into a new culture – the culture of the legally dominant Euro-Christian Canadian society (TRC 2015c, p. 1).

For over a century, the TRC declared the outcomes of compulsory education system were more than educational malpractice, rather the staggering failure of the residential schools endemically abused more than 15,000 Indian, Inuit, and Metis children that was best described as "cultural genocide" (Woolford 2009, p. 8). Over 30,000 children died either in or immediately coming from these schools (TRC 2015b, 2015c). These schools, the teachers and administrators and the government that funded them, had the intention to prevent the transmission of cultural values and identity from one generation to the next and to destroy Indigenous knowledge systems of life-long learning and languages (Moore and Deloria 2003, p. 8).

Though the last Indian residential school closed in 1996, compulsory education of Indians in Eurocentric systems has not ended; in fact, it has shifted to compulsory provincial education and in particular to their mandated curricula that continue the assimilation model and overt cognitive imperialism. Over half of First Nations and Inuit students are in provincial schools (AFN 2012) and the remaining First Nations youth are in First Nations schools, most of which are having to implement the provincial standards and curricula in reserve schools by public school law (Ouellette 2011). The Canadian Council of Ministers of Education (CCME) of the federal, provincial, and territories (2004, 2008) began addressing the resulting negative outcomes of that schooling by acknowledging the gaps created among First Nations schools (Avison 2004), noting the lower achievements and reduced graduation rates among First Nations. The provincial narrative did not, however, see the problem as their Eurocentric curricula or their mandated standards on the schools, but rather sought to ameliorate the perceived intergenerational challenges of Aboriginal youth by advocating for new initiatives to support First Nations students at various levels. The Council has made several recommendations, including recognize early childhood education as a key to improved literacy; provide clear objectives and a commitment to report results, including working closer with the Government of Canada and Aboriginal communities; institute strong teacher development and recruitment; improve accountability arrangements with Aboriginal parents and communities; share learning resources; support the elimination of inequitable funding levels for First Nations Schools; and create a National Forum on Aboriginal Education (Avison 2004,). Regrettably, the CCMEC did not focus on curricula reform by examining Indigenous knowledge and their humanities as a foundation for their future reforms.

The challenges of moving beyond the assimilation model continue to baffle provincial school authorities with the provinces continuing to apply the assumed superior standards for the failed education system rather than a transformative and responsive education that could provide a new foundation to their lives and their well-being. While provincial school systems attempt to address the concerns and issues presented to them, the lack of dialogue with Indigenous peoples and clear guidelines for curricula reform have led many to begin approaching the problem with add-ons of Aboriginal content to the current structures, increasing Aboriginal hires in the school system, and professional development in learning styles and pedagogical approaches. Without guidance and dialogue on the curricula needs however, they continue to rely on Eurocentric dispositional analysis of education, meaning that the problems of disparities in outcomes rests largely on the individual dispositions of Aboriginal students rather than focusing on a systemic analysis of the Eurocentric curriculum and structures and its narrowed conventional foundations. Meanwhile Aboriginal youth face the continuing losses to their knowledge system, languages, cultures, and livelihood, and its consequences to their outlook, self-esteem, identities, and collective well-being and their subsequent low engagement and performance in formal education, and their lack of employment after leaving schools (Battiste 2005; CCL 2009).

Literature regarding the purposes and structures of compulsory education has continued to point to the fact that schools have not been benign or politically neutral (McLaren 2015; Apple 2006; Bartolome 1994, 2008; Carnoy 1974; Friere 1973). Schools have always been embedded with power, ideologies and meanings constructed from the Eurocentric economic, political, social and cultural foundations of their societies that are further implicated with race, class and gender (Quinn 1999; Calliste and Dei 2000; Dei et al. 2000; St. Denis 2002). They have also been based solidly and definitely on a coercive assimilation path to advance Eurocentric norms through and with public funds.

In their several reports, the Truth and Reconciliation Commission (2012, 2015a, b, c) addressed the multiple layers of negative outcomes of the Indian Residential Schools and set out in their Calls to Action to urge immediate concerted individual and collective action for governments, education, medical and legal institutions, organizations, media, and general public. The TRC calls to actions (TRC 2015a) as thus stated are intended to remedy the situation created by the state apparatus of compulsory education, maligned by epistemological racism and public and state self-interest, and urged by an educated elite steeped in racism to perpetuate a deficit discourse and a racialized practice of fixing the Indians by stripping them of their Indigeneity and identity, not transform the systems of their Eurocentric superiority. The TRC pointed to the urgent need for reconciliation because the relationship between Aboriginal and non-Aboriginal peoples is and has not been a mutually respectful one. It introduced the term 'spiritual violence' in schools which was defined as occurring when "a person's spiritual or religious tradition, beliefs, or practices are demeaned or belittled". It asserted that reconciliation is about coming to terms with and ending the cultural genocide of compulsory education of the past in a manner that overcomes conflict and establishes a respectful and healthy relationship toward cognitive justice among people going forward and living together. It defined reconciliation as an ongoing process of establishing and maintaining the revitalization of Aboriginal culture, languages, spirituality, laws, governance and way of life.

Convinced by the importance of the United Nations Declaration on the Rights of Indigenous Peoples (UNDRIP 2007), the TRC affirmed that it was an appropriate framework for a holistic vision of reconciliation (2015b, pp. 20–21). UNDRIP is a 20-year dialogue document developed by and with Indigenous peoples worldwide that provides the necessary principles, norms and standards for self-determination and reconciliation to flourish in 21st century Canada. The UN Declaration's minimum standards achieved by the global consensus of Indigenous peoples are rights set out to ensure that Indigenous peoples and individuals have the right not to be subjected to forced assimilation or destruction of their culture (art. 8); have the right to establish and control their educational systems and institutions providing education in their own languages, in a manner appropriate to their cultural methods of teaching and learning (art. 14(1)); the right to all levels and forms of education of the State without discrimination (art. 14(2)); the right to the dignity and diversity of their cultures, traditions, histories and aspirations which shall be appropriately reflected in education (art. 15); have the right to "revitalize, use, develop and transmit to future generations their histories, languages, oral traditions, philosophies, writing systems and literatures" (art. 13); the right to practising and revitalizing their cultural traditions and customs (art. 11(1)); have the right to manifest, practise, develop and teach their spiritual and religious traditions, customs, and ceremonies (art. 12); and the right "to maintain, control, protect and develop their cultural heritage, traditional knowledge and traditional cultural expressions" (art 31). Moreover, Indigenous peoples have the right to the recognition, observance and enforcement of treaties and to have States honour and respect such treaties (art. 37(1)); nothing in this Declaration may be interpreted as diminishing or eliminating the rights of Indigenous peoples contained in treaties and agreements (art. 37(2)). In 2016 Canada affirmed the Declaration as part of the constitutional rights of Aboriginal peoples.

Aboriginal families have a long ways to go until the affirmations of the UNDRIP reach a sufficient level to feel that they can reconcile from their past and be secure with their future. They have suffered and fought to take back their children's lives, languages, and cultural roots and identities with the land and have not resigned themselves or their children to situations not of their making or desire. As in the treaties and for more than the last 35 years, Aboriginal families and educators in Canada have been articulating their goals for control of Aboriginal education of their children (AFN 1972, 2010; Gabriel Dumont Institute of Native Studies and Applied Research 2009; Inuit Tapiriit Kanatami 2008). This is properly understood as a reconciliation with the compulsory education law to deal with the generational traumas of the undesired past and their lasting consequences, which is focused on decolonization (Battiste 2013; Yellow Bird 2012) and cognitive justice (Santos et al. 2007). Reconciliation requires knowledge revitalization and sustainability. Since Aboriginal peoples regard their children as precious and sacred gifts, the objective of Aboriginal peoples is to take control of the constitutional right and jurisdiction over the education of their children. They want to create an educational systems and curricula based on their knowledge systems, languages, and place based activated learning that will prepare them to participate fully in their communities and in Canadian society (RCAP 1996, vol. 3, ch. 5). They expect education to be lifelong and holistic and to serve as a vehicle for their cultural and economic renewal and collective well-being (Bouvier et al. 2016). This educational system must develop the whole child, intellectually, spiritually, emotionally and physically. The current step is then for Canadian society, and its governmental structures and systems to conduct their own forms of reconciliation that begins with the recognition of their abusive socio-historic reality, inequities and racism, continuing neglect and land appropriation built into Canadian colonialism, the presumptions and assumptions based in Eurocentric superiority that have led to this damage, and the recovery of systems and structures within Indigenous worldviews and structures to rebuild, restore and regenerate Indigenous peoples collective well-being.

28.3 Constitutional Reconciliation and Education Responsibilities

Compulsory education has remained a system of injustices that needs to be constitutionally reconciled with Aboriginal peoples of Canada with the other constitutional powers of education (Battiste 2009). Section 35 of the Constitution Act, 1982 affirms and recognizes Aboriginal and treaty rights, which include the educational rights of Aboriginal nations, peoples, and parents. The Supreme Court of Canada has identified a constitutional commitment in this section to recognize, value, protect, and enhance their distinctive cultures (Powley 2003, paras. 13, 18). To ensure the revitalization and continuity of Aboriginal customs and traditions, the Supreme Court has determined that every substantive constitutional right will normally include the incidental constitutional right to teach such a practice, custom and tradition to a younger generation (Coté 1996). As a constitutional provision, Aboriginal and treaty rights have been affirmed as part of the supreme law of Canada, and the courts may declare invalid any provincial or federal law or policy inconsistent with these rights (UK 1982, s. 52(1)). This includes the compulsory school attendance laws or compulsory conventional curriculum.

A problem remains however. The existing compulsory federal and provincial school systems have not translated these constitutionally protected rights into current models of education, but rather have developed the discursive modes of neoliberal economic analysis that have led to various models of education that focus on individual Aboriginal students' or on their parents' or communities' perceived deficits while they continue to ignore systemic racism and structural failures of the compulsory educational systems and the well-being of First Nations, Métis and Inuit (Bouvier et al. 2016). This situation has yet to change, despite on-going discourses of intended changes to these structures (Harper 2008; Canada 2015) or recommendations made to this government.

The First Nation Education National Panel report (Canada AANDC 2011) concluded that the federal Indian Act sections on education (ss. 114–122) offer no guidance for First Nation schools; they deal only with compulsory attendance, truancy and sectarian rights. Moreover, the National Panel and the Canadian Human Rights Tribunal in the First Nations Child and Family Caring Society v Canada (2016) have found the governmental funding of First Nation schools on reserves – both operating funding and capital funding – is inadequate, intentional discriminatory and unequal to provincial education. The Auditor General of Canada (2004, 2010) has further noted failure on the part of the Canadian government in inadequately funding and supporting First Nations education in a sustainable and meaningful manner that has generated "a significant education gap" between First Nations people living on reserves and the Canadian population that at the current rate can only be closed within 27–28 years. The unequal funding for First Nation education requires a new fiscal framework for these essential educational services that has to match the principle of equalization programs as set out in the s. 36(2) of the Constitution Act, 1982.

Importantly, the National Panel found that Indian youth are succeeding in other forms of educational jurisdiction, those specifically under First Nations control of education, such as Mi'kmaw Kina'matnewey Agreement in Nova Scotia and the British Columbia schools under the First Nations Education Steering Committee system. These are schools in First Nations communities that have voluntarily amalgamated to negotiate and collaborate to create the needed resources and develop supportive services that serve the needs of First Nations children, such as immersion and cultural language programming, special education specialists, and other similar agreed upon servicing of their needs. One such amalgamated First Nations authority has been able to demonstrate over 88% graduation rates averaging over seven years in their schools (MK Annual Report 2016, p. 25) and is well noted across Canada for its successes, though this innovation is slow in being replicated in other areas across Canada.

Constitutional reconciliation generates a reorientation of the dialogue needed between First Nations and those seeking to rebuild relations in what has been theorized by Ermine (2007) as ethical space. Ethical space is one where positive relations between Indigenous and Western systems can be nurtured, where two cultures agree to engage in a neutral zone where two cultures can meet with respect for one another, and where the "notions of universality are replaced by concepts such as the equality of nations… [and] triggers a dialogue that begins to set the parameters for an agreement to interact modeled on appropriate, ethical and human principles" (p. 202).

The current federal government under the Liberal government platform has issued its commitment to implement all of the TRC's calls to action. It has committed to renew the nation-to-nation relations and to gradually replace the oppressive federal Indian Act. It has also expressed its commitment to increase funding and reform of K-12 education. Similarly, the Canadian Association of Deans of Education (2010) has developed an Indigenous Education Accord that is aimed at ameliorating the past neglect and omissions and recognition of the need to address the past and present of Indigenous peoples and knowledges through teacher education and professional development.

However, the common approach of provincial educational systems continues to patchwork the dam that is leaking at many places with manipulation and half measures that fail to address the system of domination that produced the cultural genocide through forced assimilation (Trouillot 2011). Gender, poverty, race, class, Eurocentric culture and language imperialism, underfunding of communities, and rural isolation continue to restrict student access to adequate schooling, while unaddressed prejudice, stereotyping and racism continue unabated in the Canadian urban and rural communities and governments. While some of these factors that generate systemic inequalities have been addressed in the studies on Aboriginal education, perhaps the one least addressed and one that is constitutionally mandated is the recognition of the Aboriginal rights and treaty rights.

Constitutional reconciliation requires that Aboriginal families, province and territorial school systems reform their compulsory educational systems and curricula to begin to effectively address the structural discrimination against Indigenous knowledge systems that have resulted in the tragic failure of educating Aboriginal students. The constitutional framework and court decisions generate an emerging need for reconciliation of Indigenous knowledge systems in learning and pedagogy that impacts all compulsory forms of education. It creates the innovative context for systemic curricular reform to include the various models of the holistic, resilient, lifelong learning paradigm in existing constitutional rights. This includes: Indigenous science, humanities, visual arts, and languages as well as existing education philosophy, pedagogy, teacher education, and practice. Reconciling the constitutional rights of Indigenous students with the core competencies of Indigenous knowledge systems and its variants in the Indigenous humanities is a way to reconcile the compulsory law that relies on assimilative and acculturative approach of education to generate curricula that is ameliorative, restorative, nurturing, respectful, and accountable.

28.4 A Way Forward: Decolonizing and Indigenizing of Canadian Educational Systems

The decolonizing of an educational system entails seeking an ethical modality for the functioning of at least two knowledge systems in such a manner that fosters active dialogue, inter-learning, and reciprocal valorization of the knowledge systems. Canadian and Aboriginal educators have begun the constitutional reconciliation and the renaissance with negotiated principles for working with Indigenous peoples, new protocols for engaging respectful relationships (Ermine et al. 2005), new foundations for curriculum change (Governments of Alberta et al. 2000), and new frameworks such as was created with Aboriginal communities through the work of the former Canadian Council on Learning (2007) and the holistic lifelong learning models for identifying success and collective well-being (Bouvier et al. 2016).

Indigenization of the curriculum at every level of the compulsory education system is another important component of constitutional reconciliation. It is the expression of the constitutional rights of Aboriginal peoples concerning educational choice. It is where cognitive healing must begin. It must recognize the expressed epistemic vision of First Nations is a return to lifelong learning in multiple knowledge systems and orientations. Their vision is that lifelong learning is a process of nurturing First Nations learners in linguistically and culturally-appropriate holistic learning environments that meet the individual and collective needs of First Nations and ensures that all First Nations learners have the opportunity to achieve their personal aspirations within comprehensive, trans-systemic learning systems (AFN 2010). The AFN National Panel's structural solutions began with returning control to the First Nation families to nurture respect, positive identity, well-being and the needs of children to prosper as distinct peoples (pp. viii, 20). This is called the Indigenization of education, a journey from cognitive imperialism and myopia to connectedness and complementarity, and cognitive justice which requires an investment in knowledge systems, languages, culture, traditions and families (Oreopoulos 2005; Sharpe and Arsenault 2009).

Indigenizing the curricula of compulsory education is another ameliorative concept that can be key in designing meaningful educational curricula for all youth in Canada that confronts the hidden standards of racism, colonialism, and cultural and linguistic imperialism in the modern curriculum. This curriculum reform is required if attendance in school is going to continue to be the compulsory. The logical place to start seeking educational improvement of Aboriginal school is through Indigenizing the curricula that will develop better schools and learning environments. Most Canadians, both Aboriginal and non-Aboriginal, have long accepted some of the Eurocentric assumptions underlying compulsory schools. The assumptions are contrary to the facts of the existing failures. The existing situation of Aboriginal students in Canada and beyond have provided dramatic evidence that compulsory Eurocentric education is cultural imperialism and genocide; it is not a form of accessibility to liberation that opens to the individual options and possibilities.

Compulsory education has been a process of normalizing Eurocentric chauvinism that fostered judgement of others, talking down to them, degrading them, colonizing their mind, heart, and resources; it has not acknowledged or respected that all knowledge systems are valid and valuable in their own right. It has generated the ideologies of oppression, which negates the process of IKS as a process of inquiry, and seeks to change the consciousness of the oppressed, not change the situation that oppressed them. Recent American research points to the significant impact of social factors such as acceptance, belonging and expectations on intellectual capacity on success in schools (Paul 2010).

Nonetheless, Indigenizing the curriculum and remedying systemic and epistemological injustices may be the most difficult problem in the restorative journey toward constitutional reconciliation. Transformation cannot come from perceptions of discretion or good will, which can easily be sidelined when times get tough and economic priorities of elites or majorities are raised. It cannot come from equity and multiculturalism, both which have an economic imperative and tolerance factor that positions Indigenous peoples on the bottom of the hierarchy of othering needs. Indigenization must most importantly be understood and discoursed under the constitutional imperative for transformation.

The constitutional rights of Aboriginal people and parents are essential to decolonizing and indigenizing the compulsory education system and curriculum. Their inherent rights of Aboriginal families and parents are further framed in the now accepted UN Declaration of the Rights of Indigenous Peoples that presents a framework for braiding Indigenous knowledges and Eurocentric knowledge system into trans-systemic curricula (Battiste 2007). Because of the constitutional rights attached to Aboriginal peoples, especially their families and parents, must be involved at all stages of Indigenizing the curriculum and in all phases of developing the weaving of the trans-systemic curricula, education planning and future governing of their education. The current challenge is not so much finding receptivity to inclusion of the synthesis among curriculum specialists, but the challenge of ensuring that receptivity to inclusive trans-systemic curricula is appropriately and ethically achieved consistent with Indigenous choice. Together the Indigenous families and educators have to eliminate and remedy the difficult systemic challenges for overcoming Eurocentrism, culturalism, racism, and intolerance and to replace them with respect for Indigenous knowledge systems of the place they are located.

References

Alberta. (2000). *Strengthening relationships. The Government of Alberta's aboriginal policy framework*. Edmonton: Alberta.

Apple, M. (2006). *Educating the right way*. New York: Routledge.

Assembly of First Nations (AFN). (2010). *First Nations control of First Nations education: It's our vision, it's our time*. Ottawa: Assembly of First Nations.

Assembly of First Nations (AFN). (2012). Summary of the report of the National Panel on First Nation Elementary and Secondary Education for Students On-reserve. *Nurturing the learning spirit of first nation students*. Rose-Alma MacDonald, author. Ottawa: AFN Education Secretariat. Retrieved September 26, 2016, from http://www.afn.ca/uploads/files/education/sr_summary_of_the_national_panel_report_feb_14_2012_final.pdf

Auditor General of Canada. (2004). *November report of auditor general of Canada, ch 5 Indian and Northern affairs Canada – Education and post-secondary student support*. Retrieved September 26, 2016, from http://www.oag-bvg.gc.ca/internet/English/parl_oag_200411_05_e_14909.html

Auditor General of Canada. (2010). *Indian and Northern Affairs Canada: Elementary and secondary education*. Report to the House of Commons, Chapter 4. Ottawa: Minister of Public Works and Government Services Canada.

Avison, D. (2004, May). *A challenge worth meeting: Opportunities for improving Aboriginal education outcomes*. Prepared Report for the Council of Ministers in Education.

Bartolome, L. I. (1994). Beyond the methods fetish: Toward a humanizing pedagogy. *Harvard Educational Review, 64*(2), 173–194.

Bartolome, L. I. (2008). *Ideologies in education: Unmasking the trap of teacher neutrality*. New York: Peter Lang.

Battiste, M. (1986). Micmac literacy and cognitive assimilation. In J. Barman, Y. Hébert, & D. McCaskill (Eds.), *Indian education in Canada: The legacy* (Vol. I, pp. 23–44). Vancouver: University of British Columbia Press.

Battiste, M. (2005). *State of Aboriginal learning*. Ottawa, ON: Canadian Council on Learning.

Battiste, M. (2007). The struggle and renaissance of Indigenous knowledge in Eurocentric education. In M. Villegas, S. Rak Neugebauer, & K. R. Venegas (Eds.), *Indigenous knowledge and education: Sites of struggle, strength, and Survivance, Harvard Education Review reprint series no. 44* (pp. 85–91). Cambridge, MA: Harvard Educational Publishing Group.

Battiste, M. (2009). Constitutional reconciliation of education for Aboriginal peoples/La réconciliation constitutionnelle des Autochtones et leurs droits éducationnels *Directions, 5*(1), 81–84.

Battiste, M. (2013). *Decolonizing education: Nourishing the learning spirit*. Saskatoon and Vancouver: Purich Press and University of British Columbia.

Bouvier, R., Battiste, M., & Laughlin, J. (2016). Centring Indigenous intellectual traditions on holistic lifelong learning. In F. Deer & T. Falkenberg (Eds.), *Indigenous perspectives on education for well-being in Canada* (pp. 21–40). Winnipeg: Education for Sustainable Well-Being Press, University of Manitoba. Retrieved March 15, 2017, from http://www.eswb-press.org/uploads/1/2/8/9/12899389/indigeneous_perspectives_2016.pdf

Calliste, A., & Dei, G. J. S. (Eds.). (2000). *Anti-racist feminism: Critical race and gender studies*. Halifax: Fernwood Press.

Canada. (1880-1936). Annual Reports, Department of Indian Affairs. (1883, May 9 *House of commons debate*. 1107–1108). Ottawa: Department of Indian Affairs.

Canada. (2008). *Prime minister Harper offers full apology on behalf of Canadians for the Indian residential schools system*. Retrieved October 11, 2010, from http://pm.gc.ca/eng/media.asp?id=2149

Canada. (2015). Office of the Prime Minister. Mandate letter. Ottawa: Minister of Indigenous and Northern Affairs Canada.

Canada. (2016). Indigenous and Northern Affairs Canada, United Nations Declaration of Rights of Indigenous Peoples. https://www.aadnc-aandc.gc.ca/eng/1309374407406/1309374458958. Accessed 16 Sept 2017.

Canada, Department of Aboriginal Affairs and Northern Development [AANDC]. (2011). The report of the national panel on first nation elementary and secondary education for students on reserve. Government of Canada.

Canadian Association of Deans of Education. (2010). *Accord on Indigenous education*. Retrieved from http://educ.ubc.ca/sites/educ.ubc.ca/les/FoE%20document_ACDE_Ac-cord_Indigenous_Education_01–12-10.pdf

Canadian Council on Learning. (2007). *Redefining how success is measured in First Nations, Inuit and Métis learning*. Retrieved from http://eboulearning.com/ccl/RedefiningSuccess/Redefining_How_Success_Is_Measured_EN.pdf

Canadian Council on Learning. (2009). *The state of Aboriginal learning in Canada: A holistic approach to measuring success*. Retrieved March 17, 2017, from https://www.eboulearning.com/ccl/StateAboriginalLearning/SAL-FINALReport_EN.PDF

Carnoy, M. (1974). *Education as cultural imperialism*. New York: David McKay Company.

Council of Ministers of Education, Canada [CMEC]. (2004). Backgrounder on the CMEC Aboriginal Education Action Plan. Retrieved from https://www.cmec.ca/Publications/Lists/Publications/Attachments/71/BackgrounderAboriginalEducation.en.pdf

Council of Ministers of Education. (2008). *Learn Canada 2020: Joint declaration provincial and territorial ministers of education*. Ottawa: CMEC Retrieved October 11, 2010, from http://www.cmec.ca/Publications/Lists/Publications/Attachments/187/CMEC-2020-DECLARATION.en.pdf

Dei, G. J. S., Hall, B. L., & Goldin Rosenberg, D. (Eds.). (2000). *Removing the margins: The challenges and possibilities of inclusive schooling*. Toronto: Canadian Scholars' Press.

Ermine, W. (2007). The ethical space of engagement. *Indigenous Law Journal, 6*(1), 193–203.

Ermine, W., Sinclair, R., & Browne, M. (2005). *Kwayask itôtamowin: Indigenous research ethics. Report of the Indigenous peoples' health research centre to the institute of Aboriginal peoples' health and the Canadian institutes of health research*. Regina: Indigenous Peoples' Health Research Centre.

First Nations Child and Family Caring Society v Canada 2016 C.H.R.T. 2.

Freire, P. (1973). *Pedagogy of the oppressed*. New York: Seabury Press.

Gabriel Dumont Institute of Native Studies and Applied Research. (2009). *Métis education report: A special report on Métis education prepared by the Métis National Council for the summit on Aboriginal education*. Retrieved November 2009, from Gabriel Dumont Institute of Native Studies and Applied Research http://www.gdins.org/documents/resources/KtMEducationReportFeb20-2009.pdf

Harper, S. (2008). *Prime minister Harper offers full apology on behalf of Canadians for the Indian residential schools system* 11 June 2008 Ottawa. Retrieved from http://www.pm.gc.ca/eng/media.asp?id=2149

Henderson, J. Y. (1995). Indian education and treaties. In M. Battiste & J. Barman (Eds.), *First Nations education in Canada: The circle unfolds*. Vancouver: University of British Columbia Press.

Indian Residential Schools Settlement Agreement. (2007). Retrieved October 4, 2016, from http://www.thecanadianencyclopedia.ca/en/article/indian-residential-schools-settlement-agreement/

Inuit Tapiriit Kanatami. (2008, April 15–17). *Report on the Inuit Tapiriit Kanatami education initiative: Summary of ITK summit on Inuit education and background research*. Inuvik/Ottawa: Author.

Mi'kmaw Kina'matnewey [MK] (2016). Annual report 2015–2016. Retrieved from http://kinu.ca/sites/default/files/doc/2014/Feb/mk_annual_report_2016.pdf

McLaren, P. (2015). *Life in schools* (6th ed.). London: Paradigm Publishers.

Moore, M., & Deloria, V., Jr. (2003). *Genocide of the mind: New Native American writing*. New York: Thunder's Mouth Press/Nation Books.

National Indian Brotherhood (NIB). (1972). *Indian control of Indian education.* Policy Paper presented to the Minister of Indian Affairs and Northern Development. Ottawa: National Indian Brotherhood.

Oreopoulos, P. (2005). *Canadian compulsory school law and their impact on education attainment and future earning*. Ottawa: Minister of Industry. Previewed 26 September 2016 http://publications.gc.ca/Collection/Statcan/11F0019MIE/11F0019MIE2005251.pdf

Ouellette, R. F. (2011). *Evaluating Aboriginal curricula using a Cree-Métis perspective with a regard toward Indigenous knowledge*. Unpublished doctoral dissertation, Laval University, Laval.

Paul, A. M. (2010, October). It's not me, it's you. *New York Times.*http://www.nytimes.com/2012/10/07/opinion/sunday/intelligence-and-the-stereotype-threat.html?nl=opinion&emc=edit_ty_20121008&_r=0

PM Justin Trudeau Speech at UN. (9-21-17). https://www.youtube.com/watch?v=W7LLCFpaUqw

Quinn, B. (1999). *Counterpoint: An analysis of Canadian native educational academic discourse*. Ph.D. thesis, Department of Education Foundations, University of Alberta, Edmonton.

Royal Commission on Aboriginal Peoples (RCAP). (1996). *Report of the Royal Commission on Aboriginal Peoples*. 5 vols. Ottawa: Canada Communication Group.

R. v. Côté, [1996] 3 S.C.R. 139.

R. v. Powley, [2003] 2 S.C.R. 207, 2003 SCC 43.

Sharpe, A., & Arsenault, J.-F. (2009). *Investing in aboriginal education in Canada: An economic perspective*. Ottawa: Canadian Policy Research Networks. Retrieved 26 September 2016 http://www.cprn.org/documents/51980_EN.pdf

Santos, B., Arriscado Nunes, J., & Meneses, M. P. (2007). Opening up the canon of knowledge and recognition of difference. In B. de Sousa Santos (Ed.), *Another knowledge is possible: Beyond Northern epistemologies* (pp. xix–lxii). New York: Verso.

Soustelle, J. (2002). *Daily life of the Aztecs: On the eve of the Spanish conquest*. Mineola: Courier Dover Publications.

St. Denis, V. (2002). *Exploring the socio-cultural production of aboriginal identities: Implications for education*. A Ph.D. dissertation, School of Education, Stanford University, Stanford.

Trouillot, M.-R. (2011). Abortive rituals: Historical apologies in the global era. *Interventions, 2*(2), 171–186. https://doi.org/10.1080/136980100427298.
Truth and Reconciliation Commission. (2015). Calls to action. Retrieved from http://www.trc.ca/websites/trcinstitution/File/2015/Findings/Calls_to_Action_English2.pdf
Truth and Reconciliation Commission. (2015c). *A knock at the door: An essential history of residential schools from the Truth and Reconciliation Commission of Canada.* Winnipeg: TRC.
Truth and Reconciliation Commission of Canada. (2012). Interim report. Ottawa. Retrieved from http://www.attendancemarketing.com/~attmk/TRC_jd/Interim%20re- port%20English%20electronic%20copy.pdf
Truth and Reconciliation Commission of Canada (TRC). (2015). Honouring the truth, reconciling for the future: Summary of the final report of the Truth and Reconciliation Commission of Canada. http://www.trc.ca/websites/trcinstitution/File/2015/Honouring_the_Truth_Reconciling_for_the_Future_July_23_2015.pdf
United Kingdom. (1867). Constitution act, 1867, 30 & 31 Victoria, c. 3.
United Kingdom. (1982). Canadian charter of rights and freedoms, part I of the constitution act, 1982, being schedule B to the Canada act 1982 (UK), 1982, c. 11.
United Nations. (2007). Declaration on the rights of Indigenous peoples UN Doc. A/61/L.67.
Woolford, A. (2009). Ontological destruction: Genocide and Canadian Indigenous peoples. *Genocide Studies and Prevention, 4*(1), 81–97.
Yellow Bird, M. (2012). Neurodecolonization: Using mindfulness practices to delete the neural networks of colonialism. In Waziyatawin & M. Yellow Bird (Eds.), *For indigenous minds only: A decolonization handbook* (pp. 57–84). Santa Fe: School for Advanced Research Press.

References

Abbott, A. (1988). *The system of professions: An essay on the division of expert labor.* Chicago: University of Chicago Press.

Abela v State of Victoria [2013] FCA 832.

Abrahams, N., Casey, K., & Daro, D. (1992). Teachers' knowledge, attitudes, and beliefs about child abuse and its prevention. *Child Abuse & Neglect, 16*(2), 229–238.

ACEI. (n.d.). *The ten pillars of a good childhood.* http://www.acei.org/decade-for-childhood/. Accessed 07 Mar 2017.

ACT Government Education & Training (ACTGET). (2013). *Taskforce on students with learning difficulties.* Canberra: ACT.

Agbenyega, J. S., & Sharma, U. (2014). *Leading inclusive education: Measuring 'effective' leadership for inclusive education through a Bourdieuian lens measuring inclusive education* (pp. 115–132). Bingley: Emerald Group Publishing Limited.

AIFS. (2016). *Child abuse and neglect statistics.* Retrieved October 31, 2016, from https://aifs.gov.au/cfca/publications/child-abuse-and-neglect-statistics

AIHW. (2015). *Australia's welfare 2015.* Australia's welfare no. 12. Cat. no. AUS 189. Canberra: AIHW.

Ainscow, M. (2004). Developing inclusive education systems: What are the levers for change. *Journal of Educational Change, 6*, 109–124.

Ainsworth, F. (2002). Mandatory reporting of child abuse and neglect: Does it really make a difference? *Child & Family Social Work, 7*(1), 57–63.

Ákos, K. (2010). Állampolgárság határon innen és túl. Beszélő Folyóirat. 15, 5 (May–June), 2010.

Al Zidjaly, N. (2015). *Disability, discourse and technology: Agency and inclusion in (inter) action.* Hampshire: Palgrave Macmillan.

K. Trimmer et al. (eds.), *The Palgrave Handbook of Education Law for Schools*,
https://doi.org/10.1007/978-3-319-77751-1

Alberta Learning. (2011). *First Nations, Métis and Inuit education policy framework*. Alberta: Edmonton.

Alderson, P. (2016). International human rights, citizenship education, and critical realism. *London Review of Education, 14*(3), 1–12. https://doi.org/10.18546/LRE.14.3.01.

Aldred, R. (2013). *Broadening the boundaries of agency: Cognitive disability, agency, and autonomy*. Doctoral dissertation, University of Calgary. Retrieved from http://theses.ucalgary.ca/jspui/bitstream/11023/822/2/ucalgary_2013_aldred_raymond.pdf

Alexander, R. (Ed.). (2009). *Children, their world, their education: Final report and recommendations of the Cambridge primary review*. London: Routledge.

Alexander, K., & Alexander, M. (2011). *American public school law* (8th ed.). Belmont: Thomson West.

Allison, G. (1983). Public and private management: Are they fundamentally alike in all unimportant respects? In J. Perry & K. Kramer (Eds.), *Public management, public and private perspectives*. Palo Alto: Mayfield Publishing.

Allmendinger, J. (1989). *Career mobility dynamics: A comparative analysis of the United States, Norway and West Germany*. Berlin: Edition Sigma.

Allmendinger, J., & Hinz, T. (2009). Occupational careers under different welfare regimes: West Germany, Great Britain and Sweden. In W. Heinz et al. (Eds.), *The life-course reader; individuals and societies across time* (pp. 63–84). Frankfurt: Main Campus.

Alvarez, R. R., Jr. (1986). The lemon grove incident. *The Journal of San Diego History, 32*(2), 116–135.

Alvarez, K. M., Kenny, M. C., Donohue, B., & Carpin, K. M. (2004). Why are professionals failing to initiate mandated reports of child maltreatment, and are there any empirically based training programs to assist professionals in the reporting process? *Aggression and Violent Behaviour, 9*, 563–578.

Alwell, M., & Cobb, B. (2006). *A systematic review of the effects of curricular interventions on the acquisition of functional life skills by youth with disabilities*. Kalamazoo: National Secondary Transition Technical Assistance Center.

Aman, A. C., & Mayton. (2014). *Administrative law* (3rd ed.). St. Paul: West Academic Publishing.

American Federation of Teachers. (2009). *The medically fragile child in the school setting: Caring for children with special healthcare needs in the school setting*. Washington, DC: American Federation of Teachers.

Anders, J. (2015). *Keeping kids in school and out of court: A study of education – Youth justice collaboration in the US, Scotland and Denmark*. Canberra: Winston Churchill Memorial Trust of Australia.

Anderson, J., & Boyle, C. (2015). Inclusive education in Australia: Rhetoric, reality and the road ahead. *Support for Learning, 30*(1), 4–22. https://doi.org/10.1111/1467-9604.12074.

Angell, M. E., Stoner, J. B., & Shelden, D. L. (2009). Trust in education professionals: Perspectives of mothers of children with disabilities. *Remedial and Special Education, 30*, 160–176.

Angelle, P., & Bilton, L. M. (2009). Confronting the unknown: Principal preparation training in issues related to special education. *AASA Journal of Scholarship & Practice, 5*(4), 5–9.

Anti-Discrimination Act 1998 (Tas).

Anti-Discrimination Tribunal of Queensland. (2006, July 11). *JC on behalf of BC v State of Queensland (ADTQ)*. Retrieved from http://www.austlii.edu.au/cgi-bin/sinodisp/au/cases/qld/QADT/2006/27.html?stem=0&synonyms=0&query=JC%20on%20behalf%20of%20BC

Apple, M. (2006). *Educating the right way*. New York: Routledge.

Arendt, H. (1954). The crisis in education. In Arendt, H. (1958). *Between past and future: Eight exercises in political thought*. London: Penguin.

Arendt, H. (1958). *The human condition*. Chicago: University of Chicago Press.

Arendt, H. (2006). *Eichmann in Jerusalem: A report on the banality of evil*. Paperback.

Arendt, L., Priem, R., & Ndofor, H. (2005). A CEO-adviser model of strategic decision making. *Journal of Management, 31*(5), 680–699.

Ariely, D. (2012). *The (honest) truth about dishonesty*. New York: HarperCollins.

Armstrong, A. C., Armstrong, D., & Spandagou, I. (2010). *Inclusive education: International policy & practice*. London: Sage.

Armstrong, D., Armstrong, A. C., & Spandagou, I. (2011). Inclusion: By choice or by chance. *International Journal of Inclusive Education, 15*(1), 29–39.

Arnardottir, O. M. (2009). A future of multidimensional disadvantage equality? In O. M. Arnardottir & G. Quinn (Eds.), *The UN convention on the rights of persons with disabilities: European and Scandinavian perspectives* (pp. 41–66). Lieden: Martinus Nijhoff Publishers.

Arnstein-Kerslake, A., & Flynn, E. (2017). The right to legal agency: Domination, disability and the protections of article 12 of the convention on the rights of persons with disabilities. *International Journal of Law in Context, 13*(1), 22–38. https://doi.org/10.1017/S1744552316000458.

Artiles, A. J., Kozleski, E. B., & Waitoller, F. R. (2011). *Inclusive education: Examining equity on five continents*. Cambridge, MA: Harvard Education Press.

Arya, N. (2014). Family-driven justice. *Arizona Law Review, 56*(3), 623–706.

Ashby, C. (2011). Whose "voice" is it anyway? Giving voice and qualitative research involving individuals that type to communicate. *Disability Studies Quarterly, 31*(4), 26. Retrieved from http://dsq-sds.org/article/view/1723/1771

Asif, M., Raouf, A., & Searcy, C. (2013). Developing measures for performance excellence: Is the Baldrige criteria sufficient for performance excellence in higher education? *Quality & Quantity, 47*, 3095–3111.

Assembly of First Nations (AFN). (2010). *First nations control of first nations education: It's our vision, it's our time*. Ottawa: Assembly of First Nations.

Assembly of First Nations (AFN). (2012a). Summary of the report of the national panel on first nation elementary and secondary education for students on-reserve. *Nurturing the learning spirit of first nation students*. Rose-Alma MacDonald, author. Ottawa: AFN Education Secretariat.

Assembly of First Nations (AFN). (2012b). Summary of the report of the national panel on first nation elementary and secondary education for students on-reserve. *Nurturing the learning spirit of first nation students*. Retrieved September 26, 2016, from http://www.afn.ca/uploads/files/education/sr_summary_of_the_national_panel_report_feb_14_2012_final.pdf

Atkins, D. (1995, December 15). A question of hardship. *The Courier Mail*, p. 6.

Atkins, D. (1996, January 19). Commonsense win or rights setback? *The Courier Mail*, p. 2.

Atkinson, R. (2002, October 2–4). Education and the law: Protecting the educational well-being of students. *Legal risk management safety security & success in education: Proceedings of the 11th annual conference of the Australia and New Zealand education law association* (pp. 2–4). Brisbane: GSM Press.

Au, W. (2007). High-stakes testing and curricular control: A qualitative metasynthesis. *Educational Researcher, 36*(5), 258–267.

Auditor General of Canada. (2004). *November report of auditor general of Canada, ch 5 Indian and Northern affairs Canada – Education and post-secondary student support*. Retrieved September 26, 2016, from http://www.oag-bvg.gc.ca/internet/English/parl_oag_200411_05_e_14909.html

Auditor General of Canada. (2010, May 12). *Opening statement to the standing senate committee on aboriginal peoples Indian and Northern affairs Canada – Education program and post-secondary student support*. Retrieved December 11, 2012, from http://www.oag-bvg.gc.ca/internet/English/oss_20100512_e_33879.html

Auerbach, S. (2010). Beyond coffee with the principal: Toward leadership for authentic school-family partnerships. *Journal of School Leadership, 20*, 728–757.

Aultman, L. P., Williams-Johnson, M. R., & Schutz, P. A. (2009). Boundary dilemmas in teacher-student relationships: Struggling with "the line". *Teaching and Teacher Education, 25*, 636–646.

Austin, J., Johnson, K. D., & Weitzer, R. (2005). *Alternatives to the secure detention and confinement of juvenile offenders*. OJJDP Juvenile Justice Practice Series. Retrieved from https://www.ncjrs.gov/App/Publications/abstract.aspx?ID=208804

Australian Bureau of Statistics. (2011, March). 4102.0 – Australian social trends. 'Year 12 attainment'. Canberra: ACT.

Australian Bureau of Statistics. (2013). *1220.0 – ANZSCO – Australian and New Zealand standard classification of occupations, version 1.2*. Retrieved from http://www.abs.gov.au/ausstats/abs@.nsf/Lookup/1220.0Chapter612013%20Version%201.2

Australia Capital Territory Schools Authority v El Sheik (2000) FCA 931 (11 July 2000).

Australian Curriculum Assessment & Reporting Authority. (2013). *Student diversity and the Australian curriculum. Advice for principals, schools and teachers.* Sydney: ACARA.

Australian Curriculum Assessment & Reporting Authority. (n.d.). *National assessment program: Disability adjustment scenarios.* Retrieved from https://www.nap.edu.au/naplan/school-support/adjustments-for-students-with-disability/disability-adjustments-scenarios

Australian Government. (1992). *Disability discrimination act.* Canberra: Governor General's Department. Retrieved from https://www.legislation.gov.au/Series/C2004A04426

Australian Government. (2005). *Disability standards for education.* Canberra: Commonwealth of Australia.

Australian Government. (2006). Disability standards for education 2005. Canberra: Commonwealth of Australia. Retrieved September 1, 2016, from http://www.comlaw.gov.au/Details/C2014C00013

Australian Government. (2006). Disability standards for education 2005. Canberra: Commonwealth of Australia. Retrieved September 1, 2016, from http://www.comlaw.gov.au/Details/C2014C00013

Australian Government [Department of Education Employment and Workforce Relations]. (2012). *Report on the review of the disability standards for education 2005.* Canberra: Author.

Australian Government [Productivity Commission]. (2004). *Review of the disability discrimination act 1992: Productivity commission inquiry report* (Vol. 1). Melbourne: Author.

Australian Government Department of Education and Training. (2005). Disability standards for education. Canberra: Attorney-General's Department, Department of Education, Science and Training. Retrieved from https://education.gov.au/disability-standards-education

Australian Government Department of Education and Training. (2009). *Compact with young Australians.* Canberra: Australian Government. Retrieved from https://www.education.gov.au/compact-young-australians

Australian Human Rights Commission Act 1986 – AustLII. www.austlii.edu.au/au/legis/cth/consol_act/ahrca1986373/

Australian Institute of Criminology. (2015). Annual report 2014–2015. Canberra: Australian Institute of Criminology. Retrieved from https://aic.gov.au/publications/annualreport/2015

Australian Institute for Teaching and School Leadership (AITSL). (2011a). *Australian professional standard for principals.* Education Services Australia, Carlton.

Australian Institute for Teaching and School Leadership (AITSL). (2011b). *National professional standards for teachers.* Retrieved from http://www.aitsl.edu.au/verve/_resources/AITSL_National_Professional_Standards_for_Teachers.pdf

Australian Institute for Teaching and School Leadership (AITSL). (2012). Australian professional standard for principals. Melbourne: AITSL Retrieved from http://www.aitsl.edu.au/australian-professional-standard-forprincipals

Australian Institute for Teaching and School Leadership (AITSL). (2015a). *Preparing future leaders: Effective preparation for aspiring school principals*. Melbourne: AITSL.

Australian Institute for Teaching and School Leadership (AITSL). (2015b). *Accreditation of initial teacher education programs: Standards and procedures*. Melbourne: Education Services Australia.

Australian Institute of Health and Welfare (AIHW). (2015a). *Youth justice fact sheet no. 54. Comparisons between the youth and adult justice systems: 2013–14*. Cat. no. JUV 73. Canberra: AIHW.

Australian Institute of Health and Welfare (AIHW). (2015b). *Youth justice fact sheet no. 47. Types of community-based youth justice supervision: 2013–14*. Cat. no. JUV 66. Canberra: AIHW.

Australian Institute of Health and Welfare (AIHW). (2016). *Youth justice*. Retrieved from http://www.aihw.gov.au/youth-justice/

Australian Institute of Health and Welfare. (2016). *Child protection Australia 2014–15*. Child welfare series no. 63. Cat. no. CWS 57. Canberra: AIHW.

Australian Senate, Workplace Relations and Education Committee. (2002). *Education of students with disabilities*. Retrieved from http://www.aph.gov.au/binaries/senate/committee/eet_ctte/completed_inquiries/2002–04/ed_students_withdis abilities/report/report.Pdf

Ávila, H. (2007). *Theory of legal principles*. Dordrecht: Springer.

Avison, D. (2004a, May). *A challenge worth meeting: Opportunities for improving aboriginal education outcomes*. Prepared Report for the Council of Ministers in Education.

Avison, D. (2004b). *A challenge worth meeting: Opportunities for improving aboriginal education outcomes*. Prepared for the Council of Ministers in Education Canada.

Ayoub v Downs (SC NSW), (Common Law Division, Yeldham J, 7 October 1982, unreported).

B.M. v State, 649 P.2d 425 (Mont. 1982).

Babie, P., Russo, C. J., & Dickinson, G. M. (2004). Supervision of students: An exploratory comparative analysis. *Australia & New Zealand Journal of Law and Education, 9*(1), 41–70.

Badri, M. A., Selim, H., Alshare, K., Grandon, E. E., Younis, H., & Abdulla, M. (2006). The Baldrige education criteria for performance excellence framework: Empirical test and validation. *International Journal of Quality & Reliability Management, 23*(9), 1118–1157.

Bae, S. H. (2007). The relationship between ISO 9000 participation and educational outcomes of schools. *Quality Assurance in Education, 15*(3), 251–270.

Baginsky, M. (2003). Newly qualified teachers and child protection. *Child Abuse Review, 12*, 119–127.

Baginsky, M. (2007). *Schools, social services and safeguarding children*. Leicester: NSPCC.

Baginsky, M., & Macpherson, P. (2005). Training teachers to safeguard children: Developing a consistent approach. *Child Abuse Review, 14*(5), 317–330.

Baldrige Performance Excellence Program (BPEP). (2015a). *2015–2016 Baldrige excellence framework: A systems approach to improving your organization's performance (Education).* Gaithersburg: U.S. Department of Commerce, National Institute of Standards and Technology.

Baldrige Performance Excellence Program (BPEP). (2015b). *2015–2016 Baldrige excellence framework: A systems approach to improving your organization's technology.* Gaithersburg: U.S. Department of Commerce, Technology, National Institute of Standards and Technology.

Balizar, A., & Korthonen, O. (1999). Ethics, morals and international law. *EJIL, 10*(2), 279–311.

Ballantine, J., & Spade, J. (2011). *Schools and society: A sociological approach to education.* Thousand Oaks: Pine Forge Press.

Ballard, S. (1990, September 17). *Ethics, public policy and civic education.* Speech delivered at the national public policy education conference, Salt Lake City, Utah.

Banaji, M. R., Bazerman, M. H., & Chugh, D. (2003). How (un)ethical are you? *Harvard Business Review, 81*(12), 56–64.

Barker, B. (2010). *The pendulum swings: Transforming school reform.* Stoke-on-Trent: Trentham Books.

Barnes, J. (2010). Towards a third generation of administrative procedure. In S. Rose-Ackerman & P. L. Lindseth (Eds.), *Comparative administrative law* (pp. 336–356). Cheltenham/Northampton: Edward Elgar.

Barry, A., Osborne, T., & Rose, N. (1996). Introduction. In A. Barry, T. Osborne, & N. Rose (Eds.), *Foucault and political reason: Liberalism, neoliberalism and rationalities of government.* Chicago: University of Chicago Press.

Bartolome, L. I. (1994). Beyond the methods fetish: Toward a humanizing pedagogy. *Harvard Educational Review, 64*(2), 173–194.

Bartolome, L. I. (2008). *Ideologies in education: Unmasking the trap of teacher neutrality.* New York: Peter Lang.

Batsányi, J. (1790). A franciaországi változásokra 1789 Magyar Museum II. évad I.kötet http://mek.oszk.hu/00600/00611/00611.htm#14

Battiste, M. (1986). Micmac literacy and cognitive assimilation. In J. Barman, Y. Hébert, & D. McCaskill (Eds.), *Indian education in Canada: The legacy* (Vol. I, pp. 23–44). Vancouver: University of British Columbia Press.

Battiste, M. (2005). *State of aboriginal learning.* Ottawa: Canadian Council on Learning.

Battiste, M. (2007). The struggle and renaissance of indigenous knowledge in Eurocentric education. In M. Villegas, S. Rak Neugebauer, & K. R. Venegas (Eds.), *Indigenous knowledge and education: Sites of struggle, strength, and Survivance, Harvard education review reprint series no. 44* (pp. 85–91). Cambridge, MA: Harvard Educational Publishing Group.

Battiste, M. (2009). Constitutional reconciliation of education for aboriginal peoples/La réconciliation constitutionnelle des Autochtones et leurs droits éducationnels Directions, *5*(1), 81–84.

Battiste, M. (2013). *Decolonizing education: Nourishing the learning spirit.* Saskatoon: Purich Press.

Bauer, S., & Bogotch, I. (2006). Modeling site-based decision making: School practices in the age of accountability. *Journal of Educational Administration, 44*(5), 446–470.

Bauman, Z. (2005). Education in liquid modernity. *Review of Education, Pedagogy and Cultural Studies, 27*(4), 303–317.

Bauman, Z. (2012). *Liquid modernity.* Cambridge: Polity.

Bauman, Z., & Haugaard, M. (2008). Culture, modernity and revolution. *Journal of Power, 1*(2), 111–130.

Bays, D. A., & Crockett, J. B. (2007). Investigating instructional leadership for special education. *Exceptionality: A Special Education Journal, 15,* 143–161. https://doi.org/10.1080/09362830701503495.

Bazerman, M. H. (2014). *The power of noticing: What the best leaders see.* New York: Simon & Schuster.

Bazerman, M. H., & Banaji, M. R. (2004). The social psychology of ordinary ethical failures. *Social Justice Research, 17*(2), 111–115.

Bazerman, M. H., & Gino, F. (2012). Behavioral ethics: Toward a deeper understanding of moral judgment and dishonesty. *Annual Review of Law and Social Science, 8,* 85–104.

Bazerman, M. H., & Moore, D. A. (2008). *Judgment in managerial decision making* (7th ed.). New York: Wiley.

Bazerman, M. H., & Tenbrunsel, A. E. (2011). *Blind spots: Why we fail to do what's right and what to do about it.* Princeton: Princeton University Press.

Bazerman, M. H., Tenbrunsel, A. E., & Wade-Benzoni, K. (1998). Negotiating with yourself and losing: Making decisions with competing internal preferences. *Academy of Management Review, 23*(2), 225–241.

Bazley v Curry. (1999). 2 SCR 534.

BBC. (2001, October 1). *School sued over poor results.* Retrieved from http://news.bbc.co.uk/2/hi/uk_news/education/1573033.stm

Beanland v State of Queensland and Queensland Studies Authority [2007] QADT 16 ('Beanland').

Beauchamp, T. (2012). *Addressing high rates of school suspension.* Paramatta: UnitingCare Children, Young People and Families.

Beaupert, F. (2017). *Freedom of opinion and expression: From the perspective of psychosocial disability and madness.* (Unpublished paper).

Beckett, F. (2007). *The great city academy fraud.* London: Continuum.

Becroft, A. J. (2006). *Youth offending: Factors that contribute and how the system responds.* Symposium child and youth offenders: What works, Te Kooti Taiohi o

Aotearoa. Retrieved from http://www.justice.govt.nz/courts/youth/publications-and-media/speeches/youthoffending-factors-that-contribute-and-how-the-system-responds

Beitsch, R. (2016, December). Special education case at Supreme court could prove costly for schools. *Stateline*. Retrieved from http://www.pewtrusts.org/en/research-and-analysis/blogs/stateline/2016/12/08/special-education-case-at-supreme-court-could-prove-costly-for-schools

Bell, J. (2005). *Doing your research project*. Maidenhead: Open University Press.

Bell v Board of Educ. of the City of W.Haven, 739 A.2d 321(Conn. Ct. App. 1999).

Belsey, B. (2007). Always on, always aware! bullying.org. 17 January www.cyberbullying.ca

Bentham, J. (1776). A fragment on government. Current edition (1988) Harrison, R. (Ed.), *Cambridge texts in the history of political thought*. Cambridge: Cambridge University Press.

Bentham, J. (1789). *An introduction to the principles of morals and legislation*. London. Current edition (1907). Oxford: Clarendon Press. http://oll.libertyfund.org/?option=com_staticxt&staticfile=show.php%3Ftitle=278&Itemid=27. Accessed 12 May 2013

Berkes, F. (2007). Understanding uncertainty and reducing vulnerability: Lessons from resilience thinking. *Natural Hazards, 41*, 283–295.

Berlin, D. F., & White, A. L. (2009). Preservice mathematics and science teachers in an integrated teacher preparation program for grades 7–12: A 3-year study of attitudes and perceptions related to integration. *International Journal of Science and Mathematics Education, 8*, 97–115.

Berliner, D. C. (1982, March). *The executive function of teachers*. Paper presented at the Wingspread conference on relating reading research to classroom instruction, Racine, WI. pp. 12–16.

Berzsnyánszky, L. (1981). Hagyományok és útkeresések az állampolgári nevelésben. Acta Paedagogica Debrecina. N 82. Debrecen.

Best, R. (2001). Where child protection systems and schools meet. (K. Lindsay, Ed.). *Australia and New Zealand Journal of Law and Education, 6*(1 & 2), 3–14.

Best, S. (2017). Education in the interregnum: An evaluation of Zygmund Bauman's liquid turn in education. *British Journal of Sociology of Education, 38*(2), 203–220.

Bhat, V. N. (2006). TQM implementation: Does the legal system matter? *Total Quality Management & Business Excellence, 17*(6), 685–690.

BI v Board of Studies [2000] NSWSC 921 ('BI').

Biffi, E. (2013). Tutela. *Pedagogia Oggi, 2*, 243–261.

Billingsley, B. S., & McLeskey, J. (2014). Role of principals in inclusive schools. In J. McLeskey, N. L. Waldron, F. Spooner, & B. Algozzine (Eds.), *Handbook of effective inclusive schools, research and practice* (pp. 67–79). London: Routledge.

Birnbaum, R. (2000). *Management fads in higher education: Where they come from, what they do, why they fail*. San Francisco: Jossey-Bass.

Bishop v Sports Massage Training School [2000] HREOC No H99/55 ('Bishop').

Black, J. (2008). Constructing and contesting legitimacy and accountability in polycentric regulatory regimes. *Regulation & Governance, 2*, 137–164.

Black, J., & Baldwin, R. (2010). Really responsive risk based regulation. *Law and Policy, 32*, 181–213.

Black, P., & Wiliam, D. (1998). *Inside the black box: Raising standards through classroom assessment*. Retrieved from http://www.pdkintl.org/kappan/kbla9810.htm website.

Blackburn, R., Tanewski, G., & Carey, P. (2010). *Advice seeking strategies: Entrepreneurs' and accountants' perspectives*. London: Kingston University.

Blaskett, B., & Taylor, C. (2003). *Facilitators and inhibitors of mandatory reporting of suspected child abuse*. Ballarat: University of Ballarat.

Bledsoe, C. H., Sherin, B., Galinsky, A. G., et al. (2007). Regulating creativity: Research and survival in the IRB iron cage. *Northwestern Law Review, 101*(2), 593–642.

Bluhm, W. T., & Heineman, R. A. (2007). *Ethics and public policy: Method and cases*. Upper Saddle River: Pearson Prentice Hall.

Blum, R. W., & Libbey, H. P. (2004). Executive summary. *Journal of School Health, 74*, 231–232.

Bohr, N. (1963). *Essays 1958–1962 on atomic physics and human knowledge*. Bungay: Richard Clay and Company, Ltd.

Bolton, B. (2002). Schools, the internet and the law. (A. Knott, & D. Stewart, Eds.). *ANZELA Reporter, 8*(1), 29–52.

Bon, S. C. (2012). Examining the crossroads of law, ethics, and education leadership. *Journal of School Leadership, 22*, 285–308.

Bon, S. C., & Bigbee, A. (2011). Special education leadership: Integrating professional and personal codes of ethics to serve the best interest of the child. *Journal of School Leadership, 21*(3), 324–359.

Bonaccio, S., & Dalal, R. (2006). Advice taking and decision-making: An integrative literature review, and implications for the organizational sciences. *Organizational Behavior and Human Decision Processes, 101*(2), 127–151. https://doi.org/10.1016/j.obhdp.2006.07.001.

Boone, R., & Higgins, K. (2007). The software checklist: Evaluating educational software for use by students with disabilities. *Technology in Action, 3*(1), 1–16.

Boscardin, M. (2005). The administrative role in transforming secondary schools to support inclusive evidence-based practices. *American Secondary Education, 33*, 21–32.

Bottery, M. (2001). *Education: Policy and ethics*. New York: Continuum.

Bou-Llusar, J. C., Escrig-Tena, A. B., Roca-Puig, V., & Beltrán-Martín, I. (2009). An empirical assessment of the EFQM model: Evaluation as a TQM framework relative to the MBQNA model. *Journal of Operations Management, 27*(1), 1–22.

Bouck, E. C. (2016). A national snapshot of assistive technology for students with disabilities. *Journal of Special Education Technology, 31*, 4–13. https://doi.org/10.1177/0162643416633330.

Bourke, A., & Maunsell, C. (2015). 'Teachers matter': The impact of mandatory reporting on teacher education in Ireland. *Child Abuse Review*. https://doi.org/10.1002/car.2379.

Bouvier, R., Battiste, M., & Laughlin, J. (2016). Centring indigenous intellectual traditions on holistic lifelong learning. In F. Deer & T. Falkenberg (Eds.), *Indigenous perspectives on education for well-being in Canada* (pp. 21–40). Winnipeg: Education for Sustainable Well-Being Press, University of Manitoba. Retrieved March 15, 2017, from http://www.eswb-press.org/uploads/1/2/8/9/12899389/indigeneous_perspectives_2016.pdf

Bowman, K. L. (2001). The new face of school desegregation. *Duke Law Journal, 50*, 1751–1808.

Boyd, R. (2016). The "gatekeeper principle". *Perspectives, 2016*(1), 3–4.

Boyle, C., Scriven, B., Durning, S., & Downes, C. (2011). Facilitating the learning of all students: The 'professional positive' of inclusive practice in Australian primary schools. *Support for Learning, 26*(2), 72–78. https://doi.org/10.1111/j.1467-9604.2011.01480.x.

Bozeman, B. (2002). Public-value failure: When efficient markets may not do. *Public Administration Review, 62*(2), 145–161.

Brackenreg v Queensland University of Technology [1999] QADT 11 ('Brackenreg').

Bradley, D., Noonan, P., Nugent, H., & Scales, B. (2008). *A review of Australian higher education: Final report*. Canberra: DEEWR.

Braudel, F. (1993). *A history of civilisations*. London: Penguin.

Briggs, F., & Hawkins, R. (1997). *Child protection: A guide for teachers and child care professionals*. St Leonards: Allen St Unwin.

Brighouse, H. (2000). *School choice and social justice*. Oxford: Oxford University Press.

British Nationality Act, 1948 (11 & 12 Geo. 6.) Chapter 56.

British Refugee Council. (2012). *Not a minor offence: Unaccompanied children locked up as part of the asylum system*. Retrieved from London www.refugeecouncil.org.uk

Brock, L., O'Cummings, M., & Milligan, D. (2008). *Transition toolkit 2.0: Meeting the educational needs of youth exposed to the juvenile justice system*. Washington, DC: National Evaluation and Technical Assistance Center for the Education of Children and Youth Who Are Neglected, Delinquent, or At Risk (NDTAC). Retrieved from http://www.neglecteddelinquent.org/nd/resources/toolkits/transition_200808.asp

Bromberg, M., & Theokas, C. (2016). *Meandering toward graduation: Transcript outcome of high school graduates*. Washington, DC: Education Trust.

Bromfield, L. M. (2005). *Chronic child maltreatment in an Australian statutory child protection sample*. Unpublished doctoral dissertation, Deakin University, Geelong.

Bromfield, L., & Miller, R. (2007). *Specialist practice guide: Cumulative harm*. Melbourne: Victorian Government Department of Human Services.

Bromfield, L., Lamont, A., Antcliff, G., & Parker, R. (2014). *Practice guide 7: Cumulative harm*. Sydney: The Benevolent Society.

Brown, D. A., & Lewis, C. N. (2013). Competence is in the eye of the beholder: Perceptions of intellectually disabled child witnesses. *International Journal of Disability, Development and Education, 60*(1), 3–17. https://doi.org/10.1080/1034912X.2013.757132.

Brown v. Board of Education of Topeka, 347 U.S. 483 (1954).

Brundrett, M., & Rhodes, C. (2014). *Researching educational leadership and management.* London: Sage.

Bruns, E. J., & Suter, J. C. (2010). Summary of the wraparound evidence base. In E. J. Bruns & J. S. Walker (Eds.), *The resource guide to wraparound.* Portland: National Wraparound Initiative.

Bryan, H. (2012, August). Reconstructing the teacher as post-secular pedagogue: A consideration of the new teachers' standards. *Journal of Values and Beliefs, 33*(2), 217–228.

Bryan, H. (2017). Developing the political citizen: How teachers are navigating the statutory demands of the counter-terrorism and Security Act 205 and the prevent duty. *Journal of Education, Citizenship and Social Justice.* http://journals.sagepub.com/doi/abs/10.1177/1746197917717841. Accessed 12 May 2018.

Buckley, S., & Maxwell, G. (2007). *Respectful schools: Restorative practices in education a summary report.* Office of the Children's Commissioner and the Institute of Policy Studies, School of Government, Victoria University, Wellington.

Buckley, H., & McGarry, K. (2011). Child protection in primary schools: A contradiction in terms or a potential opportunity? *Irish Educational Studies, 30*(1), 113–128.

Bujnowicz v Trustees Roman Catholic Church [2005] NSWCA 457.

Bullis, M., Yovanoff, P., & Havel, E. (2004). The importance of getting started right: A further examination of the facility-to-community transition of formerly incarcerated youth. *The Journal of Special Education, 38*, 80–94.

Burns, M. (2015). The 'named person' debate: The case for. *Scottish Journal of Residential Child Care, 14*(3), 64–68.

Burns, T., & Koster, F. (Eds.). (2016). *Governing education in a complex world, educational research and innovation.* Paris: OECD Publishing.

Burrows, V. K., & Garvey, T. (2011). *A brief overview of rulemaking and judicial review. CRS report for congress – Prepared for members and committees of congress.* Washington, DC: U.S. Government.

Bush, T. (2017). Governing schools and colleges. *Educational Management Administration & Leadership, 45*(1), 3–4. https://doi.org/10.1177/1741143216671044.

Butler, G. (1995, December 16). QC defends all pupils' rights. *The Courier Mail*, p. 6.

Butler, G. (1996, January 23). Row over disabled students. *The Courier Mail*, p. 3.

Butler, D., & Mathews, B. (2007). *Schools and the law.* Sydney: The Federation Press.

Butlin, M. (2014). *Legal principles for school principals: An investigation into the impact of education law on school leaders.* Unpublished master's thesis, University of Southern Queensland, Australia.

Butterfield, K. D., Trevin, L. K., & Weaver, G. R. (2000). Moral awareness in business organizations: Influences of issue-related and social context factors. *Human Relations, 53*(7), 981–1018.

Butts, R. F. (1947). *A cultural history of education: Reassessing our educational traditions*. New York: McGraw-Hill.

Byrnes, L. J., & Rickards, F. W. (2011). Listening to the voices of students with disabilities: Can such voices inform practice? *Australasian Journal of Special Education, 35*(1), 25–34. https://doi.org/10.1375/ajse.35.1.25.

Caena, F. (2014). Teacher competence frameworks in Europe: Policy-as-discourse and policy-as-practice. *European Journal of Education, 49*(3), 311–331.

Cain, M., & Hunt, A. (1979). *Marx and Engels on law*. London: Academic.

Caldwell, B. (1994). Australian perspectives on leadership: The principal's role in radical decentralisation in Victoria's schools of the future. *The Australian Educational Researcher, 21*(2), 45–62.

Callahan, R. E. (1959). *An introduction to education in American society*. New York: Alfred A. Knopf.

Calliste, A., & Dei, G. J. S. (Eds.). (2000). *Anti-racist feminism: Critical race and gender studies*. Halifax: Fernwood Press.

Cambra, J. E. (2016). *Preparing for student led IEPs*. Masters dissertation. Retrieved from http://csusm-dspace.calstate.edu/bitstream/handle/10211.3/174686/CambaJordan_Summer2016.pdf?sequence=1

Camilli, G. (2013). Ongoing issues in test fairness. *Educational Research and Evaluation: An International Journal on Theory and Practice, 19*(2–3), 104–120.

Campbell, M., Butler, D., & Kift, S. (2008). A school's duty to provide a safe learning environment: Does this include cyberbullying? (J. Cumming, & E. Dickson, Eds.). *Australia and New Zealand Journal of Law and Education, 13*(2), 21–32.

Canada, *The House of Commons, Debates*, 46 Vict. (May 9, 1883) 14: 1107–1108.

Canada. (2008). *Prime minister Harper offers full apology on behalf of Canadians for the Indian residential schools system*. Retrieved October 11, 2010, from http://pm.gc.ca/eng/media.asp?id=2149

Canada. (2016). *Indigenous and Northern affairs Canada United Nations declaration of rights of indigenous peoples*. Website Retrieved August 10, 2016, from https://www.aadnc-aandc.gc.ca/eng/1309374407406/1309374458958

Canadian Association of Deans of Education. (2010). *Accord on indigenous education*. Retrieved from http://educ.ubc.ca/sites/educ.ubc.ca/les/FoE%20document_ACDE_Ac-cord_Indigenous_Education_01-12-10.pdf

Canadian Council on Learning. (2007a). *Redefining how success is measured in first nations, Inuit and Métis learning*. Retrieved from http://eboulearning.com/ccl/RedefiningSuccess/Redefining_How_Success_Is_Measured_EN.pdf

Canadian Council on Learning. (2007b). *Redefining how success is measured in first nations, Inuit and Métis learning*. Retrieved March 17, 2017, from http://eboulearning.com/ccl/RedefiningSuccess/Redefining_How_Success_Is_Measured_EN.pdf

Canadian Council on Learning. (2009). *The state of Aboriginal learning in Canada: A holistic approach to measuring success*. Retrieved March 17, 2017, from https://www.eboulearning.com/ccl/StateAboriginalLearning/SAL-FINALReport_EN.PDF

Caraman, I., Lazar, G., Bucuroiu, R., Lungu, O., & Stamate, M. (2008). How IWA 2 helps to implement a quality management system in Bacau university. *International Journal for Quality Research, 2*(4), 305–308.

Carnoy, M. (1974). *Education as cultural imperialism*. New York: David McKay Company.

Carr v Inland Revenue Commissioners [1944] All ER 163.

Carter, D. P., Weible, C. M., Siddiki, S. N., Brett, J., & Chonaiew, S. M. (2015). Assessing policy divergence: How to investigate the differences between a law and a corresponding regulation. *Public Administration, 93*(1), 159–176.

Carter, W. J. (2006). *Challenging behaviour and disability: A targeted response*. Report to Honourable Warren Pitt MP, Minister for Communities, Disability Services and Seniors. https://www.communities.qld.gov.au/resources/disability/centre-of-excellence/carter-report-full.pdf

Catholic Education Commission NSW. (2016). *Annual report 2016*. NSW: Author

Castelli, P., & Goodman, G. S. (2014). Children's perceived emotional behavior at disclosure and prosecutors' evaluations. *Child Abuse & Neglect, 38*(9), 1521–1532. Retrieved from https://www.researchgate.net/profile/Paola_Castelli3/publication/261102978_Children's_perceived_emotional_behavior_at_disclosure_and_prosecutors'_evaluations/links/5751b41f08ae17e65ec33f20.pdf

Catherine, N., Bernard, B., & Bernard, R. (1998). Pour une anthropologie de la citoyenneté, une approche comparative France/Grande-Bretagne. In: Agora débats/jeunesses.1998/12. Jeunes en Europe: politique et citoyenneté. 43–51. p.

Catholic Education Office Archdiocese of Melbourne, Student Wellbeing Central to Learning and School Improvement. (2007, October). http://web.spgww.catholic.edu.au/documents/policies/restorativejusticeresearch.pdf

Causton, J., & Theoharis, G. (2014). How do schools become effective and inclusive. In J. McLeskey, N. L. Waldron, B. Algozzine, & F. Spooner (Eds.), *Handbook of effective inclusive schools, research and practice* (pp. 30–42). London: Routledge.

Cavendish, W. (2013). Student perceptions of school efforts to facilitate student involvement, school commitment, self-determination and graduation track. *Social Psychology of Education, 16*, 257–275. https://doi.org/10.1007/s11218-013-9212-z.

Cavendish, W., & Connor, D. (2017). Toward authentic IEPs and transition plans: Student, parent, and teacher perspectives. *Learning Disability Quarterly*. Advance online publication. https://doi.org/10.1177/0731948716684680.

Centers for Disease Control and Prevention. (2016). *Adverse childhood experiences study*. Retrieved September 20, 2016, from https://www.cdc.gov/violenceprevention/acestudy/ child abuse: An analysis of the decision to report. *Child Abuse & Neglect, 19*(9), 095–1113. Child Protection Act (Qld) 1999.

Centre for Restorative Justice. www.restorativejustice.com.au
Cerar, M. (2009). Relationship between law and politics. *Annual Survey of International & Comparative Law, 15*(1), 19–40.
CFCA. (2016). *Reporting child abuse and neglect – CFCA resource sheet.* Victoria: Australian Institute of Family Studies.
Chadwick, G. (2016). Could the named person scheme have a role in addressing mental health problems in vulnerable children? *International Journal of Culture and Mental Health, 10*(1), 1–6. https://doi.org/10.1080/17542863.2016.1250798.
Chapman, C. (2014). Becoming perpetrator: How I came to accept restraining and confining disabled Aboriginal children. In B. Burstow, B. A. LeFrancois, & S. Diamond (Eds.), *Psychiatry disrupted: Theorizing resistance and crafting the (r) evolution* (pp. 16–33). Montreal/Kingston: McGill-Queen's University Press.
Chaina v Presbyterian Church (NSW) Property Trust (No. 25) [2014] NSWSC 518.
Chen, I.-S., Chen, J.-K., & Padró, F. F. (2017). Critical quality indicators of higher education. *Total Quality & Business Excellence, 28*(1–2), 130–146.
Cheney, D., Cumming, T., & Slemrod, T. (2013). Issues and approaches in accommodating adolescent EBD students at the secondary level. In H. Walker & F. Gresham (Eds.), *Evidence-based practices for addressing school-related behaviour problems and disorders* (pp. 344–360). New York: Guilford Press.
Cheng, Y.-Y., Lyu, J., & Lin, Y.-C. (2004). Education improvement through ISO 9000 implementation: Experiences in Taiwan. *International Journal of Engineering Education, 20*(1), 91–95.
Chandler, K., Willmott, L., & White, B. (2014). Rethinking restrictive practices: A comparative analysis. *QUT Law Review, 4*(2), 90–122. https://doi.org/10.5204/qutlr.v14i2.568.
Children and Young People (Scotland) Act 2014, asp 8.
Children's Rights Director for England. (2014). *The united nations convention on the rights of the child: How children say the UK is doing.* London: OFSTED.
Children with Disability Australia. (2015). *Submission to inquiry into violence, abuse and neglect against people with disability in institutional and residential settings.* Collingwood: Children with Disability Australia. http://www.cyda.org.au/cdasubmissions#section5
Chinchen v NSW Department of Education and Training [2006] NSWADT 180 ('Chinchen').
Chinn, P. (2004). Brown's far reaching impact. *Multicultural Perspectives, 6*(4), 9–11.
Chrispeels, J. H., & Martin, K. J. (2002). Four school leadership teams define their roles within organizational and political structures to improve student learning. *School Effectiveness and School Improvement, 13*(3), 327–365. https://doi.org/10.1076/sesi.13.3.327.3430.
Christensen, C. (1996). Disabled, handicapped or disordered: "What's in a name?". In C. Christensen & F. Rizvi (Eds.), *Disability and the dilemmas of justice and education* (pp. 63–78). Buckingham: Open University Press.

Christensen, S., & Duncan, W. D. (2004). *Professional liability and property transactions.* Annandale: Federation Press.
Christensen, J., Robertson, J. S., Williamson, R., & Hunter, C. (2013). Preparing educational leaders for special education success: Principals' perspectives. *The Researcher, 25*(1), 94–107.
Christie, P., & Christie, S. (2008, October). *Family law and the school.* Paper presented at the 17th Annual Conference of the Australia and New Zealand Education Law Association, Christchurch.
Christoffel, K. K., Scheidt, P. C., Agran, P. F., Kraus, J. F., McLoughlin, E., & Paulson, J. A. (1992). Standard definitions for childhood injury research: Excerpts of a conference report. *Pediatrics, 89*(6), 1027–1034.
Chua, A. C. K. (2015). A triple-E framework on parental involvement of children with autism spectrum disorder in early intervention. *International Journal of Multidisciplinary Research and Development, 30*, 579–586. Retrieved from https://www.researchgate.net/profile/Arnold_Chua3/publication/283150879_A_Triple-E_Framework_on_Parental_Involvement_of_Children_with_Autism_Spectrum_Disorder_in_Early_Intervention/links/562cd92208ae518e348244f9.pdf
Chuang, E., & Wells, R. (2010). The role of inter-agency collaboration in facilitating receipt of behavioural health services for youth involved with child welfare and juvenile justice. *Children and Youth Services Review, 32*, 1814–1822. https://doi.org/10.1016/j.childyouth.2010.08.002.
Chugh, D., Bazerman, M. H., & Banaji, M. B. (2005). Bounded ethicality as a psychological barrier to recognizing conflicts of interest. In D. A. Moore, D. M. Cain, G. Lowewenstein, & M. H. Bazerman (Eds.), *Conflicts of interest: Challenges and solutions in business, law, medicine, and public policy* (pp. 74–95). New York: Cambridge University Press.
Chung v University of Sydney [2002] FCA 186 ('Chung').
Citizenship Education in Europe Eurodyce report. (2012). Education, audiovisual and culture executive agency (EACEA P9 Eurydice and policy support), Brussels http://eacea.ec.europa.eu/education/eurydice/documents/thematic_reports/139EN.pdf
Civil Law (Wrongs) Act 2002 (ACT).
Civil Liability Act 1936 (SA).
Civil Liability Act 2002a (NSW).
Civil Liability Act 2002b (Tas).
Civil Liability Act 2002c (WA).
Civil Liability Act 2003 (Qld).
Clark, B. R. (1983). *The higher education system: Academic organization in cross-national perspective.* Berkeley: University of California Press.
Clark, J. P. (2011). *A legislative and judicial analysis of sexual relationships between American secondary students and their teachers.* Unpublished dissertation, Kent State University.

Clarke, J., & Newman, N. (1997). *The managerial state*. London: Sage Publications.

Cleland, A., & Sutherland, E. E. (2009). *Children's rights in Scotland* (3rd ed.). W. Green: Edinburgh.

Coaldrake, P., & Stedman, L. (2016). *Raising the stakes: Gambling with the future of universities* (2nd ed.). St. Lucia: University of Queensland Press.

Cobb, J. (2017). Hernandez v. Texas: A class apart. *Bullock Museum Online*. Retrieved May 2, 2017, from http://www.thestoryoftexas.com/discover/artifacts/hernandez-v-texas-spotlight-050115

Cobb, B., Lehmann, J., Newman-Gonchar, R., & Alwell, M. (2009). Self-determination for students with disabilities: A narrative metasynthesis. *Career Development for Exceptional Individuals, 32*, 108–114. https://doi.org/10.1177/0885728809336654.

Coco v R 1994 179 CLR 427 (Austl.).

Cole, H., & Cohen, R. (2013). Breaking down the barriers: A case study of juvenile justice personnel perspectives on school reentry. *The Journal of Correctional Education, 64*, 13–35.

Cole, C. M., Waldron, N., Majd, M., & Hasazi, S. (2004). Academic progress of students across inclusive and traditional settings. *Mental Retardation, 42*(2), 136–144.

Coles, E., Cheyne, H., Rankin, J., & Daniel, B. (2016). Getting it right for every child: A national policy framework to promote children's well-being in Scotland, UK. *The Millbank Quarterly, 95*(2), 334–365.

Collier, J., & Roberts, J. (2001). An ethic for corporate governance. *Business Ethics Quarterly, 11*(1), 67–71.

Collier, M. L., Griffin, M. M., & Wei, Y. (2016). Facilitating student involvement in transition assessment: A pilot study of the student transition questionnaire. *Career Development and Transition for Exceptional Individuals, 39*(3), 175–184. https://doi.org/10.1177/2165143414556746.

Collins, E., Percy, E., Smith, E., & Kruschke, J. (2011). Integrating advice and experience: Learning and decision making with social and nonsocial cues. *Journal of Personality and Social Psychology, 100*(6), 967–982. https://doi.org/10.1037/a0022982.

Collins, K., & O'Cathain, A. (2009). Ten points about mixed methods research to be considered by the novice researcher. *International Journal of Multiple Research Approaches, 3*(1), 2–7.

Cologon, K. (2013). *Inclusion in education: Towards equality for students with disability*. Issues paper, Children and Families Research Centre, Macquarie University.

COM. (2015). 408 final. 26.8.2015, Brussels. https://ec.europa.eu/transparency/regdoc/rep/1/2015/EN/1-2015-408-EN-F1-1.PDF

ComLaw. (2016). *Disability standards for education 2005 [Cth] (DSE)*. Retrieved from http://www.comlaw.gov.au/Details/F2005L00767

Commissioner of Inland Revenue v Maxse [1919] KB 647.

Committee on the Rights of Persons with Disabilities. (2013, October 21). *Concluding observations on the initial report of Australia*, 10th session. CRPD/C/AUS/CO/1.

http://docstore.ohchr.org/SelfServices/FilesHandler.ashx?enc=6QkG1d%2FPPRiCAqhKb7yhsnzSGolKOaUX8SsM2PfxU7tjZ6g%2FxLBVYsYEv6iDyTXyNk%2BsAB%2FHgrVpAKHcEYTB%2B1t%2FH3HX1F%2F%2Bo%2Bk3O4KhxfhPoTQZ3LeS75n8PHidYHE3

Committee on the Rights of Persons with Disabilities. (2016, September 2). *General comment no 4 (2016): Article 24: Right to inclusive education.* CRPD/C/GC/4. http://www.ohchr.org/EN/HRBodies/CRPD/Pages/GC.aspx

Commonwealth of Australia (Attorney – General's Department). (2011). Disability standards for education. http://www.ag.gov.au/Humanrightandantidiscrimination

Commonwealth of Australia. (2015). *Reports of case study 6: The response of a primary school and the Toowoomba Catholic education office to the conduct of Gerard Byrnes.* NSW: Commonwealth of Australia Education (General Provisions) Act (Qld) 2006.

Commonwealth v Introvigne. (1982). 150 CLR 258.

Comte, A. (1848). Trans. Bridges, J. H. (1865); *A general view of positivism.* Trubner and Co. (Reissued by Cambridge University Press, 2009).

Connell, R. (2009). Good teachers on dangerous ground: Towards a new view of teacher quality and professionalism. *Critical Studies in Education, 50*(3), 213–229.

Connelly, G. (2012). Multi-agency working. In T. G. K. Bryce, W. M. Humes, D. Gillies & A. Kennedy. (Eds.), *Scottish education* (4th ed.). (pp. 840–849). Edinburgh: Edinburgh University Press.

Connett, D. (2017, August 25). School nurse shortage "Putting children's lives at risk". *The Guardian.*

Connolly, M., Farrell, C., & James, C. (2017). An analysis of the stakeholder model of public boards and the case of school governing bodies in England and Wales. *Educational Management Administration & Leadership, 45*(1), 5–19. https://doi.org/10.1177/1741143215607879.

Conte, A. E. (2000). In loco parentis: Alive and well. *Jurisprudence, 121*(1), 195.

Conte-Mills, K. (2010, October). *Family law issues and the school: Views from the school and court.* Paper presented at the 19th Annual Conference of the Australia and New Zealand Education Law Association, Sydney.

Conti, T. A. (2007). A history and review of the European quality award model. *The TQM Magazine, 19*(2), 112–128.

Cooper, D. (1995). Local government legal consciousness in the shadow of juridifcation. *Journal of Law and Society, 22*(4), 506–526.

Cooper, H. (2013). The oppressive power of normalcy in the lives of disabled children: Deploying history to denaturalize the notion of the 'normal child'. In T. Curran (Ed.), *Disabled children's childhood studies* (pp. 136–151). Houndmills/New York: Palgrave Macmillan.

Cooper, T. (2011). The legal literacy levels of educators in one family of schools in Ontario. M.Ed. Unpublished, Nipissing University, North Bay. Retrieved from http://search.proquest.com.ezproxy.utas.edu.au/pqdt/docview/904667231/abstract/D8047370663E496APQ/1?accountid=14245. ProQuest Dissertations & Theses A&I database (MR80926).

Corse, P. S., Edwards, V. J., Fang, X., & Mercy, J. A. (2008). Health-related quality of life among adults who experienced maltreatment during childhood. *American Journal of Public Health, 98*(6), 1094–1100.

Council of Australian Governments. (2011). *National disability strategy 2010–2020*. Retrieved from https://www.dss.gov.au/sites/default/files/documents/05_2012/national_disability_strategy_2010_2020.pdf

Council of Europe. (1950). European convention for the protection of human rights and fundamental freedoms as amended by protocol no. 11, Nov. 4, 1950, 213 U.N.T.S. 221.

Council of Ministers of Education. (2008). *Learn Canada 2020: Joint declaration provincial and territorial ministers of education*. Ottawa: CMEC Retrieved October 11, 2010, from http://www.cmec.ca/Publications/Lists/Publications/Attachments/187/CMEC-2020-DECLARATION.en.pdf

Council of Ministers of Education of Canada. (2015, June 29–30). *Aboriginal educators symposium*. Summary report. https://www.cmec.ca/Publications/Lists/Publications/Attachments/359/CMEC-Aboriginal-Educators-Symposium-2015-EN.pdf

Council of the European Union: Promoting citizenship and fundamental values through education (Followup to the Paris declaration) – Presidency discussion paper, Brussels, 2016, February 5. http://data.consilium.europa.eu/doc/document/ST-5545-2016-INIT/en/pdf

Cox v New South Wales [2007] NSWCA 471.

Cox v. State of New South Wales (2007) NSWSC 471.

Cowell v Corrective Services Commission of New South Wales 1988 13 NSWLR 714 (Austl.).

Cravens, H. (1985). Child-saving in the age of professionalism, 1915–1930. In J. Hawes & R. Hiner (Eds.), *American childhood* (pp. 415–488). Westport: Greenwood Press.

Cregor, M., & Hewitt, D. (2011). Dismantling the school-to-prison pipeline: A survey from the field. *Poverty and Race, 20*(1), 5–7.

Crenshaw, W. B., Crenshaw, L. M., & Lichtenberg, J. W. (1995). When educators confront difference? *Child and Family Social Work, 7*(1), 57.

Cresswell, J., & Plano Clark, V. (2007). *Designing and conducting mixed methods research*. Thousand Oaks: Sage.

Crimes Amendment (School Protection) Act 2002 (NSW) s 60E inserted into Crimes Act 1900 (NSW).

Crockett, J. B. (2002). Special education's role in preparing responsive leaders for inclusive schools. *Remedial and Special Education, 23*, 157–168. https://doi.org/10.1177/07419325020230030401.

Crockett, J. B., & Kauffman, J. M. (1999). *The least restrictive environment: Its origins and interpretations in special education, The LEA series on special education and disability*. New York: Routledge.

Crockett, J. B., Neely, H., & Brown, K. G. (2000, February). *Administrating special education: Is it just a matter of discipline*. Paper presented at the Eastern Educational Research Association, Clearwater, FL.

Crone, D. A., Hawken, L. S., & Horner, R. H. (2010). *Responding to problem behavior in schools: The behavior education program* (2nd ed.). New York: Guilford Press.

Cumming, J. J. (2009). Assessment challenges, the law and the future. In C. Wyatt-Smith & J. J. Cumming (Eds.), *Educational assessment in the 21st century – Connecting theory and practice* (pp. 157–179). London: Springer.

Cumming, J. J. (2012). *Valuing students with impairments: International comparisons of practice in educational accountability*. Dordrecht: Springer.

Cumming, J., & Dickson, E. (2013). Educational accountability tests, social and legal inclusion approaches to discrimination for students with disability: A national case study from Australia. *Assessment in Education Principles, Policy & Practice, 20*(2), 221–239. https://doi.org/10.1080/0969594X.2012.730499.

Cumming, J., Dickson, E., & Webster, A. (2013). Reasonable adjustments in assessment: Putting law and policy into practice. *International Journal of Disability, Development, & Education, 60*(4), 295–311. https://doi.org/10.1080/1034912X.2013.846467.

Cumming, T., Strnadová, I., & Dowse, L. (2014). At-risk youth in Australian schools and promising models of intervention. *International Journal of Special Education, 29*(3), 16–25.

Cummings, T., & Worley, C. (2014). *Organization development and change* (10th ed.). Mason: Cengage Learning.

Cunningham, H. (2005). *Children and childhood in western society since 1500* (2nd ed.). Harlow: Pearson Longman.

Cunningham, H. (2006). *The invention of childhood*. London: BBC Books.

Currie v Commissioner of Inland Revenue [1921] 2 KB 332.

D.S.W. v Fairbanks North Star Borough Sch. Dist., 628 P.2d 554 (Alaska 1981).

Dale, A. (2011, June 1). Parents must pay up – Court rules Roseville college did enough to help daughters. *The Daily Telegraph*. Retrieved from http://www.news.com.au/top-stories/parents-must-pay-up-court-rules-private-school-did-enough-to-help-daughters/story-e6frfkp9-1226066808945

DalPont, G. E. (2006). *Lawyers' professional responsibility in Australia and New Zealand* (3rd ed.). Pyrmont: Lawbook Co.

Dalsen, J. (2017). Technology, disability, and law: Then and now. *Journal of Special Education Technology, 32*, 102–108. https://doi.org/10.1177/0162643417704438.

Daly, E. (2013). *Student suspensions. A research review. Stage one. Commission for children Tasmania*. Retrieved January, 2, 2014 from http://www.childcomm.tas.gov.au/wp-content/uploads/2013/12/Student-Suspensions.A-Research-Review-Stage-One.-E.Daly-Nov-2013.pdf

Darling-Hammond, L. (2017). Teacher education around the world: What can we learn from international practice? *European Journal of Teacher Education, 40*(3), 291–309.

Darrow, A. A. (2016). The every student succeeds act (ESSA): What it means for students with disabilities and music educators. *General Music Today, 30*, 41–44. https://doi.org/10.1177/1048371316658327.

Data Protection Act 1998, ch.29.

Davidson, D. N., & Algozzine, B. (2002). Administrators' perceptions of special education law. *Journal of Special Education Leadership, 15*(2), 43–48.

Davies, A. (1997). Family law reform act, 1995. (D. Stewart, Ed.). *ANZELA Reporter, 4*(1), 3–20.

Day, C., Kington, A., Stobart, G., & Sammons, P. (2006). The personal and professional selves of teachers: Stable and unstable identities. *British Educational Research Journal, 32*(4), 601–616.

D'Cruz, C. (2016). Legal actions against schools: Is your school prepared? *School Governance, 28*, 1–4.

DCSF. (2009). *Independent review of the primary curriculum: Final report*. Nottingham: DCSF.

de Apodaca, R. F., Gentling, D. G., Steinhaus, J. K., & Rosenberg, E. A. (2015). Parental involvement as a mediator of academic performance among special education middle school students. *School Community Journal, 25*(2), 35–54. Retrieved from http://files.eric.ed.gov/fulltext/EJ1085649.pdf

de Bakker, F. G. A., & den Hond, F. (2008). Introducing the politics of stakeholder influence: A review essay. *Business & Society, 47*(1), 8–20.

De Beer v The State of New South Wales and anor [2009] NSWSC 365.

De Cremer, D. (2009). *Psychological perspectives on ethical behavior and decision making*. Charlotte: Information Age Press.

de Figueiredo, R. J. P., Jr., & Vanden Bergh, R. G. (2004). The political economy of state-level administrative procedure acts. *The Journal of Law & Economics, 47*(2), 569–588.

de Sousa Santos, B., Nunes, J. A., & Meneses, M. P. (2007). Opening up the canon of knowledge and recognition of difference. In B. de Sousa Santos (Ed.), *Another knowledge is possible: Beyond Northern epistemologies* (pp. ix–lxii). London: Verso.

de Tocqueville, A. (1994). A régi rend és a forradalom (The Old Regime and the Revolution). Translated, preface, notes, and bibliography by Hahner Péter ed. Kontler László. Circus Maximus. Atlantisz Könyvkiadó. Budapest.

Deatons Pty Ltd v Flew (1949) 79 CLR 370.

Debreczeni, J. (1998). A Miniszterelnök. Antall József és a rendszerváltozás. Osiris. Budapest.

Déclaration de Paris (2015). http://cache.media.education.gouv.fr/file/03_-_mars/66/9/2015_mobilisation_declaration_FR_401669.pdf

Degani, A., & Wiener, E. L. (1991). *Philosophy, policies and procedures: The three P's of flight deck operations*. Paper presented at the sixth international symposium on aviation psychology, April 1992, Columbus.

Degener, T. (2016). Disability in a human rights context. *Laws, 5*(35), 1–24. https://doi.org/10.3390/Lwas5030035.

Degener, T. (2017). A new human rights model of disability. In V. Della Fina, R. Cera, & G. Palmisano (Eds.), *The United Nations convention on the rights of persons with disabilities; a commentary* (pp. 41–59). Cham: Springer.

Degener, T., & Begg, A. (2017). From invisible citizens to agents of change: A short history of the struggle for the recognition of the rights of persons with disabilities at the United Nations. In V. Della Fina, R. Cera, & G. Palmisano (Eds.), *The United Nations convention on the rights of persons with disabilities; a commentary* (pp. 1–39). Cham: Springer.

Dei, G. J. S., Hall, B. L., & Goldin Rosenberg, D. (Eds.). (2000). *Removing the margins: The challenges and possibilities of inclusive schooling*. Toronto: Canadian Scholars' Press.

Della Fina, V. (2017). Article 24 [Education]. In V. Della Fina, R. Cera, & G. Palmisano (Eds.), *The United Nations convention on the rights of persons with disabilities; a commentary* (pp. 439–470). Cham: Springer.

Deloitte Access Economics. (2017). *Review of education for students with disability in Queensland state schools*. Brisbane: Department of Education and Training (Queensland). http://education.qld.gov.au/schools/disability/docs/disability-review-report.pdf

Delors, J. (1996). *Learning: The treasure within*. Paris: United Nations Educational Scientific and Cultural Organization.

DeMitchell, T. A., DeMitchell, T. A., & Gagnon, D. (2012). Teacher effectiveness and value-added modelling: Building a pathway to educational malpractice? *Brigham Young University Education and Law Journal, 2*, 257–301.

Dempsey, I. (2003). The Impact of the disability discrimination act on school students with a disability in Australia. (K. Lindsay, Ed.). *Australia and New Zealand Journal of Law and Education, 8*(1), 35–44.

Dempsey, I. (2012). The use of individual education programs for children in Australian schools. *Australasian Journal of Special Education, 36*, 21–31. https://doi.org/10.1017/jse.2012.5.

Dempsey, I., & Davies, M. (2013). National test performance of young Australian children with additional educational needs. *Australian Journal of Education, 57*(1), 5–18. https://doi.org/10.1177/0004944112468700.

Dempster, N. (2009). *Leadership for learning: A framework synthesising recent research. edVentures*. Canberra: The Australian College of Educators.

Denham, G. (2008). Mandatory reporting of child abuse requirements for medical imaging professionals throughout Australia. *The Radiographer, 55*(3), 9–12.

Department of Education. (2011). *Teachers' standards: Guidance for school leaders, school staff and governing bodies*. Retrieved from https://www.gov.uk/government/uploads/system/uploads/attachment_data/file/301107/Teachers__Standards.pdf

Department of Education. (2014). *Supporting pupils with medical conditions at school*. [online]. Available at: https://www.gov.uk/government/publications/supporting-pupils-at-school-with-medical-conditions—3. Accessed 31 Oct 2017.

Department of Health. (2002). *Safeguarding children: A joint chief inspectors' report on arrangements to safeguard children*. London: Department of Health.

Department of Health. (2004). *National service framework for children, young children and maternity services*. [online]. Available at: https://www.gov.uk/government/publications/national-service-framework-children-young-people-and-maternity-services. Accessed 31 Oct 2017.

Department of Health. (2009). *Healthy lives, brighter futures: The strategy for children and young people's health*. [online]. Available at: http://webarchive.nationalarchives.gov.uk/+/http://www.dh.gov.uk/en/Publicationsandstatistics/Publications/PublicationsPolicyAndGuidance/DH_094400. Accessed 31 Oct 2017.

Department of Education Queensland. (2016). *Student protection procedure*. Queensland: Author.

Department of Education and Training Victoria. (2016). *Child protection – Reporting obligations*. Victoria: Author.

Department of Education and Child Development South Australia. (2016). *Child protection in schools, early childhood education and care*. South Australia: Author.

Department of Education Northern Territory. (2016). *Student safety and wellbeing*. Northern Territory: Author.

Department of Education Western Australia. (2016). *Child protection*. Western Australia: Author

Department of Education, Australian Capital Territory. (2016). *Safe and supportive schools*. WA: Author.

DES. (1992). *Curriculum organisation and classroom practice in primary schools: A discussion paper*. London: HMSO.

DeVito, D. (2007). The gap between the real and the ideal: The right to education amid fiscal equity legislation in a democratic culture. *Ethics and Education, 2*(2), 173–180.

Dewey, J. (1897, January). My pedagogic creed. *School Journal, 54*, 77–80p. http://dewey.pragmatism.org/creed.htm

Dewey, J. (1915). *The school and society and the child and the curriculum*. Chicago: University of Chicago Press.

DfE. (1992). *White paper choice and diversity: A new framework for schools*. Cm 2021. London: HMSO.

DfE. (2010). *White paper: The importance of teaching*. CM 7980. London: HMSO.

DfEE. (1997). *White paper: Excellence in schools*. Cmnd 3681. London: HMSO.

DHR. (1944). International Covenant on Economic, Social and Cultural Rights (ICESCR), 1966a; International Covenant on Civil and Political Rights (ICCPR), 1966b.

Diamond, J. (1998). *Guns, germs and steel: A short history of everybody for the last 30,000 years*. New York: Vintage books.

Diana v. California State Board of Education, No. C-70, RFT, (N. D. Cal. 1970).

Dicey, A. V. (1885). *Introduction to the study of law of the constitution*. London: Macmillan.

Dicey, A. V. (1982/1915). *Introduction to the study of the law of the constitution* (8th ed.). Indianapolis: Liberty Press.

Dickson, E. (2003). Understanding disability: An analysis of the influence of the social model of disability in the drafting of the anti-discrimination act 1991 (Qld) and in its interpretation and application. (K. Lindsay, Ed.). *Australia and New Zealand Journal of Law and Education, 8*(1), 45–68.

Dickson, E. (2004). Disability discrimination, unjustifiable hardship and students with disability-induced problem behaviour. (K. Lindsay, Ed.). *Australia and New Zealand Journal of Law and Education, 9*(2), 37–52.

Dickson, E. (2005). Disability discrimination in education: Purvis v. New South Wales (Department of education and training), amendment of the education provisions of the disability discrimination act 1992 (CTH) and the formulation of disability standards for education. *University of Queensland Law Journal, 24*(1), 213.

Dickson, E. (2006). Disability standards for education and the obligations of reasonable adjustment. (J. Cumming, & E. Dickson, Eds.). *Australia and New Zealand Journal of Law and Education, 11*(2), 23–42.

Dickson, E. (2008). The inclusion and exclusion of students with disability related problem behaviour: The contrasting approaches of Australia and the United States of America. *Australia & New Zealand Journal of Law and Education, 13*(2), 49–63.

Dickson, E. (2012). The assessment of students with disabilities: The Australian law as to reasonable adjustment and academic integrity. *International Journal of Law and Education, 17*(2), 49–62.

Dickson, E. (2014). Disability standards for education 2005 (Cth): Sword or shield for Australian students with disability. *International Journal of Law and Education, 19*(1), 5–20.

Dinham, S. (2013). The quality teaching movement in Australia encounters difficult terrain: A personal perspective. *Australian Journal of Education, 57*(2), 91–106.

Disability Discrimination Act. (1992). Retrieved from http://www.austlii.edu.au/au/legis/cth/consol_act/dda1992264/

Dixon, R. M., & Tanner, K. (2013). The experience of transitioning two adolescents with Asperger syndrome in academically focused high schools. *Australasian Journal of Special Education, 37*(1), 28–48. https://doi.org/10.1017/jse.2013.5.

Dixon, R. M., & Verenikina, I. (2007). Towards inclusive schools: An examination of socio-cultural theory and inclusive practices and policy in New South Wales DET schools. *Learning and Socio-cultural Theory: Exploring Modern Vygotskian Perspectives International Workshop 2007, 1*(1), 192–208.

Dolovich, S. (2002). Ethical lawyering and the possibility of integrity. *Fordham Law Review, 70*(5), 1629–1687.

Donoghue v Stevenson [1932] AC 562.

Donohue v. Copiague Union Free Sch. Dist., 418 N.Y.S.2d 375 (N.Y. 1979).

Doubleday v Kelly [2005] NSWCA 151.

Dow, K. L., & Braithwaite, V. (2013). *Review of higher education regulation report.* Canberra: Commonwealth of Australia. Retrieved from http://www.innovation.gov.au/highereducation/Policy/HEAssuringQuality/Documents/FinalReviewReport.pdf

Dowse, L. (2017). Disruptive, dangerous and disturbing: The "challenge" of behaviour in the construction of normalcy and vulnerability. *Continuum, 31*(3), 447–457. https://doi.org/10.1080/10304312.2016.1275148.

Dred Scott v. Sandford, 60 U.S. 393 (1857).

Drumwright, M., Prentice, R., & Biasucci, C. (2015). Behavioral ethics and teaching ethical decision making. *Decision Sciences Journal of Innovative Education, 13*(3), 431–458.

Dudau, A. (2009). Leadership in public sector partnerships: A case study of local safeguarding children boards. *Public Policy and Administration, 24*(4), 399–415.

Dunleavy, P. (1980). *Urban politics analysis: The politics of collective consumption.* London: The Macmillan Press.

Dwork, D. (1987). *What is good for babies and other young children: A history of the infant and child welfare movement in England. 1818–1918.* London: Tavistock Publications.

Dworkin, R. (1986). *Law's empire.* Cambridge, MA: Belknap Press.

Dwyer, A., & Easteal, P. (2013). Cyber bullying in Australian schools: The question of negligence and liability. *Alternative Law Journal, 38*(2), 92.

Dzienkowski, J. (2016). *Professional responsibility, standards, rules and statutes, abridged (selected statutes).* Kansas: West Academic Publishing.

Eberwein, H. (2008). Raising legal literacy in public schools, a call for principal leadership: A national study of secondary school principals' knowledge of public school law. Ed.D. Unpublished, University of Massachusetts Amherst, Amherst. Retrieved from http://search.proquest.com.ezproxy.utas.edu.au/pqdt/docview/304576529/previewPDF/C5B8D3C3D11A40D7PQ/1?accountid=14245. ProQuest Dissertations and Theses A&I database (3325154).

Eckersley v Binnie. (1988). 18 Con LR 1, 80.

Eckes, S. E., Decker, J. R., & Richardson, E. N. (2012). Trends in court opinions involving negligence in K-12 schools: Considerations for teachers and administrators. *West's Education Law Reporter, 275*, 505.

Edelstein, L. (1956). The professional ethics of the Greek Physician. *Bulletin of the History of Medicine, 30*, 391.

Edleson, J., Daro, D., & Pinderhughes, H. (2004). Finding common ground in the study of child maltreatment, youth violence, and adult domestic violence. *Journal of Interpersonal Violence, 19*(3), 282–298.

Education and Training Reform Act 2006 (Vic).

Education Council. (2016). *Nationally consistent collection of data – School students with a disability: 2016 emergent data on students in Australian schools receiving adjustments for disability.* Retrieved from http://www.educationcouncil.edu.au/site/DefaultSite/filesystem/documents/Reports%20and%20publications/ED17-0046%20SCH%20NCCD%20Report%202017_ACC.PDF

'Education Department "Unaware" of Gun Incidents'. *ABC Online*, 26 June 2006. http://www.abc.net.au/news/newsitems/200606/s1671246.html

Edwards, J. (1996). Swings and roundabouts: Changing state and federal laws regulating employment and its termination. *Education, law and the future: Proceedings of the fifth ANZELA national conference* (pp. 73–84). Brisbane: Australia and New Zealand Education Law Association (Inc.) Qld Chapter.

Edwards, S. (2004). Purvis in the high court behaviour, disability and the meaning of direct discrimination. *Sydney Law Review, 26*(4), 639–652.

Ehrlich, W. (1974). The origins of the Dred Scott case. *The Journal of Negro History, 59*(2), 132–142.

Eisner, E. W. (1979). *The educational imagination: On the design and evaluation of school programs*. New York: Macmillan Publishing Co., Inc.

El Abbaddi, L., Bouayard, A., & Lamrini, M. (2013). ISO 9001 and the field of higher education: Proposal for an update of the IWA 2 guidelines. *Quality Approaches in Higher Education, 4*(2), 14–19.

Ellis, V. (2010). Impoverishing experience: The problem of teacher education in England. *Journal of Education for Teaching, 36*(1), 105–120.

Elo, S., & Kyngäs, H. (2008). The qualitative content analysis process. *Journal of Advanced Nursing, 62*(1), 107–115.

Elson, J. (1978). A common law remedy for the educational harms caused by incompetent or careless teaching. *Northwestern University Law Review, 73*, 641–771.

Elton-Chalcraft, S., Lander V., Revell, L., Warner, D., & Whitworth, L. (2017, February). To promote, or not to promote fundamental British values? Teachers' standards, diversity and teacher education. *British Educational Research Journal, 43*(1). Available at http://onlinelibrary.wiley.com/doi/10.1111/berj.2017.43.issue-1/issuetoc

Engels, F. (1884). *The origins of the family, private property and the state* (trans: West, A.). (1942). London: Penguin Classics.

Epley, N., & Dunning, D. (2000). Feeling "holier than thou": Are self-serving assessments produced by errors in self- or social prediction. *Journal of Personality and Social Psychology, 79*(6), 861–875.

Epstein, R. A. (2016). The role of guidance in modern administrative procedure: The case for *de novo* review. *Journal of Legal Analysis, 8*(1), 47–93.

Erevelles, N. (2000). Educating unruly bodies: Critical pedagogy, disability studies, and the politics of schooling. *Educational Theory, 50*(1), 25–47. https://doi.org/10.1111/j.1741-5446.2000.00025.x.

Erevelles, N. (2011). *Disability and difference in global contexts: Enabling a transformative body politic*. New York: Palgrave Macmillan.

Ermine, W. (2007). The ethical space of engagement. *Indigenous Law Journal, 6*(1), 193–203.

Ermine, W., Sinclair, R., & Browne, M. (2005). *Kwayask itôtamowin: Indigenous research ethics. Report of the indigenous peoples' health research centre to the institute of aboriginal peoples' health and the Canadian institutes of health research*. Regina: Indigenous Peoples' Health Research Centre.

Esman, M. J. (1967). *The institution building concepts: An interim appraisal*. Pittsburgh: University of Pittsburgh.

Etscheidt, S. L. (2016). Assistive technology for students with disabilities: A legal analysis of issues. *Journal of Special Education Technology, 31*, 183–194. https://doi.org/10.1177/0162643416673912.

European Commission Press release, Brussels. 31 May 2012: Citizenship education now taught in all European countries but specialist training for teachers lacking. http://europa.eu/rapid/press-release_IP-12-514_en.htm

Every Student Succeeds Act of 2015, Pub. L. No. 114–95 § 114 Stat. 1177 (2015).

Fagan, A., & Western, J. (2005). Escalation and deceleration of offending behaviours from adolescence to early adulthood. *Australian and New Zealand Journal of Criminology, 38*, 59–76.

Fairclough, N. (2000). *New labour, new language?* London: Routledge.

Fallas v Mourlas [2006] NSWCA 32.

Falvo v Australian Oztag Sports Association [2006] NSWCA 17.

Farazmand, A. (2005). Role of government in an era of Total Quality Management (TQM) and globalization: Challenges and opportunities. *Public Organization Review: A Global Journal, 5*, 201–217.

Farrell, A. (1998). Bullying in early childhood settings. (A. Knott, & D. Stewart, Eds.). *ANZELA Reporter, 5*(1), 14–17.

Farrell, A. (2001). Legislative responsibility for child protection and human rights in Queensland. (K. Lindsay, Ed.). *Australia and New Zealand Journal of Law and Education, 6*(1 & 2), 15–24.

Farrell, F. (2016). Why all of a sudden do we need to teach fundamental British values? A critical investigation of religious education student teacher positioning within a policy discourse of discipline and control. *Journal of Education for teaching, 42*(3), 280–297. Special issue: Fundamental British Values.

Fassin, Y. (2009). The stakeholder model refined. *Journal of Business Ethics, 84*, 113–135.

Federow, H. (1993). Total quality management: A survey of legal issues relating to implementation of TQM. *Commercial Law Journal, 98*, 96–116.

Felitti, V. J., Anda, R. F., Nordenberg, D., Williamson, D. F., Spitz, A. M., Edwards, V., & Koss, M. P. (1998). Relationship of childhood abuse and household dysfunction in many of the leading causes of death in adults. *American Journal of Preventive Medicine, 14*(4), 245–258.

Fels, A. (2001, July). Regulation, competition and the profession. *Industry economics conference*. Available at https://www.accc.gov.au/system/files/Fels_Industry_Economics_14_7_01%5B1%5D.pdf

Feng, J.-Y., & Levine, M. (2005). Factors associated with nurses' intention to report child abuse: A national survey of Taiwanese nurses. *Child Abuse & Neglect, 29*(7), 783–795.

Feng, J. Y., Chen, S. J., Wilk, N. C., Yang, W. P., & Fetzer, S. (2009). Kindergarten teachers' experience of reporting child abuse in Taiwan: Dancing on the edge. *Children and Youth Services Review, 31*(3), 405–409.

Feng, J. Y., Huang, T. Y., & Wang, C. J. (2010). Kindergarten teachers' experience with reporting child abuse in Taiwan. *Child Abuse & Neglect, 34*(2), 124–128.

Feng, J. Y., Chen, Y. W., Fetzer, S., Feng, M. C., & Lin, C. L. (2012). Ethical and legal challenges of mandated child abuse reporters. *Children and Youth Services Review, 34*(1), 276–280.

Findlay, N. (2007). *Ignorance of the law is no excuse: School administrators' knowledge of education law*. Regina: Saskatchewan School Boards Association.

First Nations Child and Family Caring Society v Canada 2016 CHRT 2.

Fisher, D., Sax, C., & Grove, K. A. (2000). The resilience of changes promoting inclusiveness in an urban elementary school. *The Elementary School Journal, 100*, 213–227.

Fixsen, D. L., Blase, K. A., Metz, A., & Van Dyke, M. (2013). Statewide implementation of evidence-based programs. *Exceptional Children, 79*, 243–230.

Flew, T. (2014). Six theories of neoliberalism. *Thesis Eleven, 122*(1), 49–71.

Folke, C., Colding, J., & Berkes, F. (2003). Building resilience and adaptive capacity in social–ecological systems. In F. Berkes, J. Colding, & C. Folke (Eds.), *Navigating social–ecological systems* (pp. 352–387). Cambridge: Cambridge University Press.

Ford, D. (2004, December 1). *Emil Ford & Co*. Retrieved from School excursions: Are they worth the risk? http://www.emilford.com.au/imagesDB/wysiwyg/Excursions%20Article.pdf

Forlin, P. (1995). Health and safety law in Australia: Identifying a standard of liability in Australia from an international perspective. In D. Hopkins (Ed.), *Fourth national conference of the Australian and New Zealand education law association* (pp. 120–132). Melbourne: Australian and New Zealand Education Law Association (Inc.).

Forlin, C., & Bamford, G. (2005). Sustaining an inclusive approach to schooling in a middleschool location. *Australasian Journal of Special Education, 29*(2), 172–181.

Forlin, C., Keen, M., & Barrett, E. (2008). The concerns of mainstream teachers: Coping with inclusivity in an Australian context. *International Journal of Disability, Development and Education, 55*(3), 251–264.

Foster, W. F. (1985). Educational malpractice: A Tort for the untaught? *University of British Columbia Law Review, 19*, 161–244.

Foucault, M. (2000). Governmentality. In J. D. Faubion (Ed.), *Michel Foucault: Power* (trans: Hurley, R. and others). (pp. 201–222). New York: The New Press.

Foucault, M. (2004). Naissance de la biopolitique Cours au College de France 1978–1979. Hautes Études. Gallimard Seuil.

Foucault, M. (2007/1978). *Security, territory, population: Lectures at the Collège de France, 1977–1978*. (trans: Burchell, G.). New York: Palgrave Macmillan.

Foucault, M. (2008/1979). *The birth of biopolitics: Lectures at the Collège de France 1979–1979*. In M. Sellenart (Ed.), (trans: Burchell, V.). New York: Picador.

Francis, K., Chapman, Y., Sellick, K., James, A., Miles, M., Jones, J., & Grant, J. (2012). The decision-making processes adopted by rurally located mandated professionals when child abuse or neglect is suspected. *Contemporary Nurse, 41*(1), 58–69.

Fraser, J. G., Lloyd, S., Murphy, R., Crowson, M., Zolotor, A. J., Coker-Schwimmer, E., & Viswanathan, M. (2013). A comparative effectiveness review of parenting and trauma-focused interventions for children exposed to maltreatment. *Journal of Developmental & Behavioral Pediatrics, 34*(5), 353–368.

Fredman, S. (2005). Disability equality; a challenge to the existing anti-discrimination paradigm? In A. Lawson & C. Gooding (Eds.), *Disability rights in Europe: From theory to practice* (pp. 199–218). Oxford: Oxford University Press.

Fredrickson, N., Simmonds, E., Evans, L., & Soulsby, C. (2007). Assessing the social and affective outcomes of inclusion. *British Journal of Special Education, 34*, 105–115.

Freedom of Information Act 2000, ch.36.

Freeman, S. F., & Alkin, M. C. (2000). Academic and social attainments of children with mental retardation in general education and special education settings. *Remedial and Special Education, 21*(1), 3–26.

Freire, P. (1970). *Pedagogy of the oppressed* (Current Edition 2007). London: Continuum.

Freire, P. (1972). *Pedagogy of the oppressed*. Middlesex: Penguin.

Freire, P. (1973). *Pedagogy of the oppressed*. New York: Seabury Press.

Fried, Y. (1995). TQM and the legal environment in the United States: A neglected issue in the TQM literature. *The Academy of Management Review, 20*(1), 15–17.

Friedman, M. (1955). The role of government in education. In R. A. Solo (Ed.), *Economics fox, C., and the public interest* (pp. 123–144). New Brunswick: Rutgers University Press.

Frohmader, C., & Sands, T. (2015). *Australian Cross Disability Alliance (ACDA) submission to the Senate inquiry into violence, abuse and neglect against people with disability in institutional and residential settings*. Sydney: Australian Cross Disability Alliance. http://www.pwd.org.au/issues/violence-inquiry.html

Fronius, et al. (2016). *Restorative justice in US schools: A research review*. San Francisco: Wested Justice and Prevention Research Centre.

Frooman, J., & Murrell, A. J. (2005). Stakeholder influence strategies: The roles of structural and demographic determinants. *Business & Society, 44*(1), 3–31.

Fuller, L. L. (1969). *The morality of law* (Revised ed.). New Haven: Yale University Press.

Funston, R. (1980–1981). Educational malpractice: A cause of action in search of a theory. *San Diego Law Review, 18*, 743–812.

Furlong, J. (2013). Globalisation, neoliberalism, and the reform of teacher education in England. *The Educational Forum, 77*(1), 28–50.

Gábor, P. (2013). Az állampolgárság intézményének eredetéről. Publicationes Universitatis Miskolcinensis. Sectio Juridica et Politica. Tomus XXXI. (2013).

Gabriel Dumont Institute of Native Studies and Applied Research. (2009). *Metis education report: A special report on Metis education prepared by the Metis national council for the summit on aboriginal education.* Retrieved November 2009, from Gabriel Dumont Institute of Native Studies and Applied Research http://www.gdins.org/documents/resources/KtMEducationReportFeb20-2009.pdf

Gadamer, H. G. (1976). Man and language. In E. David (Ed. and trans.), *Philosophical hermeneutics.* Berkeley: University of California Press.

Gagnon, J., & Barber, B. (2010). Characteristics of and services provided to youth in secure care facilities. *Behavioral Disorders, 36*(1), 7–19.

Gagnon, J. C., & Richards, C. (2008). *Making the right turn: A guide about improving transition outcomes of youth involved in the juvenile corrections system.* Washington, DC: National Collaborative on Workforce and Disability for Youth, Institute for Educational Leadership.

Gallant, J. (2004). Advising principals: Using law to improve schools and support school leaders. In R. Flynn (Ed.), *Law in education: Help or hindrance?* (pp. 403–429). Markham: Bluestone Print.

Garan, E. M. (2004). *In defense of our children: When politics, profit and education collide.* Portsmouth: Heinemann.

Garfinkel, L. (2010). Improving family involvement for juvenile offenders with emotional/behavioural disorders and related disabilities. *Behavior Disorders, 36*(1), 52–60.

Garvin, D. A. (1984). What does "product quality" really mean? *Sloan Management Review, 25*(1), 25–43.

Guthrie, R., & Waldeck, E. (2008). Disability standards and inclusiveness in education: A review of the Australian landscape. *International Journal of Discrimination and the Law, 9*(3), 133–162.

General Secretariat. (2012). 2012 strategic framework on human rights and democracy. Retrieved from https://europa.eu/european-union/topics/human-rights_en

General Teaching Council for Scotland. (2012a). *The standards for leadership and management.* http://www.gtcs.org.uk/web/FILES/the-standards/standards-for-leadership-and-management-1212.pdf. Accessed 07 Mar 2017.

General Teaching Council for Scotland. (2012b). *The standards for registration: Mandatory requirements for registration with the general teaching council for Scotland.* Edinburgh: GTC Scotland.

General Teaching Council Scotland. (2012). *Standards for leadership and management.*

Gerő, M., & Szabó, A. (2015). Politikai Tükör. Jelentés a magyar társadalom politikai gondolkodásmódjáról, politikai integráltságáról és részvételéről (Report on the political way of thinking, political integrity and participation of the Hungarian society). MTA Társadalomtudományi Kutatóközpont. Budapest. http://www.sociomta.hu/uploads/files/2015/poltukor_online.pdf

Gersen, J. (2007). Overlapping and underlapping jurisdiction in administrative law. *Supreme Court Review, 2006*(1), 201–247.
Geyer v Downs. (1977). 138 CLR 90.
Gillard, D. (2011). *Education in England: A brief history*. http://www.educationengland.org.uk/history/index.html. Accessed Apr 2017.
Gilligan, R. (1998). The importance of schools and teachers in child welfare. *Child and Family Social Work, 3*, 13–25.
Gino, F. (2013). *Sidetracked*. Boston: Harvard Business Review Press.
Gino, F., & Bazerman, M. H. (2009). When misconduct goes unnoticed: The acceptability of gradual erosion in others' unethical behavior. *Journal of Experimental Social Psychology, 45*, 708–719.
Gino, F., & Margolis, J. D. (2011). Bringing ethics into focus: How regulator focus and risk preferences influence (un)ethical behavior. *Organizational Behavior and Human Decision Processes, 115*(2011), 145–156.
Gino, F., Shu, L. L., & Bazerman, M. H. (2010). Nameless + harmless = blameless: When seemingly irrelevant factors influence judgment of (un)ethical behavior. *Organizational Behavior and Human Decision Processes, 111*(2), 102–115.
GIO General Ltd v Newcastle City Council. (1996). 38 NSWLR 558.
Glanville, B. (Reporter). (2017, October 9). Hundreds of complaints of abuse of disabled children. In *7.30 Report*. [Television broadcast]. Sydney, Australia: Australian Broadcasting Corporation.
Gleeson, M. (1999, May 31). *Are the professions worth keeping? (Speech) Greek-Australian international legal and medical conference*. Available at http://www.hcourt.gov.au/assets/publications/speeches/former-justices/gleesoncj/cj_areprofe.htm
Goddard, C. (1996). *Child abuse and child protection a guide for health, education and welfare professionals*. South Melbourne: Churchill Livingstone.
Goddard, C., Saunders, B., Stanley, J., & Tucci, J. (2002). *A study in confusion: Factors which affect the decisions of community professionals when reporting child abuse and neglect*. Australians Against Child Abuse, Melbourne.
Goodley, D., & Runswick-Cole, K. (2012). Reading Rosie: The postmodern disabled child. *Educational & Child Psychology, 29*(2), 53–66.
Goodley, D., & Runswick-Cole, K. (2011a). Problematising policy: Conceptions of 'child', 'disabled' and 'parents' in social policy in England. *International Journal of Inclusive Education, 15*(1), 71–85. https://doi.org/10.1080/13603116.2010.496197.
Goodley, D., & Runswick-Cole, K. (2011b). The violence of disablism. *Sociology of Health & Illness, 33*(4), 602–617. https://doi.org/10.1111/j.1467-9566.2010.01302.x.
Goodley, D., Runswick-Cole, K., & Liddiard, K. (2016). The DisHuman child. *Discourse: Studies in the Cultural Politics of Education, 37*(5), 770–784. https://doi.org/10.1080/01596306.2015.1075731.

Godfrey, A. B. (1999). Total Quality Management. In J. M. Juran, A. B. Godfrey, R. E. Hoogstoel, & E. G. Schilling (Eds.), *Juran's quality handbook* (5th ed., pp. 14.1–14.35). New York: McGraw-Hill.

Goebbels, A., Nicholson, J., Walsh, K., & De Vries, H. (2008). Teachers' reporting of suspected child abuse and neglect: Behaviour and determinants. *Health Education Research, 23*(6), 941–951.

Goldfarb, D., Goodman, G. S., & Lawler, M. (2015). Children's evidence and the| convention on the rights of the child: Improving the legal system for children. In S. Mahmoudi, P. Leviner, A. Kaldal, & K. Lainpelto (Eds.), *Child-friendly justice: A quarter of a century of the UN convention on the rights of the child* (pp. 85–109). Leiden/Stockholm: Brill Nijhoff.

Gordon, M. (2010). Student voice key to unlocking inclusive educational practices. *Canadian Journal of New Scholars in Education, 3*(2), 1–11. Retrieved from https://journalhosting.ucalgary.ca/index.php/cjnse/article/viewFile/30480/24877

Government of Western Australia. (2008). *Mandatory reporting of child sexual abuse*. Western Australia: Government of Western Australia, Department of Child Protection.

Graham, L. J., & Jahnukainen, M. (2011). Wherefore art thou, inclusion? Analysing the development of inclusive education in New South Wales, Finland and Alberta. *Journal of Education Policy, 26*, 263–388. https://doi.org/10.1080/02680939.2010.493230.

Graham, L., & Slee, R. (2008). An illusionary interiority: Interrogating the discourse/s of inclusion. *Educational Philosophy and Theory, 40*(2), 277–293.

Graham, L. J., & Spandagou, I. (2011). From vision to reality: Views of primary school principals on inclusive education in New South Wales, Australia. *Disability & Society, 26*(2), 223–237. https://doi.org/10.1080/09687599.2011.544062.

Graham, L., Proctor, H., & Dixon, R. M. (2016). *How schools are avoiding enrolling students with disabilities in the conversation yearbook 2016: 50 outstanding chapters from Australia's greatest thinkers*. Melbourne: Melbourne University Press.

Grant, A. W. H., & Schlesinger, L. A. (1995). Realize your customers' full profit potential. *Harvard Business Review, 73*(5), 59–72.

Grant Mears v Sydney Anglican Schools Corporation [2016] NSWCA 39.

Gray v Queensland (SC (Qld), Mullins J, 1993/2000, 15 December 2000, unreported).

Greco, M. (2009, September 25). Remarks to the Connecticut bar association Westbrook Connecticut.

Green, J. (2013). *Moral tribes: Emotion, reason, and the gap between us and them*. New York: Penguin Press.

Gregory v New South Wales [2009] NSWSC 559.

Griffin, M. M., Lounds Taylor, J., Urbano, R. C., & Hodapp, R. M. (2014). Involvement in transition planning meetings among high school students with autism spectrum disorders. *The Journal of Special Education, 47*(4), 256–264. https://doi.org/10.1177/0022466913475668.

Griller Clark, H., & Unruh, D. (2010). Transition practices for adjudicated youth with E/BDs and related disabilities. *Behavioral Disorders, 36*(1), 43–51.

Griller Clark, H., Mathur, S. R., & Helding, B. (2011). Transition services for juvenile detainees with disabilities: Findings on recidivism. *Education and Treatment of Children, 34*(4), 511–529.

Guthrie, J., & Schuermann, P. (2010). *Successful school leadership: Planning, politics, performance, and power*. Boston: Allyn & Bacon.

Gutmann, A., & Thompson, D. (2006). *Ethics and politics: Cases and comments* (4th ed.). Chicago: Nelson-Hall.

H v Pennell and South Australia. (1987). 46 SASR 158.

Habermas, J. (1994). Citizenship and national identity. In B. van Steenbergen (Ed.), *The condition of citizenship* (pp. 20–36). London: Sage.

Hacking, I. (1983). *Representing and intervening: Introductory topics in the philosophy of natural science*. Cambridge: Cambridge University Press.

Hacking, I. (1990). *The taming of chance*. New York: Cambridge University Press.

Hadow. (1923). *Differentiation of the curriculum for boys and girls. Report of the consultative committee*. London: HMSO.

Hadow. (1926). *The education of the adolescent. Report of the consultative committee*. London: HMSO.

Hadow. (1931). *The primary school. Report of the consultative committee*. London: HMSO.

Hadow. (1933). *Infant and nursery schools. Report of the consultative committee*. London: HMSO.

Hall, L., & Patty, A. (2012, 4 July). Student loses appeal over 99.95 HSC mark. *Sydney Morning Herald*. Retrieved from http://www.smh.com.au/national/education/student-loses-appeal-over-9995-hsc-mark-20120703-21flw.html

Hamann, T. H. (2009). Neoliberalism, governmentality, and ethics. *Foucault Studies, 6*, 37–59.

Hamilton, J. (2002). Discrimination and the enrolment process – Who is in the wrong? In D. Stewart (Ed.), *Legal risk management safety, security and success in education: Proceedings of the 11th annual conference of the Australia and New Zealand education law association* (pp. 329–350). Brisbane: GSM Press.

Hamilton, M. (2010). People with complex needs and the criminal justice system. *Current Issues in Criminal Justice, 22*(2), 307–324.

Hamilton, J., & Smith, F. (2002). The schoolyard fight: Duty of cared owed by teachers. (K. Lindsay, Ed.). *Australia and New Zealand Journal of Law and Education, 7*(1), 88–90.

Handicapped Children's Protection Act of 1986, Public Law 99–372, 20 U.S.C. [section] 1415 (1986).

Handy, C. (1994). *The empty raincoat: Making sense of the future*. London: Random House.

Hannan, E. (2006, August 15). School payout for boy's reading failure. *The Australian*, p. 1.

Hansen, J., Pigozzi, G., & van der Torre, L. (2007). Ten philosophical problems in deontic logic. In G. Boella, L. van der Torre, & H. Verhagen (Eds.), *Normative multi-agent systems Dagstuhl seminar proceedings* (Vol. 07122, p. 26). Waden: Schloss Dagstuhl Leibniz-Zentrum für Informatik GmbH (IBFI). Retrieved from http://icr.uni.lu/pubs/han07a.pdf

Harber, C. (2004). *Schooling as violence; how schools harm pupils and societies*. London: Routledge.

Harber, C., & Mncube, V. (2012). *Education, democracy and development: Does education contribute to democratisation in developing countries?* Oxford: Symposium.

Hareven, M. (1982). *Family time and industrial time*. New York: Cambridge University Press.

Harper, S. (2008). *Prime minister Harper offers full apology on behalf of Canadians for the Indian residential schools system* 11 June 2008 Ottawa. Retrieved from http://www.pm.gc.ca/eng/media.asp?id=2149

Harpwood, V. (2009). *Modern Tort law* (7th ed.). London: Routledge-Cavendish.

Harries, M., & Clare, M. (2002). *Mandatory reporting of child abuse: Evidence and options*. Perth: University of Western Australia.

Hart, H. L. A. (1997). *The concept of law* (2nd ed.). Oxford: Oxford University Press.

Harvey, L. (1995). *Quality assurance systems, TQM, and the new collegialism*. Birmingham: Centre for Research into Quality, University of Central England.

Harvey, L. (2004). The power of accreditation: Views of academics. *Journal of Higher Education Policy and Management, 26*(2), 207–223.

Harvey, L., & Green, D. (1993). Defining quality. *Assessment & Evaluation in Higher Education, 18*(1), 9–34.

Hattie, J. (2009). *Visible learning: A synthesis of over 800 meta-analyses relating to achievement*. Milton Park: Routledge.

Hawkins, R., & McCallum, C. (2001). Mandatory notification training for suspected child abuse and neglect in South Australian schools. *Child Abuse & Neglect, 25*(12), 1603–1625.

Hayden, A. (2001). *Restorative conferencing manual of Aotearoa New Zealand*. Wellington: Department for Courts.

Hayek, F. A. (1944). *The road to serfdom*. London: Routledge Classics.

Hayek, F. A. (1998/1973). *Law, legislation and liberty: A new statement of the liberal principles of justice and political economy*. London: Routledge.

Hayek, F. A. (2011/1960). The constitution of liberty. In R. Hamowy (Ed.), *The collected works of F.A. Hayek*, Volume 17: The constitution of liberty. The definitive edition. Chicago: University of Chicago Press.

Hayes, A., & Higgins, D. (Eds.). (2014). *Families, policy and the law: Selected essays on contemporary issues for Australia*. Melbourne: Australian Institute of Family Studies.

Hayibor, S., & Wasieleski, D. M. (2009). Effects of the use of the availability heuristic on ethical decision-making in organizations. *Journal of Business Ethics, 84*, 151–165.

Haysom, L., Indig, D., Moore, E., & Gaskin, C. (2014). Intellectual disability in young people in custody in New South Wales, Australia – Prevalence and markers. *Journal of Intellectual Disability Research, 58*, 1004–1014. https://doi.org/10.1111/jir.12109.

Head, M. (2012). *Administrative law: Context and critique* (3rd ed.). Anndale: Federation Press.

Health and Social Care Alliance Scotland. (2016). *Getting it right for every child parent and information pack*. Edinburgh: The Alliance Scotland.

Healy, K. (1998). *Addressing bullying at the school level through multiple systems*. (A. Knott, & D. Stewart, Eds.). *ANZELA Reporter, 5*(1), 18–22.

Heffernan, M. (2011). *Willful blindness*. New York: Walker & Co.

Hehir, T., & Katzman, L. I. (2012). *Effective inclusive schools: Designing successful schoolwide programs*. San Francisco: Jossey-Bass.

Henderson, J. Y. (1995). Indian education and treaties. In M. Battiste & J. Barman (Eds.), *First nations education in Canada: The circle unfolds*. Vancouver: University of British Columbia Press.

Henderson, J. Y. (2007). *Treaty rights in the constitution of Canada*. Scarborough: Thompson Carswell.

Hentoff, N. (1990). How Timothy W. got into school. *The Washington Post*. Published January 2, 1990. Retrieved May 1, 2017, from https://www.washingtonpost.com/archive/opinions/1990/01/02/how-timothy-w-got-into-school/c1b83691-a1b4-4a59-98f5-6976b5aebc3a/?utm_term=.24e2a0f46fd4

Heyden, M., van Doorn, S., Reimer, M., Van Den Bosch, F., & Volberda, H. (2013). Perceived environmental dynamism, relative competitive performance, and top management team heterogeneity: Examining correlates of upper echelons' advice-seeking. *Organization Studies, 34*(9), 1327–1356. https://doi.org/10.1177/0170840612470229.

Heywood, C. (2004). *A history of childhood*. Cambridge: Polity Press.

Higgins, D. (2004). Differentiating between child maltreatment experiences. *Family Matters, 69*, 50–55.

Hill v Van Erp. (1997). 188 CLR 159.

Hilton, A. J. B. (1988a). *The age of atonement; the influence of evangelicalism on social and economic thought 1795–1865*. Oxford: Oxford University Press.

Hilton, A. J. B. (1988b). *A mad bad dangerous people? England 1783–1846*. Oxford: Oxford University Press.

Hinchliffe v University of Sydney [2004] FMCA 85 ('Hinchliffe').

Hirschfield, P. J. (2014). Effective and promising practices in transitional planning and school re-entry. *The Journal of Correctional Education, 65*, 84–96.

HM Government. (2006). *English joint planning and commissioning framework for children, young people and maternity services*. [online]. Available at: http://www.regionalcommissioning.co.uk/resources/A9%20DfES%20Joint%20Planning%20and%20Commissioning.pdf. Accessed 31 Oct 2017.

Hobsbawm, E. (1962). *The age of revolution 1789–1848*. London: Abacus.

Hobsbawm, E. (1975). *The age of capital 1848–1875*. London: Abacus.

Hobsbawm, E. (1991). *The age of empire 1875–1914*. London: Abacus.

Hofferbert, R. (1974). *The study of public policy*. Indianapolis: Bobbs-Merrill.

Hoffman, E. (2003). Legal consciousness and dispute resolution: Different disputing behaviour at two similar taxicab companies. *Law & Social Inquiry, 28*(3), 691–716.

Hoffman v. Board of Educ., 424 N.Y.S.2d 376 (N.Y. 1979).

Hollenweger, J. (2011). Development of an ICF-based eligibility procedure for education in Switzerland. *BMC Public Health, 11*(Suppl 4), S7.

Hollenweger, J., & Moretti, M. (2012). Using the international classification of functioning, disability and health children and youth version in education systems: A new approach to eligibility. *American Journal of Physical Medicine & Rehabilitation, 91*(13 Suppl 1), 97–102.

Holmes, R. (2009). *The age of wonder: How the romantic generation discovered the beauty and terror of science*. London: Harper.

Holstein, J., & Gubrium, J. (1995). *The active interview*. London: Sage.

Holt, J. (1964). *How children fail*. London: Penguin.

Homburg, V., Pollitt, C., & van Thiel, S. (2007). Introduction. In C. Pollitt, S. van Thiel, & V. Homburg (Eds.), *New public management in Europe: Adaptation and alternatives* (pp. 1–9). Hampshire: Palgrave Macmillan.

Honig, M. I. (2012). District central office leadership as teaching. *Educational Administration Quarterly, 48*(4), 733–774. https://doi.org/10.1177/0013161x12443258.

Honig v. Doe, 485 U.S. 305, 108 S.Ct. 592, 98 L.Ed, 2d 686 (1988).

Hopkins, D. (2008, April). *The legal obligations of a teacher*. Retrieved from http://www.vit.vic.edu.au/SiteCollectionDocuments/PDF/Legal-obligations-of-a-teacher.pdf

Hoppey, D., & McLeskey, J. (2013). A case study of principal leadership in an effective inclusive school. *The Journal of Special Education, 46*, 245–256. https://doi.org/10.1177/0022466910390507.

Hoppey, D., & McLeskey, J. (2014). What are qualities of effective inclusive schools? In J. McLeskey, N. L. Waldron, F. Spooner, & B. Algozzine (Eds.), *Handbook of effective inclusive schools* (pp. 17–29). London: Routledge.

Horrocks, J. L., White, G., & Roberts, L. (2008). Principals' attitudes regarding inclusion of children with autism in Pennsylvania public schools. *Journal of Autism and Developmental Disorders, 38*, 1462–1473. https://doi.org/10.1007/s10803-007-0522-x.

Horton, J. O., & Moresi, M. G. (2001). Roberts, Plessy, and Brown: The long, hard struggle against segregation. *OAH Magazine of History, 15*(2), 14–16.

Houston, D. (2007). TQM and higher education: A critical systems perspective on fitness for purpose. *Quality in Higher Education, 13*(1), 3–17.

Hudson, F. (2008, March 16). Father wants refund on Brighton Grammar school fees. *Sunday Herald Sun*. Retrieved from http://www.theaustralian.com.au/news/sons-flunk-school-dad-demands-a-refund/storye6frg6n6-1111115809105

Hudson, N. (2013). *Children and young people (Scotland) bill SB 13/59*. Edinburgh: Scottish Parliament. Retrieved from http://www.scottish.parliament.uk/ResearchBriefingsAndFactsheets/S4/SB_13-59.pdf

Human Rights & Equal Opportunity Commission. (1999, July 20). *Finney v the Hills grammar school (HREOC)*. Retrieved from http://www.austlii.edu.au/cgi-bin/sinodisp/au/cases/cth/HREOCA/1999/14.html?stem=0&synonyms=0&query=Finney

Human Rights & Equal Opportunity Commission. (2000, November 13). *Purvis v state of New South Wales (Department of education) (HREOC)*. Retrieved from http://www.austlii.edu.au/cgi-bin/sinodisp/au/cases/cth/HREOCA/2000/47.html?stem=0&synonyms=0&query=Purvis

Human Rights Act 1998 (UK)

Hume, D. (1739). *Treatise of human nature: Being an attempt to introduce the experimental method of reasoning into moral subjects*. London, John Noon. Current edition (1985) London: Penguin Classics.

Hume, M. (2003, May 5). Give the NSPCC a clip around the ear, somebody. *The Times*.

Hunter v. Board of Educ. of Montgomery Cnty., 439 A.2d 582 (Md.1982).

Hurley, M. M., Padró, F. F., & Hawke, M. F. (2013). Will race to the top have the same mixed results no child left behind had on student learning and preservice teacher preparation? *Quality Approaches in Higher Education, 4*(2), 20–29.

Hurst v State of Queensland [2006] FCAFC 100 ('Hurst').

Hutt, E., & Tang, A. (2013). The new education malpractice litigation. *Virginia Law Review, 99*(3), 419–492.

Hwang, J., & Riccomini, P. J. (2014). Enhancing mathematical problem solving for secondary students with or at risk of learning disabilities: A literature review. *Learning Disabilities Research and Practice, 31*, 169–181. https://doi.org/10.1111/ldrp.12105.

I on behalf of BI v State of Queensland [2006] QADT 19 ("BI").

ICFGEO. (2016). The international commission for global education opportunity. The learning generation: Investing in education for a changing world. p. 12. Retrieved from http://educationcommission.org/about/

Indian Act. (1985). An act respecting Indians. RSC 1985, c. I-5.

Indian Residential Schools Settlement Agreement. (2007). Retrieved October 4, 2016, from http://www.thecanadianencyclopedia.ca/en/article/indian-residential-schools-settlement-agreement/

Indig, D., Vecchiato, C., Haysom, L., Beilby, R., Carter, J., Champion, U., et al. (2011). *2009 NSW young people in custody health survey: Full report*. Sydney: Justice Health and Juvenile Justice.

Individuals With Disabilities Education Act Amendments of 1997, 20 U.S.C. § 1415 et seq. (1997).

Individuals with Disabilities Education Act, 20 U.S.C. § 1400 (2004).

Individuals With Disabilities Education Improvement Act of 2004, 20 U.S.C. § 1400 et seq. (2004).

Individuals with Disabilities Improvement Education ACT (IDEA). (2004). Available from http://idea.ed.gov

International Institute for Restorative Practices. https://www.iirp.edu, Restorative practices Australia www.restorativepractices.org.au, RealJustice australia@realjustice.org

International Organization for Standardization (ISO). (2007). *IWA 2: 2007: Quality management systems – Guidelines for the application of ISO 9001:2000 in education.* Retrieved from: http://www.ips.pt/ips_si/web_gessi_docs.download_file?p_name=F799130955/IWA_2_2007.pdf

Inuit Tapiriit Kanatami. (2008, April 15–17). *Report on the Inuit Tapiriit Kanatami education initiative: Summary of ITK summit on Inuit education and background research.* Inuvik/Ottawa: Author.

Invernizzi, A., & Williams, J. (Eds.). (2008). *Children and citizenship.* London: Sage.

Iori, V. (2012). Diventare genitori nella società dell'incertezza. In G.B. La Sala & C. Rinaldi, (Eds.), *La "normale" complessità del diventare genitori.* Reggio Children. Reggio Emilia.

Iori, V., & Bruzzone, D. (2015). *Le ombre dell'educazione. Ambivalenze, impliciti e paradossi.* Milano: FrancoAngeli.

Ipp, J. (2002). *Report of the panel for the review of the law of negligence* (the Ipp report). http:revofneg.treasury.gov.au/content/reports.asp

Itkonen, T. (2007). PL 94-142: Policy, evolution, and landscape shift. *Issues in Teacher Education, 16*(2), 7–17.

IW v City of Perth (1996) 191 CLR 1 ("IW").

Jaber v Rockdale City Council [2008] NSWCA 98.

Jackson, R. (2016). *State guardian or head gardener? The imposition of state guardianship by the Scottish government.* A discussion paper. Sheffield: Centre for Welfare Reform.

Jackson, J., & Varnham, S. (2007a). *Law for educators: School and university law in Australia.* Sydney: LexisNexis Butterworths.

Jackson, J., & Varnham, S. (2007b). *Law for educators: School and university law in Australia* (1st ed.). Sydney: LexisNexis.

Jacobi v Griffiths. (1999). 2 SCR 570.

Jacobs, S. H. (2007). Current trends in the process and methods of regulatory impact assessment: Mainstreaming RIA into policy processes. In C. Kirkpatrick & D. Parker (Eds.), *Regulatory impact assessment: Towards better regulation?* (pp. 17–35). Cheltenham: Edward Elgar.

James, J. C., & Tanner, C. K. (1993). Standardized testing of young children. *Journal of Research and Development in Education, 26*(3), 143–152.

Jamieson, L. S. (1991). Educational malpractice: A lesson in professional accountability. *Boston College Law Review, 32*(4), 899–965.

János, B. (1789). A franciaországi változásokra. Magyar Museum. Kassa. http://mek.niif.hu/00600/00611/00611.htm#14

Japanese Union of Scientists and Engineers (JUSE). (2018). *The application guide for The Deming Prize/The Deming Grand Prize 2018: For companies and organizations overseas.* Retrieved from http://www.juse.or.jp/upload/files/en_oubo2018_3.pdf

Jervis-Tracey, P., Chenoweth, L., McAuliffe, D., O'Connor, B., & Stehlik, D. (2012). Managing tensions in statutory professional practice: Living and working in rural and remote communities. *Australian and International Journal of Rural Education, 22*(2), 97.

Jeszenszky, G. (2010). Antall József, a nemzetpolitikus. Sóvidék 2. évf. 2. sz. (2010, november) 62–65 p.

John, D. (1897, January). My pedagogic creed. *School Journal, 54*, 77–80.

Johnson, P. (2002). Disability discrimination law and occupational health and safety law: How to reconcile the two? In D. Stewart (Ed.), *Legal risk management safety, security and success in education: Proceedings of the 11th annual conference of the Australia and New Zealand education law association* (pp. 277–286). Brisbane: GSM Press.

Johnson, M. (2014). *Morality for humans.* Chicago: University of Chicago Press.

Jones, H. W. (1978). Lawyers and justice: The uneasy ethics of partisanship. *Villanova Law Review, 23*(5–6), 957–976.

Jones, T. M. (1991). Ethical decision making by individuals in organizations: An issue contingent model. *Academy of Management Review, 16*, 366–395.

Jones, T. M., Felps, W., & Bigley, G. A. (2007). Ethical theory and stakeholder-related decisions: The role of stakeholder culture. *The Academy of Management Review, 32*(1), 137–155.

József, R. (1997). Európa Jogtörténete (History of European law). Püski Kiadó Kft. Budapest.

József, D. (1998). A Miniszterelnök. Antall József és a rendszerváltozás. Osiris. Budapest.

Jubran, L. N. (2015). *Student voice for enhancing the quality of inclusive education.* Doctoral dissertation. Retrieved from https://bspace.buid.ac.ae/bitstream/1234/778/1/120043.pdf

Juran, J. M. (1989). *Juran on leadership for quality: An executive handbook.* New York: Free Press.

Jürgen, H. (1991). Staatsbürgerschaft und nationale Identität. Überlegungen zur europäischen Zukunft, Erker.

Justia US Supreme Court (n.d.). *Smith v. Robinson 468 U.S. 992* (1984). Author. Retrieved May 1, 2017, from https://supreme.justia.com/cases/federal/us/468/992/case.html

K v N School (No 3) [1996] 1QADR 620 ("K").

Kaczkowski, M. (2012). *A qualitative case study: Student perceptions of "voice" in the IEP process.* Doctoral dissertation. Retrieved from http://search.proquest.com/openview/c5dee189df2175348be5364e362a8488/1?pq-origsite=gscholar&cbl=18750&diss=y

Kafer, A. (2013). *Feminist, queer, crip.* Bloomington: Indiana University Press.

Kahneman, D., & Tversky, A. (1979). Prospect theory: An analysis of decisions under risk. *Econometrica, 47*(2), 263–291.

Kanji, G. K., & Asher, M. (1993). *Total quality management process: A systematic approach*. Oxford: Carfax.

Kanji, G. K., Tambi, B. A., & Wallace, W. (1999). A comparative study of quality practices in higher education institutions in the US and Malaysia. *Total Quality Management, 10*(3), 357–371.

Kant, I. (1781). *Groundwork for the metaphysics of morals*. (2002, trans/Ed. Wood, A. W.). New Haven: Yale University Press.

Kanter, A. S. (2015). *The development of disability rights under international law*. Oxon: Routledge.

Kaplan, A. (2010). Harm without recourse: The need for a private right of action in federal restraint and seclusion legislation. *Cardozo Law Review, 32*(2), 581–614.

Karatzas, K. D. (2016). Lyndon B. Johnson and the civil rights act of 1964. *Science Journal of History, Area Studies, International Relations, 21*(3), 25–33.

Karmiris, M. (2016). Breaks and ruptures: Cripping the reading of resistance. *Canadian Journal of Disability Studies, 5*(4), 205–222. http://cjds.uwaterloo.ca/index.php/cjds/article/view/319

Karmiris, M. (2017). De-centering the myth of normalcy in education: A critique of inclusionary policies in education through disability studies. *Critical Disability Discourses, 8*, 99–199. https://cdd.journals.yorku.ca/index.php/cdd/article/view/39722

Károly, K. (2009). Az állampolgárság fogalmának és jogi szabályozásának történeti fejlődése: Koncepciók és alapmodellek Európában és Magyarországon. (The historical development of the concept of citizenship: Concepts and basic models in Europe and Hungary) PhD. ELTE Állam- és Jogtudományi Kar Alkotmányjogi Tanszék – Egyetemes Állam- és Jogtörténet Tanszék. Budapest.

Kasinathan, J. (2016). Predictors of rapid reincarceration in mentally ill young offenders. *Australian Psychiatry, 23*, 550–555. https://doi.org/10.1177/1039856215597532.

Kay, E., Tisdall, M., & David, J. (2015). Children's rights and well-being: Tensions within the children and young people (Scotland) act 2014. In A. B. Smith (Ed.), *Enhancing children's rights* (pp. 214–227). London: Palgrave Macmillan.

Kayess, R., & French, P. (2008). Out of darkness into light? Introducing the convention on the rights of persons with disabilities. *Human Rights Law Review, 1*(8), 1–34.

Kean, R. B., & Dukes, R. L. (1991). Effects of witness characteristics on the perception and reportage of child abuse. *Child Abuse & Neglect, 15*(4), 423–435.

Keeffe, M. (2003). The principal's governance of inclusion and the requirements of the disability discrimination legislation: Are they words apart? (K. Lindsay, Ed.). *Australia and New Zealand Journal of Law and Education, 8*(1), 69–76.

Keeffe, M. (2004). Principal's stress: Tensions between the requirements of the disability discrimination legislation and the governance of inclusion in schools. In *Proceedings AARE annual conference*, Melbourne.

Keeton, W. P., Dobbs, D. B., Keeton, R. E., & Owen, D. G. (1984). *Prosser and Keeton on the law of Torts* (5th ed.). St Paul: West Publishing Co.

Kelsen, H. (1952). *The principles of international law*. New York: Rinehart & Company, Inc.

Kelsen, H. (1967). *Pure theory of law* (Revised ed.). (trans: Knight, M.). Clark: The Lawbook Exchange, Ltd.

Kelsen, H. (1982). The concept of the legal order. *The American Journal of Jurisprudence, 27*(1), 64–84.

Kempe, C. H., Silverman, F., Steele, B., Droegemueller, W., & Silver, H. (1962). The battered-child syndrome. *JAMA: Journal of the American Medical Association, 181*, 17–24.

Kennedy, P. (1989). *The rise and fall of great powers; economic change and military conflict from 1500–2000*. London: Fontana.

Kennedy, M. J., Thomas, C. N., Meyer, P., Alves, K. D., & Lloyd, J. W. (2014). Using evidence-based multimedia to improve vocabulary performance of adolescents with LD: A UDL approach. *Learning Disability Quarterly, 37*, 71–85. https://doi.org/10.1177/073194871350762.

Kenny, M. C. (2001). Child abuse reporting: Teachers' perceived deterrents. *Child Abuse & Neglect, 25*(1), 81–92.

Kenny, M. C. (2004). Teachers' attitudes toward and knowledge of child maltreatment. *Child Abuse & Neglect, 28*(12), 1311–1319.

Kenway, J. (2013). Challenging inequality in Australian schools: Gonski and beyond. *Discourse: Studies in the Cultural Politics of Education, 34*(2), 286–308.

Keogh, B. K. (2007). Celebrating PL 94–142: The education of all handicapped children act of 1975. *Issues in Teacher Education, 16*(2), 65–69.

Kern, M. C., & Chugh, D. (2009). Bounded ethicality: The perils of loss framing. *Psychological Science, 20*(3), 378–384.

Kesner, J. E. (2000). Teacher characteristics and the quality of child–teacher relationships. *Journal of School Psychology, 38*(2), 133–149.

Kesner, J. E., & Robinson, M. (2002). Teachers as mandated reporters of child maltreatment: Comparison with legal, medical, and social services reporters. *Children & Schools, 24*(222), 231.

Keynes, J. M. (1936). *The general theory of employment, interest, and money*. London: Macmillan & Co. Retrieved from http://cas2.umkc.edu/economics/people/facultypages/kregel/courses/econ645/winter2011/generaltheory.pdf

Kezelman Am, C., Hossack, N., Stavropoulos, P., & Burley, P. (2015). *The cost of unresolved childhood trauma and abuse in adults in Australia*. Sydney: Adults Surviving Child Abuse.

Khemani, R. S., & Shapiro, D. M. (1993). *Glossary of industrial organisation economics and competition law*. Paris: OECD.

Kidner, C. (2013). *Children and young people (Scotland) bill SB 13/38*. Edinburgh: Scottish Parliament. Retrieved from http://www.scottish.parliament.uk/ResearchBriefingsAndFactsheets/S4/SB_13-38.pdf

Kiefel v State of Victoria [2013] FCA 1398 ("Kiefel").

Kilham, C., & Watson, L. (2014, December). *The Impact of online learning about the disability standards for education on Australian school staff.* Paper presented at the Australian Association for Research in Education Conference, Brisbane.

Kim, J.-N., Grunig, J. E., & Ni, L. (2010). Reconceptualizing the communicative action of publics: Acquisition, selection, and transmission of information in problematic situations. *International Journal of Strategic Communication, 4*(2), 126–154.

Kirby, M. (1982, March 22). *Legal and social responsibilities of teachers.* Speech delivered at the education centre for Whyalla and region annual dinner, Whyalla, South Australia. Retrieved from http://www.michaelkirby.com.au/images/stories/speeches/1980s/vol9/1982/316-Education_Centre_for_Whyalla_and_Region___Legal_and_Social_Responsibilities_for_Teachers.pdf

Kirkpatrick, C. (2014). Assessing the impact of regulatory reform in developing countries. *Public Administration and Development, 24*, 161–167.

Kisteleki, K. (2011). Az állampolgárság fogalmának és jogi szabályozásának történeti fejlődése: koncepciók és alapmodellek Európában és Magyarországon. Opitz. Budapest.

Kleinhenz, E., & Ingvarson, L. (2004). Teacher accountability in Australia: Current policies and practices and their relation to the improvement of teaching and learning. *Research Papers in Education, 19*(1), 31–49.

Kleinman, C. S. (2006). Ethical drift: When good people do bad things. *JONA's Healthcare Law, Ethics, and Regulation, 8*(3), 72–76.

Klocko, B., & Wells, C. (2015). Workload pressures of principals: A focus on renewal, support, and mindfulness. *NASSP Bulletin, 99*(4), 332–355. https://doi.org/10.1177/0192636515619727.

Knerr, W., Gardner, F., & Cluver, L. (2013). Improving positive parenting skills and reducing harsh and abusive parenting in low-and middle-income countries: A systematic review. *Prevention Science, 14*(4), 352–363.

Knott, A. (1998). Bullying, harassment and violence in schools – Legal options for victims. (A. Knott, & D. Stewart, Eds.). *ANZELA Reporter, 5*(1), 23–31.

Knott, A. (2010). Regulation of the school teaching profession 1970–2010 (Mid-career reflections). In *Australian & New Zealand education law association 19th annual conference* (pp. 51–52). Sydney: ANZELA.

Knutsson, J., & Allwood, C. M. (2014). Opinions of legal professionals: Comparing child and adult witnesses' memory report capabilities. *The European Journal of Psychology Applied to Legal Context, 6*(2), 79–89. Retrieved from https://doi.org/10.1016/j.ejpal.2014.06.001.

Kocha, J. (Ed.). (2010). *Work in a modern society. The German historical experience in a comparative perspective.* Oxford: Berghahn Books.

Kohler, P. D. (1996). *A taxonomy for transition programming: Linking research and practice.* Champaign: Transition Research Institute, University of Illinois.

Kohli, M. (1986). The world that we forgot: A historical review of life course. In V. W. Marshall (Ed.), *Later life: The social psychology of aging* (pp. 271–303). London: Sage.

Kohli, M. (1987). Retirement and the moral economy: A historical interpretation of the German case. *Journal of Aging Studies, 1*(2), 125–144.

Kohli, R., Picower, B., Martinez, A. N., & Ortiz, N. (2015). Critical professional development: Centering the social justice needs of teachers. *The International Journal of Critical Pedagogy, 6*(2), 8–24.

Komulainen, K., Naskali, P., Korhonen, M., & Keskitalo-Foley, S. (2011). Internal entrepreneurship – A Trojan horse of the neoliberal governance of education? Finnish pre- and in-service teachers' implementation of and resistance towards entrepreneurship education. *Journal for Critical Education Policy Studies, 9*(1), 342–373.

Kontoghiorghes, C. (2003). Examining the association between quality and productivity performance in a service organization. *Quality Management Journal, 10*(1), 32–42.

Kopper, Á. (2010). Állampolgárság határon innen és túl. Beszélő Folyóirat. *15*, 5 (May–June).

Kretschmar v Queensland. (1989). Aust Torts Reports ¶80–272.

Krug, E. G., Dahlberg, L. L., Mercy, J. A., Zwi, A. B., & Lozano, R. (Eds.). (2002). *World report on violence and health*. Geneva: World Heath Organization.

Kuhn, T. S. (1962). *The structure of scientific revolutions*. Chicago/USA: University of Chicago Press.

Kunc, N. (1992). The need to belong: Rediscovering Maslow's hierarchy of needs. In R. Villa, J. Thousand, W. Stainback, & S. Stainback (Eds.), *Restructuring for caring and effective education*. Baltimore: Paul Brookes.

Kurth, J. (2009). *Academic outcomes in inclusive and non-inclusive special education programs for adolescents with autism spectrum disorders*. Dissertation abstracts international Section A: Humanities and social sciences, *69*(11-A), 4291.

Kyriazopoulou, M., & Weber, H. (Eds.). (2009). *Development of a set of indicators for inclusive education in Europe*. Odense: European Agency for Development in Special Needs Education.

L v Minister for Education for the State of Queensland (No. 2) [1995] 1 QADR 207 ("L").

Lai, Y., & Vadeboncoeur, J. A. (2013). The discourse of parent involvement in special education: A critical analysis linking policy documents to the experiences of mothers. *Educational Policy, 27*(6), 867–897. https://doi.org/10.1177/0895904812440501.

Lamming, W. H. (2003). The Victoria Climbié death enquiry, presented to parliament by the secretary of state for health and the secretary of state for the home department (CM 5730).

Landecker, W. S. (1952). Integration and group structure: An area for research. *Social Forces, 30*, 394–400.

Lander, M., Koene, B., & Linssen, S. (2013). Committed to professionalism: Organizational responses of mid-tier accounting firms to conflicting institutional logics. *Accounting, Organizations and Society, 38*, 130–148.

Landmark, L., Zhang, D., & Montoya, L. (2007). Culturally diverse parents' experiences in their children's transition: Knowledge and involvement. *Career Development and Transition for Exceptional Individuals, 30*, 68–79. https://doi.org/10.1177/08857288070300020401.

Landmark, L., Roberts, E., & Zhang, D. (2013). Educators' beliefs and practices about parent involvement in transition planning. *Career Development and Transition for Exceptional Individuals, 36*, 114–123. https://doi.org/10.1177/2165143412463047.

Langford, P. (1989). *A polite and commercial people. England 1727–1783*. Oxford: Oxford University Press.

Lannen, P., & Ziswiler, M. (2014). Potential and perils of the early years: The need to integrate violence prevention and early childhood development (ECD +). *Aggression and Violent Behaviour, 19*(6), 625–628.

Lanskey, C. (2015). Up or down and out? A systematic analysis of young people's educational pathways in the youth justice system in England and Wales. *International Journal of Inclusive Education, 16*, 568–582. https://doi.org/10.1080/13603116.2014.961675.

Larry P. v. Riles. 343 F. Supp 401 (N.D. CA., 1972).

Larry P. v. Riles, 495 F. Supp. 926 (N.D. Cal. 1979).

Larry P. v. Riles. United States Court of Appeals. Ninth Circuit. No. 80–427. January 23, 1984. Trial Court Decision Affirmed.

Lasswell, H. D. (1971). *A preview of policy sciences*. New York: Elsevier.

Law Reform (Miscellaneous Provisions) Act 1944 s 5.

Lawrence, E. (Ed.). (1952). *Friedrich Froebel and English education*. London: University of London Press.

Layton, R. (2003). *Child protection review*. Adelaide: Government of South Australia.

Legal Aid NSW. (2015). *A guide to bail*. Retrieved from http://www.legalaid.nsw.gov.au/publications/factsheets-and-resources/guide-to-bail

Legislation.gov.uk. (2016). *Equality Act 2010*. [online]. Available at: http://www.legislation.gov.uk/ukpga/2010/15/contents. Accessed 31 Oct 2017.

Legislation.gov.uk. (2014). *Children and Families Act from 2014*. [online]. Available at: http://www.legislation.gov.uk/ukpga/2014/6/contents/enacted. Accessed 31 Oct 2017.

Leithwood, K., & Menzies, T. (1998). Forms and effects of school-based management: A review. *Educational Policy, 12*(3), 325–346.

Leone, P. E., Christle, C. A., Nelson, C. M., Skiba, R., Frey, A., & Jolivette, K. (2003, October). *School failure, race, and disability: Promoting positive outcomes, decreasing vulnerability for involvement with the juvenile delinquency system*. College Park: The National Center on Education, Disability, and Juvenile Justice.

Levin, C. S. (2016). *Legal analysis: How far can schools go in limited student speech online?* Retrieved from http://www.splc.org/article/2016/06/legal-analysis-student-speech

Levinson, L. H. (1977). Elements of the administrative process: Formal, semi-formal, and free-form models. *The American University Law Review, 26*, 872–941.

Levy, A. (2008, November). Police chief calls to bring back a clip round the ear for naughty children. *The Daily Mail.* Accessed 3 May 2017.

Lewis, A. (2008). Silence in the context of 'child voice'. *Child & Society, 24*, 14–23. https://doi.org/10.1111/j.1099-0860.2008.00200.x.

Lilley, R. (2012). It's an absolute nightmare: Maternal experiences of enrolling children diagnosed with autism in primary school in Sydney, Australia. *Disability and Society, 28*, 514–526. https://doi.org/10.1080/09687599.2012.717882.

Lincoln, S. H., & Homes, E. K. (2007, October). *A need to know: An ethical decisions-making model for research administrators.* Paper presented at the annual society of research administrators international meeting, Nashville.

Lindahl, L. (1977). *Position and change.* Dordrecht: Reidel Publishing Company.

Lindborg, H., & Spangehl, S. D. (2011). U.S. higher education and accreditation: A quality perspective. *ASQ Higher Education Brief December, 4*(6), 1–7.

Lindsay, K. (1997). Age discrimination in education: A critique of law and policy. (D. Stewart, Ed). *Australia and New Zealand Journal of Law and Education, 2*(1), 59–68.

Lindsay, K., & Keeffe-Martin, M. (2002). Issues in Australian disability discrimination case law and strategic approaches for the lawful management of inclusion. (K. Lindsay, Ed.). *Australia and New Zealand Journal of Law and Education, 7*(2), 141–160.

Lindsey, D. (2004). *The welfare of children* (2nd ed.). New York: Oxford University Press.

Lindström, M. (2011). *Promoting agency among people with severe psychiatric disability: Occupation-oriented interventions in home and community settings.* Retrieved from https://www.diva-portal.org/smash/get/diva2:458648/FULLTEXT01.pdf

Lisa Eskinazi v Victoria (County Court (Vic), Lewitan J, No 06471/99, 20 June 2003, unreported).

Lister v Hesley Hall Ltd [2002] 1 AC 215.

Lock, G., & Lummis, G. (2014). Complying with school accountability requirements and the impact on school leaders. *Australian Journal of Teacher Education, 39*(2), 58–69.

Löffler, E. (2001). Defining and measuring quality in public administration. *Bristol Business School Teaching and Research Review, 5*(4), 15 pp.

Lonne, R., & Gillespie, K. (2014). How do Australian print media representations of child abuse and neglect inform the public system reform. *Child Abuse & Neglect, 38*(5), 837–850. https://doi.org/10.1016/j.chiabu.2014.04.021.

Loreman, T. (2014). Measuring inclusive education outcomes in Alberta Canada. *International Journal of Inclusive Education, 18*, 459–483. https://doi.org/10.1080/13603116.2013.788223.

Loreman, T., Deppeler, J., & Harvey, D. (2011). *Inclusive education: Supporting diversity in the classroom*. Crows Nest: Allen and Unwin.

Lorini, E., Longin, D., Gaudou, B., & Herzig, A. (2009). The logic of acceptance: Grounding institutions on agents' attitudes. *Journal of Logic and Computation, 19*(6), 901–940.

Lowi, T. J. (1972). Four systems of policy, politics, and choice. *Public Administration Review, 32*(4), 298–310.

Lowi, T. J. (1985). The state in politics: The relationship between policy and administration. In R. G. Noll (Ed.), *Regulatory policy and the social sciences* (pp. 67–104). Berkeley: University of California Press.

Lowi, T. J. (2002). Law vs. public policy: A critical exploration. *Cornell Journal of Law and Public Policy, 12*(3), 493–501.

Luban, D., Strudler, A., & Wasserman, D. (1992). Moral responsibility in the age of bureaucracy. *Michigan Law Review, 90*, 2348–2392.

Lucius Annaeus Seneca: Epistulae morales ad Lucilium, Libri XVII-XVIIIEpistula CVI http://www.intratext.com/IXT/LAT0230/_P2Y.HTM

Luhmann, N. (1995) *Social systems*. (trans: Bednarz, J. Jr. & Baecker, D.). Stanford: Stanford University Press.

Lundahl, B., Nimer, J., & Parsons, B. (2006). Preventing child abuse: A meta-analysis of parent training programs. *Research on Social Work Practice, 16*(3), 251–262.

Lyons, D. (2015). Restraint and seclusion of students with disabilities: A child rights perspective from Victoria, Australia. *International Journal of Children's Rights, 23*, 189–239. https://doi.org/10.1163/15718182-02301009.

M (a minor) v Newham London Borough [1994] 2 WLR 554.

Macdonald, E. (Reporter). (2016, August 11). Autism cage timeline: From Canberra classroom to the United Nations. *Canberra Times*. http://www.canberratimes.com.au/act-news/autism-cage-timeline-from-canberra-classroom-to-the-united-nations-20160811-gqqnjm.html

Machlup, F. (1962). *The production and distribution of knowledge in the United States*. Princeton: Princeton University Press.

MacIntyre, A. (2007). *After virtue: A study in moral theory* (3rd ed.). Notre Dame: University of Notre Dame Press.

Madrid, E. M. (2008). The unheralded history of the lemon grove desegregation case. *Multicultural Education, 15*(3), 15–19.

Maglan, C. (2016, October 27). Judge dismisses lawsuit challenging Minnesota teachers union protections. *Duluth News Tribune* (MN) at A 9, 2016 WLNR 32881528.

Mandeville, B. (1714). *The Fable of the bees and other writings*. (1997 ed.). Abridged and Ed. Hunert, E. J. Indianapolis: Hackett Publishing.

Maram, A. (2008). Reassessment of the application of TQM in the public sector. *International Public Management Review, 9*(2), 194–212.

March v E & M H Stramare Pty Ltd (1991) 171 CLR 506.

Margaret Thorsborne & Associates. www.thorsborne.com.au/schools-conferencing/

Mark, E. (2013). Student satisfaction and the customer focus in higher education. *Journal of Higher Education Policy and Management, 35*(1), 2–10.

Mark Oberhardt, M. (1995, December 15). School integration policy under fire. *The Courier Mail*, p. 5.

Marks, F. R., & Cathcart, D. (1974). Discipline within the legal profession: Is it self-regulation? *University of Illinois Law Forum, 2*(5), 193–236.

Marshall, A., Powell, N., Pierce, D., Nolan, E., & Fehringer, E. (2012). Youth and administrator perspectives on transition in Kentucky's state agency schools. *Child Welfare, 91*, 97–118.

Martin, J. E., Marshall, L. H., Maxson, L. M., & Jerman, P. L. (1997). *The self-directed IEP*. Longmont: Sopris West.

Martin, J. E., Van Dycke, J. L., Christensen, W. R., Greene, B. A., Gardner, J. E., & Lovett, D. (2006). Increasing student participation in IEP meetings: Establishing the self-directed IEP as an evidenced-based practice. *Exceptional Children, 72*(3), 299–316.

Maslow, A. (1943). A theory of human motivation. *Psychological Review, 50*(4), 370–396.

Mason, J., & Fattore, T. (Eds.). (2005). *Children taken seriously: In theory, policy and practice*. London: Jessica Kingsley Publishers.

Massachusetts Department of Elementary and Secondary Education (DESE). (2016). *Guidelines for program approval* (Revised ed.). Malden: Author. Retrieved from http://www.doe.mass.edu/edprep/ProgramApproval.pdf

Masters, G. (2009). *A shared challenge improving literacy, numeracy and science learning in Queensland primary schools*. Camberwell: ACER.

Mathews, B. (2011). Teacher education to meet the challenges of child sexual abuse. *Australian Journal of Teacher Education, 36*(11), 13–32.

Mathews, B. (2014). Mandatory reporting laws and identification of child abuse and neglect: Consideration of differential maltreatment types, and a cross-jurisdictional analysis of child sexual abuse reports. *Social Sciences, 3*(3), 460–482.

Mathews, B., & Bross, D. (2008). Mandated reporting is still a policy with reason: Empirical evidence and philosophical grounds. *Child Abuse & Neglect, 32*(5), 511–516.

Mathews, B., & Kenny, M. C. (2008). Mandatory reporting legislation in the USA, Canada and Australia: A cross-jurisdictional review of key features, differences and issues. *Child Maltreatment, 13*(1), 50–63.

Mathews, B., & Walsh, K. (2004). Queensland teachers' new legal obligation to report child sexual abuse. *Australia and New Zealand Journal of Law and Education, 9*(1), 25–40.

Mathews, B. (2014). Mandatory reporting laws and identification of child abuse and neglect: Consideration of differential maltreatment types, and a cross-jurisdictional analysis of child sexual abuse reports. *Social Sciences, 3*(3), 460–482.

Mathews, B., & Bromfield, L. (2012). Australian laws and policies on child neglect. In H. Dubowitz (Ed.), *World perspectives on child abuse* (pp. 61–66). Aurora: ISPCAN.

Mathews, B. P., & Walsh, K. M. (2014). Mandatory reporting laws. In A. Hayes & D. Higgins (Eds.), *Families, policy and the law: Selected essays on contemporary issues for Australia* (pp. 131–142). Melbourne: Australian Institute of Family Studies.

Mathews, B. P., & Walsh, K. M. (2015). *Submission to Queensland Law Reform Commission WP 73 Review of child protection mandatory reporting laws for the early childhood education and care sector*. Brisbane: Queensland Law Reform Commission.

Mathews, B. P., Walsh, K. M., Butler, D. A., & Farrell, A. M. (2006). Mandatory reporting by Australian teachers of suspected child abuse and neglect: Legislative requirements and questions for future direction. *Australia and New Zealand Journal of Law and Education, 11*(2), 7–22.

Mathews, B., Goddard, C., Lonne, B., Short, S., & Briggs, F. (2009). Developments in Australian laws requiring the reporting of suspected child sexual abuse. *Children Australia, 34*(3), 18–23.

Mathews, B. P., Bromfield, L., Walsh, K. M., & Vimpani, G. (2015). *Child abuse and neglect: A socio-legal study of mandatory reporting in Australia – Report for the Australian government*. Commonwealth of Australia, Canberra, A.C.T. (In Press).

Mathur, S. R., & Griller Clark, H. (2013). Prerelease planning and practices for youth with disabilities in juvenile detention. *Journal of Special Education Leadership, 26*, 82–92.

Mathur, S., & Schoenfeld, N. (2010). Effective instructional practices in juvenile justice facilities. *Behavioral Disorders, 36*(1), 20–27.

Matos, A. (2016, April 14). Lawsuit accuses Minnesota of protecting bad teachers at expense of students. Minneapolis-St. Paul, *Star Tribune*. Retrieved from http://www.startribune.com/suit-says-minnesota-protects-bad-teachers-at-expense-of-students/375609941

Mau, S., & Verweibe, R. (2010). *European societies; mapping structure and change*. Bristol: The Policy Press.

Mawdsley, R. D., & Cumming, J. J. (2008a). Educational malpractice and setting damages for ineffective teaching: A comparison of legal principles in the USA, England and Australia. *Education and the Law, 20*(1), 25–46.

Mawdsley, R. D., & Cumming, J. J. (2008b). The origins and development of education law as a separate field of law in the United States and Australia. *Australia and New Zealand Journal of Law & Education, 13*(2), 7–20.

Mawdsley, R. D., & Mawdsley, J. L. (2012). Should educational malpractice be actionable? In C. J. Russo (Ed.), *School law* (pp. 213–227). Thousand Oaks: SAGE Publications.

Maxwell, A., & Riley, P. (2017). Emotional demands, emotional labour and occupational outcomes in school principals. *Educational Management Administration & Leadership, 45*(3), 484–502. https://doi.org/10.1177/1741143215607878.

Mayer, K. U. (2000). Promises fulfilled? A review of 20 years of life course research. *Archives Europeennes de Sociologie, XLI*(2), 259–282.
Mayer, K. U., & Tuma, N. B. (Eds.). (1990). *Event history analysis in life course research*. Madison: University of Wisconsin Press.
Mazerolle, P., Legosz, M., & Finighan, P. Weapons in schools in Queensland: The nature, causes and responses (2011) Griffith University, Brisbane. www.behaviour.education.qld.gov.au/SiteCollectionDocuments/.../weapons-in-schools.pdf
McAdam, R., Reid, R., & Saulters, R. (2002). Sustaining quality in the UK public sector: Quality measurement frameworks. *International Journal of Public Sector Management, 22*(6), 478–498.
McAra, L., & McVie, S. (2010). Youth crime and justice: Key messages from the Edinburgh study of youth transitions and crime. *Criminology and Criminal Justice, 10*(2), 179–209.
McAuslan, P. (1988). Public law and public choice. *The Modern Law Review, 51*(6), 681–705.
McCann, P. (2006). Principals' understanding of aspects of the law impacting on the administration of Catholic schools: Some implications for leadership. PhD Published, Australian Catholic University, Melbourne. Retrieved from http://dlibrary.acu.edu.au/digitaltheses/public/adt-acuvp129.17052007/index.html Available from National Library of Australia Trove database (174389481).
McCarthy, J., & Prudham, S. (2004). Neoliberal nature and the nature of neoliberalism. *Geoforum, 35*, 275–283.
McDaniel, M. (2006). In the eye of the beholder: The role of reporters in bringing families to the attention of child protective services. *Children and Youth Services Review, 28*, 306–324.
McGregor, G., Mills, M., te Riele, K., & Hayes, D. (2015). Excluded from school: Getting a second chance as a 'meaningful' education. *International Journal of Inclusive Education, 16*, 608–625. https://doi.org/10.1080/13603116.2014.961684.
McKee, B. E., & Dillenburger, K. (2009). Child abuse and neglect: Training needs of student teachers. *International Journal of Educational Research, 48*(5), 320–330.
McKee, B. E., & Dillenburger, K. (2012). Effectiveness in child protection training for pre-service early childhood educators. *International Journal of Educational Research, 53*, 348–359.
McKinsey & Company. (2007). *How the world's most improved school systems keep getting better.* Washington, DC/New York: McKinsey & Company/The Wallace Foundation.
McLaren, K. (2000). *Tough is not enough – Getting smart about youth crime*. Wellington: Ministry of Youth affairs.
McLaren, P. (2015). *Life in schools* (6th ed.). London: Paradigm Publishers.
McLeskey, J., & Waldron, N. L. (2015). Effective leadership makes schools truly inclusive. *Phi Delta Kappan, 96*(5), 68–73. https://doi.org/10.1177/0031721715569474.
McLeskey, J., Landers, E., Williamson, P., & Hoppey, D. (2010). Are we moving toward educating students with disabilities in less restrictive settings? *Journal of Special Education, 46*, 131–140.

McLeskey, J., Waldron, N. L., Spooner, F., & Algozzine, B. (2014). What are effective inclusive schools and why are they important? In J. McLeskey, N. L. Waldron, F. Spooner, & B. Algozzine (Eds.), *Handbook of effective inclusive schools, research and practice* (pp. 3–16). London: Routledge.

McNaught, K. (2013). The potential impacts of 'inherent requirements' and 'mandatory professional reporting' on students, particularly those with mental health concerns, registering with university disability/support services. *Journal of the Australian and New Zealand Student Services Association, 42*, 25–30.

McSherry, B. (2016, November 29). Breaking bad: Regulating the responses of teachers to students' 'behaviours of concern', paper delivered at *Dean's Lecture Series*. Melbourne. http://education.unimelb.edu.au/news_and_activities/events/event/2016/breaking-bad-regulating-the-responses-of-teachers-to-students-behaviours-of-concern

Meadan, H., Shelden, D., Appel, K., & DeGrazia, R. (2010). Developing a long-term vision: A road map for students' futures. *Teaching Exceptional Children, 43*, 8–14. https://doi.org/10.1177/004005991004300201.

Mears v Sydney Anglican Schools Corporation [2013] NSWSC 535; Mears v Sydney Anglican schools corporation (No. 2)[2013] NSWSC 876.

Meekosha, H., & Soldatic, K. (2011). Human rights and the global South: The case of disability. *Third World Quarterly, 32*(8), 1383–1397.

Melton, G. (2005). Mandated reporting: A policy without reason. *Child Abuse & Neglect, 29*(1), 9–18.

Mendez et al. v. Westminister School District of Orange County, 64 F. Supp. 544 (1946).

Mendus, S. (2009). *Politics and morality*. Cambridge: Polity.

Messick, D. M., & Bazerman, M. H. (1996). Ethics for the 21st century: A decision making approach. *Sloan Management Review, 37*, 9–22.

Messick, D. M., & Tenbrunsel, A. E. (Eds.). (1996). *Codes of conduct*. New York: Russell Sage Foundation.

Metcalfe, A. (2010). Administrative law evolution: An administrator's point of view. *Admin Review, 59*, 59–69.

Mi'kmaw Kina'matnewey. (2015–2016). Mi'kmaw Kina'matnewey annual report 2015–2016. Retrieved at http://kinu.ca/sites/default/files/doc/2014/Feb/mk_annual_report_2016.pdf

Michel, F. (2004). Naissance de la biopolitique Cours au College de France 1978–1979. Hautes Études. Gallimard Seuil.

Middleton, R. A., Harley, D. A., & Rollins, C. W. (1999). The historical and political context of the civil rights of persons with disabilities: A multicultural perspective for counselors. *Journal of Multicultural Counseling and Development, 27*(2), 105–120.

Miles, S., & Singal, N. (2010). The education for all and inclusive education debate: Conflict, contradiction or opportunity? *International Journal of Inclusive Education, 14*(1), 1–15.

Mill, J. (1825a). *Education*. London. Encyclopedia Britannica. http://oll.libertyfund.org/index.php?option=com_staticxt&staticfile=show.php%3Ftitle=1764&Itemid=99999999. Accessed 13 May 2013.

Mill, J. (1825b). *Prisons and prison discipline*. London. Encyclopedia Britannica. http://oll.libertyfund.org/index.php?option=com_staticxt&staticfile=show.php%3Ftitle=1766&Itemid=99999999. Accessed 13 May 2013.

Miller, A. (1997). *The drama of the gifted child: The search for the true self*. New York: Basic Books.

Miller, A. (2002). *For your own good: Hidden cruelty in child-rearing and the roots of violence*. London: Macmillan.

Miller, G. E., Colebrook, J., & Ellis, B. R. (2014). Advocating for the rights of the child through family–school collaboration. *Journal of Educational and Psychological Consultation, 24*(1), 10–27. https://doi.org/10.1080/10474412.2014.870483.

Miller v South Australia. (1980). 24 SASR 416.

Mills v. Board of Education of District of Columbia, 348 F. Supp. 866 (D.D.C. 1972).

Ministerial Council on Education Employment Training and Youth Affairs. (2008). *Melbourne declaration on educational goals for young Australians*. Carlton South: MCEETYA.

Minns v State of New South Wales [2002] FMCA 60 ("Minns").

Mishra, P., & Mehta, R. (2017). What we educators get wrong about 21st-century learning: Results of a survey. *Journal of Digital Learning in Teacher Education, 33*, 6–19. https://doi.org/10.1080/21532974.2016.1242392.

Mitchell, D. (2014). *What really works in special and inclusive education: Using evidence-based teaching strategies* (2nd ed.). Milton Park: Routledge.

Mitchell, R. K., Agle, B. R., & Wood, D. J. (1997). Toward a theory of stakeholder identification and salience: Defining the principle of who and what really counts. *The Academy of Management Review, 22*(4), 853–886.

Mitchell, D. T., & Snyder, S. L. (1997). Introduction: Disability studies and the double bind of representation. In D. T. Mitchell & S. L. Snyder (Eds.), *The body and physical difference: Discourses of disability* (pp. 1–31). Ann Arbor: University of Michigan Press.

Moore, C. (2009). Psychological perspectives on corruption. In D. De Cremer (Ed.), *Psychological perspectives on ethical behavior and decision making* (pp. 35–71). Charlotte: Information Age Publishing.

Moore, M., & Deloria, V., Jr. (2003). *Genocide of the mind: New native American writing*. New York: Thunder's Mouth Press/Nation Books.

Moore, C., & Gino, F. (2013). Ethically adrift: How others pull our moral compass from true North, and how we can fix it. *Research in Organizational Behavior, 33*, 53–77.

Moore, D., Tanlu, L., & Bazerman, M. H. (2010). Conflict of interest and the intrusion of bias. *Judgment and Decision making, 5*(1), 37–53.

Moore v Vanderloo, 386 N.W.2d 108 (Iowa 1986).

Morejohn, N. B. (2006). *Reporting child maltreatment: Challenges faced by teachers.* Berkeley: California State University.

Morgan, D. (1998). Practical strategies for combining qualitative and quantitative methods: Applications to health research. *Qualitative Health Research, 8*(3), 362–376. https://doi.org/10.1177/104973239800800307.

Morgan, J. J., Boone, R., & Higgins, K. (2013). Integrating technology in content area classrooms to support reading comprehension. In R. T. Boon & V. G. Spencer (Eds.), *Adolescent literacy: Strategies for content comprehension in inclusive classrooms* (pp. 157–169). Baltimore: Brookes Publishing.

Morgan, J. J., Brown, N. B., Hsiao, Y. J., Howerter, C., Juniel, P., Sedano, L., & Castillo, W. L. (2014). Unwrapping academic standards to increase the achievement of students with disabilities. *Intervention in School and Clinic, 49*, 131–141. https://doi.org/10.1177/1053451213496156.

Morrison, B., & Vaandering, D. (2012). Restorative justice: Pedagogy, praxis, and discipline. *Journal of School Violence, 11*(2), 138.

Moylett, H. (Ed.). (2013). *Characteristics of effective early learning; helping young children become learners for life*. Berkshire: Open University/McGraw-Hill.

Murphy and Grahl v The State of New South Wales (NSW Department of Education) and Wayne Houston ('Murphy and Grahl').

Murphy, L., & Nagel, T. (2002). *The myth of ownership: Taxes and justice*. New York: Oxford University Press.

Murphy, P., & Warren, P. (2015, December 11). Good timing for new federal education law. *Viewpoints: PPIC Blog*. Retrieved from http://ppic.org/main/blog_detail.asp?i=1923

Murray, B. (1997). Failing to report: Potential action for breach of the statutory duty to report child abuse in Victoria. (D. Stewart, Ed.). *Australia and New Zealand Journal of Law and Education, 2*(1), 89–100.

Nagorcka, F., Stanton, M., & Wilson, M. (2005). Stranded between partisanship and the truth? A comparative analysis of legal ethics in the adversarial and inquisitorial systems of justice. *Melbourne University Law Review, 29*(2), 448–477.

National Assessment of Educational Progress (NAEP, 2014). *The nation's report card 2014: Technology and engineering literacy*. Retrieved from https://www.nationsreportcard.gov/tel_2014/#

National Association of School Nurses. (2011, revised 2017). *Position statement: Role of the school nurse*. [online]. Available at: https://schoolnursenet.nasn.org/blogs/nasn-profile/2017/07/28/chronic-health-conditions-students-with-the-role-of-the-school-nurse. Accessed 31 Oct 2017.

National Association of School Nurses. (2017). *Definition of school nursing*. [online]. Available at: https://www.nasn.org/home. Accessed 31 Oct 2017.

National Disability Rights Network. (2012). *School is not supposed to hurt: The U.S. Department of Education must do more to protect school children from restraint and seclusion*. Washington, DC: Author. http://www.ndrn.org/images/Documents/Resources/Publications/Reports/School_is_Not_Supposed_to_Hurt_3_v7.pdf

National Institute of Health (NIH). (1998). *NIH policy for data and safety monitoring*. Retrieved from https://grants.nih.gov/grants/guide/notice-files/not98-084.html

National Safe Schools Framework. www.education.gov.au/national-safe-schools-framework-0

Nellis, A., & Hooks Wayman, R. (2009). *Back on track: Supporting youth reentry from out-of-home placement to the community*. Washington, DC: Juvenile Justice and Delinquency Prevention Taskforce, Youth Reentry Task Force.

Nelson, N. J., Fien, H., Doabler, C. T., & Clarke, B. (2016). Considerations for realizing the promise of educational gaming technology. *Teaching Exceptional Children, 48*, 293–300. https://doi.org/10.1177/0040059916650639.

Neveu, C., Bier, B., & Roudet, B. (1998). Pour une anthropologie de la citoyenneté, une approche comparative France/Grande-Bretagne. In: Agora débats/jeunesses.1998/12. Jeunes en Europe: politique et citoyenneté. 43–51p. https://www.persee.fr/doc/agora_1268-5666_1998_num_12_1_1605

New South Wales Department of Education and Communities. (2015). *Suspension and expulsion of school students procedures – 2011*. Sydney: New South Wales Department of Education and Communities.

New South Wales Department of Education. (2016). *Guide to teaching and protecting young people*. NSW: Author.

New South Wales Department of Education and Training. (1997). *Enrolment of students in government schools: A summary and consolidation of policy*. Sydney: New South Wales Department of Education and Training. Retrieved from https://www.det.nsw.edu.au/policies/student_admin/enrolment/enrolpol/pd02_06_enrolment_of_students.pdf

New South Wales Department of Education and Training. (2006). *Collection, use and disclosure of information about students with a history of violence*, Legal issues bulletin no. 40. Sydney: Legal Services Directorate, New South Wales Department of Education and Training. Retrieved from https://www.nswtf.org.au/files/legal_issues_bulletin_no.40.pdf

New South Wales Government. (1998). *Children and young persons (care and protection) act 1998 no 157*. Sydney: NSW Government. Retrieved from http://www.legislation.nsw.gov.au/acts/1998-157.pdf

New South Wales Government. (2012). *Education act 1990 no 8*. Sydney: NSW Government. Retrieved from http://www.legislation.nsw.gov.au/inforce/fc4bcf6a-d005-68af-fa91-fd9a7d10cd09/1990-8.pdf

New South Wales Government. (2016a). *Privacy and personal information protection act 1998 no 133*. Sydney: NSW Government. Retrieved from http://www.legislation.nsw.gov.au/#/view/act/1998/133

New South Wales Government. (2016b). *Work health and safety act 2011 no 10*. Sydney: NSW Government. Retrieved from http://www.legislation.nsw.gov.au/#/view/act/2011/10/full

New South Wales v Lepore. (2003). 195 ALR 412; Samin v Queensland and Rich v Queensland (2003) 195 ALR 412.

New South Wales Government Education & Communities. (2011). *Guidelines for the use of time-out strategies including dedicated time-out rooms*. https://education.nsw.gov.au/policy-library/associated-documents/timeout_gui.pdf

New South Wales Government Education & Communities. (2012). Physical restraint of students. *Legal Services Bulletin, 9*. Reviewed June 2012. https://www.det.nsw.edu.au/media/downloads/about-us/how-we-operate/legal-issues-bulletins/number_09.pdf

New South Wales Parliament Legislative Council. (2017). *Education of students with a disability or special needs in New South Wales*, Report no. 37, Portfolio Committee No. 3 – Education. Sydney: Author. https://www.parliament.nsw.gov.au/committees/DBAssets/InquiryReport/ReportAcrobat/6114/170921%20-%20Final%20report.pdf

NO2NP (No 2 Named Person). (n.d.-a). *Supporters*. Retrieved from http://no2np.org/supporters/

NO2NP (No 2 Named Person). (n.d.-b). *Teachers concerned over demands of named persons workload*. Retrieved from http://no2np.org/teachers-concerned-unmanageable-workload-named-person-scheme/

NO2NP (No 2 Named Person). (n.d.-c). *11 reasons to say no to the named person scheme*. Retrieved from http://no2np.org

Nobrega v Trustees of the Roman Catholic Church for the Archdiocese of Sydney (No 1) [1999] NSWCA 75.

Nolan, B. C., & Spencer, J. D. (Eds.). (1997). *Schools and litigation: Developing legal policies*. Toowoomba: P.C.S. Publications.

Nolan-Spohn, H. (2016). Increasing student involvement in IEPs. *Mid-Western Educational Researcher, 28*(3), 300–308. Retrieved from http://www.mwera.org/MWER/volumes/v28/issue3/v28n3-Nolan-VOICES-FROM-THE-CLASSROOM.pdf

Noll, R. G. (1985). Government regulatory behaviour: A multidisciplinary survey and synthesis. In R. G. Noll (Ed.), *Regulatory policy and the social sciences* (pp. 9–63). Berkeley: University of California Press.

North, D. C. (1991). Institutions. *The Journal of Economic Perspectives, 5*(1), 97–112.

Norwich, B. (2014). How does the capability approach address current issues in special educational needs, disability and inclusive education field? *Journal of Research in Special Educational Needs, 14*(1), 16–21. https://doi.org/10.1111/1471-3802.12012.

Norwich, B., & Eaton, A. (2015). The new special education needs (SEN) legislation in England and implications for services for children and young people with social, emotional and behavioural difficulties. *Emotional and Behavioural Difficulties, 20*(2), 117–132.

NSW Ombudsman (NSW O). (2013). *A level playing field? HSC disability provisions*. Sydney: NSW O.

NSW Ombudsman. (2017). *NSW Ombudsman inquiry into behaviour management in schools*. Sydney: Author. https://www.ombo.nsw.gov.au/news-and-publications/

publications/reports/community-and-disability-services/nsw-ombudsman-inquiry-into-behaviour-management-in-schools-august-2017

Nunkoosing, K., & Haydon-Laurelut, M. (2012). Intellectual disability trouble: Foucault and Goffman on 'challenging behaviour'. In D. Goodley, B. Hughes, & L. Davis (Eds.), *Disability and social theory: New developments and directions* (pp. 195–211). Basingstoke: Palgrave Macmillan.

Nurcombe, B., Wooding, S., Marrington, P., Bickman, L., & Roberts, G. (2000). Child sexual abuse II: Treatment. *Australian & New Zealand Journal of Psychiatry, 34*, 92–97.

O'Connell, K. (2016). Unequal brains: Disability discrimination law and children with challenging behavior. *Medical Law Review, 24*(1), 76–98.

O'Connell, K. (2016, May 5–6). *How the DDA and the DSE have been implemented in NSW for students with challenging behaviours.* Paper presented at the Aspect Autism in Education Conference, Melbourne.

O'Connell, K. (2017). Should we take the 'disability' out of discrimination laws? Students with challenging behaviour and the definition of disability. *Law in Context, 35*(2), 108–128.

O'Connor, K. M., deDreu, C. K. W., Schroth, H., Barry, B., Lituchy, T., & Bazerman, M. H. (2002). What we want to do versus what we think we should do. *Journal of Behavioral Decision Making, 15*, 403–418.

O'Hanlon, C. (Ed.). (2017). *Inclusive education in Europe.* London: Routledge.

O'Neill, S., & Zajac, R. (2013). Preparing children for cross-examination: How does intervention timing influence efficacy? *Psychology, Public Policy, and Law, 19*(3), 307–320. https://doi.org/10.1037/a0031538.

O'Neill, S. C., Cumming, T. M., & Strnadová, I. (2017). *How juvenile justice and education support the transition of school-aged youth from within a custodial environment to the community: Lessons to be learned and celebrations to share.* Sydney: UNSW Sydney School of Education.

O'Rourke, J., & Houghton, S. (2008). Perceptions of secondary school students with mild disabilities to the academic and social support mechanisms implemented in regular classrooms. *International Journal of Disability, Development and Education, 55*(3), 227–237.

O'Toole, R., & Webster, S. W. (1999). Teachers' recognition and reporting of child abuse: Factorial survey. *Child Abuse & Neglect, 23*(11), 1083–1101.

O'Toole, R., Webster, S. W., O'Toole, A. W., & Lucal, B. (1999). Teachers' recognition and reporting of child abuse: A factorial survey. *Child Abuse & Neglect, 23*(11), 1083–1101.

OECD. (2008). *Introductory handbook for undertaking regulatory impact analysis (RIA). Version 1.0.* Paris: Author.

OECD. (2009). *Regulatory impact analysis: A tool for regulatory coherence.* Paris: Author. Retrieved from http://www.keepeek.com/Digital-Asset-Management/oecd/governance/regulatory-impact-analysis_9789264067110-en#.WSIbNH2-YSk#page4

Office for Human Research Protection (OHRP). (2010). *IRB continuing review of research.* Retrieved from https://www.hhs.gov/ohrp/regulations-and-policy/guidance/guidance-on-continuing-review-2010/index.html

Office of Educational Technology (OET, 2017). *National education technology plan.* Retrieved from https://tech.ed.gov/netp/

Ofsted. (2010). *The special educational needs and disability review. A statement is not enough.* Manchester: Ofsted.

Okolo, C. M., & Diedrich, J. (2014). Twenty-five years later: How is technology used in the education of students with disabilities? Results of a statewide study. *Journal of Special Education Technology, 29,* 1–20. https://doi.org/10.1177/016264341402900101.

Oliver, M. (1996). *Understanding disability: From theory to practice.* London: Macmillan Press.

Oliver, R. L. (1997). *Satisfaction: A behavioral perspective on the consumer.* New York: The McGraw-Hill Companies, Inc.

Oliver, M., & Barnes, C. (2010). Disability studies, disabled people and the struggle for inclusion. *British Journal of Sociology of Education, 31*(5), 547–560. https://doi.org/10.1080/01425692.2010.500088.

Olweus, D. (1991). Bully/victim problems among school children: Some basic facts and effects of a school-based intervention program. In D. Pepler & K. H. Rubin (Eds.), *The development and treatment of childhood aggression.* Hillsdale: Erlbaum.

Oreopoulos, P. (2005). *Canadian compulsory school law and their impact on education attainment and future earning.* Ottawa: Minister of Industry. Previewed 26 September 2016 http://publications.gc.ca/Collection/Statcan/11F0019MIE/11F0019MIE2005251.pdf

Organisation for Economic Cooperation and Development (OECD). (2013). *Education today 2013: The OECD perspective.* Paris: Author.

Organisation for Economic Cooperation and Development (OECD). (2014). *TALIS 2013 results: An international perspective on teaching and learning.* TALIS, OECD Publishing.

Organisation for Economic Cooperation and Development (OECD). (2017). *PISA for development assessment and analytical framework: Reading, mathematics and science. (Preliminary version).* Paris: Author.

Organization of African Unity (OAU), African Charter on the Rights and Welfare of the Child, 11 July 1990, CAB/LEG/24.9/49 (1990). Available at http://www.refworld.org/docid/3ae6b38c18.html. Accessed 4 Apr 2018.

Osher, D., Bear, G., Sprague, J., & Doyle, W. (2010). How can we improve school discipline? *Educational Researcher, 39*(1), 48.

Ouellette, R. F. (2011). *Evaluating aboriginal curricula using a Cree-Métis perspective with a regard toward indigenous knowledge.* Unpublished doctoral dissertation, Laval University, Laval.

Overseas Tankship (UK) Ltd v Miller Steamship Co Pty Ltd (Wagon Mound (No 2)) [1967] AC 617.

Oyston v St Patrick's College [2011] NSWSC 269.

Oyston v St Patrick's College [2013] NSWCA 135.

Oyston v St Patrick's College (No 2) [2013] NSWCA 310.

P v Director-General, Department of Education [1995] 1 QADR 755 ('P').

Padró, F. F. (1988a). *Quality circles and their existence in present-day school administration.* Unpublished dissertation, Tucson, AZ: University of Arizona.

Padró, F. F. (1988b). *Quality circles and their existence in present-day high schools.* Unpublished doctoral dissertation, University of Arizona, Tucson, AZ.

Padró, F. F. (2004). *Statistical handbook on the social safety net.* Westport: Greenwood Publishers.

Padró, F. F. (2009). Deming's system of profound knowledge and its application to higher education institutions. *Journal for Quality Progress, 32*(1), 10–14.

Padró, F. F. (2015). Quality in primary and secondary education. In S. M. Dahlgaard-Park (Ed.), *The SAGE encyclopedia of quality and the service economy* (pp. 592–596). Thousand Oaks: SAGE.

Padró, F. F., Hawke, M. F., & Hawke, L. M. (2016). Assessment and quality: Policy-steering and the making of a *deus ex machina*. In Bower & P. L. Thomas (Eds.), *De-testing and de-grading schools: Authentic alternatives to accountability and standardization* (Revised ed., pp. 33–50). New York: Peter Lang.

Pagliano, P., & Gillies, R. M. (2015). Inclusive practices. In A. Ashman (Ed.), *Education for inclusion and diversity* (5th ed., pp. 131–161). Melbourne: Pearson.

Palmer, S. B., Wehmeyer, M. L., & Shogren, K. A. (2017). The development of self-determination during childhood. In M. L. Wehmeyer, K. A. Shogren, T. D. Little, & S. J. Lopez (Eds.), *Development of self-determination through the life-course* (Ch. 6, pp. 71–88). Dordrecht: Springer.

Panjwani, F. (2016). Towards an overlapping consensus: Muslim teachers' views on fundamental British values. *Journal of Education for Teaching, 42*(3), 329–340. Special issue: Fundamental British Values.

Pap, G. (2013). Az állampolgárság intézményének eredetéről. Publicationes Universitatis Miskolcinensis. Sectio Juridica et Politica. *Tomus, XXXI,* 93–101.p.

Papandrea, M.-R. (2012). Social media, public school teachers, and the first amendment. *North Carolina Law Review, 90,* 1597–1642.

Parent, M. M., & Deephouse, D. L. (2007). A case study of stakeholder identification and prioritization by managers. *Journal of Business Ethics, 75,* 1–23.

Parker, C. (2010). Forum: Philosophical legal ethics, morals and jurisprudence. *Legal Ethics, 13*(2), 165–208.

Parker, D., & Kirkpatrick, C. (2005). Privatisation in developing countries: A review of the evidence and the policy lessons. *The Journal of Development Studies, 41*(4), 513–541.

Parsons, T. (1962). The law and social control. In W. M. Evan (Ed.), *Law and Sociology.* New York: Free Press.

Parsons, T. (1964). *Sociological theory and modern society*. New York: Free Press.

Parsons, T. (1976). Social structure and the symbolic media of interchange. In P. M. Blau (Ed.), *Approaches to the study of social structure*. London: Open Books.

Parsons, T. (1978). Law as an intellectual stepchild. In H. M. Johnson (Ed.), *Social system and legal process*. San Francisco: Jossey-Bass.

Paul, A. M. (2010, October). It's not me, it's you. *New York Times*. http://www.nytimes.com/2012/10/07/opinion/sunday/intelligence-and-the-stereotype-threat.html?nl=opinion&emc=edit_ty_20121008&_r=0

Paul v. British Columbia (Forest Appeals Commission), [2003] 2 S.C.R. 585.

Pawley, H., & Tennant, G. (2008). Student perceptions of their IEP targets. *Support for Learning, 23*(4), 183–186. https://doi.org/10.1111/j.1467-9604.2008.00392.x.

Payne, L. (2009). Twenty years on: The implementation of the UN convention on the rights of the child in the United Kingdom. *Children & Society, 23*, 149–155.

Pazey, B. L., Schalock, R. L., Schaller, J., & Burkett, J. (2016). Incorporating quality of life concepts into educational reform: Creating real opportunities for students with disabilities in the 21st century. *Journal of Disability Policy Studies, 27*(2), 96–105. https://doi.org/10.1177/1044207315604364.

Pearce, G. R. (1998). Teaching legal ethics seriously: Legal ethics as the most important subject in law school. *Loyola University Chicago Law Journal, 29*(4), 719–739.

Pelletier, R., Handal, B., Khalil, J., & Francis, T. (2015). Cyberbullying – When does a school authority's liability in Tort end? *The Western Australian Jurist, 6*, 93.

Pennsylvania Association for Retarded Children (PARC) v. the Commonwealth of Pennsylvania 343 F. Supp. 279 (1972).

Pepler, D. J., & Craig, W. M. (1995). A peek behind the fence: Naturalistic observations of aggressive children with remote audiovisual recording. *Developmental Psychology, 31*(4), 548–553.

Perlman, A. M. (2015). A behavioral theory of ethics. *Indiana Law Journal, 9*, 1639–1669.

Perry-Hazan, L., & Birnhack, M. (2016). The hidden human rights curriculum of surveillance cameras in schools: Due process, privacy and trust. *Cambridge Journal of Education, 48*(1), 47–64.

Personal Injuries (Civil Claims) Act 2003 (NT).

Personal Injuries (Liabilities and Damages) Act 2003 (NT).

Personal Values and Commitment GTCS, 2012: General Teaching Council for Scotland. (2012). *The standards for leadership and management*. http://www.gtcs.org.uk/web/FILES/the-standards/standards-for-leadership-and-management-1212.pdf. Accessed 07 Mar 2017.

Peter W v. San Francisco Unified Sch. Dist., 131 Cal. Rptr. 854 (Cal. Ct. App. 1976).

Peter, S. J. (2010). The heterodoxy of student voice: Challenges to identity in the sociology of disability and education. *British Journal of Sociology of Education, 31*(5), 591–602.

Peterkin, T. (2016, April 2). Revealed: What can happen when a named person reports on your children. *The Scotsman* [Online]. Retrieved from http://www.scotsman.com/news/revealed-what-can-happen-when-a-named-person-reports-on-your-children-1-4089077

Peters, S. J. (2007). 'Education for all?' A historical analysis of international inclusive education policy and individuals with disabilities. *Journal of Disability Policy Studies, 18*(2), 98–108.

Peters, S. J. (2010). The heterodoxy of student voice: Challenges to identity in the sociology of disability and education. *British Journal of Sociology of Education, 31*(5), 591–602. https://doi.org/10.1080/01425692.2010.500092.

Pfeiffer, W., & Jones, J. E. (1975). *A handbook of structured experiences for human relations training.* La Jolla: University Associates.

Phelps v Hillingdon London Borough Council [1999] 1 W.L.R. 500.

Phelps v London Borough of Hillingdon [2001] 2 AC 619.

Phillips, R. (2003). Stakeholder legitimacy. *Business Ethics Quarterly, 13*(1), 25–41.

Pierce, R. J. (1988). Two problems in administrative law: Political polarity on the district of Columbia circuit and judicial deterrence of agency rulemaking. *Duke Law Journal, 37,* 300–328.

Pinheiro, P. S. (2006). *Word report on violence against children.* Geneve: United Nations Publishing Service.

Pittarello, A., Leib, M., Gordon-Hecker, T., & Shalvi, S. (2015). Justifications shape ethical blind spots. *Psychological Science, 26*(6), 794–804.

Plessy v. Ferguson, 163 U.S. 537 (1896).

Plowden. (1967). *Children and their primary schools Report of the central advisory council for education (England).* London: HMSO.

Poed, S., Cologon, K., & Jackson, R. (2017, October). Gatekeeping and restrictive practices with students with disability: Results of an Australian survey, paper delivered at *Inclusive Education Summit.* Adelaide. http://allmeansall.org.au/wp-content/uploads/2017/10/TIES-4.0-20172.pdf

Polanyi, K. (2001/1944). *The great transformation: The political and economic origins of our times.* Boston: Beacon Press.

'Police stats reveal students taking weapons into Hunter schools' *ABC Online,* 18 May 2015. http://www.abc.net.au/news/2015-05-18/police-stats-reveal-students-taking-weapons-into-hunter-schools/6476620

Pollitt, C. (2004, November 3). *From there to here, from now till then: Buying and borrowing public management reforms.* Paper presented at CLAD ninth international conference, Madrid.

Popkewitz, T. (1994). Professionalization in teaching and teacher education: Some notes on its history, ideology, and potential. *Teaching and Teacher Education, 10*(1), 1–14.

Popper, K. (2002/1959). *The logic of scientific discovery.* London: Routledge.

Porter, T., & Ronit, K. (2006). Self-regulation as policy process: The multiple and criss-crossing stages of private rule-making. *Policy Sciences, 39,* 41–72.

Portwood, S. (1998). The impact of individuals' characteristics and experiences on their definitions of child maltreatment. *Child Abuse & Neglect. 22*(5), 437–452. Professionals. St Leonards: Allen & Unwin.

Power, M. (2010). *Organized uncertainty: Designing a world of risk management.* Oxford: Oxford University Press.

Praisner, C. L. (2003). Attitudes of elementary school principals toward the inclusion of students with disabilities. *Exceptional Children, 69*, 135–145.

Prince Alfred College Incorporated v ADC [2016] HCA 37.

Pring, R. (2004). The aim of education: Liberal or vocational? In R. Pring (Ed.), *Philosophy of education: Aims, theory, common sense, and research.* London: Continuum.

Prout, A., & Hallett, C. (2003). Introduction. In C. Hallett & A. Prout (Eds.), *Hearing the voices of children: Social policy for a new century* (pp. 1–8). London: Routledge Falmer.

Purvis v New South Wales (Department of Education and Training) 2003 217 CLR 92 (Austl.).

Pufpaff, L. A., McIntosh, C. E., Thomas, C., Elam, M., & Irwin, M. K. (2015). Meeting the health care needs of students with severe disabilities in the school setting: Collaboration between school nurses and special education teachers. *Psychology in the Schools, 52*(7), 683–701.

Pulkkinen, L. (2012). *Goals for the decade of childhood based on ten pillars of a good childhood: A Finnish perspective.* http://www.allianceforchildhood.eu/files/Book2013/QOC13-Chapter5-Pulkinnen.pdf. Accessed 07 Mar 2017.

Purvis v State of New South Wales (Department of Education and Training) (2003) 217 CLR 92 ("Purvis").

Quennerstedt, A., & Quennerstedt, M. (2014). Researching children's rights in education: Sociology of childhood encountering educational theory. *British Journal of Sociology of Education, 35*(1), 115–132.

Queensland Government. (2015). *Queensland child safety practice manual.* Brisbane: Department of Communities, Child Safety and Disabilities.

Queensland Catholic Education Commission. (2016). *Annual report 2016.* Queensland: Author.

Quetelet, A. (1835). Sur l homme et le developpement de ses facultes ou essai de physique sociale, 2 vol., Paris, Bachelier (Republished Paris, Fayard, 1991); translated as A treatise on man and the development of his faculties, London, 1842.

Quinn, B. (1999). *Counterpoint: An analysis of Canadian native educational academic discourse.* Ph.D. thesis, Department of Education Foundations, University of Alberta, Edmonton.

R v Brown 1994 1 AC 212 (United Kingdom).

R. v. Côté, [1996] 3 S.C.R. 139.

R. v. Powley, [2003] 2 S.C.R. 207.

Radin, B. A., & Coffee, J. N. (1993). A critique of TQM: Problems of implementation in the public sector. *Public Administration Quarterly, 17*(1), 42–54.

Raethel, S. (1996, April 11). Pupils sue over missing lessons. *Sydney Morning Herald*, p. 3.

Rago, W. V. (1994). Adapting Total Quality Management (TQM) to government: Another point of view, *Public Administration Review, 54*(1), 61–64.

Ramsay, I. (1988). Educational negligence and the legalisation of education. *University of New South Wales Law Journal, 11*, 184–218.

Ramsay, I., & Shorten, A. (1996). *Education and the law*. Sydney: Butterworths.

Ramsay v Larsen. (1964). 111 CLR 16.

Rattigan, K. (2004). The Purvis decision: A case for amending the disability discrimination act 1992. *Melbourne University Law Review, 28*(2), 532–563.

Rayner, M. (1996). Student's rights. *Education, law and the future: Proceedings of the fifth ANZELA national conference* (pp. 19–30). Brisbane: Australia and New Zealand Education Law Association (Inc.) QLD Chapter.

Raz, J. (1979). *The authority of law*. Oxford: Clarendon Press.

Raz, J. (1999). *Practical reasons and norms*. Oxford: Oxford University Press.

Regan, M. C. (2003). Ethics, law firms, and legal education. *Maine Law Review, 55*(2), 363–372.

Regan v Australian Capital Territory Schools Authority [2003] ACTSC 47 (13 June 2003).

Rennie, L., Venville, G., & Wallace, J. (2012). *Knowledge that counts in a global community*. Abingdon: Routledge.

Restorative Practices Australia. www.restorativepractices.org.au

Revell, L., & Bryan, H. (2016). Calibrating fundamental British values: How head teachers are approaching appraisal in the light of the Teachers' Standards 2012, Prevent and the Counter-Terrorism and Security Act, 2015. *Journal of Education for Teaching: International Research and Pedagogy, 42*(3), 341–353.

Reyes-Gonzalez v NSW TAFE Commission [2003] NSWADT 22 ('Reyes-Gonzalez').

Reynolds, S. J. (2006). Moral awareness and ethical predispositions: Investigating the role of individual differences in the recognition of moral issues. *Journal of Applied Psychology, 91*(1), 233–243.

Reynolds v Haines (SC (NSW), Common Law Division, Master McLaughlin, BC9305229, 27 October 1993, unreported).

Re F (Mental Patient Sterilisation) 1990 2 AC 1 (United Kingdom).

Rhode, D., & Luban, D. (2008). *Legal ethics* (5th ed.). New York: Foundation Press.

Richards, K. (2011). What makes juvenile offenders different from adult offenders? *Trends and Issues in Crime and Criminal Justice, 409*, 1–8.

Richards, K., & Lee, M. (2013). Beyond the 'three dogmas of juvenile justice': A response to Skaff, Kemp, Sternesky McGovern, and Fantacone (2016). Educator and parent views of the effectiveness of individualized learning plans for students with disabilities. *Career Development and Transition for Exceptional Individuals, 39*(2), 28–38.

Riehl, C. J. (2000). The principal's role in creating inclusive schools for diverse students: A review of normative, empirical, and critical literature on the practice of educational administration. *Review of Educational Research, 70*(1), 55–81. https://doi.org/10.3102/00346543070001055.

Rieser, R. (2012). Inclusive education: A human right. In M. Cole (Ed.), *Education, equality and human rights; issues of gender, 'race', sexuality, disability and social class* (3rd ed., pp. 190–216). Oxon: Routledge.

Riley, P. (2009). An adult attachment perspective on the student–teacher relationship & classroom management difficulties. *Teaching and Teacher Education, 25*(5), 626–635.

Riley, P. (2017). The Australian principal occupational, safety and well-being survey: 2016. Institute for Positive Psychology & Education, Faculty of Education & Arts, Australian Catholic University, Fitzroy.

Rioux, M. (2013). Disability rights in education. In L. Florian (Ed.), *The Sage handbook of special education: Volume 1* (2nd ed., pp. 131–147). London: Sage.

Rioux, M. H., & Riddle, C. A. (2011). Values in disability policy and law: Equality. In M. H. Rioux, L. A. Basser, & M. Jones (Eds.), *Critical perspectives on human rights and disability law* (pp. 37–55). Lieden: Martinus Nijhoff Publishers.

Risler, E., & O'Rourke, T. (2009). Thinking exit and entry: Exploring outcomes of Georgia's juvenile justice educational programs. *The Journal of Correctional Education, 60*, 225–239.

Riva, M. G. (1993). *L'abuso educativo. Teoria del trauma e pedagogia.* Milano: Unicopli.

Riva, M. G. (2014). Violence interrogates adult education today. A radical and critical reflection. In B. Käpplinger, N. Lichte, E. Haberzeth, & C. Kulmus (Eds.), *Changing configurations of adult education in transitional times* (pp. 642–653). Berlin: ESREA - European Society for Research on the Education of Adults.

Roads and Traffic Authority of New South Wales v Dederer. (2007). 234 CLR 330.

Roads and Traffic Authority v Royal [2008] HCA 19.

Robbennolt, J. K., & Sternlight, J. R. (2013). Behavioral legal ethics. *Arizona State Law Journal, 45*, 1107–1182.

Robbins Herbal Institute v Federal Commissioner of Taxation. (1923). 32 CLR 457.

Robinson, A. (2014). *Foundations for youth justice: Positive approaches to practice.* Bristol: Policy Press.

Robinson, J. (2015). The experience of the child witness: Legal and psychological issues. *International Journal of Law and Psychiatry, 42*, 168–176. Retrieved from https://doi.org/10.1016/j.ijlp.2015.08.022

Robinson, V., Hohepa, M., & Lloyd, C. (2007). *School leadership and student outcomes: Identifying what works and why.* Melbourne: Australian Council of Education Leaders.

Robinson, R., Molenda, M., & Rezabek, L. (2008). Facilitating learning. In A. Januszewski & M. Molenda (Eds.), *Educational technology: A definition with commentary* (pp. 15–48). New York: Lawrence Erlbaum Associates.

Rodger, N. A. M. (1988). *The wooden world: An anatomy of the Georgian navy.* London: Harper Collins.

Rogers, W. V. H. (2010). *Winfield & Jolowicz Tort* (18th ed.). London: Sweet & Maxwell.

Romano, N., Casey, K., & Daro, D. (1990). *Schools and child abuse: A national survey of principals' attitudes, beliefs and practices*. Chicago: National Centre on Child Abuse Prevention Research.

Rooney, T. (2010). Trusting children: How do surveillance technologies alter a child's experience of trust, risk and responsibility? *Surveillance & Society, 7*(3/4), 344.

Rosewater, A., & Goodmark, L. S. (2007). *Steps toward safety: Improving systemic and community responses for families experiencing domestic violence*. Book Gallery. Book.

Rothenbacher, F. (2002). *The European population 1850–1945*. London: Palgrave Macmillan.

Rothman, R. (2011). *Something in common: The common core standards and the next chapter in American education*. Cambridge, MA: Harvard Education Press.

Rothstein, B., & Teorell, J. (2008). What is quality of government? A theory of impartial government institutions. *Governance: An International Journal of Policy, Administration, and Institutions, 21*(2), 165–190.

Rotunda, R. D. (2002). *Professional responsibility* (6th ed.). St. Paul: West.

Rousseau, J.-J. (1762). Du contrat social ou Principes du droit politique. Paris. http://classiques.uqac.ca/classiques/Rousseau_jj/contrat_social/Contrat_social.pdf

Rowland, D. (1999). Negligence, professional competence and computer systems. *Journal of Information Law and Technology, 20*. Available at http://www2.warwick.ac.uk/fac/soc/law/elj/jilt/1999_2/rowland/#fnb3

Royal Commission on Aboriginal Peoples (RCAP). (1996). *Report of the royal commission on aboriginal peoples*. 5 vols. Ottawa: Canada Communication Group.

Ruijs, N. M., & Peetsma, T. T. (2009). Effects of inclusion on students with and without special educational needs reviewed. *Educational Research Review, 4*(2), 67–79.

Russo, C. J. (2012). *Reutter's the law of public education* (9th ed.). St. Paul: Foundation Press.

Ruszoly, J. (1997). Európa Jogtörténete (History of European Law). Püski Kiadó Kft. Budapest.

Ryan, J. (2010). Establishing inclusion in a new school: The role of principal leadership. *Exceptionality Education International, 20*(2), 6–24.

S on behalf of M & C v Director General, Department of Education & Training [2001] NSWADT 43 ("M & C").

Sabatier, P. A. (1986). Top-down and bottom-up approaches to implementation research: A critical analysis and suggested synthesis. *Journal of Public Policy, 6*(1), 21–48.

Sabatier, P. A. (1988). An advocacy coalition framework of policy change and the role of policy-oriented learning therein. *Policy Sciences, 21*, 129–168.

Sachs, J. (2003). Teacher professional standards: Controlling or developing teaching? *Teachers and Teaching, 9*(2), 175–186.

Sahney, S. (2016). Use of multiple methodologies for developing a customer-oriented model of total quality management in higher education. *International Journal of Educational Management, 30*(3), 326–353.

Sahney, S., Banwet, D. K., & Karunes, S. (2004). A SERVQUAL and QFD approach to total quality education: A student perspective. *International Journal of Productivity and Performance Management, 53*(2), 143–166.

Salidu, M. (1994). Discrimination and schools: The legislation and its effects. In D. Stewart (Ed.), *Third annual conference of the Australian and New Zealand education law association* (pp. 173–193). Brisbane: Qld University of Technology Press.

Salisbury, C. L. (2006). Principals' perspectives on inclusive elementary schools. *Research and Practice for Persons with Severe Disabilities, 31*, 70–82.

Sallis, E. (2002). *Total quality in education* (3rd ed.). London: Kogan Page.

Salmond, J. (1907). Salmond on Torts (1st ed.). London: Sweet & Maxwell. Schools should be sued for cyberbullying: Experts. *Sydney Morning Herald*, August 15 2013.

Saltmann, K. J. (2007). *Capitalizing on disaster: Taking and breaking public schools.* London: Paradigm Publishers.

Sami-Nair. (2013). Pour une herméneutique de la Charia (For the hermeneutics of the Saría), the introduction by the member of the scientific council of the Res Publica Foundation, which was presented at the seminar "What does it mean to us: Sária?" on 15 April 2013. http://www.fondation-res-publica.org/Pour-une-hermeneutique-de-la-Charia_a723.html

Sampson, G. (1921). *English for the English: A chapter on national education* (Current Edition 1952). Cambridge: Cambridge University Press.

Samuels, C. (2014). Landmark special ed. case confirming 'zero reject' rule marks 25 years. *Education Week Blog*, Published December 8, 2014. Retrieved April 29, 2017, from http://blogs.edweek.org/edweek/speced/2014/12/landmark_special_ed_case_confi.html

Sanchez, L. (2004, May 18). Before Brown. *The San Diego Union-Tribune* [Electronicversion]. Retrieved April 28, 2017, from http://signonsandiego.com/uniontrib/20050518news_1n18grove.html.

Santiago, M. (2013). Mendez v. Westminster, 1947: Teaching a new chapter of history. *The Phi Delta Kappan, 94*(6), 35–38.

Sarantakos, S. (2005). *Social research* (3rd ed.). Basingstoke: Palgrave Macmillan.

Sarre, R. (2008). Fairness in trading: Trade practices law and school governance. *AISSA School Board Governance Journal, 11*, 1–4.

Satir, V. (1994). *Peoplemaking.* London: Souvenir Press.

Sauer, J. S., & Jorgenson, C. M. (2016). Still caught in the continuum: A critical analysis of least restrictive environment and its effect on placement of students with intellectual disability. *Inclusion, 4*(2), 56–74.

Saunders, B. J., & Goddard, C. (2002). *The role of mass media in facilitating community education and child abuse prevention strategies.* Melbourne: Australian Institute of Family Studies.

Saunders, B. J., & Goddard, C. (Eds.). (2009). *Physical punishment in childhood: The rights of the child.* London: Wiley-Blackwell.

Schraven, J., & Jolly, J. L. (2010). Section 504 in American public schools: An ongoing response to change. *American Educational History Journal, 37*(1/2), 419–436.

Schiro, M. S. (2013). *Curriculum theory: Conflicting visions and enduring concerns.* London: Sage.

Scott, D. A. (2012). *Improving the measurement and surveillance of child abuse in Queensland emergency departments.* Doctoral dissertation, Queensland University of Technology.

Scottish Government. (2016). *Engagement to implement named person.* Retrieved from http://news.gov.scot/news/engagement-to-implement-named-person

Scottish Government. (n.d.). *GIRFEC briefings for practitioners: 8 of 8: Single agency and integrated chronologies.* Retrieved from http://www.gov.scot/Resource/0039/00399456.pdf

Seidman, E., Allen, L., Aber, J. L., Mitchell, C., & Feinman, J. (1994). The impact of school transitions in early adolescence on the self-system and social context of poor urban youth. *Child Development, 65*, 507–522.

Senate Employment, Workplace Relations and Education Committee, Parliament of Australia, Education of students with disabilities (2002).

Senate, Employment and Training Reference Committee. (1998). *A class act.* Senate Inquiry into the Teaching Profession.

Seneca Lucius Annaeus: Epistulae morales ad Lucilium, Libri XVII-XVIII Epistula CVI. http://www.intratext.com/IXT/LAT0230/_P2Y.HTM

Seong, Y., Wehmeyer, M. L., Palmer, S. B., & Little, T. D. (2015). Effects of the self-directed individualized education program on self-determination and transition of adolescents with disabilities. *Career Development and Transition for Exceptional Individuals, 38*(3), 132–141. https://doi.org/10.1177/2165143414544359.

Seymour, D. T. (1993). *On Q: Causing quality in higher education.* New York: Macmillan.

Sezer, O., Gino, F., & Bazerman, M. H. (2015). Ethical blind spots: Explaining unintentional unethical behavior. *Current Opinion in Psychology, 6*, 77–81.

Shaddock, A., MacDonald, N., Hook, J., Giorcelli, L., & Arthur-Kelly, M. (2009). *Disability, diversity and tides that lift all boats: Review of special education in the ACT.* Chiswick: Services Initiative.

Shaddock, A., Packer, P., & Roy, A. (2015). *Report of the expert panel on students with complex needs and challenging behaviour.* Canberra, Australia: Authors. https://www.education.act.gov.au/__data/assets/pdf_file/0003/856254/Attach-4-Expert-Panel-Report-Web.pdf

Shakeshaft, C. (2004). *Educator sexual misconduct: A synthesis of existing literature.* Washington, DC: U.S. Department of Education, Department of the Under Secretary, Policy and Program Studies Service.

Shakeshaft, C. (2013). Knowing the warning signs of educator sexual misconduct. *Phi Delta Kappan, 94*(5), 8–13.

Shapiro, S. A. (2005). *Pragmatic administrative law,* Wake forest legal studies research papers series. Research paper no, 05-02. Retrieved from http://ssrn.com/abstract=653784

Shariff, S., & Hoff, D. L. (2007). Cyberbullying: Clarifying the legal boundaries for school supervision in cyberspace. *International Journal of Cyber Criminology, 1*(1), 76.

Sharma, U., & Chow, E. W. S. (2008). The attitudes of Hong Kong primary school principals towards integrated education. *Asia Pacific Education Review, 9,* 380–3781.

Sharpe, A., & Arsenault, J.-F. (2009). *Investing in aboriginal education in Canada: An economic perspective.* Ottawa: Canadian Policy Research Networks. Retrieved 26 September 2016 http://www.cprn.org/documents/51980_EN.pdf

Shelden, D. L., Angell, M. E., Stoner, J. B., & Roseland, B. D. (2010). School principals' influence on trust: Perspectives of mothers of children with disabilities. *The Journal of Educational Research, 103,* 159–170. https://doi.org/10.1080/00220670903382921.

Shelley, M. (1991). Report on the national consultations with people with a disability. In *Disability advisory council of Australia.* Canberra: Australian Government Printing Service.

Shoemaker, D. (2010). Responsibility, agency, and cognitive disability. In E. Feder Kittay & L. Carlson (Eds.), *Cognitive disability and its challenge to moral philosophy* (Ch. 12, pp. 201–224). West Sussex: Wiley.

Shrimpton v Hertfordshire County Council. (1911). 104 LT 145.

Siaroff, A. (1999). Corporatism in 24 industrial democracies: Meaning and measurement. *European Journal of Political Research, 36,* 175–205.

Sievwright v State of Victoria [2012] FCA 118 ("Sievwright").

Simeonsson, R. J., Leonardi, M., Lollar, D., Bjorck-Akesson, E., Hollenweger, J., & Martinuzzi, A. (2003). Applying the International Classification of Functioning, Disability and Health (ICF) to measure childhood disability. *Disability and Rehabilitation, 25*(11–12), 602–610.

Simmonds, R. (2005). Is our right to privacy at risk in a technology world? In *Free speech, privacy and property rights in education* (pp. 11–35). Fremantle: Promaco Conventions Pty Ltd.

Simons, C., & Robinson, S. (2014). *Strengthening participation of children and young people with disability in advocacy: Issues paper.* Report prepared by Children with Disability Australia for the Australian Government Department of Social Services. Retrieved from http://www.cyda.org.au/strengthening-participation

Simpson, M. (2015). *Social networking nightmares.* Retrieved from www.nea.org/home/38324.htm

Sinclair, T., & Hodgkinson, K. (2001). Subjecting the initial teacher training curriculum for England and Wales to the test of child protection. *Teacher Development, 5*(1), 75–86.

Sinclair, M. F., Christenson, S. L., Evelo, D. L., & Hurley, C. M. (1998). Dropout prevention for high-risk youth with disabilities: Efficacy of a sustained school engagement procedure. *Exceptional Children, 65*(1), 7–21.

Sisters of the Holy Child Jesus at Old Westbury v. Corwin, 29 N.Y.S.3d 736 (N.Y. App. Div. 2016).

Skaff, L. F., Kemp, J. N., Sternesky McGovern, L. A., & Fantacone, J. M. (2016). Educator and parent views of the effectiveness of individualized learning plans for students with disabilities. *Career Development and Transition for Exceptional Individuals, 39*(2), 68–78.

Skinner, B. F. (1974). *About behaviourism.* New York: Alfred A. Knopf.

Skinner, R. R., & Kuenzi, J. J. (2015). *Reauthorization of the elementary and secondary education act: Highlights of the every student succeeds act* (Report no. R44297). Washington, DC: Congressional Research Service.

Slapper, G. (2011). *How the law works* (2nd ed.). Abingdon/Oxfordshire: Routledge.

Slaughter, D. (2010). *Improving transition outcomes for youth involved in the juvenile justice system: Practical considerations.* Info Brief, 25, 1–12. Washington, DC: National Collaborative on Workforce and Disability for Youth.

Slee, P. (1998). Bullying in Australian Schools. (A. Knott, & D. Stewart, Eds.). *ANZELA Reporter, 5*(1), 3–6.

Slee, R. (2008). Beyond special and regular schooling? An inclusive education reform agenda. *International Studies in Sociology and Education, 18*(2), 99–116.

Slee, R. (2011a). *The irregular school: Exclusion, schooling and inclusive education.* Abingdon: Routledge.

Slee, R. (2011b). *The irregular school: Exclusion, schooling and inclusive education.* London: Routledge.

Slee, R. (2013). How do we make inclusive education happen when exclusion is a political predisposition? *International Journal of Inclusive Education, 17*(8), 895–907. https://doi.org/10.1080/13603116.2011.602534.

Sluggett v Flinders University of South Australia [2003] FCAFC 27 ('Sluggett').

Smallbone, S., & Wortley, R. (2001). Child sexual abuse in Queensland: Offender characteristics and modus operandi. *Trends and issues in crime and criminal justice 193.* Canberra: Australian Institute of Criminology.

Smith, K. M. (2016). *Investigating transition processes for students with special needs.* Masters dissertation. Retrieved from http://opus.ipfw.edu/cgi/viewcontent.cgi?article=1037&context=grad_research

Smith, S. J., & Okolo, C. (2010). Response to intervention and evidence-based practices: Where does technology fit? *Learning Disability Quarterly, 33*, 257–272.

Smith v. Alameda Cnty. Social Servs. Agency, 153 Cal.Rptr. 712 (Cal. Ct. App. 1979).

Smith v. Robinson, 104 S. Ct. 3457 (1984).

Smyth, K. (1996). An investigation into teachers' knowledge and awareness of child sexual abuse in singe sex national schools in Dublin. *Journal of Child Centred Practice, 3*(1), 23–44.

Sneed, R., May, W., & Stencel, C. (2004). Policy versus practice: Comparison of prescriping therapy and durable medical equipment in medical and educational settings. *Pediatrics, 114*(5), 612–625.

Soustelle, J. (2002). *Daily life of the Aztecs: On the eve of the Spanish conquest.* Mineola: Courier Dover Publications.

Southwark London Borough Council v Williams 1971 Ch 734 (United Kingdom).

Southwick, J. (1997). Can the professions survive under a national competition policy? *Competition law and the professions conference,* Perth, 11 April 1997 online. Available at http://ncp.ncc.gov.au/docs/NCP%20and%20the%20professions%20-%20the%20issues.pdf. Accessed 20 Jan 2018.

Spivakovsky, C. (2017). Governing freedom through risk: Locating the group home in the archipelago of confinement and control. *Punishment & Society, 19*(3), 366–383. https://doi.org/10.1177/1462474517703968.

Squelch, J., & Goldacre, L. (2009). School prospectuses and the potential liability of private schools under section 52 of the trade practices act 1974 (Cth). (J. Cumming, & E. Dickson, Eds.). *International Journal of Law and Education, 14*(1), 39–50.

St. Denis, V. (2002). *Exploring the socio-cultural production of aboriginal identities: Implications for education.* A Ph.D. dissertation, School of Education, Stanford University, Stanford.

Stafford, N. (2004, September). *What can a school do to ensure student and staff wellbeing and safety in light of the Australian high court's decision in Purvis v State of NSW.* Paper presented at the 13th Annual Conference of the Australia and New Zealand Education Law Association, Wellington.

Starr, K. (2012). Problematizing "risk" and the principalship: The risky business of managing rick in schools. *Educational Management Administration & Leadership, 40*(4), 464–479.

State of Victoria (Department of Education and Training). (2017a). *The principles for reduction and elimination of restraint and seclusion in Victorian government schools.* East Melbourne: Author. http://www.education.vic.gov.au/Documents/school/principals/participation/15Principals.pdf

State of Victoria (Department of Education and Training). (2017b). *Restraint of students policy.* East Melbourne: Author. http://www.education.vic.gov.au/school/principals/spag/governance/Pages/restraint.aspx

Steele, L. (2015). *Submission to Senate Community Affairs References Committee Inquiry into violence, abuse and neglect against people with disability in institutional and residential settings, including the gender and age related dimensions, and the particular situation of Aboriginal and Torres Strait Islander people with disability, and culturally and linguistically diverse people with disability,* submission no. 94. https://www.aph.gov.au/Parliamentary_Business/Committees/Senate/Community_Affairs/Violence_abuse_neglect/Submissions

Steele, L. (2016). Court-authorised sterilisation and human rights: Inequality, discrimination and violence against women and girls with disability? *UNSW Law Journal, 39*(3), 1002–1037. http://www.unswlawjournal.unsw.edu.au/sites/default/files/393-4.pdf

Steele, L. (2017). Temporality, disability and institutional violence: Revisiting In re F. *Griffith Law Review, 26*(3), 378–400. https://doi.org/10.1080/10383441.2017.1436368.

Steele, L., & Dowse, L. (2016). Gender, disability rights and violence against medical bodies. *Australian Feminist Studies, 31*(88), 117–124. https://doi.org/10.1080/08164649.2016.1224054.

Sternberg, R. J. (2012a). Ethical drift. *Liberal Education, 98*(3), 58–60.

Sternberg, R. J. (2012b). A model of ethical reasoning. *Review of General Psychology, 16*(4), 319–326.

Stewart, D. (1996). School principals and the law: A study of the legal knowledge needed and held by principals in government schools in Queensland. PhD Unpublished, Queensland University of Technology, Brisbane. Available from National Library of Australia Trove database (24587328).

Stewart, D. (1998). Legalisation of education: Implications for principals' professional knowledge. *Journal of Educational Administration, 36*(2), 129–145.

Stewart, R. B. (2003a). Administrative law in the twenty-first century. *New York University Law Review, 78*(2), 437–460.

Stewart, D. (2003b). Inclusion: How far does a school have to go? Ensuring best practice: The case of 'I'. (K. Lindsay, Ed.). *Australia and New Zealand Journal of Law and Education, 8*(1), 77–86.

Stewart, D., & Cope, B. (1996). Judicious behaviour management. *Education, law and the future: Proceedings of the fifth ANZELA national conference* (pp. 173–180). Brisbane: Australia and New Zealand Education Law Association (Inc.) Qld Chapter.

Stewart, D., & Knott, A. (2002). *Schools, courts and the law: Managing student welfare.* Sydney: Pearson Education Australia.

Stewart, D., & McCann, P. (1999). Educators and the law: Implications for the professional development of school administrators and teachers. *Professional Development in Education, 25*(1), 135–150.

Stewart, P., & Stuhmcke, A. (2009). *Australian principles of Tort law* (4th ed.). Sydney: Federation Press.

Stoddart, E. (2015). The named person: Surveillance and the well-being of children and young people in Scotland. *Surveillance and Society, 13*(1), 102–116.

Stolz, S. M. (2010). *Disability trajectories: Disabled youths' identity development, negotiation of experience and expectation, and sense of agency during transition.* Doctoral dissertation. Retrieved from https://escholarship.org/uc/item/7zg9w5ht

Strahilevitz, M., Harvey, J., & Ariely, D. (2015). Understanding consumer financial behaviour: Spending, saving, investing and debt. *Advances in Consumer Research, 43*, 90–94.

Sugai, G., & Simonsen, B. (2012). *Positive behavioural interventions and supports: History, defining features, and misconceptions.* Center for PBIS & Center for Positive Behavioral Interventions and Supports, University of Connecticut. Retrieved from: http://www.pbis.org/common/pbisresources/publications/PBIS_revisited_June19r_2012.pdf

Sullivan, A., Johnson, B., Owens, L., & Conway, R. (2014). Punish them or engage them? Teachers' views of unproductive student behaviours in the classroom. *Australian Journal of Teacher Education, 39*(6), 43.

Sundell, K. (1997). Child care personnel's failure to report child maltreatment: Some Swedish evidence. *Child Abuse & Neglect, 21*(1), 93–105.

Supreme Court Act 1986 (Vic).

Sutherland, E. E. (2016, September 19). Beyond the named person service. *The Journal of the Law Society of Scotland*. http://www.journalonline.co.uk/Magazine/61-9/1022210.aspx

Svensson, I., Lundberg, I., & Jacobson, C. (2001). The prevalence of reading and spelling difficulties among inmates of institutions for compulsory care of juvenile delinquents. *Dyslexia: An International Journal, 7*, 62–76.

Swann. (1985). *Education for all report of the committee of enquiry*. Cmnd 9453. London: HMSO.

Swift, J. A., Ross, J. E., & Omachonu, V. K. (1998). *Principles of total quality* (2nd ed.). Boca Raton: St. Lucie Press.

Swiss, J. E. (1992). Adapting Total Quality Management (TQM) to government. *Public Administration Review, 52*(4), 356–362.

Swiss Teachers Association (Dachverband Lehrerinnen und Lehrer Schweiz). (2008). *Gelingensbedingungen für eine integrierte Förderung aller*. https://www.lch.ch/publikationen/stellungnahmen/dokument/gelingensbedingungen_fuer_eine_integrierte_foerderung_fuer_alle/

Tabb, W. K. (1995). *The post-war Japanese system: Cultural economy and economic transformation*. New York: Oxford University Press.

Tague, N. R. (2005). *The quality toolbox* (2nd ed.). Milwaukee: American Society for Quality Press.

Tamanaha, B. Z. (2012, December). The history and the elements of the rule of law. *Singapore Journal of Legal Studies*, 232–247.

Tan, J. (2011). Education and children's rights. In P. Jones & G. Walker (Eds.), *Children's rights in practice* (pp. 109–123). London: Sage.

Taylor, F. W. (1911). *The principles of scientific management*. Mineola: Dover Publications.

Taylor, A. S. (1997). From survival to reflection: Locating child protection in teacher education. In J. Davies & P. Garner (Eds.), *At the crossroads: Special education needs and teacher education* (pp. 61–74). London: David Fulton Publishers.

Taylor, A. (1998). Hostages to fortune: The abuse of children in care. In G. Hunt (Ed.), *Whistleblowing in the social services: Public accountability and professional practice*. London: Arnold.

Taylor, A. S., & Hodgkinson, K. (2001). Subjecting the initial teacher training curriculum for England and Wales to the test of child protection. *Teacher Development, 5*(1), 75–86.

Teacher Education Ministerial Advisory Group. (2014, December). *Action now: Classroom ready teachers*.

Teh, K. (2014). The case for legal literacy for educators. *Australian & New Zealand education law association 23rd annual conference* (pp. 387–412). Adelaide: ANZELA.

Teh, M. (2008). Schools and the law: Legal issues internationally with implications for school leaders in Singapore. PhD Published, University of Southern Queensland, Toowoomba. Retrieved from http://eprints.usq.edu.au/4439/. Available from National Library of Australia Trove database (153062505)

Teh, M. (2009). *Principals and legal risk: Complacency or concern?* Paper presentated as the 18th Annual Conference of the Australia and New Zealand Education Law Association, Melbourne.

Tenbrunsel, A. E., & Messick, D. M. (2004). Ethical fading: The role of self-deception in unethical behavior. *Social Justice Research, 17*, 223–236.

Tenbrunsel, A. E., Diekman, K. A., Wade-Benzoni, K. A., & Bazerman, M. H. (2010). The ethical mirage: A temporal explanation as to why we are not as ethical as we think we are. *Research in Organizational Behavior, 30*, 153–173.

Test, D. W., Fowler, C. H., Richter, S. M., White, J., Mazzotti, V., Walker, A. R., Kohler, P., & Kortering, L. (2009). Evidence-based practices in secondary transition. *Career Development for Exceptional Individuals, 32*(2), 115–128.

The Christian Institute and others (Appellants) v The Lord Advocate (Respondent) (Scotland) [2016] UKSC 51. Retrieved from https://www.supremecourt.uk/cases/uksc-2015-0216.html

The Directorate for Children, Older People and Social Care Services.

The Family Educational Rights and Privacy Act (FERPA). (20 U.S.C. § 1232g; 34 CFR Part 99)

The Institute for Education Leadership Ontario. (2013). *The Ontario leadership framework-a school and system leader's guide to putting Ontario's leadership framework into action*. Revised.

The International NGO Council on Violence Against Children. (2016). *10 Years on: Global progress & delay in ending violence against children – The rhetoric & the reality*.

The National Autistic Society. (2015). *Choosing a school in England*. Retrieved from http://www.autism.org.uk/about/in-education/choosing-school/england.aspx

The Royal Commission on Child Sexual Abuse. http://www.childabuseroyalcommission.gov.au/

The text of Secretary-General. Kofi Annan's statement to the opening of the World Conference of Ministers Responsible for Youth, in Lisbon, on 8 August. http://www.un.org/press/en/1998/19980810.sgsm6670.html

The United Nations. Convention on the Rights of the Child. Treaty Series, 1577, 3.

The Wallace Foundation, Perspective: The Making of the principal: Five lessons in leadership training, June 2012, New York.

Thoman, D. H. (2013). Testifying minors: Pre-trial strategies to reduce anxiety in child witnesses. *Nevada Law Journal, 14*, 236–267. Retrieved from http://scholars.law.unlv.edu/cgi/viewcontent.cgi?article=1532&context=nlj&sei-redir=1&referer=https%3A%2F%2Fscholar.google.com.au%2Fscholar%3Fstart%3D10%26q%3Dcourt%2B%2522children%2Bas%2Bwitnesses%2522%26hl%3Den%26as_sdt%3D0%2C5%26as_ylo%3D2013%26as_yhi%3D2017#search=%22court%20children%20as%20witnesses%22

Thompson, D. F. (1987). *Political ethics and public office*. Cambridge, MA: Harvard University Press.

Thompson, D. F. (2013). Political ethics. In H. LaFollette (Ed.), *International encyclopedia of ethics*. Oxford: Wiley-Blackwell.

Thornhauser, T., & Passmore, D. L. (2006). ISO 9000 in education: A comparison between the United States and England. *Research in Comparative & International Education, 1*(2), 156–173.

Thornton, M. (2009). Disabling discrimination legislation: The High court and judicial activism. *Australian Journal of Human Rights, 15*(1), 1–28.

Thorsen, D. E. (2010). The neoliberal challenge: What is neoliberalism? *Contemporary Readings in Law and Social Justice, 2*(2), 188–214.

Timmermans, S., & Epstein, S. (2010). A world of standards but not standards world: Towards a sociology of standards and standardization. *Annual Review of Sociology, 36*, 69–89.

Timothy W. v. Rochester School District, 875F.2d954 (1st Cir. 1989).

Tokic, S. (2014). Rethinking educational malpractice: Are educators rock stars? *Brigham Young University Education and Law Journal, 3*(1), 105–133.

Torres v Little Flower, 485 N.Y.S.2d 15 (N.Y.1984).

Tough, P. (2012). *How children succeed: Grit curiosity and the hidden power of character*. New York: Random House.

Trade Practices Act 1974 (Cth).

Trimble, A. (2017). Education law, schools and school principals: A mixed methods study of the impact of law on Tasmanian school principals. PhD Unpublished, University of Tasmania, Launceston.

Trimble, A., Cranston, N., & Allen, J. (2012). School principals and Education Law: What do they know, what they need to know? *Leading & Managing, 18*(2), 46–61.

Trimmer, K. (2003). *Review of the West Australian department of education regulatory framework*. Paper read at Australian Association of Research in Education Conference, Auckland.

Trimmer, K. (2011). *Non-compliance by school principals: The effects of experience, stakeholder characteristics and governance mechanisms on reasoned risk-taking in decision-making*. Thesis for award of Doctor of Business Administration, Curtin University of Technology, Australia.

Triseliotis, J. P., Sellick, C., & Short, R. (1995). *Foster care: Theory and practice*. London: Batsford.

Tronc, K. (1996). *You, your school and the law*. Brisbane: Fernfawn Publications.

Tronc, K. (1999a). *Educational malpractice. Australian professional liability–education 32-000 at 20, 303*. Sydney: CCH Australia.

Tronc, K. (1999b, September). *Schools and the law: Some backdates, updates and mandates*. Paper presented at the 8th Annual Conference of the Australia and New Zealand Education Law Association, Brisbane.

Tronc, K., & Sleigh, D. (1989). *Australian teachers and the law*. Sydney: Butterworths.

Trudeau, Prime Minister J. (2016, December 6). *Speech to assembly of first nations, Niagara*. Retrieved June 17, 2017, from http://pm.gc.ca/eng/news/2016/12/06/prime-minister-justin-trudeaus-speech-assembly-first-nations-special-chiefs-assembly

Trustees of the Roman Catholic Church for the Diocese of Bathurst v Koffman (1996) Aust Torts Reps 81.

Trustees of the Roman Catholic Church for the Diocese of Canberra and Goulburn v Hadba [2005] HCA 31.

Truth and Reconciliation Commission. (2015). *A knock at the door: An essential history of residential schools from the Truth and Reconciliation Commission of Canada*. Winnipeg: TRC.

Truth and Reconciliation Commission of Canada. (2012a). *Interim report*. Ottawa. Retrieved from http://www.attendancemarketing.com/~attmk/TRC_jd/Interim%20re-port%20English%20electronic%20copy.pdf

Truth and Reconciliation Commission of Canada. (2012b). *They came for the children: Canada, aboriginal peoples, and residential schools*. Winnipeg: Author.

Truth and Reconciliation Commission of Canada. (2015a). *Honouring the truth, reconciling the future – Summary of the final report of the truth and reconciliation of Canada*. Retrieved from http://www.trc.ca/websites/trcinstitution/File/2015/Findings/Exec_Summary_2015_05_31_web_o.pdf

Truth and Reconciliation Commission of Canada. (2015b). *Truth and Reconciliation Commission of Canada: Calls to action*. Winnipeg: Author. Retrieved from http://www.trc.ca/websites/trcinstitution/File/2015/Findings/Calls_to_Action_English2.pdf

TT v Lutheran Church of Australia Queensland District [2013] QCAT 48 ('TT').

Turmel, A. (1998). Childhood and normalcy: Classification, numerical regularities and tabulations. *International Journal of Educational Research, 27*(8), 661–672.

Tversky, A., & Kahneman, D. (1973). Availability: A heuristic for judging frequency and probability. *Cognitive Psychology, 5*(2), 207–232.

Tyler v Kesser Torah College [2006] FMCA 1 ("Tyler").

U.S. Advisory Board on Child Abuse and Neglect. (1990). *Child abuse and neglect: Critical first steps in response to a national emergency*. Washington, DC: U.S. Department of Health and Human Services and Office of Human Developmental Services.

U.S. Department of Education. (2004). *Individuals with disabilities education improvement act*. Retrieved from http://idea.ed.gov/download/statute.html.

U.S. Department of Education, National Center for Education Statistics. (2016). *Internet access in U.S. public schools and classrooms: 1994–2005 and educational technology in U.S. public schools: Fall 2008*. Retrieved from https://nces.ed.gov/programs/digest/d15/tables/dt15_218.10.asp?current=yes

U.S. Department of Labor. (1973). *National rehabilitation act of 1973 § 504*. Retrieved May 1, 2017, from https://www.dol.gov/oasam/regs/statutes/sec504.htm

Uglow, J. (2002). *The lunar men: The friends who made the future*. London: Faber and Faber.

Ulivieri Stiozzi, S. (2008). Pensarsi padre. La paternità come esperienza autoformativa. Milano. CUEM.

Ulivieri Stiozzi, S. (2013). Paper school or flesh and blood school? Pedagogic analysis of some symptoms of suffering in contemporary schools. *Society, Integration, Education. Proceedings of the International Scientifical Conference, 1*, 310–319.

UN Convention on the Rights of the Child, Australian Treaty Series 1991, no. 4, Dept. of Foreign Affairs and Trade, Canberra, Commonwealth of Australia.

UNESCO. (1990). *World declaration on education for all*. Online at http://www.unesco.org/education/efa/ed_for_all/background/jomtien_declaration.shtml. Accessed 28 July 2014.

UNESCO. (1994). *The Salamanca statement and framework for action on special needs education*. Paris: UNESCO.

UNESCO. (2000). *The Dakar framework of action*. Paris: UNESCO.

UNESCO. (2004). *The flagship on education for all and the rights of persons with disabilities: Towards inclusion*. Paris: UNESCO.

UNESCO. (2009). *Towards inclusive education for children with disabilities: A guideline*. Bangkok: UNESCO.

UNESCO International Standard Classification of Education I S C E D. (1997). http://www.unesco.org/education/information/nfsunesco/doc/isced_1997.htm

UNICEF. (2007). *Child poverty in perspective: An overview of child well-being in rich countries, Innocenti report card*. 7, 2007 UNICEF Innocenti Research Centre, Florence.

UNICEF. (2014). *Hidden in plain sight. A statistical analysis of violence against children*. New York: United Nations.

UNICEF. (2016a). *10 Years on: Global progress & delay in ending violence against children – The Rhetoric & the reality*. Report 2016, The International NGO Council on Violence Against Children.

UNICEF. (2016b). The State of the World's Children 2016: A fair chance for every child. https://www.unicef.org/sowc2016/. Accessed 07 Mar 2017.

Unicef. (1989). Convention on the Rights of the Child. *Child Labor*, 8.

United Kingdom. (1867). Constitution act, 1867, 30 & 31 Victoria, c. 3.

United Kingdom. (1982). Canadian charter of rights and freedoms, part I of the constitution act, 1982, being schedule B to the Canada act 1982 (UK), 1982, c. 11.

United Nations. (1948a). Universal Declaration of Human Rights. www.un.org/en/universal-declaration-human-rights/. Accessed 07 Mar 2017.

United Nations. (1948b). *The universal declaration of human rights*. New York: United Nations.

United Nations. (1966a). *International covenant on economic, social and cultural rights*. New York: United Nations.

United Nations. (1966b). *International covenant on civil and political rights*. New York: United Nations.

United Nations. (1969). *Declaration on social progress and development.* New York: United Nations.

United Nations. (1971). *Declaration on the rights of mentally retarded persons.* New York: United Nations.

United Nations. (1975). *Declaration on the rights of disabled persons.* New York: United Nations.

United Nations. (1983). *World program of action concerning disabled persons.* New York: United Nations.

United Nations. (1989a). Convention on the Rights of the Child. www.unicef.org.uk/Documents/Publication-pdfs/UNCRC_PRESS200910web.pdf. Accessed 07 March 2017.

United Nations. (1989b). *Convention on the rights of the child.* General assembly resolution 44/25, 20 November 1989. UN Doc. A/RES/44/25.

United Nations. (1989c). *Convention on the rights of the child.* New York: United Nations. Retrieved from URL: http://www.refworld.org/docid/3ae6b38f0.html

United Nations. (1993). *Standard rules on the equalization of opportunities for persons with disabilities.* New York: United Nations.

United Nations. (1999). *Convention on the rights of the child.* Geneva: United Nations.

United Nations. (2000a). United Nations Millennium Declaration. http://www.un.org/millennium/declaration/ares552e.htm. Accessed 07 Mar 2017.

United Nations. (2000b). *Conventions on the rights of persons with disabilities (CRPD).* Retrieved from http://www.un.org/disabilities/convention/conventionfull.shtml

United Nations. (2000c). *Conventions on the rights of the child (CROC).* Retrieved from http://www.ohchr.org/en/professionalinterest/pages/crc.aspx

United Nations. (2000a). Conventions on the Rights of Persons with Disabilities (CRPD). Retrieved from http://www.un.org/disabilities/convention/conventionfull.shtml

United Nations. (2000b). Conventions on the Rights of the Child (CROC). Retrieved from http://www.ohchr.org/en/professionalinterest/pages/crc.aspx

United Nations. (2002). A world fit for children. https://www.unicef.org/specialsession/wffc/. Accessed 07 Mar 2017.

United Nations. (2006). *Convention on the rights of persons with disabilities.* Geneva: United Nations.

United Nations. (2007). Declaration on the rights of indigenous peoples UN Doc. A/61/L.67.

United Nations. (2013). *Report of the office of the United Nations high commissioner for human rights: Thematic study on the right of persons with disabilities.* New York: United Nations.

United Nations. (2015). The Millennium Development Goals Report 2015. https://www.unicef.org/sowc2016/. Accessed 07 Mar 2017.

United Nations. (2016). *General comment no. 4 (2016) on the right to inclusive education.* New York: United Nations.

United Nations Committee on the Right of the Child. (2011). *General comment no. 13*. The right of the child to freedom from all forms of violence (CRC/C/GC/13).

United Nations Committee on the Rights of Persons with Disabilities. (2014a). *Concluding observations on the initial report of Belgium*. Geneva: United Nations.

United Nations Committee on the Rights of Persons with Disabilities. (2014b). *Concluding observations on the initial report of Ecuador*. Geneva: United Nations.

United Nations Convention on the Rights of the Child (UNCRC). (1989). United Nations, New York.

United Nations Convention on the Rights of the Child. (2001). *Report of the twenty-eight session* (CRC/C/111).

United Nations General Assembly. (1989). *Resolution no. 44/25* (A/RES/44/25).

United Nations General Assembly on the Rights of the Child. (2002). *Resolution 56/138* (A/RES/56/138).

United Nations General Assembly on the Rights of the Child. (2006). Report of the independent expert for the United Nations study on violence against children (A/61/299).

United Nations General Assembly on the Rights of the Child. (2008). *Resolution no. 62/141* (A/RES/62/141).

United Nations Human Rights. (1976). *International covenant on economic, social and cultural rights*. New York: Office of the High Commissioner Human Rights. Retrieved from http://www.ohchr.org/EN/ProfessionalInterest/Pages/CESCR.aspx

United Nations Treaty Collection. https://treaties.un.org/Pages/ViewDetails.aspx?src=TREATY&mtdsg_no=IV-15&chapter=4&clang=_en#EndDec. Accessed 16 June 2017.

United States Department of Education. (2013). Closing memorandum for file 11-000491, Steven D. Anderson, special agent in charge. Office of Inspector General, Investigative Services. Washington, DC: Author.

Uniting Church in Australia Property Trust (NSW) v Miller, Miller v Lithgow City Council [2015] NSWCA 320.

Unruh, D., Gau, J., & Waintrup, M. (2009). An exploration of factors reducing recidivism rates of formerly incarcerated youth with disabilities participating in a re-entry intervention. *Journal of Child & Family Studies, 18*, 284–293.

Unruh, D., Waintrup, M., & Canter, T. (2010). Project STAYOUT: A facility-to-community transition intervention targeting incarcerated adolescent offenders. In D. Cheney (Ed.), *Transition of secondary students with emotional or behavioural disorders. Current approaches for positive outcomes* (2nd ed., pp. 347–374). Champaign: Research Press.

Valle, J. W. (2009). *What mothers say about special education: From the 1960s to the present*. London: Palgrave Macmillan.

Valle, J. W., & Aponte, E. (2002). IDEA and collaboration: A Bakhtinian perspective on parent and professional discourse. *Journal of Learning Disabilities, 35*, 469–479. https://doi.org/10.1177/00222194020350050701.

Van Laarhoven-Myers, T. E., Van Laarhoven, T. R., Smith, T. J., Johnson, H., & Olson, J. (2016). Promoting self-determination and transition planning using technology: Student and parent perspectives. *Career Development and Transition for Exceptional Individuals, 39*(2), 99–110. https://doi.org/10.1177/2165143414552518.

Vanderstraeten, D. (2002). Parsons, Luhmann and the theorem of double contingency. *Journal of Classical Sociology, 2*(1), 78–92.

Varnham, S. (2002). Mainstreaming or Maindumping? Daniels v the attorney general. Equality of access to education for children with special needs in New Zealand. In D. Stewart (Ed.), *Legal risk management safety, security and success in education: Proceedings of the 11th annual conference of the Australia and New Zealand education law association* (pp. 239–254). Brisbane: GSM Press.

Varnham, S. (2015a, July 1). It shouldn't take legal action for schools to act on bullying. *The Conversation.* http://theconversation.com/it-shouldnt-take-legal-action-for-schools-to-act-on-bullying-43711

Varnham, S. (2015b, November). *The role of Catholic schools in Australia in educating for human rights and social justice: An overview.* Paper presented at the annual conference of the European education law association, within educating for today and tomorrow: A renewing passion, The World Catholic Education Congress, The Vatican, 18–21. (International Journal of Education Law and Policy Special Issue forthcoming).

Varnham, S., Evers, M., & Booth, T. (2014–2015a). Valuing their voices: Encouraging responsibility and citizenship through student participation in school decision making. *International Journal of Law and Education, 19*(2) & *20*(1), 23.

Varnham, S., Evers, M., Booth, T., & Avgoustinos, C. (2014–2015b). Democracy in schools: Encouraging responsibility and citizenship through student participation in school decision making. *International Journal of Law and Education, 19*(1) & *20*(1), 73.

Veltman, M. W., & Browne, K. D. (2001). Three decades of child maltreatment research implications for the school years. *Trauma, Violence, & Abuse, 2*(3), 215–239.

Victoria Department of Education. http://www.education.vic.gov.au/about/programs/bullystoppers/Pages/methodrestorative.asp

Victoria Government, Department of Human Services. (2007). *Cumulative harm: A conceptual overview.* Melbourne: Victorian Government.

Victorian Certification and Assessment Authority. (2012). *VCE chemistry assessment handbook 2010–2015.* Melbourne: VCAA.

Victorian Civil & Administrative Tribunal. (2006, June 6). *Beasley v State of Victoria Department of Education & Training* (VCAT). Retrieved from http://www.austlii.edu.au/cgi-bin/sinodisp/au/cases/vic/VCAT/2006/1050.html?stem=0&synonyms=0&query=Beasley

Victorian Equal Opportunity & Human Rights Commission (VEOHRC). (2012a). *Held back: The experiences of students with disabilities in Victorian schools.* Retrieved from http://www.humanrightscommission.vic.gov.au/media/k2/attachments/1404-VEOHRC_HeldBack_-_StudentwithDisabilityReportW3.pdf

Victorian Equal Opportunity & Human Rights Commission (VEOHRC). (2012b). *Held back: The experiences of students with disabilities in Victorian schools*. Carlton: VEOHRC.

Victorian Equal Opportunity and Human Rights Commission. (2017). *Held back: The experiences of students with disabilities in Victorian schools: Analysis paper*. Carlton: Victorian Equal Opportunity and Human Rights Commission. https://www.humanrightscommission.vic.gov.au/home/our-resources-and-publications/reports/item/1602-held-back-the-experiences-of-students-with-disabilities-in-victorian-schools-analysis-paper

Victorian Institute of Teaching, *Codes of conduct and ethics*. Available at https://www.vit.vic.edu.au/professional-responsibilities/conduct-and-ethics

Victorian Ombudsman. (2017). *Investigation into Victorian government school expulsions*. Melbourne: Author. https://www.ombudsman.vic.gov.au/Publications/Parliamentary-Reports/Investigation-into-vic-gov-school-expulsions

Villa, R. A., Thousand, J. S., Meyers, H., & Nevin, A. (1996). Teacher and administrator perceptions of heterogeneous education. *Exceptional Children, 63*(1), 29–45. https://doi.org/10.1177/001440299606300103.

Vlachou, A., & Papananou, I. (2015). Disabled students' narratives about their schooling experiences. *Disability & Society, 30*(1), 73–86. https://doi.org/10.1080/09687599.2014.982787.

Vlăsceanu, L., Grünberg, L., & Pârlea, D. (2007). *Quality assurance and accreditation: A glossary of basic terms and definitions* (Revised ed.). Paris: UNESCO.

Vollmer, H., & Mills, D. (Eds.). (1966). *Professionalization*. Eaglewood Cliffs: Prentice-Hall.

Von Hayek, F. (1944). *The road to serfdom*. Abingdon: Routledge.

W v Flinders University of South Australia [1998] HREOCA 19 ('W').

Wagner, P. A. (2012). Legal ethics no paradigm for educational administrators. *Journal of Thought, 47*(1), 21–27.

Waiton, S. (2016). Third way parenting and the creation of the "named person" in Scotland. The end of family privacy and autonomy? *SAGE Open, 6*(1), 1–13. https://doi.org/10.1177/2158244016629525.

Waldron, N. L., & McLeskey, J. (2010). Establishing a collaborative school culture through comprehensive school reform. *Journal of Educational and Psychological Consultation, 20*, 58–74. https://doi.org/10.1080/10474410903535364.

Waldron, N. L., McLeskey, J., & Redd, L. (2011). Setting the direction: The role of the principal in developing an effective, inclusive school. *Journal of Special Education Leadership, 24*(2), 51–60.

Waldron, N. L., McLeskey, J., & Redd, L. (2014). A case study of a highly effective, inclusive elementary school. *Journal of Special Education, 48*, 59–70. https://doi.org/10.1177/0022466912440455.

Walker, S. (1995). Schools and defamation. In D. Hopkins (Ed.), *Fourth national conference of the Australian and New Zealand education law association* (pp. 15–25). Melbourne: Australian and New Zealand Education Law Association (Inc.).

Walker, S. C., Bishop, A. S., Pullmann, M. D., & Bauer, G. (2015). A research framework for understanding the practical impact of family involvement in the juvenile justice system: The juvenile justice family involvement model. *American Journal of Community Psychology, 56*(3–4), 408–421.

Walker v State of Victoria [2012] FCAFC 38 ("Walker").

Walsh, K., & Farrel, A. (2004). Identifying and evaluating teacher's knowledge in relation to child abuse and neglect: A qualitative study with Australian early childhood teachers. *Teaching and Teachers Education, 24*, 585–600.

Walsh, K., & Farrell, A. (2008). Identifying and evaluating teachers' knowledge in relation to child abuse and neglect: A qualitative study with Australian early childhood teachers. *Teaching and Teacher Education, 24*(3), 585–600.

Walsh, K., Farrell, A., Schweitzer, R., & Bridgstock, R. (2005). *Critical factors in teachers' detecting and reporting child abuse and neglect: Implications for practice.* Brisbane: Queensland University of Technology.

Walsh, K., Bridgstock, R., Farrel, A., Rassafiani, M., & Schweitzer, R. (2008). Case, teacher and school characteristics influencing teachers' detection and reporting of child physical abuse and neglect: Results from an Australian survey. *Child Abuse & Neglect, 32*(10), 983–993.

Walsh, K. M., Laskey, L., McInnes, E., Farrell, A., Mathews, B. P., & Briggs, F. (2011). Locating child protection in preservice teacher education. *Australian Journal of Teacher Education, 36*(7), 1–20.

Walton, M. (1986). *The Deming management method.* New York: Perigee Books.

Wardle, D. (2006). School related law: Do principals know what they need to know? Masters of Educational Administration Unpublished, Massey University, Palmerstone North.

Warner, J. E., & Hansen, D. J. (1994). The identification and reporting of physical abuse by physicians: A review and implications for research. *Child Abuse & Neglect, 18*(1), 11–25.

Warnock. (1978). *Special educational needs report of the committee of enquiry into the education of handicapped children and young people.* Cmnd. 7212. London: HMSO.

Warren, E. (1962). *Special address to the Louis Marshall award dinner of the Jewish theological seminary, Americana hotel.* New York. November 11.

Wasserman, M. F. (2015). Defense asymmetries: Distortions in the evolution of regulatory law. *Texas Law Review, 93*, 625–679.

Watkins, B. T. (2014). *Reducing court-related stress through court education: Examining child witnesses, attorneys and parents.* Doctoral dissertation. Retrieved from http://digitalscholarship.unlv.edu/thesesdissertations/2228/

Watson, J. (2016). *The right to supported decision-making for people rarely heard.* Doctoral dissertation. Retrieved from https://www.researchgate.net/profile/Joanne_Watson/publication/258997358_Thesis_The_right_to_supported_decision-making_for_people_rarely_heard/links/5751420a08ae17e65ec149cf.pdf

Watson v Haines. (1987). Aust Torts reports 80–094.

Watts, I. E., & Erevelles, N. (2004). These deadly times: Reconceptualizing school violence by using critical race theory and disability studies. *American Educational Research Journal, 41*(2), 271–299.

'Weapons worry: Knives, guns brought by students to WA schools' 11 October 2015 news.com.au. http://www.news.com.au/national/western-australia/weapons-worry-knives-guns-brought-by-students-to-wa-schools/news-story/57c9bbc269084b6b4448be1221659d0920050518news_1n18grove.html

Weber, M. (2013). Children with disabilities, parents without disabilities, and lawyers: Issues of life experience, affinity, and agency. In B. A. Ferri & A. Kanter (Eds.), *Righting educational wrongs: Disability studies in law and education.* Syracuse: Syracuse University Press.

Weber v Land Agents Board. (1986). 40 SASR 312.

Webster, A. A. (2016). Utilising a leadership blueprint to build capacity of schools to achieve outcomes for students with autism spectrum disorder. In G. Johnson & N. Dempster (Eds.), *Leadership for learning and effective change* (pp. 109–128). Melbourne: Springer.

Webster, A. A., & Roberts, J. M. A. (2014). *Building the capacity of schools to achieve outcomes for students with autism spectrum disorders: A pilot project.* Cairns: Department of Education, Training & Employment, Far North Queensland.

Webster, A. A., & Roberts, J. M. A. (2015). *Developing a region-wide approach to supporting students with autism spectrum disorder in inclusive schools: Building autism friendly schools and communities.* Cairns: Department of Education, Training & Employment, Far North Queensland.

Webster, A. A., & Wilkinson, J. (2015). Leading school communities to implement a sustainable school-wide model leading to outcomes for students with ASD. *Special Education Perspectives, 24*, 27–37.

Webster, S. W., O'Toole, R., O'Toole, A. W., & Lucal, B. (2005). Overreporting and underreporting of child abuse: Teachers' use of professional discretion. *Child Abuse & Neglect, 29*(11), 1281–1296.

Weegen, C. (2013). Defining 'reasonable force' in the modern school environment. *International Journal of Law & Education, 18*(1), 83–97.

Wehmeyer, M. L., Davis, S., & Palmer, S. B. (2012). 10 steps to independence: Promoting self-determination in the home, *Research to practice in self-determination series,* (4), 5. Retrieved from National Gateway to Self-determination website http://ngsd.org/sites/default/files/research_to_practice_sd_-_issue_4.pdf

Wehmeyer, M. L., Shogren, K. A., & Seo, H. (2015). Promoting the self-determination and goal attainment of youth with learning disabilities and behavioral disorders. In B. G. Cook, M. Tankersley, & T. J. Landrum (Eds.), *Transition of youth and young adults* (pp. 173–196). Bingley: Emerald Group.

Weick, K. E. (1993). The collapse of sensemaking in organizations: The Mann Gulch disaster. *Administrative Science Quarterly, 38*(4), 628–652.

Weir v Geelong Grammar School (Civil Claims) [2012] VCAT 1736.

Weissbrodt, D., Maderia, W., Stewart, D., & Dikel, W. (2012). Applying international human rights standards to the restraint and seclusion of students with disabilities. *Law and Inequality, 30*, 287–307. http://scholarship.law.umn.edu/faculty_articles/365?utm_source=scholarship.law.umn.edu%2Ffaculty_articles%2F365&utm_medium=PDF&utm_campaign=PDFCoverPages

Wenger, E. (1998). *Communities of practice: Learning, meaning and identity.* Cambridge: Cambridge University Press.

West, A., & Ylönen, A. (2010). Market-oriented school reform in England and Finland: School choice, finance and governance. *Educational Studies, 36*(1), 1–12.

Whelan, J. (2017, August 31). Doctors, lawyers and ministers all take a professional pledge: Here's why teachers should too. *The Conversation.*

Whitburn, B. (2016). Voice, post-structural representation and the subjectivity of 'included' students. *International Journal of Research & Method in Education, 39*(2), 117–130. https://doi.org/10.1080/1743727X.2014.946497.

Wilczynski, A. (1995). Child killing by parents: A motivational model. *Child Abuse Review, 4*, 365–370.

Wilder, M. (2016). Whither the funnel of causality? *Canadian Journal of Political Science, 49*(4), 721–741.

Williams, P. (1995). Touching students: A legal dilemma for teachers. (A. Knott, & D. Stewart, Eds.). *ANZELA Reporter, 3*(1), 17–23.

Williams, P. (2002). Educational employers and foreseeable risks of harm. (K. Lindsay, Ed.). *Australia and New Zealand Journal of Law and Education, 7*(1), 81–83.

Williams, R., Bertsch, B., Dale, B., van der Wiele, T., van Iwaarden, J., Smith, M., & Visser, R. (2006). Quality and risk management: What are the key issues? *The TQM Magazine, 18*(1), 67–86.

Williams v. Eady. (1893). 10 TLR 41 CA.

Williams-Lewis, Y. R. (2014). *Principal leadership that creates a school culture supportive of inclusive education for students on the autism spectrum.* Doctoral dissertation. Retrieved from https://sdsu-dspace.calstate.edu/bitstream/handle/10211.3/138246/WilliamsLewis_sdsu_0220D_10674.pdf?sequence=1

Wilson, L. (2014, October 14). Frightened teachers avoiding excursions. *The Courier Mail.* Brisbane.

Wilson, A., Poed, S., & Byrnes, L. (2015). Full steam ahead: Facilitating the involvement of Australian students with impairments in individual planning processes through student-led program support group meetings. *Special Education Perspectives, 24*(1), 15–25. Retrieved from http://aase.edu.au/wordpress/wp-content/uploads/documents/SEP-Contents-Vol24-No1-18Jun15-.pdf.

Winn, B. A., & Cameron, K. S. (1998). Organizational quality: An examination of the Malcolm Baldrige National Quality framework. *Research in Higher Education, 39*(5), 491–512.

Winnicott, D. (1953). Transitional objects and transitional phenomena. *International Journal of Psychoanalysis, 34*, 89–97.

Winram, M. (2008). Lawyers and educators working together to protect schools, teachers and students from You-Tube and other websites that malign them, *Achieving excellence: Lawyers and educators working together* (pp. 133–150). Christchurch.

Winzer, M., & Mazurek, K. (2014). The convention on the rights of persons with disabilities: Notes on genealogy and prospects. *International Journal of Special Needs Education, 17*(1), 3–12. https://doi.org/10.9782/2159-4341-17.1.3.

Wirtz, V., Cribb, A., & Barber, N. (2005). Reimbursement decisions in health policy-extending our understanding of the elements of decision-making. *Health Policy, 73*, 330–338.

Wolf v. State of Utah, Civ. No. 182646 (Utah Dist. Ct. 1969).

Wolff, J. (2011). *Ethics and public policy: A philosophical inquiry*. New York, NY: Routledge.

Wollenberg, C. (1974). Mendez v. Westminster: Race, nationality and segregation in California schools. *California Historical Quarterly, 53*(4), 317–332.

Wong, D. (2007). Beyond control and rationality; Dewey, aesthetics, motivation and educative experiences. *Teachers College Record, 109*(1), 192–220.

Wong v Office of the Board of Studies NSW (No 4) [2012] NSWADT 128 ('Wong').

Wood, P., Evans, D., & Spandagou, I. (2014). Attitudes of principals towards students with disruptive behaviour: An Australian perspective. *Australasian Journal of Special Education, 38*(01), 14–33. https://doi.org/10.1017/jse.2014.5.

Woods, N. L. (2013). Educational malfeasance: A new cause of action for failure in education. *Tulsa Law Review, 14*(2), 383–409.

Woolford, A. (2009). Ontological destruction: Genocide and Canadian indigenous peoples. *Genocide Studies and Prevention, 4*(1), 81–97.

Woolley, A. (2010a). The psychology of good character: The past, present and future of good character regulation in Canada (with Jocelyn Stacey). In K. Tranter et al. (Eds.), *Re-affirming legal ethics* (p. 165–187). New York, NY: Routledge.

Woolley, A. (2010b). Legal ethics and regulatory legitimacy: Regulating lawyers for personal misconduct. In F. Bartlett et al. (Eds.), *Alternative perspectives on legal ethics: Reimagining the profession* (pp. 241–268). New York: Routledge.

Woolley, A., & Wendel, W. B. (2010). Legal ethics and moral character. *Georgetown Journal of Legal Ethics, 23*(4), 1065–1100.

World Bank. (2011). *Learning for all: Investing in people's knowledge and skills to promote development: World Bank group education strategy 2020*. Washington, DC: The International Bank for Reconstruction and Development/The World Bank.

World Health Organization. (1980). *International classification of impairment, disability and handicap (ICIDH)*. Geneva: World Health Organization.

World Health Organization. (1990). *International classification of diseases and related health problems (ICD-10)*. Geneva: World Health Organization.

World Health Organization. (2001). *International classification of functioning, disability and health*. Geneva: World Health Organization.

Wrongs Act (Vic) 1958.

Wyong Shire Council v Shirt (1980) 146 CLR 40.

Wyong Shire Council v Vairy [2004] NSWCA 247.

Wyong Shire v Shirt (1980) 146 CLR 40.
X (minors) v Bedfordshire County Council; M (a minor) and another v Newham London Borough Council and others; E (a minor) v Dorset County Council; and other appeals [1995] 2 AC 633.
X (Minors) v Bedfordshire County Council and Phelps v London Borough of Hillingdon [1995] AC 633 & [2000] 3 WLR 776.
Yee Tak On v Dr Linda Hort (ANU College) [2012] FMCA 391.
Yell, M. L. (2016). *The law and special education* (4th ed.). Upper Saddle River: Pearson.
Yell, M. L., Shriner, J. G., & Katsiyannis, A. (2006). Individuals with disabilities education improvement act of 2004 and IDEA regulations of 2006: Implications for educators, administrators, and teacher trainers. *Focus on Exceptional Children, 39*, 1–24.
Yell, M. L., Katsiyannis, A., Ryan, J. B., McDuffie, K. A., & Mattocks, L. (2008). Twenty ways to ensure compliance with the individuals with disabilities education improvement act of 2004. *Intervention in School and Clinic, 44*, 45–51. https://doi.org/10.1177/1053451208318875.
Yellow Bird, M. (2012). Neurodecolonization: Using mindfulness practices to delete the neural networks of colonialism. In Waziyatawin & M. Yellow Bird (Eds.), *For indigenous minds only: A decolonization handbook* (pp. 57–84). Santa Fe: School for Advanced Research Press.
Zarra, E. J., III. (2013). *Teacher-student relationships: Crossing into the emotional, physical, and sexual realms*. Lanham: Rowman & Littlefield Publishers.
Zarra, E. J., III. (2016). Addressing appropriate and inappropriate teacher-student relationships: A secondary education professional development model. *CLEARvoz Journal, 3*(2), 15–29.
Zermatten, J., & Krappmann, L. (2011). *Governance fit for children*. Retrieved from United Kingdom http://www.savethechildren.org.uk/resources/online-library/governance-fit-children
Zierkel, P. A. (2006). Paralyzing fear? Avoiding distorted assessments of the effect of law on education. *Journal of Law and Education, 35*(4), 461–495.
Zirkel, P. A., & Weathers, J. M. (2015). Section 504-only students: National incidence data. *Journal of Disability Policy Studies, 26*(3), 184–193.
Zygorodimos [2004] VCAT 128 ("Zygorodimos").

Legislation

Anti-Discrimination Act 1977 (NSW).
Anti-Discrimination Act 1991 (Qld).
Anti-Discrimination Act 1992 (NT).
Anti-Discrimination Act 1998 (Tas).
Australian Human Rights Commission Act 1986 (Cth).

Discrimination Act 1991 (ACT).
Education Act 1990 (NSW).
Education and Training Reform Act 2006 (Vic).
Education and Training Reform Regulations 2007 (Vic).
Equal Opportunity Act 1984 (SA).
Equal Opportunity Act 1984 (WA).
Equal Opportunity Act 2010 (VIC).
Equality Act 2010 (UK).
Fair Work Act 2009 (Cth).
Occupational Health and Safety Act 2004 (Vic) ss 21 and 23.
Occupational Safety and Health Act 1984 (WA).
Racial and Religious Tolerance Act 2001 (UK).
Sex Discrimination Act 1984 (Cth).
Work Health and Safety Act 2011 (ACT).
Work Health and Safety Act 2011 (Cth).
Work Health and Safety Act 2011 (NSW).
Work Health and Safety Act 2011 (Qld).
Work Health and Safety Act 2012 (SA).
Work Health and Safety Act 2012 (Tas).

Cases

A obo V and A v NSW Department of Education EOD [2000] NSWADTAP 14.
Achbita & Anor v G4S Secure Solutions NV [2016] EUECJ C-157/15.
Adelaide Co of Jehovah's Witnesses Inc v Commonwealth (1943) 67 CLR 116.
Al-Kateb v Godwin (2004) 219 CLR 562.
Arora v Melton Christian College (Human Rights) [2017] VCAT 1507.
Attorney-General (Vic); Ex Rel Black v Commonwealth (1981) 146 CLR 559.
Azmi v Kirklees Metropolitan Borough Council [2007] UKEA/0009/07.
Bougnaoui v Micropole Univers SA (2015) C-188/15.
Bull and Another v Hall and Another [2013] UKSC 73.
Catch the Fire Ministries Inc & Ors v Islamic Council of Victoria Inc [2006] VSCA 284.
Church of the New Faith v Commissioner of Payroll Tax (1983) 154 CLR 120.
Coy Mathis v Fountain-Fort Carson School District 8 (2013) P20130034X.
De Groen v Gan Mecachem Hendon Limited 3347281/2016.
E.T. v Hamilton-Wentworth District School Board (2016) ONSC 7313.
G.G. [Gavin Grimm] v. Gloucester County School Board; see Shapiro, I, T Burrus and D McDonald. 'Gloucester County School Board v G.G', *Cato Institute*, 10 January 2017 accessed at https://www.cato.org/publications/legal-briefs/gloucester-county-school-board-v-gg-0
Goldberg v Korsunski Carmel School [2000] EOC 93-074.

Haider v Combined District Radio Cabs Pty Ltd t/as Central Coast Taxis [2008] NSWADT 123.
HM Chief Inspector of Education, Children's Services and Skills v The Interim Executive Board of Al-Hijrah School [2017] EWCA Civ 1426.
HM Land Registry v Grant EAT [2010] UKEAT 0232_09_1504.
Islamic Council of Victoria v Catch the Fire Ministries Inc [2004] VCAT 2510.
Johns and Another, Regina (on The Application of) v Derby City Council and Another [2011] EWHC 375 (Admin).
Jones v Lee and Guilding [1980] ICR 310.
Krygger v Williams (1912) 15 CLR 366.
Miller v Wertheim [2001] FMCA 103.
Miller v Wertheim [2004] FCA 988.
Minister for Immigration and Ethnic Affairs v Teoh (1995) 183 CLR 273.
Multani v Commission Scolaire Marguerite-Bourgeoys [2006] 1 SCR 256.
Pothecary Witham Weld (A Firm) and Another v Bullimore [2010] UKEAT 0158_09_2903.
R (on the application of E) (Respondent) v The Governing Body of JFS and the Admissions Appeal Panel of JFS and others (Appellants) [2009] UKSC 15.
R (on the application of Playfoot) v Governing Body of Millais School [2007] HRLR 34.
R (on the application of Watkins-Singh) v Aberdare Girls' High School Governors [2008] EWHC 1865.
R (SB) v Governors of Denbigh High School [2007] 1 AC 100.
R (Williamson) v Secretary of State for Education and Employment [2005] 2 AC 246.
SDW v Church of Jesus Christ of Latter-Day Saints (2008) 222 FLR 84.
Sutherland Shire Council v Folkes [2015] FCA 1288.
The Interim Executive Board of X School v. Her Majesty's Chief Inspector of Education, Children's Services and Skills [2016] EWHC 2813 (Admin).
Trinity Western University v British Columbia College of Teachers [2001] 1 SCR 772.

Books and Journal Articles

Evans, C. (2009). Legal aspects of the protection of religious freedom in Australia. *Melbourne Law School.*
Evans, C. (2012). *Legal protection of religious freedom in Australia*. Sydney: Federation Press.
Evans, C., & Gaze, B. (2010). Discrimination by religious schools: Views from the coal face. *Melbourne University Law Review, 34*, 392.
Evans, C., & Ujvari, L. (2009). Non-discrimination laws and religious schools in Australia. *Adelaide Law Review, 30*, 31.
Ford, D. (2016). *Lesbian, gay, transgender and intersex students.* Retrieved from www.emilford.com.au/imagesDB/wysiwyg/LGBTIStudentsandDutyofCare-November2016PaperbyDavidFord.pdf

Schuster, M., Reisner, S., & Onorato, S. (2016). Beyond bathrooms – Meeting the health needs of transgender people. *The New England Journal of Medicine, 375*, 101–103. https://doi.org/10.1056/NEJMp1605912.

Walsh, G. (2014). The right to equality and the employment decisions of religious schools. *The University of Notre Dame Australia Law Review, 16*, 107–144.

Media Reports

Bachelard, M. (2008, February 25). At the crossroads? *The Age*. Retrieved from www.theage.com.au/news/in-depth/at-the-crossroads/2008/02/24/1203788145887.html?page=5

Christodoulou, H. (2016, November 7). Four 'extremist' schools which teach 'men can beat their wives' fighting government orders to shut down. *The Sun*. Retrieved from www.thesun.co.uk/news/2130831/four-extremist-schools-which-teach-men-can-beat-their-wives-fighting-government-orders-to-shut-down/

Conifer, D. (2017, November 19). Ministers at odds over whether to include religious protections in same-sex marriage bill. *ABC News*. Retrieved from http://www.abc.net.au/news/2017-11-19/split-in-turnbull-government-over-religious-amendments-to-ssm-l/9166360

Donnelly, K. (2013, January 17). Schools practise what they preach. *The Sydney Morning Herald*. Retrieved from www.smh.com.au/federal-politics/political-opinion/schools-practise-what-they-preach-20130116-2ctpf.html

Fyfe, M. (2009, October 4). Teacher scorned for chosen lifestyle. *The Age*. Retrieved from www.theage.com.au/national/teacher-scorned-for-chosen-lifestyle-20091003-ghbl.html

Haydar, N. (2017, April 16). Safe schools program ditched in NSW, to be replaced by wider anti-bullying plan. *ABC News*. Retrieved from www.abc.net.au/news/2017-04-16/safe-schools-program-ditched-in-nsw/8446680

Human Rights Watch. (2016, September 13). Shut out: Restrictions of bathroom and locker room access for transgender youth in US schools'. *Human Rights Watch*. Retrieved from www.hrw.org/report/2016/09/13/shut-out/restrictions-bathroom-and-locker-room-access-transgender-youth-us-schools

Hurley, L. (2017, March 7). U.S top court throws out ruling favouring transgender student. *Reuters*. Retrieved from https://www.reuters.com/article/us-usa-court-transgender/u-s-top-court-throws-out-ruling-favoring-transgender-student-idUSKBN16D1OD

Jabour, B. (2012, May 1). Teacher sacked over pregnancy. *Brisbane Times*. Retrieved from www.brisbanetimes.com.au/queensland/teacher-sacked-over-pregnancy-20120501-1xw79.html

Lipka, M. (2016). Americans are divided over which public bathrooms transgender people should use. *Pew Research Center*. Retrieved from www.pewresearch.org/

fact-tank/2016/10/03/americans-are-divided-over-which-public-bathrooms-transgender-people-should-use/

McCarriston, G. (2017, March 16). Partisan gap widens on transgender bathroom rights. *YouGov*. Retrieved from today.yougov.com/news/2017/03/16/partisan-lines-drawn-which-bathrooms-transgender-p/

Pells, R. (2016, October 14). Islamist girls' school that taught pupils gay people should be killed and men could beat their wives forced to close. *Independent*. Retrieved from www.independent.co.uk/news/education/education-news/islamist-girls-school-jamia-al-hudaa-taught-pupils-gay-people-should-be-killed-forced-closure-aliyah-a7361596.html

Rankin, J., & Oltermann, P. (2017, March 13). Europe's right hails EU court's workplace headscarf ban ruling. *The Guardian*. Retrieved from www.theguardian.com/law/2017/mar/14/employers-can-ban-staff-from-wearing-headscarves-european-court-rules

Tomazin, F. (2009, March 25). Christian school rejects teacher. *The Age*. Retrieved from www.theage.com.au/national/christian-school-rejects-teacher-20090324-98y0.html

Turner, A. (2017, March 6). BREAKING: U.S. Supreme Court remands and vacates Gavin Grimm case. *Human Rights Campaign*. Retrieved from https://www.hrc.org/blog/breaking-united-states-supreme-court-remands-and-vacates-gavin-grimm-case

Other

Human Rights and Equal Opportunity Commission Inquiry. (1998). HRC Report No 6.

James, D., & Clarke, T. (2009). Evidence to Scrutiny of Acts and Regulations Committee, Parliament of Victoria, Melbourne, *Inquiry into the exceptions and exemptions in the Equal Opportunity Act — Public hearing*. Victorian Independent Education Union, 3. Retrieved from www.parliament.vic.gov.au/images/stories/committees/sarc/EOV/transcripts/5_August__Victorian_Independent_Education_Union.pdf

NSW Education Standards Authority. (2017). *Modifications to a NESA syllabus*. Retrieved from http://rego.nesa.nsw.edu.au/registered-individual-non-government-schools/registration-requirements/curriculum/modifications-to-a-nesa-syllabus

NSW Education Standards Authority. (2017). *Registered and accredited individual non-government schools (NSW) manual*. Retrieved from http://educationstandards.nsw.edu.au/wps/wcm/connect/e9aad3a8-808b-468f-a8e1-92de94b10e31/reg-accred-individ-non-gov-manual.pdf?MOD=AJPERES&CVID

Victorian Independent Education Union. (2009). *Evidence to Scrutiny of Acts and Regulations Committee, Inquiry into the exceptions and exemptions in the Equal Opportunity Act — Public hearing*. Retrieved from http://www.parliament.vic.gov.

au/images/stories/committees/sarc/EOV/transcripts/5_August_-_Victorian_Independent_Education_Union.pdf
Williams, G. (2017). *Submission to inquiry into the status of the human right to freedom of religion or belief.*

US Laws

Americans with Disabilities Act of 1990, 42 U.S.C. § 12101.
Americans with Disabilities Act Amendments Act of 2008, Pub. L. No. 110-325.
Education for All Handicapped Children Act from 1975, Pub. L. No. 94-142.
Individuals with Disabilities Act from 1997, Pub. L. No. 105-17.
Section 504 of the Rehabilitation Act of 1973, Pub. L. No. 93-112.

US Supreme Court Cases

Irving Independent School District vs Tatro, 468 U.S. 833 (1984).
Cedar Rapids Community School District v Garret F, 526 U.S. 66 (1999).

Index[1]

A

[1] Note: Page numbers followed by 'n' refer to notes.

K. Trimmer et al. (eds.), *The Palgrave Handbook of Education Law for Schools*,
https://doi.org/10.1007/978-3-319-77751-1